Politics of Latin America

The Power Game

HARRY E. VANDEN

GARY PREVOST

New York   Oxford
Oxford University Press
2002

Oxford University Press

Oxford   New York
Athens   Auckland   Bangkok   Bogotá   Buenos Aires   Calcutta
Cape Town   Chennai   Dar es Salaam   Delhi   Florence   Hong Kong   Istanbul
Karachi   Kuala Lumpur   Madrid   Melbourne   Mexico City   Mumbai
Nairobi   Paris   São Paulo   Shanghai   Singapore   Taipei   Tokyo   Toronto   Warsaw

and associated companies in
Berlin   Ibadan

Copyright © 2002 by Oxford University Press, Inc.

Published by Oxford University Press, Inc.
198 Madison Avenue, New York, New York 10016
http://www.oup-usa.org

Oxford is a registered trademark of Oxford University Press

Library of Congress Cataloging-in-Publication Data

Vanden, Harry E.
   Politics of Latin America : the power game / Harry E. Vanden, Gary Prevost.
      p. cm.
   Includes bibliographical references and index.
   ISBN 0-19-512316-6 — ISBN 0-19-512317-4 (pbk.)
   1. Latin America — Politics and government. I. Prevost, Gary. II. Title.

JL960.V36 2002
980—dc21   2001016272

9 8 7 6 5 4 3 2 1

Printed in the United States of America
on acid-free paper

This work is dedicated to those who teach Latin American politics, with special thanks to those who showed us the way: Gary Wynia, who taught Gary Prevost, and C. Neale Ronning, John C. Honey, and Mario Hernández Sánchez-Barba, who guided Harry Vanden.

CONTENTS

iv

MAPS AND TABLES

MAPS

TABLES

FREQUENTLY CITED ACRONYMS

AD	Democratic Action, Venezuela
AID	Agency for International Development, US Department of State
AMNLAE	Association of Nicaraguan Women, Luisa Amanda Espinosa
APRA	American Popular Revolutionary Alliance, Peru
ARENA	National Republican Alliance, El Salvador
ARENA	National Renovating Alliance, Brazil
BPR	People's Revolutionary Bloc, El Salvador
CACIF	Coordinating Committee of Agricultural, Commercial, Industrial and Financial Associations, Guatemala
CBC	Christian Base Communities
CDR	Committees for the Defense of the Revolution, Cuba
CDT	Democratic Workers' Confederation, Chile
CGT	General Confederation of Labor, Argentina
CIA	Central Intelligence Agency, US
CNS	Coordinadora Nacional de Sindicatos, Chile
CONIAE	Confederation of Ecuadorean Indigenous Nacionalities
COPEI	Social Christian Party, Venezuela
CORFO	Development Corporation, Chile
CPC	Confederation of Production and Commerce, Chile
CPD	Coalition of Parties for Democracy, Chile
CTC	Confederation of Cuban Workers
CUT	Unitary Labor Central, Chile
ECLA/ECLAC	Economic Commission for Latin America/and the Caribbean
EGP	Guerrilla Army of the Poor, Guatemala
ELN	National Liberation Army, Colombia
ERP	Revolutionary Army of the People, Argentina
ERP	Popular Revolutionary Army, El Salvador
EZLN	Zapatista National Liberation Army, Mexico
FAL	Armed Forces of Liberation, El Salvador
FAR	Fuerzas Armadas Rebeldes, Guatemala
FARC	Armed Forces of the Colombian Revolution, Colombia
FDNG	New Guatemala Democratic Front
FDR	Democratic Revolutionary Front, El Salvador
FMLN	Farabundo Marti National Liberation Front, El Salvador
FREPASO	Front for a Country in Solidarity, Argentina
FSLN	Sandinista Front for National Liberation, Nicaragua
FTAA	Free Trade Area of the Americas
IFI	International Financial Institution
IMF	International Monetary Fund
ISI	Import Substitution Industrialization

M-19	April 19 Movement, Colombia
M-26 July	July 26 Movement, Cuba
MAS	Movement Toward Socialism, Venezuela
MDB	Brazilian Democratic Movement
MERCOSUR	[MERCOSUL], Common Market of the Southern Cone
MIR	Revolutionary Movement of the Left, Chile
MNC	Multinational Corporation
MST	Landless Movement, Brazil
NAFTA	North American Free Trade Agreement
NAM	Non-Aligned Movement
OAS	Organization of American States
PAN	National Action Party, Mexico
PCC	Cuban Communist Party
PDC	Christian Democratic Party
PJ	Justice [Peronist] Party, Argentina
PMDB	Brazilian Democratic Movement Party
PPD	Party for Democracy, Chile
PRD	Democratic Revolutionary Party, Mexico
PRI	Institutional Revolutionary Party, Mexico
PSDB	Brazilian Social Democratic Party
PSN	Nicaraguan Socialist Party
PT	Workers Party, Brazil
RN	National Renovation, Chile
UCR	Radical Civic Union, Argentina
UFCo	United Fruit Company
UNO	National Opposition Union, Nicaragua
UP	Popular Unity, Chile
UP	Patriotic Union, Colombia
URNG	Guatemalan National Revolutionary Union

PREFACE

This book is born from a great love and appreciation for Latin America and a fascination with how politics are conducted there. It is designed to convey a contemporary and, we hope, realistic understanding of politics and power in the region and is premised on the belief that politics in Latin America can only be understood after one gains an appreciation for the socio-economic-historical context in which the political game is played.

Our understanding of the region and its politics is far from complete, but is well informed by the scholars, writers, and teachers who have preceded us. In recognition of those on whose shoulders we stand, we dedicate this book to those professors who showed us the complexities that define politics in the region. Gary Prevost gratefully acknowledges the import of his teacher Gary Wynia and his excellent work, *The Politics of Latin American Development*. Harry Vanden expresses his profound thanks to those who guided and inspired his study of politics in the region: C. Neale Ronning, John C. Honey, and Mario Hernández Sánchez-Barba. Both authors also gratefully acknowledge the influence of a great many Latin American friends and colleagues and many excellent Latinamericanists from all of the Americas, Europe, and Asia.

We acknowledge the assistance of many people in the preparation of this book, beginning with our colleagues who wrote the country chapters: Wilber Chaffee, Nora Hamilton, Susanne Jonas, Eduardo Silva, and Aldo Vacs. We are indebted to the many scholars who provided helpful commentary on the individual chapters including Mark Amen, Carlos Batista, Dan Buchanan, Robert Buffington, David Close, María Crummett, Ed Nesman, Festus Ohaegbulam, Patrice E. Olsen, Lou Pérez, Eric Selbin, Ofelia Shutte, and Ward Stavig. Thanks are due to Ilene Frank for research and web assistance. We wish to express our appreciation to Dorothea Melcher, who not only read several chapters, but contributed significantly to sections of Chapter 2 on pre-Columbian and colonial history. Likewise, we are deeply indebted to Kwame Dixon for his assistance in the sections on slavery and Afro-Latins in Chapters 3, 4, and 5. We also gratefully acknowledge the editorial assistance of Linda Jarkesy and Lisa Grzan at Oxford University Press.

We are most indebted to Brendan Dwyer for constructing the maps in this work and to Betilde Muñoz and Patrice E. Olsen for completing the index. Kate Arroyo, Ahad Hayauddin, Betilde Muñoz, Xuan Luo, and Jennifer Nagel deserve special thanks for their important work in preparing tables and chronologies. At St. John's University Suzanne Reinert provided valuable office assistance including the typing of significant parts of the manuscript and maintenance of computer files. Erik Gerrits prepared the appendices on elections and government structures. Gary Prevost acknowledges the support of a Dillon Research Grant from St. John's University that enables him to conduct field research. Finally, we remind the reader that any errors or omissions fall on our shoulders alone.

Harry E. Vanden
Tampa

Gary Prevost
Collegeville

Notes on Studying Politics in Latin America

Latin America is a dynamic, complex, and rapidly changing reality. It ranges from small pastoral villages to the largest urban megalopolis on earth. Both democratic and dictatorial, its governments are sometimes replaced by voting in clean elections and other times by military coups. Although exciting to study, Latin America's complexity often challenges the ideas and intellectual approaches we use to study it—indeed, one approach alone is usually just not sufficient to understand what is going on there. The authors of this work maintain that it takes all the conceptual tools and insights that can be mustered to begin to understand such a complex reality. Because the political history of the nations that comprise Latin America has been quite different from that which developed in the United States, Canada, Britain, or Australia, most of us who study Latin American politics believe it is imperative to know this history because most political practices grew out of it. The authors speak of dictatorial *caudillos* and of authoritarian political culture, yet we acknowledge the great political changes and democratic reforms that have also marked Latin American history. Each nation has a political history marked by periods of dictatorship and democracy. Each nation has struggled with the need to change social and economic structures and traditional economic practices that have vested most of the land in a few families and left the vast majority of citizens with no or little land or means of adequately sustaining themselves. Latin America has experienced more revolutions than any other part of the world, yet the conditions for the lower classes in most countries are arguably not much better than they were at the end of the colonial period in the early 1800s. As reflected in the two introductory chapters on broad historical periods in Latin America (Chapters 2 and 3) and the detailed political history provided for each of the seven country case studies presented here, the authors strongly believe that one cannot begin to understand Latin American politics without knowing the region's history. Equally, they know just how great the political variations have been and thus strongly believe that one must equally study the particular historical evolution of each country to comprehend its own brand of politics and see how it conforms to and diverges from general political trends and practices in the region. Similarly, there are certain events—such as the Mexican and Cuban revolutions—and certain figures—such as Victor Raúl Haya de la Torre of Peru, Juan Perón of Argentina, or Cuba's Fidel Castro—whose historical trajectories need be studied because of their lasting influence in their own countries and the region as a whole.

It should further be noted that there are many ways of remembering or interpreting what went on before. Indeed, it has been suggested that much, or some part, of history has been written by the elite. Using the term perfected by the influential Italian thinker Antonio Gramsci, we would say that the "superstructure," or dominant classes, and the culture and institutions they control have dictated much of the history that has been written. For instance, we now know that much that was written by such patriarchical European elites was but one version of what transpired. Class, gender, race, nationality, religion, and ideology all influence how we see an event and how we evaluate it. Slavery, one imagines, will always be seen somewhat differently by slave and slaveholder. And the descendants of each may keep many of their foreparents' views of things. The chapters in this book will endeavor to present a view of the present and past that is inclusive of views of native peoples, Africans who were brought as slaves, women, dominated classes, and others who were subordinated, as well as the more standard history written from the perspective of the dominant elites in Latin America and Europe. By incorporating more diverse views, we hope to supply a better and more complete picture of how the region evolved and what it is like today.

But history is not enough. Even before we deploy specific concepts gleaned from the study of comparative politics, most students of Latin American politics believe that a great deal of the political behavior in the region has been heavily influenced by internal and international economic forces and that one cannot fully comprehend politics without understanding the economics of the region. The internal economies of the indigenous societies were totally disrupted by the conquest and the imposition of economic systems designed to export wealth to Europe and thus incorporate the Americas into the international system on terms favorable to Europe. Economic power was given to the European elite. Thereafter, the structure and functioning of Latin American nations would be heavily influenced by their trade and commercial relations with more economically developed areas; their economies, societies, and political institutions would also be transformed by this external orientation. Latin America was to fit into the system as a producer of primary (unfinished) goods such as sugar, tin, tobacco, copper, coffee, and bananas. According to classical Western capitalist theories of free trade economics, such trade was to be equally advantageous to peripheral areas such as Latin America as it was to metropolitan areas such as Europe and the United States. Yet, after World War II, a careful study of the terms of trade for Latin America by the Economic Commission for Latin America of the

United Nations suggested just the opposite—that benefits from trading patterns were accruing primarily to the developed areas, not to Latin America. As scholars of Latin America and other social scientists studied the full implication of this phenomenon, they arrived at a theory that explained the continuing underdevelopment and dependency of Latin America. Dependency theory, as the paradigm came to be called, soon heavily dominated thinking among social scientists who studied Latin America. For most scholars, it became the principal way of understanding Latin American society, politics, development, and the region's relations with the outside world. This approach predominated from the late 1960s into the 1990s, supplanting many classical economic assumptions and displacing other theories of underdevelopment, such as modernization theory, which was championed by many U.S. scholars. Chapter 9 explores dependency theory in greater detail and makes the general argument that since economic and political power is so closely entwined in Latin America, an approach that combines both—political economy—is necessary.

But even if, as Karl Marx believed, economic relations form the basis for social structures, it is still necessary to examine those social structures carefully. Nor can economic relations be fully comprehended until elements of social, gender, race, and class relations are introduced. Family and gender relations, race, and subordination have all played key roles in the development of Latin American politics and economics. The subordinate position of indigenous peoples, Afro-Latins, and women has conditioned politics and been conditioned by them. Class is of equal importance, given the hierarchical nature of the societies that developed. The authors believe familiarity with these issues is necessary and thus have included one chapter on indigenous and African peoples (Chapter 4) and a second that explores the status of women and gender roles (Chapter 6).

The rise of fundamentalism in domestic politics in the United States, the Islamic resurgence in a variety of Muslim countries, and the rise of religious parties in India have once more brought religion to the center of the political stage. Yet in Latin America, the role of the Catholic Church and religion has always been an important factor in politics. For five centuries, the Church has remained the bulwark of the status quo in most countries. Yet, there have always been radicals in the Church who were not afraid to challenge entrenched political interests, even though most of the Church hierarchy usually worked hand and glove with the state. Such was the case in the sixteenth century with Chiapas Bishop Bartolomé de las Casas, who became a crusader against the enslavement of indigenous people. At the beginning of the nineteenth century two progressive priests waged the first phase of the mass-based independence movement in Mexico. Standing Marx on his head, the most original Marxist thinker in Latin America, José Carlos Mariátegui, argued that religion could be a revolutionary force. Stimulated by his thought and progressive theological trends in Europe, the Peruvian priest Gustavo Gutiérrez developed a radical new theology of liberation. The advent of liberation theology and growing support for the radical transformation of socioeconomic structures by the Conference of Latin American Bishops after 1968 made religion a major political force for change in many countries in the region. Priests supported guerrilla groups, resisted dictatorships, became guerrillas themselves, and, in the case of four priests in Nicaragua, became part of the Sandinista government. Lay people formed participatory Christian Base Communities and used their faith as a potent political force. Meanwhile, more conservative Protestant evangelical groups converted millions of the faithful. The new flock was often exhorted not to be involved in (radical) politics or to support fellow Protestant (and usually conservative) candidates. It is difficult to comprehend the dynamics of Latin American politics without understanding the religious forces and factions at work there. Thus the authors have also included a chapter on religion (Chapter 6).

Chapters 1–9 provide the context in which Latin American politics are played out. Different readers and instructors may choose to emphasize different areas; others may opt to also read an accompanying novel like Isabel Allende's *House of the Spirits, El Señor Presidente* by Miguel Angel Asturias, or Gabriel García Márquez's *One Hundred Years of Solitude*. Films and videos also illustrate many of these factors and bring figures like Juan and Eva Perón to life (*Evita*). The authors believe that astute students of the political game in Latin America must develop some appreciation for such background factors before they begin to focus on politics.

Most political scientists believe that politics concerns power and influence—how resources are allocated in a society. In his classic work, *Politics, Who Gets What When, How,* Harold Lasswell suggests that the study of politics is the study of influence and the influential. In a context that is particularly relevant to Latin America, he states that the "influential are those who get the most of what there is to get" and further adds that those who get the most are the elite, and the rest are the masses (Lasswell 1958, 13). He further invokes the early political economist David Ricardo to the effect that the distribution of wealth suggests one of the principal avenues of influence in a given society. Thus Lasswell notes that in the early part of the twentieth century, 2500 individuals in Chile owned 50 million of the 57 million acres of privately held land in the nation (17). That is, the large landowners were dominant economically and could use this base to influence—if not dominate—the political process. The study of politics and the subfield of comparative politics has evolved considerably since the time Lasswell originally wrote these pages (the 1930s). At that time he and other social scientists in the United States were more willing to focus on concepts of class and the domination of wealth. That was before the advent of the Cold War and the dichotomization of the world into two opposing camps, with social science often reflecting each camp's dominant values. Social science in Latin America has been much more willing to use class and Marxist concepts in its study of the Latin American reality. This is reflected in the work of many Latin Americanists outside the region as well. In the United States comparative politics evolved from traditional-legalistic approaches that looked at history and constitutions to behavioral approaches that looked at interest groups and voting behavior and other quantifiable political actions to explain politics, to postbehavioral approaches that came to include policy analysis, aspects of dependency theory, and world systems analysis, as well as a postmodern literary/cultural deconstructionist analysis. Currently, political scientists in the United States are focusing a great deal of interest on rational choice theory. Yet, those conceptual tools most frequently employed by Latin Americanists who focus on politics do not usually include deconstruction (although there are exceptions among literary-oriented Latin Americanists and Latin American intellectuals) or rational choice theory. Conceptual approaches most often and most successfully employed include elitist analysis, a pluralistic analysis of interest groups, mass organizations and others who exercise power in the political process, analysis of voting and political preferences where conditions allow for relatively clean elections and free expression of opinion, dependency analysis and political economy, and a careful consideration of powerful groups like the military or armed guerrilla groups that have the capacity to use force to take power or heavily influence policy decisions. All of these are employed in this work. The authors also rely on the approach to understanding Latin American power relations developed by Gary Wynia in *The Politics of Latin American Development*.

Latin Americanists have followed their own evolution. As suggested earlier, they have found political history to be of great importance. From this they extracted useful political concepts such as those of *caudillismo, golpe de estado* (coup d'état), and *junta*. These and similar concepts like authoritarianism and machismo are, nonetheless, explained well by the concept of political culture as developed in comparative politics in the 1960s, during the time when behaviorism was dominant. In that political values and beliefs in Latin America are generally so different from those found in Anglo-American political cultures, special treatment is given to general outlines of Latin American political culture in Chapter 5. Linking the development of political values to family, gender, race, and class relations as well as historic factors, the authors begin to define Latin American political culture in the second part of this chapter. Yet they do so in the confines imposed by class, authoritarian rule, and the use and abuse of power by those who rule. Later, the country chapter authors make frequent use of these concepts as they analyze the politics of individual countries. Of equal importance is a fundamental subtext in most writing about Latin American politics: Power rules, and absolute power rules absolutely. This is manifest in the title of a highly respected work on Guatemala by Richard Adams, *Crucifixion by Power*. Frequently it is not what the constitution says, it is the power of the dictator or the president to ignore the constitution, have congress amend it, or simply arrange for the nation's supreme court to make a favorable interpretation. Ultimately it may not be the constitution, elections, public opinion, civilian politicians, or the party system that decide the issues. Rather it may be a coup, as in Ecuador in 2000, or a political understanding with the military that allows the president to dismiss congress and the supreme court and rule on his own, as in Peru in 1992. In most Latin American countries there is always the possibility that naked power can and will be used. This has been the case since the conquistadores established their rule through brute force. Naked power—violence—can be used by the government to suppress the rulers' political enemies, by the military to take over the government or threaten to do so, or by armed opposition groups that contend for power through the use of arms. One is here reminded of Mao Zedong's oft-quoted dictum—"power flows out of the barrel of a gun." Even when democratic processes are being followed, the threat of the use of force is often present. Thus the military can often veto policy decisions by a civilian government, as was the case in El Salvador and Guatemala for many years; the oligarchy can threaten to mobilize their friends in the military on their behalf; or, as is the case in Nicaragua and Colombia, the opposition groups that grew out of revolutionary organizations can threaten to take up arms again. At the local level the amount of power a large landowner can wield may be a more important factor in local politics than the election of a reformist in the last election or the composition of the government. The local notable's power allows him to manipulate the policy process, control public officials, pay off the local police, or hire his own armed guards and also heavily influence the electoral process—indeed, most likely the reformer would have never been elected. Yet his power could be challenged by a well-organized popular organization like the Landless in Brazil or neutralized by the presence of an active guerrilla group like the Fuerzas Armadas Revolucionarias de Colombia (FARC) in Colombia.

In Latin America politics are dictated by power and the powerful. This book examines those who play the power game in separate chapters on political actors and political institutions (Chapter 8) and revolutions (Chapter 9). The way the game is played is conditioned by the historic, social, and economic factors mentioned previously, but it also has developed its own rules and practices. They are explored in these chapters, beginning with a discussion of how the constitution is often best described as an ideal to strive for rather than a basis for the rule of law.

Country chapters on Guatemala, Mexico, Argentina, Brazil, Chile, Cuba, and Nicaragua follow. They provide specific examples of how the power game is played in seven different Latin American nations. This is a representative—but not inclusive—sampling of the Latin American political reality. Each of the Latin American nation-states has developed its own way of conducting politics. Reference is made to some key events in the countries not included in the case studies, but it was not possible to fully explore the particular political nuances of all aspects of national politics in each country. Those who carefully study general trends and how they develop in the case studies will, however, have a good basis to explore how politics are conducted elsewhere in Latin America.

Bibliography

Adams, Richard. *Crucifixion by Power*. Austin: University of Texas Press, 1970.

Allende, Isabel. *House of the Spirits*. New York: A. Knopf, 1985.

Asociación Latinoamericano de Sociología, Centro de Estudios sobre America, Editorial Nueva Sociedad. *Sistemas políticos: poder y sociedad (estudios de caso en América Latina)* [Political Systems: Power and Society (Latin American Case Studies)]. Caracas: Editorial Nueva Sociedad, 1992.

Asturias, Miguel. *El Señor Presidente*. New York: Antheneum, 1987.

Eckstein, Susan, ed. *Power and Popular Protest, Latin American Social Movements*. Berkeley and London: University of California Press, 1989.

García Márquez, Gabriel. *One Hundred Years of Solitude*. New York: Harper & Row, 1970.

Lasswell, Howard D. *Politics: Who Gets What, When, How*. New York: Meridian Books, The World Publishing Company, 1958.

Mills, C. Wright. *The Power Elite*. New York and London: Oxford University Press, 1956.

Wynia, Gary. *The Politics of Latin American Development*. New York: Cambridge University Press, 1990.

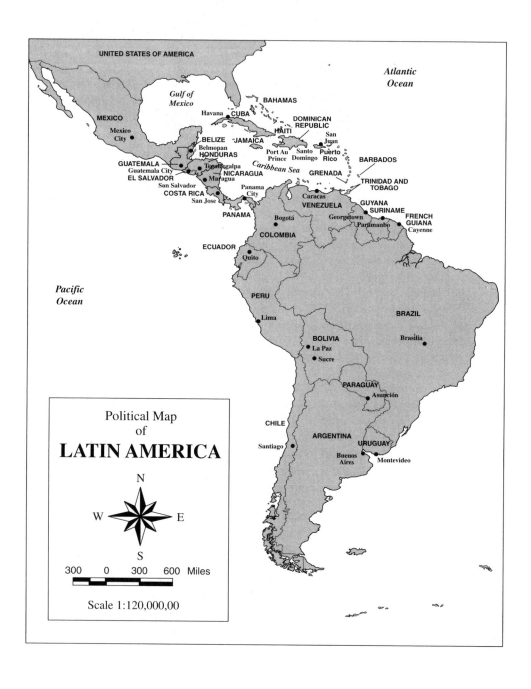

UNITED STATES OF AMERICA

Atlantic Ocean

Gulf of Mexico

BAHAMAS

Havana ● CUBA

DOMINICAN REPUBLIC

MEXICO

Mexico City ●

BELIZE   JAMAICA

HAITI

San Juan

Belmopan

Port Au   Santo   Puerto

Prince   Domingo   Rico

BARBADOS

HONDURAS

GUATEMALA

Caribbean Sea

GRENADA

Guatemala City   Tegucigalpa

EL SALVADOR   NICARAGUA

TRINIDAD AND TOBAGO

San Salvador   Managua

COSTA RICA

Panama City

San Jose

PANAMA

Caracas

VENEZUELA

GUYANA

SURINAME

FRENCH GUIANA

Bogotá   Georgetown

Paramanbo   Cayenne

COLOMBIA

ECUADOR

Quito

Pacific Ocean

PERU

Lima

BRAZIL

Brasília ●

BOLIVIA

La Paz ●

● Sucre

PARAGUAY

Asunción ●

CHILE

ARGENTINA

URUGUAY

Santiago ●

Buenos Aires

Montevideo

Political Map
of
LATIN AMERICA

N

W ✦ E

S

300   0   300   600   Miles

Scale 1:120,000,00

ONE

AN INTRODUCTION TO LATIN AMERICA (AS IT IS)

Latin America—a term coined by a Frenchman—is not a homogeneous part of the world that just happens to lie South of the border that runs from Florida to California. It is an immense world region that is striving to establish its place in the new global order.

A diverse area of thirty-four nations and peoples that includes Mexico, Central America, the Caribbean nations, and South America and surrounding islands, Latin America is home to some 500 million people (10 percent of the world's population) who well represent the rich racial and cultural diversity of the human family. Its people include Amero-Indians from pre-Colombian civilizations, such as the Incas, Aztecs, and Mayans; Europeans from such countries as Spain and Portugal (but also England, France, Holland, Italy, Poland, and Germany); Africans from West African areas such as what is now Nigeria, the Congo, and Angola, Jews from Europe and elsewhere; Arabs and Turks from countries such as Lebanon, Syria, Egypt, and Turkey; Japanese; Chinese; and different peoples from the Indian subcontinent. These and other racial and cultural groupings have combined to create modern nations rich in talent and variety. The dynamic way that the races have combined in Latin America even led one observer to predict that the Latin American region would be the birthplace of the fusion of the world's major racial groupings into a new *raza cosmica*—a cosmic race.

Latin America is a place where an Indian woman from Guatemala can be awarded the Nobel Prize, a Japanese president from Peru can receive the highest approval ratings in recent history, and an Arab can be elected president of Ecuador only to be replaced briefly by his female vice president.

Latin American still has places where the siesta follows the large mid-day meal. More commonly, the modern Latin American has a heavy meal in an urban setting and returns to the job for a full afternoon of work. The rapid pace of urbanization, commercialization, industrialization, and political mobilization continue to radically change the face of the region. Colombia, Nicaragua, Brazil, and Costa Rica still gear much of their economies around

Table 1. Basic Statistics for Latin America, Canada, and the United States

Countries	Estimated Total Population (Thousands) (1998)	Annual Population Growth Rate (%)	% Urban Population	Cities with 100,000 or More Inhabitants*	Per Capita Gross National Product (1998) (US$)†	Life Expectancy (Years)	Literacy Rate (%)	Female Economically Active Rate (%)†	Infant Mortality (per 1000 live births)
Argentina	36,123	1.3	88.9	32	8030	73.3	96	41	20.9
Bolivia	7957	2.3	63.1	7	1010	61.7	83	60	59
Brazil	165,158	1.3	80.1	189	4630	67.2	85	53	39.8
Chile	14,824	1.3	84.3	20	4990	75.4	95	36	11.1
Colombia	37,685	1.6	74	28	2470	71	91	54	24
Costa Rica	3650	2.1	50.9	3	2770	76.9	95	39	11.8
Cuba	11,115	0.4	77.1	11	—	76.1	97	41	7.2
Dominican Republic	8232	1.7	63.9	2	1770	71	82	41	45
Ecuador	12,175	2	61	15	1520	69.9	90	52	39.4
El Salvador	6059	2.3	46	8	1850	69.6	79	41	40
Guatemala	11,562	2.6	39.8	3	1640	67.4	64	24	37.7
Haiti	7534	2.1	33.7	3	410	54.5	45	49	74
Honduras	6147	2.7	45.7	3	740	69.9	80	40	42
Nicaragua	4464	2.6	63.7	1	370	68.4	66	34	47
Panama	2767	1.6	56.9	2	2990	74	91	43	16.1
Paraguay	5222	2.6	54.6	4	1760	69.8	91	53	36
Peru	24,797	1.7	72	17	2440	68.5	90	56	43
Puerto Rico	3807	1	74.4	14	—	76.6	90	37	9
Uruguay	3239	0.6	90.9	1	6070	72.9	97	49	17.5
Venezuela	23,242	2	86.8	41	3530	72.9	93	46	22
NAFTA Countries									
Canada	30,194	0.9	76.9	66	19,170	79	99	58	5.6
Mexico	95,831	1.63	74	78	3840	72.6	90	39	23.4
United States	273,754	0.8	81.8	210	29,240	76.8	99	60	7

Source: Pan American Health Organization, *Basic Country Health Profiles for the Americas,* 1999 (online: http://www.paho.org/english/sha/profiles.htm)

*United Nations Statistical Division, *Capital Cities and Cities of 100,000 or More Inhabitants,* 1995 (online: http://www.un.org/Depts/unsd/demog/index.htm)

†World Bank, *World Development Indicators,* 2000 (online: http://worldbank.org/data/wdi2000/pdfs/ta1_1.pdf)

the export of excellent coffee. Meanwhile, Mexico is making more and more cars and automobile components for the new North American Free Trade Agreement (Mexico, Canada, and the United States); Brazil is selling its passenger planes, jet trainers, and modern fighter aircraft on the international market; new clothing assembly plants are moving to Nicaragua; and Costa Rica is exporting software for hospital administrations.

Latin America and the Caribbean constitute an enormous and extremely rich region. The area ranges from the Bahamas, Cuba, and Mexico in the North to Argentina and Chile's southern tips in Tierra del Fuego some 7000 miles to the south. *El continente*, as the region is called by many of its Spanish-speaking inhabitants, is extremely diverse in geography and population. It encompasses hot humid coastal lowlands, steamy interior river basins, tropical rainforest, highland plateaus, coastal deserts, fertile lowlands, and high mountain peaks of some 8000 meters (24,000 feet).

The term *Latin America* is an ingenious attempt to link together most of this vast area. Strictly speaking, it refers to those countries in the Western Hemisphere south of the United States that speak Spanish, Portuguese, and French.[1] In a more general sense, it also includes the English- and Dutch-speaking Caribbean and South America and Belize in Central America.[2] The focus of this book will be on the Latin part of the region, although the English- and Dutch-speaking countries will be included in many of the maps and tables and are occasionally referred to for the sake of comparison.

Geography

Latin America is huge and diverse; it runs from 32.5° North latitude to 55° South latitude. With a total area of 8 million square miles (20 million km^2), it is one of the largest regions of the world. Taken on whole, it is almost as large as the United States and Canada combined and is larger than Europe.

The climatic and topographic diversity of Latin America is remarkable. Its range of environments is greater than in North America and Europe: rainforests, savanna grass lands, thorn scrub, temperate grass lands, coniferous forests, and even deserts. Plateaus extend down from the United States into Mexico and Central America. The Andes are found from the Caribbean island of Trinidad to Tierra del Fuego in the southern tip of South America and are the largest mountain chain on earth. They are most prominent as they parallel the West Coast of South America. Many peaks are over 18,000 feet; Mount Aconcagua in Northern Chile reaches 24,000 feet and is the highest point in the Western Hemisphere. Snow-capped peaks can be found from Venezuela in northern South America to Argentina and Chile in the south. A fault line that runs from California through the middle of Mexico and Central America and down the West Coast of South America makes the region prone to earthquakes. Volcanoes are found in Mexico, the Caribbean, and Central and South America. Other major geographic areas include the Guiana Highlands in northern South America, the Brazilian highlands, and the pampas in the south. River systems include the Orinoco in the north, the

Physical Map
of
LATIN AMERICA

N

W — E

S

400   0   400   800 Miles

Scale 1:120,000,00

Río de la Plata in the south, and the mighty Amazon in the middle of the South American continent.

Even at the same latitude, one can find very different climates. Altitudinal zonation, as this phenomenon is called, refers to the range in altitude from sea level to thousands of feet that occurs as you travel as few as fifty miles horizontally. It makes for very different climates. Land from sea level to 3000 feet is termed *tierra caliente*; from 3000–6000 feet, *tierra templada*; from 6000–12,000 feet, *tierra fría*; and above 12,000 feet, *tierra helada*, which experiences frost, snow, and ice through all or most of the year. Even close to the equator, the temperature cools 3.7° F for each 1000 feet of altitude. Although at the same latitude, Quito, the capital of Ecuador at 9300 feet, has an average annual temperature of 54.6° F, while Ecuador's largest city, Quayaquil, located on the coast, has an average temperature of 78.2° F. Each zone is suitable for different crops. *Tierra caliente*, when it is humid, is usually ideal for tropical fruits, while *tierra templada* is suited for growing crops like coffee, potatoes (which can be grown up to 11,000 ft), corn, and coca plants. Because of the temperature variation, crops requiring very different climates, such as bananas (humid tropical lowlands) and coffee (cooler shaded highlands), can be grown in the same Caribbean island (Jamaica) or small Central American nation (Costa Rica, Nicaragua, or Guatemala). It is interesting to note that there are some crops that are extremely adaptive and can grow at variety of altitudes. Corn is grown throughout Mexico, Central America, and the Andean region and formed an essential part of the classical Aztec, Mayan, and Incan economies. Coca cultivation has remained an essential part of agriculture in the area occupied by the Incan empire (concentrated in Peru, Bolivia, and Ecuador, but extending into Colombia, northern Chile, and Argentina). The cultivation and consumption of coca leaves was an essential part of indigenous culture in most of the Andean region since pre-Incan times. The coca plant can live up to forty years and produces the best leaves for chewing when grown at altitudes of 3000–4000 feet. Coca thrives on the shaded areas of the eastern Andean slopes, but it also can be grown at much higher altitudes or in the dryer mountainous region such as the eastern Colombian Andes. It will also grow in hot humid rainforests at much lower elevations. The leaves are not as good from these latter locations, but this is a less important consideration when they are used for a newer economic activity—the production of cocaine.

The Amazon is the second longest river in the world, carrying more water than any other. It runs from the jungles of eastern Peru for some 3900 miles to its mouth on the Atlantic Ocean. Large riverboats and many ocean-going ships with a draft of fourteen feet or less can go as far as Iquitos, Peru, where they still transport all the heavy cargoes for that jungle city.

Once There Were Rainforests

During the first century, tropical rainforests covered 5 billion acres on our planet and represented 12 percent of the land surface. In the last 100 years alone, more than half that forest has been actively destroyed. The deforestation is extensive. According to one study, the size of the deforested areas rose from 78,000 square kilometers in 1978 to 230,000 square kilometers in 1988. By the mid 1990s, the annual deforestation rate was 15,000 square kilometers per year and may be continuing to rise. As we begin the new millenium, over 50 million acres of tropical rainforest are lost every year. In Latin America, the Amazon basin alone houses the largest tropical rainforest in the world and contains one-fifth of the earth's fresh water, 20 percent of the world's bird species, and 10 percent of the world's mammals. More than 50 percent of the planet's oxygen is produced by the trees and plants in the area.

In 1964 a military government staged a coup and displaced the civilian government in Brazil. During their two decades in power the development-minded military leadership built the trans-Amazon highway and embarked on a policy of exploiting the resources in the Amazon basin and encouraging settlement. During the 1960s, Peru's civilian president Fernando Belaunde Terry tried a similar developmentalist strategy for Peru's jungle area that lay on the eastern side of the Andes. However, most of the Peruvian settlers found the jungle's Green Wall[3] much more impenetrable than did their Brazilian counterparts. In Brazil the migration into the Amazon was enormous. In 1960, there were 2.5 million people living in Brazil's six Amazon states. By the early 1990s, the population had grown to 10 million. There are more than 18 million landless people in Brazil. Thousands of landless peasants, rural workers, urban slum dwellers, entrepreneurs and well-healed Brazilian and foreign businessmen arrived each day to see how they could carve a fortune from the land and resources in the forest. The land is often crudely torn open to search for gold, iron ore, or other minerals in places like the huge open pit gold mine at Serra Pelada. Indigenous populations like the Yanomami are pushed further into the jungle and even shot if they resist the encroachment on their ancesteral lands. When other local inhabitants, like rubber trapper Chico Méndes, try to resist the brutal destruction of the rainforest they are often bullied by local officials, *fazenderos* (large landowners), or their hired henchmen or, as was Chico's fate, assassinated.

The rainforest problem in Brazil alone is enormous. In 1998 the Brazilian government released figures indicating that destruction of the Amazon rainforest reached record levels in the mid-1990s. In 1994 and 1995, for example, an area larger than the state of New Jersey (7836 square miles) was destroyed. Not only is the rainforest cut down, but in classical slash-and-burn fashion, the vegetation is burned to prepare the land for agriculture or pasture. This means that not only are thousands of oxygen-producing trees lost every year, but enormous amounts of carbon dioxide are released into the atmosphere when the biomass is burned. This process is also accelerating in Central America and the rainforest in southern Mexico. Since 1960 almost 50 percent of Central American forests have been destroyed. Environmentalists see the resultant drastic reduction in oxygen production and dramatic increase in carbon dioxide as significant causal factors in the greenhouse effect linked to global warming.

As Latin America strives to develop and as its population grows, its ecosystems are put under increasing stress. In Haiti the ecosystem has suffered severe stress because of the intense population density. Most of the trees have been cut down for building materials and firewood, and the number of birds and other dependent species has been reduced drastically. In Haiti and elsewhere, the commercialization of agriculture, demographic pressure, and policies that favor large commercial producers over small peasant farmers are also combining to increase land degradation. Deforestation, overgrazing, and overexploitation of the land are endangering entire ecosystems throughout the region. Desertification is advancing. It has been estimated that desertification and deforestation alone have affected about one-fifth of Latin America. As of 1995, some 200 million hectares of land—almost a third of the total vegetated land—were moderately or severely degraded.

The People

Latin America is endowed with enormous human resources. Its more than 500 million people come from all corners of the globe and are rich in their diversity and skills. Fertility rates are high in Latin America, and population growth rates have been some of the highest in the world. Currently these rates have declined to about 2 percent per year. Even at this rate, the population will double approximately every thirty-five years.

The original inhabitants of the region crossed to the Western Hemisphere on the Bering land and ice bridge that once united Asia and North America. This happened some 20,000–35,000 years ago during the Ice Age. The Asian migration flowed into North America and then spread into the Caribbean and through Central America to South America. Varied indigenous civilizations grew up throughout the region. By the time the Spaniards and Portuguese arrived in the late 1400s and early 1500s at least 50 million indigenous people lived in the region (some estimates are more than double this figure). Population concentrations included the Aztec civilization in Central Mexico, the Mayans in southern Mexico and northern Central America, and the Inca empire in the west coast central Andean region in South America. Other groupings could be found throughout the region, including the Caribs, Tainos, Arawaks, Guaraní, and Araucanian. These peoples and their civilizations will be discussed more fully in the following chapter.

The Spanish and Portuguese were the first Europeans to arrive in Latin America. As they came in ever-increasing numbers they began to populate the region as well. Informal and formal unions between Iberian men and indigenous women soon produced offspring who came to be known as *mestizos*. Later, as the native Amero-Indian population was drastically decimated and additional inexpensive labor was needed, Africans were brought to the hemisphere as enslaved peoples. At least 7 million survived the Middle Passage from western and southern Africa to Latin America and the Caribbean. The culture, religion, and cuisine they brought with them would forever change the face of the societies they helped to form. Indians, Europeans, and Africans populated Latin America during the first centuries. The fact that early Spaniards and Portuguese came without their families and claimed access to women in subordinant positions began a process of racial melding that continues to the present day. These pairings and their children were thrown together in dynamic new societies. *Mestizos, mulattos,* and *zambos* (the children of unions between Indians and Africans) appeared in growing numbers.

Most Latin Americans trace their ancestory to Amero-Indian, Iberian, and/or African ancestory. However, by the middle of the nineteenth century, there was a general realization that new laborers, artisans, and those with other skills could add to the growing nations. Most nations had outlawed slavery by the time of the Civil War in the United States. Brazil was the last; slavery was outlawed there in 1888. Thus other sources of abundant and inexpensive labor were often needed. Chinese laborers were brought into Peru in the later part of the nineteenth century. Thousands of Italians were lured to Argentina and southern Brazil to supply the labor for the growing agriculture and industrial production. Workers and indentured servants from India and the Chinese mainland were brought to the British Caribbean. Many Europeans came to their colonies or former colonies, or from other nations to make their way in these new societies. French, Germans, Swedes, Irish, Poles, and others from Europe arrived on Latin American shores to make a better life or as refugees from famine, uprising, and revolution. European Jews came to seek opportunity and escape pogroms and persecution. Japanese came to southern Brazil and to other countries like Peru for better opportunities, often with their passages paid by the Japanese government (which wanted to alleviate population pressures on the home islands). Turks and Arabs came to explore new horizons. As the United States expanded its economic sphere into Latin America and the Caribbean, some U.S. citizens chose to stay in the lands where they went to make their fortunes. One, an early aviator who came to Peru, stayed to found what was that nation's best known private airline—Faucett. The Spanish Civil War began a new wave of immigration from Spain and other countries taken over by the Fascists. Many Jews and others targeted by the Nazis owe their lives to the liberal immigration and visa policies of Latin American nations. (Ironically, as World War II was ending, Nazis, Fascists, and accused war criminals were often able to take advantage of these same liberal immigration policies and Argentine neutrality during World War II to make their way to countries like Argentina or Paraguay.) Today, new immigrants from the former Soviet Union and elsewhere continue to arrive to make their places in these dynamic new societies.

The Land

When the first Europeans arrived in the Western Hemisphere they found abundant land and resources. Most of the native peoples incorporated the concept of the Incan earth mother Pachamama, the giver of all life. The land was a sacred trust to be used with respect and care and was not the property of any one person. Land either existed in a state of nature or was used or owned collectively by and for the whole community. It was never to be harmed or destroyed and was always to be used for the benefit of all creatures. Thus the native people used but did not abuse the land. Early reports suggest that food was in abundance and was generally well distributed to the entire population.

The regime that the Iberians brought was far different. The crown, not the earth mother, was sovereign. Lands that had been inhabited by native peoples for thousands of years were unhesitatingly claimed for Spain and Portugal. Those who had been living on the land and working it were thought to have only those rights granted by the crown. Europeanization had begun. Hereafter, the land was to be used, owned, and abused for the benefit of the crown or its subjects. The native peoples, their needs, and their descendants were and would continue to be secondary and subordinate. The land and the people who lived in harmony with it would no longer be respected. There were empires to be carved and fortunes to be made.

At the time of the conquest Spain and Portugal were very much dominated by feudal institutions. The landowning system was no exception. Both countries were dominated by huge feudal estates and powerful landlords. The peasants were poor and subordinate. This would be the basis of the system brought to the newly conquered lands. Initially the Spanish and Portuguese monarchs gave huge land grants and grants to use the native peoples in a specific area. The *mercedes* (land grants; *sesmarias* in Brazil) and *encomiendas* (right to use the native peoples and the land on which they lived as long as the *encomendero* took responsibility for Christianizing the natives) were given to the *conquistadores* and others to whom the crown owed favors or debts. Thus Europeans soon established domain over huge stretches of land and the people who lived on them. These initial grants were later turned into large landed estates, or *latifundios*, which were not too different from the huge feudal landed estates in the Iberian peninsula. Often ranging for hundreds of thousands of acres, they were frequently larger than whole counties. They were ruled over by the *patrón* and his family who were the undisputed masters. The lowly *peon* was like a feudal serf and had little if any power or recourse, even after protective laws had been enacted. From colonial time to the present, the land tenure system reflected the nature and power configuration of the whole society. Well into the twentieth century the subordinate status of the peasant and agriculture laborer was maintained. Vestiges of this system were still in evidence in the 1970s. In many areas the humble *campesino* was expected to approach the *patrón* with eyes cast down, bowing and scraping. As late as the 1960s, there were still instances of what had became a widespread practice in colonial times: *primera noche/prima nocta*, the right the landlord had to spend the first night with newly married women on his estate.

In time many of the *latifundios* were divided or otherwise changed and became modern-day large landholdings: *haciendas, fazendas* (in Brazil), and *estancias* (in Argentina). Still owned by one family and comprising hundreds if not thousands of hectares (1 hectare = 2.47 acres), these farms still control a disproportionate amount of the land and resources in the countryside. Their continued existence attests to the concentrated nature of land ownership in Latin America.

The original indigenous population and later the mestizos, Africans, mulatoes and Europeans who became *campesinos* (anyone who owns or has control over the small or medium-size land parcels they work) were left with the rest. Their holdings were never large and were further reduced by division through inheritance, illegal takings by large landowners, or the need to sell off part of the land to survive. The resulting small land holdings, or *minifundios*, were and are the most common type of agricultural unit. Comprising less than ten hectares (24.71 acres), these small family farms afford a meager living during good times and near starvation during bad. In Colombia, traditionally they accounted for 73 percent of the farms, yet they covered only 7.2 percent of the agricultural area. In Ecuador in 1954, .04 percent of the landholdings accounted for 45.2 percent of the farmland; in contrast, the *minifundios* comprised 73 percent of the landholdings, but only had 7 percent of the land. In Guatemala as per the 1979 agrarian census, less than one-tenth of 1 percent of the landholdings comprised 22 percent of the land, while the largest 2 percent of the farms had 65 percent of the land. In El Salvador in 1971 4 percent of the landowners (the *latifundistas*) owned 64 percent of the land, and 63 percent of the landowners (the *minifundistas* and *microfundistas*) had only 8 percent of the land. At the beginning of the 1980s 40.9 percent of rural families were landless altogether. And land concentration is still continuing in many areas. In Brazil 70 percent of the rural population did not own any land at all, but 1 percent of the country's farms (*fazendas*) occupied 43 percent of the arable land in the 1950s. This inequity continued and later engendered a growing movement of the Sem Terra— the Landless—in the 1980s. Their occupations of unused land have often met with brutal repression by local authorities and the *fazendero's* hired gunmen. (See Table 2.) The conflict was so intense that some 1600 Brazilians have been killed in land disputes since 1985.

The process of the fractionalization of small holdings has continued. The *microfundio*, a very small farm of less than two hectares, is unable to sustain a family. The food and income from this small holding must be supplemented by income from outside labor by one or more family members. The capitalization and commercialization of agriculture have put even greater stress on the *microfundistas* and many of the *minifundistas*. The reduction in demand for rural labor has forced many to abandon their holdings and flee to the cities in hope of better opportunities. In recent times, large-scale agricultural production has undergone a transformation. The heavy reliance on cheap labor and abundant land in the absence of mechanization is rapidly giving way to more capital-intensive production that relies on mechanization and more intensive use of irrigation (where necessary), chemical fertilizers, and the application of insecticides by aerial spraying. As has been the case in U.S. agriculture, land is also in the process of being consolidated into

Table 2. *Minifundios* and *Latifundios* in Select Countries: Traditional Landholding Patterns (1970)

	Minifundios		Latifundios	
	% of farms	% of land	% of farms	% of land
Argentina	43.2	3.4	0.8	36.9
Brazil	22.5	0.5	4.7	59.5
Colombia	64.0	4.9	1.3	49.5
Chile	36.9	0.2	6.9	81.3
Ecuador	89.9	16.6	0.4	45.1
Guatemala	88.4	14.3	0.1	40.8
Peru	88.0	7.4	1.1	82.4

Source: Michael Todaro, *Economic Development in the Third World*, 2nd ed. (New York: Longman, 1985), p. 295.

larger units that can most benefit from the efficiencies of large-scale production. This has signaled a move from the traditional agricultural economy to an integrated capitalist mode of production.[4] The large plantations and commercial farms devote more and more of their production to cash crops that are sold on the world market, while the production of basic foodstuffs for local consumption more frequently occurs on the small farms. Not surprisingly, the production of corn and grains for local consumption is decreasing amidst growing malnutrition. Fewer of the poor have the funds to augment their consumption of staples. Groups such as OxFam, Bread for the World, and Food First have noted the decrease in protein consumption among the poor with increasing alarm. More and more land is being used for the production of beef for export. Yet few of the poor are able to afford beef or other meats more than a few times a year.

Although Latin America is industrializing and urbanizing at an amazing rate, agriculture is still very important. In 1990 agriculture still accounted for 40 percent of the exports for the region. The capitalization of agriculture that has buttressed the consolidation and reconcentration of the land has radically decreased opportunities for labor and sharecropping in the countryside. Thirty-nine percent of the rural population in Brazil is now landless. There are also high incidences of landlessness is Colombia, Ecuador, Guatemala, and Peru. Consequently there are fewer opportunities for peasants and landless laborers to sustain themselves. Currently more than 60 percent of the rural population live in poverty. Global economic forces are driving people off the land in record numbers. In Brazil many flee to the Amazon region to mine gold or engage in a cycle of slash-and-burn agriculture that pushes them ever farther into the virgin forest. More generally, new rural refugees flock to the cities, where they try to establish themselves in the growing shantytowns that ring large urban centers.

The Cities Explode: Urbanization

Latin America is no longer the land of sleepy peasants and small villages. It has changed dramatically. Some three-quarters of the population now live in urban areas (see Table 1), compared to 41.6 percent in 1950. There are three cities in Latin America that are now larger than New York City. Mexico City alone has more than 20 million people and is the largest city in the world. São Paulo, Brazil, has 16 million, and Buenos Aires, the capital of Argentina, has more than 12 million. By 1990 Latin America had forty cities with 1 million or more inhabitants. This was more than Canada and the United States combined. More than 130 million Latin Americans live in these modern megalopolises, as compared to fewer than 100 million in the United States. Urban areas in Latin America continue to explode with new people as more children are born and as millions flock to the bright city lights each year. Municipal services can in no way keep up with the steady stream of new arrivals. The streets are clogged with all types of vehicular traffic, and the air is polluted by the thousands of cars, trucks, and buses. Mexico City has some of the most polluted air in the world. Oxygen is sold at booths on the street. Thousands suffer and many die from pollution-induced respiratory problems. With more than 20 million residents, Mexico City is immense and unmanageable. The quality of life for all too many of its residents is marginal. Nor is it easy to escape. It can take more than two hours to traverse it. With more than 16 million residents, São Paulo, Brazil, suffers from the same problems and has an even higher urban crime rate. Other cities seem headed in this direction. As the growing middle class exercises its consumers' right to own private vehicles, gridlock is the norm in rush hour and parking is often near impossible. The impoverished masses endure long hours on crowded buses and vans. The congestion is sometimes alleviated by subways, but they rarely cover more than a few areas of the city and cannot keep up with the growing number of new neighborhoods and urban squatter settlements.

Often a third or more of the population in the large cities live in slums and shantytowns. Of the 22 million people in greater São Paulo, close to 8 million live in the *favelas*, as the urban slums are called in Brazil. Because many of these new agglomerations often grow up quickly as unused land is illegally occupied, city services are often minimal or unavailable altogether. Living conditions are frequently horrible, with no running water, sewer, or trash collection (see Table 7 in Chapter 5). Sometimes the only electricity is provided by illegal taps to lines that run close to the neighborhood. Crime and violence are often at uncontrollable levels. Little if any police protection is available in most of the larger slums, and poor neighborhoods are often infiltrated by drug gangs and other types of organized crime. These areas are referred to as *barriadas, pueblos jovenes, villas de miseria,* or *tugurvios* in different Spanish-speaking countries and as *favelas* or *mocambos* in Brazil. They continue to grow dramatically. In these places, there is an abundance of misery, and hope is often in short supply.

Originally towns in Spanish America were planned around gracious central plazas, often called the *Plaza de Armas* or *zócalo*. Here one would find a pleasant plaza with the church or cathedral, government buildings, and the palaces of prominent officials ringing it. Others of means and social standing would occupy neighborhoods adjacent to the center. The outskirts of the cities were reserved for the poor and marginalized. However, the once-majestic colonial centers are now generally overwhelmed with traffic problems and pollution. Towns in Portuguese America were not always planned affairs; often they grew up around a fort or business center and then just grew. In all of Latin America, the worst slums are still generally found on the periphery of the cities, although poor neighborhoods and scattered makeshift dwellings can also be found inside traditional cities, as is the case in Rio de Janeiro. Many of the wealthy and upper middle class have also begun to flee the centers to populate more removed attractive, exclusive neighborhoods characterized by high-walled luxurious houses and high-rise condominiums staffed by numerous servants, well-armed private guards, and easy access to the newest in Latin American consumerism—the mall. Suburban-style *urbanizaciones* are also being constructed to cater to the housing needs of the rest of the growing middle class, which is also flocking to shopping centers and malls in growing numbers. The contrast between the lives of the urban poor and their middle- and upper-class fellow urbanites becomes ever more stark each day.

Ironically, many are afraid to shop outside of the privately guarded malls and shopping centers. Fed by deteriorating socioeconomic conditions for the poor, urban crime and delinquency have grown dramatically in recent years. One can see the homeless and the hustlers living and sleeping on the streets in most of the major cities. Many middle- and upper-class drivers are even afraid to stop at traffic lights—particularly at night—in many areas for fear they will be robbed at knife or gunpoint or even by street children who threaten with broken shards of glass. Sometimes the merchants and the police take matters into their own hands. Brazil in particular has become infamous for the way street children have been beaten, run off, and even killed in groups to clear the area and discourage their perceived criminal activity. Some 5 percent of Brazil's children live in the streets. Of these, more than 4000 were murdered between 1988 and 1991. Even Charles Dickens' impoverished souls would find life hard in the modern Latin American city.

Throughout Latin American society crime and violence are growing. Economic and social disparities, the suffering caused by International Monetary Fund–dictated economic adjustments and austerity, the ravages of globalization, narco-trafficking, and the fallout from the guerrilla wars that have raged throughout the region all add to the general level of violence, which is now very high. For instance, El Salvador has one of the highest murder rates in the world at 140 per 100,000 per annum. Colombia is close behind at 80 murders per 100,000, while Brazil has 20 per 100,000. The cost in human suffering and lives is horrendous, and the economic cost is staggering. In 1998 the head of the Inter-American Development Bank reported that violence cost the region about $168 billion per year, or 14.2 percent of the regional economic product. Just in Brazil, the cost was $84 billion, or 10.5 percent of the gross domestic product. The figure for Colombia was 24.7 percent. The resultant personal insecurity and added economic expense weigh heavily on the region's future and cloud its growing dynamism. The problem, and its causes, will need to be addressed before the region can realize its full potential.

Yet the growing personal insecurity and environmental degradation that the region is suffering would seem to contradict an essential tenet of Latin American life—"*Hay que gozar de la vida*": Life is to be enjoyed. Many Latin Americans note that North Americans (meaning those of us who are from the United States) live to work and worry much too much about things. In contrast, Latin Americans work to live and *no se preocupan tanto*—don't worry so much. Whenever there is a bare modicum of economic security—and sometimes even when there is not—they live very well indeed. Life is an enjoyable experience to be savored. One rarely turns down an invitation to a social gathering and frequently enthusiastically dances till dawn at a *fiesta*. Of those with any means, it is common practice to stop for a coffee or lunch with friends and family, and most business meetings begin with a *cafecito* and talk of family and friends. Indeed, work is generally not the all-consuming activity it has become in the United States, Japan, and parts of Western Europe. But when the pollution from the street makes it difficult to sit in sidewalk cafés and the frequency of attacks on nocturnal travelers make it dangerous to go out at night, the very essence of the Latin American existence is challenged. Many are even afraid to leave their houses unattended or in the hands of poorly paid servants because of the frequent break-ins and house takeovers. In countries like Colombia, Guatemala, and El Salvador and in cities like Mexico City any person of means or position must also live in fear of kidnapping for ransom. Thus rapid urbanization, industrialization, and the persistence of unresolved social and economic problems such as high unemployment, exploitation, and economic injustice have combined with rapid social and cultural change to produce conditions that threaten the very essence of the Latin American lifestyle. And yet the indomitable Latin American spirit and passion for life propel the continent ever onward.

Notes

1. Latin here refers to modern languages that were derived from classical Latin: Spanish, Portuguese, and French in this case. Haiti is included as part of the region (indeed, it was the first country to gain independence—in 1804) and receives its fair share of attention and interest. Those areas still under French colonial rule receive much less attention. French colonies in Latin America include the Caribbean islands of Martinique, Guadeloupe, Saint Martin, and Saint Pierre and Miquelon and French Guyana (site of Devil's Island) on the South America continent.

2. Although we will generally not include those areas that do not speak Spanish, Portuguese, or French in our study, it should be noted that the English-speaking part of the region includes not only Belize in Central America and Guyana in South America but also the Caribbean countries of the Bahamas, Barbados, Dominica, Grenada, Jamaica, Saint Kitts-Nevis, Saint Lucia, Saint Vincent and the Grenadines, and Trinidad and Tobago; English-speaking territories include Anguilla, Bermuda, Cayman Islands, the Faukland Islands (Argentina claims as Islas Malvinas), Monserrat, Turks and Caicos Islands, the British Virgin Islands, and the U.S. Virgin Islands. Dutch is spoken in the South American nation of Surinam and in the Caribbean Dutch islands of islands of Aruba, Curaçao, Bonaire, Saba, Saint Eustatius, and Saint Martin.

3. See the award-winning 1970 Peruvian film *La Muralla Verde* (written, produced, and directed by Armando Robles Godoy and Mario Robles Godoy) for a graphic depiction of the struggle with the jungle.

4. Because of the feudal nature of the original *latifundio* system and the way many small producers were primarily subsistence farmers who sold little if any of their production for the world market, many spoke of a dual rural economy with aspects of both feudal and capitalist modes of production. The integration into the capitalist world system that authors like Andre Gunder Frank emphasized in his *Capitalism and Underdevelopment in Latin America* (1967) has now become almost universal as the large farmers and plantations become ever more oriented to the production of cash crops for export and more and more of the smaller farmers are forced to sell their labor in the globalized national economy in order to survive.

Bibliography

Black, Jan Knippers, ed. *Latin America, Its Problems and Promise*. 3rd ed. Boulder, CO: Westview Press, 1998.

Blouet, Brian W., and Olwyn M. Blouet. *Latin America and the Caribbean, A Systematic and Regional Survey*. 3rd ed. New York: John Wiley and Sons, 1997.

Burch, Joann J. *Chico Mendes, Defender of the Rain Forest*. Brookfield, CT: Millbrook Press, 1994.

Dimenstein, Gilberto. *Brazil: War on Children*. London: Latin American Bureau, 1991.

Elkin, Judith. *The Jews of Latin America*. New York: Holmes and Meir, 1997.

Frank, Andre Gunder. *Capitalism and Underdevelopment in Latin America*. New York: Monthly Review, 1967.

Garrett, James L., ed. *A 2020 Vision for Food, Agriculture, and the Environment in Latin America*. Washington, DC: International Food Policy Research Institute, 1995.

Haralambous, Sappho, ed. *The State of World Rural Poverty, A Profile of Latin America and the Caribbean*. Rome: International Fund for Agricultural Development, 1993.

Hillman, Richard, ed. *Understanding Contemporary Latin America*. Boulder, CO: Lynne Rienner Publishers, 1997.

Janvry, Alain de. *The Agrarian Question and Reformism in Latin America*. Baltimore: Johns Hopkins Press, 1981.

Klich, Ignacio, and Jeffrey Lesser. *Arab and Jewish Immigrants in Latin America, Images and Realities*. London: F. Cass, 1998.

Levine, Robert. *Tropical Diasphora; the Jewish Experience in Cuba*. Gainesville: University Press of Florida, 1993.

Page, Joseph A. *The Brazilians*. New York: Addison-Wesley, 1995.

Preston, David, ed. *Latin American Development: Geographical Perspectives.* 2nd ed. Burnt Mill, Harlow, England: Longman, 1996.

Rifkin, Jeremy. *Biosphere Politics: A New Consciousness for a New Century.* New York: Crown Publishers, 1991.

Skole, D. L., and C. J. Tucker. "Tropical Deforestation, Fragmented Habitat, and Adversely Affected Habitat in the Brazilian Amazon: 1978–1988." *Science* 260:1905–1910. 1993.

Trigo, Eduardo J. *Agriculture, Technological Change, and the Environment in Latin America: A 2020 Perspective.* Washington, DC: International Food Policy Research Institute, 1995.

Vandermeer, John, and Ivette Perfecto. *Breakfast of Biodiversity, The Truth about Rainforest Destruction.* Oakland, CA: Food First, 1995.

Vasconcelos, José. *The Cosmic Race: A Bilingual Edition.* Baltimore: Johns Hopkins University Press, 1997.

FILMS AND VIDEOS

Bye, Bye Brazil. Brazil, 1980. A madcap introduction to Brazil.

Like Water For Chocolate. Mexico, 1992. Excellent portrait of Mexican family, food, and the daughter who stays at home to care for her mother.

Mexican Bus Ride. Mexico, 1951. Classic film by Spanish director Luis Buñuel on Mexico, life in Latin America and the institution of the bus in Mexico and Latin America.

La Muralla Verde/The Green Wall. Peru, 1970 (video, 1990). An excellent film about a young Lima family that fights the bureaucracy and the jungle's green wall to colonize the Peruvian Amazon.

Pejote. Brazil, 1981. Gives a glimpse of the life of street children in a large Brazilian city. For more general city life, *Central Station*, Brazil, 1998.

WEB SITE

http://lanic.utexas./edu   Latin American Center Homepage, University of Texas.

TWO

EARLY HISTORY

For many years people in the Western Hemisphere widely celebrated Columbus' 1492 "discovery" of what the Europeans called the "new world." Accordingly, Columbus Day is celebrated as a national holiday in the United States. More broadly, throughout the Americas the year 1992 was celebrated as the 500th anniversary of the discovery of "New World." But not all celebrated. Many native Americans banded together to solemnly mark the same period as 500 years of mourning because of the many injustices that the European invasion wrought on their people. Indeed, in the first 100 years of colonization, European rule attacked native religion and culture, razed temples and cultural centers to the ground, and forbade the practice of native religions. In so doing the colonists attacked the very essence of the original Americans, called Indians because Columbus and the original explorers mistakenly believed they had reached the East Indies. Colonization was, as the French Antillean author Frantz Fanon suggests, a brutal, violent imposition of European on native. The effect of European rule was so devastating to the native peoples of Latin America that their numbers were reduced by as much as 90 percent during the first 100 years of European occupation.

There are several versions of how the Iberians treated the native people they encountered. The indigenous version is one of conquest, domination, and subordination. Yet Spain maintained that it brought Christianity and Western civilization to the world *it* found. In contrast, England long propagated the Black Legend about the cruelties of Spanish colonial rule in the Americas and attributed much of the native population's decline to the barbarities they suffered at the hands of the Spaniards. Another explanation of this precipitous decline is found in several recent studies that make an ever stronger case for the disease theory of population decline—that is, the main cause of the radical decline in population of the original Americans was not the undeniable cruelty practiced by many of the Spaniards, but the unstoppable epidemics of smallpox, measles, typhus, and other diseases that swept through the native population. The first Americans had not, it seems, acquired any natural immunities to these and other diseases the Europeans brought with them. Thus they were ravaged by them. Many also argue this was the principal factor in the Spaniards' astounding conquest of millions of people with a few hundred *conquistadores*. Indeed, the diseases often spread so rapidly that they arrived before the Spaniards. Evaluating these different perspectives one might conclude that the story does indeed sometimes change over time, but that each new version adds to our understanding of the past. Not surprisingly, then, we find that our historical views of what happened in the sixteenth century are heavily colored not only by the cruelty that gave rise to the Black Legend, but also by our present understanding of epidemiology.

People in the Americas before the Conquest

To understand the historic context in which political power is exercised in Latin America we need to briefly trace the human past as it developed in the Americas. Human history did not begin when Europeans began arriving in the Western Hemisphere in large numbers after 1492. Indeed, the common ancestry of all racial groups who found their way to the Americas was neither European nor Asian. Currently, it is believed that the earliest humans emerged on the shores of Lake Victoria in Eastern Africa some 3 million years ago. The famous Leakey family of anthropologists' discovery of tools and bone fragments from our most ancient human predecessors suggests the African birthplace of our species. From there, it is believed, humans spread south in Africa and north to the Middle East, Asia, and eventually Europe. Later they crossed the land and ice bridge that spanned the Bering Strait during the Ice Age to move into the Americas.

INDIGENOUS CIVILIZATION

The movement of peoples from Asia to North America occurred in waves and began as early as 40,000 years ago. It continued until about 8000 B.C.E. These immigrants first populated the Western Hemisphere and were the first Americans. They swept down from Alaska and spread across North America and into the Caribbean and Central America; from there they spread down the west coast of South America and then eastward across the continent. As their productive forces increased, they moved from a nomadic existence to one of sedentary agriculture. By 1500 B.C.E. there were villages of full-time farmers. Corn, beans, and squash became staples in Mesoamerica (the Southern two-thirds of Mexico, all of Guatemala, and most of El Salvador, Belize, Honduras, and Nicaragua), while potatoes, manioc, and amaranth were dominant in areas of South America. The large numbers of different ethnic groups practiced sedentary or semisedentary agriculture. As they further developed their productivity they formed larger groups: tribes, chiefdoms, and states. This also led to more concentrated political power.

Native American settlements were scattered throughout the region. The population did, however, become concentrated in three areas: present-day Central Mexico, southern Mexico and northern Central America, and along the Pacific Coast and in the Andean highlands in what is now Peru, Bolivia, and Ecuador. Here agriculture production was sufficiently advanced to sustain a large, relatively concentrated population. Each of these areas eventually developed a dominant, centralized state civilization that came to be known respectively as Aztec, Mayan, and Incan. Smaller political groupings developed elsewhere.

Many aspects of these empires have influenced the culture and even the political organization of subsequent polities in these areas. In that little about these civilizations is usually included in most general courses, the following section presents a rudimentary description of their key aspects.

Large draft or meat animals that could be domesticated were not available to the native civilizations. In the west coast civilization in South America the guinea pig was domesticated as a source of food, and the llama was used as a pack animal and as a source of wool and meat. The Aztecs bred a small mute dog for food in Mexico. Unlike in Europe, there were no cattle, horses, or oxen.

The use of baskets and of stone, bone, and wood gave way to the development of pottery and more sophisticated stone (obsidian) weapons and tools and eventually to the use of bronze in the Aztec and Inca empires. In the first more developed societies to emerge such as the Olmecs and Toltecs in Mexico and the Mochica in coastal Peru, large temple-centered cities emerged. They were beautifully designed and employed sophisticated stone and adobe construction. Only in the thirteenth and fourteenth centuries did these city-centered societies begin to expand to form empires. They were still in a process of expansion when the Europeans arrived.

Our knowledge of these societies is incomplete, in part because there were few chronicles and inscriptions in Inca and pre-Inca civilizations on the west coast of South America and because many of the written texts, inscriptions, and chronicles that did exist for the Aztecs and Mayans were destroyed by the Europeans. The story of these peoples is only now being reconstructed through the laborious work of archaeologists and ethnologists from around the world.

The Mayans. Mayan Civilization flowered between 300 B.C.E. and 1100 A.D. During this time Europe witnessed the disintegration of the Roman Empire, the rise of the Holy Roman Empire, and the beginning of the Middle Ages. Mayan civilization consisted of a series of city-states that developed in the Petén region of northern Guatemala, the Yucatan, and Chiapas. Their cities later spread into Belize and part of Honduras and eventually numbered about fifty. The Mayans developed what was then a very sophisticated native civilization. Their political-social organization was, however, hierarchical, with a king, nobles and priests on top and the common people and slaves on the bottom; decision making was authoritarian.

In the original Mayan states the common people lived in thatched roof huts not unlike those of the poor Mayan peasants of today and nourished themselves on a balanced diet consisting of beans, corn, and squash. These crops could be cultivated in the same field. Planting the corn first ensured that it grew upward toward the all-important sun; the beans then used the stalk of the corn to follow the same path, while the broad leaves of the squash spread out on the ground to shade the soil from the desiccating rays of the sun and inhibit the growth of weeds. Further, the beans added nitrogen to the soil as the corn and squash removed it. The Mayan calendar also specified times when the land was to lie fallow. Terraces were used in highland areas to increase land area and stop soil erosion.

It is currently believed that the Mayan peasants paid tribute to the political and religious rulers in the cities. They in turn engaged in warfare with other city states to gain more riches and obtain additional tribute. They also established extended commercial relations with civilizations to the North, and even used the sea as a trade route.

In about 900 Mayan civilization suffered a rapid decline. The major cities and ceremonial centers were eventually abandoned to be reclaimed by the jungle. Current research suggests the causes for this disaster were probably the increasing wars among the Mayan states, civil wars, and soil exhaustion from overfarming, which had been induced by what evidently became unsustainable population density.

The Mayans' accomplishments in astronomy, mathematics, ideographic writing, architecture, and art and their highly sophisticated calendar mark them as one of the most developed civilizations of their time. They had incorporated advances in time-keeping from the Toltec and Olmec and employed the resultant extremely accurate 365-day calendar of eighteen twenty-day months and five additional days or dead days (which were considered unlucky). Their mathematical system used units of one, five, and twenty (which could be written as dots for ones, dashes for fives, and twenties denoted by position) and included a place value system employing a sign for zero. During their classical period, their calendar, astronomical observations, and use of zero as a place in written numbers marked their civilization as more advanced than any in Europe in these areas. Their hieroglyph-type writing recounted great events in their history and mythology and was carved or painted on their temples, pyramids, or upright stone *stelae* or was recorded in their bark paper *codices*. Recent research suggests symbols for syllables were also sometimes used to phonetically sound out words. Although only four of the original glyph codices survived, an early Spanish transcription of the Quiche Mayan creation story, the *Popol Vuh*, is now part of world literature. Mayan civilization thrived in the classic period from A.D. 250 to 900 in the lowlands in northern Central America and southern Mexico. Great city state centers like Tikal, Palenque, and Copan flourished.

Although there were occasional female rulers, the societies were patriarchal and the royal succession was decided through primogeniture. The kings and the nobles made up the ruling class but worked closely with the priests, who were also the astronomers and chroniclers as well as the theologians. Human sacrifice and blood-letting were integral parts of the ceremonial functions, with special importance placed on blood derived from puncturing the royal penis. The losers in a version of Mayan soccer were often beheaded or rolled down the steps of the great pyramids after being tied together as human balls.

Rising some 45 meters out of the jungle in the Petén region of Guatemala, the Temple of the Jaguar in Tikal is one of the greatest Mayan structures. Apparently used for ceremonial purposes, it dates from the Classical Mayan period and was constructed about 700 A.D. *(Photo by H. Vanden)*

Post-classical Mayan civilization lived on in the Yucatan centers like Chichén Itzá and Uxmal after other Mayan lands were conquered by the Spaniards beginning in 1527. As had been the case with the Aztecs, much of the remaining Mayan culture was destroyed by the Spanish authorities, who, despite some initial efforts by priests to preserve Mayan culture, eventually burned many invaluable Mayan *codices* as works of the devil, thus depriving the Mayan people of a good part of their history and heritage. Perhaps because of the strength and sophistication of culture, Mayan resistance to European domination lived on in more remote areas for centuries and bubbled to the surface occasionally. The Caste Wars in the Yucatan in the nineteenth century (isolated pockets of rebellion lasted into the twentieth century), the indigenous support for some guerrilla groups in the Guatemalan highlands in the 1980s, and the Zapatista uprising in Chiapas in the 1990s were more recent manifestations. Mayan languages are still spoken in these areas, and some religious practices are still honored.

The Aztecs. The Aztecs replaced previous native civilizations like that of Teotihuacan and the Toltecs in central Mexico and the Olmecs in eastern Mexico and incorporated many of the values, knowledge, and technology of their predecessors' cultures. By the time Cortés arrived in central Mexico in 1519, there were perhaps 25 million inhabitants in the region (there is some controversy as to the exact number here and elsewhere in the region). The Aztecs, who migrated from northern Mexico, arrived in the Valley of Mexico in the early 1200s. They were relegated to marshy land not occupied by any other ethnic group. There they established their capital, Tenochtitlán, on an island in Lake Texcoco about 1325. As their myths explain, they picked the spot because they saw the promised sign of an eagle clutching a snake perched atop a cactus (this symbol graces the Mexican flag).

The Aztec capital became very populous; it had between 150,000 and 200,000 inhabitants by the time of the conquest. As many as 60,000 came to an open air market each day. Aztec civilization was characterized by military prowess that extended control beyond the mountains ringing the Valley of Mexico through most of Central Mexico and as far south as the Guatemalan border. Once they subjugated other peoples, the Aztecs forced them to pay tribute, but did not directly occupy them save in times of rebellion. Their frequent military campaigns provided many prisoners from the loose-knit empire. Aztec traders and merchants ranged far and wide. The thriving merchant class lived well. There were large houses for the nobility and the priests, palaces for the emperor, monumental limestone-covered pyramids, temples and other public buildings, and thatched roof huts for the commoners. Agriculture and trade provided the economic base for the society, which had also developed a well-respected artisan class. The common people consumed corn, beans, and vegetables garnished with chili sauces as their daily meals. The nobility and emperor had diets that included abundant fowl, venison, and the drink reserved solely for them—chocolate. Aztec civilization excelled in engineering, architecture, astronomy, and mathematics. Based on earlier achievements of the Toltecs and Maya, the Aztecs adopted the same 365-day calendar, divided into eighteen months of twenty days, with five additional or hollow days added. The calendar also marked the beginning and end of religious rituals. A type of pictorial writing had been developed that was linked to some phonic elements and was found in their *codices*, or paperlike books. They did elaborate metal work in gold and silver, but not iron. Like other civilizations in the Americas, the Aztecs had not yet learned how to work hard metals and did not use the wheel, nor as noted before, had nature provided draft animals or beasts of burden.

Power was concentrated and vertical. The Aztec polity was a hierarchical theocracy headed by an emperor who was assisted by four great lords. Next came the politically powerful priests and nobles. The power of the ruler was not unlike that exercised by Mexican leaders in the last two centuries. The ruler exercised power absolutely and often despotically. The new Aztec emperor was chosen by a tribal council where priests, state officials, and warriors dominated. He was chosen from among the sons, brothers, or nephews of the previous ruler. When Hernán Cortés arrived in 1519 and began to subjugate the Aztecs, Moctezuma II was the ruler. He had succeeded his uncle.

By the late fifteenth century the number of private estates belonging to the nobles had begun to grow, with the subsequent conversion of small farmers into farm workers and tenant farmers. Slavery was a recognized institution and, as in African society, was used as a punishment for a variety of offenses. There was continuing incentive for the frequent wars and uprisings that occurred within the empire. The continuing conflicts provided an almost constant flow of prisoners, who were sometimes sold as slaves to be used as forced labor but were most often sacrificed in large numbers to Aztec deities like Huitzilopochli, the God of War.

Conflicts within the Aztec Empire hastened its demise. With the help of the Tlaxcalans and other Aztec enemies, the Spaniards (whose numbers never exceeded 600) finally defeated the last Aztec emperor, Cuauhtemoc, in 1521. This signaled the formal end of what had been a great, although autocratic, civilization. When the capital had been stripped of its gold and silver, Cortés ordered the temples burned and the city of Tenochtitlán razed. As a way of legitimizing European rule, orders were given to have Mexico City built on the ruins of the old city. It can be argued, however, that the hierarchical power configurations, brutality of those who ruled, and political patriarchy were part of the legacy that did survive and that they left indelible marks on subsequent society and the polities that emerged in the centuries that followed.

The Incas. The third great pre-Colombian civilization in the Americas at the time of the conquest was the Inca Empire. The Incas date their early development back to the 1200s but did not begin to expand into an empire until the middle of the fifteenth century. This expansion was led by a series of extremely capable Inca rulers. Outstanding among these was Pachacuti Inca Yupanqui (ruler from the late 1400s to 1525), who many consider one of the great rulers and conquerors in the annals of history. The empire was centered in the Andes mountains around the valley of Cuzco in southern Peru and eventually extended from what is now Colombia's southern border for 2250 miles through Ecuador, Peru, and Bolivia into northern Chile and northwest Argentina. At its zenith in the early 1500s, it was tied together by an excellent system of often narrow stone roads that facilitated communication and troop movement. A system of relay runners could carry messages at the rate of some 150 miles a day. The llama was used as a pack animal, but the wheel was not part of their technology. There was no written language, and history and events were kept by official memorizers. Also employed was the *kipu,* a memory device composed of a handle with cords of different colors attached to it. Knots were tied in the different color strands at different lengths to signify quantity and events.

The land was intensively tilled, and terraces were built in the highlands to improve and expand the fields. The cultivation of a variety of different types of potatoes (which originated in the Andes) was highly perfected, as was the cultivation of corn. The common people primarily ate potatoes and corn. The latter crop was also collected by the rulers as a form of tribute. A portion of the grain harvest was given to the state to be kept in state storehouses. It was distributed to the elderly, the infirm, and the widowed or dispensed to villages in times of famine or natural disaster. Coca leaves (which are still used today), beans, amaranth, and other crops were also grown.

The state was more developed than other pre-Colombian civilizations and was ruled by a semi-divine hereditary king called the Inca. Power was centralized in his hands, and he was assisted by other members of the royal family, the nobility, and the royal administrators who were responsible for running the far-flung empire. A lesser nobility also existed. The artisans and agriculturists were on the bottom of the social pyramid and lived in humble, adobe-sided thatched roof huts with simple furnishings. Priests and public officials also received grain from the storehouses, as did those pressed into public labor. The state owned or administered most of the society and could require voluntary labor on roads, other public works, or the land of the Inca or estate holders. Writers like the Peruvian indigenist thinker José Carlos Mariátegui have characterized this as a form of state socialism. Even today, there is still a strong communal heritage in the Indian villages in the Andes.

Some have also noted the importance of the collection of tribute in this system and have further suggested that, as was the case in the Aztec Empire, the tradition of tribute made it very easy for the Spaniards to also extract tribute from the indigenous population.

The Incan empire was administratively divided into four parts, with each part subdivided into provinces. The basic unit was the *ayllu*, which was organized around the extended family. Villages were formed by a collection of *ayllus*, and a grouping of these were ruled over by a *curaca*, or ethnic lord.

Like their Mayan and Aztec counterparts, the Incas had a developed theological system. They had a pantheon of gods beginning with Viracocha, the creator, and Inti, the sun god. Also included was Tumi, the god invoked in human sacrifice. They gave special attention to events like the summer solstice, which occasioned great ceremony and feasting. This is still a major festival in the Peruvian highlands.

The Incas excelled in pottery and weaving and had the proficiency to open the skull in a form of brain surgery. Their architecture was impressive and marked by their ability to move huge stones (on wooden rollers) that weighed tons and then carefully cut and fit them together without mortar. The Cuzco fortress of Sacsahuaman is an excellent example of this. In metallurgy they were quite proficient in their production of gold, silver, and copper, and they even made some of their tools from bronze. They did not, however, utilize iron.

Less Centralized Societies. There were many other less centralized native civilizations as well. These societies were based on hunting, gathering, and agriculture. When they did grow foods, they often practiced slash-and-burn agriculture. Their social organization was much more decentralized than that of the Aztecs, Incas, or Mayans. Carib (the origin of the word Caribbean), Taino, and island Arawak peoples populated Antilles islands like Hispaniola, Cuba, and Puerto Rico and were the first native people to have contact with the Spanish explorers. At the time of Colombus' arrival, there were Arawak settlements extending from Florida to the Amazon basin. Also of importance were the Tainos, who were a native people found in Puerto Rico, Cuba, Hispaniola, and elsewhere in the Caribbean. Their treatment by the Europeans and susceptibility to disease caused them to virtually disappear during the first generation after the conquest.

Other less politically centralized groups fared better. The Araucanians of Chile and Argentina offered such spirited and sustained resistance to the European invaders that they were not completely conquered until 1883. Similarly, the Apaches of northern Mexico battled on until the last decades of the nineteenth century.

The Conquest

The first clash of European and native American civilizations occurred when the Spanish explorers and *conquistadores* consolidated their power in the Caribbean in the 1490s and early 1500s. Santo Domingo and later Havana in particular had become major staging areas for expeditions to other areas. Native people in the Caribbean were rapidly subjugated and the conquerors looked elsewhere for gold and glory. By the second decade of the sixteenth century, rumors of a rich civilization in central Mexico reached the new colonial rulers in the Caribbean.

Like many of the *conquistadores*, Hernán Cortés was a poor noble, or *hidalgo*, who came to the new world to make his fortune. Commissioned by the colonial authorities to explore the Mexican gulfcoast, he led an expedition of 600 men from Cuba to Mexico in 1519. Violating orders established by the Governor of Cuba, Cortéz landed on the coast, and soon made allies with local tribes that had been forced into tributary status by the Aztecs. He was given a resourceful native woman by one of the chiefs. Malinche (Marina), or la Malinche as she was called by subsequent generations, became Cortés' translator, advisor, and eventually his mistress. Because of this collaboration she has often been equated with the betrayal of Latin American culture and autonomy and is sometimes seen as a symbol of selling out to outside interests. Others note that a more complex reading of her life reveals her to be a woman trying to survive in a complex time in which both indigenous and European society cemented relationships through the use of native women.

Cortés sent some of his force back to Cuba for more proper authorization and reinforcements and left other men installed in the newly formed municipality of Vera Cruz on the coast. He then ordered his ships burned and directed his main force toward the Aztec capital. They were greatly aided not only by their horses (which were unknown to the natives), diseases, steel swords, steel armor, guns, and cannons, but also by an Aztec myth. Cortés was coming in the year that was foretold for the return of the deposed plumed serpent king Quetzalcóatl. The Spanish leader was seen by the Aztec ruler Moctezuma II as Quetzalcóatl returning to claim his throne, and his arrival was not resisted, although Aztec resistance did spring up once the avaricious nature of the Spaniards became evident and the indecisive Moctezuma was replaced by more aggressive rulers.

Christopher Columbus landed in Central America in 1502 on his forth voyage to the Americas. After Bilbao crossed the isthmus and discovered the Pacific Ocean in 1513, settlements were set up on the Caribbean side of Panama. They were later used as transit points between the two oceans. On the Pacific Coast, Panama City was not founded until 1519. As expeditions went north from Panama into what is now Costa Rica and Nicaragua, no large, centralized civilizations were encountered and the indigenous groups were soon subjugated. By the second decade of the sixteenth-century, Cortés was sending expeditions south from Mexico. By this time the Mayans in Central America were not highly organized in city-states, although there were heavily populated areas in Guatemala. Guatemala City, founded in 1524, eventually became the administrative center for the part of Central America north of Panama. From the time of the earliest European arrivals, there were rivalries among different groups and leaders and a great deal of conflict. Indeed, within two years of the founding of the cities of Granada and Leon in present-day Nicaragua, the two centers were engaged in a conflict that might be best described as a civil war. This pattern of behavior has persisted in most of the Central American isthmus to the present.

After reports of the riches of the empire to the south had reached the Spanish settlement in Panama, considerable interest in conquest developed. After going back to Spain for special authorization to colonize the great civilization in South America, Francisco Pizarro sailed from Panama with a band of some 200 *conquistadores*. They landed on the Peruvian coast in 1532. The Inca Empire was then at the height of its territorial expansion and encompassed more than 10 million people. However, at that time it was engaged in civil war. The last Inca, Huayna Capac, had died without naming his successor, and his two sons, Huáscar and Atahualpa, were both competing for the throne. Atahualpa had just captured Huáscar as the Spaniards arrived, but many followers of the latter were still ready to continue the conflict. Pizarro arranged a meeting with the victor in Cajamarca, but used the occasion to capture Atahualpa and slaughter many of his surprised followers. Atahualpa ordered the execution of Huáscar lest he mobilize his supporters and soon offered his Spanish captors a surprising ransom to gain his freedom. Realizing the Spaniard's obsession with gold, he offered to buy his freedom by filling the room where he was kept with gold to the height of his raised arm. As pack trains of llamas were bringing the ransom from the far corners of the empire, Atahualpa's cruel captors nonetheless executed him by garrote. From there Pizarro and his men went on to capture and loot the Inca capital Cuzco, despite the heroic resistance led by the new Inca, Manco Copac. By 1535 the empire was, for all intents and purposes, under Spanish control.

How Could They Do It?

One question remains unresolved: How could a few hundred Spaniards conquer empires of millions? One reason would surely be the seemingly indomitable Spanish spirit forged in the crucible of Iberian culture, where for centuries men had symbolically pitted themselves against huge bulls and reveled in the seemingly impossible victory. It is difficult to explain all the reasons for the ease of the conquest, but authors like Benjamin Keen note some of the following:

1. The Spaniards and Portuguese had honed their fighting and tactical skills in the 700-year reconquest of the Iberian peninsula from the Moors.
2. The Spaniards came outfitted as the soldiers of the great power of the time and enjoyed the latest in military armament and technology: steel swords and armor from foundries like those in Toledo, guns and cannons, horses, cavalries, and huge attack dogs. The Amero-Indian armies had neither steel nor guns and had never seen horses at all. Further, their notion of war was more limited and their tactics were generally more ritualistic and emphasized advance warning of attack and capturing the enemy so as to increase the pool of sacrificial victims. The Europeans focused on swift, sure victory and dispensed their enemies quickly.
3. As suggested earlier, the diseases that the Europeans brought wiped out whole native populations and greatly debilitated the native armies.
4. The Indian peoples often first saw the Spaniards as gods or demigods and were initially reluctant to destroy them.
5. The three most highly advanced indigenous civilizations had become quite sedentary over the years and could not think of fleeing their agricultural land to regroup elsewhere.
6. The hierarchical and often cruel nature of the political leadership in the native civilization had accustomed the common people to authoritarian decision making and arbitrary acts from above and had conditioned the common people not to rebel against the current leaders or those who wielded power. The Spaniards were at least initially perceived as just one more ruling group that had taken over.

Early Colony

The conquest was a joint endeavor between the crown and private entre-preneurs. The conquistador leader was expected to equip his band with the necessary arms and supplies or find financial backers who would. In turn, he and his mates had a royal license to hunt treasure and native peoples who had not embraced Christianity for their own profit. The only require-ment was that they pay the royal fifth, or *quinto real*. Much of the nature of the early colony was dictated by the conditions of the conquest. The Spaniards came for gold, glory, and God and competed fiercely for the for-mer. Many were poor nobleman or *hidalgos,* but most came from more hum-ble origins. The wealth from looted native cities and civilizations was shared among the members of the conquering military bands. *Encomiendas* and ti-tles were handed out later but usually just to the captains and leaders. Cortés, for instance, proved to be as successful in business as he was in the con-quest. He amassed a series of large and very profitable holdings in Mexico and proved very apt in his business dealings.

But only a few of the *conquistadores* achieved the fortunes they desired, and many remained disappointed and bitter. After the initial years of the conquest, more and more Spaniards came in search of fortune at a time when there were few additional native civilizations to loot. In Peru much of the early sixteenth century was spent in fighting, assassination, and intrigue among the conqueror, Francisco Pizarro; his brother; and other Spaniards. Treachery and betrayal were common. The native peoples were often com-pletely brutalized in the plundering of their societies and were at best seen by most as instruments of lucre and occasionally lust: slaves to capture and sell, laborers to exploit, owners of land or property to be seized, women to be used. And the colonialists often rose in rebellion when reforms were attempted.

The Spaniards conquered an area forty times the size of Spain. They and the Portuguese had the power and the audacity to enslave the better part of the population on two continents. They did not come as equals, but as force-ful conquerors. It was their belief that they were morally superior, possessed of the true faith (which was to be imposed more than practiced), and pre-sented with the opportunity of their lives for fame and wealth. The nature of the colony was foretold by Columbus' action on the island of Hispaniola during his second voyage. Anxious to prove the economic viability of the lands he had found, he began to force the natives to bring him a tribute of gold dust. When they refused and rebelled against their would-be masters, Columbus gave the orders to have large numbers of the locals captured and held. As a way of continuing to extract value from the natives, he sent sev-eral hundred to Europe as slaves. To placate the gold-starved settlers on the island, he distributed most of the remaining prisoners to them as a form of bounty. As was to be the case throughout the region, the original Ameri-cans would be enslaved outright or divided among the European settlers who took their land and then forced them to contribute their labor to the new European enterprise. The original inhabitants of Hispaniola declined rapidly because of disease and the harsh treatment handed out by the Europeans. From several hundred thousand inhabitants on Hispaniola at the time of Columbus' arrival, only some 29,000 were alive two decades later. By the mid-1500s hardly any natives were left.

Ironically, the original *conquistadores* also proved to be an endangered group as well. They were soon removed from power and replaced by direct representatives of the king whose loyalty to the crown was unquestioned. In this and other areas, European institutions began to replace the military structures and unbridled civilian power that marked the conquest. Thus the Iberian colonial bureaucracy began to replace the arbitrary rapaciousness of the conquerors.

Establishing a New Social Structure: The Castas

Spanish legislation created a complicated system of social classification consisting of the *castas,* defined by descent and color. On the top were the recently immigrated white Spaniards, the peninsular whites; below them were the descendants of the white colonists, called white *criollos.* After them came the brown people, the *pardos* or *mestizos* who consisted of people with mixed ancestry. As time went on the ranks of the lower and middle class were bolstered by *mestizos, mulattoes,* and *zambos.* The social pyramid that resulted from the conquest and the colonization consisted of a small group of powerful and usually wealthy Europeans or their descendants on top, a large number of natives and, soon, African slaves on the bottom, and a few Spanish artisans, soldiers, or small merchants as a wisp of a middle class.

The society that the Europeans brought with them from the Iberian peninsula was feudal in nature. Land tenure and many of the social institutions of the colony were more feudal than modern. The early colony still labored under the medieval philosophical doctrine of scholasticism. Thus considerable time was spend debating the true nature of the Indian population and the comparability of their souls with those of the Europeans. Moral argument and ethical debate were, however, rarely a match for the immense influence of a powerful person in the new world. Like the grand seigneur in Spain or Portugal, he (rarely she) was the unchallenged master of his domain. His will could be imposed in high and low places. Judges would listen, and peons, his to use as he saw fit, had very few practical rights (as contrasted to often extensive unrealized legal rights).

Women and Power

Few European women came in the earliest years of the colony. Those who did were subject to the strict traditional mores of the Iberian peninsula. However, women unprotected by both class (upper) and race (white) might well be available to the person of power to *coger* (generally meaning to grab or seize, although in parts of Latin America it came to mean to have sexual relations). Thus lower-class women of color were often at the disposition of men of lighter caste and higher class. In mostly Indian Bolivia, for instance, many *latifundistas* or large landowners were able to exercise the *derecho de pernada* (the sexual right to women on their estate) well into the twentieth century. Most upper-class women were strongly subordinated to male members of the family. There are, however, cases of a few women running large estates and even participating in colonial administration. There are more cases of women being the owners of record for huge amounts of land or other forms of wealth. Many of these inherited their wealth and prestige from a husband or father who had passed on. In more general transgender terms, their power and strength were respected (although not necessarily liked or even accepted whenever an opportunity for noncompliance or rebellion presented itself). In that women were socialized to be meek they were at a distinct disadvantage. Further, domination in many forms was omnipresent, and it colored the colony and subsequent social and political relations in Latin America in gender relations, politics, and many other areas.

LABOR

Persons of importance in Spain and Portugal did not engage in manual labor in large part because they were nobles or aspired to be like them. This attitude was carried over into the American colonies and permeated the societies with a disdain for manual labor that is perhaps most poignantly manifest in the low wages and lack of respect it still engenders and the hesitancy to engage in it carried by most members of the upper class and many in the middle class. The initial abundance of free Indian labor heightened this characteristic, as did the subsequent importation of large numbers of African slaves. Over time these labor pools were augmented by the progeny of often illicit unions of Europeans and Amero-Indians (*mestizos*) and Europeans and Africans (*mulattoes*).

Symbolic of the exploitative use of Amero-Indian labor and land was the *encomienda* (*sesmaria* in Brazil). The *encomienda* originated in a Spanish practice of granting jurisdiction over lands and peoples captured from the Moors to one of the warriors who led the reconquest. In Spanish and Portuguese America it came to be the assignment of a group of native people to a conquistador or other colonist. He would oversee them and the land on which they lived and be responsible for their proper Christianization. They in turn were to serve him with their labor and by paying him tribute. This form of forced semi–slave labor was often supplemented with the labor of Indian slaves. The Dominicans and church officials like Bishop Bartolomé de las Casas championed Indian rights and endeavored to stop some of the worst practices against the indigenous population. In 1512 the crown responded with the Leyes de Burgos to outlaw some of the worst abuses of the native Americans and make Indian slavery illegal. In 1549, the *encomendero's* right to demand labor from his *tributarios* was also outlawed. Both practices did, however, continue well beyond these dates in some areas.

After the decline of the *encomienda*, land, mine, and *obraje* (textile workshop) owners were forced to rely on the *repartimiento* for their free labor. The *repartimiento* was the practice of requiring the Indian population to provide a set amount of free labor to the landowners, the owners of the mines, the workshop or *obraje* operators, or the state for public works. In Peru, where the *repartimiento* was known by the old Inca term *mita*, as much as six months to a year of service could be required from each male every seven years. The Indians were often horribly exploited (thousands died at mines like Potosí, in what is now Bolivia) even though they did receive a token wage. But, as historian Benjamin Keen observes, "the repartimiento like the encomienda was a disguised form of slavery." Indeed, there were harsh penalties for those who avoided service and for community leaders who could not provide the required quotas of laborers.

SLAVERY AND OTHER FORMS OF ORGANIZATION

As is the case in the United States, Latin America is still feeling the effects of slavery. It is not possible to understand society or working conditions in Brazil, Cuba, Haiti, the Dominican Republic, or the other Latin American societies without understanding the lasting effects of this institution. As suggested by the popularity of a Brazilian *telenovela* (soap opera) bearing her name, Brazilian society is still reverberating from the adoration a rich Brazilian miner showered on Xica da Silva, the mulatto slave woman he called his African queen. Yet one of the worst aspects of the process of colonization was enslavement. The Eurocentrism and racism of the European colonizers initially allowed them to see the native peoples as non-Christian pagans who were inferior and, like the rest of what they found, there to be used by the colonizers. Slavery existed in Europe, North Africa, and the Middle East from long before the conquest. From this the practice of enslaving native people spread to the Americas. In the initial years of the colony, raiding parties were sent out to find slaves to be used for forced labor. Thus thousands of the original inhabitants of the Americas were enslaved in the first century of colonization. As the native population was rapidly depleted and as more laws to protect the indigenous population were passed and sometimes enforced by the crown, landowners needed to look elsewhere for exploitable labor. The outlawing of Indian slavery in 1542 accelerated this process.

As with other areas, slavery was also an institution in Africa, but it was tied to specific functions. It was, for instance, a way of punishing incorrigible criminals in societies that had mores against drawing blood from their own clansmen. Slavery became a recognized institution in Middle Eastern Muslim societies. So it was that there was a growing slave trade in Arab lands and from northern African societies that were conquered by them. Slave traders were soon penetrating further south into Africa from the area around the Sudan and elsewhere. The proximity of the market for African slaves in the Middle East and North Africa helped to establish the slave trade as an international activity.

Seeking a route to the Far East that did not have to pass through the Muslim controlled Middle East, the Portuguese began to penetrate further and further south on Africa's west coast. Spurred on by advances in navigation that were supported by Prince Henry the Navigator after 1450, they eventually circumnavigated the African continent to establish sea routes to the Indies. As they did this, Portuguese settlements were established all along the African coast and trade was begun. Soon the Portuguese took over islands off the Atlantic African coast (Madeira, Cape Verde Islands). Later they colonized several of the areas where they had settlements (Angola, Guinea Bissau, and Mozambique).

Stimulated by the strong market for sugar in Europe, Arabs had begun the cultivation of sugar in North Africa. Slave labor was used to supply the intense labor needed in the sugar cane cutting and milling process. When the Portuguese decided to cultivate sugar in their Atlantic Islands, they copied the Arab use of slave labor. The Portuguese then began to use their outposts in west Africa and southern Africa to capture or buy slaves. When the Portuguese took the cultivation of sugar to their colony in Brazil in the 1500s they also installed the plantation system based on slave labor. As the Dutch, English, and French adopted this crop in their Caribbean possessions, they too relied on a system of slave labor. On arriving in the Americas, the European colonists were faced with tremendous expansions of land available to them. It soon became clear that they needed to find crops and the labor to cultivate them if they were to turn their new possessions into paying propositions. In northern Brazil and the Caribbean, native slavery failed, and the native peoples would not otherwise provide the abundant labor needed. The superutilization of native peoples and their understandable dislike for the European system combined with factors like their rapid depletion by European-born diseases (particularly in the Caribbean) and the natives' ability to flee further into the interior in Brazil to minimize the number of available workers. This ensured that the Europeans' voracious appetite for cheap and easily exploitable labor could not be satisfied by the local supply in these areas. The use of indentured servants was also to became part of colonial life, but this source of cheap labor also proved insufficient for the demand. Nor did the well-to-do European landowning elite have any intention of farming the land themselves. They were much more prone to use the labor of others to accumulate their wealth and finance trips to London or stays in Madrid or Lisbon.

Slaves, then, had initially been acquired by Portuguese and Arab raiding parties and traders. Later, the Portuguese used their trade connections, outposts, and a series of slave forts to buy more and more slaves for the growing market in the Americas. During the first century of the colony they enjoyed a monopoly on the importation of slaves in the Spanish colonies and Brazil. In this way the transatlantic slave trade was begun. As the trade in humans grew, England and other countries also engaged in the lucrative business. The triangular trade took guns, rum, metal tools, and whiskey to Africa, where these were traded for slaves. Those who survived the horrendous Middle Passage were in turn sold in the slave markets in Havana and elsewhere and the ships loaded with tobacco, rum, and indigo for the trip back to Europe. From here the journey began anew. More than 7 million souls were brought to the Portuguese and Spanish colonies in this way.

The African diaspora had a major demographic and cultural impact on all areas of Latin America and the Caribbean, from Mexico to the Bahamas, Martinique, Grenada, Guatemala, Cuba, and Brazil. The arrival of black slaves to the Americas started roughly in 1502. African slaves were imported to substitute for the rapidly diminishing indigenous population. These first groups of slaves came from the slave markets of Spain. The slave markets in Seville, while relatively small, were the most active in Europe during this time. With colonization of the Americas the demand for slave labor increased dramatically. Europeans were looking to satisfy their labor demands in the New World. After 1519 slaves were taken directly from Africa by European slave ships. The modern day transatlantic slave trade dated from 1519 to 1867; by 1530 the Spanish crown had authorized the spread of slavery to Puerto Rico, Cuba, and Jamaica.

Law and Slavery. Spanish law legitimized the practice and ownership of other persons in the Caribbean and Latin America. The foundation of Spanish jurisprudence acknowledged the legality of the institution of slavery even while declaring it contrary to natural law. These laws protected the enslaved person from serious abuse by their masters and gave them the right to marry, inherit property, and be manumitted. Spanish slave law was developed from Roman slave codes. The French had no slave laws on the books in France, so they eventually enacted the Code Noir, a 1685 compilation designed to regulate slavery in the French Caribbean. Like Spanish Law, the Code Noir accorded the slaves basic rights such as marriage, manumission, and judicial recourse in the case of mistreatment. The British had no tradition of slavery in their land and had no elaborated slave codes to define relations between slave and master. This reality left the English slaveholders in the Caribbean to their own devices. They developed slave codes that essentially gave all of the power to the slave masters.

Comparative Slave Thesis. In the areas of the New World where there were more carefully elaborated slave codes and laws, as in the Spanish colonies, one theory holds that the nature of slavery was more humane or less dehumanizing. The slave—according to the argument—had a legal personality and was recognized by the law. Thus slaves could learn to read and even buy their freedom. Along with the process of miscegenation—the mixing of the races—some scholars believe that the Spanish slave codes created a far different life for slaves.

In contrast to the Spanish-speaking Caribbean, the English had no elaborated slave codes and had to make them up as they went along. Thus in British slave codes the slave was not recognized as a person but as property. They were accorded no rights: Slaves were strictly forbidden to learn how to read or write and strictly forbidden to own property. Moreover, miscegenation was less frequent.

Nonetheless, the massive degradation and exploitation of millions of human beings uprooted from their homes in Africa combined with the treatment of the native American population imbued the Spanish and Portuguese colonies with a deep-seated racism, institutionalized callousness toward laborers (particularly when they were of color), and a proclivity toward (often brutal) exploitation that remains today.

Not all exploited the indigenous or African population with the same degree of harshness. The settlements that the Jesuits set up in Paraguay and elsewhere were notable exceptions, although they too enforced cultural assimilation of native peoples like the Guaraní. The Spanish and Portuguese crowns did not take kindly to the independent power of the Jesuits in these or other matters. Further, many of the powerful in the colonies resisted and sharply criticized the protective role progressive sectors in the Catholic Church played in regard to Indian rights. The *encomendero* turned priest and Indian advocate, Bishop Bartolomé de las Casas, was repeatedly rebuked and threatened. Bishop Antonio Valdivieso was threatened and eventually assassinated for his pro-native stances in the area that is now Nicaragua. The Spanish crown did eventually decree minimal protection for indigenous peoples starting with the Law of Burgos (1512) and outlawed practices like Indian slavery. However, the Jesuits were later expelled from the colonies by the Portuguese in 1757 and the Spanish in 1767. African slavery continued into the nineteenth century in the remaining Spanish colonies in the Caribbean and in Brazil until 1888. The status of enslaved or horribly exploited Africans did not attract the attention of enlightened Church officials. Even Bartolomé de las Casas recommended the use of African slave labor to free the indigenous people from slavery. Further, given the power and prerogative of local notables and their influence on local public officials, many of the worst practices toward the natives and former slaves continued on well after being outlawed. One could draw parallels between these practices and the way sectors of the old elite in the American South were able to exploit and deny fundamental rights to former slaves and their descendants in rural areas of Mississippi and Louisiana.

The Indian and African slaves and laborers were, it seemed, to be used and exploited (at times to the point of extinction) to achieve the production necessary to enrich the European owners and to funnel wealth and products back to the metropolitan centers of power and wealth in Europe. As pointed out by many observers, the conditions in the mines, workshops, and farms were often horrendous. They were reflective of the callousness of many of the powerful to the condition and suffering of those more lowly than they.

Production, Trade, and Extraction of Riches

The native gold and silver was quickly expropriated and sent back to Spain in fleets of gold- and silver-laden galleons. The crown always got its *quinto real*. After the existing riches in gold, silver, and gems were depleted by the first conquerors, the Spanish administration began to foster the establishment of durable production of mercantile goods and the introduction of trade in Indian societies that had not yet begun to exchange their products for money. Of primary interest to the mercantilist leadership were precious metals, such as gold or silver, and pearls or precious stones. Where these were not found the colonial leadership sought to grow commercial goods such as dyes, sugar cane, tobacco, or cocoa. Soon after the conquest, they discovered rich silver mines in Mexico and in the Potosí mountain in the Andes in Upper Peru (Bolivia). The extraction of silver and gold in Mexico and Peru stimulated the colonizers' keen interest in the lands of the former Aztec and Inca empires. In the regions surroundings these centers, the production of food and other necessary supplies began to determine how the land was used. In Chile the land was used to produce wheat for Spanish bread; in northern Argentina the land was used to breed cattle, horses, and mules for the work in the mines and for hides for leather. The beef was dried and salted to make *charqui*, jerked meat.

Tremendous amounts of wealth were removed from the colonies in the form of preexisting gold and silver. Next the conquerors turned to mining, often expending thousands of Indian lives each year to extract the precious metal (as suggested earlier, the mines at Potosí are reputed to have consumed as many as 8 million native lives over three centuries). Between 1531 and 1600 over 33 million pounds of silver were exported back to Spain. By the last quarter of the sixteenth century silver bullion accounted for about 90 percent of Latin American exports. Some three-fifths came from mines in what is now Peru and Bolivia. The silver mine in Potosí was legendary. The town attracted so many fortune seekers that it was the largest city in Latin America (160,000) at the beginning of the seventeenth century.

The silver produced by the miners was extracted and shipped to Spain in different ways. First, the crown took the *quinto real* of gross production. The other 80 percent stayed in the hands of the miners and was used to pay the workforce and for materials, animals for transportation, food, and luxury products for the rich miners. Here the merchants who worked in the colony itself dominated, as did those who had the exclusive rights to export goods from Spain to the American possessions. This later group principally resided in the center of Spanish colonial administration in Spain, Seville. Furthermore, the Spanish crown levied taxes on all imported goods. The capacity of the Spanish state to add more, higher taxes on colonial commerce was astonishing. The consequence was that the goods became very expensive because of the excessive taxation imposed by Spain's colonial monopoly.

As a way of ensuring increased consumption of such imported goods, the *repartimiento de mercancias* was introduced as a way to tax native Americans who were not or were only marginally incorporated in the market economy. Under this system the *corregidor* or other local official was able to oblige each household in his charge to buy some Western merchandise at a substantial (and usually highly inflated) price. The colonial official became the monopoly supplier to a captive market.

The high taxes on all imported and exported goods caused considerable discontent among the *criollo* producers and merchants in the colonies, and they were soon ready to evade them by trading with nonauthorized merchants from other countries. Their trade was principally with Dutch, British, and French *contrabandistas*. The whole of colonial history is characterized by the efforts of the Spanish authorities to eliminate smuggling, by patrolling the coasts, controlling the accounts of the merchants, or forming monopolistic companies such as Guipuzcoana in Venezuela. These efforts never enjoyed much success because the smuggled goods were much cheaper than those coming from Spain.

The Church

The Catholic Church was a major political institution in the colony and was in charge of (Catholic) Christianization and education. It was in charge of the Spiritual Conquest of the Americas. It acted as an agent for the crown, incorporating native peoples into the European world and European economy through participating in and paying for the acts of baptism and other rites and the still popular street processions celebrating Church holy days and the lives of favorite saints and local madonnas. The Church's power was exercised in concert with the state and was utilized to extend European control and influence. Its autonomy was mitigated by the fact that in 1508 then Pope Julius II granted the Spain monarch the *patronato real*—the right to nominate all church officials, collect tithes, and found churches and monasteries in the Spanish Americas. This allowed the state a great deal of control over the church and helped to fuse the two. Nonetheless, the Church did engage in a variety of different activities, amassed considerable wealth, and was often the largest landowner in different regions of the colony.

The cultural and political evolution of Spanish America was also influenced by an instrument employed to purify the Catholic faith. The Spanish Inquisition persecuted alleged heretics (mostly Jewish and Muslim converts) and was in large part responsible for the mass exodus of non-Christians from Spain in the late fifteenth and sixteenth centuries. In 1569 the institution of the Inquisition began in Latin America in Lima and Mexico City. It was charged with investigating signs of heresy. Later it spread to other Spanish (but not Portuguese) possessions and became a license to search out any deviant or different thinking or innovation. Although indigenous people were exempted from the Inquisition after the 1570s and its victims were relatively few in number, it did have the effect of enforcing a certain heterodoxy in thought and suppressing an unfettered spirit of inquiry. Some have even seen it as the forerunner of the infamous secret police employed by Latin American dictatorships and military governments. Others speculate that the lax enforcement of the inquisition in the Portuguese territories helps to account for the less constrained approach to thinking and social and business relations that developed in Brazil. The Museum of the Inquisition in downtown Lima attests to the chilling nature of the interrogation and brutality of the instruments of torture employed to induce confessions in Spanish America.

Colonial State Organization

Political power was highly concentrated in colonial governmental structures as well. A *virrey*, or vice-king (viceroy), headed the colonial administration, ruling as the king's representative in his designated area. The region was first divided into the Spanish viceroyalties of Nueva España (Mexico, Central America, and the Caribbean) and Lima (all the Andean countries, present-day Panama, Argentina, Paraguay, and Uruguay) and the Portuguese viceroyalty of Brazil. Later the viceroyalties of Nueva Granada (present-day Venezuela, Colombia, and Ecuador) and Río de la Plata (present-day Argentina, Uruguay, and Paraguay) were broken off. Unlike the English colonies in North America, there were no representative assemblies in Latin America. Laws and decrees came from the Iberian monarchs or the Council of the Indies in Seville, Spain, and were implemented by colonial authorities from Spain and Portugal. Communication was slow, imprecise, and greatly filtered by the interests of the powerful. The colonists often felt that they were living under orders or laws imposed from afar that did not respond to their needs. This led to one of the most famous dictims during the colony—"*Obedezco pero no cumplo*": I obey but I do not comply. I will yield to your orders and authority, but you will be hard-pressed to make me carry them out. The colonial elite that emerged amassed considerable wealth and power. They were all too willing to employ both to frustrate laws or decrees they found objectionable or impractical. The large landowners in Brazil were perhaps the most independent—a tradition that continues to the present. In Spanish and Portuguese America laws like those that protected the native peoples were often unenforceable because of the concerted power of local elites. There was also a fault line between the newly arrived colonials from Spain and Portugal, the *peninsulares*, and the sons and daughters of the earlier arrivals from the Iberian peninsula, the *criollos*. The *criollos* resented the fact that the best positions in the colonial administration and the church went to the *peninsulares* even though they had just stepped off the boat and did not have the *criollos'* history, family, or wealth in the Americas.

The viceroy was indeed the king's representative and could truly rule. Executive, military, and some legislative power were combined in such a way as to establish the cultural model of the all-powerful executive that has permeated Latin American political (and business) culture to the present day. Captains general were appointed to rule over smaller and usually more distant divisions of the viceroyalties and governed in much the same way. Thus the captain general of Guatemala ruled Central America (excluding present-day Panama) from his headquarters in Guatemala City but was ostensibly subordinate to the viceroy of New Spain in Mexico City. The captains general in colonial Brazil were given even greater power over their domains and enjoyed greater autonomy from the crown and the viceroy.

The viceroyalties of New Spain and Peru were further subdivided into *audiencias*, or advisory councils, that were presided over by judge-presidents and composed of appointed judges, or *oidores*. They were established in Santo Domingo, Mexico City, Panama, Lima, Guatemala, Guadalajara, Santa Fe, La Plata, Buenos Aires, Quito, Santiago, Cuzco, and Caracas. Beneath the *audiencias* were the governors, and at the local level the notoriously corrupt *corregidores* and mayors (*Alcaldes*). At the higher levels of government, the judicial, legislative, and executive functions were mixed with the viceroys generally also in charge of the military. Functions and powers often over-lapped in a system that was designed to encourage mutual suspicion, spy-ing, the checking of a potential rival's power, and thus the supremacy of the power of the crown. The *cabildo*, or town council (*câmara* in Brazil), was one of the few political structures with any degree of popular participation or democracy. Many councils were all or partly elected and were truly repre-sentative of the population. Many others of these were dominated by pow-erful and often corrupt political appointees. Offices were, however, fre-quently sold, and corruption and intense exploitation of the native population were all too often the norm. The official who did not use his of-fice to accumulate a fortune to take back to the Iberian Peninsula might well be considered the exception. Conditions did improve somewhat after the late eighteenth century Bourbon reforms, but many of the worst practices had by then become ingrained.

Historical Time Line in the Americas

40,000 B.C.E.–8000 B.C.E.   Migration of Asian people to North America through the Bering Strait

1500 B.C.E.–A.D. 1000   Mayan civilization develops in the Yucatan Peninsula, Guatemala, and parts of Honduras and El Salvador

1150 B.C.E.–A.D. 500   Olmec culture flourishes in Mesoamerica

1000   Incan culture emerges in the Cuzco Valley of South America

1200   The Aztecs arrive to the central plateau of Mexico

1466   The last Aztec emperor, Moctezuma Xocoyotzín, is born in Mexico

1492   Christopher Columbus arrives at what he called San Salvador Island in the Caribbean and encounters Native American culture

1494   Treaty of Tordesillas signed by Spain and Portugal, establishing a line of demarcation from pole to pole 370 leagues west of the Cape Verde Islands; Spain received the right to colonize all territory to the west of that line; Portugal colonized lands to the east

1500   Pedro Alvares Cabral arrives in Brazil and claims it for Portugal

1508   In Hispaniola, the first sugar mill is constructed

1509   Pope Julius II authorizes the Spanish Catholic monarchs to propagate the Catholic Church in the Americas; Patronato Real gave power to crown to appoint Church officials

1510   Two-hundred and fifty slaves are imported to the Americas to work in the gold mines in Hispaniola

1512   The Laws of Burgos are promulgated to protect the native Americans from the worst ravages of Spanish conquest

1516 Bartolomé de Las Casas is named the official Protector of the Indians
1519 Hernán Cortés marches into Tenochtitlán and takes Montezuma prisoner
1521 The Spaniards complete conquest of Aztec Empire
1521 Conquistador Gil González de Avila converts 30,000 Indians to Christianity in the area called Nicaragua, and sends some 500,000 as slaves to other parts of Spanish Empire
1524 The Council of the Indies is established by King Charles V
1532 Francisco Pizarro invades the Incan Empire, captures and executes Emperor Atahualpa, and conquers the Incas
1538 The first university in the Americas is established: St. Thomas Aquinas in the city of Santo Domingo
1541 Francisco de Orellana discovers the headwaters of the Amazon River in what is now Ecuador
1542 The New Laws of the Indies are issued by Spain, officially eliminating the *encomienda*
1551 In Mexico and Lima, new universities are created
1554 Araucan Indian chief Caupolican, allied with Chief Lautaro, defeats Spaniards, kills Pedro de Valdivia, and defeats the forces of Francisco de Villagrá de Chile
1767 King Charles III expels the Jesuits from the Spanish Empire
1780 Incan descendant Túpac Amaru leads a two-year rebellion against authorities on behalf of the Indians.

Bibliography

Adelman, Jeremy. Colonial Legacies: *The Problem of Persistence in Latin American History*. New York: Routledge, 1999.

Bakewell, Peter. *A History of Latin American Empires and Sequels, 1450–1930*. Malden, MA, and Oxford: Blackwell Publishers, 1997.

Burkholder, Mark A., and Lyman L. Johnson. *Colonial Latin America*. Fourth edition. New York: Oxford University Press, 2001.

Conniff, Michael, and Thomas Davis. *Africans in the Americas: A History of the Black Diaspora*. New York: St. Martin's Press, 1994.

Davis, Darien, ed. *Slavery and Beyond: The African Impact on Latin America and the Caribbean* (Jaguar Books on Latin America, No. 5). Wilmington, DE: Scholarly Resources, 1995.

Fagan, Brian. *Kingdoms of Gold, Kingdoms of Jade: The Americas Before Columbus*. London: Thames and Hudson, 1991.

Keen, Benjamin. *A History of Latin America, Volume 1, Ancient America to 1910*. Boston and Toronto: Houghton Mifflin Company, 1996.

Leon-Portilla. Miguel, ed. *The Broken Spears: The Aztec Account of the Conquest of Mexico*. Translated by Lysander Kemp. Boston: Beacon Press, 1992.

Kicza, John E., ed. *The Indian in Latin American History, Resistance, Resilience and Acculturation*. Wilmington, DE: Scholarly Resources, 1993.

Ohaegbulam, Festus U. *Toward and Understanding of the African Experience from Historical and Contempory Perspectives*. Lunham, MD: University Press of America, 1990.

Newson, Linda. "The Latin American Colonial Experience." In David Preston, ed., *Latin American* Development. 2nd ed. Burnt Mill, Essex, England: Longman, 1996.

Rosenberg, Marc A., A. Douglas Kincaid, and Kathleen Logan, eds. *Americas, An Anthology*. New York and Oxford: Oxford University Press, 1992.

Schele, Linda, and David Freidel. A Forest of Kings: *The Untold Story of the Ancient Maya*. New York: William Morrow and Company, 1990.

Smith, Carol. *Guatemalan Indians and the State: 1540 to 1988*. Austin: University of Texas Press, 1990.

Soustelle, Jacques. *Daily Life of the Aztecs, on the Eve of the Spanish Conquest*. Stanford, CA: Stanford University Press, 1970.

Stavig, Ward. *The World of Túpac Amaru: Conflict Community and Identity in Colonial Peru*. Lincoln: University of Nebraska Press, 1999.

FILMS AND VIDEOS

The Burried Mirror. Reflections of Spain in the New World, Part two: The Conflict of the Gods. U.S. 1991. Video version of Carlos Fuentes' insightful commentary on the indigenous world conquered by Spain and the transposition of the new belief system.

The Mission. U.S. 1986. An excellent feature-length film starring Robert De Niro; graphically depicts the colonization process among indigenous peoples above the Iguassú Falls in southern Brazil.

Popol Vuh. U.S. 1991. An animated video that portrays the creation myth of the Mayas.

Prayer of Virachocha. U.S. A beautifully animated indigenous lament to the Incan god Virachocha at the time of the conquest.

Quetzalcoatl. A vision of the Mesoamerican winged serpent god.

The Spanish Conquest of Mexico. U.S. 1999. Tells the story of how the Aztec empire was conquered.

Sword and Cross. U.S. 1991. Tells the story of the conquest.

Xica. Brazil, 1976. The embellished story of Xica da Silva.

THREE

REPUBLICS AND THE STRUGGLE TO EMPOWER THE PEOPLE

Nineteenth- and Twentieth-Century History

Independence

The independence movements that created most of the nation-states that currently make up Latin America developed during the first twenty-five years of the nineteenth century as the result of events occurring in both Europe and Latin America. By the time independent states were established in Latin America in the 1820s, the local elites had largely succeeded in transferring political power into their own hands outside of the control of Madrid or Lisbon. However, the underlying systems of social and economic power inherited from the colonial era were largely intact. Further, the authoritarian tradition inherited from Spanish and Portuguese colonialism would plague Latin America into the twenty-first century. There was a continual and generally unresolved tension between authoritarian rule learned from years of heavy-handed, top-down colonial (and often pre-colonial) practice on the one hand and the democratic ideals and inspiration that the independence movements chose to rely on to explain and set up the state structures in the independent nations on the other. Nonetheless, the end of direct colonialism did initiate a nation-building process that would eventually modernize governmental structures and bring Latin America closer to the world economic system. The political change also produced a legitimacy crisis that led to nearly a century of political struggle and the eventual hegemony of liberalism. These more profound changes for the Americas began in the last twenty-five years of the nineteenth century, when the region's long-standing social and economic structures were challenged by the arrival of the industrial revolution and market capitalism. These forces eventually weakened the traditional elites and laid the groundwork for the political struggles of the twentieth century.

To better understand the independence movements of the early nineteenth century in Latin America it is necessary to look to Europe. By the beginning of the eighteenth century, the Spanish empire was already well into a decline that proved to be permanent. However, as was suggested in the last chapter, the Bourbon monarchs of Spain, whose family had assumed the crown in 1713, had embarked on a series of political and economic reforms in their American colonies that they hoped would solidify that rule. In reality these reforms contributed to the eventual triumph of the independence movements. Inspired by Enlightenment political and economic thought, the Bourbons sought to reform the existing overlapping systems of authority by centralizing political power. They created new administrative units at New Grenada (1717) and Buenos Aires (1776). More importantly, Charles III, who ruled from 1759 to 1788, established a new administrative system that resulted in the appointment of local governors by the crown in Madrid. These rulers, called intendants, were almost all Spanish-born rather than American *criollos*. This approach marginally solidified the hold of the monarchy over the colonies but brought the crown into more direct conflict with the local elites who had prospered under the previous system of less intrusive rule from Madrid. In one significant example, the monarchy sharply reduced *criollo* control of the administrative and court system, which it had originally established in the late seventeenth century by purchasing judgeships. Charles III also strengthened his hand by taking greater control of the Church. In his boldest move, he expelled the Jesuits from all Spanish colonies in 1767. Charles saw the Jesuits as an independent power base, so he removed them and profited from the sale of their lands. The Spanish crown also engaged in economic reform that freed the various ports of the empire to trade with other ports in Spanish America and in Spain itself. Illegal trade had long flourished on the forbidden routes, with most of the profits staying within the Americas, but now the Spanish crown was gaining a greater share of the wealth through the collection of customs duties. These economic reforms resulted in a more prosperous colonial economy where new ports such as Buenos Aires flourished, but their most important long-term effect was the resentment generated among *criollos*, who saw the moves as a plot to undermine their status and power. This resentment, more than any other factor, fueled the independence movements of the early nineteenth century.

Ironically, another reform instituted by the Spanish crown unwittingly aided the cause of American independence. During the eighteenth century the monarchy had authorized the creation of colonial militias as a protection against feared British and French invasions, by 1800, 80 percent of the soldiers serving in Spanish America were American-born. Military careers were one of the few remaining avenues of advancement for socially ambitious *criollos*. These forces provided the core of the local forces that would later fight for independence.

THE FRENCH REVOLUTION AND INDEPENDENCE

Events in Europe determined the timing of the independence movement. The French revolution of 1789 launched ideas of freedom and equality throughout the French Empire, and cries of *liberté, egalité,* and *fraternité* fell on receptive ears among the slave population in Haiti. In 1791 a slave uprising was led by Toussaint L' Ouverture, an extremely able, self-educated freed slave. After a series of successful battles against opposition forces that included a formitable contingent of Napoleon's army in 1802, the popular forces triumphed. Haiti gained its independence from France in 1804 and thus became the first independent Latin American nation. In other parts of Latin America a few, like the Afro-Venezuelan José Leonardo Chirinos, even spoke of proclaiming a republic of the "law of the French" in 1795. Meanwhile, the Spanish monarchy had tried to save their Bourbon counterparts during the French Revolution in 1789, but having failed that, Spain allied itself with Napoleon Bonaparte in 1796. However, in 1808 Napoleon turned on his Spanish allies and occupied Madrid, placing his brother Joseph on the Spanish throne. This act by Napoleon was the catalyst for rebellion in Spain and the Americas that would eventually lead to independence for most of Spanish America. Some historians do argue, however, that the resistance of indigenous peoples in the latter part of the eighteenth century was the real catalyst. In 1780 Tupac Amaru II, claiming lineage to the ancient Inca empire, led a revolt that mobilized more than 80,000 mostly indigenous fighters and lasted for two years in southern Peru and Bolivia before it was defeated by the Spanish army. This movement is important in the history of indigenous struggles but is probably better understood outside the context of the independence movements. With radical demands for land reform and indigenous rights, the political thrust of these movements was not supported by the *criollo* independence leaders of the early nineteenth century. In fact, the Peruvian rebellion and the later rebellion in Mexico led by Hidalgo frightened the *criollo* into making common cause with the Spanish-born elites and delayed independence in both Mexico and Peru. It also meant that, outside of Haiti, rebellions against colonial rule by the masses (who were predominantly people of color) did not triumph.

The *criollos,* born in America, increasingly longed to wrest political power from the *peninsulares.* In the late eighteenth century the *criollos* began to look outward for guidance, increasingly to France. As a result, the French Revolution had more impact than the American Revolution. As suggested earlier, the most dramatic example of the influence in Latin America was in Haiti. Of course, the majority of creoles were not Jacobin revolutionaries. They wanted to reform the local political systems to give themselves power, but they were in no way interested in revolution or in giving all the power to the common people. Napoleon's invasion of Spain in 1808 provided that opportunity.

In the wake of the Napoleonic invasion, the Spanish king Ferdinand was imprisoned, and the Braganzas, Portugal's royal family, escaped to Rio de

Janeiro. The Brazilians received their royal family warmly and celebrated their extended stay in Rio de Janeiro. In contrast, the initial instincts of Spanish Americans was to pledge loyalty to Ferdinand, but fairly quickly the creole elites began to realize their own power, and by 1810 the creoles had moved from tentative autonomy to open declarations of independence. However, despite the fortuitous circumstances for independence, the events that followed were not preordained to lead to independence for most of Latin America during the ensuing twenty-five years.

ARGENTINA, 1806–1810

One of the earliest examples of the capacity of resistance by the local population came in Buenos Aires. In 1806 the British occupied the city, forcing the viceroy to flee to Córdoba. The British, however, were driven out by a locally organized citizens' army, which also successfully defended against a counterattack in 1807. This local action independent of Madrid set a powerful example for future actions. The viceroyalty of Buenos Aires was also able to negotiate a better deal in the arena of free trade after the expulsion of the British forces. Ironically, it involved the desire of the local commercial elite to trade directly with the British, who provided the most promising market for their growing production of hides and salted beef. In 1809 Spain granted Buenos Aires limited freedom of trade with nations allied to Spain or neutral in the Napoleonic Wars. This agreement helped to strengthen the self-confidence of the local elites.

Early Drive for Independence in Hispanic America

The first phase of the Spanish American independence movements occurred between 1810 and 1814. In 1810 Napoleon's forces completed their victory over the Bourbons and established a liberal constitution for Spain, but in 1814 Ferdinand VII returned to the Spanish throne and annulled the liberal constitution. In 1810 Argentine local elites came together to create a provisional government of the provinces of the Río de la Plata. Prior to their declaration of independence of 1816, these local elites pledged their allegiance to Ferdinand VII. But the pattern of local initiative, first shown in the rebellions against the British, was institutionalized.

Venezuela was the scene of a movement similar to that in Buenos Aires. In Caracas, a local council expelled the Spanish governors and organized a new government under Ferdinand VII. The most well-known of the leaders was Simón Bolívar. Born into a wealthy Caracas family and tutored by the great Latin American liberal thinker Simón Rodríguez, Bolívar was educated in Spain and came in contact with the ideas of the Enlightenment (especially Rousseau and romanticism); in 1805 he committed himself to the independence of his homeland. In 1811 the local Caracas authorities, under his influence, declared Venezuela's independence. After an initial series of military defeats, the exiled Bolívar returned to Venezuela and defeated the

Spanish army in a series of exceptional military victories earning him the title "The Liberator" (El Libertador).

In the provinces of New Spain (Mexico) this time period also saw exceptional developments. By 1810 a group of *criollos*, including priest Miguel Hidalgo, began plotting to seize authority in the name of Ferdinand. When the plot was discovered by the Spanish authorities, Hidalgo led a popular uprising centered in the village of Dolores—thus the famous "grito de Dolores." A powerful response came not from the local elites but rather from the impoverished mestizos and indigenous people. Uniting under the banner of the long-adored dark-skinned Virgin of Guadalupe, they comprised a fighting force of 50,000. In a decision whose motivation has been debated ever since, Hidalgo turned away from a probable victory over the Spanish authorities in Mexico City and moved to the north. In 1811 his army was defeated near Guadalajara, leading to his capture and execution.

Following Hidalgo's death, leadership of the independence forces was taken by José María Morelos, another priest even more strongly committed to radical social reform, including the end of slavery. A republican, Morelos believed that the whole population should participate in political affairs. In 1813 the Congress of Chilpancingo declared Mexico's independence from Spain and decreed that slavery should be abolished. The congress' liberal constitution of 1814 created a system of indirect elections and a powerful legislature. However, it was never enacted because Morelos' guerrilla army did not control enough territory to seriously threaten Spanish authority.

In 1814 Napoleon's defeat restored Ferdinand VII to power in Spain. The colonial authorities used this fortuitous event—along with military reinforcements—to regain control in the face of the developing independence movements. Ferdinand annulled the liberal Spanish constitution of 1812 and reestablished himself as an absolute ruler. The king's return divided *criollo* leaders, with many concluding that there was no reason to continue their rebellions. By 1816, with the exception of Buenos Aires, Spanish rule had been reestablished throughout the empire. In Venezuela even the victorious Bolívar saw his support significantly reduced; he was forced into exile on the English island of Jamaica. The independence movement in New Spain also suffered serious setbacks. In 1815 Morelos was captured, tried, and executed as the Spanish military commanders regained the upper hand and blocked the implementation of the liberal constitution that had been enacted the previous year. Only the government in Río de la Plata survived the reconquest. It struggled to survive and had not yet become a full-blown independence movement.

The Spanish reconquest was short-lived. In 1816 Bolívar returned to Venezuela from his exile on Jamaica and launched a new campaign for the independence of his country. His new ally was José Antonio Páez, the leader of the *llaneros* (cowboys) who had fought alongside the royalists during the previous struggles. In 1819 Bolívar mounted an army of 4000 and succeeded in defeating the Spanish and their royalist collaborators. Meanwhile in the south, José de San Martín initiated a significant military campaign. San

Martín, the son of a Spanish military officer, entered the service at age eleven. In 1812 he offered his services to the junta in Buenos Aires. Over the next five years he developed the rebel forces into an army and then led 5000 soldiers across the Andes in a surprise attack on the loyalist forces in Chile. The Spaniards were defeated in the battle of Chacabuco, and San Martín entered Santiago triumphantly. San Martín's next target was the liberation of Peru; in 1820 he prepared for the attack on Lima, the capital of the viceroyalty. San Martín faced a city where the monarchist sentiment was quite strong. Both the *criollos* and the *peninsulares* favored the continuation of Ferdinand's rule. Wary of a defeat, San Martín withheld his attack.

At that point decisive events in Spain again intervened. Ferdinand reversed his political course and abruptly embraced the previously annulled Spanish liberal constitution of 1812. Monarchists throughout Spanish America were shocked by the turnabout, which abolished the Inquisition, thus unacceptably weakening the power of the Church. The changes in Spain suddenly altered the climate for independence in both Lima and Mexico City, where the monarchists held sway. The monarchists now viewed independence as a means of preserving the status quo, which would uphold traditional values and social codes. As a result of this sudden change of perspective, in 1821 the municipal council of Lima invited San Martín to enter the city; on July 28 he formally proclaimed the independence of Peru. Meanwhile in the north, Bolívar, after defeating the Spanish forces in New Grenada, attempted to create a new State of Gran Columbia, uniting Venezuela, New Grenada, and Ecuador under republican principles. This effort received little support, so Bolívar moved south, hoping to confront and defeat more of the royalist forces as he sought to achieve his vision of a united continent independent of colonial control and organized along republican principles.

Antonio José de Sucre was sent by Bolívar to liberate Ecuador. Sucre led the combined Ecuadorian, Colombian, and Venezuelan forces against the Spanish and finally defeated them in the Battle of Pichincha in 1822. In Ecuador Bolívar met with San Martín and declared that they were "the two greatest men in America." Personal and political differences, however, precluded the consummation of an alliance. Bolívar rejected San Martín's proposal for a monarchy in Peru and San Martín's offer for Bolívar to serve under his command. Further, Bolívar's plans for the union of Gran Columbia were rejected by San Martín. Disillusioned and unwilling to split the revolutionary forces, San Martín soon after resigned his post and retired to France, where he died in 1850. But even San Martín's departure did not slow the independence movement. In late 1823 Bolívar's forces confronted the large Spanish force that had retreated inland from Lima, and a year later the royalists were defeated decisively at the battle of Ayacucho, effectively ending three centuries of Spanish rule in the Americas. In 1825 Bolívar entered Upper Peru to press the idea that the two Perus should form a single nation. The leaders of Upper Peru, however, having already struck an independent course, declared their own republic and named it Bolivia in honor of Bolívar. Over the next five years Bolívar tried unsuccessfully to promote his idea of political union. His ideas were resisted by the local elites, including some of his own lieutenants, who feared the reinstatement of centralized control. In 1826 Bolívar tried to implement his vision of a united Spanish America by convening the Congress of Panama to begin to implement such a plan. His efforts were not successful, and in 1830, the Liberator died a bitter man who failed to achieve a united Latin America and saw many of his democratic dreams languish. Toward the end of his life he concluded that he and the other independence leaders "had plowed the sea."

Simultaneous to these events in South America the conservative independence movement went forward in Mexico. The royal government was disintegrating; Agustín de Iturbide, the creole commander of the army in Mexico, seized the moment to declare Mexican independence with little bloodshed on September 28, 1821. Only the Spanish garrison in Veracruz held out against Iturbide's proclamation. It was a conservative revolt that even many Spaniards supported. The new regime was marked by three conservative principles: constitutional monarchy, official Catholicism, and equality of *peninsulares* and *criollos*. Iturbide had himself proclaimed emperor only when "no suitable European monarch could be found." Central America, with its traditional strong ties to Mexico, followed suit and declared its independence from Spain in 1821. In 1822 the Central American landowners, fearing liberal dominance in Spain, transferred their loyalty to royalist Mexico. However, the Mexican monarchy lasted only two years. In 1823 when Iturbide abdicated, the modern-day Central American states from Guatemala to Costa Rica became the Independent United Provinces of Central America. With the independence of Mexico and Central America, Spanish control in the Western Hemisphere was reduced to Cuba and Puerto Rico.

Brazilian Independence

Brazilian independence was achieved in a manner very different from that of Spanish America. The differences were rooted in the character of the Brazilian state and economy and in the special role played by Britain in the context of the Napoleonic Wars. When the Napoleonic army invaded Portugal in 1807, the entire royal family was able to flee to Brazil with the assistance of the British Navy. The royal family ended Portugal's commercial monopoly by opening Brazil's ports. Soon after 1810 Britain gained privileged access to Brazil through low tariffs, a commitment to the gradual end of the African slave trade, and extraterritorial privileges for British citizens living in Brazil.

When Napoleon was decisively defeated, the Portuguese monarchy was free to return to Lisbon; initially they did not, and instead Dom João proclaimed Brazil to be a coequal kingdom with the same rank as Portugal. Dom João, however, did eventually return to Lisbon and left his son Dom Pedro behind with the prerogative to declare Brazil independent. The new king declared independence on September 7, 1822, with the full support of the Brazilian elites and with only token resistence from a few Portuguese garrisons. In sharp contrast to much of Spanish America, independence was achieved in Brazil without significant bloodshed and without the development of a strong military caste. The nation also remained united despite some small-scale regional revolts. Furthermore, Brazil did not see a strong republican/monarchist split because the overwhelming majority of the local elite sided with monarchism. Brazilian sugar barons were dependent on the slave trade and thus on the monarchy, which lasted only a year beyond the abolition of slavery in 1888.

Early Years of Independence

And so it was that the Latin American nations became independent of European rule. It was, however, a much longer struggle to liberate themselves from their inherited political and cultural traditions. Foremost among these was the authoritarian proclivity that was strongly ingrained in political culture. Thus, for instance, Bolívar, the great Liberator, frustrated with regionalism and the assertion of political autonomy by various leaders in the Republic of Gran Colombia, often forsook formal democracy and reverted to dictatorial rule in order to try to hold the republic together. Much of the early history of the early republics was filled with such local and national *caudillos*—by men on white horses. An even more telling example is that of Dr. Francia. Soon after independence in Paraguay the then-leader of the country, Dr. José Gaspar Rodríguez de Francia, proclaimed himself dictator in perpetuity. His rule from 1816 to 1840 set a pattern for extended dictatorial rule that would continue to plague Paraguay until 1989. This and similar traditions of extented authoritarian rule continued to haunt many other Latin American countries through the nineteenth and twentieth centuries. Indeed, authoritarian rule would predominate in Paraguay, Bolivia, and Haiti through the nineteenth and twentieth centuries. The military-style leaders would dominate the period up until 1855 in most countries, including Mexico, Argentina, and Peru. The seeds of democracy had been planted, but the early years of republican history seemed to justify Bolívar's previously noted conclusion the "we have plowed the sea."

The aftermath of independence was a difficult time for most of Latin America. The newly independent nations faced terrible obstacles as they sought to move forward economically, politically, and socially. It was a considerable struggle to establish national control and move beyond the regionalism that was so strong in most of the nations. Further, politics were generally dominated by the upper-class landowning elite. With the primary exception of Brazil, the new leaders took over power in the context of the physical devastation brought by the wars for independence. Devastation was particularly heavy in Mexico and Venezuela, but everywhere the burden of supporting the large armies of liberation was significant. Economic activity was also greatly affected by the continuous wars. Trade had almost ceased during the period. Trade with Spain ceased, of course, but inter-American trade was also adversely affected. Communication almost completely broke down among the new countries. The economics of the newly independent countries also faced challenges related to their very nature. Based almost exclusively on mining and agriculture, the colonies had been marginally integrated into the world economy before independence, but they now faced new challenges freed from their previous colonial commitments. The failure to achieve political unity meant that each new country faced the challenge of creating its own national economy. There were also regional differences; Mexico had a fairly well-developed national economy, but most of the other countries did not. As countries sought to develop themselves, they often faced internal divisions as well as interference from outside political and economic influences. Most new regimes lacked the financial assets even to equip a national army, let alone embark on significant national economic development. Mechanisms for tax collection and other standard methods of revenue collection were simply not sophisticated enough to meet the new nations' considerable needs. As a result, many countries, including Mexico and Argentina, turned to loans from foreign banks as a way out of their crises. Foreign governments, especially Britain, eagerly provided money in hopes of significant returns. These loans, made more than 150 years ago, began a dependence that has persisted to the present day.

The era of free trade was also launched during this time period, as Latin America slowly adapted itself to the world economy. Exports to the United States and Europe began to increase—nitrates from Chile, hides and salted beef from Argentina, sugar from Cuba, and coffee from Brazil. The growth in exports was also accompanied by a corresponding rise in manufactured imports, especially textiles. Latin American artisans and small producers were often driven out of business in the exchange. This time also saw the arrival of a small number of foreign merchants who took up key positions in the fields of shipping, insurance, and banking. The pattern of losing out to foreign competitors was primarily the result of the technological superiority of the Europeans, but the local elites exacerbated the problem with misguided political choices. The traditional landowning elites first ensured that their holdings were secure and then retreated to the security of their *haciendas* and *fazendas*, not particularly concerned about maximizing production or contributing to the economic modernization of their countries. Political power was left largely in the hands of military men who had become *caudillos*, among them, Juan Manuel de Rosas, the governor of Buenos Aires province; Antonio López de Santa Anna, the president of Mexico; and a lieutenant of Bolívar, José Antonio Páez. These military governments, without significant streams of revenue, were vulnerable to being overthrown and were incapable of sustaining local economic growth. Some leaders recognized the dangers inherent in a weak central state, so in many countries conflict developed between locally based power brokers and the centralizers. These struggles were to be the forerunners of later battles for political power between Conservatives and Liberals.

One group negatively affected by independence was the indigenous peoples. They had not been a consistent force for elite-led independence and therefore were not seen by the new governments as important allies. As a result, they lost whatever protections they may have had under colonial administrations. Their land became increasingly vulnerable to takeover and their condition made even more impoverished. The immediate aftermath of the independence movement also saw the Mexican-American War of 1846–1848. This conflict reestablished a pattern of foreign intervention in Latin America and cost Mexico nearly half of its national territory.

1850–1880

The second stage of Latin America's integration into the world economy occurred between 1850 and 1880. National unification became the political theme as local *caudillo* rulers were slowly supplanted by national leaders who began to construct the apparatus of the modern state. Liberal reform leaders like Benito Juárez in Mexico, Domingo Sarmiento in Argentina, and Justo Rufino Barrios in Guatemala appeared.

As Latin American nations were ever more integrated into the commercializing world economy, Liberal political (and economic) reforms and modernization that began in the 1850s continued. The epic Argentine struggle between the rural *gaucho* and remaining Indians on one hand and the Europeanized *porteño* (port) elite from Buenos Aires on the other was indicative of this trend. The 1853 defeat of the *gaucho* dictator Juan Manuel de Rosas by reformist forces ushered in a new regime that opted for the "civilizing" influence of the port city over the rural land owners, the *estanciaros*. The government and economy were modernized, and massive European immigration (mostly from Italy) began. European capital, science, and technology were interjected into the development process. Liberal reforms set the stage for the emergence of other sectors in Argentine society. The meatpacking and grain-exporting industries gradually facilitated the emergence of an industrial proletariat and the beginning of a middle class. Argentina became ever more closely tied to England through the sale of its beef and the influx of British investment.

Meanwhile, peasants were beginning to feel the squeeze as their countries were further incorporated into the world market. Economic pressures and social upheaval fomented political restructuring as well. As a result, the region began to witness the emergence of reformist parties like the Radical Civic Union in Argentina, where this party held sway for most of the second and third decades of the twentieth century.

Periods of democratic rule began to appear, and political participation was slowly widened in many countries to begin to include common people. The transformation was in part driven by the slow rise of Latin America's export trade and the need to have a national infrastructure to support such trade. This era saw the beginning of efforts by national governments to transform long-standing land tenure arrangements that were dominated by largely unproductive *latifundios* and government land. This was the era of liberal ascendency almost everywhere in Latin America. During this period there were significant efforts to undermine Church authority and establish secular, public education. Liberal ideas also made their way into the prison system and even military organizations. All of these Liberal reforms and nation-building occurred in the context of the penetration of North American and European capital.

To transport the region's coffee, sugar, nitrates, and other primary products to Europe and elsewhere, there was a strong need to replace the region's antiquated transportation system with new roads, canals, railroads, and docks. The traditional landowning elites had no need for infrastructure development to prosper, so they had not built it and were indifferent to its construction. The impetus for such development came primarily from abroad. European industrialization created a great thirst for everything from foodstuffs to fertilizers to metals. The developing European industries also sought out new markets for their manufactured goods. These twin European needs laid the groundwork for the next phase of Latin American development. Latin American countries willing to do business with Europe gained rising political power and wealth that challenged the traditional elites. However, the character of this economic arrangement—Latin American primary goods traded for European finished goods—established the pattern of Latin America's role in the world economy that persists to this day. The countries saw very little growth of domestic industry, as European producers of machinery, weapons, and other light manufactured goods often blocked the development of indigenous industries. Competing with European entrepreneurs would have been difficult given their head start in technology; nor were Latin American governments of the time inclined to set up tariff barriers to spur local development. Generally they were more than happy to welcome unrestricted foreign trade in return for their share of the profits. The era of 1850–1880 was one of laying the groundwork for even more dramatic changes that occurred in the last twenty years of the nineteenth century.

1880–1910

The needs of European industrialization that had been developing slowly throughout the nineteenth century came to a head after 1880. The demand for food by Europe's industrial workers and for raw materials to fuel factories was insatiable. Several key Latin American countries were transformed by this demand. Argentina became a great producer of beef, wool, and wheat. Brazil and El Salvador became the world's primary producers of coffee, satisfying Europe's newfound addiction, with Peru, Mexico, and Cuba supplying the sugar. Mexico provided Europe and North America with a variety of raw materials, including hemp, copper, and zinc. Thus, the pattern established in earlier decades of Latin American countries producing primary goods in exchange for European manufactured goods was deepened.

European countries also became invested in Latin America during this period. Britain was by far the dominant investor, with almost two-thirds of the total investment by 1913. Railroads and mining were the two key sectors into which Europeans and North Americans placed their money. American investment also began to increase dramatically after 1900. Only modest amounts of Latin American capital went into these sectors, so the pattern of economic control by foreign powers became well established. Thus, Latin American prosperity became increasingly tied to the health of the European and North American economies. It also meant that most of the key decisions about the economic direction of Latin America were not being made in Rio de Janeiro or Buenos Aires but rather in New York, London, and Paris.

The new economic reality was justified and validated by the growing predominance of liberal ideology in most parts of Latin America. Free trade political liberals who favored less centralized state rule formed Liberal parties, while traditional agricultural interests and pro-Church conservatives formed Conservative parties. Local political leaders and their foreign counterparts extolled the virtues of free trade and open borders. It was viewed as simply "unnatural" to stand in the way of the economic and social progress that such arrangements were supposed to bring. Even the traditional landed elites in large measure cooperated in the modernization process, providing generous concessions to foreign companies while relying on traditional labor practices. To local governments it seemed only logical to collect some government revenue from commercial trade that during colonial times had flourished illegally outside their control. Of course, it was only a tiny slice (less than 5 percent) of the populations that benefitted from these free trade agreements. Local elites, who viewed the native populations as significantly inferior, excluded them systematically from national political life. Where elections were held in Latin America in the nineteenth century, fewer than 10 percent of the population was eligible to vote. Most of the countries were organized as republics, but it was in form only. Political participation was limited and democracy was weak.

Elitist domination of politics persisted through the end of the nineteenth century, but in a different form. The dominance of the local *caudillo* was over. National governments were now dominant, epitomized in the Porfirio Díaz regime in Mexico, 1876–1880 and 1884–1911. In some ways leaders like Díaz were mirror images of the local *caudillo*. Usually military men, they were no longer doing the bidding of a local hacienda owner. Instead they were representing the interests of commercial farmers and merchants whose economic success was predicated on foreign trade and a national infrastructure. To achieve the national power they needed, local authorities had to be put in line, a process that was consummated in Argentina and Mexico during this period. All such national regimes had a law-and-order focus designed to achieve political stability and therefore attract foreign investment.

The turn of the twentieth century saw the beginning of the consolidation of the modern nation-state in Latin America. As suggested earlier, this process had begun with Liberal reforms in Mexico under Benito Júarez in the 1850s and by Bartolomé Mitre and Domingo Sarmiento (1862–1874) in Argentina. In each country the consolidation of power by newly emerging commercial elites was tied to increasing trade with the industrializing world. This movement of power away from more traditionally oriented elites would continue in the region through the 1940s.

Late nineteenth-century Brazil and Mexico saw the strong influence of developmental thought associated with Auguste Comte's philosophical positivism. Indeed, it was positivism that inspired the modernization of the Brazilian state and the foundation of the Brazilian Republic in 1889. Thus the new elites in both of these countries began to rely on science and technology and tried to organize their societies to conform to the scientific law of progress. Following the advice of his positivist scientific advisors, or *científicos*, Díaz consolidated the commercial integration of Mexico into the world economy and was responsible for the massive foreign investment and improved infrastructure that characterized his rule. As with elite-run regimes in virtually all Latin American countries save Argentina, these new regimes did little to enfranchise the peasant and laboring masses economically. Indeed, the economic conditions of the common people had changed little since independence, and conditions that favored the emergence of a substantial middle class developed at a slow pace.

Post-1910

By 1910 Latin America was being integrated ever more strongly into the world capitalist economy, assigned the role of peripheral producer of primary goods and consumer of industrialized goods from the developed nations at the center of the system. Further, there was increasing investment in plantations like those that grew sugar in Cuba or bananas in Central America and mines in countries like Mexico (silver), Chile (copper), and Bolivia (tin). Likewise, British and American financial capital sought even more investment opportunities in the expanding Latin American economies. The Great Depression temporarily halted the integration of Latin America into the international capitalist economic system, but the pace of integration continued and quickened in the second half of the century.

As we suggest in the chapter on economics (Chapter 7), increased demand for the export commodities and increasing imports helped commercialize Latin American economies. Import substitution industrialization (ISI) further changed the face of Latin America, as did the subsequent phase of export-led growth and the growing production and export of manufactured goods. The 1970s saw Latin American countries borrow more and more capital from outside the region, greatly increasing their external debts in the process. Debt and debt repayment remained a poignant problem into the twenty-first century. The last decades of the twentieth century witnessed the transformation of the region from what at the beginning of the century was a rural area where wealthy landowners and poor peasants or rural laborers predominated to a modern, urbanized area where three-quarters of the people lived in cities. By the turn of the twenty-first century the largest class in most countries was the urban working class, which included a growing informal sector. Likewise, a significant middle class had developed and cut its political teeth. As these new classes were joined by new segments of the upper class tied to industrialization and commercialization and the increased involvement of multinational corporations and foreign investors, new political forces were mobilized and new political coalitions developed.

THE MEXICAN REVOLUTION

These and other factors led to the development of the first great revolutionary movement of the twentieth century—the Mexican Revolution. The dominance of traditional landowners, the Church, and the Díaz dictatorship kept developing social and political forces in check for many years. However, the struggle for change finally erupted in 1910 and spread throughout the society. The mostly rural masses soon mobilized with cries of *"pan y tierra"* (bread and land) and participated full force in the many revolutionary armies that fought for the next seven years under such generals as Pancho Villa and Emiliano Zapata. It was indeed a revolution won by *los de abajo*, those from below, to use the term of Mariano Azuela. The radical constitution of 1917 manifested many of the new ideas of the revolutionaries, set the stage for the development of modern Mexico, and infected the rest of Latin American with new ideas and expectations. Hereafter land reform, legislation protecting workers, secular education, reduction of the power of foreign investors, and the Church's power and influence—as well as the ability to break with overly European models in favor of those that recognized the culture, history, and ethnicity of the masses—began to filter through Latin America. They soon combined with ideas from the second great revolution of the twentieth century (in Russia in 1917) to stimulate the development of new, more progressive social movements and political parties that would endeavor to forge a very different Latin American reality. The rest of the twentieth century witnessed myriad struggles between the conservative political and economic forces and mobilized classes and coalitions advocating significant reformist or revolutionary change.

Forces favoring reform and revolution would hereafter battle conservative forces and those tied to the existent system. After the Russian Revolution and subsequent spread of more radical forms of socialism and Marxism, these struggles would often become more class-oriented and often quite bloody as the dominant classes fought tooth and nail to preserve their status and privilege.

DEMOCRATIC REFORMISM IN URUGUAY

The modern reformist era arrived in Uruguay at the turn of the century. Like Argentina, Uruguay had an urban working class and the beginning of a middle class whose interests were quite different from those of the traditional landholders. The dynamic leader of the liberal Colorado party, José Batlle y Ordóñez, chose his 1903 election as president to enact a series of extensive economic and political reforms that would turn Uruguay into a modern social democracy and welfare state by the 1920s. Further, in a fascinating experiment with less autocratic forms of rule, Uruguay was even governed by the *colegiado,* or collective presidency (where power was shared among members of a presidential council and the titular head of state rotated) from 1917 to 1933 and 1951 to 1967. Thus from 1903 until 1973 Uruguay was regarded as the Switzerland of Latin America and as an example of just how democracy and enlightened social democratic-style rule could triumph in a Latin American state.

Later, conditions changed in Uruguay, and the threat of even greater popular mobilizations and the threat to the domestic upper class and foreign capitalists posed by the often popular Tupamaro guerrillas mobilized conservative forces against further change. Thus, even in democratic Uruguay, the rising tide of bureaucratic authoritarian military governments in the 1970s undermined their hard-won democratic political culture and the working and middle-class benefits and liberties that had been achieved. This experiment with reformist democracy and a fully developed welfare state was cut short when the military staged a coup in 1973. The military controlled the country for the next twelve years. Full democratic rule was not restored until 1985, but the *colegiado* was no longer employed and the working and middle class were forced to accept government cutbacks and other structural adjustments. More recently, a progressive coalition, the *Frente Amplio,* has become a major power contender.

DEMOCRACY AND DICTATORSHIP IN ARGENTINA

It was suggested earlier that in the nineteenth century Argentina evolved from the gaucho dictatorship of Juan Manuel de Rosas to the reformist civilian rule of presidents like Domingo Faustino Sarmiento. By the turn of the century Argentine beef and wheat were flooding into Europe, and British investment was pouring into Argentina. The South American nation was developing rapidly and had a higher per capita income than several European nations. It soon spawned a proletariat and a nascent middle class. These groups became the base for a newly formed, European-inspired Radical party, which promised to bring enlightened democratic rule to Argentina. Before Argentina could experience sustained economic or political development, the Great Depression dashed Argentina's hope for continued economic development, and the weakening of the Radical party and a subsequent coup d'état in 1930 plunged the nation back into a military dictatorship.

After oligarchic-inspired conservative rule in most of the 1930s and early 1940s, a group of officers again intervened to take over the government in 1943. The junta they formed was eventually dominated by Colonel Juan Domingo Perón, who was later able to consolidate his power with the help of Eva Duarte and successfully ran for president in the 1946 elections. Peronism, as his political movement came to be called, became the dominant political party and political movement in Argentina. Peronism displace the Socialist party as the party of the masses and remained the largest political party for the rest of the twentieth century. Juan Perón was a dynamic, charismatic, and often dictatorial leader who was famous for his mass rallies and ties to the Argentine labor movement. Eva Perón became the darling of the masses and greatly bolstered the Peronist project. Eva died in 1952 and Juan Perón was ousted from power in 1955, yet their influence would linger; when again allowed to run for president in 1973 Juan Perón was reelected with his then wife María Isabel Martínez Perón as his vice president. He died the next year, and Isabel Perón become the first woman president in Latin America, only to be overthrown by a military coup in 1976.

From 1955 to 1966 Argentina was characterized by frequent alternation between military regimes and weak democratic governments. The country was industrializing and engaging in successful policies of import substitution, but it continued to be plagued by high inflation and a growing foreign debt. Strikes, labor actions, and guerrilla warfare challenged the oligarchy and the government. The military ruled outright from 1966 to 1973 and instituted a brutal "dirty war" against leftists and other political enemies from 1976 to 1983. After the military government initiated and lost the Falkland Islands war in 1982, elections brought a return to civilian government in 1983. Although initially threatened by barracks revolts and plagued by economic difficulties that allowed rightist Peronist President Menem to impose unpopular austerity measures, democracy continued through the rest of the century.

AUTHORITARIANISM, APRISMO, MARXISMO, AND DEMOCRACY IN PERU

In Peru, that nation's defeat in the War of the Pacific (1879–1883) caused a national reexamination that began the process of the consolidation of the modern nation-state and unleashed new social and political forces. Critical writers like Manuel González Prada spawned the radical reformist movements that eventually led to state centralization and consolidation under subsequent presidents and radical political movements like Victor Raúl Haya de la Torre's Alianza Popular Revolucionaria Americana (American Popular Revolutionary Alliance) (APRA) and José Carlos Mariátegui's Peruvian Socialist party (later the Peruvian Communist party).

Haya de la Torre, heavily influenced by the Mexican as well as the Russian Revolution, came to believe in a necessary political, economic, and social restructuring of all of Latin America. He founded APRA while visiting Mexico in 1924 and began a lifelong struggle to found political movements that would enfranchise the masses, promote land reform, improve treatment of indigenous Americans, and resist the dominance of the United States. This movement led to the formation of the APRA in Peru (which was kept from power by conservative and then reformist military forces until Alan García's presidency in 1985) and similar political movements in other countries. These movements represented the aspirations of the toiling masses—particularly indigenous peoples—and many sectors of the emerging middle classs. The groups were often characterized as national revolutionary parties even though they were generally more reformist than revolutionary by the time they came to power. They came to be dominant parties in Venezuela (Acción Democrática, founded by Rómulo Betancourt), Costa Rica (Liberación Nacional, founded by José Figueres), Bolivia (Movimiento Nacionalista Revolucionario—the National Revolutionary Movement, MNR—founded by Victor Paz Esstensoro), Puerto Rico (the Popular Democratic Party—PDP—founded by Luis Muñoz Marín) and the Dominican Republic (Partido Revolucionario, founded by Juan Bosch).

Coming from a more modest background than the aristocratic Haya de la Torre and more specifically focused on the Indian peasants and rural laborers, miners, and the small urban proletariat, the self-educated Mariátegui was heavily influenced by his reading of González Prada, the indigenist movement in Peru, Marxist literature, Lenin and the Russian Revolution, and the Mexican Revolution. He supported indigenous rights and the workers' movement in Peru and went on to found the Peruvian Socialist Party, which soon affiliated with Communist International. In so doing he stimulated the development of a Marxist-Leninist movement in Peru and gave impetus to revolutionary struggle in Peru and elsewhere. Indeed, he argued for a Latin American socialism that was "neither copy or imitation" of any other. But his early demise in 1930 and strong criticism from the Soviet-controlled Communist International limited his influence for many years. Marxists in Peru and Latin America rarely followed his independent stance, and Communist parties were generally subordinate to European influences and Soviet control.

Substantial structural change did not come to Peru through a socialist movement or through APRA; rather, it arrived with a reformist military takeover in 1968 that maintained power until 1980. Thus it was the military—not reformist or radical civilian politicians—who instituted a comprehensive system of land reform in Peru (although they did not set up sufficient financial mechanisms to empower poor peasants and agricultural workers who were the beneficiaries of this reform) and began to address the conditions of the workers.

Previously, Peru's political history had been marked by dictators like Augusto Leguía (1919–1930) and Manuel Prado (1949 and 1956–1962) and by intermittent periods of democracy.

There was a return to democratically elected governments after 1980, but the struggle against severe economic conditions for the masses and the rise of the guerrilla group Sendero Luminoso stretched the democratic institutions beyond their limits. By the mid-1990s, the 1992 *auto-glope* (self-coup) of elected president Alberto Fujimori had greatly diminished the practice of democracy. This trend was continued with the 2000 fraudulent reelection of Fujimori for a constitutionally prohibited third term, though he was forced from office in 2001 and new elections were held.

Democracy, Socialism, and Dictatorship in Chile

Political reform came to Chile earlier. It began with the formation of a Parliamentary Republic (1891–1924) and came to include the formation of a proletariat and a nascent middle class. The predominance of copper mines owned by foreign corporations sparked the formation of a strong socialist-oriented union movement, and the large number of socialist immigrants helped create a political socialist movement in Chile. Like Mariátegui in Peru, labor leader Luis Emilio Recabarren championed a Marxist party in Chile. Building on the newly developing political forces unleashed by a nitrate boom, the parliamentary republic, and the development of copper mining, Chile continued to evolve, experiencing a short-lived socialist republic under Marmaduke Grove in the early 1930s.

Along with more traditional parties, a substantial socialist movement developed. As its support among the miners and urban working class and sectors of the middle class grew, it was challenged by a strong, reformist Christian Democratic party that had also created a union movement tied to their party. The Christian Democrats headed off the leftist challenge, mobilized workers, and, with support from the United States and their Christian Democratic allies in Europe, won two important election in the 1960s and went on to establish themselves as a major reformist party. Even greater structural change began when the Socialist party, in coalition with the Communist and Radical parties, finally achieved power in 1970 with the election of Salvador Allende as president. This was a clear triumph of the popular classes.

Up to this point Chile, like Uruguay and Costa Rica after 1948, was considered a nation where the seeds of democracy had taken root and flowered. Indeed, many thought that the thoroughgoing socialist restructuring proposed by Allende might actually be carried out by peacefully, constitutional means. Some significant progress was made during the first years of Allende's Popular Unity government from 1970 to 1973, but Chilean society became increasing polarized. The United States and conservative sectors in Chile made every effort to destabilize the newly elected government. United States military aid to the Chilean military was, interestingly, continued. Finally, Chilean democracy was shattered by a brutal military coup in September 1973. The workers had lost. The coup displaced all progressive forces and instituted a repressive military regime run by August Pinochet that lasted until 1990. A return to free market economics was one of the primary goals of the military dictatorship. As the country came to terms with the brutality of the military dictatorship in the post-Pinochet period, three democratic elections were held and a socialist once again became president in 2000, although the country had become a model for neoliberal economics.

CUBA, COLONIALISM, AND COMMUNISM

Much of the inspiration for the democratic attempt at a constitutional socialist revolution in Chile was derived from the Cuban example as well as from Chile's own socialist and democratic tradition. Indeed, the event after the Mexican Revolution that inspired the most attempts at radical change in Latin America was the revolution that took place in Cuba in 1959. As it evolved toward a socialist path that eventually embraced Marxism-Leninism, Cuba became a model for radical change throughout the region.

Cuba, like Mexico, was an example of change delayed. Even independence had come late to Cuba; Cuban patriots lost the Ten Years War (1868–1878), and slavery was not abolished until 1886. Spanish colonial rule endured until 1898 and independence was not achieved until 1902, and then only under U.S. tutelage. The system that ensued was dominated by sugar plantations and sugar refineries (*centrales*) that were increasingly owned or controlled by U.S. businesses as American investment capital flooded into the island in the first decades of the twentieth century. A Cuban upper class centered in sugar production also developed, while the masses were generally relegated to positions as cane workers and *guajiros*—peasants. Poverty and seasonal unemployment characterized rural agricultural labor, as did de facto subordination of people of color. A monocrop economy and dependent nation par excellence, Cuba became closely tied to the United States for sugar sales and the importation of finished goods. Indeed, it was often suggested that the American ambassador to Havana was nothing less than a proconsul.

By the 1920s Cuba had already experienced its first dictatorship (Gerardo Machado, 1924–1933). A second coup was led by a noncommissioned officer, Sergeant Fulgencio Batista, in 1934. Batista maintained good relations with the United States and, promoted to Colonel, was elected to the presidency in 1940 as a reformer. In 1952 he executed another coup and established what became a brutal and unpopular dictatorship that was eventually overthrown by Fidel Castro's 26th of July movement. Supported by peasants and agricultural workers, segments of the Cuban upper class, and many from the middle class that had emerged in Havana, the revolutionaries took power in 1959 and went about reforming the country, basing many of their ideas on the reformist constitution of 1940. The guerrilla war that put them in power became immortalized in fellow guerrilla leader Ernesto "Che" Guevara's manual on *guerrilla* fighting, *Guerrilla Warfare*.

The example of the Cuban revolution and the power and example of forming guerrilla groups to wrest power from dominant elites was of immediate interest to the Latin American left. The Cuban revolution became Marxist after the United States organized the Bay of Pigs invasion in 1961 and thus also became an example of the revolutionary transformation of a Latin American society. The notion of overthrowing the status quo with a band of guerrilla fighters and going about addressing the economic and social injustices and foreign control that had characterized the region was widely acclaimed by progressive forces. A variety of Fidelista guerilla groups were organized throughout Latin American and set about the task of emulating the Cuban example and fighting their way down from the hills into the corridors of power in the nations' capitals. Guerrilla movements like the FSLN in Nicaragua, the Armed Forces of National Liberation (FALN) in Venezuela, and the Movement of the Revolutionary Left (MIR) in Peru and Chile began to operate from Mexico and Guatemala in the north to Argentina and Chile in the south. Radical change and socialist revolution through violent struggle were now added to the political mix. The revolutions were not led or fomented by Latin American Soviet-oriented Communist parties, which generally had very limited success, frequently criticized the young Fidelista revolutionaries, and often did not support the movements. Cuba became the revolutionaries' mecca and source for moral and sometimes material support. The radical regime continued in power into the twenty-first century.

Earlier Attempts at Change: Bolivia and Colombia

Before the Cuban Revolution, other less radical attempts at change had been tried in Latin America in the post–World War II period. The MNR in Bolivia was inspired by the philosophy and example of the Peruvian-based APRA and the Mexican Revolution. Led by Victor Paz Estensora, MNR radicals had led the strongly indigenous and heavily unionized radical tin miners, indigenous peasants, and middle-class supportors to seize power in 1952. They soon nationalized the tin mines and engaged in a major agrarian reform that distributed large amounts of land to impoverished peasants. Difficult economic conditions and the hostility of the United States made it difficult to maintain the reformist project. The experiment was cut short in 1964 when the vice president took power through a military coup. A series of military governments followed.

The movement to enfranchise the masses in Colombia was manifest in the figure of progressive Liberal politician Jorge Gaitán. He represented the progressive wing of the Liberal party and promised better conditions for the labor movement and for peasants. Before he could mobilize support for such badly needed reforms, he was assassinated in Bogotá in April 1948. Those committed to change took to the streets and days of violent rioting followed. Know as the Bogotazo, the violent actions in the capital soon spread throughout the country, where bands of Liberals attacked Conservatives, whom they believed had denied them the change they so badly needed. Soon the entire country was caught up in a decade of fighting known as La Violencia. It was finally ended by the formation of the National Front—a common front based on a political pact between the political elite in the Conservative and Liberal parties whereby they agreed to share power among the mainstream elements of the two parties. The pact lasted until the early 1970s.

In the meantime, those desiring more fundamental change gravitated to a variety of guerrilla groups that began to operate in Colombia from the 1960s onward. Many of these gained such power that they were able to ne-

gotiate special agreements with the government, one of the original and surviving guerrilla groups, the Fuerzas Armadas Revolucionarias de Colombia
(FARC), even managed to negotiate a temporary cease fire with the Colombian government that gave them control over part of Colombian territory.
They and other guerrilla groups had been greatly strengthened in the 1990s
by agreements with several Colombian drug cartels that guaranteed protection and economic well-being for the peasants in their areas and gave the
cartels certain protection from the armed forces as long as they paid their
taxes to the guerrilla organization. By 2000 the eroding power and legitimacy of the government, the growing strength of FARC and the Ejercito de
Liberación Nacional (ELN) suggested that change in Colombia could still
come through a revolutionary takeover. This, and the continuing power of
the drug cartels, prompted the United States to greatly increase military,
anti-drug, and economic aid to Colombia in 2000.

BRAZIL AND THE NATIONAL SECURITY STATE

Like Cuba, change and social restructuring came late to Brazil. From independence in 1821 until 1889 Brazil was an empire under the control of emperors from the Portuguese royal family. Brazil did not see the consolidation of the modern nation-state until Getúlio Vargas' takeover of the federal
government in the revolution of 1930 and his subsequent establishment of
the New State in 1936. Vargas and his personal style of populism dominated
Brazilian politics until his suicide in 1954. Through the efforts of many progressive political movements, change again occurred in the late 1950s.
Juscelino Kubitschek was elected in 1955 by promising to move the country
forward. His dynamic approach to government action and the founding
of the new capital of Brasília helped heighten expectations for a brighter
future.

After 1960, the United States became increasingly concerned with political mobilization of the masses and political movements that might, as had
occurred in Cuba, become radicalized as they struggled to break away from
the stultifying economic and social structures that had condemned the vast
majority of Latin Americans to poverty and suffering. U.S. policy toward
Latin America in the 1960s was twofold: Foment gradual change and restructuring through the Alliance For Progress and related activities (this
would undermine the political base of more revolutionary movements), and
support the development of counterinsurgency and the national security
states to fight and defeat the radical guerrilla movements that did appear.
To that end, military training in places like the School of the Americas in
the Panama Canal Zone and aid to Latin American militaries was greatly
increased. Soldiers and lower-level officers were trained in counterinsurgency tactics. Command officers were imbued with a version of the national
security doctrine that suggested that the Latin American governments and
especially the military were responsible for protecting the nation and state
from the threat posed by guerillas, leftist political movements, and communism. Since many Latin American military leaders already thought of

themselves as guardians of the nation, this training—which was replicated and emphasized in national war colleges—served as a further impetus to intervene when there was danger of uncontrollable popular mobilization or unchecked guerrilla activity. In 1965, President Lyndon Johnson even enunciated the Johnson Doctrine (a corollary to the Monroe Doctrine) to explain the need of the United States to intervene in its sister republics to stop the spread of communism.

The shadow of the Cuban revolution, peasant mobilization, worker militancy, and domestic radicals who might opt for violent revolution—all seen through the lens of national security doctrine—convinced the Brazilian military and conservative forces that they were facing a revolutionary situation. The United States had already expressed concern and was communicating with the military and sympathetic politicians. A military coup was staged in 1964, and a long period of authoritarian military rule was initiated.

The military regime that took power did not, however, stabilize the situation and then hold elections, as was often the case when military juntas took over. Rather, it usurped power from civilian politicians, closing congress, arresting some leftist leaders, banning traditional political parties, and generally arguing that the Brazilian military could develop the country much better than the civilian politicians could. The peasant mobilization and worker militancy that helped spark the revolution were suppressed, as were radical groups. There would be no revolution in Brazil. Instead, a long period of military rule (lasting until 1985) was initiated and the military took it upon itself to guide Brazil in achieving its *grandeza* (greatness) by developing along more conservative, state-directed capitalist lines. *Fazendas* were continued, foreign capital was invited in, the government went into joint business ventures with multinational corporations, the Amazon was thrown open for development, and indigenous people were seen as expendable in the rapid developmental process that ensued. Growth and development were expected; socioeconomic restructuring and income redistribution were unaccceptable. This long-term economically and politically involved military rule and the resultant national security state designed to stop political or social revolutions like that which occurred in Cuba came to be called *bureaucratic authoritarianism*. Brazil was the prototype.

The Cold War and Change

THE DOMINICAN CASE

In early 1965 political instability and the possibility of the mobilization of the Dominican masses by Juan Bosch and his APRA-style Dominican Revolutionary Party raised the specter of a reformist party taking power but, like the 26th of July movement in Cuba, then becoming radicalized as it endeavored to effect change in an economy heavy with U.S. investment. Red flags went up in the White House and the Pentagon, and in April 1965 25,000 Marines were dispatched to Santo Domingo to restore order and staunch any leftist threat. No more Cubas would be tolerated. Conservative rule was restored and continued into the 1930s.

CENTRAL AMERICA

The quest for change in Central America came more slowly. American involvement in the region dated from William Walker's intervention in Nicaragua in the 1850s (he took power and declared himself president in 1855). American investment grew through the later part of the nineteenth century and all during the twentieth. Initial attempts to consolidate the Nicaraguan state by Liberal president José Santos Zelaya were eventually met with a landing by the U.S. Marines in 1909. In Nicaragua, these efforts to initiate change, enfranchise more of the mostly peasant masses, and gain a greater degree of autonomy from the United States were led by nationalists like Benjamin Zeledón and the famous guerrilla leader Augusto César Sandino. But these were stymied by the continuing presence of the United States and the installation of the Somoza family dictatorship in the 1930s. The state was never modernized under Somoza family rule. Modernization and change did not reappear until the Frente Sandinista de Liberación Nacional (FSLN) defeated the dictatorship in 1979. The Sandinistas ruled until 1990 and were able to institute a major land reform program and greatly improve health care and education, although the degree and quality of governance remained mixed. The United States–inspired contra war put great pressure on the Sandinista government, exacerbated economic problems, and contributed to the adoption of austerity measures that undermined Sandinista popularity. U.S.-backed opposition candidate Violeta Chamorro won the presidential election in 1990, ending Sandinista rule. An even more conservative president was elected in 1996.

Other attempts were also made to transform the traditional reality of Central America. For instance, from 1944 to 1954, reformist forces in Guatemala attempted to consolidate a modern nation-state and make economic and social reforms that would economically and politically empower the peasants, banana workers, and majority indigenous population for the first time. However, the new government soon found itself in a heated dispute with the Boston-based United Fruit Company, which had very strong ties to the U.S. government. Before the land reform program could be completed, the Revolution of 1944 was overthrown by a CIA-organized military coup in 1954. A virtual civil war erupted in the 1960s as Cuban-inspired guerrillas tried unsuccessfully to overthrow the military and conservative forces. The struggle continued into the 1990s and claimed some 200,000 Guatemalan lives.

In El Salvador a small oligarchy reigned as fourteen families ruled and used brutal repression to maintain their virtual monopoly on wealth and power (as in the Matanza of 1932). The families frequently used their military allies to maintain an unjust status quo. Military rule predominated in the 1960s and 1970s, and pressure for change grew by 1979. Rather than allow needed land and other reforms the rulers once again opted for repression. This led to strong civilian opposition and the eventual formation of the

Faribundi Martí Front for National Liberation (FMLN). A civil war developed in the 1980s as a coalition of reformers and revolutionaries battled the military and the U.S.-backed civilian government. More than 70,000 lives were lost in the civil war in El Salvador; the United States supplied more than $5 billion in military and economic aid to stop the revolution. A negotiated peace was finally arranged in the 1990s, and the FMLN was transformed into a major political party.

Events were different in Costa Rica. The victory of José Figueres and his National Liberation forces in the Costa Rican civil war of 1948 and the subsequent establishment of a modern social democratic state in the 1950s marked the only example of progressive change to endure in the region. Figueres' strong ties to the United States and his American wife helped facilitate the success of the Costa Rican experiment, which turned into a two-party dominant democracy that valued honest elections and electoral competition. The country opted for a European-style social democracy that achieved high levels of education, health care, and sanitation.

As was mentioned earlier, the Cold War and the socialist turn of the Cuban Revolution encouraged the United States to suppress progressive political movements throughout the second half of the twentieth century, lest they lead to communism or Cuba-like revolutions. This often buttressed the most conservative forces and the status quo at the expense of much-needed reforms. Indeed, it sometimes served to kill hope for those who tried to effect change. U.S. policy makers encouraged their military and civilian allies in Latin America to think in terms of the national security state. Thus the United States sponsored counterinsurgency training for Latin American militaries at the School of the Americas in the Panama Canal Zone and at U.S. military bases such as Fort Bragg, North Carolina. Since the U.S. intervention in Guatemala in 1954, there has been significant U.S. military or political involvement in Cuba (Bay of Pigs, 1961), the Dominican Republic (Marines in Santo Domingo, 1965), Chile (destabilization and overthrow of Allende, 1973), Jamaica (destabilization of Manley government, 1980), El Salvador (continued political and military involvement, 1980–1992), Nicaragua (U.S.-inspired Contra war, 1981–1990), Grenada (military invasion, 1982), Panama (military invasion, 1989), and Colombia (aid and military advisors, 2000 on). Thus reform, revolution, and change often had to be played against a backdrop of real or potential involvement by the United States. As civil wars and guerrilla movements wound down in the 1990s, the United States continued to exert strong pressure on the internal politics of Latin American countries. The end of the Cold War and the new international order, however, made for less violent forms of economically focused intervention.

The 1991 demise of the Soviet Union, the main socialist rival to the ascending hegemony of the United States, and the resultant difficulties for Cuba and the Cuban revolutionary model meant that neither communism nor Cuba was perceived as an immediate threat in Latin America. This, in turn, relaxed the emphasis on the national security state and counterinsurgency in Latin America. Further, the end of bureaucratic authoritarian regimes by the early 1990s signaled a return to greater formal democracy. The triumph of capitalism in Eastern Europe further stimulated the process of free-market capitalist globalization. In Latin America, nationalist economic policies that protected and promoted import substitution industrialization and the growth of national businesses were rapidly abandoned in favor of free markets, free trade, and the free flow of investment capital. Latin America now seemed to be a safe place for international capital to do business. By 2000 Colombia was the only country to have any significant radical groups contesting power through the use of force and challenging the new Pax Americana. Throughout the region, increasing pressure came from international financial institutions like the International Monetary Fund (IMF) to globalize and set aside policies that would directly transfer benefits, income, or wealth to the still-suffering masses of Latin Americans. The new focus was not on socioeconomic change, restructuring, or income redistribution; rather, it was on capitalist growth that would—Latin Americans were told—benefit all. Those suspicious of the continuing intervention of the United States believed that Marine uniforms and guns may well have given way to business suits and IMF portfolios. Others felt that Latin America nations might now finally be able to compete in the international economic arena on more equal ground because the globalization of their economies would force them to modernize and become more competitive.

VENEZUELA: DICTATORSHIP, DEMOCRACY, AND THE POST–COLD WAR BOLIVARIAN REPUBLIC

The combination of these conditions generated a movement led by a progressive army officer in the country where Simón Bolívar had started the movement for independence in South America. In 1810 Bolívar and the junta in Caracas struggled to establish democracy in Caracas and the rest of what is now Venezuela. Yet the march toward democracy was not always easy in Bolívar's homeland. The nation saw its share of dictators in the remaining years of the nineteenth century and experienced a long period of dictatorial rule in the first part of the twentieth century. Indeed, the dictatorship of Juan Vicente Gómez (1908–1935) is one of the most notorious in Latin American history. Before Gómez Venezuela almost experienced another wave of European intervention. At the turn of the century several European states led by Germany wanted to take over the customs operations of the nation to get funds to repay debts owed by Venezuela. This plan was frustrated by the U.S. invocation of the Monroe Doctrine, but even so, Germany, England, and Italy did manage to engage in a naval bombardment of Puerto Cabezas in 1903. These economic problems were resolved with the beginning of petroleum production under the Gómez dictatorship.

Modern democracy came to Venezuela with the APRA-inspired Acción Democrática takeover in 1945 and the election of civilian president Rómulo Gallegos in 1947. But he too was overthrown by another coup in 1948. From 1952 to 1958 Venezuela suffered the military dictatorship of Pérez Jiménez. Led by Rómulo Betancourt, Acción Democrática instituted an open democracy, political competition (mostly with the Christian Democratic COPEI Party) that lasted until 1998. A founding member of the Organization of Petroleum Exporting Countries (OPEC), Venezuela was able to build a governmental and physical infrastructure from its increasing petroleum revenues. Although many lived well, the proceeds from petroleum production were concentrated in the middle and upper class and a few well-paid unionized petroleum workers. The vast majority continued to live in poverty despite the petroleum bonanza. Strong civilian government and a stable two-party system did, however, develop. This system suffered its first challenge when major riots broke out after IMF-inspired austerity measures were met with massive rioting by the poor in Caracas in 1989. The inability of the governments and increasing corruption led to two serious coup attempts by reformist military officers in 1992 and the eventual emergence of one of the coup leaders as a challenger to the old political system. After serving two years in prison, Hugo Chávez assembled an opposition movement (Fifth Republic Movement) and successfully ran for the presidency in December 1998. He defeated the candidates fielded by the two main parties and swept many of his supporters into office throughout the nation. The two long dominant parties lost legitimacy in the face of the traditional system's breakdown and Chávez's promises to confront neoliberalism and the conditions that were keeping the masses in poverty. Further, he charged the old political structures with corruption and of only benefitting the elite. He spoke of the need for structural change and made favorable references to the achievements of the Cuban revolution and Fidel Castro after his visit to the island. In 2000 Chávez managed to have a much revised constitutional system passed in a national plebiscite and to again hold elections at all levels to legitimize his mandate. The newly restructured state was dubbed the Bolivarian Republic of Venezuela.

As was the case in Venezuela, by the 1990s most Latin American economies experienced a wide gap between upper-class beneficiaries of globalization and the still-prevalent misery of the masses. In many cases income distribution even widened. However, a few countries, such as Costa Rica and Chile, after 1990 developed sufficient social welfare programs to at least soften the savage capitalism that globalization had unleashed in Latin America. It remains to be seen if this new direction in economic policy will engender sufficient benefits to satisfy the masses—or if the people will mobilize behind new political leaders and political movements that promise greater economic equality.

Nineteenth-Century Time Line

1804 Following mass slave rebellion led by Toussant L'Ouverture, Haiti becomes the first independent republic in Latin America

1807 Napoleon Bonaparte invades Spain and Portugal; Ferdinand VII abdicates Spanish throne, Napoleon names his brother as successor; In the Americas, creoles begin plotting the independence of their Spanish

American countries; The Portuguese court escapes and, with the British Navy's help, flees to Brazil

1810 Mexico declares independence from Spain under the leadership of Father Miguel Hidalgo

1811 Venezuela declares its independence by forming a junta that expels the Spanish governor of Venezuela

1813 Father José María Morelos revives the Mexican independence movement; José de San Martín and the Army of the Andes liberate Argentina

1816 The United Provinces of the River Plate declare their independence

1817 Chile is liberated by Bernardo O'Higgins; Spain outlaws the slave trade in all of its provinces to the north of the equator

1819 The United States buys Florida for $5 million

1821 On July 28, San Martín proclaims Peru independent; Dom Pedro defies summons of the Cortes by remaining in Brazil, creating the only durable monarchy in Latin American history; Stephen F. Austin and other settlers move into Texas; Mexico and Central America gain independence

1822 Agustín de Iturbide is crowned emperor of Mexico

1823 The Central American Federation is established; The Monroe Doctrine is announced by U.S. President James Monroe; Peru passes its constitution

1824 The defeat of the Spanish Army in Ayachuyo, Peru, marks the end of Spanish rule in the Americas

1825 Bolivia gains its independence

1825–1828 War between Brazil and United Provinces of the Rió de la Plata (present-day Argentina); the peace treaty created the independent state of Uruguay

1826 Congress of American Republics held in Panama

1826 Independence leaders sign concordats with the Vatican making Catholicism the state religion

1830 In Chile, beginning of the "Conservative Republic"; the Conservative Party holds power for thirty years

1835 Texans revolt

1836 Texans declare independence from Mexico

1845 U.S. Congress annexes Texas

1846 War between the United States and Mexico begins

1848 The Treaty of Guadalupe Hidalgo brings end to war between United States and Mexico; the United States gains approximately half of Mexico's territory

1855 U.S. citizen William Walker and former troops from the Mexican-American War invade Nicaragua; Walker declares himself president and holds power until 1857

1857 In Mexico the Laws of Reform are promulgated by Benito Juárez

1864 Maximilian given Mexican throne by Napoleon III

1867 President Juárez expels the French and marches into Mexico City

1868–1878 The Ten Years War; Nationalist Cubans lose fight for independence from Spain

1871   Chilean constitution is changed, disallowing consecutive presidential terms; Brazil passes "law of the free womb"—all children born to Brazilian slaves are considered free; also in Brazil, ex-Liberals found the Republican party

1876–1880; 1884–1911   General Porfirio Díaz rules over Mexico

1879–1883   War of the Pacific between Chile, Peru, and Bolivia; Bolivia loses land access to sea

1886   Slavery ends in Cuba

1887   In Chile, the Democratic party is founded

1888   Brazil passes "golden law," which frees all slaves without compensation

1889   On November 16, Brazil is declared a republic as Emperor Dom Pedro II and his family leave in exile

Contemporary Time Line

1910–1917   Mexican Revolution

1911   Madero elected president of Mexico

1912   Universal male suffrage granted in Argentina; The U.S. military intervenes in Nicaragua; U.S. troops stay until 1925

1913   Madero killed

1914   Panama Canal opens

1915–1934   United States occupies Haiti

1916–1922   U.S. Marines occupy Dominican Republic

1916   Hipólito Yrigoyen, leader of the Unión Cívica Radical (UCR, or Radicals), elected president of Argentina; Worker's compensation laws passed in Chile

1917   Chile passes employer liability laws; Venustiano Carranza assumes presidency in Mexico; a new constitution is written; U.S. military intervenes in Cuba; Puerto Rico is legally annexed to the United States; Puerto Ricans given U.S. citizenship

1919   Chile passes retirement system for railway workers in the same year that 100,000 workers march past presidential palace; Emiliano Zapata murdered

1922   Communist party formed in Brazil; Oil found in Venezuela

1924   Military junta in Chile; Alianza Popular Revolucionaria Americana (APRA) formed by Victor Raúl Haya de la Torre

1925   Sandino returns to Nicaragua to fight with Liberals; begins guerilla war against newly occupying U.S. forces

1926–1929   Mexican Church suspends worship protesting state harassment; Many priests and civilians killed in the Cristero rebellion

1926   Democratic party founded in São Paulo, Brazil

1929   Ecuador the first Latin American country to grant suffrage to women

1930   On September 6, the military of Argentina overthrows the Yrigoyen government; October coup in Brazil; Getúlio Vargas takes over government

1932   Brazil and Uruguay grant suffrage to women; Chaco War between Bolivia and Paraguay; Paraguay gains more territory; Uprising in El Salvador is brutally repressed in "la Matanza"

1933   U.S. troops leave Nicaragua; Anastasio Somoza begins to take power; U.S. president Franklin Roosevelt announces "Good Neighbor Policy"

1934   Lázaro Cárdenas becomes president of Mexico; during his term he redistributes 44 million acres of land to landless Mexicans; Sandino murdered

1938   Mexican oil industry nationalized under Cárdenas

1939   El Salvador grants suffrage to women

1943   Juan Perón and other military officers take over in Argentina

1944   Democratic Revolution in Guatemala

1945   Modern democratic era begins in Venezuela with takeover by APRA-inspired Acción Democrática, led by Rómulo Betancourt; Guatemala and Panama grant suffrage to women

1946   Juan Perón elected president of Argentina; Eva "Evita" Duarte Perón becomes first lady

1947   Argentina and Venezuela grant women suffrage

1948   José Figueres and APRA-inspired Liberación Nacional party lead reformist revolution in Costa Rica and establish modern democratic social welfare state; Costa Rican army banned by its new constitution; Bogotazo in Colombia; La Violencia begins

1949   Chile and Costa Rica grant women suffrage

1952   Evita Perón dies of cancer; Fulgencio Batista takes direct power in Cuba; Puerto Rico becomes a commonwealth of the United States; Marcos Pérez Jiménez stages coup in Venezuela, initiating a dictatorship that lasts until 1958; Bolivia grants women suffrage; Bolivian revolution led by Movimiento Nacionalista Revolucionario (MNR) and Víctor Paz Estenssoro

1954   Alfredo Stroessner takes over as president of Paraguay; rules until 1989; In Guatemala, CIA-organized coup deposes constitutional President Jacobo Arbenz and begins three decades of often brutal military rule; United Fruit regains land nationalized in land reform program during 1944 revolution

1955   Juan Perón ousted from power by the military; goes into exile; Honduras, Nicaragua, and Peru grant women suffrage

1956   Juscelino Kubitschek de Oliveira inaugurated president of Brazil; Construction of Brasília begins

1957   François "Papa Doc" Duvalier elected president of Haiti; Colombia grants women suffrage

1958   Dictator Pérez Jiménez ousted in Venezuela; Acción Démocratica's Rómulo Betancourt elected president, beginning modern democratic era

1959   Batista flees Cuba; Fidel Castro and the 26th of July movement take power

1960   Construction of Brasília completed

1961   Paraguay the last Latin American country to grant suffrage to women; The United States organizes unsuccessful Bay of Pigs invasion by Cuban exiles

1962–1965   The Second Vatican Conference commits the Church to work for human rights, justice, and freedom

1962   Peronists again allowed to run for office in Argentina; Cuban Missile Crisis; Jamaica gains independence from Britain

1963   Rural unionization legalized in Brazil; peasant leagues grow

1964   Eduardo Frei elected president of Chile; Military coup in Brazil; bureaucratic authoritarian military stays in power until 1985

1965   U.S. Marines invade the Dominican Republic

1966   Brazil's government unveils "Operation Amazonia" a plan to develop the Amazon Basin

1967   Ernesto "Che" Guevara dies in Bolivia

1968   October 2 student massacre in Tlatelolca, Mexico City; Meeting of Latin American bishops in Medellín; Columbia adopts a "preferential option for the poor" under the influence of liberation theology; Reformist military leaders take over in Peru under Juan Velasco Alvarado

1970   Salvador Allende elected president of Chile; he is the first freely elected Marxist president in Latin America; The Communist Party of Peru—Sendero Luminoso (PCP-SL) emerges after an ideological split in Peru's Communist party; origins of the group can be traced to a study group formed in the early 1960s by Professor Abimael Guzmán Reynoso at the University of San Cristoból de Huamanga; Sendero Luminoso, the Shining Path, later takes the form of a revolutionary movement

1971   Haitian president "Papa Doc" Duvalier dies; his son, Jean Claude "Baby Doc" Duvalier, takes control; U.S. Peace Corps, accused of sterilizing Indian women without their knowledge, expelled from Bolivia

1973   Juan Perón reelected president of Argentina; his wife Isabel becomes vice president; Salvador Allende killed in a September 11 military coup in Chile; General Augusto Pinochet initiates a brutal military dictatorship that rules until 1990

1974   Juan Perón dies; Isabel Perón becomes first female president of a Latin American country

1975   UN Conference on Women held in Mexico City, kicking off the Decade for Women; Cuba passes law requiring men and women to share responsibilities for housework and child-rearing

1976   Argentine military ousts Isabel Perón; General Jorge Rafael Videla takes power, and the "Dirty War" begins; The Mothers of the Disappeared begin to hold weekly vigils challenging the military government's human rights abuses

1978   John Paul II becomes Pope; the Catholic Church becomes more conservative; conservative Church leaders begin to attempt to eliminate liberation theology

1979   Somoza regime collapses; the Frente Sandinista de Liberación Nacional (FSLN), or Sandinista National Liberation Front takes power

1980 Archbishop Oscar Romero of San Salvador assassinated; four American church women murdered by Salvadoran military; Farabundo Martí National Liberation Front formed in El Salvador

1981 U.S. inspires contras to war against Nicaraguan government; 30,000 die before 1990

1982 Falklands/Malvinas War begins between Argentina and Britain; Brazil elects first freely elected governors since 1965; General Efrain Rios Montt becomes Latin America's first evangelical dictator in Guatemala, and embarks on a brutal counterinsurgency that often targets entire Indian communities

1983 U.S. Marines land in Grenada

1985 Brazil elects Tancredo Neves as first freely elected president; the night of his inauguration he has surgery and never recovers; Vice President José Sarney becomes president

1986 "Baby Doc" Duvalier flees Haiti

1988 Amidst well-documented charges of election fraud Institutional Revolutionary Party (PRI) candidate Carlos Salinas defeats Cuauhtémoc Cárdenas and Party of the Democratic Revolution (PRD) to gain presidency of Mexico

1989 Carlos Menem elected president of Argentina; Patricio Aylwin elected president of Chile, the first elected president of Chile since Allende took power; Pinochet maintains his position as Commander-in-Chief of the Chilean Armed Forces and as Senator-for-life; In Brazil, Fernando Collor de Mello elected president, defeating Workers' Party (PT) leader Inacio "Lula" da Silva; U.S. troops invade Panama to oust Manuel Noreíga; Six Jesuit priests assassinated in El Salvador by U.S.-trained troops after the Faribundi Martí Front for National Liberation (FMLN) overruns much of San Salvador; Announcement of austerity package in Venezuela causes riots; 276 die

1990 Alberto Fujimori elected president of Peru; stays in office until 2001; President Salinas of Mexico announces his intent to negotiate the North American Free Trade Agreement (NAFTA) with the United States; Jean-Bertrand Aristide elected president of Haiti; a military coup prevents him from taking power; Violeta Barrios de Chamorro elected president of Nicaragua, defeating FSLN candidate Daniel Ortega

1991 Jorge Serrano of Guatemala becomes Latin America's first elected evangelical president

1992 In Brazil, Collor is impeached and Vice President Itamar Franco becomes president; Fujimori closes congress in an *auto-golpe*, or self-coup; leader of the Sendero Luminoso, Abimael Guzmán, captured; World Summit on the Environment and Development held in Rio de Janeiro; Guerrilla war ends in El Salvador; Two military coup attempts occur in Venezuela

1993 Eduardo Frei (son of the president from 1964–1970) elected president of Chile; Carlos Andrés Pérez forced to step down in Venezuela

1994 Fernando Henrique Cardoso elected president of Brazil; NAFTA goes into effect on January 1; Zapatista National Liberation Army revolts in

Chiapas; Ernesto Zedillo elected president of Mexico after first PRI candidate is assassinated

1995	Menem reelected president of Argentina; Fujimori reelected president of Peru; United States occupies Haiti; Aristide assumes presidency; New quota in Argentina making sure that one in four congresspeople are women; Mercosur, or Southern Cone Common Market, is founded; nations included are: Argentina, Brazil, Uruguay, and Paraguay; they are later joined by Bolivia and Chile

1998	Pinochet loses post as Commander-in-Chief of Chilean Armed Forces; Cardoso reelected president of Brazil, once again defeating Lula; Former coup leader Hugo Chávez elected president of Venezuela, ending domination by two traditional parties, Acción Democrática and the Social Christian Party (COPEI)

1999	Mireya Moscoso elected first woman president of Panama

2000	Socialist Ricardo Lagos elected president of Chile as the Concentación candidate; Confederation of Indigenous Nationalitites of Ecuador (CONAIE) and military officers briefly take over congress in Ecuador; Fujimori reelected in Peru after forcing constitutional changes allowing him to run for a third term, forced out of office in 2001; Opposition candidate Vicente Fox elected president of Mexico, breaking seven decades of presidential domination by the PRI; In Venezuela, president Hugo Chávez reelected for six-year term under new constitution

Bibliography

Azuela, Mariano. *The Underdogs* (*Los de abajo*). New York: Penguin, 1962.

Beezley, William H., and Judith Ewell, eds. *The Human Tradition in Latin America.* Wilmington, DE: Scholarly Resources, 1997.

Bethell, Leslie, ed. *The Cambridge History of Latin America.* Vols. IV and V. Cambridge, England: Cambridge University Press, 1986.

Blum, William. *Killing Hope: U.S. Military and CIA Interventions since World War II.* Monroe, ME: Common Courage Press, 1995.

Bulmer-Thomas, Victor. *The Economic History of Latin America since Independence.* New York: Cambridge University Press, 1994.

Burns, E. Bradford. *Latin America, A Concise Interpretive History.* 6th ed. Englewood Cliffs, NJ: Prentice Hall, 1994.

Cortés Conde, Roberto, and Shane J. Hunt, eds. *The Latin American Economies: Growth and the Export Sector, 1880–1930.* New York: Holmes and Meier, 1985.

Galeano, Eduardo. *Open Veins of Latin America.* New York: Monthly Review Press, 1997.

———. *We Say No: Chronicles 1963–1991.* New York: W.W. Norton, 1992.

Keen, Benjamin. *A History of Latin America: Independence to the Present.* 5th ed. Boston: Houghton Mifflin, 1996.

LaFeber, Walter. *Inevitable Revolutions.* 2nd ed. New York: W.W. Norton, 1992.

Langley, Lester. *The Americas in the Age of Revolution 1750–1850.* New Haven, CT: Yale University Press, 1996.

Leo Grande, William. *Our Own Back Yard: The United States in Central America, 1977–1992*. Chapel Hill: University of North Carolina Press, 1998.

Lynch, John. *The Spanish-American Revolutions 1806–1826*. New York: Norton, 1986.

Macauley, Neil. *The Emergence of Latin America in the Nineteenth Century*. New York: Oxford University Press, 1988.

Rodríquez O., Jaime E. *The Independence of Spanish America*. Cambridge University Press, 1998.

Russell-Wood, A. J. R. *From Colony to Nation: Essays on the Independence of Brazil*. Baltimore: John Hopkins University Press, 1975.

Schoultz, Lars. *Beneath the United States: A History of U.S. Policy Toward Latin America*. Cambridge, MA: Harvard University Press, 1998.

Skidmore, Thomas E., and Peter H. Smith. *Modern Latin America*. 5th ed. New York: Oxford University Press, 2000.

Smith, Peter H. *Talons of the Eagle: Dynamics of U.S.–Latin American Relations*. New York: Oxford University Press, 2000.

FILMS AND VIDEOS

The Battle of Chile. Chile, 1976.

Evita. U.S., 1997.

Missing. U.S., 1983.

The Official Story. Argentina, 1985.

Que Viva Mexica. Russia/USSR, 1931.

Reed: Mexico Insurgente. Mexico, 1971.

Romero. U.S., 1989.

State of Siege. U.S., 1982.

FOUR

THE OTHER AMERICANS

Details of the Spanish and Portuguese colonization of Latin America were provided in earlier chapters in this volume. The purpose of this chapter is to explore the contemporary consequences of that conquest on the indigenous peoples of the Americas who lived in the region prior to 1492 and also to examine the fate of the more than 10 million Africans who were brought to the Caribbean and Latin America as slaves.

In 1992, the 500th anniversary of the first voyage of Columbus provided renewed focus on the current conditions of those segments of Latin American society who have been often ignored and marginalized by governments and scholars alike. It is estimated that more than 40 million indigenous people are alive today. Indigenous people constitute clear majorities in Guatemala and Bolivia, close to half of the population in Peru and Ecuador, and a substantial minority in countries such as Mexico, Brazil, El Salvador, Nicaragua, and Colombia. In the 1980s conflict and then negotiation between the revolutionary government of Nicaragua and the peoples of the Atlantic Coast focused international attention on the region's indigenous people. In recent years the indigenous people have become more politically active in both Latin America and worldwide. In 1990 a nationwide indigenous uprising paralyzed Ecuador. A decade later the national indigenous group, the Confederation of Indigenous Nationalities of Ecuador (CONAIE), was one of the primary political actors in a government takeover that forced out President Jamil Mahuad. In 1994 an indigenous-based guerrilla movement, the Zapatistas, drew international attention to the southern Mexican state of Chiapas. In many countries indigenous movements have been in the forefront of struggles over the control of natural resources and the environment and have begun to move from the position of marginalization to one of centrality in Latin American society.

In 1492 Spain turned westward in search of wealth and empire. That same year the Spanish monarchy had recovered Grenada from the Moors, the culmination of a struggle that had lasted seven centuries. It was an era of reconquest for Spain, undertaken in the context of its Christian vision. Queen

74

Isabella became the patroness of the Inquisition, which was designed to root out all alien religions (Judaism, Islam, and so forth) in Spain. Pope Alexander VI, who was Spanish, ordained Isabella as the master of the New World. Three years after the discovery, Columbus directed a military campaign against the native population in Hispaniola. His cavalry decimated the native inhabitants, and more than 500 were shipped to Spain and sold as slaves. Most died within a few years. Throughout the conquest of the Americas, each military action began with the Indians being read a long narrative (in Spanish, without an interpreter) exhorting them to join the Catholic faith and threatening them with death or slavery if they did not comply. The brutality of the proselytization notwithstanding, in many ways the religious arguments were only a cover for the primarily commercial basis of the conquest.

The newly powerful Spanish government had decided to establish its own direct links to the east, hoping to bypass the independent traders who up until that time monopolized the trade there for spices and tropical plants. The voyages also sought precious metals. All of Europe needed silver. The existing sources in Central Europe had largely been exhausted. In the Renaissance era gold and silver were becoming the basis of a new economic system, mercantilism. Those nations that had supplies of these precious metals could dominate the Western world. Despite that, most of the expeditions that came to the Americas in search of wealth were not sponsored by governments (Columbus and Magellan were the exceptions), but by the *conquistadores* themselves or by businessmen who backed them. The *conquistadores* did indeed find gold and silver in large quantities, but in order to mine it they needed local labor. That drive for labor produced what Eduardo Galeano has called the Antillean holocaust. He writes:

> The Carribean island populations were totally exterminated in the gold mines, in the deadly task of sifting auriferous sands with their bodies half submerged in water or in breaking up the ground beyond the point of exhaustion, doubled up over the heavy cultivating tools brought from Spain. Many natives of Haiti anticipated the fate imposed by their white oppressors: they killed their children and committed mass suicide.

The civilizations confronted by the Spaniards in Mexico and Peru were large and prosperous ones. The Aztec capital, Tenochtitlán (present-day Mexico City), with 300,000 people was then five times larger than Madrid and double the population of Seville, Spain's largest city. Tenochtitlán had an advanced sanitation system and engaged in sophisticated agricultural techniques in the marshland around the city. It was a majestic city dominated by the Templo Major, its most sacred site.

When the conqueror Pizarro arrived in South America, the Inca empire was at its height, spreading over the area of what is now Peru, Bolivia, and Ecuador and including parts of Colombia and Chile. The third great civilization was that of the Mayans, who inhabited the Yucatan Peninsula of

Mexico and south into Guatemala. The Mayans were skilled astronomers and mathematicians who had developed the concept of the number zero.

Despite their high level of civic and scientific development, the indigenous people in the Americas were defeated by a variety of factors that favored the European invaders. The European military commanders were also quite skillful in exploiting divisions among the indigenous people. In Mexico Cortés allied with the Tlaxcalans against Montezuma and the Aztecs of Tenochtitlán. Pizarro also succeeded in exploiting family disputes among the Incas to foster his advantage in Peru.

The brutality of their conquest was unlimited. They took the gold and melted it into bars for shipment to Spain. Sacred temples and other public places were simply destroyed. Later in Mexico City, the Spanish would build their metropolitan cathedral and government buildings on the foundations of the primary religious and political buildings of the old Aztec capital, as if to symbolize the total subjugation of the original inhabitants. Pizarro's forces in Peru did the same, sacking the Temple of the Sun in Cuzco, the capital of the Inca empire.

The Europeans also brought with them diseases not found in the Americas—smallpox, tetanus, leprosy and yellow fever. Smallpox, the first to appear, had devastating consequences. The indigenous people had no defenses against these plagues and died in overwhelming numbers. As much as half of the existing population may have died as the result of the first contact.

As suggested in Chapter 2, the scope of the genocide against the indigenous people of the Americas is staggering. There were probably upward of 70 million people living in the Americas when the Europeans arrived, between 30 and 40 million in Mexico alone. By the middle of the seventeenth century that number had been reduced to 3.5 million. In some countries such as Cuba the native population had been completely exterminated, while in one region of Peru where there had been more than 2 million people only about 4000 families survived. Over the course of three centuries the silver-producing area of Potosí consumed 8 million lives.

In addition to such dramatic loss of life through forced labor, the mining system also indirectly destroyed the farming system. Forced to work in the mines or as virtual slaves on crown lands, the indigenous people were forced to neglect their own cultivated lands. In the Inca empire the Spanish conquest resulted in the abandonment of the large, sophisticated farms that had grown corn, peanuts, yucca, and sweet potato. The irrigation systems that had been built over centuries were neglected and the land reverted to desert, a condition that persists today.

European Justification

While millions of indigenous people perished, Europeans engaged in marginalized debates over the legal status of their victims. The Spanish court in the sixteenth century acknowledged in principle their legal rights and entitlement to dignity. Various religious leaders spoke out against the inhumane treatment that the native people received, but these legal statements and religious proclamations ultimately had no meaning because the exploitation of indigenous labor was essential to the functioning of the colonial system. In 1601 Philip III formally banned forced labor in the mines, but in a secret decree allowed it to go forward; his successors, Philip IV and Charles II, continued the exploitation.

The ideological justifications for the exploitation of the indigenous people were many and varied. Political and religious leaders often characterized the native people as "naturally wicked" and viewed their back-breaking work in the mines as retribution for prior transgressions. Many religious leaders offered the opinion that as a race indigenous people lacked a soul and therefore could not be "saved" by the Church in the traditional sense. Many Church leaders never accepted Pope Paul III's declaration of 1537 that the indigenous people were "true men." Others viewed them as natural beasts of burden better suited for much of the region's manual labor than its four-legged creatures. The Spanish and Portuguese colonizers were not alone in consigning the indigenous to a subhuman status. Some European intellectuals of the Enlightenment, such as Voltaire and Montesquieu, refused to recognize them as equals.

The indigenous population of the Americas, though conquered and defeated by the Spanish and Portuguese during the sixteenth century, continued their resistance on an ongoing basis. Probably the most dramatic example of that resistance occurred in Peru near the end of the eighteenth century. At that time Spanish pressures and demands on the Peruvian Indians increased considerably. In particular, under the *repartimiento de mercancias* the natives had to purchase goods from the Spanish traders whether or not the item was useful. Locals were often unable to pay for these purchases and as a result were forced from their villages to earn money in mines or on haciendas, neglecting their own productive enterprises. During this time the Spanish rulers also sought to dramatically increase silver production at Potosí and did so with harsh forced labor programs. These conditions fostered a strong desire among the indigenous population to return to the glories of the Inca Empire of three centuries earlier. Their aspirations led to the great revolt of 1780–1781. These dramatic events had many forerunners; 128 rebellions took place in the Andean area between 1730 and 1780. From 1742 to 1755 a native leader, Juan Santos, waged partisan warfare against the Spaniards. The memory of his exploits was still alive when the revolt of José Gabriel Condorcanquéa erupted. A well-educated, wealthy mestizo descendant of Inca kings, Condorcanquéa took the name of the last head of the neo-Inca state and became Tupac Amaru II. His actions began with an ambush of a hated local Spanish commander; by early 1781 the southern highlands of Peru were in full revolt. The objective of Amaru's revolt was the establishment of an independent Peruvian state that would be essentially European in its political and social organization. His vision was that caste distinctions would disappear and that the criollos would live in harmony with Indians, blacks, and mestizos. The Catholic Church was to

Table 3. How Many Native People?

	Estimated Population	% of Total Population
Mexico	10,537,000	12.4
Peru	8,097,000	38.6
Guatemala	5,423,000	60.3
Bolivia	4,985,000	71.2
Ecuador	3,753,000	37.5
United States	1,959,000	0.8
Canada	892,000	3.4
Chile	767,000	5.9
Colombia	708,000	2.2
El Salvador	500,000	10.0
Argentina	477,000	1.5
Brazil	325,000	0.2
Venezuela	290,000	1.5
Panama	194,000	8.0
Honduras	168,000	3.4
Paraguay	101,000	2.5
Nicaragua	66,000	1.7
Guyana	29,000	3.9
Costa Rica	19,000	0.6
Belize	15,000	9.1
Surinam	11,000	2.9
French Guiana	1,000	1.2
Uruguay	0	0.0
Total	**39,317,000**	**5.8**

Computed from: Enrique Mayer & Elio Masferrer, "La Población Indígena de América," *América Indígena,* Vol. 39, No. 2 (1979); World Bank, *Informe sobre el desarrollo mundial* (New York: Oxford 1991; U.S. and Canadian census, 1990).

remain the state church. However, the Indian peasantry who responded to his call for revolt had clearly more radical goals—no less than a total inversion of the existing social order and a return to an idealized Inca empire where the humble peasant would be dominant. The peasants exacted their revenge on all those viewed as European, including the Church hierarchy and its priests. These actions frustrated Amaru's strategy of forming a common pro-independence front of all social and racial groups. Some Indian leaders, fearing the radical direction of the revolt, threw their support to the Spaniards. Despite some initial successes the rebel movement soon suffered a complete rout. Amaru, members of his family, and his leading captains were captured and brutally executed in Cuzco. While the most spectacular indigenous rebellion of that era, it was not unique. The revolt of the Comuneros in New Grenada in 1781–1782 had its origins in intolerable economic conditions. Unlike the Peruvian upheaval it was more clearly limited in its aims. Its organization and its effort to form a common front of all colonial groups with grievances against Spanish authority was an advance over Amaru's rebellion. A central committee elected by thousands of peasants and artisans directed the insurrection, which carried out an assault on Bogotá. Negotiations followed the rebellion, and an apparent agreement reached in June 1781 satisfied virtually all of the rebels' demands. However, the Spanish commissioners secretly voided the deal and, following the demobilization of the rebel army, regained control by crushing the leadership of the Comuneros.

The exploitation of the indigenous population did not end with Spanish and Portuguese colonial rule. The continuing oppression was never more graphic than in Bolivia, which always had one of the highest percentages of indigenous people. Well into the twentieth century *pongos*, or domestic servants, were being offered for hire as virtual slaves. As they had in colonial times, the locals acted as beasts of burden for the equivalent of a few pennies. Throughout much of the continent they continued to be marginalized, driven from the little good land they had been able to maintain during colonial times. In the latter part of the nineteenth century and the early part of the twentieth century the dramatic expansion of commercial farming fell heavily on those indigenous communities that had survived the earlier genocide of the mining operations.

The Role of Sugar and Slavery

Gold and silver were the primary targets of the conquest, but on his second voyage Columbus brought sugarcane roots from the Canary Islands and planted them in what is now the Dominican Republic, where they grew quite rapidly. Sugar was already a prized product in Europe because it was grown and refined in only a few places (Sicily, Madeira, and the Cape Verde Islands). Over the next three centuries it would become the most important agricultural product shipped from the Western Hemisphere to Europe. Cane was planted in northeast Brazil and then in most of the Caribbean colonies— Barbados, Jamaica, Haiti, Santo Domingo, Guadeloupe, Cuba, and Puerto Rico. In the places where the sugar industry was developed it quickly became dependent on the importation of slaves from Western Africa. This industry became central to the development of significant parts of Latin America and left a legacy of environmental destruction and racism that still influences the reality of the region.

This is not to say that all slave systems in the Caribbean and elsewhere were based on the sugar plantation. Also, not all black people in the Americas are descendants of slaves, and not all slaves worked on sugar plantations. An important exception is the role slaves played in the extraction of gold in Brazil, which will be discussed later. However, it was the development of the sugar plantations of Brazil and the Caribbean in the seventeenth century that provided the impetus for the massive importation of Africans throughout the Americas. A full-blown transatlantic slave trade began after

1518 when Charles I of Spain authorized the direct commercial transfer of Africans to his possessions in the New World. It took some time for slavery to develop as we would come to know it, but eventually it is estimated that the slave trade moved more than 10 million Africans into various parts of the Americas between 1518 and 1870. Of those 10 to 11 million, more than 4 million wound up in the Caribbean islands. Brazil was the only area of the Americas to receive more slaves than did the Caribbean, with more than 5 million. The North American colonies received less than 1 million. Brazil was the first place where a slave society was established in the Americas, and it was the last country in the Western Hemisphere to abolish slavery, doing so only in 1888, two years after it was ended in Cuba and twenty-three years after it came to an end in the United States.

The contemporary condition of northeast Brazil is a testament to the destructive power of the sugar industry. From the beginning of Portuguese colonization early in the sixteenth century, Brazil was the world's largest producer of sugar; initially in the Spanish colonies it was only a secondary activity. Brazil would remain the largest producer of sugar for over 150 years; from early on it required the importation of African slaves because of scarce local labor and the large-scale loss of life among the native population. The sugar industry was labor intensive, needing thousands of workers to prepare the ground and plant, harvest, grind, and refine the cane. Ironically, although the Portuguese crown initiated the colonization of northeast Brazil, Dutch entrepreneurs actually dominated the sugar industry, including participation in the slave trade. In 1630 the Dutch West India Company conquered northeast Brazil and took direct control of sugar production. From there the sugar production facilities were exported to the British in Barbados. Eventually a sharp competition developed between the two regions, with the Caribbean island eventually winning out as the Brazilian land began to deteriorate. The land was left permanently scarred by the 150 years of the sugar monoculture. It had been a vast and fertile area when the colonists arrived, but the agricultural methods used were not sustainable. Fire was used to clear the land, and as a result considerable flora and fauna were permanently destroyed. The condition of life for the African slaves who worked on the plantations was horrendous. No food was grown; all had to be imported, along with luxury goods, by the owners of the plantations. In this way the plantation workers were totally dependent on the landowners. The result was chronic malnutrition and misery for most of the population. The current legacy of the sugar monoculture is that northeast Brazil is one of the most underdeveloped regions of the Americas, inhabited by more than 30 million people who are primarily the descendants of African slaves brought there more than four centuries ago. Sugar remains an important crop for the region, but today less than 20 percent of the land is used for sugar production; much of the rest is simply unusable because of environmental degradation. Other regions of Brazil have gone on to produce more sugar. As a result, this once fertile region must import food from other parts of Brazil, and more than half of the people in the region live below the poverty line.

Northeast Brazil is not the only region to be permanently scarred by the production of sugar and the slavery that accompanied it. The islands of the Caribbean have suffered much the same fate. The Spanish had originally grown sugar cane in Cuba and Santo Domingo but on a relatively small scale. Barbados under Dutch entrepreneurship became the first great sugar experiment in the Caribbean, beginning in 1641. In just twenty-five years Barbados had 800 plantations and over 80,000 slaves. The island's previously diverse agricultural production was slowly destroyed as virtually all good land was given over to sugar production. However, before long, the island's ecology was destroyed and its sugar production was no longer competitive, leaving behind a destitute people. From Barbados, sugar production shifted northward to Jamaica, where by 1700 there were ten times as many slaves as white inhabitants; by the middle of the eighteenth century its land had also become depleted. In the second half of the eighteenth century sugar cane production shifted to Haiti, where more than 25,000 slaves per year were being imported to increase the size of the industry to meet growing European demand. Haiti soon ceased to be the center of Caribbean sugar production, not as the result of an ecological disaster, but rather as the result of revolution.

Revolution erupted in Haiti in 1791, and over the course of the next twelve years the sugar economy of the island was devastated. The rebellious slaves eventually succeeded in driving out the French army in 1803 and establishing Haiti as an independent nation. However, independence had high costs, including an embargo by both the United States and France. Although Haiti eventually won its recognized independence from France in 1825, the island's economy was devastated by continual attacks by French expeditionary forces and because of a large cash indemnity paid upon recognition of independence. As a result, Haiti ceased to be at the center of the sugar production; that focus shifted northward to Cuba.

After the Haitian rebellion and subsequent reduction in production, the price of sugar in Europe doubled, and after 1806 Cuba began to sharply increase its production. Sugar production had begun its shift toward Cuba in 1762 when the British briefly took control of Havana. To expand the sugar industry, the British dramatically increased the number of slaves brought into Cuba. During the eleven-month British occupation, Cuba's economy turned toward sugar. Previously vibrant Cuban production of fruit, beef, and light manufactured goods were largely set aside for the growth of the sugar industry. This period also saw the destruction of Cuba's forests and the beginning of the process of degrading the fertility of Cuban soil. Following the Haitian revolution, Cuban sugar production was also given a boost when Haitian sugar producers fled with their slaves to set up production in eastern Cuba. The doubling of the capacity of the Cuban sugar industry after 1806 also required the continued importation of slaves over the ensuing decades even as the slave trade was gaining more and more international condemnation. More than 1 million Africans were brought to Cuba as slaves and in the process transformed the face of the Cuban society forever. Today close to 50 percent of the Cuban population is of African heritage.

Resistance to Slavery

Similar to the long history of indigenous resistance to colonialism, Africans who survived the voyage and were sold into slavery did not willingly accept their fate. Marronage (flight from slavery) was a recorded fact almost from the first days that Africans were brought to the island of Hispaniola. Indigenous people and slaves fled into the inaccessible mountains of the interior, sustaining a condition of liberation and keeping alive a sense of independent identity. In 1514 on the island of Puerto Rico two Taíno Arawak chiefs and their people allied with black Africans against the representatives of the Spanish crown. A second uprising occurred seventeen years later when the enslaved black population rose up against their oppressors. In 1522 an uprising in Santo Domingo began with the revolt of forty sugar mill workers. Although these uprisings were eventually defeated and no full-scale rebellion would succeed prior to 1803, marronage was common throughout the Americas where large numbers of African slaves were concentrated. As Michel Laguerre observed, "Wherever there were slaves, there were also maroons. . . . [L]iving in free camps or on the fringes of port cities, they were a model for the slaves to imitate, embodying the desires of most of the slaves. What the slaves used to say in Sotto Voce on the plantations, they were able to say aloud in the maroon settlements." These maroon communities were common through four centuries of slavery in the Americas. Known by a variety of names (*palenques, quilombos, mocombos, cumbes, ladeiras,* or *mambíses*), these communities ranged from tiny, ephemeral groupings to powerful states encompassing thousands of members and surviving for generations or even centuries. Such maroon communities were generally well organized. They had political and military organization and were not, as is sometimes said, groups of wild, runaway, disorganized, blacks. Some of these maroon communities were so powerful that they were able to negotiate treaties with European powers. These free and independent communities forged autonomous societies and protected their freedom and liberty. They rejected any outside domination.

In some places throughout the Americas these communities still exist, often maintaining their cultural heritage and bearing living witness to the earliest days of African presence in the Americas. One of the best examples of such a community are the maroons of the cockpit country of northwestern Jamaica, who trace their roots back to the sixteenth century and have survived as a community to the present day. Today their early leaders are recognized as national heroes by the Jamaican government. The maroons of Jamaica are probably the most well known group in North America, but many other similar communities exist throughout the Americas. Palenque, San Baslio, located near Cartagena de India, Colombia, is a surviving example. There the inhabitants of the ex-maroon community speak a mixture of Spanish and Bantu commonly called Palenquero, a dialect that fuses Spanish and elements of several west African (Bantu) languages. Most black people of the Pacific lowlands of Panama, Columbia, and Ecuador do not see themselves as so directly connected to Africa. They lay full claim to their own homeland—the coastal section of this tropical rainforest. They are similar in outlook to maroons in the interior of Suriname and French Guiana who maintain their distinct cultural heritage.

In Brazil, fugitive slaves organized the black kingdom of Palmares in the northeast and throughout the eighteenth century successfully resisted military expeditions of both the Dutch and the Portuguese. The independent kingdom of Palmares was organized as a state, similar to many that existed in Africa in the seventeenth century. Encompassing an area one-third the size of Portugal, it boasted a diversified agriculture of corn, sweet potatoes, beans, bananas, and other foods. Land was held in common and no money was circulated. The ruling chief was elected from the ranks of the tribe and organized a defense of the territory that successfully protected it for several decades. When the Portuguese finally conquered Palmares in 1693 it required an army of several thousand, the largest colonial army of the time. Ten thousand former slaves fought to defend the kingdom in the final battle, but they were defeated by superior firepower.

The slave trade, which left its lasting legacy on the Americas, was driven in large measure by the profits it generated in Europe. Britain is probably the best example of that profiteering. Queen Elizabeth I was reportedly opposed to the slave trade on moral grounds when the first English slave traders landed in Britain, but she quickly changed her perspective when shown the financial benefits that could flow from the trade. Once the lucrative nature of the trade was clear, the British moved quickly to overcome the Dutch dominance of the early trade. A key factor in the success of the British was in the concession of the trade monopoly granted to them by the weakened Spanish. The South Sea Company, with significant investment from Britain's most powerful families, including the royal court, was the chief beneficiary of the monopoly. The impact of the slave trade on Britain's economy was significant. Traffic in slaves made Bristol Britain's second most important city and helped make Liverpool the world's most important port. Ships left Britain for Africa with cargoes of weapons, cloth, rum, and glass, which served as payment for the slaves who were obtained in West Africa and then shipped to the Americas. The African chiefs who cooperated in the slave trade used the weapons and the liquor to embark on new slave-hunting expeditions. Conditions on the ships were horrific, and often as many as half of the people on board died during the voyage. Many died of disease while others committed suicide by refusing to eat or throwing themselves overboard. Those who survived the voyage but were too weak to impress buyers were simply left on the docks to die. The healthy survivors were sold at public auction.

Despite the losses at sea, the trade was highly lucrative, as the ships sailed back to Britain with rich cargoes of sugar, cotton, coffee, and cocoa. Liverpool slave merchants were making more than £1 million profits per year, and there was considerable spinoff to the rest of the economy. Liverpool's dockyards were improved considerably to handle the increased commerce. Banks in Britain's largest cities prospered through the trade. Lloyd's of London became a dominant force in the insurance industry, covering slaves, ships, and plantations. Almost 200,000 textile workers labored in Manchester to provide the needed products for the Americas, while workers in Birmingham and Sheffield made the muskets and knives. Although initially dominated by the Portuguese, it was the slave trade that positioned Britain to be the dominant world power by the end of the eighteenth century. At the start of the nineteenth century, Britain turned against slavery, not primarily out of any newfound moral revulsion but through a calculation that its growing industrial production needed wage earners throughout the world to buy its products.

The British were by no means alone as a nation that participated in the slave trade. Equally important were the Portuguese, who supplied the millions of Africans necessary for the exploitation of their primary colony, Brazil. In addition to providing slaves for the sugar industry the Portuguese also developed gold extraction in Brazil using slave labor. From 1700 onward the region of Minas Gerais in central Brazil was the focal point of the extraction. For more than a century gold flowed out of the region with Portuguese and British slave traders gaining massive profits. The region itself was left destitute—a condition that persists today for the descendants of those slaves who worked the mines. Subsistence farming replaced the mines and, as in northeast Brazil, became, in Galeano's words, "the Kingdom of *fazendas.*"

Concept of Race

Race must be understood as a socially constructed, not biologically determined, concept. According to Michael Hanchard, race in Latin America determines status, class, and political power. In this respect, race relations are power relations. Being black in Brazil generally signifies having a lower standard of living and less access to health care and education than whites have, but in the minds of many it also signifies criminality, licentiousness, and other negative attributes considered to be related to African peoples. It follows, then, that the meaning and interpretation of racial categories are always subject to revision, change, and negotiation. Most importantly, racial constructs are dynamic and fluid, insofar as racial groups are not categorized in isolation, but in relation to other groups who have their own attendant values of class, status, and power. The concepts of blackness and race have long been controversial in Latin America, and only in recent years have scholars and political activists for black and indigenous rights begun to create a dialogue that can shed light on the process of understanding the issues. The term "black" is an adjective derived from Latin, meaning in a literal sense "sooted, smoked black from flame." In practical terms in Latin America it has been defined in terms of being "not white" and in having a connection to Africa. As in North America, blackness can equally be the target of unrelenting racism or the basis of deeply held religious and aesthetic attachment to a heritage of struggle, survival, and achievement. The dominant, lighter-skinned ruling elites of Latin America historically have viewed the population of African descent with a mixture of fear and hatred. The blacks who lived free in isolated areas such as the Cauca Valley of Colombia have been the targets of campaigns of fear labeling them as subhuman beasts who had brought a "primitive" culture with them from Africa. Such historical labeling meant that these groups in Colombia were marginalized from national political life.

The racism of the dominant classes of the Americas comes through in the historical treatment of the greatest of Latin America's heros, Simón Bolívar. In the wars of liberation led by Bolívar between 1813 and 1822 black troops from revolutionary Haiti helped overthrow colonial governments in the territory of what became the Republic of Gran Colombia. The liberation of these territories helped foster an era of black consciousness among the indigenous black communities. It has often been speculated that Bolívar may have had black ancestors, but this idea is generally rejected in Colombia and Venezuela by white and mestizo biographers who were clearly uneasy about the implications of such a possibility.

Race is a powerful ideological concept in contemporary times throughout the Americas. There are two competing concepts that vie for recognition. *Mestizaje* is the ideology of racial mixture and assimilation, which is the adopted perspective of most of the political elites of the region. *Négritude*, on the other hand, is a concept that celebrates the positive features of blackness. At the national government level only in Haiti is *négritude* the explicit national ideology. In most countries where there is a significant population of African heritage, the concept of *négritude* has been both the basis of societal discrimination and a symbol of racial pride for the oppressed. Of course, such pride is often seen by the dominant political culture to be a threat to the sovereignty and territoriality of the nation.

When reviewing their own history and social movements black social activist and movement leaders in Latin America inevitably raise the comparison with the U.S. civil rights movement and state with deep regret that black Latin America never had an equivalent movement. However, black-based social movements over the years have gained momentum and are now challenging centuries of domination. For example, black social movements are gaining strength in Brazil, Colombia, Ecuador, Venezuela, Uruguay, Nicaragua, Costa Rica, Honduras, and other Latin American countries (see Dixon). These movements are fighting for social inclusion and development, equality before the law, human rights protections, and democratic reform.

Table 4. Statistics on the Black Population

Country	Population (Thousands)		% of Total	
	Min.	Max.	Min.	Max.
Brazil	9477	53,097	5.9	33.0
United States	29,986	29,986	12.1	12.1
Colombia	4886	7329	14.0	21.0
Haiti	6500	6900	94.0	100.0
Cuba	3559	6510	33.9	62.0
Dominican Republic	847	6468	11.0	84.0
Jamaica	1976	2376	76.0	91.4
Peru	1356	2192	6.0	9.7
Venezuela	1935	2150	9.0	10.0
Panama	35	1837	14.0	73.5
Ecuador	573	1147	5.0	10.0
Nicaragua	387	559	9.0	13.0
Trinidad and Tobago	480	516	40.0	43.0
Mexico	474	474	0.5	0.5
Guyana	222	321	29.4	42.6
Guadaloupe	292	292	87.0	87.0
Honduras	112	280	2.0	5.0
Canada	260	260	1.0	1.0
Barbados	205	245	80.0	95.8
Bahamas	194	223	72.0	85.0
Bolivia	158	158	2.0	2.0
Paraguay	156	156	3.5	3.5
Suriname	146	151	39.8	41.0
Saint Lucia	121	121	90.3	90.3
Belize	92	112	46.9	57.0
Saint Vincent and the Grenadines	94	105	84.5	95.0
Antigua and Barbuda	85	85	97.9	97.9
Grenada	72	81	75.0	84.0
Costa Rica	66	66	2.0	2.0
French Guiana	37	58	42.4	66.0
Bermuda	38	39	61.0	61.3
Uruguay	38	38	1.2	1.2
Guatemala	*	*	*	*
Chile	*	*	*	*
El Salvador	†	†	†	†
Argentina	0	†	0	†
Total	**64,859**	**124,332**	**9.0**	**17.2**

*Very small black population, but specific figures not available; †Information not available.
Compiled by: Rodolfo Monge Oviedo, *NACLA: Report on the Americas*, February 1992.

Black organizations in Brazil are some of the best organized and politically developed in the region. The black movements in Brazil are not monolithic and are quite diverse in scope, practice, and philosophy. Like all social movements there are basic points of convergence and divergence.
However, most of the progressive black movements agree that racism is an

obstacle to Afro-Brazilian progress. One of the most powerful examples of a movement that has promoted black liberation is Brazil's black consciousness movement, a loosely linked network of nearly 600 organizations that has the goal of preserving ethnic heritage and fighting against the discrimination and poverty of contemporary Brazil. The groups are not united by a single ideology, and they pursue their campaign against racism using a variety of methods. Some organizations focus almost exclusively on culture, believing that the rediscovery of African roots can transform the consciousness of Brazil's black population. Other groups, such as the São Paulo–based Unified Negro Movement (MNU), are politically focused, arguing that racism must be combated through changes in political, social, and economic structures. The groups have demonstrated against police violence and have fought in the courts for the enforcement of existing laws against discrimination in the workplace. During the writing of Brazil's constitution in the 1980s, MNU was instrumental in convening a National Convention of Blacks for the Constitution. The grassroots debates of this initiative, together with the efforts of Carlos Alberto Oliveira and Benedita da Silva, two black congresspeople elected in 1986, resulted in the inclusion of a constitutional amendment that outlawed racial discrimination. The activity of the black consciousness movement has also forced the traditional Brazilian political parties to react with statements against racism and to make commitments to include blacks among their lists of political candidates and appointments to public office. These efforts have borne some fruit with the appointment of a number of blacks to key appointed positions by the Centrist Brazilian Democratic Movement Party (PMDB), but there are only a handful of black deputies in the national legislature. Pressure on the political elites has helped break down the long held elite-generated myth that Brazil is a "racial democracy."

However, the black movement is currently far from the mass political phenomenon that it aspires to be. Part of the limitation of the movement is its narrow social base. Black consciousness groups are composed primarily of professionals, intellectuals, and upwardly mobile students. The movement is relatively small in total numbers, with probably 25,000 sympathizers out of an Afro-Brazilian population of some 70 million. Despite these limitations, the movement does represent an important contribution to the cause of racial justice in the continent's largest country. African Colombians have also struggled for equality and have modestly succeeded in raising consciousness on their separateness from the majority of the Colombian nation.

Contemporary Struggle of the Indigenous People

The history of exploitation of the indigenous people at the time of the conquest and the century that followed is generally not disputed. Rather, it is the history that follows that is controversial. Even those who have sympathy and understanding for the oppression of the indigenous people have tended to avoid a systematic understanding of its contemporary reality.

There has been a common wisdom that native American cultures are primarily relics of the past, doomed to be abandoned as modernity spread to the deepest regions of rural Latin America. To the degree that indigenous cultures survived it would be as rural, isolated communities clinging to traditional ways of life. Although such communities exist, they make up only a tiny fraction of the approximately 40 million native peoples who live in the Americas today. Because the stereotype of the isolated rural community is not actually the norm, our understanding of the issues and needs of this population must change.

The indigenous people who survived the conquest recovered their numbers slowly but steadily. Contrary to the predictions of assimilative policies, native peoples have remained demographically stable; bilingualism has increased without the disappearance of native languages. The native peoples have not been defeated or eliminated. Indigenous peoples still live in nearly all of the regions where they lived in the eighteenth century. They have expanded into new territories and established a presence in urban, industrialized society that challenges the stereotypical image of indigenous peasants. Indigenous squatters are prominent throughout the major cities of the continent.

ECUADOR

One of the strongest contemporary movements of indigenous peoples is CONAIE. A strong nationwide organization that has sought to represent the native peoples of Ecuador, who make up between 37 and 40 percent of the population—the fourth largest percentage of indigenous people in the Hemisphere—CONAIE initially reached great strength in June 1994, when it sponsored a strike that shut down the country for two weeks. The target of the protest was the Ecuadoran government's Agrarian Development Law, which when approved by the Ecuadoran congress, called for the elimination of communal lands in favor of agricultural enterprises. The 1994 protests in Ecuador also demonstrated the ability of the indigenous movement to link up successfully with other nonindigenous social and political movements. Commerce was brought to a halt throughout Ecuador when CONAIE set up road blocks and boycotted marketplaces. Trade unions joined in the action by calling a general strike and stopped the delivery of goods into the cities. In parts of the Amazon, indigenous communities took over oil wells to protest the privatization of Petroecuador, the state-owned oil company.

CONAIE succeeded in getting a broad range of organizations to unite behind its own progressive agrarian reform proposal, which called for the modernization of communal agriculture but not through the government's plan of commercialization. Rather, CONAIE's proposal called for government support for sustainable, community-based projects that emphasized production for domestic consumption rather than foreign export. CONAIE also proposed the use of environmentally sound farming techniques. At the heart of their counterproposals was the idea that organized groups of civil society in the countryside would play a central role in implementing the new law.

The protests and counterproposal met stiff resistance from the government of Sixto Durán Ballin, which viewed the Agrarian Development Law at the center of its broader package of neoliberal reforms. The government declared a state of emergency and put the armed forces in charge of dealing with the protests. The armed forces arrested protest leaders and violently suppressed street demonstrations. The army occupied many indigenous communities, destroying homes and crops. However, the repression was not fully successful in stopping the protest movement. The government was forced to negotiate with CONAIE and ultimately to make modifications in the agrarian reform law that limited its potentially worst features. However, probably the most important result of the 1994 protests was the recognition that the indigenous movement is a significant actor in contemporary Ecuadorian politics. CONAIE and the indigenous people as a whole achieved this position through their mobilizations and successful linking with nonindigenous groups and their dynamic formation of political demands.

Provincial and regional indigenous organizations were created in the 1970s. In 1980 the Confederation of Indigenous Nationalities of the Ecuadorian Amazon (CONFENAIE) was founded to represent the indigenous population of the Oriente, an important step toward a national organization. In the highlands indigenous organizations dated back to the founding of the Ecuadorian Indigenous Federation (FEI) in the 1940s. In 1980, The Confederation of Indigenous Nationalities of the Ecuadorian Amazon (CONFENAIE) was founded to represent the indigenous population of the entire oriente region. CONAIE was established in 1986 to form a single, national organization. In the 1970s and 1980s the organizations tended to have a local focus, but in the 1990s the movement adopted a broader agenda, the right to self-determination, the right to cultural identity and language, and the right to economic development within the framework of indigenous values and traditions. Land became the focal point for the indigenous movement in Ecuador. It has also been the issue on which it has connected most successfully with nonindigenous groups.

Indeed, land was the focal point of CONAIE's first national actions in 1990. After weeks of organizing and stagnated discussions with the national government, CONAIE orchestrated an uprising that paralyzed the country for a week. The protests ended when the government agreed to national-level negotiations with CONAIE. While not succeeding in most of its demands, CONAIE did win the right to name the national director of bilingual education programs and the granting of some significant tracts of land to indigenous organizations. These mobilizations laid the groundwork for the larger and more powerful actions of 1994. However, the demand for more equitable distribution of land faces a long and difficult road. According to 1994 data, in the highlands, 1.6 percent of the farms occupy 43 percent of the land, while on the coast 3.9 percent of the farms occupy 55 percent of the land. Communal lands are acknowledged and theoretically defended in the Ecuadorian constitution, but they represent only 4 percent of the land in the highlands.

In January 2000 CONAIE organized several thousand indigenous people to protest the government's handling of an economic crisis and to call on the president, Jamil Mahaud, to resign. Working with cooperative members of the military, the protesters occupied the national parliament and declared a new government headed by a three-person junta including indigenous leader Antonio Vargas. However, their victory was short-lived. Under pressure from the United States and the Organization of American States (OAS) the military withdrew from the junta and conceded the presidency to Mahuad's vice president Gustavo Noboa. CONAIE was defeated in the short term in its efforts at radical reform, but its considerable power was made dramatically evident to the country's traditional rulers.

BRAZIL

In Brazil, the issue that most marks the indigenous struggle is the contest for land. Land is the subsistence base of indigenous groups, whether they are hunters or gathers in the Amazon or small farmers in the northeast. It is the issue that unites Brazil's 206 indigenous societies.

Brazil's indigenous people are only 0.2 percent of the national population, speaking 170 languages, with legal rights to about 11 percent of the national territory. Much of the indigenous land is rich in natural resources. Nearly 99 percent of the indigenous land is in the Amazon region, occupying more than 18 percent of the region, but little more than half of the indigenous population lives there. In the other densely populated parts of the country, almost half of the indigenous population lives on less than 2 percent of the indigenous land.

The current struggle over land is not a new one. Expropriation of indigenous lands and decimation of the indigenous population have usually paralleled the drive by Europeans for a particular raw material, whether it be timber, gold, sugar, or rubber. A contemporary case of the devastation of an indigenous group occurred with the isolated Canoé and Mequens peoples in the Amazonian State of Rondonia. Fewer than fifteen people from these two groups have survived. Over the last decade ranchers in the region may well have killed most of the two groups and destroyed their livelihood to make way for cattle pasture. There is evidence of some fifty-three still isolated groups, probably small remnants of larger groups that moved in response to the Brazilian government's massive resettlement programs. The administration of President José Sarney (1985–1990) was especially aggressive in moving forward with Amazonian development projects. The army's Northern Tributaries Project, begun in 1987, had as its goals the reduction of indigenous land areas and the subsequent opening up of large new areas for both farming and mining. As a result between 1987 and 1990 the Yanomami's 23.5-million-acre territory was reduced by 70 percent and divided into nineteen different unconnected parcels of land. The Yanomami people were devastated by the activity of almost 50,000 freelance gold diggers. The gold diggers drove 9000 Yanomami from their lands, and 15 percent of the population died from diseases introduced by the gold miners.

Mercury contamination down-river and mercury vapors released into the atmosphere had serious environmental consequences. Protests at the 1992 Earth Summit led to the creation of land reserves by the governments of both Brazil and Venezuela. Despite the newly created reserves, conflict between the gold miners and the Yanomami continued. In 1993 many Yanomami were massacred in an attack by the miners and with no effective intervention by the Brazilian government. The 1988 Brazilian constitution contained progressive provisions for environmental protection and indigenous peoples' rights, but the reality was that they were generally not implemented. Powerful private economic interests moved forward with their projects, often buying off government officials with large bribes. The government itself moved forward with environmentally questionable projects such as the planned Paraná-Paraguay River seaway.

However, sole focus on these devastated and isolated groups would miss an important part of the story. In the last thirty years the indigenous people have begun to change their situation through political organization. The demographic decline reached its low point in the mid-1970s, and the population has risen ever since. The first complete indigenous census, in 1990, counted about 235,000 indigenous people. By the year 2000 the number grew to 300,000. Between 1990 and 1995 the area of indigenous land with complete legal documentation increased more than fourfold.

The most recent drive of the Brazilian government into the indigenous lands in the Amazon region was initiated in the 1940s but took on full force in the 1960s and 1970s. The military government that came to power in 1964 was motivated by an almost messianic desire to conquer these supposedly undeveloped lands so that Brazil could take its place among the world's most important countries. As a result, the Brazilian government conceived and executed the development of an infrastructure (roads, dams, and hydroelectric stations) that preceded the actual economic development of the region.

Because the concept of privately held land was largely nonexistent in the Amazon region, it was necessary for the government to step up mechanisms for the demarcation of land based on private ownership. Private investors were willing to enter the region only after such procedures had been established. From the beginning, the approach of the Brazilian government toward the indigenous groups was to limit their land ownership to relatively small areas so that their ambitious development plans could proceed on the rest. In 1967 the Brazilian government created the National Indian Foundation (FUNAI) as the agency responsible for indigenous people and their land. While it had not been the intent of the government to create a rallying point, FUNAI has become exactly that. For thirty years its headquarters in Brasília has been the focal point for indigenous groups rallying to register land claims and to forestall the projects of the developers. Using FUNAI as a target, the indigenous groups developed their own organizations in the 1970s with the assistance of the wider society. The first organizations came from within the church community—The Indigenist Missionary Council (CIMI), the indigenous rights organization of the Catholic Church, and the Ecumenical Center for Documentation and Education (CEDI). Indigenous groups took a large step forward in 1978 with the formation of the first national organization, The Union of Indigenous Nations (UNI). The UNI was able to make important links both domestically and internationally. In the late 1970s and early 1980s during the height of the movement against the military dictatorship, the indigenous groups were able to make links with students and intellectuals. As a result, the issue of indigenous land rights made it to the agenda of the broad movement for the restoration of political democracy.

At the same time, the Brazilian indigenous movement also made important links in the international community, most especially with the environmental community. During the 1980s there developed among environmentalists internationally a significant consciousness over the destruction of the Amazon rainforest. In developing international attention about the problem in Brazil, groups like Greenpeace and the World Wildlife Fund made common cause with Brazil's indigenous groups. Both sets of groups began to speak the same language—sustainable development. The indigenous peoples and the environmentalists both argued that the rainforest was not a wilderness to simply be preserved but rather an area that was inhabited and contained important resources for the world that the people who currently lived there could provide—medicines, rubber, foodstuffs. The activists argued that the kind of development being projected and carried out by the Brazilian government—primarily slash-and-burn agriculture—was inappropriate for the fragile character of the land. They pointed to vast tracts of land that had been exploited in the 1960s and 1970s and were now worthless semidesert. Considerable international attention was also brought to the region by the work of Francisco "Chico" Alves Méndes, leader of the National Council of Rubber Tappers, who was assassinated in 1988 after his organization, The Alliance of the Peoples of the Forest, organized to block further dam construction and defend the environment. Internationally consciousness has clearly developed on this and related environmental issues and has placed significant pressure on the Brazilian governments since the mid-1980s. However, this has not stopped the government from moving forward with its development plans. Often the government has successfully created a nationalist backlash against international pressure by characterizing it as a form of neocolonialism.

Mexico

On January 1, 1994, a rebellion led by the Zapatista National Liberation Front (EZLN) began in the state of Chiapas in southern Mexico. This rebellion, more than any other indigenous political action in the 1990s, captured the attention of scholars and political activists alike. On that day, within a few hours after the takeover of San Cristóbal de las Casas, computer screens around the world sparked with news of the uprising. The Zapatista uprising was the world's first on-line rebellion, as the EZLN communicated its cause directly and electronically. The indigenous explosion in Chiapas, in which several hundred people lost their lives in twelve days of fighting, was only the beginning. Seven years later the rebellion continued and numerous dialogues and logistical agreements were made between the Mexican government and the Zapatista rebels, but no definitive political settlement was reached in 2000.

Little is known about the development of the EZLN prior to 1994, but they burst on the scene as NAFTA went into effect. The roots of their rebellion ran very deep. The indigenous people of Chiapas, mostly Mayan, have labored under conditions of semislavery and servitude for centuries. The state is the principal source of the nation's coffee, and just over 100 people (0.16 percent of all coffee farmers) control 12 percent of all coffee lands. The large coffee farms have the best land, most of the credit, and the best infrastructure. Even more important are the cattle lands. Some 6000 families hold more than 3 million hectares of pastureland, equivalent to nearly half the territory of all Chiapas rural landholdings. Many of these vast cattle ranches were created through violent seizures of community and national land. The current struggles here date back to the early period of this century when the local oligarchs resisted any attempt at land reform. The program of PRI President Lázaro Cárdenas, which distributed millions of acres of land elsewhere in Mexico in the 1930s, was not implemented in Chiapas. In 1974 the local elites harshly repressed indigenous efforts at political organizing for land reform. The massive repression of the 1970s was followed by a more selective repression, consisting of the assassination of several peasant leaders. The peasants responded by creating networks of self-defense, but the authoritarian PRI governors responded with harsh tactics. The state repression was carried out by a combination of the federal army, state and local police forces, and so-called "white guards"—hired security forces at the service of the big landowners. PRI leaders deliberately provoked conflicts among peasants, between peasants and small proprietors, and between PRI village leaders and opponents of the regime. The local PRI leadership has operated through a loose organization known as the "Chiapas Family." The Family is made up primarily of big ranchers, owners of coffee farms, and lumber barons who control the local elected offices. The control is enhanced by the cooption of local indigenous leaders, many of whom are bilingual teachers. Operating through PRI-dominated organizations like the National Peasant Council (CNC), the local leaders are given economic advantages that are passed on to their closest supporters in the communities. This divide-and-conquer strategy led to many violent confrontations in the period of the Zapatista uprising.

Despite the dominance of the region politically and economically by the PRI and its supporters, an independent civil society began to develop after 1975. Organizers from the outside participated in the organizing, including liberation theology–inspired Catholic clergy and members of Mexican leftist parties. Two grassroots organizations formed in the 1970s exist today—

the Union of Ejido Unions and the Emiliana Zapata Peasant Organization (OCEZ). The organizations use a variety of tactics, including direct action, to press their grievances against the Mexican government. A new phase in the impact of civil society began on October 12, 1992, with a demonstration in San Cristóbal de las Casas to commemorate the 500th anniversary of indigenous resistance to the European conquest. Thousands of people from different ethnic groups took over the colonial capital and destroyed the statue of conquistador Diego de Mazarzriegos. In hindsight the event was the turning point in the militancy of the grassroots movement and helped to create the conditions of the EZLN uprising a little more than one year later.

The more immediate catalyst for the 1994 uprising was the reform of Article 27 of the Mexican constitution announced by President Carlos Salinas de Gortari in 1992. This reform, for the first time since the programs of Cárdenas, permitted the sale of communal lands that up until that time had been protected. For the peasants of Chiapas this reform meant the end of agrarian reform, which up to that point had been slow and arbitrary but was now effectively dead. The peasants felt that they could no longer turn to the government as a mediator in land disputes. For the landowners the reform was a green light to end once and for all the peasant resistance to their plans for greater commercialization of agriculture in the region. In addition to the changes to Article 27, a new woodlands law also galvanized resistance. The law privatized lands that had long been accessible to the public, punishing the state's poorest peasants and freeing the timber companies to expand their production. The privatization of the woodlands led to confrontations between peasants and military patrols at the beginning of 1993. Government troops first confronted a column of Zapatistas in May 1993, but the Salinas government, in the midst of an intense effort to win support for NAFTA, did not wish to tarnish its image by the admission of the existence of a significant armed challenge within its borders. It was in that context of political change and resistance that the Zapatistas burst onto the scene.

From the beginning of their appearance, it was clear that the EZLN, made up of several thousand indigenous people from the highlands and the jungle, was a different kind of political movement than the traditional guerrilla armies that preceded them in Mexico and Central America. From the beginning they were a civil resistance organization seeking reformist goals using revolutionary tactics. EZLN never claimed as a goal the overthrow of the Mexican state. Rather, it called for the immediate resignation of Salinas, subsequent fall elections, and the expansion of peaceful, popular political participation. From the beginning its actions were the catalyst for generalized civil resistance throughout Chiapas.

Within one month of the launching of the Zapatistas' war, the National Mediation Commission (CONAI) headed by Bishop Samuel Ruiz brokered a cease fire between the warring parties and began a process of negotiations that have continued on and off to the present day. The government broke the truce in February 1995 with an army offensive that unsuccessfully attempted to capture the Zapatista leaders. The 1995 offensive was made possible by a massive deployment of 60,000 Mexican soldiers into the region. The army, with U.S., Argentinian, and Chilean advisors, employed counterinsurgency tactics honed during Latin America's guerrilla wars of the previous three decades. Since 1994 the United States has sold and donated to Mexico over $235 million in arms and equipment, including 103 helicopters that can be used in counterinsurgency operations. The Mexican army cooperated on its southern border with the Guatemalan army, well trained in counterinsurgency warfare. During its February 1995 offensive the army destroyed the basic resources of a number of villages suspected of collaborating with the Zapatistas. The offensive forced the EZLN to retreat into more remote areas, but the Mexican government was not able to destroy the EZLN in part because of the presence of many international human rights observers in the area and the mounting of large demonstrations on behalf of the EZLN in Mexico City. Unable to destroy the EZLN militarily, the government returned to negotiations and in February 1996 the government and the EZLN signed accords on the rights of indigenous communities. The San Andrés accords included two key demands of the EZLN—official recognition of the right of indigenous communities to choose their own leadership and to control the natural resources in their territory. However, in reality the Mexican government did implement these measures. The primary point of conflict centered around the autonomous municipal councils created by the Zapatistas since 1994. In scores of communities local councils were elected only to be denied recognition by the Mexican government, which continues to recognize local government structures dominated by the PRI as the legitimate governing authority. As a result, many towns have been divided into pro-PRI and pro-EZLN factions. Despite the lack of official recognition these councils no longer recognize the official judicial system and have established alternative methods of conflict resolution. They have also set up community development projects such as community corn and coffee fields and vegetable gardens. These alternative institutions have gained some financial backing from international nongovernmental organizations (NGOs) in sympathy with the Zapatistas. The powerful logging and oil interests have also opposed the San Andrés concession to the indigenous communities with the result that the accord has not been implemented.

The end of the 1990s saw a dramatic increase in violence in the Chiapas region, much of it carried out by paramilitary organizations with links to the government. The most horrific incident occurred on December 22, 1997, when forty-five residents of the Tzotzil indigenous town of Acteal were killed in an attack on their chapel by a heavily armed paramilitary gang. Those killed at Acteal included thirty-six women and children, and an additional twenty-five were seriously wounded. It has been reported that one group, the Anti-Zapatista Indigenous Resistance Movement (MIRA), received $1250 a month from the PRI-led state government. Two weeks after the Acteal massacre state police fired on local citizens protesting the massacre, killing an indigenous woman and wounding two children.

Seven years after the dramatic appearance of the EZLN and their leader, Subcommander Marcos, the Chiapas region remains a dramatic example of the renewed indigenous political and social consciousness. The Mexican government has been blocked by the continued high level of local organization from either destroying the EZLN or marginalizing the mobilized civil society of the indigenous communities. The government's attempts to win over Zapatista supporters are regularly rebuffed. Survivors of the Acteal massacre refused material assistance from the Mexican government, arguing that they could not accept aid from the government that organizes the paramilitaries against them. As a result, the region is likely to remain a focal point of indigenous resistance that will be modeled elsewhere in the Western Hemisphere.

Conclusion

As Latin America enters the twenty-first century its image as a continent populated only by Spanish- and Portuguese-speaking mestizos is gone forever. The indigenous peoples of the region and the descendants of the African slaves have clearly asserted their claim to a role in the future of the region. No longer forgotten and marginalized, these groups will likely grow in their political and social roles in the coming years.

Bibliography

Benjamin, Medea, and Maisa Mendoça. *Benedita da Silva. An Afro-Brazilian Woman's Story of Politics and Love.* Oakland: Food First, 1997.

Conniff, Michael, and Thomas Davis. *Africans in the Americas: A History of the Black Diaspora.* New York: St. Martin's Press, 1994.

Cook, Nobel David. *Born to Die, Disease and New World Conquest, 1492–1650.* Cambridge, England: Cambridge University Press, 1998.

Davis, Darien, ed. *Slavery and Beyond: The African Impact on Latin America and the Caribbean.* Jaguar Books on Latin America, No. 5. Wilmington, DE: Scholarly Resources, 1995.

Díaz Polanco, Héctor. *Indigenous Peoples in Latin America.* Boulder, CO: Westview Press, 1997.

Dixon, Kwame. *Race, Class and National Identity in Ecuador: Afro-Ecuasdoreans and the Struggle for Human Rights.* Ph.D. Dissertation, Clark Atlanta University, 1996.

Freyre, Gilberto. *Masters and Slaves, A Study in the Development of Brazilian Civilization.* Berkeley: University of California Press, 1986.

Graham, Richard, ed. *The Idea of Race in Latin America 1870–1940.* Austin: University of Texas Press, 1990.

Hanchard, Michael. *Orpheus and Power: The Movimento Negro of Rio de Janeiro and São Paulo, Brazil, 1945–1988.* Princeton, NJ: Princeton University Press, 1994.

Hemming, John. *Amazon Frontier: The Defeat of the Brazilian Indians.* London: Macmillan, 1987.

Kicza, John E., ed. *The Indian in Latin American History, Resistance, Resilience and Acculturation.* Wilmington, DE: Scholarly Resources, 1993.

Klein, Herbert. *Slavery in Latin America and the Caribbean*. New York: Oxford University Press, 1986.

Menchú, Rigoberta, *I Rigoberta Menchú: An Indian Woman in Guatemala*. Ed. Elizabeth Burgos-Debray. London: Verso, 1984.

Morner, Magnus. *Race Mixtures in the History of Latin America*. Boston: Little, Brown, 1967.

Olson, James. *The Indians of Central and South America: An Ethnohistorical Dictionary*. Westport, CT: Greenwood Press, 1991.

Price, Richard, ed. *Maroon Societies*. Baltimore: Johns Hopkins University Press, 1986.

Smith, Carol. *Guatemalan Indians and the State: 1540 to 1988*. Austin: University of Texas Press, 1990.

Twine, France. *Racism in a Racial Democracy: The Maintenance of White Supremacy in Brazil*. New Brunswick, NJ: Rutgers University Press, 1998.

Urban, Greg, and Joel Sherzer, eds. *Nation-States and Indians in Latin America*. Austin: University of Texas Press, 1991.

Wade, Peter. *Blackness and Racial Mixture: The Dynamics of Racial Identity in Colombia*. Baltimore: Johns Hopkins University Press, 1993.

Wearne, Philip. *Return of the Indian: Conquest and Revival in the Americas*. London: Latin American Bureau, 1996.

FILMS AND VIDEOS

Blood of the Condor. Bolivia, 1909.
How Tasty Was My Little Frenchman. Brazil, 1969.
Quilombo. Brazil, 1984.

FIVE

SOCIETY, GENDER, AND POLITICAL CULTURE

The social milieu in Latin America is a fascinating, complex, and often magical reality that frequently seems to defy description. Societies in the region were forged over five centuries from a multitude of diverse, dynamic influences. Foremost among these are the European values and social institutions the colonialists brought with them. To these are added those of the preexisting native societies as well as thoses influences of the African cultures carried to the Americas by enslaved West and Southern Africans. They have blended in different ways to form societal characteristics that have evolved over the centuries and are manifest in a fascinating array of different forms in each country. They have been molded and modified by land tenure, subsequent immigration, trade and commercialization, industrialization, intervention, the modern media, and, now, globalization. There are, however, some constants that will help us understand this reality.

To gain some insight into Latin American society one can look at how competition among groups and individuals is carried out on the playing field. One needs to see how the game is played. Sports are often an excellent reflection of culture—by understanding athletic interactions one can often better understands other forms of societal relations.

Like politics, *futbol* (soccer) is an area of great passion in most Latin American countries. *Futbol* unifies regions, classes, racial groupings, and even gender in ways few other activities can. When the national team is competing for World Cup standing, it provides a focus, a commonality and a sense of community much more strongly that most other activities, save a real or possible foreign military threat. World Cup victories are also used by governments to bolster their legitimacy.

Regional and team rivalries also exist. Fans show their spirit and team allegiance by wearing team colors, driving with team banners flowing, and engaging in rhythmic chants through the course of the game. Passions run so high that the field and the players are protected by high barbed wire fences and water-filled moats. In 1969 passions exploded after a game at a regional World Cup match between El Salvador and Honduras; the event became the spark that ignited long-standing tensions to create the so called Soccer War.

Like football and basketball in the United States, hockey in Canada, and soccer in Great Britain and continental Europe, *futbol* has provided a way out of slums and poverty. *Futbol* further offers one of the few ways to transcend classism and the omnipresent barriers to socioeconomic mobility. To carry the analogy further, it could be argued that the soccer field is one of the few places in society where one is not excluded from play or at least handicapped by class, color, or lack of connections to the powerful.

Traditionally, soccer was a male domain and there were few opportunities for young women to learn or play the game, although women were welcome to watch, cheer, and support the men who played. Only in recent years has the internationalization of women's sports begun to change this; the Brazilian women's soccer team did make it to the 1999 World Cup semifinals before being defeated by the U.S. women's team.

These analogies are equally valid for baseball in those societies where the ongoing (usually military) presence of baseball-playing North American men has made the U.S. pastime the primary national sport: Cuba, Nicaragua, Panama, and the Dominican Republic. The presence of U.S. and Canadian oil technicians introduced baseball in Venezuela, where both baseball and *futbol* are played. The ease of baseball assimilation suggests not only the strong U.S. cultural influence but also the instant enthusiasm displayed by Latin Americans when they too could compete on a level playing field with occupying military forces or technologically sophisticated foreign workers. Their success is brought home by the presence of growing numbers of Latin American players in the U.S. major leagues. This was underscored when Cuban-born Sammy Sosa of the Chicago Cubs engaged in a dramatic duel for the home run record with Mark McGuire in the 1998 baseball season. Male success notwithstanding, at present women are not often invited to play baseball, nor are women's softball teams yet popular.

The popularity of the ball game dates back to indigenous civilizations in Mexico and Central America, although the current version of soccer was brought from Europe. Hotly contested matches were played for as long as days, and the winners could enjoy great success as bestowed by the wealthy and powerful. The losers were, however, often killed or sacrificed.

Like the losers of ball games in pre-Colombian times, those in Latin American society who cannot win the wealth-status-power game (the poor) suffer from powerlessness and repression and are frequently sacrificed to poverty, exploitation, humiliation, malnutrition, and occasionally torture and death. Their blood, it could be argued, flows to satisfy the new—now globalized—gods of the day. Why do the poor lose so often? Culture defines much of the playing field and most of the rules of the game. Latin American culture is quite distinct from that in the United States, Canada, Great Britain, or Australia. The sections that follow discuss some of the key aspects of Latin American cultures.

Colonial Latin American Society

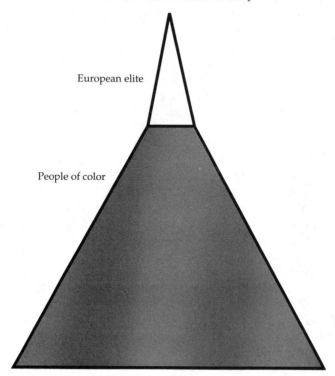

Figure 5-1.

From classical Mayan times to the present, the rules of the game have been dictated by those with power and wealth. This began with the Incas, Aztec emperors, Mayan kings, and aristocrats and priests—those who ruled. After the conquest, new hierarchies and dominant classes developed. Society in colonial times could be described as a sharply pointed upper-class pyramid seated on a broad base of indigenous and African peoples (see Figure 5-1). The small European elite enjoyed wealth, status, privilege, and power—they became the new ruling class. Even European artisans enjoyed a status well above virtually all of the indigenous masses. The exceptions to these classifications would be the *mestizo* sons and daughters of the Spanish and Portuguese elite and native women (who sometimes came from pre-

Colombian royal families). Also in this category would be the mulatto children of Portuguese colonists and Africans in Brazil. But, the African and indigenous masses enjoyed neither wealth nor privilege and could exercise little power. They were the lower class. As the subaltern, those who were subjected to elite power, they most commonly led lives characterized by economic deprivation and exploitation.

This basic structure set the tenor for Latin American society. A few continued to have it all while the darker masses suffered the vicissitudes of poverty and powerlessness. With few exceptions, the elite upper class, or *oligarchy* as it is sometimes called, still make the rules of the game and dominate the lives of the many. Lighter generally rules darker, and male typically dominates female. At the beginning of the twenty-first century those living in poverty accounted for between 40 and 60 percent of the population in most Latin American countries. Even by the rather optimistic statistics used by the regions' governments, some 40 percent still lived in poverty as of the mid-1990s. Indeed, in 1999 the newly elected populist president of Venezuela, Hugo Chávez, spoke of the 80 percent of Venezuelans who lived in poverty. Conversely, the wealthy and the super wealthy—the upper class—live very well indeed. For instance, it is estimated that the wealthiest 10 percent of the population receive close to 50 percent of the income, while the bottom half of the society only get about 4 percent of the income. The richest 20 percent of the Brazilian population receives an income that is thirty-two times the income received by the poorest 20 percent. Official statistics for urban households show much the same pattern. (See Table 5.)

The inequitable distribution of wealth and power continues to plague Latin American societies, which have always belonged to the powerful. In pre-Colombian times it was the Aztec, Mayan, and Incan royalty and nobility; later the *conquistadores*, the viceroys, the *encomenderos*, and the *latifundistas* ran the game. Still later power was monopolized by the rural landowners (the *hacendados*, *estanciaros*, and *fazendeiros*), *caudillos*, and Church leaders. By the twentieth century, it was not only the wealthy—the oligarchy—but also the military leaders, dictators, and civilian politicians who frequently shared and held absolute power on a recurring basis, using their political-military power to consolidate their place in the upper class. They were joined by emerging commercial, financial, and industrialist elites and by multinational corporations and their foreign managers. Power, like wealth, remained concentrated—often absolutely. Indeed, some observers suggest that a requisite for belonging to the ruling class is to know, to have, and to exercise power. This was not only true with the hierarchical native civilizations. It has been so since colonial times, when a small European elite allocated resources for larger societies whose majorities were made up of indigenous, African, mestizo, and mulatto majorities. For the sake of simplicity, one could argue that up to 1950 most of Latin America outside of a few major cities like Buenos Aires was comprised of an upper class comprised of *hacienda*, *fazenda*, *plantation*, or mine-owning *patrones* and a lower

Table 5. Distribution of Income in Urban Households, by Quintile (Percentages)*

Country	Year	Quintile I (poorest)		Quintile 2	Quintile 3	Quintile 4	Quintile 5 (richest)	
		Decile 1	Decile 2				Decile 9	Decile 10
Argentina†	1980	2.8	4.0	10.6	15.7	21.7	14.4	30.9
	1990	2.3	3.9	8.7	14.2	20.9	15.2	34.8
	1994	2.1	2.9	8.8	14.1	21.0	16.9	34.2
	1997	2.1	3.3	9.5	13.4	19.9	16.1	35.8
Bolivia	1989	0.7	2.7	8.7	13.1	20.6	16.1	38.2
	1994	2.0	3.4	9.9	13.5	19.8	15.9	35.6
	1997	1.6	3.1	9.0	13.6	20.5	15.3	37.0
Brazil	1979	1.3	2.6	7.9	12.2	20.0	16.9	39.1
	1990	1.1	2.2	7.0	11.1	19.4	17.4	41.8
	1993	1.2	2.6	7.8	10.9	18.2	16.1	43.2
	1996	1.1	2.3	7.2	10.4	18.2	16.6	44.3
Chile	1987	1.6	2.8	8.3	12.8	19.4	16.5	39.6
	1990	1.7	3.0	8.7	12.1	18.7	15.8	39.2
	1994	1.7	3.0	8.7	12.4	18.7	15.2	40.4
	1996	1.7	3.0	8.7	12.6	19.2	15.4	39.4
Colombia	1980	0.9	2.5	7.6	11.3	18.9	17.5	41.3
	1990	1.5	3.1	9.0	13.6	21.0	16.9	34.9
	1994	1.1	2.6	7.9	12.4	18.9	15.3	41.9
	1997	1.4	2.9	8.6	13.0	19.3	15.2	39.5
Costa Rica	1981	2.3	4.5	12.1	16.7	24.5	16.9	23.2
	1990	1.6	4.1	12.1	17.0	24.5	16.1	24.6
	1994	1.9	3.9	11.6	16.4	22.7	16.0	27.5
	1997	1.9	4.2	11.3	16.8	23.7	15.4	26.8
Ecuador	1990	2.1	3.8	11.3	15.5	21.5	15.3	30.5
	1994	1.5	3.5	10.6	15.8	22.2	14.7	31.7
	1997	2.3	3.5	11.2	15.1	21.6	14.4	31.9
El Salvador	1995	2.1	4.1	11.1	15.3	21.4	14.3	31.7
	1997	2.1	4.0	11.1	15.2	21.3	15.2	31.1

	Year							
Guatemala	1986	1.2	2.7	8.6	14.0	21.5	15.6	36.4
	1989	1.0	2.6	8.4	13.1	21.3	15.6	37.9
	1990†	1.7	3.0	8.6	12.7	20.8	16.1	37.1
Honduras	1990	1.5	2.5	8.9	12.8	20.0	16.1	38.9
	1994	1.3	3.1	8.9	13.8	20.4	15.3	37.2
	1997	1.4	3.1	9.7	13.8	20.3	14.9	36.8
Mexico	1984	3.2	4.7	12.3	16.8	21.9	15.4	25.8
	1989	2.5	3.7	10.1	13.4	19.0	14.4	36.9
	1994	2.9	3.9	10.0	13.9	19.7	15.3	34.3
	1996	2.9	4.1	10.6	14.4	19.7	14.6	33.7
Nicaragua	1997	1.3	3.2	10.0	14.0	20.2	15.9	35.4
Panama	1979	1.2	3.5	10.8	15.9	22.7	16.8	29.1
	1991	1.1	2.8	9.4	14.3	22.0	16.3	34.2
	1994	1.6	3.0	9.2	14.3	20.4	14.2	37.4
	1997	1.4	2.9	9.0	13.3	20.6	15.4	37.3
Paraguay	1986	2.2	3.6	10.6	14.5	20.2	17.1	31.8
	1990	2.7	4.1	11.8	15.7	21.4	15.4	28.8
	1994	2.4	3.7	10.1	13.6	20.4	14.6	35.2
	1996	2.6	3.9	11.0	15.1	9.8	14.6	33.1
Dominican Republic	1997	1.5	3.3	10.1	14.5	20.4	14.7	35.5
Uruguay	1981	2.7	4.1	10.9	14.7	21.2	15.2	31.2
	1990	3.5	4.7	11.9	15.4	19.1	13.3	31.2
	1994	3.7	5.2	12.8	16.8	21.5	14.6	25.4
	1997	3.7	5.3	12.9	16.5	21.1	14.6	25.8
Venezuela	1981	2.0	4.4	13.2	17.1	24.9	16.0	21.8
	1990	2.0	3.7	11.1	15.9	22.8	16.2	28.4
	1994	2.5	3.7	10.5	15.6	21.3	15.0	31.4
	1997‡	1.8	3.2	9.7	14.4	21.4	16.8	32.8

*Ordered according to per capita income.

†Metropolitan areas.

‡National total.

Source: ECLAC/CEPAL, Statistical Yearbook for Latin America. (Santiago, Chile: United Nations, 1999).

class composed of peasant or rural laborer *peones*, or plantation or mine workers. Indeed, much of the basic social-political structures of Latin America harken back to the traditional large estate, plantation, or mine run by European or mostly European owners who commanded absolute or near absolute power over the masses of people of color toiling on their property. In this hierarchical, authoritarian system, the peasants, laborers, servants, and even the overseers were strongly subordinated to the *patrón.* The difference in power, wealth, and status was extraordinary. The basic structure of the system was most often brutal for those on the bottom. Most struggled on in grinding poverty; a few fled to the interior like the runaway slaves (maroons); and occasionally there were local rebellions. In what became a classic part of Latin American society, some decided that they could best survive and maximize their lot by formalizing their position in a classical *patron-client* relationship. In this way they made their well-being in large part a function of the paternalism of the *patrón* and his family. In return for their loyalty and support, the power and influence of the *patrón* would—they hoped—be employed to protect and promote them. Leaving the area or enlisting in reform or revolutionary movements were less frequently exercised options.

Yet there have been changes. The advent of urbanization, industrialization, and the diffusion of advanced technology, as seen in the proliferation of televisions, cellular phones, computers, and cars, has stimulated the growth of new groups. There were hardly any members of the middle class through the nineteenth century in Latin America, yet their numbers have increased drastically in recent decades. They now account for as much as a quarter of the population in many countries and have lifestyles that are not totally unlike their North American or European counterparts. Further, the middle class has the added advantage of access to very affordable domestic help. Limited employment horizons for lower-class women and men, low wages, and a tradition of subordination make domestic help plentiful and affordable for most middle- and all upper-class households. Industrialization, *maquiladora*-style assembly plants, and a growing demand for services have burgeoned throughout the region, stimulating demand for middle-class positions in the clerical, supervisory, and technical fields. The social pyramid is now a little flatter and might look more like Figure 5-2.

As the new century begins, the vast majority of Latin Americans are urban workers of different types and peasants. As Latin America has industrialized in recent years, the number of industrial workers has skyrocketed and the number of peasants has fallen. Indeed, Karl Marx's vision of a large, brutally exploited, poorly treated proletariat driven from the land and unable to change its lot without total revolution could be coming to pass in Latin America in the twenty-first century. Unlike the nineteenth-century Europe of Marx, in most of Latin America neither reformers nor the labor movement have been able to change the working conditions of most workers to any appreciable extent. Many still work for less than $5 U.S. a day (the minimum wage was $3.50 a day in Mexico in 1999), and few make more than

Latin American Social Pyramid

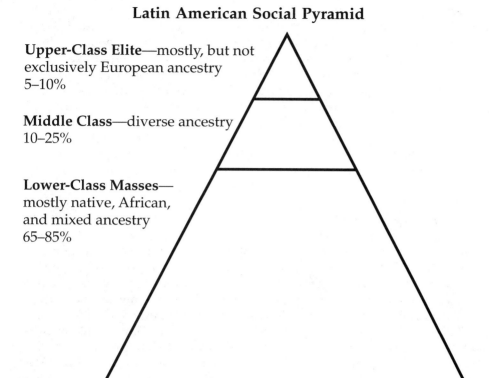

Upper-Class Elite—mostly, but not exclusively European ancestry
5–10%

Middle Class—diverse ancestry
10–25%

Lower-Class Masses—mostly native, African, and mixed ancestry
65–85%

Figure 5-2.

$10. The boss is still very much the authoritarian figure; the workers are very much subordinate.

This domination of the many by the few has not changed as more women enter the formal workforce. In Brazil 53 percent of women are employed in the formal sector; in Mexico the figure is 39 percent (see Table 7). If informal sectors (street vendors and in home producers) are added, the figures would be 72 percent for Brazil and 62 percent for Mexico. Women are thought to be less apt to resist management decisions—or to strike—and more willing to work for lower wages. Further, the proclivity of predominantly male management to hire female workers in the *maquiladoras* has also helped reinforce authoritarian control systems and feminize some of the worst worker poverty. It has also exposed a new generation of younger Latin American women to new forms of patriarchy and sexual harassment that are outside of the protective familial and community contexts in which they grew up.

As the new millennium begins, the conditions in which most Latin Americans live are very difficult indeed. Although literacy rates have improved, educational levels are still low, and basic indicators like infant mortality reflect a great deal of suffering (see Table 1, p. 2). Out of every 1000 live births in Bolivia, seventy-five infants die in their first year of life. In Haiti, eighty-seven of every 1000 children die in their first year. Cuba is the only Spanish-, Portuguese-, or French-speaking country in the Hemisphere to have an infant mortality rate lower than ten per 1000 live births (nine as of 1993). Elsewhere in Latin America, thousands of children live on the streets and must struggle to survive each day. More than 7 million children live on the streets in Brazil alone. Large numbers die of neglect, disease, or outright murder each year, and many are eliminated as nuisances by merchant-paid death squads or off-duty policemen.

As can be seen in Table 6, many who have dwellings do not even have water in their homes, and fewer still have sewer services. Conditions are hard for the masses. Caloric intake and the availability of protein (see Table 7) is low among many, and malnutrition is a severe problem for the poorer sectors in most Latin American countries. Cuba was one of the few countries to radically improve such conditions. Even there, as late as 1950 30–40 percent of the general population and 60 percent of the rural population were undernourished. Twenty years after the revolution malnutrition had been lowered to 5 percent, although it began to again grow in the 1990s as a result of the decrease in Soviet and Eastern European trade and aid and the stiffening of the U.S. trade embargo to include food and medicines.

The health care that most Latin Americans get is poor. The public hospitals that serve the great majorities are generally of very low quality outside of a few countries such as Cuba and Costa Rica (see Table 8). Good health care is usually in short supply and is rationed by wealth and power. The combination of lack of health care, poor sanitation, and malnutrition fed a major cholera epidemic that appeared in Peru in the early 1990s and then spread throughout the region. As with wealth, health care is also very poorly distributed in the region. The bulk of the best physicians and medical facilities are for the wealthy and the middle class and are concentrated in the capital and largest cities. Many—particularly in rural areas—do not have access to modern health care at all and either simply suffer or die or seek relief from practitioners of folk or traditional medicine. Yet the medical care provided for the upper classes in exclusive private clinics is often quite good, although many prefer to go to the United States for specialized treatment.

Conditions for the upper class rival or exceed upper-class lifestyles in industrialized, northern nations; conditions for the masses in areas like Brazil's northeast, Haiti, much of Bolivia, and Nicaragua rival those of the poor in less developed nations in Africa and parts of the Indian subcontinent. It could well be argued that this inequality of wealth and disparity of power and influence are Latin America's greatest curses and are at the root of many of the developmental, social, and thus political problems that continue to plague the region. Yet if varied social strata have very different economic realities, a series of cultural similarities and interconnecting social relations tie them together into national societies that share many common characteristics, as well as a few differences. To fully understand the complexity of these relations one needs to understand the nature and importance of the family and gender roles in Latin American society.

Table 6. Population and Social Conditions

	Estimated Total Population (Thousands)	Annual Population Growth Rate (%)	Life Expectancy at Birth (Years)	Population with Access to Drinking Water Services (%)	Population with Access to Drinking Water Services (%) (Urban)	Population with Access to Drinking Water Services (%) (Rural)	Population with Access to Excretal Disposal Services (%)	Female Economically Active Rate (%)*
Argentina	36,123	1.3	73.3	65	71	24	75	41
Bolivia	7957	2.3	61.7	61	88	24	46	60
Brazil	165,158	1.3	67.2	69	80	28	67	53
Chile	14,824	1.3	75.4	85	99	47	98	36
Colombia	37,685	1.6	71	80	90	77	66	54
Costa Rica	3650	2.1	76.9	100	100	100	66	39
Cuba	11,115	0.4	76.1	92	98	75	100	41
Dominican Republic	8232	1.7	71	65	91	46	90	41
Ecuador	12,175	2	69.9	70	84	51	83	52
El Salvador	6059	2.3	69.6	49	82	26	57	41
Guatemala	11,562	2.6	67.4	67	97	48	59	24
Haiti	7534	2.1	54.5	43	29	41	27	49
Honduras	6147	2.7	69.9	77	91	66	82	40
Nicaragua	4464	2.6	68.4	37	93	12	42	34
Panama	2767	1.6	74	88	99	73	91	43
Paraguay	5222	2.6	69.8	39	59	7	32	53
Peru	24,797	1.7	68.5	70	81	33	74	56
Puerto Rico	3807	1	76.6	—	—	—	—	37
Uruguay	3239	0.6	72.9	89	100	6	51	49
Venezuela	23,242	2	72.9	79	79	79	72	46
NAFTA Countries								
Canada	30,194	0.9	79	100	100	100	99	58
Mexico	95,831	1.63	72.6	85	93	57	73	39
United States	273,754	0.8	76.8	—	99	—	—	60

*World Bank, V (http://worldbank.org/data/wdi2000/pdfs/ta1_1.pdf) World Development Indicators, 2000.

Source: Pan American Health Organization. Basic Country Health Profiles for the Americas, 1999. (http://www.paho.org/english/sha/profiles.htm)

Table 7. Nutrition and Health Care

	Availability of Calories Per Day (1998)*	Availability of Protein Per Day (Grams) (1998)*	Physicians Per 10,000 Population	% of Births Attended by Trained Personnel	AIDS Deaths, Cumulative Total	Cholera Deaths (1996)	National Health Expenditure Per Capita (US$)
Argentina	3144	99	24.9	95	1624 (1996)	—	795
Bolivia	2214	57	12.9	28	123 (1996)	—	48
Brazil	2926	76	12.6	92	103,262 (1997)	—	280
Chile	2844	79	10.6	95	1456 (1996)	—	331
Colombia	2559	61	11.6	96	7776 (1996)	—	140
Costa Rica	2780	76	14.1	97	—	—	224
Cuba	2473	52	52.9	100	—	—	106
Dominican Republic	2277	50	21.5	95	—	—	77
Ecuador	2725	54	16.9	59	608 (1996)	—	71
El Salvador	2522	63	10.4	67	1789 (1984–1996)	—	158
Guatemala	2160	56	9.3	35	1371 (1996)	—	56
Haiti	1876	43	0.76	46	4967 (1996)	—	9
Honduras	2343	58	8.32	54	6005 (1996)	14	44
Nicaragua	2208	53	7.4	87	114 (1996)	82	35
Panama	2476	65	12.1	89	1044 (1995)	—	253
Paraguay	2577	72	5.1	36	253 (1986–1996)	—	85
Peru	2420	62	11.4	56	6443 (1996)	—	128
Puerto Rico	—	—	17.5	100	19,625 (1997)	0	—
Uruguay	2866	87	37	99	851 (1983–1997)	—	516
Venezuela	2358	61	2.4	95	—	50	229
NAFTA Countries							
Canada	3167	99	21.1	99	12,513 (1994–1996)	—	1899
Mexico	3144	86	17.5	84	29,962 (1997)	—	160
United States	3756	115	26.5	95	530,397 (1996)	—	3858

*FAO, *Faostat Nutritional Database*, 2000 (http://apps.fao.org/cgi_bin/nph_db.pl?subset=nutrition)

Source: Pan American Health Organization. *Basic Country Health Profiles for the Americas Summaries*, 1999. (http://www.paho.org/english/sha/profiles.htm)

Table 8. Women in National Government, 1987, 1994, and 1996

	Women Occupying Parliamentary Seats (Number)			Women in Decision-Making Positions in Government Ministries (%)				
	Mono-Cameral or Lower Chamber		Upper Chamber	Ministerial Level			Sub-Ministerial Level	
Country	1987	1994	1994	1987	1994	1996*	1987	1994
Argentina	5	16	2	—	—	0	3.1†	3.0
Bolivia	3	7	4	—	—	4	5.0†	7.7
Brazil	5	6	3	3.4	4.5	0	4.1†	10.8
Chile	—	8	7	—	13.0	14	3.8†	—
Colombia	—	11	7	6.7	11.1	13	—	5.6
Costa Rica	1	14	7	—	9.5	11	13.6†	9.1
Cuba	34	23	—	2.9	—	3	—	9.1
Dominican Republic	5	—	—	—	—	4	—	14.3
Ecuador	1	5	—	—	5.6	6	—	#†
El Salvador	3	11	—	—	10.0	6	—	6.7†
Guatemala	7	5	—	14.3	18.8	13	4.2	6.5
Haiti	—	4	—	—	13.3	29	8.3	9.5†
Honduras	5	8	—	—	10.5	10	5.4†	21.7†
Mexico	11	8	5	—	5.0	16	2.0†	5.0
Nicaragua	15	16	—	5.0	10.0	16	3.2	8.0
Panama	6	8	—	—	13.3	17	8.3†	15.4
Paraguay	2	3	11	—	—	7	—	3.3
Peru	6	9	—	—	5.6	6	2.8†	11.1
Uruguay	—	6	9	13.3	—	7	#†	5.0
Venezuela	4	6	8	—	10.7	11	14.3	#†

*As of January.

†May not include all subministerial levels; #: zero or negligible numbers.

Source: Women in the Americas: Bridging the Gender Gap. Washington, DC: InterAmerican Development Bank, 1995, table 11; United Nations Children's Fund, *Progress of Nations,* 1997, p. 47, as cited in the *Statistical Abstract of Latin America,* Vol. 35 (Los Angeles; UCLA, 1999).

Family and Gender Roles

Throughout Latin America the family is of fundamental importance. The family and family ties are the basis of identity and orientation to the greater society and political system. Much of one's life revolves around the family, and young people (especially but not exclusively women) have usually stayed with the family at least until they were married, even if this did not occur until their late twenties or even later for men. Unmarried daughters often stay in the family house and, according to some traditions—as depicted in the Mexican film *Like Water for Chocolate*—are to stay and care for their parents in their old age. Government and private pension systems are often unreliable in Latin America. Children, in fact, may be the main or only pension system that aging parents have.

Personal ties and relationships form the basis for much of Latin American society and politics, and these personal ties begin with the family. If the world outside the family unit is often perceived as hostile and dangerous, the world within is seen as safe and secure. It is a given that family members help and protect each other. And in Latin America the traditional family has been large. Most early social interaction occurs within the sphere of the extended family, which includes not only father, mother, and children but also grandparents on both sides, aunts, uncles, and first and second cousins. As beautifully depicted in novels like *One Hundred Years of Solitude* by Gabriel García Márquez or *House of the Spirits* by Isabel Allende, three or even four generations often live in the same household. Nor has the nuclear family been small. Families of eight to ten children were not uncommon in rural areas; now four or five children are still common and double that number are still seen—although less so in urban areas. Treasured, doted upon, and highly valued, children generally receive special attention from all adults. Cultural values and the adamant stand of the Catholic Church against artificial means of contraception and abortion have combined with traditional practices of measuring a woman's or a man's worth by how many children they have, to maintain large families. Yet as Latin America becomes increasingly urbanized (about 75 percent), financial pressures and the increasing need for a second income have begun to reduce family size, but not necessarily the importance of the family unit.

Patriarchy is strong in Latin America and is even manifest in the old Roman term *patria potestas* (powerful patriarch). Frequently found in Latin American constitutions and legal codes, it means that the father is all-powerful in the family and in family matters. The term preceded *pater familias* in Roman times and originally meant that the father had unrivalled authority in the family and even held life and death power over other family members. Property for the family was most commonly held in the elder male's name (although there have been significant exceptions since colonial times) and women often had to go through fathers or brothers to exercise property-owning rights. Today, fathers and husbands enjoy a great deal of power in the Latin American family. Male prerogative often seemed unbounded. While the woman was expected to come to the marriage pure and virgin and to protect the family honor by remaining above reproach, it was expected that the male would have considerable sexual experience before the marriage. Further, any extramarital affairs he might have were considered by the general society to be something that men did and most typically would not be seen as sufficient to jeopardize the marriage or to besmirch the family's reputation or honor. Mistresses were maintained, often openly, and the tradition of the *casa chica* (the little house or second household) continued over time. Wealthy and not-so-wealthy men often maintained an entire second family in a second household, acknowledged their children, and gave them their name. Eva Duarte (Evita) Perón was the product of such a union. Even today one still hears of well-known public figures being seen with their mistresses. But the dual standard suggests a very different code of behavior for married women. For instance, in rural areas of Brazil and elsewhere in the region, a husband who comes upon his wife in bed with another man and shoots them dead may argue that his actions were necessary to protect family honor. Many a judge and jury have found this sufficient grounds for acquittal. In a similar vein, daughters are carefully guarded and protected by their fathers and brothers.

Men in general and male heads of household in particular have a great deal of power and prerogative in Latin American society. Most Latin Americans are socialized into households where a strong man ostensibly rules (strong women often head single-parent households or use indirect, yet no less effective, means of control in two-parent families). Thus effective political action in the greater society is often equated with the strong, dominant, uncompromising ruling style that most Latin American patriarchs display. The traditional expectation for the Latin American politician, or *político*, is that he exhibit characteristics most often identified with the strong, dominant male—the *macho*. Strength and resolve are valued; weakness and an overly conciliatory orientation are not. Indeed, when a country is passing through a time of crisis, one can frequently hear the oft-repeated opinion that what is needed is a *mano dura*, a strong hand, and someone with the maleness to exercise it. Yet in family and politics alike, the leader is expected to have a great deal of grace and style and not to be crude or coarse—at least until driven to it. Even so, the heavy-handed use of power may be grudgingly accepted if it is clear that the leader is intent on and competent enough to impose his will.

Machismo, or maleness, is very much a part of Latin American culture and clearly defines traditional male-female relations. In the 2000 presidential election in Mexico the successful opposition candidate, Vicente Fox, frequently asserted his macho image in the campaign and even impugned the masculinity of his less forceful PRI opponent. In its worst forms machismo rationalizes total male dominance and even domestic violence. In its less violent form, it frequently robs women of their confidence and independence by socializing them to believe they need a male to protect them, do things for them, provide for them economically, and guide them in their daily lives and development. From an early age, the socialization of male children is much different than that of female children. Males are taught to be assertive and their aggressiveness is tolerated if not encouraged, while female children are most often taught to not cause a commotion, not challenge authority frontally, and to at least appear to be submissive.

Also of importance is *marianismo*, the glorification of the traditional female role. The term comes from the cult of the pure, Virgin Mary (María)–like woman who is expected to be the bastion of family honor, the submissive woman and long-suffering family anchor. Yet even in the traditional family, the woman often skillfully employs her role as mistress of her own home in child-rearing, social engagements, and religion to guide and even manipulate the ostensibly dominant male.

It has further been suggested that Latin American women traditionally have been limited to the *private space* of the house and family while the *public space* outside the home was the sole preserve of the male. Traditionally, the woman's place was in the home with the children. She was to support her spouse in his endeavors in external public space. While this was generally true, it should be noted that Latin American women have sometimes used their traditional roles to penetrate public space. Thus a very competent, ambitious Mexican noble woman of the seventeenth century joined a convent and became Sor Juana Inés de la Cruz so that she could pursue her studies and be free to write some of the best (and most passionate) poetry and prose of the colonial era. Yet the fact that she felt obliged to take this path suggests how limited the options were for education and public expression for women. Indeed, the Latin American universities started as seminaries and excluded women for many years. Only toward the middle of the twentieth century was it possible for women to pursue university education in large numbers, and most were concentrated in traditionally female fields like education, nursing, and social work.

Women have been controlled and inhibited. Courting—particularly for women of some status—was often supervised by the omnipresent chaperon in the form of the grandmother, aunt, or other female relative. Women were often expected to stay in the home and not work outside, while the man was to go forth in the outside world to gain bread and fortune. Later when it was more permissible for women to work outside the home, many occupations were closed and remuneration was markedly inferior to that of men. Nor has it been easy for women to occupy positions of authority or supervise large numbers of men. In the political sphere, those women who did aspire to public position often used their upper-class position or ties to a famous father or husband to gain access (as was the case for Violeta Chamorro in Nicaragua). Talented women like Eva Perón or President Mireya Moscoso of Panama sometimes traded on their husband's position to acquire visibility and power in their own right. Aside from a few such famous personages, competent *políticas* were, however, all too often assigned "female" posts, such as Minister of Education or Minister of Social Welfare. (See Table 8.)

Violeta Chamorro, campaigning in her successful bid for the Nicaraguan presidency in 1990. Note her white dress and hair and motherly outstretched arms. *(Photo by Bill Gentile/CORBIS)*

Many have observed that some of the most assertive political actions by women have come from their traditional, private roles as mothers or wives. This was seen in the weekly protests begun by the Mothers of the Disappeared during the dirty war in Argentina in the late 1970s and early 1980s. The Madres de la Plaza de Mayo, as they came to be known, became politically active as they sought to find and if possible save their children and other family members. They marched every week in the Plaza de Mayo in the center of Buenos Aires carrying pictures of their disappeared relatives. In Chile, women publicized the disappearance and murder of their family members by sewing together *ampilleras*—quilts that told the stories of their loved one. When Violeta Chamorro emerged as a presidential candidate and then president in Nicaragua in 1990, she did so as the wife of a martyred hero in the struggle against the dictator Somoza and as the reconciling mother who could unite her politically divided children and the Nicaraguan nation itself. She arrived at her culminating political rally in Managua symbolically dressed all in white, white hair flowing, riding in the white Pope mobile that John Paul had used on his historic visit to Nicaragua a few years before.

The Nicaraguan figure of Sandinista guerrilla Comandante Dora María Téllez, however, suggests the emergence of more independent and directly public roles for women. Women comprised some 33 percent of the Sandinista combatants, and women like Téllez and Mónica Baltodano were Sandinista comandantes in the struggle against the Somoza dictatorship. Many of their stories are told in *Sandino's Daughters* by Margaret Randal. The situation was similar among the insurgents in the civil war in El Salvador. As underlined by these examples, the emergence of other prominent female politicians such as 1998 Venezuelan presidential candidate and then governor Irene Saez, and statistics on the percent of economically active women (Table 7), the traditional role of the woman in Latin America is rapidly being redefined. This process is being moved forward by:

- Women who work outside the home.
- Women who exercise more independence by having their own apartments and entering into a relation with a *compañero*, exploring the full dimension of their sexuality.
- Revolutionary women like guerrilla comandantes in El Salvador and Nicaragua and the third of the Sandinista combatants who were women.
- The emerging figure of *La Presidenta*. With the election of Mireya Moscoso in Panama in May 1999, Latin America witnessed the election of its second female president (Violeta Chamorro was the first). Elected as vice president, Isabel Perón also served as president of Argentina for more than a year after husband Juan Perón died in office. Three other Latin American women served as unelected chief executives in Bolivia, Haiti, and Ecuador for shorter periods.

Two Zapatista guards at entrance to EZLN encampment in Chiapas, 1996. As with other mass and revolutionary organizations in Latin America, more and more women are participating in all aspects of activity. *(Photo by H. Vanden)*

Table 9. Women in High-Level and Decision-Making Occupations, 1990 and 1995

Country	Professional and Technical Occupations 1990*	Administration and Management Positions 1990*	Ministry Posts and Higher Occupations 1995 (%)
Argentina	—	—	3.2
Bolivia	72	20	9.1
Brazil	—	—	13.1
Chile	108	21	—
Columbia	72	37	24.7
Costa Rica	81	30	20.8
Cuba	—	—	8.4
Dominican Republic	—	—	11.5
Ecuador	79	35	9.8
El Salvador	76	22	18.4
Guatemala	82	48	18.2
Haiti	65	48	—
Honduras	100	38	17
Mexico	76	24	6.7
Nicaragua	—	—	10
Panama	103	41	10.7
Paraguay	105	19	3.3
Peru	69	28	9.7
Uruguay	157	26	2.9
Venezuela	123	23	6

*Per 100 men.

Source: United Nations Children's Fund, *Statistics for Latin America and the Caribbean*, 1997, p. 44, as cited in *Statistical Abstract of Latin America*, Vol. 35 (Los Angeles: UCLA, 1999).

- Radical feminists who challenge many vestiges of machismo and maintain a coherent line through their creative work, writing, magazines, journals, organizing, and personal example.
- Ever stronger national women's movements such as the Association of Nicaraguan Women Louisa Amanda Espinosa (AMNLAE) in Nicaragua.
- The new generation of young women who politely but persistently decide not to be bound by the same constraints that restricted the occupational and relational horizons of their mothers and grandmothers.

There is growing participation by women in education, the professions, government, and business. (See Table 9.) Gender roles are rapidly and radically being redefined. Feminism and women's movements have grown substantially in recent decades. There are a variety of women's organizations and feminist publications in Mexico, Argentina, Chile, Brazil, and the other larger countries. Strong women's movements can also be found in Nicaragua and Costa Rica as well as Cuba. Women's groups are also active in the smaller countries and in cities and intellectual centers throughout the region. It should, however, be noted that feminism in Latin America is well rooted in Latin American culture and can be quite distinct from North American or European feminism. Thus most Latin American feminists would define the female role as eventually including a role as spouse or *compañera* and mother. Attitudes on abortion—but not birth control—can also be quite divergent from those held by most feminists in the United States. Indeed, as the new century begins Latin American women are seeking and gaining empowerment in a variety of ways that they define on their own terms.

Class, Gender, Race, and Mobility

Even though women are gaining power at an ever increasing rate, their mobility is still limited. Cuba is one of the Latin American counties with the highest degree of equality. Socialist Cuba legislated legal equality some years ago and even went on to pass the Cuban Family Code in 1975. It requires men and women to share household tasks and child-rearing equally. In a trend that is beginning to spread throughout the region, women can enter most career paths and most professions. Although conditions for women in Cuba are very good in comparison to most Latin American countries, their mobility is limited. Although thousands belong to the ruling Communist party in Cuba, their representation is less than equal in the Party Congresses. As one moves upward to the Central Committee and higher levels of government one finds that the representation of women diminishes even further. Although women generally experience higher levels of equality at the lower levels, the higher women go in the political and party structure the greater the barriers to their upward mobility. This is even more the case in most other Latin American countries. In countries where capitalism is dominant women have generally found it very difficult to obtain management positions and even more so to rise to positions of power or prominence. Positions in the government bureaucracy or educational institutions have been easier to obtain. Not surprisingly, gender is frequently a barrier to upward mobility even in Cuba and Costa Rica (which has also passed progressive legislation guaranteeing legal equality), not to mention other more traditional areas of Latin America. But gender is not the only impediment to equality or upward mobility. Racism and a rigid class structure pose equally formidable barriers.

The class system in most of Latin America is fairly rigid, and it is very difficult for most to experience very much upward mobility. As was suggested in the discussion of Amero-Indian and African peoples in Chapter 4, race has also remained a barrier to acceptance and mobility. There have been examples of successful indigenous Latin Americans, such as Benito Júarez of Mexico who ascended to the presidency of the republic without ever repudiating his native heritage. More commonly, native peoples have had to assimilate to some extent to occupy positions of responsibility outside their native communities. Even in countries like Guatemala and Bolivia, which are predominately inhabited by native peoples, Hispanicizing family names, the predominant use of Spanish, and adoption of Western dress are generally necessary for upward mobility. Indeed, many native people feel obliged to pass as mestizos (*ladinos* in Guatemala). As suggested by the testimony of Domitila Barrios de Chungara in *Let Me Speak* (Bolivia) and Rigoberta Menchu (*I Rigoberta*) in Guatemala, indigenous peoples are still second-class citizens, particularly when they come from the working class. When they are also female, they suffer even more discrimination.

The lot of Afro-Latins has also been fraught with difficulty. Racial discrimination in Latin American was never as institutionalized as it was in the United States, but it nonetheless existed. Slavery continued in many countries until the second half of the nineteenth century. When it ended, black Latin Americans emerged from slavery into societies where official segregation was not legislated but was practiced in more subtle forms. Some observers have noted that most of the governments of Latin American have espoused a philosophy of racial democracy but have simultaneously instituted a social order that in large part excluded their African populations from many key aspects of national life. As suggested by the eloquent testimony of Brazilian congresswoman Benadita da Silva, lower-class origins and being female make the struggle of people of color even more difficult. Afro-Latin women have made a significant contribution to the women's movement in Latin America and have played a key role in social transformation. There is, however, a paucity of literature and research in this area.

Black women—like indigenous women—are at the bottom of the social pyramid in Latin America. Afro-Latin women have had to form their own organizations in order to address issues of specific concern. Indeed, many black women in Latin America complain that mainstream white organizations do not understand the intersection of race and gender. For many black women's organizations this nexus provides a much-needed framework of understanding. Field research by Kwame Dixon suggests that in the human rights area, this framework allows researchers to see the racial and gender bases for many rights violations. For instance, as a result of the war in Colombia, displaced persons tend to be disproportionately female and Afro-Colombian or indigenous. This suggests the intersection of multiple forms of discrimination. There are also distinct forms of discrimination that occur against a person when gender and race or ethnicity intersect. That is, women who are black or indigenous are more apt to suffer discrimination than either a white woman or a black or indigenous man.

As noted in Chapter 4, there is, however, growing black consciousness and movements in several countries to pass legislation prohibiting racial discrimination. Currently black women's organizations are developing frameworks that incorporate race, class, and gender. Within the black community in Brazil, one finds several groups that also focus on gender inequality. Among these are the Geledés Instituto da Mulher Negra and the Centro de Referencia da Mulher Negra in Bahia.

Initial colonial society set up a rigid system in which classism and elitism in many forms were pervasive. Even today, one is still often judged by her or his birth and family name. Indeed, the Iberian tradition of using the paternal as well as the maternal maiden name is still in practice; for example, José Sánchez Lopéz is the son of his father Sánchez and his mother whose father's name is López. Thus mobility and entrance to social circles or employment opportunities are often defined more by who you are in terms of class, race, and gender and the circles in which your family travels than by your actual accomplishments and abilities. Indeed, it may take a generation or two for a family to gain access to social institutions like the Club Nacional in Peru, even if they have achieved economic or artistic success in their time. This process may take even longer in some countries if a person is primarily of indigenous or African ancestry. Some have even suggested that a process of whitening by wealth, great success (e.g., Pelé in Brazil), or substantial power (e.g., Batista in Cuba or Somoza in Nicaragua) must occur first. Indeed, many of the competent professionals who immigrate to the United States do so because they find that they have a much better chance of being hired or accepted for their actual accomplishments and demonstrated abilities rather than being prejudged by class, race, gender, or family. In this and other areas, cultural norms and mores strongly precondition perceptions.

CLASSISM CHALLENGED: MASS ORGANIZATIONS

If rule by the powerful oligarchy or upper class have dominated Latin American society and politics, it has not been unchallenged. As noted in previous chapters, Túpac Amaru led the indigenous masses of the Andean highlands in open—although unsuccessful—revolt against the Spanish authorities in the early 1780s. Miguel Hidalgo led a similar revolt in Central Mexico in 1810 and almost succeeded in establishing a mass-based independent Mexico. In Haiti a successful slave rebellion led by Toussaint L'Ouverture overthrew French colonial rule and laid the basis for the Haitian republic. Similar mass uprisings occurred in other Latin American countries, such as El Salvador. Although often under the thumb of the elite, the masses have found ways to assert themselves. Sometimes led by elitist figures such as Túpac Amaru or Hidalgo, other times they were led by sons and daughters of the lower classes, such as L'Ouverture and the great Mexican revolutionary Emiliano Zapata.

Similar movements bubbled up in the nineteenth and twentieth century, such as those that resulted in a major peasant uprisings in El Salvador in 1832 and—assisted by Faribundo Martí and the Salvadorean Communist Party—1932. Thus there is a long and well-developed tradition of popular uprisings and resistance movements. In more recent times these have coalesced in mass organizations and NGOs that take advantage of the increased political space that new regimes and democratization have provided to assert their strength and push for their objectives. Latin American women's and feminist movements are but one example of this. Likewise, there are urban slum-dweller movements such as those in Mexico City and movements of rural workers such as the Landless Movements (Sem Terra) in Brazil. The reemergence of indigenous peoples' movements, such as CONAIE in Ecuador, is also of particular significance. Indeed, Alvarez, Dagnino, and Ecobar argue that social movements are revitalizing civil society in their important *Cultures of Politics, Politics of Culture, Re-visioning Latin American Social Movements.*

Political Culture and Key Political Concepts

To better understand the very unique context of politics in Latin America, it is necessary to understand not only general aspects of Latin American society and culture but also those specific beliefs and views that affect how Latin Americans see, judge, and participate in politics. To understand how Latin American politics are conducted, a concept that focuses on the political beliefs and values that are embedded in a particular culture can be employed. Developed through the study of comparative politics, *political culture* is defined as those *attitudes and beliefs that affect the way we think about, engage in, and evaluate politics and political events.* That is, our particular political culture defines the way we see, judge, and participate in politics. Thus the strong-man rule that is so common in Latin America might be totally unacceptable in Great Britain, Canada, or the United States, where moderation and compromise are more highly valued. Or, conversely, the political vacillation for which U.S. President Bill Clinton became famous would be little tolerated in a Latin American president, even though his personal indiscretions might.

The way in which politics are done in Latin America developed over many centuries, with the most remote origins in the pre-Colombian hierarchical and authoritarian rule that characterized the governing process among the Aztecs, Mayas, Incas, and other indigenous groups. To this was added the authoritarian, hierarchical, and often dictatorial forms of governing that developed in the colonial and early republican era. Of particular note is the unchecked power of the viceroy and other governmental leaders in the colonies and the fusion of political and military power in the viceroy's hands. Similarly, there was little experience with democracy during the colonial period. There were no legislatures or popular representative bodies where the people could make their views known above the municipal level. In many areas the town council, or *cabildo*, did allow some degree of participation and democracy in many—but not all—municipalities. This lack of experience with democracy led one astute student of Latin America, Mario Hernádez Sánchez-Barba, to observe that the democratic constitutions patterned on the United States and France that were enacted in Latin America during the early eighteenth-century independence struggles were attempts to impose a democratic framework on a very authoritarian reality. It was perhaps a little like introducing cricket and cricket rules to players who have never seen the game and have been playing soccer all their lives. Although some countries took to the new game faster than others, all underwent a long period of assimilation that witnessed periods of play much more like the old game. As was suggested in Chapter 3, nineteenth- and twentieth-century Latin American history saw ongoing pendulum swings between periods of democratic and authoritarian rule. Indeed, it might be argued that Latin American political culture in most countries is characterized by a nominal commitment to the practice of democracy and a deep-seated reverence for authoritarian rulers with the strength to govern effectively. On the other hand, in Costa Rica and, to a lesser degree, Venezuela and Colombia, the commitment to democracy and democratic means is much more pervasive. This was the case in Uruguay and Chile before they were beset by long periods of bureaucratic authoritarianism in the 1970s and 1980s, when the military ruled.

Other than authoritarianism and macho political roles, *individualism* is also strong in Latin American political culture. The individual does not like to be subordinated by government or other powerful political forces and will only accept such control when there is sufficient power to sustain such rule. Yet when power weakens or countervailing power can be invoked, rebellion often follows and the will of another group or individual may become dominant. Political leaders also sometimes individualize their rule. Power is used by the individual ruler and oftentimes for the individual benefit of the ruler, or by or for the group to which the individual belongs.

A commonly held view among many is that—like the colonial rulers—those who hold power will use it in ways that will directly benefit them or their political or socioeconomic group and that this will be done at the expense of the general population. This may make for pork barrel projects for home regions or political or business friends or—at times—outright corruption.

Ideological values are often polarized between those advocating a political agenda inspired by socialism or leftist nationalism and those advocating a political agenda based on different conservative ideologies. The wide gap between these positions and the lack of consensus on common objectives (and sometimes the rules of the game) make for a political culture that in most instances is not consensual (Costa Rica since 1948 is one notable exception). As suggested by the title of Kalman Silbert's well-respected work, *The Conflict Society*, Latin American society and political culture have strong conflictual elements. Indeed, conflict is often taken to the extreme. Like a high-stakes poker game, there is a willingness on the part of many to take their political struggle to the wall. Politics is seen as a winner-take-all game, and losing often means losing power and thus being forced to fold and cash in one's chips. Players gamble with the power chips they have to win the game. The pot is not to be split. There are winners and losers. Power is to be used to the maximum. In the last hands of the game, push may come to shove—and that means you play all your power chips. This may mean buying votes, closing opposition strong polling places, mobilizing friendly army garrisons, or executing a full-blown coup d'état. In such situations there is frequent resort to violence or the threat of violence. The willingness at times to take the political struggle to such intense and passionate levels means that violence is regularly employed through intimidation, repression, assassination, rebellion, guerilla warfare, coups, or even civil war.

Other key elements of Latin American political culture include some of the following.

ELITISM

Elites have dominated Latin America since the Mayan monarch and nobles ran the Mayan states in pre-classical Mayan times. As suggested earlier, there have been a variety of economic, political, and social elites. Similarly, there are intellectual elites, cultural elites, and even elites that dominate leftist parties and guerrilla movements. The conscious or unconscious belief that an elite should lead, decide, dictate, or otherwise rule has greatly butressed authoritarian practices in politics and many other areas of society.

PERSONALISM

Personal relations are valued in Latin America. One is defined by ties to family and friends. Since the time of the early *hildagos* (less-well-off noblemen) and upper-class representatives of the crown, a charming personal veneer has been deemed necessary for successful civil relations. A charismatic manner and personal warmth are highly valued commodities that are prerequisites for higher-level positions. Men embrace each other if they are friends or close business associates (the *abrazo*), and opposite-sex and female-female greetings in the same circles include a kiss on one cheek (Hispanic America) or both cheeks (Brazilian and French Latin America). For new introductions and less-well-known acquaintances, one *always* shakes hands. Even in formal business dealings one usually begins by discussing the family or common friends and interests and eases into the business at hand once all are assured of their personal importance to each other. One makes friends or renews friendships *before* one does business. To coldly rush into the business matters at hand might be considered a breach of etiquette or a sign of crassness that only a boor or an insensitive Anglo Saxon might be capable of. The more grace and charm a person displays, the higher his or her presumed social status.

Such is equally the case in politics. *Personalismo* is a valued commodity among politicians. Much of their popularity and following may well be based on their personal charm and warmth. A leader is expected to be able to inspire a personal commitment from his or her following, and this is done in large part through their *personalismo*. In this context the term takes on a meaning closer to charisma and has defined some of the region's most successful political leaders: Victor Raúl Haya de la Torre of Peru's APRA, Juan Domingo Perón of Argentina, or Fidel Castro of Cuba. Each of these leaders was capable of exuding an immense personal charm in virtually all social contacts, be it a private meeting with an individual or small group or a speech to an assembled throng of thousands. Fidel Castro became known for his ability to hold an audience's attention in speeches that lasted hours.

STRONG-MAN RULE: *CAUDILLO, CACIQUE,* AND *CORONEL*

We have established that political leadership in Latin America has often tended to be authoritarian, with the political leader exercising a great deal of power and control. Military dictators who can employ the force and power to maintain their position are tolerated or at least endured until time passes or they can be overthrown. Brutal rulers such as Augusto Pinochet (the military dictator in Chile from 1973 until 1990) have not always had the *personalismo* of most civilian politicians. Pinochet simply relied on overwhelming force. Since before the conquest, the tradition of the strong local leader became well established. The *cacique* came to mean a local indigenous leader who could be best described as a political boss. In his local community and among his own people his power base was strong, but it diminished rapidly as he moved away from it. After colonial rule was put in place other strong men developed. The *caudillo* initially was a regional political leader or boss who might exercise absolute or near-absolute power in his region. Often a local landowner or other local notable, he usually had an independent base for economic-political power. As time went on the *caudillo* and *caudillismo* also came to refer to strong, if rather authoritarian, national political leaders such as Juan Perón of Argentina. In the rural areas of traditional Brazil the large landowners or *fazendeiros* were often given the rank of *colonel* in the state militia. This also came to be a honorific title given to a powerful local notable who was a power to be reckoned with. Like the Southern colonels in the post-bellum American South, *coroneis* were, and sometimes still are, powerful political players in much of rural Brazil. It would be difficult to understand politics in rural Brazil without referring to *coronelismo* or realizing the power and impunity of the *coronel*.

CUARTEL, CUARTELAZO, GOLPE DE ESTADO, AND THE *JUNTA*

Political culture in Latin America is also influenced by the tendency of the military to leave their military barracks, or *cuartel*, to intervene in the political process, the *cuartelazo*. Indeed, when the government is indecisive, ineffective, overly corrupt, or leaning too far to the left, many civilians call on the military to intervene. Military intervention has been an ongoing phenomenon in most Latin America countries. With few exceptions, such as Costa Rica since the 1948 revolution and the subsequent abolition of the armed forces and Mexico since the 1920s, the militaries have engaged in *golpismo*. Believing themselves to be defenders of the constitution, upholders of national honor, or defenders against subversion, corruption, or tyranny, the Latin American military has staged more than 200 coups d'état, or *golpes de estado*, since most of the nations became independent in the early part of the nineteenth century. After the successful *golpe*, the dominant military coup makers, or *golpistas*, typically set up a military junta to rule until civilian government is restored. Most commonly, the junta is made up of upper-level officers from the army, navy, and air force. The period of rule can range from the time it takes to elect or appoint a new civilian president (usually a few months) to more than a decade, as was the case in Brazil (1964–1985) and Chile (1973–1990). This later type of extended military governance came to be called *bureaucratic authoritarianism* (see Guillermo O'Donnel) and was used to refer to the extended period of military rule where the military actively ran the bureaucratic governmental apparatus. Such bureaucratic authoritarianism characterized many of the governments in South America during the 1960s (beginning with the coup in Brazil in 1964), 1970s, and 1980s. Nations under such rule included not only Brazil, Chile, and Argentina, but also Bolivia and Uruguay. A progressive Nasserite (a nationalist military government patterned after that led by Gamal Abdel Nasser in Egypt from 1952 to 1970) ruled Peru from 1968 to 1980. A conservative form of extended military rule characterized Guatemala from 1954 until 1985, and the military dominated politics well into the 1990s. In Paraguay a traditional military *caudillo*, General Alfredo Stroessner, ruled from 1954 to 1989.

OTHER *POLÍTICOS*

Professional politicians are *políticos*. In fact, all those who engage in politics could be described as *políticos*, or *políticas* if they are women. One does not, however, need to be authoritarian to qualify. Different countries have different political cultures. In Brazil the tradition of the *chefe político* emerged. It came to have special meaning and refers to a *político* with special powers and attributes who could best be described in English as a political boss. The figure of the political bosses also existed in Spanish-speaking America and could be referred to as a *jefe político*, although the connotation of power might not be quite so strong.

CORPORATISM

Another aspect of Latin American society that strongly influences the political system is *corporatism*, the tendency to divide society into different bodies (corpus) or corporations according to specific function or profession. The identity of individuals to their particular body is oftentimes stronger than to the nation. Thus military officers in particular frequently display more loyalty to their military institutions than to civilian government or national civilian leaders. This tendency has also traditionally been strong among members of another important societal institution—the Catholic Church.

PATRON-CLIENT, CLIENTELISM, AND OTHER SPECIAL RELATIONS

As was suggested earlier, there is often great disparity in power and prerogative in Latin America. Those who do not have power seek protection from those who do. Thus alliances between the powerful and the not-so-powerful are often made. Indeed, this practice began on the large landed estates between the *patrón* and the *peon*, his humble employee. As with patrons and their supporters and followers elsewhere, this type of relationship spread throughout the society. The *patron-client relationship* refers to the special ties of personal loyalty and commitment that connect a powerful person with those below him. The *patrón* will look after his followers and personally intervene to make sure they are well treated or to assist them in a time of trouble, even paying for medical treatment for a family members from personal funds. As the *patrón* rises or falls, his retainers rise or fall with him. The followers give unswerving support to their leader and can always be counted on because of their personal loyalty. This has characterized many political movements as well. Indeed, it has been suggested that many Latin American political parties are personal parties grouped around the party leader. Many observers have also noted the existence of personal factions or groups within parties and government—public administration in particular is often rife with these personal groupings.

Compadres and Comadres Everywhere

Another important social relationship that spills over into business and politics is that of the *compadre* and the *comadre*—the godparents of one's children. Given the traditional importance of the Church, it is not surprising that those who stand with the parents at the christening of their child should play an important role in the life not only of the child, but also of the parents. The *compadre* or *comadre* is someone with whom one's relationship has been cemented. Like a blood relative, they generally are someone who can be counted on. *Compadres* protect each other, as do *comadres*. They can gain access or special favors and can always count on one's help. If amenable, a person of a higher social status, like the *patrón*, may be chosen as a *compadre* or *comadre*, thus creating a special tie to the *patrón* for the whole family.

Camarillas and Other Small Groups

Personal or professional networks are always significant. The importance of the small group, or *grupito*, cannot be underestimated. The *camarilla*, or clique, is pervasive in Mexican society and politics. In the political context it specifically refers to a self-promoting political group that maximizes the power and position of its members through concerted collective action. In Brazil friends or associates often form a *panelinha* so they can do business with each other or be assured of contacts through people they know they can trust.

Finally, finesse and the ability to improvise are greatly valued. One hopes to move things along with the same deftness that world-famous soccer player Pelé moved the ball down the field. Indeed, the Brazilians have a special word for such adroitness, *jeito*. To give a *jeito* is to finesse something, to manage it, to make things happen.

The conduct of politics in Latin America is a complex process that occurs in a reality far different from that found in the United States, Canada, Great Britain, or elsewhere. In political and social interactions, all the factors we have discussed—and many others—come into play. Ultimately power rules, but it is exercised through the culturally based concepts, rules, and techniques that define the power game in Latin America. Further, the nuanced nature of the role these factors play is often the deciding factor in many key political and other events. Their importance in business or economics cannot be underestimated; in the game of politics their comprehension is essential.

Bibliography

"!Adelante! The New Rural Activism in the Americas." *NACLA: Report on the Americas.* Vol XXXIII, No. 5. March/April, 2000.

Alvarez, Sonia E., Evelina Dagino, and Arturo Escobar. *Cultures of Politics, Politics of Culture, Revisioning of Latin American Social Movements.* Boulder, CO: Westview, 1998.

Barrios de Chungara, Domitila, with Moema Viezzer. *Let Me Speak! Testimony of Domitilia, a Woman of the Bolivian Mines.* New York: Monthly Review, 1978.

Benjamin, Medea, and Maisa Mendoça. *Benedita da Silva, an Afro-Brazilian Woman's Story of Politics and Love.* Oakland, CA: Institute for Food and Development, 1997.

Bose, Christine E., and Edna Acosta-Belén, eds. *Women in the Latin American Development Process.* Philadelphia: Temple University Press, 1995.

Bouvard, Margarite Guzman. *Revolutionizing Motherhood: The Mothers of the Plaza de Mayo.* Wilmington, DE: Scholarly Resources, 1994.

Caipora Women's Group. *Women in Brazil.* London: Latin American Bureau and New York: Monthly Review Press, 1993.

Cubit, Tessa. *Latin American Society.* 2nd ed. Burnt Mills, Essex, England: Longman Scientific and Technical, and New York: Wiley, 1995.

Dixon, Kwame. Field notes shared with H. Vanden, September 2000.

Dore, Elizabeth, ed. *Gender Politics in Latin America: Debate in Theory and Practice.* New York: Monthly Review, 1998.

Dore, Elizabeth, and Maxine Molyneux, eds. *Hidden Histories of Gender and the State in Latin America.* Durham, NC: Duke University Press, 2000.

Eckstein, Susan, ed. *Power and Protest: Latin American Social Movements.* Berkeley: University of California Press, 1989.

Farnsworth-Alvear, Elizabeth. *Dulcinea in the Factory, Myths, Morals, Men, and Women in Colombia's Industrial Experiment, 1905–1960.* Durham, NC: Duke University Press, 2000.

Galeano, Eduardo. *Open Veins of Latin America, Five Centuries of the Pillage of a Continent.* 25th Anniversary Edition. New York: Monthly Review Press, 1997.

Grandin, Greg. *The Blood of Guatemala: A History of Race and Nation.* Durham, NC: Duke University Press, 2000.

Green, Duncan. *Faces of Latin America.* 2nd ed. London: Latin American Bureau, 1997.

Hanchard, Michael, ed. *Racial Politics in Contemporary Brazil.* Durham, NC: Duke University Press, 1999.

Hillman, Richard S., ed. *Understanding Contemporary Latin America.* Boulder, CO: Lynne Rienner, 1997.

Imaz, José Luis de. *Los Que Mandan* [Those Who Rule]. Translated by Carlos A. Astiz. Albany: State University of New York Press, 1970.

January, Alain de. *The Agrarian Question and Reformism in Latin America.* Baltimore: Johns Hopkins University Press, 1988.

Jesus, Carolina María de. *Britita's Diary: the Childhood Memories of Carolina María de Jesus.* Armonk, NY: M.E. Sharp, 1998.

Kuppers, Gaby, ed. *Compañeras: Voices from the Latin American Women's Movement.* London: Latin American Bureau, 1994.

Loveman, Brian, and Thomas M. Davies, Jr. *The Politics of Anti-Politics, The Military in Latin America.* Wilmington, DE: Scholarly Resources, 1997.

Levine, Daniel, ed. *Constructing Culture and Power in Latin America.* Ann Arbor: University of Michigan Press, 1993.

Minority Rights Publishing. *No Longer Invisible: Afro-Latins Today.* London: Minority Rights Publishing, 1995.

Roseberry, William, and Lowell Gudmundson. *Coffee, Society and Power in Latin America.* Baltimore: Johns Hopkins University Press, 1995.

Thiesenhusen, William C. *Searching for Agrarian Reform in Latin America.* Boston: Unwin Hyman, 1989.

Windance Twine, Francis. *Racism in a Racial Democracy: The Maintenance of White Supremacy in Brazil.* New Brunswick, NJ: Rutgers University Press, 1998.

FILMS AND VIDEOS

Americas 4, Mirrors of the Heart. U.S., 1993.

Black Orpheus. Brazil, 1958.

Eles ñao usam Black Tie. Brazil, 1980.

Buenos Días Compañera: Women in Cuba. Cuba, 1974.

Central Station. Brazil, 1998.

Details of a Duel: a Question of Honor. Chile/Cuba, 1988.

The Double Day. U.S., 1975.

Like Water for Chocolate. Mexico, 1992.

Los Olvidados. Mexico, 1950.

Mexican Bus Ride. Mexico, 1951.

Portrait of Teresa. Cuba, 1979.

Shoot to Kill. Venezuela, 1990.

We're All Stars. Peru, 1993.

SIX

RELIGION IN LATIN AMERICA

Treatments of contemporary Latin American politics often pay relatively little attention to the role of religion. Such an omission is a serious one because from the era of the great Meso-American civilizations to the present time spiritual factors have had great impact on the political scene. This chapter will explore that evolution over time. The Roman Catholic Church will be a major focus but not to the exclusion of other religions, especially the rapid rise of evangelical Protestantism in the last twenty-five years.

The primary perception of the religious character of Latin America is Roman Catholic. For nearly five centuries the Catholic Church had a virtual monopoly on religious life. During that time religious and political authorities were tightly bound together. The North American concept of separation of church and state was not known in Latin America until almost the twentieth century. Today's reality in Latin America is somewhat different, although close to 70 percent of the population still identify themselves as Roman Catholic. During the last twenty-five years the most important development in Latin American religiosity is the exponential growth of evangelical Protestantism. In 1970 only 2–3 percent of the population in most Latin American countries were evangelicals; today that number has reached close to 15 percent. The last thirty years has also witnessed significant turmoil within the Catholic Church. Following the historic Vatican Council in the early 1960s the region's bishops began meeting regularly; in 1968 at a meeting in Medellín, Columbia, they issued a ground-breaking document that seemed to commit the Church to a much greater role in promoting social justice. If the Medellín document had been fully implemented it would have marked a dramatic reversal of the historical role played by the Catholic Church as the ally of the wealthy and powerful. However, the promise of Medellín to stand with the poor brought resistance from the more conservative clergy in both Latin America and Rome, leaving a divided Church that has been vulnerable to inroads from Protestantism. It is also inaccurate to view the totality of Latin American religion as falling within the scope of Protestantism and Catholicism. A variety of spiritist cults and movements also continue to exist in the region, many with their roots in the large number of slaves brought to the Western Hemisphere from Africa in the seventeenth century. In many cases, the indigenous peoples of the Americas have also maintained a spiritual identity independent of Western religions.

Historically religion and politics have been deeply intertwined in Latin America. This interconnection began with the role the Roman Catholic Church played in the military conquests of the Spanish and Portuguese in the fifteenth and sixteenth centuries. Church authorities came ashore with the *conquistadores* in search of souls to convert and provided ideological justification for the military conquests and for monarchical rule. Ultimately the Church was rewarded for this role with vast amounts of wealth and power. The Church set up parallel institutions to the royal administration. They were granted significant tracts of land from which they generated wealth and were given free reign to develop the region's educational system.

The relationship between religion and politics is a complex one. Strong religious communities help set the value structure of a society by stating what is important in life. In doing so religious values help frame what the citizenry expects out of their lives and therefore on one level what they may expect from government authorities. For example, traditional Roman Catholic teaching, which emphasized the glories of eternal salvation rather than the material pleasures of one's current life, seemed to dampen the expectations of the citizenry and therefore reduce the pressure on the political authorities to provide for the good life in the here and now. Catholic theology rooted in Thomas Aquinas also provided a direct justification for monarchy and elite rule. All humans were deemed to be born in original sin, and it was only through God's grace that some people were better suited to rule than others. The essence of politics was then to elevate such people to power so that they could be responsible to God's will, not to the will of the people. This reasoning was used to provide justification for the Spanish and Portuguese monarchies. Religious authorities can also play a more direct role in politics by influencing their followers to support a particular political leader or party. In recent times, Argentina and Chile have shown contrasting examples of Church policy. In Argentina the Catholic hierarchy actively supported the two military regimes that ruled between 1966 and 1983. Such support was important in a country where military rule had earlier been supplanted by constitutional parliamentary governance. In contrast, the Catholic hierarchy became an outspoken critic of the Chilean military regime during the 1980s. That opposition helped pave the way for the defeat of a military-sponsored referendum in 1988 and the return to civilian rule in 1990. Despite these contrasting examples, historically most interventions by the Church have been to support the status quo. There are numerous examples in Latin American history of the Catholic Church playing such a role.

The question of separation of church and state has long been a contentious one, with the establishment of such a principle being slow to arrive in Latin America in comparison with the United States. As elsewhere, the impetus for such a separation came from those who sought independence in spiritual matters from an overbearing government that gave favors only to persons from a particular religion. In Latin America the challenge to the tight relationship between the church and state came from the Liberal political movements of the nineteenth century. In response the Church closely allied itself with the Conservatives in an attempt to maintain its historically privileged position. When Liberal regimes came to power the Church was usually "disestablished," meaning that the hierarchy lost its direct control over political matters. The dates of disestablishment range from the initial case of Colombia in 1848 to Mexico in 1857 and Brazil in 1889. Unlike the Liberal establishment in the United States, which granted freedom of religion and then largely stayed out of Church affairs, the Latin American Liberals granted official freedom of worship but then proceeded to seek to interfere in the affairs of the Church by attempting to compel priests to marry and reorganize diocesan boundaries. By 1910 virtually all of the Latin American countries, with the exception of Colombia, which reversed its disestablishment from 1886 until 1930, had granted formal religious liberty. As a result the Catholic hierarchy ended its sole association with the Conservatives and broadened its relations to include the Liberal elites with whom they had fought so bitterly. The terms of their dealings with the state were now different, lacking the legal and financial privileges of the previous centuries.

In the early twentieth century the Catholic Church also faced for the first time a significant thrust of Protestant missionary work into the region. However, the Catholics retained a strong position based on their large following and the rootedness of their ideas in the popular culture. Also, as the fierce anti-clericism of the nineteenth century began to fade, the Church, without official representation in government, began to regain its political influence with the elites as newer, more powerful challenges from revolutionary movements united Liberal and Conservative elites. The church concentrated its political efforts on protecting its own position in society by pushing for mandatory religious education and public funding of Church organizations and projects. The new tactic of accommodating both Liberal and Conservative elites and even the populist leaders in Brazil and Argentina actually succeeded in winning back some privileges previously lost and in guaranteeing the Church a prominent societal position through education and public festivals.

Today Roman Catholicism remains the dominant religion of Latin America, but it is facing an increasing challenge from both evangelical Protestantism and the overall secularization of society. In several countries Protestants may surpass Catholics in numbers of adherents if the current trends continue. Philip Berryman has observed that because of the relatively low percentage of Catholics attending mass regularly, the number of churchgoing Protestants may be roughly equal to that of Catholics. As Protestantism grows the political implications of this development are unclear. Many of the evangelical movements are closely connected with right-wing political movements based in the United States, but overall the evangelical movement is quite pluralistic and represents a liberalizing trend in comparison to the most conservative forces within the Catholic Church. This chapter will analyze all of the religious movements in greater depth with an emphasis on their relationship to politics.

From its first appearance in the New World, the Catholic Church was an essential element in the conquest and colonization of the native peoples by Spain and Portugal. From the beginning, the Catholic Church established a privileged position as the holder of considerable economic and political power. It provided ideological justification for the subjugation of the native peoples encountered by the conquerors. As a reward for its role, the Church was granted significant landholdings and a central role in the new colonial societies as the primary providers of education. The Church viewed the local populations as people who could be converted to the Catholic faith, thus augmenting the Church's ranks worldwide. The Church had no respect whatsoever for the existing spiritual beliefs of the native peoples. For example, when the Spanish conquered Tenochtitlán, the capital of the Aztecs, they destroyed the chief temple of the Aztecs and constructed the metropolitan cathedral of Mexico City directly on top of its foundations. This aggressive and intolerant Catholicism reflected that era when the Spanish monarchy defeated the Moors in southern Spain and expelled the Jews. The early sixteenth century was also marked by Catholicism's vigorous reaction to the Protestant Reformation. The Church's stature was further enhanced when Pope Alexander VI in 1494 adjudicated the division of the continent between Spain and Portugal and conferred on their monarchies the right and duty of propagating the Catholic faith. The model of social order the Iberian conquerors brought was that of "Christendom." Ironically this model arrived in Latin America just as it was beginning to unravel in Europe. Philip Berryman has called the Latin American form "colonial Christendom." Under this system of patronage the Spanish and Portuguese monarchs exercised full administrative control over the churches in their territories. This set the stage for struggles over church-state relations during the independence period when the new leaders assumed that their governments would retain the administrative powers previously held by the monarchies.

In many ways, the role played by the Catholic Church in Latin America was simply an extension of the role that it had played in Europe. After its first four centuries as a movement that struggled to survive in the face of hostile secular authorities, the Church succeeded in gaining recognition from the political and economic elites who allowed it to carry out its spiritual mission without significant interference from government authorities. It protected its position by endorsing governments and social systems that were willing to further Catholic values and protect Church interests. The Church always had an ambivalent view toward secular life. It tended to view the difficult human existence of the majority of the people as a burden to be endured in the hopes of a glorious afterlife. Secular authorities were viewed with a skeptical eye, but as long as they permitted the Church authorities to carry out their pastoral mission the Church leaders gave their backing to the political and economic leaders.

The Latin American Catholic Church adopted this model and applied it throughout the New World, but it is important to note that from the beginning of the Church's presence in Latin America there were missionaries who protested the cruelty of the conquest. The most famous is Dominican priest Bartolomé de las Casas, who came to Hispaniola in 1502. Although he initially held Indian slaves, las Casas experienced a conversion and spent the remainder of his life arguing that the indigenous people should be treated with respect and won over to Catholicism with the power of the gospel rather than the force of arms. He wrote in *In Defense of the Indians*, "With what swords and cannons did Christ arm his disciples when he sent them to preach the gospel. Devastating provinces and exterminating natives or putting them to flight, is this freely sharing the faith?" Many Dominican bishops followed las Casas in the defense of the Indians. The tradition continues today with Church leaders like Bishop Samuel Ruíz defending indigenous peasant interests in contemporary Chiapas. The primary motivation for such actions may well be moral, but they are also aimed at preventing the government from interfering with the Church's efforts to increase the size of their ranks.

Independence Movements

In the first twenty-five years of the nineteenth century Latin America broke away from Spain and Portugal. The independence movement and its aftermath created a crisis for the Catholic Church. Most of the bishops had sided with the Spanish crown, and popes had made pronouncements against independence in 1816 and 1823. Some clerics, including Mexican priests Hidalgo and Morales, were leaders of the independence movement, but for the most part the Church found itself on the losing side of the political change. The Vatican only began to recognize the new states in 1831 and in many countries the clergy left, leaving some dioceses vacant. Those clerics who remained in most case allied themselves with the newly created conservative parties, who pledged to support the historic role of the church in Latin society. In societies where the Conservatives held sway the Church was able to prosper, albeit in a more limited way. However, in those countries where the Liberals came to power, the Church faced new laws that enabled the government to confiscate their lands. In the eyes of the Liberals the Church represented an obstacle to their vision of progress and development. The nineteenth century also saw the rise of Free Masonry in Latin America as a challenge to the dominance of the Church in secular matters. As a result of attacks from the Liberals and Free Masons, the Catholic Church was thrown into crisis in much of Latin America in the nineteenth century. The Church came to rely on a steady flow of priests from Europe, as they could not recruit enough clergy from within the region. Even today Catholic clergy are primarily foreign in many Latin countries, including Guatemala, Venezuela, and Bolivia.

The Catholic Church entered the twentieth century in considerable disarray, weakened by attacks from Liberal governments and facing an increasingly aggressive Protestant challenge. The Protestant missionaries began arriving in the last decades of the nineteenth century and often received favorable treatment from the Liberal governments, who saw them as a useful tool in breaking the hold of the Catholic Church. Inroads in Catholic dominance did occur, but most Latin Americans continued to view themselves as Catholic. In the early twentieth century, the Catholic hierarchy did initiate changes in response to the challenges it faced. The Church embraced new values as it sought to maintain its hold on a population that was also undergoing significant change. Religious freedom was embraced, and there was a limited recognition of the principle of separation of church and state. The latter was limited because Catholic schools continued to receive government subsidies and Catholic teaching was promoted in public schools. The Church also embraced the concept of social justice as it sought to relate the gospel to people's actual living circumstances on this earth as opposed to being only concerned with heavenly salvation. Church leaders also began to speak out on a variety of universal issues, such as freedom, equality, and women's rights. This era was marked by serious efforts to combat what the Church saw as "alien" influences on its traditional followers. The Church created organizations like Catholic Action to resist the influence of Liberalism, Masonry, and Marxism. Catholic Action especially targeted university students and middle-class youth who were seen as the likely future leaders.

The Vatican originally developed Catholic Action to combat socialism among working-class Europeans, but Pope Pius XI saw benefits in the Latin American incarnation. The organization was firmly rooted in such early social encyclicals as Rerum Novarum, but its success in Latin America was limited because the sectors to which it was targeted were so much smaller than in Western Europe. One exception to this pattern was in Chile, where the efforts of Catholic Action contributed to the formation of the Christian Democratic Party as a centrist alternative between the Conservatives and the Socialists and Communists.

The Church also organized competing unions or "workers' circles" to directly compete with socialist- and communist-led unions that were gaining significant influence in the Latin American working class. Anthony Gill, an expert on the Roman Catholic Church in Latin America, points out that the turn to organizing workers did not represent a significant ideological shift for the Church because it was limited to those places and groups that were being seriously courted by socialist ideologies. In this period the rural poor were largely ignored. In another break with tradition the Church hierarchy also sanctioned a much greater role for lay people within the activities of the Church. These changes occurred very slowly over the early decades of the century, but the pace of change accelerated in the 1950s and 1960s as the Latin American Church increasingly shaped its teaching and practice of Catholicism to the particular conditions of Latin America.

The first plenary meeting of the Latin American Bishops' Conference (CELAM) occurred in 1955 in Rio de Janeiro. This conference would become influential in shaping the direction of the Church over the remainder of the century. The Latin American Church had been moving closer to greater acceptance of a role in social change and social justice, but the Second Vatican Council in Rome (1962–1965) accelerated the process. The documents produced by the Council committed the Church to oppose governments that restricted religious or political freedoms and to acknowledge the significance of working for social justice in a variety of settings. During the early 1960s the Catholic Church became involved in various reform movements that sought agrarian reform, expanded voting rights, and greater government spending on health and education. The Church also became the direct vehicle for improving people's lives through health training, literacy programs, and production cooperatives. Such programs contributed to a wider movement for nonviolent reformist-oriented change.

In addition to promoting social justice Vatican II also articulated a more collegial model for the bishops. Rather than simply being subordinates of the pope, bishops came to be seen as peers who needed to work together to address concerns in their particular geographical area. Although the Vatican Council was an important turning point, socially conscious activity by the Church pre-dated the Council in some places. In Brazil in the late 1950s the Catholic hierarchy united with the government of reformer Juscelino Kubitschek to oppose the country's landowning oligarchy. The Church was instrumental in the formation of a development agency for northeast Brazil. Kubitschek used the Christian language of social justice to justify his reforms. It was in this era that Paulo Freire, a Catholic educator in the northeast, developed a new method for teaching literacy. Catholic action movements of students and workers organized in many places to promote a progressive agenda. The activities of Catholic action led to discussion of the need for political action to change the basic structural inequalities that were limiting the effects of reform and social work. Before these discussions were fully consummated, the 1964 Brazilian military coup occurred, placing the Church and its activists in a more defensive mode and setting the stage for its next important contribution to Latin American political life. During the 1950s bishops in Chile became involved in programs of land reform, literacy, and rural cooperatives. These efforts went beyond the Church's traditional social work and, as a result, brought the Church in conflict with the traditional elites.

A New Political Role

From the 1960s through the 1980s the Catholic Church became a focal point in many areas of resistance to military rule. In Brazil after the military coup of 1964 the Catholic hierarchy broke from its traditional role of absolute defenders of the status quo. This stance in Brazil contrasted with the role that the Catholic Church had played during the Cuban revolution. The Church had stood with the Batista dictatorship to the end and few Catholic activists had been involved in the revolutionary movement. After the 26th of July movement took power the Church became the focal point of resistance to the new government and suffered significant repression, including the expulsion of foreign priests, which further debilitated an already weak Cuban Church. As a result of the Cuban revolution the Latin American hierarchy saw the potential danger to the future of the Church in an uncompromising stand toward revolution and radical reform. In societies under dictatorial rule, like Brazil, the Church was just about the only institution that could provide a haven against the overwhelming power of the state. Aided by the Church's organizational and financial resources, local parishes were able to provide material and legal assistance for those who were repressed. Agencies established by the Church monitored human rights violations and provided lawyers for those accused of political crimes. The Church also set up programs that distributed food and clothing to the families of those who were imprisoned, and upon release from jail political prisoners received assistance from the Church in the form of counseling and employment assistance.

In many countries Catholic clerics and lay people became part of nonviolent resistance movements that argued for the restoration of civilian rule. Catholic leaders not only criticized specific military governments but also rejected authoritarianism as a method of rule, a significant break from the past. In the context of that ferment the Latin American Bishops Conference (CELAM) met in Medellín, Columbia, in 1968. The conference came on the heels of the historic Second Vatican Council, which had turned the Church to a social justice vision and also encouraged the regional conferences of bishops to look more closely at the specific challenges of their areas. The Latin American bishops picked up this challenge and in the process produced a document that has influenced the Church's work ever since. In 1967 Pope Paul VI's encyclical *On the Progress of Peoples* focused on Third World development issues, containing a mild rebuke of the existing international economic order. Soon after the Pope's encyclical, groups of bishops and priests began to lay out a program for Latin America in advance of the conference. A group of eighteen bishops, half from Brazil, went beyond the Pope's statement while also drawing heavily upon it. They wrote approvingly of both revolution and socialism. In Argentina, Peru, Columbia, and Mexico new groups of priests formed to press a progressive agenda as the gap between the rhetoric of the Vatican Council and the reality of everyday life in Latin America became more obvious. They raised fundamental questions about the wealth of the Church, its historic support for the status quo, and the need for political action to achieve change. These groups did not speak for anywhere near a majority of the clergy, but their ideas were shaking up the complacency of the Church and dominated the discussion leading into the conference.

The task of those at CELAM was to apply the work of the Second Vatican Council to Latin America, but they met at a particularly significant moment in the history of the struggle for social change. The year had been one of dramatic developments—students had occupied universities in the United States, factory workers and students had united in France, Mexican police had repressed student demonstrations, and the Soviet invasion of Czechoslovakia had ended the drive for reform in that country. Combined with the force of Pope Paul's encyclical, these events pushed the bishops to produce a philosophy and plan of action that would be more progressive than its conservative past and probably more radical than most were actually prepared to carry out in practice. The documents emerging from the conference were striking in that such topics as justice, peace, and education received greater attention than did the traditionally dominant topics of pastoral work and Church structures.

At its most basic level the bishops called for Catholics to be involved in the transformation of society. "Institutionalized violence" in the form of poverty, repression, and underdevelopment was decried and was categorized as "sin." Such a categorization represented a significant expansion of the concept beyond its traditional meaning of individual transgression. The document called for "sweeping, bold, urgent, and profoundly renovating changes." Revolutionaries were presented in a very positive light and were not tainted with an identification to use violence. The Church made a number of commitments that included the defense of human rights and the sharing of the conditions of the poor. The conference also raised the idea of neighborhood-based, lay-led ecclesial communities (CEBs) that would soon begin springing up all over Latin America. The term "liberation" was used often and was placed primarily in human rather than spiritual terms. However, the document stopped short of endorsing the right of the oppressed to fight for their rights. Some feared being labeled as condoning violence, while others remained committed in a principled way to nonviolence. The conference came to grips with the realization that Catholic theology needed to emerge from the Latin American condition. Theology was no longer viewed as universal and could not simply be imported from Europe or North America. A key figure in the development of liberation theology, as it came to be called, was Peruvian theologian Gustavo Gutiérrez. Gutiérrez had first used the term liberation theology shortly before Medellín, and soon afterward Gutiérrez and Brazilian theologian Hugo Assmann published full-length books on the subject. From the early 1960s Catholic theologians had begun to discuss the necessity of developing a specific Latin American theology, but they were slow to break with the long-standing tradition of a universal theology. Ultimately the pressure of events resulted in the breakthrough works of Gutiérrez and Assmann. For decades Catholicism had struggled to be relevant to the modern world, but with liberation theology it sought to find in Christianity guidance for the struggle for change. As Berryman states, "It is a critique of how social structures treat the poor and how Christians and the church itself operate."

As Anthony Gill points out, a key element of liberation theology is the reliance on Marxist methodology. The theologians based their understanding of Latin American poverty on dependency theory, a perspective that views poverty and oppression in the Third World as a direct consequence of the world capitalist economy dominated by Western Europe and the United States. Some theologians, such as Ernesto Cardenal of Nicaragua, also embraced the Marxist idea of class struggle and from that justified participation in revolutionary movements. In the wake of the 1968 conference Catholic clergy and lay people throughout Latin American increasingly took up the Church's call for greater attention to matters of social justice and greater political involvement. Thousands of Catholic nuns and priests moved out of traditional convents and religious houses and into poor neighborhoods, where they shared the difficult living conditions of the poor. Part of the motivation was to make the Church more relevant to its majority poor constituency. Traditionally the Church had devoted the great proportion of its time and resources to the middle and upper classes and had sustained itself in significant measure through the tuition payments it received to educate the sons and daughters of the wealthy. The move to the poor neighborhoods was seen by those who did it as a means to better carry out their religious vocation. Although the moves did involve some personal hardship, the nuns and priests who engaged in this new form of pastoral work were freer than their counterparts who remained in traditional roles as parish priests and educators.

Most of the clergy who went into the poor neighborhoods adopted the educational approach of Brazilian educator Paulo Freire, called *concientización* (consciousness-raising), detailed in his classic work *Pedagogy of the Oppressed*. Rather than imparting their wisdom to the people in the neighborhoods, the clergy saw their role as drawing out conclusions through group reflection. These discussions were often carried out in what became known as ecclesial base communities, meetings in homes to read and discuss the scriptures with the purpose of drawing conclusions about their relevance to everyday life. Those leading the discussion, religious or lay, urged people to search for the underlying causes of their poor situation. In rural areas these discussions would often move from immediate problems toward matters such as land ownership and from there to class structures. Similar developments occurred in urban settings, where people would seek to understand the root problem for poor sanitation or poor public transportation in their neighborhoods. More often than not the consciousness-raising led to the formation of groups that had a variety of purposes—soup kitchens, peasant associations, cooperatives, and so forth. Some were primarily self-helping in their focus, while others were more oriented toward political action. Self-help activities included programs to teach job skills or to serve as Alcoholics Anonymous centers. Political activities ranged from voter registration to serving as centers for revolutionary organizing in Nicaragua and El Salvador.

Impact of Liberation Theology

The impact of liberation theology and the work of nuns, priests, and lay people in advancing an agenda for social change was considerable, but it never succeeded in fully transforming the historic role of the Church as a bastion of the status quo in Latin America. Within five years of the historic confer-ence at Medellín, conservative Latin American bishops, especially in Brazil and Mexico, began a systematic counterattack against liberation theology. As the first step in their strategy they took control of CELAM, the very or-ganization that had initiated the progressive changes. Their counterattack was not initially a frontal assault. For example, no attempt was made to re-peal the documents that were passed in Colombia. However, the conserva-tives were given a large lift with the ascension of Pope John Paul II in 1978. John Paul had been archbishop of Kraków, Poland, and a staunch anti-communist. It was natural that he would side strongly with those in the Latin American Church who saw themselves as working against the influ-ences of Marxism within the Church. The papacy's assault on liberation the-ology proceeded on many fronts during the 1980s. In 1984 the Vatican is-sued a document that strongly criticized liberation theology; in the same time period Rome was successful in marginalizing the influential Brazilian theologian Leonardo Boff. The revolutionary government in Nicaragua, which contained several priests sympathetic to liberation theology, was sin-gled out for harsh criticism during a papal visit in 1983. Those priests in the Nicaraguan government were prevented from carrying out their religious duties. However, the papacy's strongest role against liberation theology may have been its appointment of new bishops who would hold steadfastly to Rome's conservative stance. Archbishop Helder Camera of Recife, Brazil, one of the region's harshest critics of military rule and a strong proponent of the strategy of working with the poor, was replaced by a conservative who moved almost immediately to reverse the fruits of Camera's work. In Cuernavaca, Mexico, there was a high concentration of base Christian com-munities as the result of the work of Bishop Méndes Arceo, but when he re-tired in the late 1980s the Vatican appointed a conservative to replace him and the grassroots work suffered. Overall, the counterattack of the conser-vative forces in the Church was directly related to the growing strength of the Left and the high stakes that were involved. In Brazil the PT was on the verge of winning the national presidency in the late 1980s and only a united front of all the conservative forces succeeded in defeating their candidate, Luis Inacio da Silva, in the 1989 election. In Central America throughout the 1980s revolutionary forces were on the upswing in Nicaragua, El Salvador, and Guatemala. The revolutionary shock waves were felt as far north as Mexico. In that context the papacy weighed in on the side of the anti-communist forces, a decision that dovetailed with the foreign policy initia-tives of the United States. Progressive Church forces came to be seen as part of a revolutionary upsurge that had to be suppressed.

The diminishing impact of liberation theology in the 1990s cannot be blamed exclusively on the counterattack by the Vatican. Part of the failure of liberation theology to fully transform the Church lies within the move-ment itself. Liberation theology initiatives never really succeeded in be-coming a mass movement within the Church. Fewer than 10 percent of the nuns and priests actually moved into communities to work directly with the poor. CEBs did arise in significant numbers in some select places, such as in Brazil during the military government in the 1970s, but they never did come close to their goal of transforming the manner in which the Church functioned. In Brazil close to 100,000 CEBs developed by the mid-1980s, but that accounted for only about 2.5 percent of the Catholic population. Significant lay leadership was involved in the CEBs, but most remained dependent on the leadership of clergy, which limited the CEBs' ability to grow into a mass movement. However, one very positive result of the work of the CEBs was a significant increase in the proportion of women in leadership roles in comparison to the past. The CEBs also gave the Catholic Church a significant presence in working-class neighborhoods that had been previously ignored. The decline of liberation theology, acknowledged by Guittérez in 1994, was also the result of a changing political climate. Born in the era of 1960s revolutionary idealism, liberation theology has declined with the assault on the progressive agenda marked by the collapse of East European socialism and the defeat of the Sandinista revolutionary project in Nicaragua. These setbacks led many within the progressive Church community to scale back their short-term expectations for dramatic social change and to work for more reformist goals within the existing system. The restoration of democratic systems throughout the region in the 1980s facilitated this change in strategy.

The horizons of the reformers may have been limited by world events and their own shortcomings, but their political legacy has not been unimportant. In several key situations in the 1980s, progressive Roman Catholic bishops played an important political role as mediators. In El Salvador, Archbishop Arturo Rivera y Damas, who assumed the leadership of the Church after the military assassinated outspoken Archbishop Oscar Romero, made numerous attempts to bring an end to that country's devastating civil war. The military initially rejected such appeals as treason, but the archbishop's efforts eventually contributed to the 1992 peace agreement. The Guatemalan bishops played a similar role against the wishes of the military to help broker the eventual agreement in that country that ended a forty-year civil war in 1997. Chilean bishops were also instrumental in bringing about a negotiated end to the Pinochet regime. In the current conflict in Chiapas in southern Mexico, Bishop Samuel Ruíz has played an important role as a mediator between the Mexican government and the Zapatistas. During the 1970s and 1980s scores of human rights monitoring organizations were formed in the region often with the protection and funding of the Church. Under different political circumstances, most of these organizations are now independent of the Church, but their work continues and they represent an important legacy of the movement for liberation theology.

Pentecostalism

The most important development in the Latin American religious sector in the last twenty years is the remarkable growth of Pentecostalism. Less than twenty years ago the groups made up no more than 2–3 percent of the population, but today they have reached the significant level of 15 percent continentwide, with a much greater presence in countries such as Guatemala. It also should be pointed out that a focus on absolute numbers is misleading because in comparison to those who identify themselves as Catholic, the evangelicals tend to be more active in church life than their Catholic counterparts. Pentecostal churches were founded mostly in the early part of the twentieth century. They are often connected to Charles Parham's spiritual revival in Topeka, Kansas, in 1901 and a subsequent revival in Los Angeles in 1906. From those revivals came churches such as The Assemblies of God, The Church of God, and The Church of God in Christ.

It is important to not place any single label on the Pentecostal churches, which are quite diverse in both their religious and political practice. Some such as the Universal Church and the Deus e Amor Church are not built around fixed church structures, but instead draw followers to tents and warehouses where the emphasis is on singing and spiritual healing. Their services are dramatic with considerable moaning, screaming, and crawling on hands and knees. The object of the services is to drive out the demons that have "infected" its members. These churches also have a considerable presence on the radio, with hundreds of hours of programming in countries such as Brazil. The Universal Church tends to draw a middle-class constituency, while the Deus e Amor Church is overwhelmingly poor. The largest single Pentecostal group in Latin America is the Assemblies of God, who have 8 to 12 million followers and 35,000 churches in Brazil alone. In contrast to lack of institutionalism in the previously discussed evangelicals, the Assemblies of God, with their origins from North America, are highly organized and have considerable financial resources. Although the majority of their members are very poor, the level of professionalism and wealth belies their North American ties.

Author Philip Berryman has attributed the appeal of the Pentecostals to a simple message of love and prayer that provides community and a sense of self-respect. Another basis of the success of the movement among the region's poorest citizens is that most evangelical ministers come from the same social class as their congregants. In contrast, most Catholic priests, even those who espouse liberation theology, come from middle- and upper-class backgrounds. It is also very difficult to characterize the political impact of the evangelical movement. Unquestionably some churches, such as the Word of God movement in Guatemala, have directly promoted right-wing politics through the born-again leader Ríos Montt, who carried out massive repression in the early 1980s. Later Jorge Serrano based his Guatemalan presidential campaign on evangelical votes, and Alberto Fujimori reached out to evangelicals in his 1990 run for the presidency in Peru. Evangelical representatives are an important voting bloc in the Brazilian congress. However, beyond those examples the evangelicals have not really developed anything close to a clear coherent political message. Not all evangelicals are politically conservative. The Brazilian PT has many evangelicals within its ranks, including one of its congressional leaders, Benedita da Silva, an active member of the Assemblies of God. Many Pentecostals consciously reject any significant involvement in politics.

Spiritism

The third religious tradition in Latin America after Catholicism and Protestantism is Spiritism. This religious trend is present to some degree throughout the continent but is especially prevalent in countries such as Cuba, Haiti, and Brazil, where millions of slaves were imported from West Africa. The Africans brought their spiritual beliefs with them and have maintained them for more than three centuries in the face of efforts by both political and religious authorities to marginalize them. Another branch of Spiritism that exists to the present day is the spiritual beliefs of the descendants of the indigenous people of the Americas. In many instances the spiritist beliefs have comingled with Catholic and Protestant spirituality to form a hybrid usually refered to as syncretism. Generally speaking, Spiritists believe that the dead continue to live and communicate with the world through a variety of means. They believe that these spirits influence the manner in which the living exist, sometimes for good and other times for evil.

One of the strongest Spiritist movements is the voodoo of Haiti, which developed among the slave population and was influential in the abolitionist and independence movements at the end of the eighteenth century. It also would later become a tool of Duvalier dictatorships from the 1950s to the 1980s. Voodoo spirits are called *loas,* and the objective of the religion is to connect the living with the *loas.* The spirits' help is sought to cure ailments and to provide advice for solving daily problems. Priests, called *hougans,* facilitate the connection between the spiritual world and the followers of voodoo. The priests have an authority that can be based on their charisma or in conjunction with the patrimony of a local political or military leader.

Following an instrumental role in achieving Haitian independence in 1804, the voodoo movement was largely driven underground for the next 150 years at the behest of the country's white and Catholic elite. However, a strong underground network of priests and their followers was constructed in Haiti's poorest communities and the religious beliefs were passed on from generation to generation. Then in the late 1950s these local voodoo organizations became the power base for the political movement of François Duvalier, who won the 1957 elections and later established a harsh dictatorial rule that was eventually passed on to his son. The feared Tonton Macoute militias organized by Duvalier for use against his political foes were organized from his voodoo power base. The younger Duvalier was driven from power in mid-1980s, but voodoo retains a strong spiritual following in the contemporary Haiti without, however, the politicization that it had during the Duvalier period.

A less well known but equally important spiritist movement called Santería has a very important presence in contemporary Cuba and Puerto Rico, and is part of the changes occurring in socialist Cuba. Like voodoo, Santería has its origins in the African slaves brought to Cuba to harvest sugar cane. Santería came from the Yoruba people of what is today Nigeria. Like voodoo,

Santería provided a link to their African past and some respite from the brutality of slavery. As in Haiti, the bonds of the Santería communities helped pave the way for independence and abolitionist movements that developed in the latter part of the nineteenth century in Cuba. However, in contrast to voodoo, Santería, out of its instincts for survival in strongly Catholic Cuba, often linked its rituals and spirits to those of the Roman Catholic Church. The key figures of the Catholic Church, such as Jesus and various saints, were taken as equivalents of Yoruba spirits. The Santerístas also timed their main festivals to those of the Catholic Church, such as Easter and Christmas. Such accommodation simply reflected the relationship of forces that existed in Cuba and Puerto Rico during the long years of Spanish and Catholic rule. However, it was a very successful accommodation because it allowed the spiritual beliefs of the Afro-Cuban population to survive into the twentieth century. The movement went into decline with the advent of the revolutionary government in Cuba in 1959, but has undergone a revival in the 1990s with the more tolerant attitude toward religion by the government. The Cuban Catholic Church has even complained that the Santería movement is the favored religion of the current government. Santería is also practiced in the U.S. where there are heavy concentrations of Cubans and Puerto Ricans.

Brazil is another country where Spiritist movements have a significant following. Spiritism has two major variants within the country. Umbanda shares the practice with Santería of pairing its deities of those of the Catholic Church. Similar to voodoo and Santería, Umbanda's followers seek advice from the spirits on problems of everyday life. There are many Umbanda centers, especially in Rio de Janeiro, which holds full schedules of cultural activities alongside exercise programs and social services. The intermediaries between the people and the spirits, called mediums, often obtain a large personal following. Even more akin to Santería is Candomblé, also brought by slaves from the Yoruba region of West Africa. Like Santería it links its deities with those of the Catholic religion (e.g., the spirit Oxala is identified with Jesus). Candomblé is less religious than Umbanda and generally appeals more to the poorer classes. The spirits are also less connected to practical advice and more to pageants of dancing and eating. The Spiritist movements in Brazil have probably been less directly political than similar movements in Haiti and Cuba, but they can be credited with helping the poorer classes in Brazil maintain their cultural identity in the face of the dominant white and Catholic culture.

Discussion of the spiritual and religious beliefs of the indigenous peoples of the Americas is a complex one. It is necessary to analyze the spiritual beliefs of the indigenous as they existed at the time of the Spanish and Portuguese conquest and then to analyze to what extent and in what forms they have persisted to the present time. There is a rich literature in the study of the concept of syncretism. Syncretism describes the process whereby indigenous people simply continued to consciously worship their gods under the guise of Catholic images. The best-known cases of syncretism are actually not of indigenous groups but rather of the previously discussed of Santería in Cuba and Candomblé in Brazil. However, there are numerous anecdotes from Meso-American civilizations where the people hid their idols within the Catholic Church so as to continue the worship of their traditional spirits.

What are the traditional spirits of the indigenous people? Jean Schobinger argues that indigenous religious practice as it evolved to the time of the conquest was significantly different from that of European religious tradition. He argues that indigenous religion was intuitive, open to nature, communitarian, and tending to see everything visible as a symbol of something greater on which they depended. This religious tradition was seen as contrasting with the more individualistic thrust of European religion. Religious rites became more sophisticated over time and practices were passed from one generation to the next and from one civilization to the next. Several high points are worth noting. The classic Mayan period from 300 to 900 A.D. in what is today southern Mexico and Guatemala was governed by a priestly elite who was inspired by dieties. The civilization was sophisticated in that there was both an official religion of the upper classes and a popular spiritualism. This spiritual divergence may help us understand the painful nature of the encounter between the two civilizations.

Anthropological research on the indigenous civilizations of the Americas demonstrates a broad evolution of religious and spiritual practices. Our knowledge of these activities comes primarily from wall art and carvings that survived to the twentieth century, when the majority of research was done. The pattern that can be observed is the growing religiosity of the lower classes. The spiritual life was constructed around both official ceremonies or feast days and series of myths and stories that framed their view of the world.

Mayan religious life was centered around their magnificent stepped pyramids, which symbolically reached toward the cosmic world. Their world view was embodied in the story of the Popol Vuh, whose basic idea was that there had been four ages previous to the one they were then living in. Each previous one had been brought to a cataclysmic end by gods dissatisfied with the imperfections of humans. Life was focused on activities and rites designed to convince the gods not to bring their civilization to an abrupt end. The ceremonies were elaborate and proceeded by strict fasts. Sacrifices played an important part, but in the classic Mayan period human sacrifice was not involved. That practice only emerged later; it originated in Mexico with the Toltecs and was then adopted by Mayans under their influence.

The arrival of the Spanish and Portuguese conquerors had a devastating impact on the spiritual life of the indigenous civilizations, especially the ones that were at the height of their development in the sixteenth century, the Aztecs and the Incas. The conquerors often destroyed the public religious buildings and, through the missionaries who accompanied them, forcibly converted the local population to Catholicism. Perhaps the most blatant example of this was in the capital of the Aztecs, Tenochitlán, where the Spanish conquerors constructed the Catholic metropolitan cathedral on top of the foundations of the destroyed Templo Mayor of the Aztecs, destroying the official and public form of indigenous religions. Indigenous leaders were subjugated and, with that, the ability to conduct the festivals that had dominated their religious practice. This approach by the conquerors led to two parallel phenomena, the maintenance of indigenous religious beliefs through popular culture and the practice of syncretism as a way to maintain traditional practices in the face of a superior power.

Judaism

Any discussion of religion in Latin America should make mention of the region's Jews. They are not large in number, probably under 500,000 in the region as a whole, with the largest communities in Argentina (240,000), Brazil (100,000) and Mexico (35,000). Most Jews who live in Latin America came as part of nineteenth- and twentieth-century immigration, but they have faced persistent anti-Semitism and marginalization that dates to the time of the conquest.

By the fifteenth century Jews had lived in Spain for 1000 years. Always a minority, the Jews were often caught in the battle between Catholicism and Islam and manipulated by both. Over the thousand years there were periods of great Jewish contribution to Spanish life alternated with periods of persecution and forced conversion. Their situation worsened after 1391 when pogroms broke out, first in Seville and then throughout Spain. In 1492 the Spanish crown expelled the Jews from Spain and soon established a series of laws that excluded all Jews, even those who had converted to Catholicism from Spanish public life. Anyone who had any Jewish or Moorish "blood" was excluded from positions in the professions, the Church, the military, and the government. This indelible labeling of those with Jewish ancestry, converted or not, led to the widespread labeling of Jews as a race, a perspective that was imported to Latin America and continues to the present time.

The exclusion of Jews from Spain was extended to Spanish lands in the Americas. In her first instruction to the governor of Hispaniola, Queen Isabella forbade Jews and New Christians (as the converts were called) from settling in the Indies. This legal prohibition continued throughout Spanish rule into the nineteenth century. Many New Christians and some Jews did succeed in settling in the Indies by subverting the law. However, the local missionaries laid the groundwork for long-term anti-Semitism among the native population. Jews were singled out as the tormentors and killers of Christ. Primary among the charges leveled against Jews was subversion. Popular opinion blamed converted Jews for the Dutch defeat of the Portuguese in Brazil in 1630. It was alleged that the New Christians assisted the invaders because they hoped to reestablish Judaism under more tolerant Dutch rule. The stereotype of Jews as subversives persists in Argentina, the country with the largest Jewish population. The generals who carried out

Argentina's Dirty War in the 1970s attacked Jews as subversives and Marxists. Their most famous target was the Jewish journalist Jacabo Timmerman, but the campaign revived anti-Semitism in contemporary Latin America.

Conclusion

As the twenty-first century begins in Latin America, the impact of religion on society is more complex than ever before. The absolute hold of Catholicism on the region is now part of history, and, despite the Church's attempts to remake itself in the last thirty years there will likely be no return to its former dominance. Protestantism has made great strides in recent years, especially with the rapid growth of evangelical sects. However, it should be remembered that these groups claim the allegiance of fewer than one in five Latin Americans. The political impact of the rapid growth of Protestantism is difficult to measure. Some groups are avowedly conservative in their political thrust, but most discourage social activism in their theology. Although generally critical of liberation theology, the evangelicals have largely failed to develop their own strategy for confronting the region's ongoing social ills. That failure may yet derail the long-term growth of the evangelical movement.

It would seem that the work of liberation theology begun in the 1960s has run its course in the current dominant political climate in the region, but that does not mean that its future impact will be marginal. The Catholic Church's commitment to social justice seems to have been firmly established. Pope John Paul's visit to Mexico in early 1999 underscored this fact. Twenty years earlier in his first visit to Mexico he spoke harshly of liberation theology and emphasized his opposition to communism of any kind. That message inevitably bolstered the status quo and by implication was a pro-capitalist message. In the 1999 visit the Pope's message was strikingly different. In reference to the contemporary emphasis on neoliberalism and free markets he said, "The human race is facing forms of slavery which are new and more subtle than those of the past." The Pope has called on both governments and international organizations to carry out plans aimed at Third World debt relief and wealth redistribution. Some have called this perspective post–liberation theology. The long-term impact of the Vatican's new emphasis is yet to be seen. It will likely take a new generation of theologians and Church activists to fully articulate a new vision of social change. The diversity of views within the Protestant sector definitely leaves the field open for a theological alliance that could bridge the two different traditions.

Bibliography

Berryman, Philip. *Stubborn Hope, Religion, Politics, and Revolution in Central America.* Mary Knoll, NY: Orbis Books, 1994.

———. *Religion in the Megacity: Catholic and Protestant Portraits from Latin America.* Mary Knoll, NY: Orbis Books, 1996.

Cleary, Edward, and Hannah Stewart-Gambino. *Power, Politics, and Pentecostals in Latin America*. Boulder, CO: Westview Press, 1997.

Efunde, Agun. *Los Secretos de la Santería*. Miami, FL: Ediciones Cubamerica, 1983.

Fleet, Michael, and Brian Smith. *The Catholic Church and Democratization in Latin America: Twentieth-Century Chile and Peru*. Notre Dame, IN: University of Notre Dame Press, 1996.

Gill, Anthony. *Rendering unto Caesar: The Catholic Church and the State in Latin America*. Chicago: University of Chicago Press, 1997.

Hess, David. *Samba in the Night: Spiritism in Brazil*. New York: Columbia University Press, 1994.

Languerre, Michael S. *Voodoo and Politics in Haiti*. New York: St. Martin's Press, 1989.

Levine, Daniel. *Popular Voices in Latin American Catholicism*. Princeton, NJ: Princeton University Press, 1992.

Martin, David. *Tongues of Fire: The Explosion of Protestantism in Latin America*. London: Basil Blackwell, 1990.

Stevens-Arroyo, Anthony M., and Andrés I. Pérez y Mena, *Enigmatic Powers: Syncretism with African and Indigenous Peoples' Religions among Latinos*. New York: Bildner Center for Western Hemispheric Studies, 1995.

FILMS AND VIDEOS

Americas 6, Miracles Are Not Enough. U.S., 1993.
From Faith to Action in Brazil. United States, 1984.
Onward Christian Soldiers. United States, 1985.
Remembering Romero. United States, 1992.

SEVEN

THE POLITICAL ECONOMY OF LATIN AMERICA

On Economics and Political Economy

In Latin America, one cannot fully understand the political game without understanding its economic underpinnings. The initial encounter between the old world and the Americas resulted from Iberian desire for the economic advantage gained from new trade routes to the East Indies. From the onset, the Americas were an economic enterprise for European colonizers; subsequently, local elites have used the region for their gain. Since the conquest, the economic good of the masses has frequently been sacrificed for the enrichment of foreign and domestic interests. Political power and economic power have generally reinforced each other in Latin America. Those with the wealth have written the political rules. Thus, an understanding of the economics of the region enriches our understanding of its politics and vice versa.

We note that the discipline of economics studies the allocation of scarce resources—how goods and services are produced, distributed, and consumed. It has its immediate origins in the eighteenth century in works such as Adam Smith's *An Inquiry into the Nature and Causes of the Wealth of Nations* (1776). In more recent times economists—like political scientists—often have tried to separate the study of politics and economics. Yet this was not the original intent of Smith, his fellow political economist David Ricardo, or a subsequent student of political economy, Karl Marx. Indeed, if we go back to the original writings of Adam Smith and David Ricardo, we find that they preferred the concept of *political economy* because such an approach took into account the complexity and unity of political and economic phenomena.

Modern students of political economy thus believe that an approach that encompasses both politics and economics is much more effective in studying how scarce resources are allocated and how political values and political power affect that allocation. Given the considerable concentration and interconnection of economic and political power in Latin America, a more comprehensive approach would seem in order.

When Adam Smith was writing in the late 1700s, the dominant economic system for Great Britain, Spain, Portugal, and the American colonies was *mercantilism*, in which the state implemented a policy of increasing exports and acquiring bullion and raw materials through carefully restricted commerce. This was a politically directed policy that used state control of trade and colonization. The government exercised considerable control by regulating production, directing foreign trade and tariffs, and exploiting commerce, particularly with a European nation's colonies. Thus Smith and Ricardo realized the fundamental role of the state and the political power that defined the policy-making process. Indeed, they hoped to induce the state to exert less control over economic interactions. As the discipline of economics evolved over the years, the difficulty in understanding economic phenomena led some commentators to refer to economics as the dismal science. Yet by looking at economics and politics jointly and taking into consideration historical context and sociological factors, a more comprehensive approach to understanding resource and power allocation in different nations can be achieved. This is very much the case in Latin America. Such an approach will be employed in this text.

The Latin American Economy

As in the rest of the world, economies in the Americas began as small, local spheres that were isolated from events outside their valley, village, or small region. As time and productive forces progressed, this initial isolation slowly began to break down in many regions. Civilizations such as the Olmec in eastern Mexico (1500–400 B.C.E.), the early Maya (1500 B.C.E.–300), and the Mochica (400–1000) in northern Peru appeared and began to tie the hithertofore isolated population clusters together. As the Aztec and Incan empires grew, trade and commerce over much wider regions developed. Such economic intercourse was, however, limited to regions and did not extend far beyond the actual political entities (polities). Latin America's integration into the world economy only began when the Europeans arrived. However, even after centuries, one could still find isolated villages and valleys that were only marginally integrated into the world economy. During colonial times and well into the twentieth century, haciendas were often near self-contained economic units with minimal contact with the outside, save the sale of one or two cash crops for national consumption or export to Europe or North America. Indeed, a few native Amazonian groups such as the Yanomami were only being integrated into the world economy as the twentieth century ended.

A substantial sector of agriculture made up of Native American and other subsistence farmers who used the bulk of their production to feed themselves and their families were only slowly integrated into the international system. Their growing need for goods that they could not produce themselves led to their gradual integration into the national and international economy as they sold small amounts of a cash crop, handicraft, or their labor to landowners, plantations, or tourist enterprises. Yet as the sad history of the Yanomami in recent times suggests, integration into the international economic system did not necessarily benefit those who were losing their isolation. Indeed, as their consumption and nutritional patterns changed, they were more likely to suffer from malnutrition.

Latin America was integrated into the world economy after 1500. Due to improvements in navigation and seafaring, Portugal and Spain established world trade routes that circumnavigated Africa and eventually came to include the Americas. From Columbus' second voyage on, the Americas were used to extract wealth for European powers—beginning with gold and silver bullion and slaves. As suggested previously, a pattern was soon established whereby land, people, and resources were used to benefit nations outside the region and for the advantage of the local European or mostly European elite, rather than the native masses. As gold and silver stocks were eventually depleted, new crops and minerals were found to export to Europe and other industrializing areas such as the United States. Indigo, cacao, brazilwood, and sugar were exported in colonial times, as were rubber, nitrates, copper, and tin in the nineteenth century and coffee, grains, beef, bananas, and petroleum in the twentieth century.

As time passed, Western and Western-trained economists came to believe in the economic doctrine of *comparative advantage,* whereby a country that is especially well endowed by climate, resources, soil, or labor can produce a product comparatively better and more efficiently than any other. Coffee exports from Colombia are an example. By specializing in the production of that product and trading it in the international market for products that other countries could produce better and more cheaply because of their comparative advantage, the producing country can maximize revenues in world trade. That is, Colombia currently produces coffee cheaply and uses the money from the sales of the coffee to buy, for example, computers and stereos from Japan, where these products are produced best and most cheaply. This view holds that it would be expensive, inefficient, and all but impossible for Japan to produce coffee and difficult and costly for Colombia to produce stereos and computers. Both countries, it is argued, gain when they specialize in the production of one or a few products that they are best able to produce. After World War II, the Latin American experience with international trade and the pioneering work of the Economic Commission for Latin America (ECLA) challenged this view. But, before this view is explored, a more thorough explanation of the production and export of commodities will be offered.

After 1500, Latin America became tied to the Western economic system that had become the basis for the international economic system in two distinct ways: First, products were exported according to the demands of the market and development in Europe; and second, the region became an outlet for European products. Much like the old South in the United States, most of the local economy revolved around the production of one crop and most of the infrastructure was geared to getting that commodity to ports where it could be loaded on boats and shipped out. (See Table 10.) As cotton was

Table 10. Two Major Exports of Latin American Nations, 1985 and 1998 (More than two commodities given for 1998 when closely ranked)

		% of Total Exports	
Country	Commodity	1985	1998
Argentina	Wheat	13.5	—
	Corn	9.1	—
	Vegetable oils	—	7.4
	Passenger cars	—	6.3
Bolivia	Natural gas	59.8	—
	Tin	29.9	—
		(58 in 1958)	
	Zinc	—	11.9
	Aircraft	—	11.2
Brazil	Coffee	9.2	4.6
	Soybeans and products	9.9	—
	Iron ore	—	6.4
Chile	Copper and ore	46.1	35.0
	Wine and grapes	—	6.1
Colombia	Coffee	50.2	17.5
	Petroleum	—	19.1
Costa Rica	Coffee	32.2	—
	Bananas	22.1	12.2
	Office machine parts, transistors and flow regulators	—	18.8
Cuba	Sugar	74% (1987)	—
Dominican Republic	Sugar	25.9	—
	Ferronickel	16.4	—
	Coffee and cocoa	16.6	—
Ecuador	Crude petroleum	62.8	18.8
	Bananas	—	25.5
	Shrimp/shellfish	—	20.8
El Salvador	Coffee	66.9	25.6
	Sugar	—	5.1
	Medicines	—	4.3
Guatemala	Coffee	42.5	22.7
	Cotton	6.89	—
	Sugar	—	12.3
Haiti	Coffee	26.0	—
	Bauxite	8.6	—
Honduras	Bananas	31.1	12.9
	Coffee	22.7	44.3
Mexico	Petroleum	66.6	5.5
	Passenger vehicles	—	9.4
	Insulated wire	—	4.4
	Television receivers	—	4.2
Nicaragua	Cotton	34.1	—
	Coffee	30.4	29.8
	Shrimp/shellfish	—	13.1

(continued)

Table 10.　Two Major Exports of Latin American Nations, 1985 and 1998 (More than two commodities given for 1998 when closely ranked). *Continued*

Country	Commodity	% of Total Exports 1985	% of Total Exports 1998
Panama	Bananas	23.3	20.2
	Shrimp	17.8	23.3
Paraguay	Cotton	48.9	7.4
	Soybeans	33.2	43.4
	Beef	—	6.5
Peru	Petroleum (crude and products)	21.8	—
	Copper	15.6	11.0
	Zinc	9.1	—
	Gold	—	16.8
Uruguay	Wool	19.2	5.1
	Meat	13.8	14.0
	Rice	—	7.3
	Leather	—	6.4
Venezuela	Petroleum and products	84.3	70.6

Sources: James Wilkie, ed., *Statistical Abstract of Latin America*, vol. 27 (Los Angeles: UCLA Latin American Center, 1989); ECLAC/CEPAL, *Statistical Yearbook for Latin America and the Caribbean* (Santiago, Chile: United Nations, 1999).

king in the antebellum South, so sugar was king in northern Brazil, Cuba, the Dominican Republic, Haiti, and much of the rest of the Caribbean. Coffee and bananas became the prime export crop in Central America and Colombia. Economies also revolved around the extraction and export of minerals: copper in Chile, tin in Bolivia, and oil in Venezuela. Luxury goods for the landowning elite or for mineowners came from the advanced industrialized areas, as did the tools and most of the finished products that could not be made by the local blacksmith or carpenter. There are even tales of Brazilian planters sending their shirts to Europe for proper cleaning and pressing. During colonial times, manufacturing was often outlawed (in 1785 all manufacturing was prohibited in Brazil) and was usually discouraged. Thus, most all of the finished products came from outside. Indeed, such practice was consistent with the free trade concepts of specialization and comparative advantage. There was very little industry in Latin America until well into the twentieth century—after World War II in most countries— and very little interregional trade existed within countries or among them, given the external orientation of the infrastructure.

A new group of merchants sprung up as part of these trade patterns. The *comprador class* made their living from selling finished goods that were imported from the outside. From importer to wholesaler to distributor to merchant, each made a considerable markup on each product sold. This tendency toward high markup was also passed on to the local merchants and was even greater among those who transported the products to remote areas where choice was very limited. The idea of mass retailing to reduce unit cost came slowly and late to Latin America. The state also charged high import taxes on imported goods, particularly if they were classified as luxuries. Monopoly was not uncommon, and personal and political ties helped secure import licenses, exclusive rights, and favorable terms. The little manufacturing that existed was usually protected by power and privilege and was not forced to compete directly with foreign products. The quality of products was often well below similar products on the world market.

Agrarian Production

Until the second half of the twentieth century, most of Latin America was agrarian. Traditional landed estates (*latifundios, haciendas, fazendas*) produced crops such as cotton, cattle, sugar, or coffee. Their feudal-like origins in the Iberian peninsula often meant very traditional forms of production as well as social relations. Workers were subordinated to the *patrón* (landlord) and his family, paid poorly, generally treated miserably, and often held in debt peonage through the monopolistic sale of necessary goods at high prices at the estate store. Armed guards and control over the roads into and out of the estate were—and sometimes still are—used to further control the labor force. The original landed estates were not overly efficient, relying principally on abundant land and inexpensive labor. The earnings from the sale of cash crops were generally used more to support the upper-class lifestyle of the family than for capital improvements on the estate. The owners often spent a considerable amount of their time in their city home in the regional or national capital or in Europe and thus were absentee landowners. The more abundant small farmers, or *minifundistas*, had very little land and thus had to use very labor-intensive forms of cultivation. Nor did they have capital or credit to invest in their land. The abundance of land (often left fallow or otherwise unused) in the hands of the landed elite and the paucity of land for the *campesinos* (farmers or tenant farmers) and rural landless laborers have perpetuated the disparity of income derived from the original distribution of land and power. Of equal importance, these inequities fueled demands for land reform and economic restructuring, and occasionally for revolution. In more recent times small farmers had to increasingly turn to paid labor outside their own land (usually for large landowners or commercial farms or plantations) to survive. Pressured by debt and intense poverty, they often sell what little land they have, become rural laborers, or move to urban areas.

As the national economies developed, regions and often whole nations became what is referred to as *monoculture* or *monocrop economies*—dedicated to the production of one crop or commodity. (See Table 10.) As late as 1985, more that 50 percent of Colombia's official export earnings were derived from the sale of coffee on the international market. In El Salvador the focus on coffee was even greater—67 percent. Mexico also derived some 67

Traditional, labor-intensive agricultural methods are still used in most of Latin America, as suggested by this toiling farm worker in Rancho Ancihuácuaro, Michoacán,
Mexico, 1987. *(Photo by Devra Weber)*

percent of its export earnings from the sale of one commodity—petroleum.
In Venezuela that figure is more than 84 percent for the same product. Chile
derived 46 percent of its export earnings from the sale of copper. Reliance
on one export commodity was even higher in previous decades. For instance,
in 1958 the Bolivian economy centered around the production of tin; 58 percent of its export earnings derived from the sale of that commodity. Since
the latter part of the nineteenth century, coffee and bananas have been big
in Central America. By the middle of the twentieth century in Honduras,
more than 50 percent of export earnings were derived from bananas (31 percent) and coffee (23 percent). Nor do radical political transformations necessarily change the basic production of a nation. In the last 100 years Cuba
has changed from a Spanish colony to a capitalist country closely linked to
the U.S. economy and dependent on it to a socialist state closely tied to the

economies of the U.S.S.R. and its Eastern European allies to a socialist state going it alone. Only in the 1990s did Cuba's dependence on sugar change dramatically. In the 1920s roughly 75 percent of Cuba's exports were in sugar production. That number had grown to 83 percent in 1958 on the eve of the revolution. Thirty years of a revolutionary government that sought to diversify the countries' economy saw a decline to only 79 percent as Cuba assumed the role of sugar producer to the East European socialist countries at above–world market prices. Only in the 1990s with the collapse of the Soviet Union has Cuba's dependence on sugar decreased dramatically. By 1997 sugar fell to just 47 percent of Cuba's export earnings. The dramatic drop was brought about by sharply reduced sugar production and prices and the dramatic increase in the role of tourism in the Cuban economy. However, the impact of centuries of monocrop dependence on sugar production places great burdens on the Cuban government as it is forced to close sugar production facilities and retrain workers for other occupations.

Foreign Investment and Enclave Production

Mining and sugar and banana plantations have often been dominated by foreign investment, as they are much more capital intensive and strongly employ U.S. and Canadian concepts of business efficiency. Initially, these foreign corporations created types of *enclaves*, where the company, upper-level management, and even middle-level management were all foreign and often lived in a special compound fenced off from local inhabitants. Tools, explosives, fertilizers, and other elements in the productive process were all shipped into the country and taken directly to the mine or plantation. Products were shipped directly out of the country—often on foreign-owned railroads—and profits were sent back to corporate headquarters in New York, Boston, or London. More local people and products were eventually incorporated into local production, but ownership, upper-level management, and the end source for profit remission (the countries where the profits ended up) remained foreign. An example would be a company known to much of North America—Chiquita Banana. United Brands (formerly United Fruit Company) started as a Boston-based company founded by a New England sea captain in the 1880s. It grew to become a huge producer and exporter of bananas and one of the largest multinational corporations (MNCs) operating in Central America. It conducted operations in Guatemala, Honduras, Nicaragua, Costa Rica, and Panama and also came to exercise considerable power over local governments—particularly in Honduras and Guatemala. Union movements sometimes challenged United's treatment of the workers, and bitter strikes and repression often ensued, as was the case in Guatemala and Costa Rica in the 1930s. The CIA-organized coup against the constitutional government in Guatemala in 1954 was directly related to United Fruit's pressure on the U.S. government to stop the expropriation of its unused land by the reformist Arbenz government.

Dependency and Underdevelopment

The problems with monocrop or near monocrop are twofold. By making the entire economy dependent on one primary product, the nation's economic health becomes heavily tied to the fortunes of that product in the international market. Boom periods are often followed by devastating busts. Coffee trees planted during a time of high coffee prices often mature a few years later when the coffee price is depressed. When their beans are sold on the international market, the excess supply only depresses coffee prices further. A dip of a few cents in the international price for coffee, or sugar or copper, can mean a recession or worse in the national economy. For instance, copper prices fell to 5 cents a pound during the Depression and rose steadily in the 1940s, only to fall 4 cents a pound in 1950. When this occurs, the resultant worsening economic conditions often stimulate unrest and have contributed to the downfall of many presidents and other political leaders in Latin America.

Attempts to organize producers into international cartels or producers' associations have generally had only the most minimal effect on the stabilization or maintenance of commodity prices. Attempts have been made to organize international associations of coffee producers to maintain the price of coffee. In the early 1960s, an International Coffee Agreement was signed and later, the International Coffee Organization was established. Production quotas were assigned to all producing members in an effort to control the supply of coffee and thus the price. However, in part because of the resistance of African nations, who preferred to set their own production quotas, these efforts failed and coffee continues to be subject to market fluctuations. OPEC, of which Venezuela was a founding member, was for many years the only producers' association that was able to influence the price of their product. Yet by the late 1990s petroleum prices had fallen significantly. These falling prices helped put considerable strain on the long-dominant Democratic Action and COPEI parties in Venezuela. As Venezuelan petroleum prices fell to a low of less than $10 per barrel at the end of 1998 (from a high of $35 a barrel in the early 1980s), the presidential election campaigns of candidates from these parties wilted in the face of the newly organized Patriotic Pole coalition formed to back Hugo Chávez. Both parties even abandoned their candidates in the last two weeks of the electoral campaign to back the candidate of the newly formed Project Venezuela movement. But the opposition candidate and political outsider could not be stopped. Former coup leader Chávez won with 57 percent of the vote. Fortunately for his administration, prices for oil again rose to $30 a barrel by the second half of 2000, a result of the new OPEC agreement. However, it is not yet clear how long the OPEC agreement can sustain higher prices.

Many national leaders and thinkers have wondered why Latin America has remained less developed than their neighbor to the North, the United States. Most Latin American nations have abundant resources and sufficient land. Gradually, national leaders and scholars have learned the same bitter

THE CROP THAT COULD

Since Latin America was brought into the international system as a producer of primary products, the region has sought a product that could demand a good price on the world market and that its farmers could produce using traditional production methods without making huge investments. In this way small and large farmers could easily grow the crop and earn a good living from its sale. They needed a crop that would hold its value in the markets in the North and could be turned into a finished product in the South with minimal investments in equipment and technology. To date, the only major crop to fill that bill has been coca. And unlike any other commodity, cocaine's manufacture, transport, and distribution in the North is controlled by Latin American based business organizations (cartels) that bring most of the profits back to their home countries. Further, the coca leaves from which cocaine is made have been part of traditional indigenous culture for more than a thousand years and are thought to have special spiritual and medicinal qualities by large parts of the populations of Peru, Bolivia, and Ecuador. In these Andean nations chewing the coca leaf is legal and common among indigenous peoples in the highlands. The leaves are also used to make tea or are moistened and applied directly to heal sore or swollen eyes. Thus it is difficult for the local population to conceive of many of the pernicious effects of the highly refined extract of the coca leaves—cocaine.

It is estimated by the U.S. Drug Enforcement Agency (DEA) that drug trafficking in the U.S. is more than a 200-billion-dollar business each year. A great deal of this figure results from the sale of powdered or crack cocaine. South America exports some 600 metric tons of cocaine each year. As with other products from the region, the primary markets are the United States, Canada, and Western Europe. Using a minimal U.S. street value price of $14,500 per kilo, this would mean that sales of South American cocaine earn $8.7 billion a year. A great deal of this goes back to Latin America. For instance, it is estimated that Colombia alone exports 555 metric tons of cocaine each year (165 metric tons made from 101,000 metric tons of Colombian coca leaves, 390 metric tons made from Peruvian and Bolivian leaves). Using the street value price, this would mean that cocaine exports for Colombia account for some $8.05 billion per year. If only half of that amount stayed in the country, that would be more than four billion dollars. The official figure for all goods and services exported from Colombia was 15.765 billion dollars in 1998 (drug sales are not reported and thus not part of official figures). About half of this resulted from the sale of coffee. Using these figures, one could deduce that the revenue for the export sale of cocaine could be as much as half that for the sale of Colombian coffee.

Unlike the production of most other Latin American products, all who work in production are relatively well paid, from the peasant who grows the leaves to the pilot who flies it into the United States. It is only as the finished product begins to be consumed in the producing countries that the full extent of the hazard becomes known. Nor do many in the producing countries see the negative effect on tourism and investment or the damage done to legitimate businesses that are crowded out of the market by enterprises that sell on a very low or negative profit margin to launder huge amounts of money.

Efforts by the U.S. government to eradicate Latin America's most lucrative export commodity have been less than successful for the above reasons, and also because many local and national police officers usually make less than 200 dollars per month and are hard put to make ends meet. One way to increase income has been to accept payments for not reporting traffic or other violations, or for simply looking the other way. Commanders and military officers make relatively modest salaries, as do most judges. Governmental officials and politicians seem particularly susceptible to bribes and campaign donations. Even former Colombian President Samper was accused of taking a large campaign donation from a drug cartel. The corruption has also spread into transshipment points in Central America, the Caribbean and especially into Mexico. In that country, drug induced corruption has spread widely. Many police officers, and upper level officials, military officers, and governmental officials have been indicted for accepting bribes. In 1988, Mexico's drug czar was removed from office and indicted for being on a Mexican cartel's payroll. Throughout these countries the amounts of money available to bribe or otherwise induce local and national officials to ignore certain activities, or give intelligence on impending government actions is many times more than most officials make in a year, if not a lifetime. The temptation is too great for many. And for those who will not be bought there are always other ways.

lessons that U.S., Canadian, and many European farmers have found to be all too true—if unprotected by government price controls, prices for primary products fluctuate greatly and rise very slowly. Like the farmers, Latin Americans have produced more and more at ever greater efficiency, but have received comparatively less and less for it—while paying increasing prices for cars, machinery, and other finished goods from industrial, more developed national and international centers.

Raúl Prebisch and the ECLA

Such an economic understanding by the Latin Americans was stimulated greatly by the pioneering work of ECLA and its director, Raúl Prebisch. Prebisch, an Argentine-born and -educated economist, had previously held high-level economic positions in the Argentine government. In the late 1940s, he gathered a team of Latin American economists at the Santiago, Chile, headquarters of ECLA. He and his fellow economists made extensive stud-

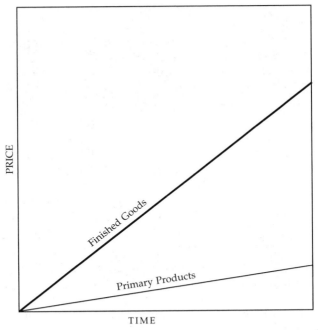

TIME

Figure 7-1.

ies of the prices for primary products exported by Latin America and compared them to those of the finished goods that were imported. Their studies indicated that the relationship between these product prices, or the terms of trade, were unfavorable to Latin America. Posited as the now-famous *Prebisch thesis,* the theory argued that there is a structural tendency for Latin American terms of trade to deteriorate over time because of the concentration of exports in primary commodities. As suggested by Figure 7-1, over time the price for finished goods rises much faster than the price for primary goods.

These findings, which were initially considered controversial by Western economists from industrialized nations, called into question the argument for specialization in the production of any one primary product in the international market. Interestingly, later studies by the Economic Commission for Africa of the United Nations Economic and Social Council found that the terms of trade for African primary exports vis-à-vis finished imports from Europe and the United States were also unfavorable to Africa. ECLA's findings were one of the principal reasons that the organization so strongly advocated import substitution industrialization (ISI) for Latin America.

Dependency Theory

ECLA's work and the Prebisch thesis were fascinating examples of how Latin American economists working from a perspective grounded in their own reality could see how their relationship with the industrialized center (Europe and United States) was less than satisfactory. This gave great impetus not only to new economic policy direction in the Latin American nations but also to the development of a whole new way to view Latin American development—*dependency theory*. The ECLA studies were symbolic of the post–World War II decolonization process and the subsequent willingness to assign negative consequences to the relations imposed by actual or formal colonial masters on the development of native peoples. This also represented a significant break with metropolitan theorists and economists who saw underdevelopment as inherent to Latin America and other Third World nations and caused primarily by economic, social, or cultural patterns that had developed within those societies.

The late 1940s also provided alternative explanations for the lack of development in Latin America, Africa, and Asia. Basing their understanding in large part on V. I. Lenin's classic Marxist work, *Imperialism, the Highest Stage of Capitalism* (1916), scholars familiar with this form of Marxist analysis argued that the colonies were used as places to invest surplus capital and sell goods from the colonizing countries and as sources of cheap raw materials and cheap labor. Indeed, according to this view the high return on investment and low prices paid for raw materials and labor meant that value was extracted from the colonized countries and exported to the developed countries, where it further fueled their development. It was further argued that such surplus value was the difference between what was paid and what it would have cost if fair value had been paid at the industrial center. As with the initial taking of gold bullion in the colonial era, this extracted wealth helped continue the impoverishment of the colonized country and made the colonial country rich.

This thesis was updated by African leader and intellectual Kwame Nkrumah. The first president of Ghana and intellectual author of Pan-Africanism argued that imperialism had taken on a new but equally pernicious form—neocolonialism. In his work *Neocolonialism, the Last Stage of Imperialism* (1965), Nkrumah argued that former colonizers now controlled their former colonies and other former colonies by less direct means. They established economic spheres of influence, pound or franc areas where the former colonial currency and its financial sector dominated; dominated the area by investment and a foreign economic presence; and bought the same raw materials at the same prices and sold the same finished goods. Further, the former colonizers were aided in this endeavor by native politicians and pro-Western elements of the native bourgeoisie, who often did the bidding of the former colonial masters and generally helped maintain their neocolonial dominance in the face of any radical reformers or revolutionaries who attempted to change the subordinate nature of this relationship. Latin

American intellectual Eduardo Galeano labeled this group "the Commission bourgeoisie." Foreign aid and missionaries were but more subtle means of continuing neocolonial control. Political and economic control was exercised in a more indirect way than under direct colonialism, but the effect was very similar for the native people. The title of a book by Guyanese intellectual Walter Rodney is most evocative of this view—*How Europe Underdeveloped Africa*. Such views clearly helped shape the intellectual climate in the Americas.

Other advocates of dependency theory argued that Latin America was maintained in a neocolonial state under the tutelage of the United States and European powers. Given that the Latin American nations had been independent much longer than the African states, the mechanisms of control were different and often more subtle. Thus one finds more discussion of cultural imperialism in Latin America. It is often asserted that economic relations, foreign aid and diplomacy, and the media and other forms of control were employed to keep Latin America subordinate. Neocolonialism was thus manifest throughout Latin American society, as could be seen in U.S. movies, television series, religious evangelization, the spread of Western consumption patterns, the canonization of Mickey Mouse and Donald Duck, and the mass pilgrimage to Miami and Florida's Disney World by Latin America's elites.

Andre Gunder Frank's *Capitalism and Underdevelopment in Latin America* brought dependency theory to the fore. As suggested earlier, Frank and other dependency theorists argued that the relationship between the developing area (satellite or periphery) and the developed area (center or metropol) was one of dependency. Thus, the *dependentistas* argued that underdevelopment in Latin America resulted from the region being brought into the capitalist system to satisfy the economic needs of the metropolitan powers. Decisions as to when and where to develop mines, plantations, or infrastructure were made according to the requirements of the metropolitan powers, not the Latin American nations. From colonial times on, economic decisions responded more to the needs of the industrializing center than to the needs of the agrarian periphery. Over time, the national economic systems in Latin America thus became dependent on the production and export of primary products to Europe and the United States (the industrialized center or metropol). The economic and political elites that emerged also became tied to this system and dependent on it for their well-being. Although they did not accumulate as much wealth per product unit as did their counterparts in the metropolitan nations, they were able to exploit the native labor force and take advantage of the abundant access to cheap land and minerals to accumulate their wealth. As more foreign corporations arrived to exploit these factors of production themselves, the national upper class often worked with or for them and became even more closely tied to the economic interests of the center.

It is argued, then, that the economic development and even the political autonomy of Latin American nations became *dependent* on the outside forces of the metropolitan powers. They did not possess full independence and thus were dependent on and subordinate to outside forces. Latin American underdevelopment was thus a result of the exploitation and control of forces outside the region. As Latin America had been incorporated into the international capitalist system, it had lost its wealth and autonomy. The plundering of the gold and silver of the region was symbolic of how the capitalist system had served the interests of the Latin American nations. Indeed, capitalism and economic penetration by the metropolitan capitalist powers were responsible for a great deal of Latin American underdevelopment. Frank and others argued that even the feudalistic *latifundios* had been incorporated into the international system and were part of the worldwide spread of capitalism. Latin America's problems thus resulted from the nature of capitalism itself and the way it subordinated classes in nations and even developing nations themselves. Some further expanded this concept to argue that the capital cities in the region acted as metropolitan areas that extracted value from the peripheral countryside.

The dependency perspective also contradicted what had become a common view about Latin American economies. The *dual economy* view held that the economies were divided into two sectors. One was comprised of near-feudal social and economic relations on the *latifundio* and in landowner-sharecropper relations and subsistence agriculture; the other was centered in the modern export sector that tended to employ modern capitalist practices. Each national economy was divided in two—one traditional and feudal-like, and the other modern and capitalist. The *dependistas* saw only one economy well integrated into the world capitalist system. Frank and the early dependency writers thus focused on external linkages and the international capitalist system in particular to explain Latin underdevelopment.

There were, however, later dependency writers who enriched this perspective by also looking more closely at the specific historical, social, and economic configurations of nations such as Brazil and Argentina. They examined such internal factors as class and intraclass competition to further explain the complex phenomenon of development in the region. Foremost among these was Brazilian social scientist Fernando Henrique Cardoso, who, together with Chilean sociologist Enzo Faletto, wrote *Dependency and Development in Latin America* in 1971. The more subtle analysis of internal class formations and historic development patterns and the role of multinational corporations made this one of the most useful analyses of the Latin American reality.

Import Substitution Industrialization

As these new perspectives stimulated a rethinking of how development should be pursued, policies began to change more rapidly. ECLA recommended ISI as a way to reduce the importation of finished goods. From the 1930s on several of the larger nations had begun to focus on what became known as *inward-looking development*, reasoning that the path to development was through developing internal economic capacity—including industrial capacity—while continuing to export primary products. ECLA now recommended strongly that internal industrialization be pursued. This would mean that less of the foreign exchange earned through the sale of primary products would be expended on finished goods and more capital would stay in the country. In this way the negative effects of the terms of trade would be minimized. Latin American domestic manufacturing was officially and continually encouraged. A growing number of new industries began to produce for the domestic market. Sporadic industrialization had occurred in some of the large countries, such as Mexico, Argentina, and Brazil—particularly in the times of World Wars I and II and even the Depression, when Latin America was cut off from its external supplies of finished goods. This time, however, ISI became official policy and was pursued vigorously through increasing domestic manufacturing. Domestic entrepreneurs were encouraged to set up new industries and expand old ones, and MNCs were invited to set up plants to supply the domestic market. Even car companies set up assembly plants, as was with the case with Volkswagen in Mexico and Brazil and Fiat in Argentina. Chrysler also began assembling cars in Latin America and was joined by Toyota in the 1970s. Panasonic, Motorola, and other electronics companies began to manufacture in Latin America as did most of the major pharmaceutical companies and even food processors like Nabisco and Nèstlé.

Attempts were made to control the national content of the components used in the finished product, the percent of nationals in middle- and upper-level management, and the amount of profit that could be remitted to the home office of the MNC each year. These attempts to assert national sovereignty met with varying success and were often skillfully circumvented by sophisticated multinationals. From the late 1940s on, Mexico required that 51 percent of all companies doing business in Mexico be owned by Mexican nationals or Mexican corporations (the dropping of this provision after NAFTA caused some controversy in Mexico). There was some nationalization of foreign corporations by Latin American governments (Bolivian tin mines after 1954, foreign assets in Cuba after 1960, copper mines in Chile in the 1960s and 1970s, and the International Petroleum Company in Peru in 1968), but the general trend was for more and more foreign investment to flock to the region. This wave of investment was particularly strong after military coups in Brazil in 1964 and Chile in 1973. Manufacturing and multinationals became part of the economic panorama in Latin America. Smaller and relatively less developed nations such as Guatemala, El Salvador, Costa Rica, and even Honduras experienced increases in manufacturing and the arrival of multinationals that produced finished products. The formation of the Central American Common Market in 1959 attracted new manufacturing plants, as was the case with Firestone in Costa Rica and Van Heusen Shirts in Honduras. The trend was also encouraged by U.S. government policies beginning with the Alliance for Progress programs after 1961.

Export Orientation

Industrial production was initially destined for internal national markets or those of neighboring nations who had entered into an agreement such as the Central American Common Market, the Latin American Free Trade Association (1960), or the Andean Pact (1967). This was a great stimulus for the industrialization of Latin America; for example, Mexico and Brazil further developed their own steel and automobile industries. The nature of production also changed. Domestic manufactured products became more similar to those manufactured for Western consumer taste. Gradually, as the domestic demand for manufactures faltered, Latin American nations began to take on an externally oriented perspective. Hereafter, manufacturing and crop diversification would be done with an eye toward external sales as well as the domestic market.

The influx of international capital, more sophisticated technology, and the opening up of internal markets made for more and better manufactured goods. The entrance of the MNCs drove some local producers out of business, and others were forced to upgrade the quality of their products. Of those local producers who survived, many soon realized that they too could enter the global market with their more sophisticated products. Nor were the products limited to those produced by sophisticated MNCs and high-technology national producers. Other domestic industries also grew—weaving and handcraft in Guatemala, wine in Chile, shoes in Brazil. Indeed, the Brazilian shoe industry eventually became one of the largest producers of footwear on the world market. As another way of gaining more foreign exchange, many countries encouraged the production of *nontraditional exports*, not only producing more finished goods that could be exported but also diversifing production of primary products. Such was the case in Colombia, where a vigorous export industry in flowers developed. As this process occurred over the 1960s, 1970s, and 1980s, Latin America became more integrated into the international economic system, primarily through ties to industrialized capitalist nations—the United States, Western Europe, and later Japan.

The transformation of Latin American economies could be seen in the following:

- More extensive use of capital-intensive technology.
- Increased training in manufacturing-related engineering and for those who employed and replicated technology in capital-intensive techniques used in advanced industrial nations. Many engineering students were sent to the United States or Europe and brought back advanced capital-intensive technology with them.
- Lack of development of appropriate technology that could take advantage of Latin America's abundant and inexpensive labor supply.
- The spread of Western-style consumerism to the upper, middle, and lower classes.

- State intervention to encourage and protect export-oriented domestic industries and sometimes to nationalize them or, as in the case of Brazil, to set up key industries such as aircraft production.
- The growth of middle sectors who worked in management and technologically sophisticated aspects of production (e.g., engineers, skilled technicians, accountants).
- The growth of an industrial proletariat.

Increasing Foreign Debt and the Debt Crisis

Newer plants created in Latin America were often copies or near copies of standard plants from a particular MNC—although often using the less advanced technology and relatively outdated standards that operated in the developed world, where capital was plentiful and labor was expensive. The employment created for such plants was modest, but the investment in new machinery and patented processes was not. This type of production used up local sources of capital quickly. Thus even as there were more goods to export, it became necessary to borrow money from abroad to satisfy these capital needs. The growing demand for Western consumer goods also meant that more and more products were being imported to keep consumers satisfied. This also used up scarce foreign exchange. These two processes and the acquisition of expensive military hardware by countries like Peru, Chile, Brazil, and Argentina meant that more external borrowing was necessary to compensate for the net outflows of funds. This caused what came to be called *debt-led growth*. The result of this outward-directed orientation and debt-led growth was that the external indebtedness of Latin American nations began to grow. Brazil is a prime example of this.

Prior to 1970 most of the Latin American external debt was owed to individual states or to multilateral lending institutions such as the Inter-American Development Bank. Interest rates were minimal. The petroleum crisis of 1973–1974 changed this. First, it meant that those Latin American nations that were net importers of petroleum were forced to use more of their foreign exchange to pay for the hydrocarbons they imported. Second, it meant that petroleum-producing countries began to amass significant foreign exchange surpluses and needed to find places to invest these funds. Most of these petrodollars ended up in Western banks, which soon had more than ample funds for lending but, because of the stagnation in developed countries, could not find borrowers in those countries. Large banks like Chase Manhattan and Bank of America began to make large loans readily available to private and public borrowers in Latin America. These factors combined to radically increase the external debt in Latin America, which jumped from less than $30 billion in 1970 to more than $230 billion in 1980. By the beginning of the 1980s, debt service payments alone were some $18 billion per year. Drops in commodity prices and world recessions in the 1980s did not improve this picture. Economic growth slowed in most countries and shrank in a few. Indeed, the 1980s were referred to as the *lost decade* because

Table 11.　Total Disbursed External Debt, 1997

Country	Amount (Millions of Dollars)
Argentina	109,359
Bolivia*	4232
Brazil	192,892
Chile	26,775
Colombia	31,345
Costa Rica	3305
Cuba	—
Dominican Republic*	3502
Ecuador	15,099
El Salvador*	2667
Guatemala*	2131
Haiti*	1025
Honduras	4095
Mexico*	149,700
Nicaragua*	6001
Panama*	5051
Paraguay	1438
Peru	28,278
Uruguay*	5618
Venezuela*	32,984

*Public external debt only.

Source: ECLAC/CEPAL, *1998 Statistical Yearbook for Latin America and the Caribbean* (Santiago, Chile: United Nations, 1999).

growth rates were so abysmal in most of Latin America, for many countries only 1 or 2 percent per year. A few countries even experienced negative growth rates.

Mexico and Brazil had both experienced high levels of economic growth in the 1960s and 1970s; each had periods of economic growth during this time that were referred to as economic miracles. Both, however, continued to borrow from abroad. Their indebtedness grew, and both Mexico and Brazil acquired external debts in excess of $110 billion. (See Table 11.) By 1982 Mexico declared that it could not meet all the loan payments that were due. This caused considerable concern in the international investment community. Large banks in the United States were particularly concerned and sought relief from the Reagan administration. After some discussion, the U.S. government tendered an emergency loan package to Mexico to stop it from defaulting. Other countries came close to defaulting as well; Peru, under the Alan García presidency, even declared a moratorium on repaying its external debt. The prospect of widespread default created near panic among many large banks in the United States and Europe, since many of them had made very high percentages of their loans (mostly unsecured) to Latin American public and private institutions. Since a large portion of their capital had been loaned out and could not be called back, they were, in bankers' language, "overexposed." There was also talk of the Latin American nations joining together and negotiating terms of debt repayment or even refusing to pay altogether. Despite official encouragement from Cuba and Fidel Castro, this movement never materialized. Instead, Western nations and international financial institutions such as the IMF and the World Bank were instrumental in renegotiating more favorable repayment packages, reducing interest rates, and even formulating debt-for-nature agreements, where debt is forgiven if environmental protection is guaranteed for parts of the national territory.

As the Latin American nations became even more dependent on external sources to solve their financial problems, the role of international financial institutions such as the IMF, the World Bank, and the Inter-American Development Bank became ever stronger. This was also true for the role of the Agency for International Development (AID) of the U.S. Department of State. In addition to the growing importance of AID, the United States and its Western capitalist allies were able to exercise a tremendous amount of control over decision making in these international bodies. Further, pursuant to the victory of the conservative economic policy embodied in Thatcherism in the United Kingdom and the Reagan revolution in the United States, the policies advocated by AID and the international financial institutions became ever more conservative. Indeed, the free market free trade ideas of Milton Friedman and the Chicago School soon began to appear as policy recommendations.

Structural Adjustment and the Move to Neoliberalism

As conditions for continued borrowing, international financial institutions began to first suggest and then insist on economic *structural adjustments* to the national economies. Indeed, more and more of the loans were conditional on such adjustments. It was argued that the Latin American nations must take the bitter pill of austerity through these structural adjustments. Government costs and inflation had to be reduced through such measures as fiscal reform, monetary restraint, cutting back jobs and services in the public sector, and stopping government subsidies for basic goods or petroleum. Likewise, wages were to be held down as a way of checking inflation and keeping wage costs at bay in the ever more important export industries. Orthodox economic thought became more widely accepted, and the ISI advocated by ECLA fell from favor.

As Eastern European socialism weakened and then began to disappear in the late 1980s and as the Soviet Union's break-up moved the world from the Cold War and a strong bipolar system to one dominated by Western capitalism and the United States, economic policy recommendations became ever more dominated by the orthodox capitalist economic thinking advocated by the conservative governments in power in the United States and United

---

KEY COMPONENTS OF NEOLIBERALISM AND THE WASHINGTON CONSENSUS

1. Radically reducing government size and spending by cutting back on government jobs and programs—especially social programs.
2. Fiscal and monetary reform.
3. Minimizing government regulation in economic matters (deregulation).
4. Liberalizing commerce through the reduction and eventual elimination of all tariff barriers and trade restrictions.
5. Opening up the national economy to foreign investment and allowing the free flow of capital.
6. Privatization of government-owned corporations, industries, agencies, and utilities.
7. Eliminating government subsidies for essential consumer goods, such as bread or tortillas and petroleum products.

Kingdom. Keynesian economics and its advocacy of state intervention in the market economy and deficit spending to stimulate business activity was no longer in favor. Rather, the free market and free trade ideas championed by economists like Milton Friedman became popular. Indeed the conservative economic thought of opponents of state intervention and planning, such as Friederich A. von Hayek, became influential. By the early 1990s such thought was dominant in the IMF, the World Bank, the Inter-American Development Bank, and AID. Since the headquarters of all of these organizations are located in Washington, DC, this thinking became referred to as the *Washington Consensus*.

In Latin America this type of economic policy was characterized as *neoliberalism* because it seemed to be a new version of the classical eighteenth-century economic liberalism of Adam Smith and other earlier economic liberals. Classical economic liberals believe that the magic hand of the market, not government control or trade barriers, should regulate the economy. Indeed, political liberalism in nineteenth century Latin America included a belief in increasing commerce through free trade.

Globalization

Other factors were at work as well. The success that a variety of MNCs, such as Nike, had with moving all or part of their production to plants they established in Asia became widely known. More and more assembly plants, or *maquiladoras,* were established first just across the U.S. border in northern Mexico, then spread throughout the Caribbean Basin and into some South American countries, such as Ecuador. Electronic components, the unsewn pieces of cloth that make up clothing, and other unassembled parts in other industries were manufactured in the United States, Japan, Western Europe, and even Taiwan and assembled in Latin America. Regular manufacturing for export production was also encouraged, and multinationals came to Latin America in increasing numbers to take advantage of low wages, lax labor and environmental protection, minimal regulation and taxation, and generally sympathetic governments. Free trade zones were also set up, where companies could be completely free of any governmental regulation. The process of globalization, it was argued, would be beneficial for all; thus all were expected to expedite its implementation.

As the world became increasingly subject to economic globalization, capital and production plants became ever more fluid, moving freely from one country to another according to who offered the most favorable terms. The new wisdom was for each nation to produce everything it could as efficiently as possible and to export as much of it as possible to maximize export earnings. This allowed the nation to keep up with external debt payments, pay for an expanding number and amount of imports, and hopefully have some foreign exchange earnings left over to add to foreign exchange reserves. The national borders were to be open to imports so that national consumers could get the lowest prices on the goods they consumed. If some national industries could not compete with the increased number and variety of imported goods, they should be closed and capital and labor shifted to those industries that could compete and also export their goods.

Privatization

The new mantra was globalize, globalize, globalize, and in Latin America it was combined with the specifically neoliberal mantra of privatize, privatize, privatize. As suggested earlier, mines had been nationalized in Bolivia and Chile, and considerable state-owned industry existed in Brazil and elsewhere. Most of the states owned all or part of the national telephone and telecommunication companies, and many had autonomous state-owned agencies, such as the Peruvian national fishing company PescaPeru. In Mexico all aspects of petroleum production had been nationalized since 1936; the resulting state-owned enterprise, PeMex, is one of the largest national companies. It was also thought that it might be possible to privatize some governmental infrastructure, such as new highways. Thus much new superhighway construction in countries like Brazil and Mexico was financed by private capital and/or was run by private companies through their direct administration of the roadways and collection of tolls.

The movement toward privatization was especially strong in Latin America because state-owned entities had generally been little more efficient than the government bureaucracies themselves. Often, they had been subject to cronyism, bloated employment practices to accommodate payback for political or personal support, and corruption. Thus one could easily wait up to two years for the installation of a phone line (unless phone company employees were "motivated" through monetary inducements) or could suffer frequent loss of electricity or water service.

As Latin American nations returned to international lending agencies (the IMF in particular) for additional short- and long-term loans, they found that the imposed conditions (*conditionality*) included the privatization of major public enterprises, such as the telephone companies. They were to be sold or auctioned off and a substantial part of the proceeds were to be used to pay off part of the external debt. This led to increasing pressure on the political leaders to sell off these enterprises (usually to foreign corporations or consortia) to meet the conditions of the loans. However, utility rates were generally very low for consumers and thousands of jobs were at stake. Not surprisingly, there were substantial popular and political mobilizations, union strikes, and job actions to resist the sales. Nonetheless, many of these entities were partially or wholly sold off, frequently at bargain prices. The lucrative entities that made good profits attracted considerable investment interest and sold rapidly, whereas those that lost money and were government liabilities went begging for buyers. This in turn led to the perception on the part of some that decisions were once again being made because of foreign influence and for the benefit of foreign corporations, not the national populace. As will be discussed later, these and other factors lead to growing political discontent and new political mobilizations.

Regional Integration, NAFTA, and the Globalization Process

In 1826 Simón Bolívar convened the Congress of Panama to foster the uniting of Spanish America into one political-economic entity. He dreamed of a united Latin America to rival the growing power of the United States in North America, but his proposal failed. Others had visions of unity in Central America. From 1824 to 1840 the Central American states that were part of the Captaincy General of Guatemala in colonial times (Guatemala, El Salvador, Honduras, Nicaragua, and Costa Rica) were united in the Central American Federation. But the Central Americans could not remain united. Their shattered dreams of unity lay dormant until after the Europeans were able to begin a process of regional economic integration out of the ashes of World War II. The beginnings of a united Europe and the creation of the European Common Market in 1957 proved to be a catalyst for Latin American efforts at economic integration.

Encouraged by the ECLA and the United States, the Central American Common Market was formed in 1960. Its common tariff walls were to encourage import substitution and internally-oriented economic growth within the region. Promoted more by Latin American initiative, the Latin American Free Trade Association was also founded in 1960, and the Andean Pact (1967) was forged with the same expectations. However, internal political pressure and vested national economic interests made it difficult to reduce tariffs among the respective member nations. None of these pacts had any appreciable success. The next stage in regional integration was not forged until the era of globalization.

In 1989 President George Bush launched the Enterprise for the Americas Initiative. This plan envisioned a common area of economic cooperation for the Americas extending from the frozen north in Canada to Tierra del Fuego in southern South America. All the Americas would move toward one gigantic economic zone that could easily rival a united Europe. Unlike the European Union, however, no attempt would be made to gradually integrate while ensuring that all member states had similar costs of production and approximately the same labor and political rights. Under this plan Canada and the United States would combine with their less powerful sister republics in the South on the assumption that free trade and increased commerce could cure all ills and benefit all member nations. The first concrete action in this process developed among the United States, Mexico, and Canada. NAFTA was signed in 1992 and went into effect on January 1, 1994, following ratification by the legislatures of the three governments. Building on a bilateral U.S.-Canada agreement initiated in 1989, NAFTA created one of the two largest trading blocs in the world, with a population of 370 million and a combined economic production of $6 trillion, a worthy rival to the European Union. NAFTA also removed most restrictions on cross-border investment and allowed the free flow of goods and services. All tariffs on goods traded among the three are to be eliminated by 2005. The agreement was vigorously pursued by the Salinas administration in Mexico in the hope that increased investment in Mexico and a greater North American market for its products would stimulate the Mexican economy and create jobs for the millions of unemployed and underemployed Mexicans. In contrast, the U.S. labor movement feared that thousands of jobs would head south, where wage rates were approximately one-tenth of what they were in the United States and labor rights and safety regulations were minimal. The movement convinced presidential candidate Bill Clinton to oppose the agreement in the 1992 election campaign. However, once in office President Clinton bowed to pressure from large U.S. corporations who wanted to set up more factories and retail stores in Mexico and investment firms and business interests that saw lucrative investment opportunities. Clinton led a difficult, but successful battle for ratification of the agreement that had been negotiated by President Bush. After the agreement went into effect many more U.S. firms moved their plants to Mexico to set up regular factories and *maquiladoras.* They took thousands of jobs with them, although new jobs were created in the United States to supply the now open Mexican market. There was, however, a net loss of U.S. jobs. Ford, General Motors, and Chrysler set up factories in Mexico to manufacture cars for Mexico, the United States, and Canada that were not only put together locally but also were made mostly from parts manufactured in Mexico, including the engines and transmissions.

In Mexico many small- and medium-sized industries and businesses were not able to compete with their larger U.S. or Canadian counterparts and went bankrupt. These and related events caused considerable political turmoil in all three countries. In Mexico, they led to charges that the Mexican elite was selling out the country to U.S. corporate interests, especially since most of the jobs created were at or around the minimum wage of less than U.S. $4 per day. Many in both Canada and the United States feared that their political leaders entered into an agreement that will be more a net exporter of jobs than a bonanza for the common people. As with the general process of globalization and the implementation of neoliberal reforms elsewhere, the benefits of growth have been distributed very unevenly. (See Table 12.) As labor, political groups, and mass organizations have mobilized against the negative effects of many of these changes in a variety of countries, including Venezuela, Ecuador, Costa Rica, Nicaragua, Argentina, and Brazil, political leaders have felt internal pressure against neoliberal changes while still being pressured by the international financial institutions and the United States to make them.

Buoyed by the successful implementation of NAFTA at the beginning of 1994, the Clinton administration promoted and hosted the Summit of the Americas in Miami in December 1994. Attended by thirty-four heads of state, with the conspicuous absence of Fidel Castro, it was the first such hemispheric gathering since 1967. The 1994 meeting represented an assurance from the United States to Latin America that it would not be neglected in the twenty-first century. The primary achievement of the meeting was to create a framework of negotiations for the creation of a hemisphere-wide customs union—the Free Trade Area of the Americas (FTAA) by 2005.

Clinton's statement that the gathering was "a watershed in the history of the continent" was overblown. As a first step, Chile was to be integrated quickly into NAFTA, then Clinton—with renewed "fast-track" negotiating authority from the U.S. Congress—would lay the groundwork for the FTAA. In the years since the Miami summit the prospects for hemispheric economic integration have dimmed. President Clinton failed to get renewed negotiating authority. As a result, Chile's entry into NAFTA was not secured and, while the framework for the creation of an FTAA remains in place, little progress has been made. It seems unlikely that this will change under the Bush administration.

Difficulties for the FTAA project and the expansion of NAFTA began at the end of 1994. At that time the Mexican peso had to be sharply devalued and was only rescued from disaster by a multibillion-dollar bailout from the IMF spearheaded by the United States. The bailout stabilized NAFTA, but it undercut political support within the U.S. Congress for making new trade agreements and potential commitments for further financial bailouts. As a result an anti-FTAA coalition developed in the U.S. Congress with support in both major parties; this coalition succeeded in both 1997 and 1998 in blocking attempts by FTAA supporters to grant renewed "fast-track" negotiating authority to the president. Without such authority foreign governments are unwilling to negotiate agreements with the United States for fear that they will be significantly altered by the U.S. Congress. Until a U.S. president regains this authority, progress toward the FTAA is unlikely. In 2001 President Bush recommitted to the FTAA project and began the process of lobbying Congress for the renewed "fast track" authority.

Table 12.   U.S. Income Inequality (1967–1998)

Household Shares of Aggregate Income
by Fifths of the Income Distribution: 1967–1998

Year	Fifths					Top 5 Percent
	Lowest	Second	Middle	Fourth	Highest	
1998	3.6	9.0	15.0	23.2	49.2	21.4
1997	3.6	8.9	15.0	23.2	49.4	21.7
1996	3.7	9.0	15.1	23.3	49.0	21.4
1995	3.7	9.1	15.2	23.3	48.7	21.0
1994	3.6	8.9	15.0	23.4	49.1	21.2
1993	3.6	9.0	15.1	23.5	48.9	21.0
1992	3.8	9.4	15.8	24.2	46.9	18.6
1991	3.8	9.6	15.9	24.2	46.5	18.1
1990	3.9	9.6	15.9	24.0	46.6	18.6
1989	3.8	9.5	15.8	24.0	46.8	18.9
1988	3.8	9.6	16.0	24.3	46.3	18.3
1987	3.8	9.6	16.1	24.3	46.2	18.2
1986	3.9	9.7	16.2	24.5	45.7	17.5
1985	4.0	9.7	16.3	24.6	45.3	17.0
1984	4.1	9.9	16.4	24.7	44.9	16.5
1983	4.1	10.0	16.5	24.7	44.7	16.4
1982	4.1	10.1	16.6	24.7	44.5	16.2
1981	4.2	10.2	16.8	25.0	43.8	15.6
1980	4.3	10.3	16.9	24.9	43.7	15.8
1979	4.2	10.3	16.9	24.7	44.0	16.4
1978	4.3	10.3	16.9	24.8	43.7	16.2
1977	4.4	10.3	17.0	24.8	43.6	16.1
1976	4.4	10.4	17.1	24.8	43.3	16.0
1975	4.4	10.5	17.1	24.8	43.2	15.9
1974	4.4	10.6	17.1	24.7	43.1	15.9
1973	4.2	10.5	17.1	24.6	43.6	16.6
1972	4.1	10.5	17.1	24.5	43.9	17.0
1971	4.1	10.6	17.3	24.5	43.5	16.7
1970	4.1	10.8	17.4	24.5	43.3	16.6
1969	4.1	10.9	17.5	24.5	43.0	16.6
1968	4.2	11.1	17.5	24.4	42.8	16.6
1967	4.0	10.8	17.3	24.2	43.8	17.5

Source: *U.S. Census Bureau Current Population Survey*, March 1968–1999.

Even if U.S. leadership for an agreement is renewed, it is no longer clear that Latin American presidents are as ready to follow as they were in 1994. Ultimately it can be said that the break in momentum for the FTAA occurred at least as much in Latin America as it did in the United States. By the middle of the 1990s political leaders fully committed to trade liberalization were in power throughout the region, but by the end of the decade those leaders were gone and their successors were not as committed to the earlier belief.

A very different response to the perceived need to integrate economically occurred in South America. Brazil, Argentina, Uruguay, and Paraguay formed Mercosur in 1994, hoping to create an increase in trade and commerce among themselves without becoming part of any trade association with the United States. Brazil in particular viewed its interests as quite different from those of the United States. It wished to maintain its balanced trade relations with both Europe and Asia and not become too closely tied to the U.S. economy. Mercosur has not fulfilled all of its promises, but it is clearly part of a regional process of economic integration that is taking hold in Latin America. In addition to Mercosur other significant integration efforts include the Andean Pact (Bolivia, Peru, Ecuador, Colombia, and Venezuela), the Group of Three (Columbia, Venezuela, and Mexico) and the Caribbean Community (CARICOM). This building block approach to regional unity is now favored by most Latin American leaders, but the approach is not shared by Washington and stalemate seems likely.

Economic Legacy

Structural adjustments, neoliberal reforms, and the globalization process generally did have considerable effect on the Latin American economies. In the 1990s they generally recovered from the lost decade of the 1980s and began to experience growth in the early and mid-1990s, although growth did begin to slow in many economies by decade's end. Another clear area of success was the reduction of inflation to single-digit figures in most of Latin America. This was particularly noteworthy in Brazil and Argentina, which had both experienced inflation in excess of 1000% per year in past decades. (See Table 13.) Real wage rates for the vast majority of workers did not, however, improve. Unemployment remained a severe problem in most countries, and growing numbers of workers were forced to go into the informal sector to survive. Indeed, the number of those selling all manner of fruits, vegetables, clothing, household products, and auto products on the streets and at traffic lights in larger cities all over Latin America increased exponentially. A new type of dual economy may be developing where the working class is forced to buy its necessities in the markets and on the streets, where quality and prices are lower, while the upper and upper middle class go to supermarkets, spe-

Table 13. Latin American Inflation by Decade (Average annual change in CPI)

	1900s	1910s	1920s	1930s	1940s	1950s	1960s	1970s	1980s	1990–95
Argentina	3	7	−3	0	36	31	21	142	787	43
Bolivia				17	69	6	20	203	12	
Brazil	−2	7	3	2	13	21	45	37	605	1270
Chile	8	6	2	7	18	38	27	175	20	19
Colombia	20	12	2	4	13	7	12	21	24	25
Costa Rica				10	2	2	11	27	19	
Cuba	2	4	−2	−1	10	1	NA	NA	NA	NA
Dominican Rep.					10	1	2	11	26	16
Ecuador			15	2	4	13	37	40		
El Salvador			10	3	1	11	19	13		
Guatemala			11	1	1	10	15	16		
Haiti				0	3	12	7	19		
Honduras			6	2	2	8	8	21		
Mexico	7	62	−2	2	11	8	3	17	69	12
Nicaragua			15	5	4	14	5121	749		
Panama			6	1	1	7	2	1		
Paraguay			25	33	3	13	22	17		
Peru		11	−2	1	15	8	9	32	1224	113
Uruguay		1	5	17	48	59	63	62		
Venezuela	3	7	−4	−3	8	2	1	9	25	45

Source: Thorp, Rosemary. *Progress, Poverty and Exclusion: An Economic History of Latin America in the 20th Century.* (Baltimore, MD: The Johns Hopkins University Press, 1998.)

cialty shops, and the growing number of malls to make their purchases. The lower segments of the middle class may frequent all of these places depending on their precise need, income that month, and interest in being seen in the right place. More consumer goods of better quality are available at better prices, but many cannot begin to afford them. Poverty and misery continue and have increased in some countries. Income and wealth have become even more concentrated in the hands of the wealthy few, although the spread continues to the middle class. Many argue that the social costs of this form of development are too high. This consensus is spreading as far as the international financial institutions (IFIs) themselves, as suggested by the title of a recent book by the InterAmerican Development Bank, *Facing Up to Inequality in Latin America, Economic and Social Progress in Latin America, 1998–99 Report.* Even the World Bank has begun to insist that loan packages contain programs specifically designed to improve living conditions for the masses and mitigate some of the worst aspects of the reforms. It remains to be seen, however, if such concerns are sufficient to prompt a reevaluation of the neoliberal model by the IFIs that are advocating it.

Political Legacy

The economic scene is changing radically in Latin America. One sees major stock exchanges in São Paulo, Mexico City, Lima, Santiago, and Buenos Aires; more and more manufactured goods or key components are being made in the region; and modern aspects of Western consumption such as computers, cable TV, mass retail stores, and the omnipresent auto are inundating national societies. Brazil is already the eighth largest economy in the world, and more and more products on the world market come from Brazil and other countries in the region. Although conditions for the masses in Mexico are still bleak, Mexico is generating more and more millionaires and now counts some of the wealthiest people in the world among its population. On an international scale, Brazilian managers are among the very best paid. Yet globalization and the neoliberal reforms imposed on Latin America have only added to the highly inequitable distribution of wealth and income that have historically characterized the region. And indebtedness has continued to grow, with Brazil and Mexico's external debt growing to more than $158 billion and $222 billion, respectively in the 1990s. Argentina's external debt increased to $118 billion. As much as 40 percent of the value of several countries' exports is used just to make debt payments. The austerity measures that have become part of structural adjustments and IMF conditionality have fallen heavily on the poor, women, and many in the middle class. These measures have become very unpopular at times, as when there was major antigovernment rioting in Venezuela in 1989, only to be followed by an almost successful coup in 1992 and the election of the coup leader to the presidency in 1998. Indeed, Venezuelan president Hugo Chávez has promised not to abandon the common people in the face of dictates from the IMF. Inequality and continued marginality for the masses have spawned major Leftist parties that have won many local and congressional elections and have come close to taking power in both Brazil and Mexico. In 1999 Ecuador also experienced widespread riots as the president tried to implement austerity measures called for by neoliberal reforms; further protests forced him out of office in 2000. The many negative effects of globalization and neoliberalism and the popular reaction to them continue to put considerable pressure on the national political leaders who are obliged to implement them as a condition for new loans from the IMF and World Bank. After more than a decade of this medicine, the miraculous cure for the misery of the masses does not seem to be forthcoming, although many of the better off have clearly benefited. Meanwhile, there has been growing mobilization against these measures. For example, in September 1999, the Brazilian Catholic Church organized the "Cry of the Excluded Ones," a series of protests against the government's neoliberal economic policies. Church leaders were joined by leaders of Brazil's powerful protest organization, the Landless Movement (MST). One archbishop noted, "Neoliberalism is a system that devours itself . . . and the worst thing is it also kills people." A bishop from Rio de Janeiro went on to say that current economic policy only created misery and that it was generating a serious social crisis. Believing that the millions used to pay the external debt would be much better spent helping the masses, the Brazilian Council of Bishops issued a call for a national plebiscite on whether to continue paying the foreign debt at all. It remains to be seen if there will be sufficient popular political pressure to force new policy directives for Brazil and the rest of Latin America or if the economic conditions will bolster the development of mass organizations and political movements that will take on power themselves to alter the economic and social policies they find less and less acceptable. It is clear that economic conditions will continue to be strong political motivators for many groups in society.

Bibliography

Baran, Paul A. *The Political Economy of Growth*. New York: Monthly Review, 1957.

Berry, Albert, ed. *Poverty, Economic Reform, and Income Distribution in Latin America*. Boulder, CO, and London: Lynne Rienner, 1998.

Blumer-Thomas, Victor. *The Economic History of Latin America since Independence*. Cambridge, New York, and Melbourne: Cambridge University Press, 1994.

———, ed. *The New Economic Model in Latin America and Its Impact on Income Distribution and Poverty*. New York: St. Martin's Press in association with the Institute of Latin American Studies, University of London, 1996.

Cardoso, Eliana, and Ann Helweg. *Latin America's Economy: Diversity, Trends, and Conflicts*. Cambridge, Massachusetts, and London: The MIT Press, 1995.

Cardoso, Fernando Henrique, and Enzo Faletto. *Dependency and Development in Latin America*. Berkley and London: University of California Press, 1979. [First published as *Dependencia y desarrollo en América Latina*, 1973.]

Drug Enforcement Agency. Information supplied from DEA Statistical Unit, Dr. Mark M. Eiler, Director, and *Major Coca & Opium Producing Nations, Cultivation and Production Estimates, 1994–98*. Washington, DC: Inter-Agency Narcotics Control Reports, 1999.

ECLA. *Study of Inter-American Trade*. New York: United Nations, 1956.

———. *Towards a Dynamic Development Policy for Latin America*. New York: United Nations, 1963.

Frank, Andre Gunder. *Capitalism and Underdevelopment in Latin America*. New York: Monthly Review, 1967.

Hadjor, Kofi Buenor. *Dictionary of Third World Terms*. London: Penguin, 1993.

Handelman, Howard, and Werner Baer. *Paying the Costs of Austerity in Latin America*. Boulder, CO, and London: Westview Press, 1989.

Hillman, Richard S., ed. *Understanding Contemporary Latin America*. Boulder, CO: Lynne Rienner, 1997.

Jameson, Kenneth P., and Charles Wilber, eds. *The Political Economy of Development and Underdevelopment*. 6th ed. New York: McGraw-Hill, 1996.

Lenin, V.I. *Imperialism, The Highest Stage of Capitalism*. New York: International Publishers, 1979.

Nkrumah, Kwame. *Neo-Colonialism; the last Stage of Imperialism*. London: Nelson, 1965, and New York: International Publishers, 1965.

Rodney, Walter. *How Europe Underdeveloped Africa*.

Salvucci, Richard J. *Latin America and the World Economy, Dependency and Beyond*. Lexington, MA, and Toronto: D.C. Heath and Company, 1996.

Smith, William C., and Roberto Patricio Korzeniewicz, eds. *Politics, Social Change, and Economic Restructuring in Latin America.* Miami, FL: North-South Center Press, University of Miami, 1997.

United Nations Human Development Program. *Human Development, 1999.* New York: Oxford University Press, 1999.

Veltmeyer, Henry, James Petras, and Steve Vieux. *Neoliberalism and Class Conflict in Latin America, a Comparative Perspective on the Political Economy of Structural Adjustment.* Houndsmills, Hampshire, England: Macmillan, and New York: St. Martin's, 1997.

FILMS AND VIDEOS

Unless otherwise noted, all films are available from the Filmmakers Library, New York.

Amazonia: The Road to the End of the Forest. Canada, 1990.

The Battle of the Titans. Denmark, 1993.

Coffee: A Sack Full of Power. U.S., 1991.

Deadly Embrace, Nicaragua, the World Bank and the International Monetary Fund. U.S., 1996. (Available through Ashley Eames, Wentworth, NH, 03282.)

The Debt Crisis. U.S., 1989.

Lines of Blood—The Drug War in Colombia. U.S., 1992.

Mama Coca. U.S., 1991.

Traffic. U.S., 2000. (Studio release.)

WEB SITE

www.eclac.org.cl   Economic Commission for Latin America

EIGHT

POLITICS, POWER, INSTITUTIONS, AND ACTORS

Power moves politics in Latin America, and naked power often rules. As we suggested in Chapter 5, politics in Latin America has to do with powerful political and economic actors. Powerful *políticos* (and the ocassional *política*) have dominated most Latin American societies since classical Mayan and Aztec times. Dictators such as Santa Anna in Mexico, Juan Perón in Argentina, and Anastasio Somoza in Nicaragua have ruled absolutely. Oligarchies such as the fourteen families in El Salvador have dominated politics and brutally suppressed those who challenged them. Military juntas have monopolized power, cancelled elections, imprisoned and sometimes eliminated the opposition, and ruled for decades. The military and other groups have ignored constitutions and seized power forcefully, as when the Chilean military bombed the presidential palace to overthrow Salvador Allende in 1973. And power can also come from the mobilized masses, demonstrations, or general strikes that force a government out of office or a dictator to resign. There have been more than 200 extra constitutional assumptions of power in Latin America since the republics became independent. Indeed, it has been the constellation of power and not constitutional constraints that has conditioned the conduct of politics during most of Latin American history. It is the powerful individual, group, institution, or party that most often rules. Only those who know how to use power can be serious players.

Yet as Latin American societies have become more complex, those who rule do so through the apparatus of the state and its interaction with political parties, political movements, individuals, and interest groups. Those who aspire to power must take over the apparatus of the state and use it to rule. This can be done by a coup d'état, a fraudulent election, a political agreement among political or economic elites to share power, or a relatively honest election with some real political competition. However the state apparatus is taken over, any discussion of the nature of political systems in Latin America must begin with a realization of the greater role that has been traditionally assigned to the state, particularly as compared to classical models of liberalism. John Locke and other classical liberal thinkers believed that the best government was that government that governed least. They were reacting to that absolutist configuration of the state that monarchies like Spain used to rule domestically and over their colonies in the sixteenth, seventeenth, and eighteenth centuries. Yet it was precisely this absolutist state that served as the model for Latin American rule. Its use and misuse in Latin America have been quite different than the way the liberal state developed in Great Britain or the United States.

When the Latin American nations gained their independence in the early nineteenth century there was a serious struggle over the political forms that would be adopted by the newly independent nations. During the colonial period the region experienced different forms of authoritarian rule and state absolutism. The traditional elites who retained power, now independent from Madrid and Lisbon, had little if any democratic experience. Indeed, since the conception of the state that was projected from Madrid or Lisbon was absolutist during the colony, the elites had to find informal, noninstitutional (and not institutionalized), more personalistic ways to assert their authority and adapt to local conditions. They were short on practical democratic models. Indeed, after independence, several countries experimented with monarchical and/or dictatorial rule.

The constitutional structures of the newly independent states were nominally democratic and modeled on the liberal constitutions of France, the United States, and the Spanish liberal constitution of 1812. Yet political practice and political culture tended to be authoritarian and absolutist, even for committed democrats like Simón Bolívar. Gradually, new groups emerged and democratic practice engendered more democratic and less absolutist attitudes—although the latter have persisted to the present day. As a result, a strange hybrid resulted. Most countries adopted a republican, democratic form of government, but in reality traditional authoritarian patterns were most often employed by the elites and suffrage was very limited. In the century and a half after independence, suffrage was gradually expanded, but there was frequent reversion to authoritarian politics and elitist, if not dictatorial, rule. Much of the course of Latin American history has been an alternation between the authoritarian tendencies that were acquired during colonial and even pre-colonial times and the democratic ideas and ideals that were interjected at the time of independence. Democracy has been gaining ground in recent years, but reversions to authoritarian rule are frequent and decision-making practices continue to reflect the authoritarian aspects of the political culture.

Constitutions

Jurisprudence is a highly developed art in Latin America. Legal documents are beautifully written and comprehensive. Latin American constitutions are no exceptions. They tend to be long, detailed, flowery documents with a large number of articles (the Mexican constitution of 1917 has well over 100 articles) covering a great many specific situations. As such, they frequently need to be modified or replaced. Based on code law, they are not open to case-based interpretation, as is the case with Anglo Saxon case law. Nor is legal precedent part of the judicial system. Constitutions have historically been more a norm to strive toward than a strict basis for the rule of law. Presidential power and prerogative are often more important than specific constitutional provisions or prohibitions.

Like the idealism of Don Quijote that permeates the culture, Latin American constitutions represent an ideal to which those who govern and are governed aspire. There have been times and places in Latin American history where they have been carefully followed (Costa Rica from 1950 to the present, Uruguay and Chile in the 1960s), but they are frequently subordinated to the power of the strong executive, dictator, or military junta. Those who rule have and use power and are less likely to be constrained by the constitution or other legal codes, although they may pay lip service to them. Like Franklin Delano Roosevelt in the 1930s, they are more likely to find ways to massage the courts and the constitution to achieve desired policy results. The political tradition in most of Latin America is of strong-man rule and the subordination of law and the courts to the executive and other powerful political and economic actors. The concept of the rule of law and protection of the individual against the arbitrary power of the state (through government) that classical liberals from Hobbes on espouse is not well developed in most of Latin America. Rather, power and the powerful have generally ruled.

Only in recent decades have supreme courts become apt at delimiting presidents' interpretations of what is permissible under the constitution. It should be noted, however, that the process of democratization based on Western concepts of classical liberal democracy that has recently spread through the region has strengthened democratic aspects of political culture in all countries where it is practiced and has begun to place a greater emphasis on the subordination of power and the powerful to the law. Nonetheless, practice is often contradictory. In 2000 the Chilean Supreme Court stripped former President Augusto Pinochet of his congressional immunity so he could be tried for human rights violations during his brutal dictatorship—as had been the case earlier for a former general who ruled Argentina during the Dirty War—but Peruvian president Alberto Fujimori was inaugurated for his third term after fraudulent elections were held after he forced the Peruvian Supreme Court to exempt him from a constitutional prohibition against third terms.

Like the constitution in the United States, Latin American constitutions almost universally created three branches of government: executive, legislative, and judicial. However, very rarely are they coequal—even in the constitutions. Two realities common to Latin American systems are a granting of greater power to the executive branch over the legislative branch and the general lack of significant judicial review. Further, while most Latin American constitutions contain a significant listing of human, civil, and political rights, they also include provisions whereby those rights can be suspended in an emergency or time of crisis by the executive. A *state of siege* (*estado de sitio*) or *state of emergency* may be invoked by most Latin American presidents (usually with the consent of the legislature) for a given period of time usually ranging from thirty to ninety days. It allows the president to suspend most constitutional guarantees, such as freedom of speech and assembly and habeas corpus, and to legislate by decree. After the initial period runs out, it may be renewed. This has often been an avenue by which presidents acquired dictatorial powers. Latin American constitutions are also often contradictory on the question of the military, asserting in one place the primacy of the civilian rule but in another granting the military a special responsibility for protecting national sovereignty and maintaining domestic order.

Like Continental law, the legal systems in Latin America are based on code law. Most analysts of Latin American constitutions and laws stress that the systems are based not on the flexible notions of British common law but rather on strict interpretation of extensive legal codes. Rather than building on a series of case law decisions, Latin American law is deductive. This code based law has its origin in Roman law, Catholic traditions, and the Napoleonic Code that have long dominated the region. The influence of Roman traditions can be traced to the long Roman domination of the Iberian peninsula, which left more than just its language. This tradition emphasized the importance of a comprehensive, written law that is applicable everywhere, in contrast to the medieval traditions of law on which the English system is based, with its emphasis on limits. What was clearly missing from the Iberian ideas of law transported to the New World were the notions of social contract developed in the English ideas of Hobbes and Locke, which laid the groundwork for the idea of a rule of law based on the consent of the governed.

John Peeler argues that another feature of Latin American constitutionalism drawn from earlier traditions is *corporatism*. In contrast to the more individualist ideas of the social contract, the Iberian tradition is more corporatist, with a great emphasis on the sociability of humans and their collectivity. Latin American constitutions are more likely to acknowledge the legitimacy of the interests of collective groups than of individuals. It is therefore interesting that in contemporary Latin American politics the struggle is often over which groups should have their interests acknowledged. For example, some of the constitutions (Argentina, Brazil, Colombia, and Mexico) specifically acknowledge the rights of indigenous groups, children, senior citizens, workers, women, and so on. (See Tables 14 and 15 on women's political rights.)

Table 14. Women's Constitutional Guarantees

Country	Legal Text	Statement of Equality
Argentina	Political constitution of 1994	All inhabitants are equal before the law. No privileges of blood or birth are recognized, nor personal exceptions nor titles of nobility.
Bolivia	Political constitution of 1967	All human beings enjoy guarantees and rights regardless of race, gender, language, religion, or any other form of discrimination. Men and women are equal in rights and obligations.
Brazil	Federal constitution of 1988 and state constitutions of 1989	Men and women are equal in rights and obligations.
Chile	Political constitution of 1980	Men are born free and equal in dignity and rights.
Colombia	Political constitution of 1991	All people enjoy the same rights, without discrimination based on gender or other reasons.
Costa Rica*	Political constitution of 1949	All men are equal before the law and cannot commit any discrimination contrary to human dignity.
Cuba	Political constitution of 1976	Women enjoy the same rights as men.
Dominican Republic	Political constitution of 1966	Does not expressly relate the equality of rights between women and men.
Ecuador	Political constitution of 1979	Women have the same rights and opportunities as men.
El Salvador	Political constitution of 1983	All people are equal before the law.
Guatemala	Political constitution of 1985	Men and women have the same opportunities and responsibilities.
Honduras	Political constitution of 1965	All Hondurans are equal. Any discrimination based on gender is prohibited.
Mexico	Political constitution of 1917	Men and women are equal before the law.
Nicaragua	Political constitution of 1987	All people are equal. Discrimination based on birth, race, nationality, origin, or other factors is prohibited.
Panama	Political constitution of 1972	There are no personal exceptions or privileges, nor discrimination by reason of gender, race, social class, religion, or political beliefs.
Paraguay	Political constitution of 1992	Men and women have equal rights. The state should concern itself with making equality a reality and with facilitating the participation of women in all arenas of national life.
Peru	Political constitution of 1993	No one should be discriminated against for reasons of origin, gender, race, language, religion, or other.
Uruguay	Political constitution of 1967	All people are equal before the law.
Venezuela	Political constitution of 1961	Discrimination based on gender, race, creed, or social condition is prohibited.

*The constitution of Costa Rica establishes that mothers, children, and the elderly enjoy special protection by the state.

Source: Statistical Abstract of Latin America, Vol. 35 (Los Angeles: UCLA, 1999).

Table 15.   Women's Political Rights

Country	Year Right to Vote Granted	Right to Be Chosen through Popular Election	Year CEDAW* Ratified
Argentina	1947	Since 1991, candidate lists for popular elections must include women in a minimum of 30% of elected positions.	—
Bolivia	1952	Same for men and women.	1960
Brazil	1932	Same for men and women.	1984
Chile	1949	Same for men and women.	1989
Colombia	1954	Same for men and women.	1981
Costa Rica	1949	Same for men and women.	1984
Cuba	1934	Same for men and women.	—
Dominican Republic	1942	Same for men and women.	1982
Ecuador	1929	Same for men and women. The law establishes the obligatory inclusion of 25% of women on candidate lists in multiperson elections.	1981
El Salvador	1950	Same for men and women.	1981
Guatemala	1945	Same for men and women.	1982
Honduras	1955	Same for men and women.	1983
Mexico	1953	Same for men and women.	—
Nicaragua	1955	Same for men and women.	—
Panama	1946	Same for men and women.	1981
Paraguay	1961	Same for men and women.	1986
Peru	1955	Same for men and women.	1981
Uruguay	1932	Same for men and women.	1981
Venezuela	1947	Same for men and women.	1982

*Convention on the Elimination of All Forms of Discrimination Against Women, adopted by the United Nations in 1979.

Source: Mujeres Latinoamericanas en Cifras, 1995, pp. 138–139, as cited in *Statistical Abstract of Latin America,* Vol. 35 (Los Angeles: UCLA, 1999).

Institutions

THE PRESIDENT

Latin American republics are based on the strong presidential form of government. Chile did experiment with parliamentary government around the turn of the twentieth century but has since employed presidential rule. Like France, Haiti does have both a president and a prime minister, but most power resides with the president, who appoints the prime minister. The single most distinctive political feature of Latin American rule is the power of the executive. Contemporary Latin American presidential power is deeply rooted in the autocratic traditions of the colonial period. Presidential power

Elecciones Nacionales 1998
Presidente

Sample ballot from the 1998 presidential election in Venezuela. Thirty-six different parties competed, but Fifth Republic Movement candidate Hugo Chávez easily won the election with close to 60 percent of the vote.

in the twentieth century has many different underpinnings that are post-colonial, including populist and revolutionary mobilizations, but the continuity with the past is strong. Also, the contemporary Latin American president wears many hats: chief executive, commander-in-chief, head of state, and head of party, to name a few. Multiple powers are not unique to Latin American presidents, just as U.S. and French presidents share similar multiple roles. In Latin American these multiple roles only further strengthen an already strong presidency, especially because of the president's ability to invoke broad emergency powers. Even during the last decade, when democratic rule predominated in the region, ruling presidents have occasionally assumed dictatorial power, the most dramatic case being Peruvian president Alberto Fujumori's *auto-golpe* of 1992. Latin American presidents often tend to continue in office—*continualismo*. This is often how elected presidents have evolved into dictators. As a way of curbing this aspect of presidential power, many Latin American constitutions—including those of Peru and Argentina—limit the time in office to two terms. The Mexican constitution of 1917 goes one step further, limiting the president to one six-year term. Several other states also limit the president to one term.

The president is also the personification of the state, as manifest in the presidential sash worn on formal occasions. His or her figure commands a great deal of respect and authority. Some observers place considerable emphasis on the role of the Latin American president as the national patrón, replacing the local landowners and *caudillos* of the past, arguing that the president is the symbol of the national society and is seen as responsible for the well-being of the country. Consistent with the classic definition of politics, the president is seen as responsible for the allocation of resources through presidential favors and patronage. Another side of this practice is that such a personification of power may lead to corruption; it is not unusual for Latin American presidents to leave the office considerably richer than when they arrived.

LEGISLATURE

In polar opposite to a parliamentary system of government, where the legislature is the dominant branch of the political system, or the government of the United States, where the legislature is seen as coequal, in Latin America the legislative branch is seen as clearly subservient, often acting as an advisory body to the executive or occasionally as a rubber stamp. Most of the legislatures in Latin America are bicameral, with a Chamber of Deputies or Chamber of Representatives and a Senate. However, all Central American states (not including Belize) follow the model of the Central American Federation and have unicameral legislatures, usually called Legislative or National Assemblies. The legislature's budgets are relatively small and their staff support minimal. In many states, the legislators may have to share a secretary and basic office equipment. The committee system is neither strong nor well developed, nor have Latin American legislatures usually retained the ability to veto acts of the executive or to initiate programs. They have served more modest goals of providing a locus for the political opposition and special interests or for refining laws for implementation. It is too early to definitively declare a new trend for Latin American legislatures, but with the region's wide reestablishment of democratic rule in the 1990s, legislatures in some countries have begun to assert their power and independence. Most significantly, in 1992 and 1993 legislatures in Brazil and Venezuela removed sitting presidents from office on the basis of official corruption while trying to reassert their prerogatives in countries such as Mexico, Argentina, Chile, and Uruguay. Such actions were virtually unprecedented. The Costa Rica Legislative Assembly has remained strong during past decades.

Legislators are most commonly elected to four-year terms for the lower house or unicameral legislature and four- or six-year terms for the upper house. Legislators are usually elected from single-member constituencies, although there has been some experimentation with forms of proportional representation in countries such as Chile. The legislative sessions have historically been short and have been known to last as little as a month. Legislative debate is often acrimonious, with walkouts, protests, and sharp denunciations. Compromise and consensus are often in short supply. As a form of protection against abuse or coercion by the powerful, Latin American legislators enjoy a special right—immunity from arrest or prosecution while the legislature is in session.

COURTS

The organization of the legal system in Latin America is not unlike that of the United States, with a supreme court, appeals courts, and local courts. Judges are generally appointed, although the national legislatures may be involved through nomination or, in the case of Costa Rica, in the election of the supreme court justices. Supreme court justices are not, however, appointed for life, as is the case in the United States. Rather, they serve for a fixed term and must have their term renewed by appointment or election. A tradition of a strong, independent judiciary is not well developed in Latin America. From the supreme court down, the judiciary has tended to be susceptible to political pressure from the executive or other powerful groups. Further, certain crimes, such as terrorism or actions by military officers, may not be within the purview of civilian courts. Rather, such cases are referred to special military courts. In recent times, Latin American courts, although still weak, have begun to seek more effective ways of attacking official corruption and protecting individual rights. Symptomatic of this trend is the increasing use of the *writ of amparo*. Used in both Mexico and Argentina, it allows the individual to protect his rights by making a special appeal to the judicial system. It is a way the individual can protect himself or herself from the power of the state.

GOVERNMENT STRUCTURE AND LOCAL GOVERNMENT

Most Latin American states are unitary, meaning that there are no state-level governmental organizations with autonomous power or independence. The only federal states are Mexico, Brazil, Argentina, and Venezuela. The other nations are divided into provinces or departments, with the national government usually appointing prefects or other administrative heads to rule over them. Municipalities exist at the lowest levels and may elect their mayors and councils (although the national government may appoint some council members as well). The organization of the four federal systems is similar to that in the United States, with elected state governors and legislatures and municipalities at the lowest level. Further, any discussion of the relative weights of central and local authorities in Latin American political systems must recognize a certain evolution over time. During the colonial period the monarchies were largely ineffective in controlling the interiors of their vast empires. Local authorities were generally appointed by the crown, but after appointment they largely functioned in an autonomous way. In rural Latin America prior to the middle of the nineteenth century, local landowners and *caudillos* were the de facto rulers. Later, the process of nation-building in the last half of the nineteenth century focused primarily around the communication system—roads, rail, and so on. These systems allowed central governments to exercise their authority over the hinterlands, thus replacing the rule of the *caudillos*. Most Latin American countries generally adopted unitary governmental structures with national/local relations similar to that of France, with almost all authority flowing from the top down—from the central government to local authorities. The local *caudillos* were eventually supplanted as national armies and bureaucracies were created late in the nineteenth century. Rudimentary systems of national taxation were established, although no formal authority to raise taxes was given to local authorities (this general lack of revenue-generating authority poses a major problem for local governments today).

This pattern of centralization was the clear intent of most national rulers in the nineteenth century, but three countertrends of the twentieth century must be mentioned lest one be left with the impression that Latin American politics has been marked only by centralized rule. First, four countries have adopted federal systems that have devolved some powers to the states—Brazil, Argentina, Venezuela, and Mexico. (Much of the autonomy of the states in Brazil and Argentina was, however, undermined by the long periods of bureaucratic authoritarianism in the 1960s, 1970s, and early 1980s.) Second, the sheer remoteness of some regions in countries like Brazil, Mexico, Argentina, and Colombia has significantly slowed down the integration process, although much of this regional remoteness has disappeared in the last twenty-five years. Finally, local leaders ranging from revolutionary chiefs and guerrilla leaders to drug traffickers and entrenched large landowners have often used the remoteness of their zones of activity to maintain relative independence from the central government. That combination is probably most evident today in Colombia.

ELECTORAL TRIBUNALS

In that their electoral systems have at times been highly susceptible to influence and manipulation, many Latin American nations have established a separate branch of government to oversee elections. Called supreme electoral councils or supreme electoral tribunals, these independent bodies are charged with overseeing the electoral process and guaranteeing honest elections. They have separate budgets and are not under the control of any other branch of government. In countries like Costa Rica they became quite strong and independent and have helped ensure electoral integrity. In other instances, they too proved to be vulnerable to powerful influences. As democracy continues to develop in the post-1990s period, their existence is a very positive factor in maintaining honest elections and open political competition.

THE BUREAUCRACY

Political scientists have long acknowledged the importance of another part of government—the administrative sector, or bureaucracy. Bureaucracies in Latin America have tended to be large, poorly paid and administered, and unmotivated. Staffing is often done as a form of political favor to political supporters of winning candidates or ministerial or agency appointees (one form of quid pro quo in a patron-client relationship). Professionalism and motivation are low, and the susceptibility to corruption or being suborned is often great. Indeed, the bribe, or *mordida* (little bite in the hand), is frequent in Mexico and most other countries. Costa Rica is the only Latin American country to have a professional civil service system. Elsewhere, each ministry or agency may have its own recruitment criteria and job classification system, with no general standardization or means of doing cross-agency comparisons. Nor are programs or university training in public administration widespread. Government offices are often only open in the mornings or until 1:00 or 2:00 P.M., and many workers have other jobs in the afternoons. In most cases, resources are very scarce. Similarly, phones go unanswered; lines are frequently long, service poor, and the ability to have a request processed or problem resolved minimal. One frequently hears stories of requests simply not being processed until an extra inducement is added to the application.

Knowledge of the bureaucratic sector is absolutely crucial to an understanding of Latin American politics. The implementation of government policy and programs is totally dependent on different segments of the bureaucracy. Bureaucratic functioning needs to be understood because many casual observers of the region are unfamiliar with the extensive role of government entities in the economy. In reality, most of the large Southern Cone countries, in pursuit of national development in the twentieth century, established significant state sectors to control everything from steel mills to coffee plantations. As in a socialist system, state employees set wages, prices, and production quotas. In the case of Argentina, under Perón a government corporation (IAPI) was established to purchase all agricultural products from the farmers and then to sell them on the international market with all proceeds going to the government. In some instances more than 50 percent of the gross national product (GNP) was generated in the public sector. Such large-scale government intervention in the economy allowed many governments to establish significant social welfare programs in education, health, and social services—each with their own administrative bureaucracies. These large bureaucracies provided central governments with vast amounts of patronage that could be used to reward friends and co-opt opposition groups. The bureaucracies generally have lacked significant legislative oversight and in many cases have been both highly inefficient and corrupt, allowing both bureaucrats and those who appoint them to become wealthy. The nature and efficiency of these organizations help legitimize neoliberal characterizations of a bloated, inefficient government apparatus that needed to be downsized. In the last two decades, however, processes of privatization and downsizing of the state have resulted in a significant decline in the size and role of the bureaucracy in most of Latin America.

NEW DIRECTIONS

As Latin America enters the twenty-first century, important questions are being asked about the direction of the region's political systems. The history of the region, as discussed in Chapters 2 and 3, saw the emergence of a wide range of governments: monarchies, rule by a *caudillo* or strong man, civilian and military dictatorships, oligarchic democracies, parliamentary democracies, populist-corporatist regimes, and, in the case of Cuba, a communist-led state. It is difficult to generalize about the location of the different types of regimes except to say that the parliamentary or Westminister-style governments only developed in countries such as Belize and Jamaica, which were formerly under British rule. Monarchical rule had some presence in the immediate post-independence period in the Latin countries, but by the latter part of the nineteenth century the trend toward republican forms of rule, albeit with limited suffrage and strong elite rule, was well established. However, for most of the twentieth century the trend toward democracy in the major countries of the region was blunted by a series of countertrends. The most pervasive was the short-circuiting of democratic rule by powerful leaders—both civilian and military. Mexico is a good case example of this pattern. After initial flirtation with monarchical rule in the 1820s, republicanism flourished in the middle of the nineteenth century under Benito Juárez as a system was established with limited suffrage and regular elections. However, in the late 1870s this trend was blocked by the emergence of a classic *caudillo*, Porfirio Díaz, who gained power by legitimate electoral means only to terminate the process and be continuously reelected through fraud and repression. He ruled for over thirty years, only being defeated and driven from office in 1910 by the powerful forces of the Mexican Revolution. After years of turmoil in the wake of the revolution, Mexico returned to a form of democratic rule with a federal republic in the 1930s. However, Mexican democracy was limited over the ensuing decades by a form of populist and corporatist rule that maintained the same political party, the PRI, in power through a combination of popular mobilization, clientelism, repression, and voting fraud.

But the Mexican PRI is not the only twentieth-century example of limitations on democracy that have occurred from regimes operating on a populist and corporatist model. Such regimes have mobilized popular support behind the government from the masses—especially the urban dwellers and working class—by attacking the traditional elites and promising significant increases in the standard of living for the majority classes. The classic examples of such regimes were those of Getúlio Vargas in Brazil and Juan Perón in Argentina. It would be unfair to classify these regimes as simply a continuation of Latin American trend of strong-man rule, although there clearly was an element of that in them. However, they often did operate within an electoral framework and did bring about significant democratic reforms in the areas of social welfare and education. At the same time, limitations on civil liberties and political opposition prevent the placing of such governments completely under the banner of democracy.

Yet populist or corporatist rule has not been the primary impediment to democratic rule in Latin America in the last 100 years; that has come from the military. In virtually every country of the region, with the exception of the British colonies that became independent in the last forty years, the military has assumed dictatorial powers, short-circuiting democratic rule for shorter or longer periods of time. The most recent strong intervention of the military into the region's political systems came in the 1960s and 1970s in prominent countries in South America and the almost continual dominance over the last half-century of military regimes in most of Central America (except Costa Rica).

In the late 1950s, many analysts of Latin America were arguing that the era of tyrannical rule was coming to an end. They pointed to long-standing democratic regimes in countries such as Chile and Uruguay and to emerging democracies in Venezuela, Brazil, and Argentina. However, these predictions proved to be short-lived. A military coup in Brazil in 1964 that would begin twenty-one years of dictatorship started a process that would be repeated in Argentina (1966 and 1976), Peru (1968), and Uruguay and Chile (1973). In addition, efforts at achieving political democracy in El Salvador, where the military had ruled for decades, came to an abrupt end in 1972 when the military blocked the election of Christian Democratic José Napoleon Duarte. As the 1970s came to an end, the great majority of Latin American countries were under military dictatorships. The 1980s were dubbed the "lost decade" in Latin America because of dramatic economic declines and rampant social problems. Military rule came to an end throughout the region in large measure because the military governments had proven themselves incapable of dealing with economic and social woes. In 2000 no country in Latin America was under military rule, the last regime falling in Haiti in 1995 under the threat of a U.S. invasion.

It is generally acknowledged that five countries in Latin America stand out for the length and stability of their democratic experiences—Chile, Uruguay, Costa Rica, Colombia, and Venezuela. However, only Costa Rica has not suffered a serious setback or rupture of democratic rule in the period since 1948. What these countries generally have in common is that at some point in their history the economic and political elites found a way to act cooperatively for the purpose of staving off more radical demands for political and economic restructuring. In fact, when democratic rule broke down as it did in Chile and Uruguay in 1973, it was because the elites came to the conclusion that revolutionary forces could not be contained by constitutional means.

Liberal democratic regimes were established in Uruguay and Chile between 1918 and 1932; Costa Rica established its regime in 1948. Colombia and Venezuela came close to establishing democratic rule in the late 1940s but only fully succeeded a decade later. Peeler argues that the key to the establishment of democracy was an agreement among the competing elites on the process of expanding political participation. He argues by counterexample that the failure to achieve such an agreement in Argentina after Perón's fall in 1955, marked by the continued exclusion of the Peronists, doomed the democratic process in that country.

All five countries conducted elections in the nineteenth century, but these elections were not the principal means of changing governments. Once in power through elections, individuals or parties regularly manipulated the system to maintain themselves in office, often forcing their opponents to turn to force to remove them. If elections were not a sufficient condition for democracy in the nineteenth century, how did that change in these five countries in the twentieth century? Chile may provide the best case example. In the nineteenth century, Chile did enjoy a high level of political stability interrupted only by a civil war in 1891. The basis of the stability was the political domination of an agro-export oligarchy that ruled through a series of limited suffrage elections. By the 1930s Chile had developed a clear, tripartite system of Liberals, Conservatives, and Radicals. Although some parties would change, this tripartite division has persisted to the present. Key to the system is a center party that often holds the presidency—the Liberal party until 1912, the Radical party from 1938 to 1952, and the Christian Democrats from 1958 to 1973 and again from 1990 to 2000.

Chilean politics in the twentieth century has been the most openly class-divided of any country in the region. It is argued that the traditional Liberal/Conservative alliance ruled until 1920 and then regained power during Pinochet's military rule. Otherwise, in the twentieth century the oligarchy has protected its interests not by direct rule of its political party but rather by maneuvering within Chile's tripartite system and using the checks and balances established in the 1925 constitution, which was not fully implemented until 1932. Such checks continue today through the Chilean senate, whose appointed Conservative faction acts as a check on radical action by the governing, Center-Left administration. Various Center and Center-Left governments ruled during the unbroken forty-one years of democratic rule between 1932 and 1973. These governments promoted a series of reforms supporting labor union organization and the creation of an extensive social welfare system. However, they never attacked the serious interests of the traditional oligarchy. There were never any actions to enfranchise rural workers or to redistribute rural property. In fact, the traditional landowners actually gained the cooperation of several reform governments in their efforts to directly obstruct the organization of the rural workers. A variety of constitutional means, including six-year presidential terms with no re-election, a congress chosen on proportional representation, and judges insulated from direct political control served to deny any sector the possibility of centralizing power and implementing their full agenda. In essence it was a guarantee for the traditional oligarchy that their fundamental economic power would not be challenged. In return, the oligarchy supported the democratic system and did not turn to the military to defend their interests. The limitations to this system as a guarantor of democracy was demonstrated in 1973 when the oligarchy supported a military coup out of the fear that Popular Unity President Salvador Allende had set in motion political forces that could ultimately lead to the expropriation of their wealth. Democracy was only reestablished in 1990 when the oligarchy was convinced that the radical Left was in full retreat and that power could again be placed in a trusted center party, the Christian Democrats, who had successfully mediated class interests prior to Allende's rule. The Chilean example demonstrates that democratic rule in Latin America in the twentieth century has been based on cooperation among elites. Only when the traditional oligarchy has been willing to support democracy have there been long periods of rule without military intervention to protect their wealth and property. Whether that pattern will persist into the twenty-first century remains to be seen.

Political Actors

Powerful actors dominate the political game in Latin America. We would agree with the definition of these players offered by Gary Wynia: "any individual or group that tries to gain public office or influence those who do." In Latin America, as elsewhere in the world, the list of such actors is a long one—landowners, businesspeople, peasants, industrial workers, civil servants, and military officers, to name just a few. However, these labels are not sufficient to fully understand the different groups or their interaction. It is important to analyze each and to ascertain the role of each within the Latin American context. Wynia also makes some important observations about Latin American politics in comparison to other parts of the world. For instance, he notes that Latin America's political systems are not replicas of those in North America and Western Europe. They have more varied rules and there is often not as much consensus among the political actors. Further, many interest groups are not as strong or well financed as in the United States or Europe.

We have previously discussed individual actors like dictators and the strong president; next we turn to groups. Looking at each group, we need to ask: Who are the people involved, and from what social class, region, or ethnic group do they come? It is also necessary to ask what if anything they want from the political process and when and how they hope to get it. We must also realize that there may be groups that largely wish to be left alone by the political process. However, by and large we will focus on groups that seek to utilize the political process to their advantage. Another important variable to be studied is the resources that are available to each group—those that can be utilized to influence the political process. Resources can range from sheer numbers, organizational cohesion, and dedication to wealth and strategic presence in the economy, or the capacity to engage in violent activity.

TRADITIONAL LARGE LANDOWNERS—*LATIFUNDISTAS*

In all of the countries of Latin America, with the exception of Costa Rica and Paraguay, the Spanish and Portuguese monarchies granted lands to a group of large landowners during colonialization. Initially the monarchies had primarily been interested in the extraction of gold and silver from the Americas, but as time passed the grant of royal lands for the cultivation of foodstuffs became more the norm for their penetration into the new world. These plantations took on some of the forms of the feudalism of medieval Europe. The local populations were forced to work on the land as virtual slaves. The workers were not paid in wages but rather lived on the *latifundio, hacienda,* or *fazenda* and were given a small piece of land to grow their own food in return for their free labor on the *patrón's* land. The *hacendados* and *fazendeiros* came to be the dominant class of the colonial period, both politically and economically. They were generally not interested in any significant involvement in the central national government or the distant monarchy in Lisbon or Madrid. All that they needed was the loyalty of local politicians and a local police force that could be called in the case of worker unrest.

At the time of independence early in the nineteenth century this group, made up of *criollo* descendants of the early European settlers, eventually took the lead in breaking ties with Spain and Portugal, taking advantage of the relative weakness of those governments at the time. In the years since independence this once-dominant class has seen its political and economic power eroded throughout the region. In countries such as Mexico, Bolivia, and Cuba dramatic twentieth-century revolutions almost eliminated their class altogether. In most countries, over the last century the large landowners slowly lost political power to the emerging commercial farmers and industrial elites. Beginning in the latter part of the nineteenth century land ownership and cultivation practices began to change, bringing forward a new class of commercial entrepreneurs who ran their landowning operations as businesses. In some instances the traditional large landowners transformed themselves into commercial farmers, but in the majority of cases their lands were eroded by land reform and the cultivation of new land by the commercial farmers reduced their political and economic influence. The changes in the rules of politics over time also cut into their power. But as long as dictatorship and military rule prevailed, the playing field favored the elites, especially the traditional large landowners. Later, as republican forms of government emerged in the nineteenth century with greater and greater extension of suffrage the influence of this group began to erode.

However, this erosion of influence has been a slow one because of the enormity of the power once held. In countries where the large landholders continued to dominate the economic landscape, such as El Salvador, they have continued to wield significant political power to the present time. *Fazendeiros* still have tremendous power in much of rural Brazil, as do their commercial counterparts.

BUSINESS AND INDUSTRIAL ELITES

While it is correct that rural elites held a dominant position politically and economically in most of Latin America well into the twentieth century, wealth has never been monopolized by them. Beginning in colonial times businesspeople who engaged in a wide range of commercial enterprises, from trading to banking, have been a part of the political scene. The turning point for the industrial elites came with the Great Depression of 1929. The Depression devastated the region economically, but it also opened the door to entrepreneurs producing goods that were no longer being supplied by depressed European economies. Many of the emerging entrepreneurs in countries like Brazil, Argentina, and Venezuela were new immigrants who generated considerable wealth within one generation. In these large countries the manufacturing sector began to grow and eventually contributed a greater share of national wealth than agriculture did. The process of becoming more economically independent from Europe was further enhanced by the isolation generated by World War II. As their contribution to national wealth grew, industrial entrepreneurs sought and gained important concessions from the national governments. Unlike the rural elites, who largely favored the import of foreign finished goods without any significant tariff protection, the burgeoning industrialists sought to have their growing industries protected from foreign competition. In addition to government subsidies the industrial entrepreneurs also sought government support for the subordination of organized labor. For obvious reasons, the entrepreneurs generally did not want the interference with their management prerogatives or profits that labor unions generally attempt. Industrialists have had only mixed success in this arena. While military dictatorships like those in Chile, Brazil, and Argentina in the 1970s and 1980s repressed the labor movement, other governments have been less willing to blunt the power of the unions because of their ability to deliver votes, engage in demonstrations, and disrupt the economy.

All members of the business elite do not have the same economic interests or policy agendas. Some elements of the commercial elite have been more engaged in buying and selling traditional primary goods and importing and distributing finished goods. Their interest in ISI was thus muted. Further, smaller national industries and banks were often at odds with those interests that allied themselves with MNCs engaging in manufacturing and finance. The specific financial interests of each group defined their political position. Such elites, since they are few in number, generally did not seek to influence the government through the traditional political process; rather, they served on government boards and commissions or appealed directly to government officials. In many instances these entrepreneurs sought to bribe government officials for favors for their individual firms. Such bribes were often an accepted part of the political process; however, when such payments came to light, as in Brazil in the 1990s, officials were indicted or forced to resign, as was the case with President Fernando Collor de Mello. Industrialists also sought and gained such overt favoritism as easy credit, export subsidies, and government purchase of only domestically produced manufactured goods. Although some businesspeople espoused the ideology of free trade, very few were actually prepared to go without government subsidies. Until the 1980s this protectionist mantra generated by the ISI model was largely accepted without question by the governments of the large countries of the region—Mexico, Brazil, and Argentina. This perspective was bolstered by the ideas of economist Raúl Prebisch and ECLA. However, the revival of the free trade ideology under the banner of neoliberalism resulted in some profound changes. Begun first under the Chilean dictatorship of Augusto Pinochet in the 1970s and 1980s, neoliberal ideas took hold in Argentina, Brazil, and elsewhere in the 1990s. As a result, tariff walls have been lowered and government subsidies of industry have been reduced. New competition from North American, Asian, and European entrepreneurs has weakened the economic and political position of many of the local industrial elites or has forced them to become associated with foreign investors. Commercial business elites may be able to adapt to the new sources of supply, but they may also be challenged by foreign chains like Wal-Mart.

THE MIDDLE OR INTERMEDIATE SECTORS

This is an important and pivotal group in the Latin American political scene. We use the term *intermediate sector* to distinguish it from the concept of middle class that is prominent in the analysis of North America and Europe. Unlike the middle classes in these countries, who gained prominence and stature through their economic activity following the Industrial Revolution and industrialization, Latin American intermediate sectors are primarily professional functionaries such as government bureaucrats, doctors, lawyers, shopkeepers, managers, accountants, middle-level military officers, and some teachers. This group is marked by their relatively high level of education and their centrality to the functioning of society, especially in the era of urbanization. Their numbers, small until Latin America began to industrialize and urbanize, have grown significantly in recent years. In comparison to the middle classes of Europe and North America, they generally developed less class consciousness and have remained a diverse and fragmented community. Their diversity and specific interests have at times made them forces for change, as was the case with their support for the reformist Radical party in Argentina during the twentieth century. At other times they have not been a force for societal change, being largely dependent on the landed and industrial elites that dominated Latin societies. Most sought to emulate the lifestyle and consumption patterns of upper classes rather than to supplant them, and they have definitely been much less entrepreneurial than their counterparts in the North.

The relationship of the intermediate sectors to the political process has been an interesting one. Not surprisingly, what they have demanded from the political system are resources that further the position of their group— government funds for education, industry, and communication infrastructure. They can move into or out of a particular political camp depending on how well they think their goals can be achieved. They have not been universally consistent in their support of any particular form of government. However, in the twentieth century more often than not the intermediate sectors have been strong supporters of political reform and multiparty democratic systems. In those situations where these movements have come to the fore, they have clearly favored the expansion of the franchise and the development of defined civil liberties. The intermediate sectors can be connected directly to the development and prosperity of such political parties as the Radicals in Argentina and the Colorados in Uruguay. However, their support for democracy has not been an unflagging one. The Mexican middle sectors have always given strong support to the one-party domination of the PRI, and in the 1960s and 1970s the middle sectors generally supported the military regimes of Chile, Brazil, and Argentina. Generally they fear radical or revolutionary movements because the success of such movements might herald the end of their hard-won standard of living. They are horrified by the prospect of slipping into the poverty of the masses. Their ambivalence is partially the result of what resources they bring to the table. In most Latin American countries this sector has not been large enough to act as a definitive voting bloc, although this is changing in some countries. Instead, they bring to the political process their organizing skills and their central position as cogs in the government, industrial, and business/ financial bureaucracy. Such positions lead them to be more comfortable in bargaining with the elites than in mobilizing the masses to achieve their political ends.

ORGANIZED LABOR

Labor organizing began in Latin America in the 1890s but had relatively little success in its early years. Much as in the United States, it was hampered by divisions among immigrant workers, who often spoke different languages, and by opposition from government authorities, allied with entrepreneurial elites in their implacable opposition to workers organizations of any kind. The workers' movement may have seemed even more threatening in Latin America than in the United States, as it was led almost entirely by political radicals espousing either socialist or anarchist ideas for the complete reorganization of society and the expropriation of the property of the ruling circles. In Argentina the labor movement organized hundreds of thousands of workers in response to the abysmal working conditions of the time. However, the strong influence of labor was broken by severe repression early in 1919. Hundreds of workers were killed by the police and the army, and the militant leadership was broken. A similar situation occurred in Brazil during the same time period, as socialist and anarchist labor leaders were jailed and deported.

Regionwide there was little successful union organizing in the 1920s. Only in the 1930s in Latin America did labor begin to become a large enough force in the most industrializing countries to become a significant political factor. During the 1930s significant labor struggles emerged again in Brazil and Argentina and in Colombia, El Salvador, Bolivia, and Venezuela. However, even as labor succeeded in organizing many workplaces, the owners of industry and their representatives in government refused to recognize the legitimacy of their organizations or to grant them a significant political role. One exception was in Mexico, where the regime of Lazaro Cárdenas (1934–1940) included the labor movement as part of a wider populist strategy aimed at further transformation of Mexican society in the wake of the 1910 revolution. The labor movement has had significant influence to the present time within the ruling PRI. Argentina is also an interesting case of labor influence. By 1943 Argentine labor had recovered from the earlier repression to organize 500,000 workers into its ranks. After initial attempts by the military to repress the movement Colonel Juan Perón emerged to harness the power of the labor movement behind his nationalist and populist political program. With the support of the labor movement, Perón easily won the 1946 presidential election despite active opposition by the United States. Perón responded by delivering tangible benefits to Argentina's working class over the following decade in the form of higher wages and significant government spending on health care and education. Perón was removed in a 1955 military coup, but the party he created has retained significant labor union support to the present time. In other countries unions have been allied with other parties.

In contemporary Latin America, the labor movement has many resources at its disposal. While the labor movement does not represent all of the working class, but rather its aristocracy, in a democratic context it has the ability to mobilize considerable votes for its candidates. Yet women and racial minorities are often underrepresented in leadership positions (see Table 16— Women on Executive Boards of Nationwide Unions). Between elections organized labor exercises important economic influence through strategic control of industrial enterprises. Strikes in industries such as transportation, banking, or mining can have great leverage in a society. In extraordinary situations the labor movement can also be a catalyst for a more far-reaching general strike or even an armed insurrection. Most labor unions are organized into national labor federations like the General Federation of Labor or General Confederation of Labor and are affiliated with Communist, Socialist, Christian Democratic parties or with strong nationalist parties like the PRI in Mexico or the Peronists in Argentina. A few unions have been formed with the help of the U.S. AFL/CIO and are heavily influenced by the less political U.S. labor model.

Table 16. Women on the Main Executive Board of Nationwide Unions, Selected Years, 1983–1994

Country	Year	Both Sexes	Women N	Women %	Level	Organization
Argentina	1994	24	0	0	National Directing Council	General Confederation of Labor (CGR)
Bolivia	1994	37	1	2.7	Executive Committee	Central Union of Bolivian Workers (COB)
Brazil*	1991	25	2	8.0	National Executive	Unified Central Union of Workers (CUT)
Chile	1992	59	5	8.5	National Direction	Unitary Central Union of Workers (CUT)
Cuba	1990	17	4	23.5	XVI Congress Secretarial	Central Union of Cuban Workers (CTIC)
Dominican Republic[†]	1991	11	2	18.2	Executive Bureau	Unitary Central Union of Workers (CUT)
Mexico	1991	47	2	4.3	National Direction	Confederation of Mexican Workers (CTM)
Nicaragua[‡]	1993	12	3	25.0	National Direction	National Confederation of Workers (CNT)
Paraguay[§]	1990	15	1	6.7	National Direction	Unified Central Union of Workers (CUT)
Peru[¶]	1983	41	1	2.4	National Direction	General Central Union of Peruvian Workers (CGTP)
Uruguay	1993	17	3	17.6	Executive Secretariat	Intersyndical Plenary of Workers / National Convention of Workers (PIT-CNT)
Venezuela	1990	17	1	5.9	Executive Committee	Confederation of Venezuelan Workers (CTV)

*The main trade union.

[†]There are several other trade unions in the country.

[‡]Trade union with the longest history.

[§]Trade union with the most members.

[¶]Corresponding to the strongest trade union.

Source: Social Watch, *The Starting Point*, 1996, p. 41, as cited in *Statistical Abstract of Latin America*, Vol. 35 (Los Angeles: UCLA, 1999).

Rural Poor

The rural poor have often received considerable attention from scholars, but historically this group has been the most marginalized from political power. First of all, it is necessary to state that this group is not homogeneous and that its role in Latin American society has evolved over time as the result of both land reform programs and economic transformation. The term *campesino* has been used to label those low-income agricultural producers who have some attachment to the land in rural Latin America. *Rural laborers* comprise another group made up of landless agricultural workers. In many ways the basic conditions of their lives has changed very little over the course of several centuries. The great majority of both groups have lived in dire poverty, barely earning enough for their survival and reproduction with little chance for advancement. Most people born as *campesinos*, or *rural laborers*, died in the same social situation and passed that legacy on to their children and grandchildren. While sharing common characteristics, it is also important to see the significant differences between various groups of the poor based on their different circumstances of employment.

The first group is known as *colonos*. They work on the large plantations described earlier as the haciendas and fazendas. Whether they are tenant farmers or sharecroppers, they are all too often bound to the plantation by generations of debt. This group is generally not paid in wages but is allowed a small plot of land to grow food for their sustenance and is provided the other basic necessities of life by the owner of the plantation in return for labor. In the best of situations this group can be said to be protected from the greatest uncertainties of harsh rural life by the *patrón*. As one might expect, their political position is especially precarious. Since they are wholly dependent on the *patrón*, they have often been either marginalized from politics or manipulated by the *patrón*'s dictates. In a context of democratic elections, *colonos*, *campesinos*, or *rural laborers* can be coerced into voting for the chosen political candidates of the estate owner. Because of its numbers, this group could be a significant political force. However, because they were traditionally isolated from one another on different estates and in different villages, their organizing power was often muted. Organizing efforts were often resisted with force by local owners and their allies among the police and judiciary. Currently, better opportunities for exchange of information and interaction are offered by the expanding modern communication infrastructure, but the forced commercialization of farming is rapidly forcing this group off the land into the cities or to become landless rural laborers.

The second important group is the *rural wage laborer,* who has become increasingly dominant through the economic transformation of Latin America in the twentieth century. These are the workers on Latin America's commercial farms and plantations who are hired first to plant and then later to harvest the region's primary cash export crops—cotton, coffee, sugar cane, and bananas. Many of the wage laborers may own small plots of land, but are forced to sell their labor to supplement their income in order to survive.

In many places they are migrants because they often have to travel great distances to find enough work to survive throughout the whole year. North Americans are somewhat familiar with this class of Latin Americans because many work each year, both legally and illegally, in the agricultural fields of the United States. Like the *colonos*, this group is largely marginalized from the Latin American political process. The combination of their constant travel and their precarious economic situation makes it difficult for them to become involved in politics, either as voters or as protestors, but there are important exceptions. Banana workers in Honduras, Costa Rica, Panama, and Guatemala have been very political at times with involvement in both elections and protest actions. In recent times many rural labors have joined the Landless Movement (Movimento dos Trabalhadores Rurais Sem Terra) in Brazil and have begun to exert greater political pressure. Likewise, much of the organizational base of the Zapatistas in Mexico and Ecuador's CONAIE is rural.

The third group are the subsistence farmers, the *minifundistas* and *microfundistas*. As was pointed out earlier, there may be overlap between the last two categories, as many subsistence farmers supplement their income with wage labor. The land that they occupy, sometimes with legal title and sometimes as squatters, is usually less than ten acres. The crops are grown largely without mechanization or fertilizers because the use of either is out of the financial reach of the cultivator. In good times the farmer grows enough for the family to survive and sells a small surplus at a local market. If there is crop failure due to storms or drought there may not be a surplus and the family is driven toward the wage labor/migrant situation. In difficult economic times the small farmer is also vulnerable to foreclosure if they owe money. This category of existence is generally preferred to that of wage labor, but it faces pressures from many directions. Proponents of land reform programs have often viewed this group's level of economic production as marginal and inefficient, so they have been targeted for elimination, with the hope that their labor can become available for the more efficient larger farms. Others have argued that giving them more land, irrigation, and agricultural credit and technical assistance would resolve much of rural poverty and increase the efficiency of production.

The rural poor have definite grievances to pursue with the political authorities. The *colonos* generally want the opportunity to improve their own lives and that of their children, usually by gaining the opportunity to work their own land. The wage workers want higher wages but are generally frustrated with the government's unwillingness to help them. Those that own small farms seek credit and technical support from the government and protection from their creditors.

For most of Latin American history the rural poor were not in a strong position to pursue their grievances, divided as they were by both geography and differing interests. However, the twentieth century has seen a significant change in their political importance. In Mexico and Venezuela mass political parties succeeded in organizing the rural poor into the political process as voters behind a clear political agenda. They have been even more important in revolutionary movements, playing a key role in such movements in Cuba, Bolivia, El Salvador, Guatemala, Peru, Colombia, and Nicaragua. In addition, the growth of grassroots movements such as the Peasants League and Landless Movement in Brazil underscore their growing political importance.

THE MILITARY

The armed forces must definitely be treated as a singularly important group in the political history of Latin America, although that prominence needs to be tempered by the fact that as Latin America enters the twenty-first century for the first time in its modern history no country is under military rule. Such a situation represents a stark contrast to the 1970s and 1980s, when more than half of the region's governments were military led. However, a strong process of democratization beginning in the mid-1980s brought civilian governments to power across the region, led by Peru in 1980, Argentina in 1983, Brazil in 1985, and Chile in 1989. Today, the discussion of the role of the military in much of Latin America revolves around its role as a significant bureaucratic interest group. Acceptance of the legitimacy of civilian rule and the subordination of the military to civilian political rule has seemingly become the norm in much of Latin America. Yet the military still holds veto power in countries such as Guatemala and Chile and are still able to operate with impunity in some aspects of civil society. The military remains as an active force in contemporary politics, and their current position flows from their longstanding power.

Since World War II, and with the strong backing of the government of the United States, Latin American militaries have been competent, professional organizations with considerable modern weaponry. Not surprisingly the region's largest country, Brazil, has the largest armed forces, with close to 300,000 soldiers in uniform. Brazil spends over $3 billion a year maintaining its forces, which include an aircraft carrier and more than 200 combat aircraft. Other countries that have maintained significant military forces in recent years include Mexico, Argentina, Chile, and Cuba. (Cuba significantly reduced its forces in the 1990s after maintaining close to 50,000 soldiers in Africa, with Soviet help, during the 1970s and 1980s.) Yet the primary role of most militaries in Latin America has been the maintenance of internal order. However, the size and sophistication of military forces is not in reality the prime determinant of political influence in Latin America or elsewhere. Throughout the twentieth century the U.S. and British militaries have been powerful forces but have never challenged control by civilian authority. In contrast, relatively weak and small military establishments in Latin America have usurped civilian authority and sought to dominate the political process.

The involvement of the Latin American military in politics has its roots in the military nature of the conquest and early settlement, the class character of the military families throughout the course of Latin American history, and other factors. Over the course of Spanish and Portuguese colonial rule, the military officer corps were deeply intertwined with political rulers and the landowning elites. They were often one and the same, as leading military people also controlled large tracts of land. If the military leaders did not happen in a given instance to own significant land, they acted as an important ally against any forces that sought to challenge the landed oligarchy. As a result, the military entered the age of democratic reforms in the twentieth century in a position deeply suspicious of forces that would have curtailed the political and economic power of the old political and economic elites through democratic political means. With few exceptions the political stance of the military as an enemy of democracy and reform was well established entering the twentieth century. Understanding the military in the twentieth century and especially in the last fifty years becomes a more complex problem. During that time the class character of military officers has changed considerably, as fewer of the children of the military continued the family tradition and as the modern, more professional militaries often became an important avenue of social mobility for those who aspired to become members of the middle class or improve their relative standing in it.

The education system for military officers has long been an important determinant of their orientation toward politics. Military leaders have maintained their system of officer corps education independent and isolated from the civilian education system. Traditionally, most military education focuses on technical warfare training with little time devoted to the humanities or the social sciences. The Centro de Altos Estudios Militares (CAEM) in Peru, which trained the Nasserite military officers who formed the reformist government of Juan Velasco Alvarado (1968–1975), is an exception; likewise, the training at the National War School of Brazil viewed strategy as involving some degree of social involvement. Yet in all military schools, to the degree that matters of history and society are treated, the ideological content very often views the military as the only institution of society that is unambiguously dedicated to the nation's welfare. All civilian politicians are treated with some suspicion, especially those of a Center or Left persuasion. On the other hand certain interest groups, especially labor unions, are viewed as detrimental to the national interest. At least until recently there has been little or no shift in this approach to education, which has definitely contributed to the military's willingness to carry out coups against civilian governments.

If military education has provided an ideological justification for certain forms of military intervention, then their disciplined and hierarchical forms of organization provided both the ability to carry out the overthrow of civilian governments and the ability to place themselves at the head of government bureaucracies previously headed by civilians. Military leaders in the 1960s and 1970s in countries such as Brazil argued that their hierarchical forms of organization could bring new levels of efficiency to government bureaucracies previously plagued by bad organization and chaos. This type of military government came to be termed *bureaucratic authoritarianism*. In general, claims that the military could be more effective rulers than civilians proved untrue and contributed to the downfall of military governments in the latter part of the 1980s.

GOVERNMENT BUREAUCRATS

Some have suggested that government bureaucrats should not be treated as a distinct and separate actors within the Latin American political process because they simply carry out the wishes of whatever political leaders are in power. However, this view is insufficient for Latin America or most any other region of the world. The key factor in understanding the significant power of government bureaucrats is that while elected politicians serve distinct terms and military leaders can be driven from power at any time, the great majority of bureaucrats stay in their positions for lengthy time periods. In Latin America, government bureaucrats have wielded considerable power because of the post–World War II trend of large-scale government involvement the ownership of important economic enterprises—banks, airlines, oil refineries, railroads, steel plantations, and many more—leading to the emergence of the nation of "technocrats" who played important political roles, particularly during the authoritarian periods in the 1960s and 1970s, in countries like Brazil, Argentina, Chile, and Uruguay. Privatizations within the last decade have reduced the government's role in countries like Argentina and Brazil, but public ownership remains formidable. A recent acknowledgment of the power of one segment of bureaucracy came in Venezuela where in 1999 elected populist President Hugo Chávez spoke of the need to trim the size of the giant bureaucracy of the state-run oil company, PDVSA. Chávez acknowledged the power of its bureaucracy, calling it a "government within a government." Other presidents have talked of reducing the size of the bureaucracy at all levels.

This sector has engaged in a significant amount of self-promotion to boost its importance. In contrast to military officers, who stake their right to political office on their duty to country and their organizational skill, government bureaucrats advertise their skill as technocrats who can rise above the squabbling or corruption that may plague elected leaders. Increasingly many Latin American technocrats are trained at foreign universities in Britain, France, and the United States. Oftentimes they return to their homelands with strong beliefs that their newfound technical skills have given them the right to a say in the political and economic direction of their nation, not just as administrators. In Mexico the previous four presidents all came from the ranks of these *tecnicos*.

Government bureaucrats, like those in other sectors, may well be motivated by selfless and patriotic concerns, but those who manage government institutions share many interests in common. First, they desire to continue their influence over public policy. Second, they seek to administer their agencies with as little interference as possible. Third, they enjoy the power and in some instances the wealth that comes from providing goods and services that those in the private sector need.

The means to achieve these ends are fairly well known. The reality is that elected officials are dependent on administrators to carry out their economic and political development plans. If an administrator disagrees with a particular policy initiative they definitely have the ability to sabotage its implementation. While such sabotage may need to be subtle to succeed, the elected officials usually lack the legal authority to remove recalcitrant officials from their posts. It is not yet clear whether the trend toward smaller government bureaucracies promoted by neoliberal reformers in the 1990s will significantly reduce the power of this sector. Ultimately the sector may well turn out to be an insurmountable barrier to the full implementation of privatization plans or other government reforms. Likewise, oversized bureaucracies have become a fiscal problem that fuels inflation.

POLITICAL PARTIES

The role of political parties is evolving in Latin America. Wynia argued that political parties have traditionally played at least three separate and distinct roles in Latin American society. Like political parties in the United States and Western Europe, they participate in elections with the aim of gaining state power. In a few countries like Costa Rica and Venezuela, political parties have played this role for decades, almost exclusively concentrating their energies on winning periodic contests for power. In countries where elections have been the norm, Ronald McDonald argues that parties tend to serve four functions—political recruitment, political communication, social control, and government organization and policy making. However, until the 1990s this role was sporadic in many countries either because there were no elections, only military rule, or because their role was limited by the lack of constitutional norms. Beyond elections, there are two other roles for political parties—the role of conspirators and the creation of political monopoly.

The category of conspirator describes those parties that do not accept the results of elections or operate in the absence of regular elections. These parties generally operate in the extraparliamentary arena, often turning to the use of force to gain power. Such parties could be coming from a variety of political positions, but most often they are movements that have been denied power through legitimate channels that turn to armed struggle to achieve their goals. Classic examples of this form of political activity occurred in Cuba, when activists in the Orthodox party, denied the opportunity of gaining power through the 1952 elections because of Fulgencio Batista's cancellation of those elections, formed an armed organization (the 26th of July movement) that challenged Batista and eventually defeated him.

Parties creating a political monopoly are those that seek to remain in power on a permanent basis. Latin America has two excellent contemporary examples of this type of political movement—The Cuban Communist Party (CCP) and Mexican Institutional Revolutionary Party (PRI). Both have been very successful in their efforts but have used different methods. The Cuban communists have succeeded in part through the establishment of formal rules of the game whereby the constitution enshrines the CCP as the country's only legal party; through its legitimacy as the party of the 1959 revolution; and through its social achievements. The PRI has dominated the Mexican political scene for over seventy years, keeping the presidency in PRI hands up to the year 2000, when it finally suffered its first defeat in a presidential election. The PRI constructed a system where opposition parties compete for power but were limited in their real opportunities for victory by a series of PRI policies, including patronage, co-optation, voter fraud, and, occasionally, repression. Both movements were born in revolutionary conflict and maintained power in part by presenting themselves as the party of the revolution and as the only political force capable of moving forward the ideals of their revolutions. The success of such movements is not easy and is usually dependent on some measure of popular support together with the support of the military, although in both Mexico and Cuba the military remained subordinated to civilian politics and heavily influenced by the dominant party.

Latin American political parties emerged in the nineteenth century when most of the region's nations adopted republican forms of government with limited suffrage. Two primary political currents emerged during this time period—the Liberals and the Conservatives. The latter were drawn primarily from the traditional rural elites of the *latifundio* system, who primarily sought from the government a preservation of the economic and political patterns that were established during the colonial period. The Liberals represented the emerging modern upper classes of the nineteenth century, the owners of commercial agriculture and other newly founded activities. The Liberals wanted the government to undertake a more active role in breaking up traditional landowning patterns, separating church from state, and promoting foreign commerce. Latin American liberals were not as committed to the political side of liberalism with its emphasis on constitutional rule and freedom of thought. Elections in Latin America were largely an elite matter throughout the nineteenth century, involving only about 5 percent of the adult male population. These parties engaged in electoral contests but also were often the basis for armed conflict as both sides often refused to recognize the results and turned to violence to achieve their political ends.

Representative of elite dominance and patriarchy, women and minorities still struggle for adequate representation in party leadership positions (see Table 17). Internal decision making is frequently authoritarian and often based on *personalismo*.

Traditional Parties. As pressure for increased suffrage succeeded in widening the electoral base and new immigrant groups swelled the Latin American population in the early part of the twentieth century, two distinct patterns of political party loyalty developed that have persisted to the present day. In some countries, Colombia and Honduras being the best examples, the Liberal and Conservative parties, despite being elite-driven, suc-

Table 17. Women in National Directive Bodies of Selected Political Parties, Selected Years, 1990–1994

Country	Year	Party	Both Sexes	Women N	Women %
Argentina	1990	Radical Civic Union	24	0	0
Bolivia	1991	Movement of the Revolutionary Left	9	1	11.1
		Free Bolivian Movement	16	1	6.3
		National Democratic Action	13	2	15.4
Brazil	1991	Workers' Party	82	5	6.1
		Liberal Front	121	2	1.7
		Social Democrats	121	2	1.7
		Labor Democrats	119	11	9.2
		Brazilian Democratic Movement	121	4	3.3
		Brazilian Social Democrats	121	8	6.6
Chile	1991	Christian Democratic Party	40	5	12.5
		Socialist Party	19	4	21.1
		Party for Democracy	20	5	25
		Independent Democratic Union	26	2	7.7
		National Renovation	15	2	13.3
Colombia	1993	Liberal Party	3	1	33.3
		Democratic Alliance, M-19	5	1	20
Costa Rica	1990	Christian Social Unity	17	1	5.9
		National Liberation	25	3	12
Cuba	1991	Cuban Communist Party	25	3	12
Dominican Republic	1993	Christian Social Reform Party	39	10	25.6
		Dominican Revolutionary Party	297	30	10.1
		Dominican Communist Party	22	1	4.5
		Dominican Workers' Party	27	1	3.7
El Salvador	1993	ARENA	15	1	6.7
		Christian Democratic Party	40	3	7.5
		National Democratic Union	10	4	40
		National Revolutionary Movement	9	1	11.1
		Farabundo Marti Front for National Liberation	50	7	14
Mexico	1992	Revolutionary Institutional Party	34	4	11.8
		National Action Party	28	5	17.9
		Democratic Revolution Party	32	7	21.9
Nicaragua*	1994	Sandinista National Liberation Front	27	6	22.2
		Social Christian Party	58	12	20.7
		Liberal Independent Party	121	20	16.5
		Communist Party of Nicaragua	103	15	14.6
Panama	1991	Christian Democratic Party	4	1	25
		Authentic Liberal Party	14	0	0
		National Republican Liberal Movement	31	4	12.9
		Panamanian Party	9	1	11.1
		Labor Party	5	0	0
		Democratic Revolution Party	5	0	0

(continued)

Table 17.   Women in National Directive Bodies of Selected Political Parties, Selected Years, 1990–1994. *Continued*

Country	Year	Party	Both Sexes	Women N	Women %
Paraguay	1994	National Republican Association	72	6	8.3
		Radical Authentic Liberal Party	46	5	11.1
		Febrerista Revolutionary Party	30	6	20
		National Encounter	38	5	13.2
Peru	1990	Peruvian Aprista Party	4	1	25
		United Left	6	0	0
		National Front of Rural Workers	20	3	15
		Change 90 Now Majority	5	0	0
Venezuela	1992	Democratic Action	33	7	21.2
		Christian Social Party	35	3	8.6
		Socialist Movement	34	4	11.8

*Regional Directive Council.

Source: Social Watch, *The Starting Point*, 1996, p. 40., as cited in *Statistical Abstract of Latin America*, Vol. 35 (Los Angeles: UCLA, 1999).

ceeded in gaining electoral support from the newly enfranchised rural and urban masses. This support has basically continued throughout the twentieth century, leaving these countries with essentially two-party systems unchanged over time. The Liberals and Conservatives who succeeded in transforming themselves did so by a variety of means. Hacienda-owning Conservatives, using the strong bonds of the *patrón*-client relationship, have often been able to secure the support of their *colonos* through a combination of reward and punishment. Wage-paying commercial farmers associated with the Liberals may not have had as direct control of their employees, but many did succeed in convincing rural workers that their self-interest lay with support for the Liberal cause. Both parties succeeded in gaining strong familial loyalty to their movements, a connection that has now been passed on through multiple generations.

However, the cases where Liberals and Conservatives succeeded in transforming themselves into broad-based electoral machines were the exception. In some cases, such as Chile's, Liberals and Conservatives were forced to unite (Chile's National Party) to be able to confront new challenges to elite domination. In the majority of countries, the traditional parties rebuffed the demands of the newly emergent groups with the result that new political parties emerged on the scene after 1900. The most interesting were the Chilean Radical Party, the Argentine Radical Civic Union, and the Uruguayan Colorado Party. Modeled after the French Radical Party, these movements stood for suffrage, expanding public education and other government services, and the protection of workers' rights from the power of oligarchies, both urban and rural. Radical politicians succeeded in getting themselves elected in all three countries, drawing primarily on an immigrant and urban constituency, including the emerging proletariat and intermediate (middle) sectors. The Radicals generally did greater damage to the Liberals, who in some ways had attempted to appeal to the same constituency. As the Radicals eclipsed the Liberals, in some countries it turned the primary electoral battlefield into one of Radicals against Conservatives. In some instances the elite former supporters of the Liberals turned to the Conservatives to form an oligarchic alliance. The heyday of the Radicals was relatively short-lived, although the Argentine party has undergone a rebirth in the last fifteen years. The Radical parties faced increased pressure in the 1930s and, unable to deal with the economic challenges of the Great Depression, were either overthrown by the military representing the traditional oligarchy or faced increasing pressure from both populist and socialist movements. They are still important political actors in Argentina and Chile, and the Colorados won the presidential election in 2000 in Uruguay. The Liberals have remains relatively strong in Colombia.

Populist Parties. The 1930s and 1940s saw the emergence of populist parties in both Brazil and Argentina. Each was organized around a single charismatic leader, Getúlio Vargas in Brazil and Juan Perón in Argentina. The populist movement founded by Vargas did not outlive him, but in the case of Argentina a Peronist party still plays an influential role in Argentine politics to this day. It is important to understand that the roots of Latin American populism were clearly different from those in the United States, where the movement was primarily a rural-based protest against the railroad monopolies. The success of Latin American populists in the 1930s and 1940s was with the growing urban industrial working class, whose needs were largely ignored by the dominant parties of the time—Conservatives, Liberals, and Radicals. Unlike the other political parties discussed here, the populists are harder to pin down as the movements were uniquely shaped by their leaders. As movements, they did not concentrate as much as the other parties on building organizational entities. Instead, they depended on the mobilizing power of the leaders themselves and, in the case of Perón, on his popular spouse, Eva. To underscore the centrality of personal rule, Vargas did not launch his populist movement's political party until he had been in power for almost fifteen years.

The heterogeneous political philosophy of the populists concentrated its attacks on the old order, the traditional *latifundistas*, but also on the commercial elites that had come to the fore in the beginning of the century. The populists were not revolutionaries; rather, their philosophy was to gain a greater share of the national wealth for their supporters within the framework of capitalism. It was also a nationalistic philosophy that sought to achieve national development without significant involvement of foreign investors, a stance that angered the foreign powers who had long dominated the region and those who had hoped to capitalize on the new opportunities.

They were also supporters of rapid industrialization and state intervention in the economy.

The populists saw themselves as the archenemies of the Socialist and Communist parties that were seeking to appeal to the same constituency—urban industrial workers. However, unlike the Conservatives and Liberals, the populists believed that it was possible to defeat the prospect of revolution by creating government-sponsored worker organizations, which could yield worker discipline in return for better wages and working conditions.

Even before creating a populist movement Vargas had linked Latin American populism with European fascism through his concept of the *Estado Novo* (new state), a corporatist idea that combined strong government involvement in economic activities with the organization of workers into government-controlled unions. In the case of Brazil, the *Estado Novo* meant a centralizing of political power against the interests of regional authorities who dominated the country's politics prior to 1930. Vargas organized the Brazilian Labor Party in 1945 as a mass organization when his opponents in the traditional oligarchy tried to drive him from power. The Labor party proved to be an effective vehicle for Vargas, winning the presidency for him in both 1945 and 1950. However, his role as a ruler who sought to mediate the diverse interests of Brazilian society was a failure. Vargas was hounded into suicide in 1954 by his political enemies, especially the military. Successors of Vargas such as Juscelino Kubitschek sought to continue elements of the populist program, but the Brazilian Labor Party did not succeed in becoming a permanent feature of Brazilian political life.

The populism of Juan Perón in Argentina had many similarities to that of Vargas, but there were also some differences. Perón also incorporated elements of Italian fascism, but, unlike Vargas, who first gained power and then later created a movement to sustain his power, Perón gained power through the transformation of the Argentine General Labor Confederation into his personal instrument and the incorporation of Conservative, Radical, and Socialist groups into his political movement. When the military and the traditional oligarchy sought to block his ascendancy to the presidency by arresting him, Perón and his future wife, Eva, mobilized his forces to gain his release and pave the way for his victory in the 1946 presidential election. In power Perón's strategy was similar to that of Vargas. He implemented programs that delivered social services and a higher standard of living to the urban workers while guaranteeing entrepreneurs labor peace through tight control of the unions. Like Vargas, his rule took on strongly nationalist tones, and policies of economic protectionism were implemented. The government took a strong hold on the economy, the most dramatic example being the creation of a government monopoly over agricultural commodity trading, a strategy that captured the considerable profits of this section entirely for the government. He also nationalized the railroads, airlines, public utilities, and the financial system, among other strategic sectors. In typical populist fashion, Perón did not move in any way to redistribute rural land as a revolutionary would have done, but rather to simply bring the rural elites under government control. Perón used the profits from this scheme to finance industrialization, social welfare programs, and the takeover of the country's utilities from foreign owners. Once the Peronist economy strategy began to fail in the early 1950s, Perón fell victim to the power of the old elites, who engineered a military coup in 1955 and sent him into exile.

However, unlike the populist movement of Vargas that largely ended when he fell from power, the Peronist Party remained strong, in part inspired by its leader in exile in Spain. Fearing their power, the military prevented the Peronists from competing in elections or nullified the results if they favored the Peronists throughout the eighteen years of his exile. Only in 1973 did the military allow a Peronist candidate to run for president and Perón to return in a desperate attempt to stem a growing revolutionary tide. His party swept the elections of 1973, only to have him die a year later. The party continued on under the leadership of Perón's third wife, Isabel, but the military ended that rule with a coup in 1976 and seven years of subsequent dictatorial rule. However, the Peronist Party, retaining its working-class base and nostalgia for the golden days of the late 1940s and early 1950s, succeeded in winning back control of the political system in both 1989 and 1995 under the leadership of Carlos Menem. Ironically, Menem shifted the ideology of the party almost completely away from that of its founder, embracing widespread privatization, free markets, and large-scale foreign investment. As a result, other political movements began to erode the electoral base of the Peronists, calling into question their influence into the next century.

It has been suggested that Alberto Fujimori represented a new type of right wing populism. Likewise, some see Hugo Chávez as representative of a type of leftist nationalist populism in Venezuela.

Reform Parties. Another type of political party that emerged during the same era as the populists was the democratic reform parties. Basically there are two types of reform parties—secular and religious. The traits that they shared in common were based on a rejection of both the populists and revolutionaries. The democratic reformers did not accept the tendency toward demagoguery and the use of strong-arm tactics against political opponents but did embrace the populist strategy of maintaining capitalist, free enterprise systems. The democratic reformers, while sharing some of the short-term desires for social justice with the Socialist and Communist parties, obviously broke with them over the vision of a classless socialist society.

The secular reform movement began with the popular American Revolutionary Alliance (APRA) founded by Peruvian Raúl Haya de la Torre in the 1920s. Their movement was inspired by a range of political ideas, including socialism. Long persecuted and marginalized in Peruvian politics, APRA only achieved government power under Alan García for a brief period in the 1980s. Today APRA has returned to its traditional position as part of a splintered opposition. However, similar political movements inspired by Haya de la Torre in Venezuela and Costa Rica have enjoyed considerable long term success. The Democratic Action Party (AD) of Venezuela first governed in the late 1940s and has held the presidency of the country for the great majority of the last forty years. In a similar fashion, the National Liberation Party of Costa Rica has held the presidency of that country five times since its founding at the time of the Costa Rican civil war in 1948.

Religious reformers are grouped in the Christian Democratic movement, which originated in Western Europe after World War II. Drawing heavily on Catholic thought, the Christian Democratic parties emerged as alternatives to the powerful Communist, Socialist, and Labor parties. The rise of Christian Democrats was especially important in Germany and Italy, where earlier pro-capitalist parties had been irredeemably tainted by their association with fascism. In the Latin American context these parties emerged in countries where populism never took significant hold and as an alternative to the revolutionary parties. Latin American Christian Democrats came to embody very similar political programs to the secular reformists, embracing political democracy in opposition to military rule and a package of reform proposals, especially in the agrarian sector. In contrast to the secular parties, they drew their inspiration from progressive papal encyclicals and reform movements within the Church. Christian Democrats sought to organize throughout the region but ultimately have only achieved full success in Chile and Costa Rica and limited success in Venezuela and El Salvador. In Chile the Christian Democrats first gained power in the 1960s as a middle ground between the Conservatives and the Socialist/Communist coalition that became Popular Unity (UP). Defeated by the latter in 1970 and then driven underground by the 1973 military coup, the Christian Democrats emerged in a postmilitary period in 1989 as the country's leading political force in association with the moderate socialists. The party has since won reelection in 1993 and is well positioned for long-term dominance with its centrist reform-oriented policies and Chile's relative economic stability. Christian Democratic parties elsewhere have been less successful. Only in two other countries have they enjoyed political power—two presidential terms in Venezuela in the 1970s (COPEI) and brief rule in El Salvador in the 1980s under José Napoleon Duarte at the height of the civil war as the recipient of considerable U.S. economic and military aid.

Left Reform Parties. A contemporary reform party that clearly bridges the religious and secular boundaries is the Brazilian Workers' Party (PT). The PT emerged in the late 1970s during the growth of opposition to the military dictatorship. From the beginning the PT had both Marxist and Catholic leadership, the latter being drawn from the powerful ecclesial base communities. The most popular leader was the leader of the resurgent metalworkers union, Inacio da Silva, known simply as "Lula." The PT grew in strength rapidly despite many obstacles thrown in its way, including the jailing of Lula in 1981. With the return of electoral democracy in 1985 the

PT established itself as a primary opposition party, supplanting older, more established Left parties. In November 1988 the PT's Luiza Erundina de Souza was elected mayor of São Paulo, Brazil's largest city. The party also demonstrated its mobilization powers through powerful industrial strikes in 1988 and 1989. The PT's high point of political power came in the 1989 presidential elections, when Lula nearly won the presidency in a runoff election against Fernando Collor de Mello, whose well-financed campaign defeated the PT leader by a scant 6 percent. The PT, seeking a more centrist image, voted at its 1991 convention to affirm its commitment to a mixed economy and democracy while retaining socialist ideals. Delegates representing the party's 600,000 members also voted to grant women a minimum of 30 percent of leadership positions. Initially favored in the polls leading up to the 1994 elections, Lula eventually finished a distant second to the well-funded campaign of centrist Fernando Henrique Cardoso, and again when Cardoso was reelected in 1999. The PT has succeeded in becoming the country's leading opposition party and holds local government control in numerous areas, but it has not been able to win the biggest prize, the presidency, or a majority in Congress.

The PRD in Mexico is also representative of this new brand of leftist party, as is the Frente Amplio in Uruguay.

Revolutionary Parties. The final group of parties to be discussed are the revolutionary parties. Revolutionary movements are discussed in far more detail in Chapter 9, but it is necessary to briefly discuss the revolutionary parties in the wider context of other political parties. Two different types of revolutionary parties are usually acknowledged in the Latin American context—those whose origins are in Marxist thought and those whose roots are elsewhere. However, it is also necessary to note that not all parties that begin their existence as revolutionary ones remain so. We must also discuss in this context those original revolutionary parties that have become thoroughly reformist in their behavior.

Communist and Socialist parties had their roots in the ideas and political activities of Karl Marx and Friedrich Engels in the last few decades of the nineteenth century in Europe. Initially the Marxist movement was united, but the 1917 October Revolution in Russia was a turning point. Most European Socialist parties had abandoned the possibility of revolution in favor of the achievement of socialism by parliamentary means, but the success of the first socialist revolution in Russia under the leadership of the Bolshevik Party inspired the creation of an alternative set of revolutionary parties, called Communist, that accepted the international leadership of the Soviet Union. Because Latin America industrialized considerably after Europe, the development of Socialist or revolutionary parties along Marxist lines was slow to occur. However, during the 1920s and 1930s these parties did begin to emerge largely among intellectuals, students, and industrial workers. Overall, these parties did not fare particularly well in the region, as they faced wholesale repression from the established governments and fierce competition to organize workers from both the Radicals and the populists. The primary exception was in Chile, where the Marxist parties succeeded in gaining a large following in the working class and entry into coalition governments during the 1930s.

By the 1950s the Socialist and Communist parties had largely ceased to be revolutionary in orientation. Where possible, in countries such as Guatemala, they sought to work through the political process, working with non-Marxist reform parties to obtain programs for workers' rights and land reform. However, the conservatism of these Communist parties only served to open political space to their left, which was soon filled by a new generation of revolutionary parties inspired by the success of the 26th of July movement in Cuba. Basing themselves on Marxist ideology and co-opting the old, reformist Cuban Communist party, movement leaders were soon at the head of a new generation of revolutionary parties that came to include the Sandinista National Liberation Front (FSLN) in Nicaragua, the Farabundo Martí National Liberation Front (FMLN) in El Salvador, and the Revolutionary Armed Forces of Columbia (FARC).

The best example of a non-Marxist revolutionary party is the PRI of Mexico. Founded in 1929, twelve years after the triumph of the revolutionary forces over the traditional oligarchy, this party has been one of the most successful in the twentieth-century history of political parties. From its founding in the late 1920s, the PRI won every presidential election in the twentieth century and held an absolute majority in the national legislature until the most recent election in 1997. Some dispute whether the PRI was ever a revolutionary party, but during the rule of Lázaro Cárdenas (1934–1940) the party used tactics of mass mobilization of workers and peasants to secure the gains of the 1910 revolution in the face of continued oligarchic resistance. After the period of Cárdenas' rule the party became more traditional, maintaining its power through a variety of means ranging from repression to voter fraud to co-optation to maintain its absolute domination of the Mexican political system.

Common Characteristics. Despite their obvious ideological differences, Ronald McDonald argues that Latin American political parties share some important characteristics, primarily elitism, factionalism, personalism, organizational weakness, and heterogeneous mass support. The elitism revolves around the centralization of decision making within a small core of (male and mostly European) party leaders who are usually drawn from the upper and middle classes. Some parties engage in a facade of democracy through the conduct of public primaries, but in reality decisions are retained by the core leadership. The latest party to follow this more transparent approach was the Mexican PRI with its first-ever presidential primary in 1999. New parties like the PT and PRD also display a greater degree of leadership diversity and internal democracy.

Factionalism has also been an enduring problem in Latin American parties. Such factionalism is often most associated with the Left, but bitter splits among party leaders on both personal and ideological lines has been common across the political spectrum. Only in the case of the existence of a strong figure, such as Fidel Castro in the Cuban Communist Party, Juan Perón in the Peronist Party, or Haya de la Torre in the APRA movement, was serious factionalism avoided. When the latter died his party split into several warring factions.

McDonald also argues that Latin American parties have tended to more often be organized around personalities than ideologies. The roots of personalism are deep in Latin American history from the era of the *caudillos*, but they have been sustained throughout the twentieth century despite the development of party ideologies and structures. Beyond the obvious examples of Vargas, Perón, and Castro many other abound, including recently elected former army officer Hugo Chávez in Venezuela. As party leaders these personalities in some cases are willing to quickly change their party's position to ensure continuation in office. The identification with a single leader has often proven easier than connection to party symbols and doctrines, especially in the case of the less-well-educated populations.

Latin America does have some significant examples of well-organized parties—the Mexican PRI, APRA up to the 1980s, the Cuban Communist Party, Argentina's Radical Party, Uruguay's Colorado and Blanco parties, and Venezuela's Democratic Action, but these are the exception rather than the rule. Most Latin American parties are more similar to the U.S. Democratic and Republican parties, coming to life primarily at the time of election, lacking strong ties to grassroots movements, and without a large number of formal members. Some of these parties are sustained by a relatively high level of party identification among the voting public, but in general party identification is weak in Latin America compared to Western Europe and the United States.

Class characteristics do tend to carry some weight in Latin American party identification but less so than in Western Europe because of the relatively late development of labor unions. An obvious exception to this rule is the Brazilian PT, which has a very clear worker and peasant allegiance. However, more common in Latin American politics are parties like the Mexican PRI, the Uruguayan Colorados, the Chilean Christian Democrats, and the Argentine Peronists, whose long-running electoral success is based on the creation of a multiclass constituency. Another basis of party identification in Latin America is region. Regional party identification has its roots in the nineteenth century, when warring Liberal and Conservative parties developed regional strongholds. Such patterns continue today in countries like Colombia, Uruguay, Honduras, Peru, and Mexico. In the latter, the opposition National Action Party (PAN) has developed a power base in the Mexican states nearest to the U.S. border, likely influenced by the tradition of the two-party system in its neighbor to the north.

MASS ORGANIZATIONS

The growth and development of mass organizations have also introduced a new category of political actor in the political scene. As suggested previously, powerful indigenous groups like CONAIE in Ecuador or rural groups like the Landless Movement in Brazil have proved themselves capable of mounting major mobilizations and demonstrations on a national basis. A series of mass organizations also demonstrated considerable power in El Salvador in the early 1980s, before being brutally repressed by security forces. Women's organizations, such as AMNLAE in Nicaragua, are also able to mobilize and to focus considerable attention on specific issues. Likewise, organizations representing Afro-Latins in countries such as Colombia and Brazil are also developing strong regional and national power bases. Indeed, as suggested by the underrepresentation of women in all levels of government (see Table 18 on Participation of Women in Government) mass organizations may be the best hope of gaining greater power and influence for underrepresented and marginalized groups. They and the new political parties may also be the primary base for emerging political movements.

Conclusion

The issue facing Latin America today is whether or not democratic rule will continue. Can the large steps taken in the last fifteen years be sustained? To do so would clearly represent a significant break with Latin America's past. The most daunting issue may be whether or not democratic governments can be maintained in the face of deep socioeconomic problems that will not be solved overnight. As was discussed more fully in Chapter 7, in the 1990s most democratically elected governments carried out programs of economic austerity that sought to improve foreign direct investments. These programs have had mixed results. Growth rates have recovered from the low points of the 1980s, but in many instances poverty has been increased and the gap between rich and poor has been widened. The installation of democratic regimes has clearly raised the levels of expectation of the Latin American citizenry. Since the expectations have generally not been met for the majority of the citizenry, the potential for significant political unrest exists. Latin American citizens in the last three years have begun to reject the neoliberal policies of the recent past not just in street demonstrations or strikes but through the support of opposition candidates in countries such as Argentina and Venezuela. New parties and mass organizations increasingly challenge the status quo. Nor are prospects for a return to military rule high—there is little support even among the business or industrial elites for a return to circumstances of widespread repression and denial of civil liberties. Further, there are also fewer illusions among the people that military rule offers an answer to the country's social and economic problems.

Table 18. Participation of Women in Government, 1994

Country	Ministers	Under-Secretaries	Provincial or Departmental Governors	Local Officers	Senators	Deputies	Single-House Congress	Supreme Court	Court of Appeals	Judges
Argentina	0	9.8	0	3.6	4.2	13.2	—	0	15.3	29.9
Bolivia	0	5.4	—	10	3.7	7.7	—	0	—	—
Brazil	3.7	—	3.7	2.4	6.2	7.4	—	0	—	45.8
Chile	14.3	7.1	9.8	7.2	6.4	7.5	—	0	20.2	49.3
Colombia	13.3	13	3.7	5.6	4.9	11.5	—	0	7.7	45.7
Costa Rica	9.5	26.3	71.4	0	—	—	15.8	9.1	30.1	43.8
Cuba	2.6	9.4	0	5.3	—	—	22.8	39.3	14.3	35.4
Dominican Republic	14.3	12.9	28	4.9	0	11.7	—	0	30.7	—
Ecuador	0	7.9	11.1	3.1	—	—	5.6	0	4	11.7
El Salvador	10	8.8	—	11.1	—	—	10.7	13.3	0	14.7
Guatemala	23.1	12.5	—	1.2	—	—	7.5	11.1	11.5	11.7
Honduras	7.7	29.4	11.1	12.7	—	—	7	11.1	11.1	63.5
Mexico	17.6	—	3.2	2.9	11.8	13.8	18.5	19.2	1.5	34.7
Nicaragua	10	10.3	—	9.8	—	—	9	11.1	25	46.2
Panama	16.7	0	22.2	9	—	—	—	22.2	26.3	40.7
Paraguay	9.1	8.3	0	4.9	11.1	2.5	—	0	9	12.8
Peru	13.3	20	—	6.2	6.7	5.6	—	8.3	20.1	17.5
Uruguay	7.7	7.7	0	15.8	6.5	7.1	—	0	16.3	52.8
Venezuela	8.3	0	4.5	6.3	6.1	6.5	—	26.7	30	53

Source: Social Watch, *The Starting Point,* 1996, p. 24, as cited in *Statistical Abstract of Latin America,* Vol. 35 (Los Angeles.: UCLA, 1999).

Table 19. Overview of Latin American Electoral Systems

Country	Presidential System	Legislative System	Governors and Municipalities	General Electoral Information
Argentina	The president is elected for a four-year term with the possibility of one successive term. If none of the candidates receives 45% or more of the votes in the first round of voting, a second round is held.	Bicameral congress. The 257 deputies are elected for four-year terms and may be reelected. Half of the Chamber of Deputies is renewed every two years. The 48 senators are elected according to procedure established in local provincial constitutions. One-third of the Senate is renewed every two years.	Governors and local authorities are elected according to the 25 provincial constitutions.	In December of 1983, Argentina returned to a democracy and since then has had free and fair democratic elections. In April 1994, elections were held to form a constituent assembly. The assembly modified the 1953 constitution with several reforms, including reduction of the president's term—from six to four years, with the possibility of a second term—and the adoption of a second round of voting if no candidate receives 45% in the first round. In addition, the reforms abolished the electoral college system.
Bolivia	Beginning in 1997, the president was elected for a five-year term without the possibility of consecutive reelection. The president may run for office again after one term has passed. If no candidate receives a majority, the Congress	Bicameral congress. The 130 deputies and 27 senators are elected for five-year terms without the possibility of reelection.	Bolivia is divided into departments; there is one *prefecto* (governor) per department. The *prefectos* are elected for five-year terms and have general executive powers. Municipal councils, which in turn elect mayors, are elected	Two successive congresses must pass the same bill in order to reform the constitution. Many reforms to the constitution were passed in August 1994: the voting age was lowered from 21 to 18 years and the terms of office for the president and both houses of

	President	Congress	Subnational	Recent Changes
	chooses the president from among the top three candidates in a secret ballot.		every two years. Mayors are elected for five-year terms.	congress were increased from four to five years. Bolivia is also in a process of decentralization. In April 1994, a "popular participation" law was passed that gave local governments more control over their communities. In December 1995, reforms were passed to give more power to the prefects of the departments.
Brazil	The president is elected for a four-year term without the possibility of reelection. If none of the candidates receives a majority in the first round of voting, a second round is held.	Bicameral congress. The 513 members of the Chamber of Deputies are elected from party lists for four-year terms and may be reelected. When elections are held, all of the 513 seats are up for election at the same time. The 81 senators are elected to serve eight-year terms and may be reelected. Two-thirds of the Senate is renewed at one time and four years later the remaining one-third is renewed. Members of both houses are elected by a system of proportional representation.	All state legislators and governors are elected for four-year terms. Mayors and city council authorities are directly elected for four-year terms.	In 1993, a popular referendum was held to choose among moving to a parliamentary system, returning to monarchy, or keeping the presidential system. A great majority of those people who voted supported the existing presidential system. In 1994, an amendment to the constitution reduced the term of the president from five to four years.

(continued)

Table 19. Overview of Latin American Electoral Systems. *Continued*

Country	Presidential System	Legislative System	Governors and Municipalities	General Electoral Information
Chile	The president is elected for a six-year term with no possibility of reelection. If no candidate receives a majority of the votes, a second round of voting is held.	Bicameral congress. There are 120 members of the Chamber of Deputies. They are elected from party lists for four-year terms and may be reelected. There are 46 members of the Senate. The senators are elected for eight-year terms and may be reelected. Every four years half of the senate seats are renewed. Thirty-eight of the 46 senators are elected and eight are appointed. Of the eight senators who are appointed, three are selected by the armed forces, two by the president, two by the supreme court, and one by the National Security Council. All are appointed for eight-year terms. In addition to the eight senators who are appointed, all former presidents are automatically members of the senate.	Chile is divided into regions with one *intendente* (governor) per region. *Intendentes* are appointed by the president for a six-year term and may be replaced at any time during their tenure. Municipal authorities are directly elected for four-year terms and appoint the mayors.	In October 1988, a plebiscite defeat ended Pinochet's military dictatorship. In July 1989, a referendum approved 64 reforms to the constitution. The measures increased the number of directly elected senators from 26 to 38, reduced the president's term from eight to six years, and prohibited reelection of the president. In November 1991, congress approved constitutional changes to local government that provide for the replacement of centrally appointed local officials with directly elected representatives. Tensions with the military continue, and the executive does not have full power over military affairs. For example, the military is constitutionally subordinate to the president through the defense minister, but the president must have

				approval of the military's National Security Council to remove service chiefs.
Colombia	The president is elected for a four-year term without the possibility of reelection. If none of the candidates receives a majority of votes in the first round of voting, a second round of voting is held.	Bicameral congress. The 161 members of the House of Representatives and the 102 members of the Senate are elected for four-year terms and may not be reelected to consecutive terms.	Governors are elected for four-year terms. Since 1988, mayors have been elected for two-year terms.	In July 1991, the new constitution was approved which granted rights to minorities and introduced many political reforms aimed at decentralizing authority. In May 1994, vice presidential elections were held for the first time. Indigenous peoples have been allotted two seats in the Senate.
Costa Rica	The president is elected for a four-year term without the possibility of reelection. If one candidate receives more than 40% of the vote, no second round voting is held.	Unicameral congress. The 61 members of the National Assembly are elected for four-years and may not be reelected for consecutive terms.	Governors are named by the president for four-year terms. Municipal authorities are elected for four-year terms.	Elections have been regular and democratic in Costa Rica since 1949.
Dominican Republic	The president is elected for a four-year term without the possibility of consecutive reelection. The president may run for office again after one term has passed. If none of the candidates receives a majority of the votes, a second round of voting is held.	Bicameral congress. There are 120 members of the Chamber of Deputies and 30 members of the Senate. All members of congress are elected for four-year terms and may be reelected.	The governors of the 29 provinces are appointed by the president. The *síndico* (mayor) of each province is elected. Both serve four-year terms.	In May 1994, the Dominican Central Electoral Board declared President Balaguer the winner in a contest international observers cited as plagued by "serious problems and irregularities" that may have affected its outcome. PRD opposition

(continued)

Table 19. Overview of Latin American Electoral Systems. *Continued*

Country	Presidential System	Legislative System	Governors and Municipalities	General Electoral Information
				candidate Francisco Peña Gómez officially lost by only 22,000 votes. After lengthy negotiations between parties and candidates. Congress reduced President Balaguer's term to two years and prohibited the consecutive reelection of future presidents.
Ecuador	The president is elected for a four-year term without the possibility of consecutive reelection. The president may run for office again after one term has passed. If no candidate receives a majority, a second round of voting is held.	Unicameral congress. The 82 deputies of the Chamber of National Representatives are elected by a system of proportional representation. There are 12 national deputies elected for four-year terms at the national level and 70 provincial deputies elected for two-year terms at the provincial level. All deputies may be reelected.	Governors are appointed by the president for two-year terms. Municipal authorities are elected for four-year terms.	In May 1996, congressional elections were held and the Social Christian Party won a majority in congress. A party representing the indigenous groups in Ecuador also won six seats. Prior to 1995, two constitutional reforms passed that have influenced the election of the president. The first reform revokes a previous law, which required that candidates for political office must belong to a political party, now allowing independents to run for any office. The second reform

	President	Congress	Local government	Notes
El Salvador	The president is elected for a five-year term without the possibility of consecutive reelection. If none of the candidates receives a majority of the votes, a second round of voting is held.	Unicameral congress. The 84 members of the National Assembly are elected for three-year terms and may be reelected.	At the municipal level, local authorities are elected for three-year terms.	allows the president to run for reelection after one term has passed. In 1994, national and international observers judged the elections as having been generally free, fair, and nonviolent despite some irregularities. The former guerrilla movement FMLN participated as a political party in the elections in alliance with reformist groups and it became the second-largest political group in congress; however, it did poorly in local elections. The National Republican Alliance (ARENA) won a landslide victory.
Guatemala	The president is elected for a four-year term without the possibility of reelection. If none of the candidates receives a majority of the votes, a second round of voting is held.	Unicameral congress. The 80 members of congress are elected by proportional representation. The candidates are elected by a national and a departmental list procedure. Of the 80 candidates in the last election, 16 were elected from the national lists and 64 were elected from the departmental lists. Votes are	Governors are appointed by the president. The duration of their terms is also decided by the president. Mayors are directly elected for terms of four years.	In 1993, former President Jorge Serrano was constitutionally deposed after he attempted to seize full power. As a result of the crisis congress elected Ramiro de León Carpio to be president and finish out Serrano's term. In 1994, the president held congressional elections and presented a referendum of

(continued)

Table 19. Overview of Latin American Electoral Systems. *Continued*

Country	Presidential System	Legislative System	Governors and Municipalities	General Electoral Information
		cast separately for the national and departmental lists.		constitutional changes to the Guatemalan people. The level of voter participation in the referendum was extremely low, but the constitutional reforms were approved. These reforms reduced the president's term from five to four years and the number of deputies in congress from 116 to 80.
Honduras	The president is elected for a four-year term during one round of voting and may not be reelected.	Unicameral congress. The 134 members are elected for four-year terms and may be reelected. Members of congress are elected on a proportional basis, according to votes cast for the presidential candidate of their party.	Governors are appointed for four-year terms. Municipal authorities are elected for four-year terms.	November 1997 marked the fifth consecutive election of a civilian president since 1982, when Honduras returned to civilian rule. In January 1995, the police force came under the direction of the civil government while the technical judicial police (i.e., federal investigative police) came under the direction of the attorney general. In May 1995, an all-volunteer military was put in place that ended forced conscription. In addition to these changes, many judicial changes are also under way.

Mexico

The president is elected for a six-year term and may not be reelected. There is only one round of voting.

Bicameral congress.
The 500 members of the Chamber of Deputies are directly elected for three years; 300 are elected from single-member constituencies and 200 chosen under a system of proportional representation. The majority party will hold no more than 300 seats.

In 1994, a six-year period of transition began that culminated in the formation of a new system for electing senators in the year 2000. This new system guarantees that at least 25% of the seats in the Senate will belong to members of minority parties. In the 2000 elections three senators were elected by direct vote in each state, and a fourth senator was allotted to the majority opposition party within the state.

Governors are elected for six-year terms according to the organization and calendar of each state. The constitution allows for the replacement of governors by reelection during the first two years of their terms and by presidential appointment after that time. Municipal authorities are elected for three-year terms. The mayor of the federal district was elected, not appointed, for the first time in 1997.

Until 2000, the official party, PRI, won every presidential election since 1929. Measures have been taken in Mexico to open up the electoral process to other political parties. In recent years, through the reforms to the Mexican congress in late 1993, as well as the creation of the autonomous Federal Electoral Institute (IFE) to oversee federal elections, opposition parties have steadily expanded their representation in the political system.

The 1994 elections were seen as critical because prior to the election the country was plagued by a series of crises, including the assassination of PRI presidential candidate Luis Donaldo Colosio. For the first time, the Mexican government asked the United Nations to train Mexican electoral monitors.

(continued)

Table 19. Overview of Latin American Electoral Systems. *Continued*

Country	Presidential System	Legislative System	Governors and Municipalities	General Electoral Information
Nicaragua	The president is elected for a five-year term, and may not run for reelection. If none of the candidates receives 45% or more of the vote, a second round of voting will be held.	Unicameral congress. The 92 members of the National Assembly are elected for five-year terms by proportional representation and may be reelected.	The office of governor does not exist in Nicaragua except in the autonomous Atlantic and South Atlantic regions. Municipal authorities are elected for five-year terms.	In March 1994, congress reduced the future terms of the president, members of congress, and mayors from six years to five years. Congress has also prohibited the election of the president's close relatives.
Panama	The president is elected for a five-year term and may not be reelected. There is only one round of voting; the candidate who receives a plurality of the votes becomes president.	Unicameral congress. The 72 members of the National Assembly are elected for five-year terms.	Governors of the nine provinces are named by the president and may be removed at any time. Municipal authorities are also appointed by the president and serve five-year terms.	On May 8, 1994, Ernesto Pérez Balladares of the PRD defeated Mireya Moscoso, widow of former President Armulfo Arias of the Arnulfista Party, and salsa singer Rubén Blades of the Papá Egoró Party. International observers found the elections to be free, fair, and nonviolent. Moscoso was elected in 1999.

Paraguay

The president is elected for a five-year term and may not be reelected. If no candidate receives a majority in the first round of voting, a second round is held.

Bicameral congress. The 80 deputies and 45 senators are elected for five-year terms and may be reelected.

Governors are elected for five-year terms. Municipal authorities are elected for five-year terms.

In February 1989, the overthrow of General Alfredo Stroessner initiated a transition to democracy in Paraguay. The elections of May 1993 were the first free and uncontested elections with an all-civilian slate of candidates since 1928. On June 20, 1992, a new constitution was approved that created the office of the vice president and prohibits the president and vice president from succeeding themselves. The constitution also established an electoral tribunal headed by three ministers of electoral justice who must be confirmed by congress. Municipal authorities are now elected and no longer appointed by the president. All parties reached a decision by consensus to postpone the municipal elections until the end of 1996 in order to give the new electoral tribunal adequate time to prepare for the elections. In April 1996, the commander of the armed

(continued)

Table 19. Overview of Latin American Electoral Systems. *Continued*

Country	Presidential System	Legislative System	Governors and Municipalities	General Electoral Information
				forces, General Lino César Oviedo, attempted an unsuccessful coup d'état. Argentina, Brazil, Uruguay, and the United States responded with strong support for President Wasmosy. In addition, the Paraguayan people protested the general's attempt by supporting the president.
Peru	The president is elected for a five-year term and may be reelected for a consecutive five-year term. If no candidate receives a majority in the first round of voting, a second round is held.	Unicameral congress. The 120 members of Congress are elected for five-year terms and may be reelected.	The office of governor does not exist. The constitution of 1993 dissolved regional government. Peru is organized into departments and its authorities are named by the president. Municipal authorities are elected for a three-year term.	In April 1992, President Fujimori dissolved congress and called for new congressional elections. The new 80-member congress served for two years and drafted a new constitution approved by a nationwide referendum in October 1993 by 52% of voters. The new constitution dissolved regional government and created a larger 120-member unicameral congress. The new constitution also permits the president to run for reelection.

Uruguay	The president is elected by a party list procedure for a five-year term without the possibility of consecutive reelection. The president may run for office again after one term has passed. There is one round of voting in the election.	Bicameral congress. The 99 deputies and 30 senators are elected by a system of proportional representation for five-year terms and may be reelected.	Governors and municipalities are elected for five-year terms.	Since the end of military rule in 1985 three presidents have been elected. In May 1996, the Senate voted on an amendment to the constitution that will change the process of electing the president by including a primary election. This change has not yet been approved.
Venezuela	The president is elected for a six-year term by the people. The executive vice president is appointed by the president. There is no second round of election for president.	Unicameral Chamber of Deputies. The 203 members are elected in this manner: 200 elected by party list vote from multi-seat states, 2 elected by plurality vote from single-seat territories, 5 awarded to realize proportional representation, 5 year term.	Governors and municipal authorities are elected for a three-year term.	Venezuela has a long-standing history of democratic rule, which began in 1958. However, in 1992 there were two coup attempts and in 1993 President Carlos André Pérez was impeached. After Hugo Chávez was elected president in December of 1998, a Constituent Assembly was convened to draft a new constitution which established a unicameral Chamber of Deputies and a 6 year presidential term. Chávez won new election in 2000 and his supporters gained dominance in the Chamber of Deputies.

Sources: Georgetown University and Organization of American States Political Database of the Americas, *http://www.georgetown.edu/pdba/*; Wilfried Derksen, "Elections around the World." *http://www.agora.stm.it/elections/election.htm*

Bibliography

"Adelante! The New Rural Activism in the Americas." *NACLA: Report on the Americas*, XXXIII, no. 5 (March/April 2000).

Asturias, Miguel Angel. *El Señor Presidente*.

Black, Jan Knippers, ed. *Latin America: Its Problems and Its Promise*. 3rd ed. Boulder, CO: Westview, 1998.

Cleary, Edward. *The Struggle for Human Rights in Latin America*. Westport, CT: Praeger, 1997.

Close, David, ed. *Legislatures and the New Democracies in Latin America*. Boulder, CO: Lynne Reinner, 1995.

Dominguez, Jorge. *Democratic Politics in Latin America and the Caribbean*. Baltimore: Johns Hopkins Press, 1998.

Liss, Sheldon. *Marxist Thought in Latin America*. Berkeley: University of California Press, 1984.

Loveman, Brian, and Thomas Davies, eds. *The Politics of Antipolitics: The Military in Latin America*. Wilmington, DE: Scholarly Resources, 1997.

Mainwaring, Scott. *Building Democratic Institutions: Party Systems in Latin America*. Stanford, CA: Stanford University Press, 1995.

Malloy, James, and Mitchell Seligson, eds. *Authoritarians and Democrats: Regime Transition in Latin America*. Pittsburgh, PA: University of Pittsburgh Press, 1987.

McDonald, Ronald, and J. Mark Rubl. *Party Politics and Election in Latin America*. Boulder, CO: Westview Press, 1989.

Peeler, John. *Building Democracy in Latin America*. Boulder, CO: Lynne Reinner, 1998.

Tulchin, Joseph, ed. *The Consolidation of Democracy in Latin America*. Boulder, CO: Lynne Reinner, 1998.

Wiarda, Howard, and Harvey Kline, eds. *Latin American Politics and Development*. Boulder, CO: Westview Press, 1996.

Wynia, Gary. *The Politics of Latin American Development*. 3rd ed. Cambridge, England: Cambridge University Press, 1990.

FILMS AND VIDEOS

Confessing to Laura. Colombia, 1990.
Death of a Bureaucrat. Cuba, 1966.
Death and the Maiden. U.S., 1994.
Evita. U.S., 1997.
Doña Barbara. Mexico, 1943.
Missing. U.S., 1983.
La Paz. Bolivia, 1994.
The Seven Madmen (Los Siete Locos). Argentina, 1973.
State of Siege. U.S., 1982.

NINE

REVOLUTION IN
LATIN AMERICA

The vision of the total transformation of oppressive societal structures that revolution implies has continued to inspire political leaders in Latin America. Indeed, many have argued that only through revolution can long-standing problems such as massive poverty, inequality, and malnutrition be remedied. Thus each new revolutionary attempt at thoroughgoing change has been met with utopian enthusiasm by supportive sociopolitical group-ings: in Mexico from 1910 to 1917, in Guatemala from 1944 to 1954, in Bo-livia from 1952 to 1964, in Cuba from 1959 on, in Nicaragua from 1979 to 1990, and in El Salvador during the revolutionary struggle from 1980 to the peace accords in 1992. Nonetheless, the resort to authoritarian methods and the many internal and external difficulties to achieving such revolutionary visions dampened much of the initial enthusiasm and occasioned many de-fections from the revolution. Yet the vision remains.

To many analysts the defeat of the Sandinistas in the 1990 Nicaraguan elections, coming in the context of the collapse of the Communist party–led governments in Eastern Europe, marked the end of an era of revolution in Latin America that had begun with the triumph of the Cuban Revolution in 1959. Many of the same observers noted the flagging fortunes of the revo-lutionary movements in Guatemala and El Salvador in the early 1990s and predicted the early demise of Fidel Castro's government in Cuba. Others are far less certain that the era of revolution in Latin America has ended. Armed insurgencies continued in countries such as Colombia, Mexico, and Peru. Further, in the cases of El Salvador and Nicaragua the revolutionary move-ments have not been destroyed. The FSLN of Nicaragua and the FMLN of El Salvador are the leading political force in their national legislatures. Such a position is far short of the revolutionary goals that each of them sought, but given the forces that were arrayed against them and the long history of dictatorship and repression in each of the three countries, their current sta-tus is in some ways remarkable.

To understand the current state of revolutionary movements in Latin America, it is necessary to review the development of those movements, tracing the demise of revolution in Latin America to the ascending of political democracy throughout the region and the seeming political dominance of the ideology of free enterprise embodied in the programs of structural adjustment. As the century ended, obituaries written for revolutionary change needed to undergo some revision. The heady days for revolutionaries experienced in the late 1970s are clearly not in evidence at the present time, but some of the obituaries of revolution may have been premature. Contrary to expectation, the Cuban Communist Party has not been driven from power, nor have the principles of socialism been renounced. Yet at the beginning of the twenty-first century the Cuban system was being transformed with significant concessions to the principles of a market economy, yet the island remained an inspiration to those political forces in Latin America that have sought to put forward an alternative politics to the neoliberal dominance.

On January 1, 1994, the world witnessed the emergence of a new revolutionary force when the armed guerrillas of the Zapatista National Liberation Front (EZLN) seized several towns in the southern Mexican state of Chiapas. They condemned NAFTA, which went into effect that day, and the "dictatorial" Mexican government that had negotiated the agreement with the United States. Seven years later the Zapatista movement, despite significant government repression, remained an armed political force in the country. The EZLN also represented a new face of revolution in Latin America. The movement has not stated openly socialist goals, nor has it projected the total overthrow of the Mexican state. Rather, the Zapatistas have been a voice for the indigenous people of Chiapas and have called for the radical reform of the Mexican political system.

New and renewed revolutionary struggles have not been limited to the survival of the socialist government of Cuba or the appearance of the EZLN. In December 1996 the Tupac Amaru rebel movement in Peru seized and held the Japanese ambassador's residence in Lima for several months. The occupation ended in disaster for the rebels when the Peruvian government stormed the building and killed all of the rebel force. Yet this action rekindled the prospect for revolutionary change in Peru soon after the Fujimori government had seemingly extinguished the revolutionary flame with the virtual defeat of the Shining Path guerrillas following the 1992 capture of their leader Abimael Guzmán.

As the 1990s ended the most significant revolutionary challenge seemed to be developing in Colombia, where a low-level civil war has percolated for almost forty years. Several armed groups headed by the FARC became increasingly bold in challenging the Colombian government, which was weakened by scandal and its inability to solve the country's basic economic and social problems. By linking up in some instances with the revenue-producing coca industry, the guerrillas were able to sustain themselves when other revolutionary movements had been marginalized. Finally, it should be noted that the revolutionary movements that dominated the 1980s, the FSLN of Nicaragua, the FMLN in Salvador, and the Guatemalan National Revolutionary Union (URNG) of Guatemala, have emerged in the renewed political democracies of their countries as significant political forces.

Marxism

Any discussion of the role of revolution in Latin American history must focus in significant measure on the ideas of Karl Marx and those political practitioners who acted on his ideas. Marxism in Latin America did not just begin with Fidel Castro or the guerrilla movements of the 1960s. It has its own long and fertile tradition that dates back well over 125 years. José Martí, the apostle of Cuban independence, read and was influenced by Karl Marx long before the turn of the century. In his "On the Death of Karl Marx" Martí observed that Marx was not only a "titanic mover of the anger of European workers, but a profound observer of the reason for human misery and destiny and a man consumed by the desire to do good." Given the immense poverty and sharp class divisions that have marked Latin American history, it is little wonder that Marxism has excited so much interest and generated so much intellectual and political upheaval for the better part of the last hundred and twenty-five years. Marxism was not the first revolutionary ideology to appear on the scene. That role was played by democratic ideals in the nineteenth century, which were adopted by progressive Latin Americans to try to change their harsh reality. However, the liberation of the continent from Spanish rule and the institution of nominal democracy did not transform the grim socioeconomic reality. In a cogent analysis of the failure of the bourgeois-democratic revolutions to produce social justice in the Latin American context, Marx observed that the aristocratic class origins of the independence movement leaders would make it very hard indeed for them to actually empower the poverty-stricken masses of Latin America.

Even before Martí wrote of Marx's death in 1883, Marxism had already begun to shape the way Latin Americans viewed their world. During the 1860s a small number of Argentine intellectuals became aware of the ideas of the First Workingman's International, for which Marx wrote the declaration of principles. These Argentine intellectuals spread Marx's ideas to Chile, Cuba, and Mexico. European immigrants exposed to the Paris Commune, working-class movements in Italy, and the Spanish antimonarchy struggles brought with them a knowledge of both anarchist and socialist ideas. In the early 1870s sections of the First International were established in both Argentina and Uruguay. However, in this period radical ideas remained marginalized. This changed in the 1890s with a greater influx of European immigrants, who came to provide a labor base for the new industries and carried with them radical ideas. Dominant among them were anarcho-syndicalists, who looked to improve the workers' economic situation and advocated strikes to achieve the abolition of capitalism. These socialist-oriented workers organized, ran candidates for public office, and argued for welfare programs and social insurance legislation. In the process they laid the foundations for the political and economic struggles of the twentieth century. Between 1900 and 1910 European-inspired socialism gained adherents in the region with particular strength among workers in Brazil, Chile, Colombia, Cuba, Mexico, and Uruguay. The Socialist parties focused on the eight-hour working day, safer working conditions, the right to strike, and universal free education.

The October 1917 Russian revolution renewed interest in Marxism among Latin American thinkers and workers. In countries where Socialist parties were strong, intellectuals and workers expressed support for the successful Russian revolution. By 1919 Lenin's writings were translated and circulated throughout Latin America. After World War I Latin American thinkers began to utilize Marx and Lenin to analyze the region's problems as based on U.S. and British domination of basic economic sectors. The Communist International, formed in Moscow in 1919, actively promoted world revolution and by 1922 Communist parties existed in Argentina, Bolivia, Brazil, Chile, Mexico, and Uruguay. Marxist thought in Latin America became divided between Marxism-Leninism (communism) and socialism, associated with more reform-oriented parties. While most Communist party leaders took their cue from Moscow, those like Peruvian José Carlos Mariátegui resisted outside directives from Moscow and insisted on constructing a truly Latin American Marxism that was not "copy or imitation of any other." Marxism in Latin America was to be developed in the national and regional context, and thus fit local conditions, not those of the Soviet Union. But such independent interpretations did not win out against the centralization of Marxist thinking and planning in the Soviet Union. After 1928, the Communist International, like the Soviet Union itself, soon came under the control of Joseph Stalin and the bureaucratic, unimaginative dogmatism that he represented. Indeed, representatives of the Communist International rejected most of the original formulations that Mariátegui and the representatives of the Peruvian Socialist Party set forth at the first meeting of Latin American Communist Parties in Buenos Aires in 1929. This trend, which continued over the better part of the next three decades through the Communist International, Comintern, and Cominform, worked against the creation of national Marxist movements as had occurred in Russia itself and that later developed in China and Vietnam.

Marxism was generally dominated by the official Communist party in each country, which was in turn closely tied to Moscow and heavily influenced by it. This often facilitated the rise of less original, more bureaucratic party leaders whose prime aim was to follow the current line and purify the party of any elements who might have been contaminated by alternative ideas. Independent analysis and creative praxis were not at a premium. Victor Codovilla, the long-time Secretary General of the Argentine Communist Party, was perhaps the most significant example of such leadership. It is little wonder that the party in that country was never large, or that it was Peronism and not Marxism that captured the imagination of the Argentine masses and even dominated the General Workers' Confederation. There were, however, a few significant party leaders, such as Faribundo Martí, who was captured and executed in early 1932 when he helped lead a popular uprising in his native El Salvador. And in Chile, socialists and communists managed to develop a more successful appeal to the masses and even founded a short-lived Socialist Republic in 1933.

As the century progressed, Marxism became increasingly popular among Latin American intellectuals, who found that it offered a cogent explanation for the poverty, outside domination, and oligarchic rule that bedeviled the region. After Russian revolutionary Leon Trotsky founded the Fourth International and moved to Mexico in the 1930s, there were small groups of his followers in many countries in the region. Although many of them also came under the influence of rigid thinking, Trotskyist ideas did provide an alternative Marxist viewpoint and allowed many independent Marxist intellectuals in the region another vision of Marxism on which to base their interpretations.

Although Trotskyists and disciples of the Peruvian Mariátegui worked hard to counter the increasingly reformist and nonrevolutionary ideas coming from Moscow, their efforts were largely unsuccessful. Thus those thinkers and activists who favored the development of original, autonomous Marxism were usually criticized, marginalized, or driven from the official parties altogether. As a result, from the 1920s until the 1960s communist movements became well established throughout Latin America and often had political influence in certain circles, especially among urban industrial workers and intellectuals, but they did not develop into a revolutionary force. One reason this nonrevolutionary trend developed was because the Moscow-oriented Communist parties almost universally marginalized the role of the peasantry in favor of the classical role of the proletariat, which often represented no more than a few percent of the population. As a result, prior to the Cuban revolution there were no important Marxist-inspired peasant movements in Latin America.

Cuba

Cuba's revolution, under the leadership of Fidel Castro and the 26th of July movement (discussed in more detail in Chapter 12), was a watershed event in Latin American revolutionary history. Following the cancellation of the scheduled 1952 national elections by Fulgencio Batista, Fidel Castro and several dozen followers organized an attack on an army barracks in Santiago, hoping to incite a nationwide uprising against the dictatorship. That attack failed, but three years later it led to the formation of the movement, named for the date of the 1953 failed attack. Drawing in part on the earlier experiences of Augusto César Sandino in Nicaragua in the late 1920s, the Cuban revolutionary movement based itself in the isolated mountains of eastern Cuba and sought to build a revolutionary army from the ranks of the local peasants. Given the history of rebellion of that region, the tactics proved successful as the rebel army flourished and eventually engaged in several successful battles against the conscript army of the dictator Batista. Aided by other revolutionary actions in Cuba's cities and the flagging support for Batista both domestically and internationally, the 26th of July Movement succeeded in taking power on January 1, 1959. In the ensuing months the revolutionary government, with the support of mass mobilizations of workers and peasants, transformed Cuban society. The economy was placed largely in the hands of the state, and by 1961 Fidel Castro had committed Cuba to the socialist path of development, the first country in the Western Hemisphere to do so. Given the popularity of Fidel Castro and the other Cuban rebels, it is not surprising that there was soon a proliferation of self-declared Marxist guerrilla groups through much of Latin America. This proliferation of the Fidelista theory of revolution through armed struggle (*foquismo*) marked what Regis Debray termed the revolution in the revolution (a revolution in the Marxist theory of revolution in Latin America).

Although the subsequent wave of guerrilla activity in the region and the virtual canonization of Ché Guevara helped free Latin American revolutionary thought from the dogmatic, static orientation that had come to characterize it during Stalin's rule, the unyielding emphasis on armed struggle effectively foreclosed a broader examination of the doctrine and the search for more effective ways to mobilize the masses. This new vision of revolution effectively challenged the now bureaucraticized orthodox Communist parties, but it did not produce any successful guerrilla movements in the 1960s or well into the 1970s. It did, however, spawn a series of urban and rural guerrilla movements across Latin America and also generated a great deal of literature by and about these new Marxist revolutionaries. The introduction of Maoism and Chinese-oriented Communist parties in countries such as Colombia and Brazil further stimulated the development of new forms of radical Marxism. However, the subsequent growth in Marxist parties and movements also provided an excellent rationale for the creation and implementation of the U.S.-inspired national security doctrine, counterinsurgency training, and its concomitant strong anti-communism. The U.S.-inspired counterinsurgency defeated most of the original guerrilla movements by the early 1970s. Most significantly, Ché Guevara was killed in Bolivia by U.S.-trained soldiers while fighting with a Bolivian revolutionary group. Guerrilla groups did, however, manage to struggle on in Guatemala, Colombia, and Nicaragua.

By 1970, several innovative approaches to Marxist thought were emerging. In Peru, Hugo Blanco was breathing new life into the Trotskyist movement through his work with the highland peasants. In Chile, socialists and communists were contemplating the realization of a peaceful revolution under the leadership of constitutionally elected socialist president, Salvador Allende. The far left Movement of the Revolutionary Left (MIR) did, however, argue that rightist forces would never allow such a transition. In Argentina, leftist theorists began to apply and adapt the theory to their own specific reality. A radical brand of Marxist-inspired Peronism (or Peronist-inspired Marxism) ensued and eventually led to a Marxist faction within Peronism (Juventud Peronista) and the formation of the radical Peronist Montonero guerrilla group. The Montoneros and the Revolutionary Army of the People (ERP) eventually confronted Argentina's military government in an intense struggle. In Uruguay, the Robin Hood–like Tupamaros hoped to foment a popular revolution. Although gains were made toward less dogmatic interpretations and in political education, the lingering emphasis on armed struggle over political education or organization eventually led to intense conflict and violent repression, which the left was ultimately unable to resist. Revolutionary and socialist movements were profoundly affected by the results of Allende's Popular Unity socialist experiment in Chile. Allende sought to make radical changes in Chilean society (land reform, wealth redistribution, increased political participation) within the parliamentary process. Some progress was made during the three years he was in power (1970–1973), but the reformist socialist experiment was largely thwarted by Allende's lack of majority control of the legislature. The entrenched power and opposition by the country's elites, together with international isolation engineered by a hostile U.S. government, disrupted the country's economy and set the stage for a military coup. Allende's rule came to a bloody end in September 1973 when the Chilean military stormed the presidential palace and killed Allende and thousands of his supporters. A military government under General Augusto Pinochet was established and held power for seventeen years. The primary impact of the Chilean events was to convince most of the Latin American left that reform-oriented efforts at achieving socialism were fruitless. These views were also bolstered by the 1973 military coup in Uruguay and the subsequent coup in Argentina in 1976. By 1976 military rule had become the norm throughout the region, and the combination of dictatorial rule and unsolved social and economic problems spawned a series of revolutionary upsurges that were strongest in Nicaragua, El Salvador, Colombia, and Peru. Each had its own characteristics and should be viewed individually, although there were many similarities.

Nicaragua

Nicaragua's leading revolutionary movement, the FSLN, was formed in 1961 and was directly inspired by the success of the Cuban revolution. Its early leaders Carlos Fonseca and Tomás Borge abandoned the reformist-oriented Nicaraguan Socialist Party (PSN) to form the FSLN. With direct Cuban assistance, the FSLN sought to replicate the Cuban experience and also that of their namesake, Augusto Sandino, by establishing a guerrilla army in the mountains of northern Nicaragua that could eventually challenge the power of the dictator Anastasio Somoza. Another element crucial to the revolutionary philosophy of the FSLN was its emphasis on will and the belief that to some degree revolution could be improvised. They turned to the writings of Sandino, Mariátegui, and Italian Antonio Gramsci to craft a philosophy based on revolutionary action, the importance of the subjective factor in making revolution, and the role of ideology in motivating the masses.

In its early stages the FSLN consisted of just twelve people, including Colonel Santos López, a veteran of Sandino's earlier struggle. Fonseca fought successfully for the inclusion of Sandino's name in the organizational label, but the lack of unanimity on this shows that a variety of revolutionary influences were at work in the early 1960s. Led by Fonseca the small group studied Sandino's writings and tactics as they prepared for their first guerrilla campaigns in 1963. Those campaigns, like many other similar ones in Latin America at the time, were a failure. The new Sandinistas had failed to do what their namesake had done so well—mobilize the local populace on the side of the guerrillas through well-planned political and organizational activities coordinated with and part of the armed struggle. Over the ensuing years the FSLN managed to survive by realizing its mistakes and broadening its political work to include neighborhood organizing in the poorest barrios of the capital, Managua. However, the National Guard of the Somoza dictatorship was a powerful force, and it exacted many defeats on the Sandinistas during the 1960s. The Sandinistas survived and slowly built their organization, especially by reaching out to progressive forces in the Catholic Church who had been inspired by liberation theology. The FSLN was the first revolutionary organization in Latin America to welcome Christians within its ranks, a position that would bear considerable fruit in the late 1970s.

Between 1967 and 1974 the FSLN carried on what it termed "accumulation of forces" in silence, largely recruiting members in ones and twos and carrying out few armed actions. The silence was broken in a spectacular way with the December 1974 seizure of the home of a wealthy Somoza supporter. An FSLN commando unit held more than a dozen foreign diplomats and top Nicaraguan government officials for several days, finally forcing Somoza to release key Sandinista political prisoners, pay a large sum of money, and broadcast and publish FSLN communiques. This dramatic act reinserted the FSLN into the political scene at an important time. Popular sentiment against the dictatorship had been growing since it had greedily profited from the devastating 1972 earthquake that had further impoverished more Nicaraguans. However, even as the FSLN reemerged its own divisions had become clear. By 1975 the organization had split into three tendencies on the basis of tactical differences. The Prolonged People's War group was basically Maoist in orientation. Their strategy and concrete work emphasized rural guerrilla warfare. Relatively isolated in the countryside, they were probably the slowest to realize that a revolutionary situation was developing in the country. The Proletarian tendency based itself in large measure on dependency theory and the traditional Marxist emphasis on the industrial working class. This tendency saw the Nicaraguan revolution as unfolding along more traditional lines as a confrontation between the bourgeoisie and the proletariat. Nicaragua's urban working class, small as it was, was seen as the main motor force of the coming revolution. Political work in the cities was emphasized, and this group also built a base among students. The Insurrectionalist, or Tercerista, tendency was the last to emerge. In reality it did not represent an entirely new approach; rather, it served primarily as a mediator between the two existing tendencies. The Terceristas (or third force) did not draw a sharp distinction between a rural and urban emphasis, seeing the need for action in both arenas. Its main and most controversial contribution was its alliance strategy. While not the first group in the FSLN to propose such an orientation, they were the first in the era of Somoza's decline to place it at the center of political work. There was also ample historic precedent for it in the strategy of both Sandino and the 26th of July movement in Cuba. Both earlier movements incorporated heterogeneous elements while maintaining a revolutionary position. The Insurrectionalists believed strongly that it was necessary to mobilize a broad-based coalition to overthrow the dictatorship while still maintaining the organizational integrity of the FSLN.

The separation into tendencies did not mean the disintegration of the FSLN. Each current pursued their political work in their own sector and as the crisis of the dictatorship deepened all achieved successes. Efforts by the leaders to reestablish unity did not cease, although they were hampered by the imprisonment of key figures such as Borge and the death of Fonseca in combat in November 1976. The three tendencies finally began to converge in the upsurge of mass anti-dictatorship activity in late 1977 and early 1978 in the wake of the death of popular opposition newspaper editor, Pedro Joaquin Chamorro. In 1978 the three tendencies collaborated to establish the National Patriotic Front (FPN), which created an anti-Somoza front encompassing trade unions, the Moscow-oriented Nicaraguan Socialist Party, student groups, and some small middle-class parties like the Popular Social Christians—all under FSLN hegemony.

In September 1978 the FSLN, led by the Terceristas, carried out an insurrection, which while not successful laid the groundwork for the dictatorship's defeat. Drawing on the lessons learned from the September 1978 action and with the organization formally reunited in March 1979, the FSLN launched its final offensive in the late spring of 1979. Somoza's National Guard fought hard to defend the dictator, who desperately ordered the bombing of Sandinista strongholds in the cities, but in July 1979 Somoza fled the country and the FSLN assumed power at the head of a provisional revolutionary government. The success of the Sandinistas in defeating the dictatorship and embarking on the fundamental restructuring of Nicaraguan society was a watershed event for Latin America, a second potential socialist revolution. As described in detail in Chapter 13, the Nicaraguan revolution has not fulfilled its promises, but that did not change the significance of the events that unfolded at the end of the 1970s in one of the region's poorest countries.

El Salvador

Nicaragua was not the only Central American nation convulsed by revolution in the 1970s and 1980s. Neighboring El Salvador witnessed a bloody confrontation between the military and that revolution that cost 75,000 lives between 1975 and 1992 and sent more than 500,000 Salvadorans into exile in the United States. The revolutionary period ended with a United Nations–brokered peace agreement that rewarded the revolutionary coalition, the FMLN, with a prominent role in Salvadoran politics as the country's primary political opposition group. The Salvadoran military, while still a major political force, stepped down from the controlling position that it had held for more than half a century.

It is not surprising that revolutionary forces came to the fore in El Salvador, for no Latin American country better fit the profile for revolutionary change. The events of the 1970s and 1980s followed directly from dramatic confrontations of the early 1930s and the fifty years of direct military rule that followed. By 1932 Salvador was the most class-polarized society in the region. In the latter part of the nineteenth century El Salvador had become one of the world's largest coffee producers, meeting the ever-growing European demand with the development of ever-larger coffee plantations dominated by a few wealthy families. The coffee boom enriched a series of oligarchic families who came to dominate Salvadoran society while it further reduced the peasant population to seasonal labor and marginal lands. From 1907 to 1931 political power rested in the hands of a single family, the Meléndez clan. The peasantry who were driven off their communal lands during the latter half of nineteenth century did not accept their fate passively and engaged in several uprisings, both armed and unarmed, from 1870 onward. The conflict between the ruling oligarchy, made up of coffee farmers, foreign investors, military officers, Church leaders, and landless peasants came to a head in 1930–1932. The Great Depression had further impoverished both the remaining small farmers and the plantation laborers as the price of coffee fell precipitously. The possibility of revolution developed very quickly. In 1930, a May Day demonstration in San Salvador against deteriorating economic conditions drew 80,000. Liberal reformer Arturo Araujo won the presidential election in 1931 with the support of students, workers, and peasants. The new government attempted to broaden the political spectrum by announcing that it would permit the newly formed Communist party, under the leadership of Farabundo Martí, to participate in the 1931 municipal elections. However, the military under the leadership of Maximiliano Hernández Martínez seized power in December 1931, and the following month Martí led a premature, mostly peasant rebellion that succeeded in murdering a few landlords and seizing control of some small towns, primarily in the northwestern part of the country.

The response of General Hernández to the uprising was swift and brutal. Known ever since as La Matanza (The Massacre) the joint actions of the military and oligarchy killed between 30,000 and 60,000 people, a huge toll in a nation of only 1.4 million. The repression was both selective and widespread. Using voter rolls the military hunted down and killed virtually everyone affiliated to the Communist party, including Martí. At the time the military's actions took on the character of a race war, as indigenous people were also singled out for attack.

La Matanza did not end resistance to the rule of the oligarchy, but it reduced it significantly for the next forty years. A series of military leaders ruled the country into the 1960s without even the façade of democracy. In that decade a reformist challenge to the military did develop under the leadership of the Christian Democratic Party and José Napoleon Duarte. Duarte, educated in the United States and the spirit of the Kennedy's Alliance for Progress, developed a strong following among intellectuals, students, and a growing middle sector. Duarte's reformist challenge ended with a probable victory in the 1972 presidential elections, but the military voided the results and continued in power. Duarte and other Christian Democratic leaders went into exile, but other more radical leaders saw the military's actions as proof that the reformist path was not viable in El Salvador. This view was reinforced by the fact that the U.S. government did not intervene, even to promote their seeming prototype for a centrist reformer like Duarte against the Salvadoran generals. As guerrilla groups began to form in the rural areas of the country, other factors also promoted revolutionary prospects. By 1975 about 40 percent of the peasants had no land at all, compared to only 12 percent in 1960. The other surprising force for revolutionary change that developed in the latter half of the 1970s was the Roman Catholic Church. The combination of the reform-oriented ideas of the 1968 Medellín Conference of Latin American Bishops and the repression of the Salvadoran military against the Church itself propelled the clergy and its followers into a central role in the political opposition to the military. The leader of the Salvadoran Church, Archbishop Oscar Romero, was a conservative at the time of his leadership appointment, but the death of a close friend at the hands of the military, combined with the growing polarization in the country, led him to the unusual position of supporting the right of armed rebellion. In response, the military assassinated Archbishop Romero in 1980 in the midst of growing civil and revolutionary resistance to the military regime.

In 1980 most of the revolutionary guerrilla groups that had begun armed activities in the 1970s came together to form the FMLN. The two primary organizations in the FMLN were the ERP and the Armed Forces of Liberation (FAL). The ERP was founded in 1971 by Marxist and Christian forces that were motivated by the *foco theory* of revolution inspired by Ché Guevara. The FAL was the armed wing of the outlawed Communist party that developed into a significant force only in the late 1970s. The primary significance of the FAL was that it is one of the few cases where a reformist-oriented Communist party opted to participate in an armed struggle. Also important in the revolutionary equation was the Democratic Revolutionary Front (FDR), an umbrella alliance also founded in 1980 that encompassed all major popular organizations, labor groups, and community groups. From the beginning it served as the political arm of the FMLN and after 1982 was recognized internationally as a legitimate political force. The heart of the FDR was the People's Revolutionary Bloc (BPR), the largest of the popular organizations. It was formed in 1975 by diverse organizations of shantytown dwellers, workers, students, teachers, and practitioners of liberation theology. By the late 1970s, despite the severe repression of the military, the organizations of the BPR had succeeded in many places in the country in establishing alternative governing bodies.

Following the decisive triumph of the Sandinista revolutionaries in the summer of 1979, the possibility of revolution in El Salvador seemed very real. Popular mobilizations spread throughout the country. Factories were occupied in San Salvador, and 1980 was declared to be the "year of the liberation." Fearing a repetition of the Nicaraguan revolution, a section of the Salvadoran elites and the government of the United States carried off a military coup designed to forestall the revolutionary process by appearing to instigate significant reform. On October 15, 1979, a new military junta took power promising reform. The new government even encompassed figures from the Left, including Social Democrat Guillermo Ungo and a minister of labor from the small Communist party. The new junta promised to reform the security forces, institute land reform, and recognize trade unions. However, the political practice of the new government was far different from its rhetoric. Within a week of taking power the government security forces broke up strikes, occupied rebellious towns, and killed more than 100 people. In January 1980, Ungo and the entire civilian cabinet quit their posts, acknowledging that the military was already making all key political and security decisions. Three weeks later the military opened fire on a massive demonstration of 150,000. In March Romero was assassinated, and the military attacked his funeral procession of 80,000. Thirty people were killed. By March 1980 it was clear to most political activists in El Salvador that open legal political activity in opposition to the military was impossible. Many political moderates, including a sizeable part of the Christian Democrats, joined with the revolutionary left. This movement soon coalesced into the FDR and FMLN. Christian Democratic Duarte assumed leadership of the junta, claiming to be in the political center between left- and right-wing forces. In reality Duarte was a figurehead who ruled on behalf of the traditional elites.

In January 1981, on the eve of President Reagan's inauguration, the FMLN launched an insurrection that was intended to take power. However, the Salvadoran military with significant resupply by the United States defeated the offensive and set the stage for a protracted armed conflict. The FMLN had hoped to gain victory before the Reagan administration took office. It gambled that the Carter administration would not resume aid to the Salvadoran government, which had been suspended one month earlier in the wake of the killing of four North American churchwomen by Salvadoran security forces. However, the FMLN's judgment proved to be wrong. Citing proof of Nicaraguan Sandinista support for FMLN rebels on January 17, 1981, President Carter authorized the shipment of $5 million of military equipment and twenty additional U.S. military personnel. Three months later, the U.S. Ambassador in El Salvador at the time of the shipments, Robert White, revealed that there was no real evidence of Nicaraguan involvement, but the shipment announcement had served its purpose. The Salvadoran military had been reassured that despite obvious human rights violations even against U.S. citizens, the government of the United States was fully committed to preventing a victory by the Salvadoran revolutionaries. There was not going to be another Nicaragua in Central America.

The civil war continued for ten more years. The FMLN showed considerable resilience in the face of a concerted effort by the Salvadoran army and its U.S. backers to eliminate the guerrilla challenge. At the high point of assistance in the late 1980s, El Salvador was receiving close to $1 billion per year in U.S. aid, ranking behind only Israel and Egypt. Total U.S. aid during this period exceeded $5 billion. The FMLN was a substantial force with several thousand soldiers in arms. They controlled more than one-third of the Salvadoran territory and carried out regular attacks in all but two of the country's fourteen provinces. However, throughout the 1980s the Salvadoran revolutionaries faced the dilemma that even if they could mount an insurrection that challenged the hold of the Salvadoran military, they faced the prospect of a massive U.S. intervention that would deny them the victory that they sought. As a result, from about 1982 onward the FMLN argued that the only solution to the civil war would be a negotiated settlement. Sporadic negotiations did occur throughout the 1980s, but the political situation both inside and outside of El Salvador prevented a successful conclusion. To ensure continued support from a reluctant U.S. Congress, the Reagan administration pressed the Salvadorans to hold elections, even though it was clear that they could not be fully democratic in the context of the civil war. There was little freedom of the press and no candidates of the left could participate without risking assassination by right-wing "death squads." With significant American backing Christian Democrat Duarte won the 1982 presidential election but was largely a figurehead. Throughout the 1980s, real political power lay with the Supreme Army Council and Roberto D'Aubuisson's ultra-right National Republican Alliance (ARENA), which controlled the Salvadoran legislation. Duarte was allowed by the military to remain in power as long as he permitted them free reign against the FMLN. Obviously such an arrangement did not allow for any real dialogue or hope for a settlement between Duarte and the FMLN. In 1989, with Duarte dying of cancer and the Christian Democratic Party deeply divided, ARENA candidate Alfredo Christiani won the presidency, further entrenching the hold of the far right on Salvadoran politics. The new ARENA government vowed a rapid campaign to defeat the FMLN, but the latter responded in the fall of 1989 with a significant military offensive that reached all the way into the capital. These events served to underscore the fact that after a decade of fighting, the civil war was a stalemate with no end in sight.

However, regional and international events intervened to bring about a negotiated settlement within two years. The electoral defeat of the FSLN in Nicaragua in 1990 and the rapid changes in the Soviet Union and Eastern Europe between 1989 and 1991 weakened the position of the FMLN but also put pressure on the U.S. government and its Salvadoran allies to come to the bargaining table. Under United Nations auspices, brokered settlements moved forward in Cambodia, Angola, Mozambique, and Namibia, placing

additional pressure on Central America. In 1990–1991 the FMLN made several concessions toward peace that went largely unreciprocated. In the March
1991 national legislative elections the FMLN and its sympathizers fielded
candidates. Despite significant pressure against the left and intimidation of
voters, the left managed to win eight seats and ARENA was denied majority control. In November 1991 the FMLN declared a unilateral cease fire that
was to last until a peace agreement was signed. In January 1992, under
mounting international pressure, the ARENA government signed an agreement with the FMLN. The agreement called for the removal of more than
100 military officers implicated in human rights violations during the civil
war. The army was to be reduced by 50 percent, the National Intelligence
Directorate dismantled, a new police force created to include members of
the FMLN, 1980 agrarian reform completed, democratic elections held, and
the FMLN disarmed in exchange for land and resettlement compensation
for its troops and the right to become a political party.

This agreement was clearly far short of the thoroughgoing social revolution that the FMLN had committed to a decade earlier, but it did represent
a partial victory for the revolutionaries and a setback for Salvador's traditional oligarchy. Since the signing of the agreement, El Salvador has remained a contradictory nation. The traditional oligarchy has worked hard
to undermine the agreement. The Christiani government was reluctant to
purge high-ranking military officers and to disarm the notorious army and
police units. In March 1993 a U.N.-appointed Truth Commission named
sixty-two Salvadoran officers responsible for the worst massacres, tortures,
and murders of the twelve-year war. It called for the immediate dismissal
of forty of them. The U.S. Army School of the Americas had trained forty-
seven of them. It eventually did so, but only after the pressure from a united
opposition within El Salvador and a temporary suspension of aid by the
Clinton administration in 1993.

Elections held under the aegis of the accords, especially the first one in
1994, were marked by significant fraud emanating from the government and
periodic armed attacks against candidates and supporters of the left. The
Christiani government used its control of the Supreme Electoral Tribunal to
prevent opposition voters from registering. Especially in the 1994 elections
this fraud definitely denied the FMLN several seats in the National Assembly and control of the local government in several cities. Despite these obstacles the FMLN succeeded in creating political space for the left that was
unprecedented in Salvadoran history. In the March 1997 national and municipal elections the FMLN fared quite well. They won the mayoralty of San
Salvador—the most important political office after the presidency—as well
as other key departmental municipalities. Of the country's 262 municipalities the FMLN governed fifty-three, covering 45 percent of the population.
On the congressional front, the FMLN won twenty-seven out of eighty-four
seats, just one fewer than ARENA, which was forced into a government
coalition with other conservative parties. The FMLN achieved its success in
local elections based on its work in the fourteen municipalities it controlled

from the 1994 elections and the role it has played in the national legislature as an opponent of the government's unpopular economic policies. In 2001, the FMLN was well on its way to completing its transformations from revolutionary army to an effective political party.

Guatemala

The discussion of revolution in Guatemala must encompass a long period of time and does not involve transcendent events like the Cuban Revolution of 1959 or the Sandinista Revolution of 1979. The high point of revolutionary forces in Guatemala may well have been in 1944, when an armed uprising succeeded in driving the long-time dictator Jorge Ubico (1931–1944) from power. The movement against Ubico began with a student strike and escalated into a general strike that forced Ubico's resignation in June 1944. However, the resignation was a front for the continuation of Ubico's system, and it soon led to an armed rebellion of students, workers, and dissident army officers. The rebel movement won an easy victory and set up a junta government known as the October Revolution. The rebellion paved the way for elections that brought Juan José Arévelo to power in 1945. Once in power the Arévelo government pursued a reformist strategy rather than a revolutionary one. There was unprecedented government spending on schools, hospitals, and housing, and workers were allowed to unionize and engage in collective bargaining. However, rural Guatemala, which held 90 percent of the country's population, was largely untouched by the reforms. Arévelo was followed in office by Jácobo Arbenz, who deepened his predecessor's reform program but still maintained Guatemala fully within the framework of capitalism. In fact, in 1950 Arbenz declared that his primary intent was to make Guatemala "a modern capitalist country." His primary extension of Arévelo's reforms was to carry them to the rural sector by inaugurating a modest land reform that challenged the most blatant policies of the U.S.-owned United Fruit Company. Arbenz also legalized the Communist party, a reform-oriented organization with significant influence among the unionized workers. These reforms, although modest in character, were too much for the country's oligarchy and the government of the United States. In 1954 Arbenz was removed from power in a military coup strongly backed by the United States through the actions of the CIA. The newly installed government of Castillo Armas cracked down hard on anyone suspected of revolutionary activity. This witch hunt succeeded in setting back the possibility of a Guatemalan revolution by many years. The military coup ushered in a 30,000-strong armed forces that brutally repressed any opposition political movements over the ensuing forty years. Peaceful forms of protest were routinely outlawed, and rural villages were often attacked by army patrols seeking to capture "subversives."

The revival of an armed resistance to the Guatemalan military began with the November 1960 revolt of army officers against President Fuentes. The revolt was crushed when the United States sent Cuban exiles being trained for the ill-fated Bay of Pigs invasion. However, several rebel leaders escaped and established low-grade guerrilla warfare against the regime. One of the guerrillas' first leaders was Marco Antonio Yon Sosa, originally trained by the United States. Yon Sosa was killed in combat, but guerrillas who survived helped form the Guerrilla Army of the Poor (EGP) in 1972. Inspired by liberation theology, they built a base among the highland Indians, the first revolutionary movement to do so. By 1980 the EGP and other smaller groups had more than 5000 members. The growing strength of the rebel movement alarmed the Guatemalan oligarchy, and fierce repression was unleashed against the rural areas in the early 1980s. The military's strategy was to destroy the guerrillas' base of operations by terrorizing the civilian population.

During General Romero Lucas Garcia's rule (1978–1982) there were numerous massacres. With financial support from the U.S. government, the military evacuated Indians from the northern highland guerrilla strongholds in Quiche and Huehuetenango departments and organized them in "model villages," a strategy developed by the United States in Vietnam. The military offered the local population a stark choice: Work with us and be housed and fed, or die. In 1982 Lucas García was replaced in a coup by General Efraín Ríos Montt, a "born-again" Christian. Montt declared a state of siege and dramatically increased the level of repression. On July 6, 1982, more than 300 Indian residents of Finca San Francisco in Huehuetenango were massacred outside of their local church. Between 1981 and 1983 it is estimated that 100,000 Indians in 440 villages lost their lives at the hands of government forces. More than 1 million people were displaced from their homes. The repression resulted in the growth of the revolutionary movement. In 1982 the four main guerrilla groups, headed by EGP, united to form the Guatemalan National Revolutionary Union (URNG). With stepped-up covert U.S. assistance, the Guatemalan military escalated its war against the guerrillas. Newer, more sophisticated weaponry, including helicopter gun ships, forced the URNG into retreat by 1983, a move that the Guatemalan government falsely labeled as a defeat of the revolutionary forces. The revolutionary movement survived throughout the 1980s and was bolstered by the growth of strong social protest movements in Guatemala's cities led by labor unions and human rights organizations. In 1987 the labor organizations formed a coalition with the Group of Mutual Support (GAM, an organization of relatives of the victims of repression) and the Peasant Unity Committee (CUC) to demand improved wages, an accounting for the victims of the repression, and land distribution. These forces of civil society, viewed by the military as allies of the guerrilla movement, also faced harsh repression. Despite the repression, the civil society organizations survived and participated in the 1992 U.N.-brokered negotiations started between the URNG and the government and military. The negotiations occurred because the guerrillas, with their numbers reduced to less than 3000, realized that military victory was unlikely and the Guatemalan government was under pressure from the Bush administration's preference for reduced emphasis on military aid programs and more emphasis on consolidating a regional trading bloc. However, given the depths of Guatemala's repression and the reluctance of the oligarchy to accept cooperation with the revolutionaries, the peace settlement did not come easily. In 1993 President Jorge Antonio Serrano attempted to reimpose military rule and return to tactics of harsh repression. However, his coup attempt was reversed by a combination of street demonstrations and opposition from the Clinton administration. Serrano was replaced by Ramiro De León Carpio, the parliament's human rights adviser. His appointment put the stalled negotiations back on track and a peace settlement was finally achieved on December 27, 1996, bringing an end to Central America's longest civil war. The peace agreement formally ended the civil war but did not end violent conflict in the country, nor did the settlement significantly address the long-standing social inequalities that have long fueled the conflict. Most importantly, there was little change in the pattern of land tenure, with 65 percent of the country's arable land remaining in the hands of just 2.6 percent of the population. The peace agreements called for peaceful settlements of land claims and the return of thousands of displaced families, but the administration of President Alvaro Enrique Arzú, with the support of the country's traditional oligarchy did little to further those aspects of the accords. The former revolutionaries, the URNG, operating as part of the civil opposition now use the courts and public protest to press their reform agenda but at this time the relationship of forces is against them.

Colombia

Another of Latin America's most important contemporary revolutionary movements is the FARC. In 1999 the FARC had a presence in more than 60 percent of Colombia's municipalities. Although under sharp attack from well-armed paramilitaries and the Colombian government, the FARC sustained itself for more than three decades and contributed significantly to that country's continuing political unrest. The origins of the FARC lie in the peasant struggles of more than a half century ago. Facing harsh living and working conditions the workers on coffee plantations began to organize around labor demands and broader political concerns. The movement was most active in central Colombia but faced brutal repression by the army. The peasants responded with armed self-defense groups as early as the 1940s. In 1948 a ten-year period known as La Violencia was sparked by the assassination of populist leader Jorge Gaitan. The Colombian Communist Party was very active in this time period and assisted in the organization of self-defense and guerrilla groups. With the triumph of the Cuban revolution in 1959, the concepts of self-defense began to be transformed into the idea of the pursuance of guerrilla warfare with the goal of achieving state power for the purpose of social revolution. It was in this political context that the FARC was founded in 1964.

The organization began among communities of displaced peasants who had settled uncultivated lands in the hopes of fleeing the repression of the state. Those who were fleeing state violence traveled in large groups protected by armed self-defense units, a process known as "armed colonization." These settlements were strongly under the influence of the Communist party. It was these communities that later became the base of the FARC. The nature of national politics in Colombia also contributed to the development of a revolutionary movement. Two political parties, the Liberals and Conservatives, totally monopolized political power and prevented the development of any role within the system for legal means of dissent. To move competition from more violent forms and share power through alternation they signed a power-sharing agreement in 1956. This alliance, known as the National Front from 1958 to 1974, has dominated the Colombian political scene to the present. Until the implementation of a new constitution in 1991, these two parties ruled under a permanent state of siege designed to curtail virtually all social protest. By blocking almost all possibility of a democratic left, the state created conditions for the emergence of an opposition that was outside of the parliamentary framework.

The FARC was not the only revolutionary group to be founded in this context. The National Liberation Army (ELN) was formed in 1964, the Popular Liberation Army (EPL) in 1965, and the April 19th Movement (M19) in 1973. Smaller urban groups were also formed in this time period. In its early years, the growth of the FARC was slow. By the late 1970s it had established a marginal presence in the central and southern parts of the country. But in the early 1980s the FARC grew rapidly as the result of a government crackdown on legal opposition. Up until that time it had operated primarily in the political arena but now began to more clearly articulate its role as a military vanguard. It acquired the organizational structure of an army and developed an autonomy from the Communist party. By 1983 it had expanded its military activity to eighteen fronts.

The FARC was committed to fundamental societal transformation through the armed achievement of state power, but it also pursued a flexible tactical position. In 1983 the government of Belisario Betancur made a significant peace overture. Departing sharply from the political stance of his predecessors, Betancur acknowledged many of the socioeconomic demands of the FARC. A cease fire was arranged and the possibility of a political revolution of the conflict became real. In the context of the cease fire, the FARC formed the Patriotic Union (UP), a political front in which the Communist party played a significant role. The FARC was preparing for a possible electoral role but did not dismantle its military apparatus.

The possibility of a political settlement was scuttled by Betancur's opposition in the congress, which rejected the reforms proposed in the accords. The political opposition represented the traditional oligarchy and its allies in the military. When a new government under Virgilio Barco came to power in 1986 the government's overture to the armed opposition officially ended. It refused to recognize the demands of the opposition as legitimate and im-

mediately launched harsh repression against the rebels and their supporters in civil society. During 1988 alone close to 200 UP leaders were assassinated and in a decade of repression nearly 3000 UP members, including
mayors, municipal council members, and senators were killed, virtually
eliminating the organization. Despite this repression the FARC did not officially return to a stance of war until 1991 after the military occupied the
town of Casa Verde, the home of the FARC leadership. Although brief peace
talks were conducted in mid-1991, the war intensified from that time onward. A constitutional assembly convened in 1991, and FARC blamed the
government for missing an opportunity to incorporate the political opposition through that process.

As the decade of the 1990s wore on, FARC and other armed rebel groups
found themselves at the center of political unrest in the country. The central
government in Bogotá was increasingly unable to govern the country effectively as it battled the increasing influence of both drug cartels and rebel political movements. Unable to control the country by normal means, the government turned to paramilitary organizations to deal with problems by sheer
force. In essence it privatized the war against the FARC and the ELN and
in the process served to delegitimize the state. As the result, the 1990s saw
great ongoing costs in terms of human lives and property. The weakness of
the central government opened the door for the FARC to implement a strategy of undermining local ruling structures by its tactic of "armed oversight."
By gathering detailed information on local government financing and spending, the guerrillas were able to both target and expose corrupt local officials
while also steering some government revenues toward FARC-sponsored
projects.

The ongoing crisis of agriculture also contributed to the growing strength
of the FARC. As traditional agricultural production declined the rebels have
built support among those sectors hardest hit by the decline. The FARC successfully attracted unemployed youth from the countryside into its ranks.
As the peasants increasingly looked to coca production to make up for the
decline in other production, the FARC stepped forward with protection for
those communities. Such actions helped finance the FARC's activities while
also raising their political legitimacy among the poorest sectors. The support of the coca growers has contributed to the growing polarization of the
society as the government ignored the real socioeconomic issues and sought
with the support of the U.S. government to place the rebels activities within
the militarized scope of the war on drugs.

The relationship between the FARC and the political process has been
more problematic. In 1996, in the midst of sharp conflict between the coca
growers and the central government the FARC organized a highly successful boycott of the municipal elections in the areas where their influence was
strongest. In some cities mayors were elected by as few as seven votes but
were prevented from taking office by popularly convened local councils.
However, the ability of the guerrillas to protect those communities that have
defied the central government was limited. The government authorized cam-

paigns of terror against these communities carried out by private paramilitaries. Such growing polarization and the growing importance of the ELN made the prospect of a political settlement to Colombia's long-running insurgent rebellion unlikely in the near future. Heightened U.S. involvement through Plan Colombia further escalated the conflict.

Peru

One of Latin America's most interesting revolutionary movements is Peru's Sendero Luminoso (Shining Path) of José Carlos Mariátequi. In the late 1980s and early 1990s they were the most active rebels in Latin America and were seen as seriously challenging state power against an increasingly weak central governments in Lima. A decade later, with most of its key leaders either in jail or dead, Sendero was reduced to a marginal position in Peruvian politics. Its relative demise provided some interesting insight on revolution and revolutionary movements.

Shining Path was founded in 1980 by Abimael Guzmán, a philosophy professor at the university in Ayacucho. He had been doing preparatory work in the area for some years before. For the next thirteen years the Communist party of Peru, known as Shining Path, was a central actor in Peruvian politics. Founded on the Maoist principle of a peasant-based revolution that would gain control of the countryside and eventually encircle and overwhelm the central government, Sendero was quite successful in reaching out from its original student base to gain widespread influence among the indigenous people of the Ayacucho region, long ignored by the central government in Lima. The rebels burst on to the scene by assassinating local officials who refused to cooperate with their efforts and by seeking to create armed, liberated communities out of the reach of the central government. Their political strategy was fiercely sectarian, rejecting all other political movements as part of the status quo. Sendero was willing to use violence against any reformist forces that refused to cooperate with their strategy— trade unionists, neighborhood organizers, other leftists, or priests or nuns engaged in community organizing. This harsh sectarianism eventually contributed to the movement's decline. Initially, the government's response was almost entirely counterproductive. In the 1980s the government carried out a military occupation of the highlands region where the Shining Path was based. The army's draconian actions did not succeed in defeating the revolutionaries in their strongholds, and popular reaction to the government repression actually helped to spread the revolution to other provinces. Between 1989 and 1992 Shining Path stepped up its armed activity in Lima and engaged in a highly effective car- and truck-bombing campaign, badly shaking the government's confidence. However, upon a thorough review of its earlier counterproductive repression, the government began to reformulate its counterinsurgency strategy. Playing on the divisions in the rural communities that were created by Sendero's sectarian tactics, the government began to succeed in getting rural inhabitants to join government-backed armed self-defense groups. It was a testament to Sendero's brutality that the government began to succeed despite its own previous brutality. Shining Path's war became one of *campesinos* against *campesinos*. Shining Path's base of support generally did not grow beyond the most marginalized people— students, teachers, and unemployed youth from the shantytowns. It became more a sect than a broad-based popular movement.

In 1992 through stepped-up intelligence activities the police were able to arrest a number of key intermediate-level officials, weakening the organization's internal structures. This increased repression occurred in the framework of President Alberto Fujimori's auto-coup, or assumption of dictatorial powers, under the guise of fighting Sendero. Fujimori's efforts culminated later in 1992 with the arrest of Sendero's leader, Guzmán. Soon after his capture Guzmán called off the armed struggle and sought political dialogue with the government. However, in 1994 several key Sendero leaders denounced Guzmán's call for negotiations and vowed to continue the armed struggle. Most of them were later arrested. Shining Path has not been completely destroyed, but as the decade ended it sought to remain politically relevant in the wake of its disunity and numerous defeats at the hands of the government.

Conclusion

Political scientist Eric Selbin has suggested that given Latin America's 500-year-old tradition of rebellion and revolution we should be wary to dismiss the possibility of future revolutions there. An understanding of why revolution and serious study of it must remain integral to our study of Latin America is rooted in the fact that the recent growth of democratic political forms and economic restructuring have done relatively little to eliminate the social inequalities and political disenfranchisement that have plagued Latin America in the twentieth century.

As U.S. President John F. Kennedy observed in the formulation of the Alliance for Progress, the stifling of reforms make the violent struggle for change inevitable. It is true that some important strides have been made in respect of democratic procedures and human rights, often as the result of political work by revolutionary forces, but the progress has been conditional. Contemporary democratic regimes, as Selbin notes, rely far too often on pacts among elites and the marginalization of the indigenous population. The fragility of Latin American democracy was often shown during the 1990s. The military coup against Jean Bertrande Aristide in Haiti in 1991 and the auto-golpe of Alberto Fujimori are the two most dramatic examples. Recent violent turnovers of power in Ecuador and Paraguay have underscored the fragility of democracy in those countries. On a less dramatic note, the changing of electoral rules to allow the continued rule of Fujimori in Peru, Menem in Argentina, and Cardoso in Brazil threaten the practice of constitutional government.

However, the greater harbinger for the continued probability of revolutionary upsurges in Latin America comes from the fact that as the region

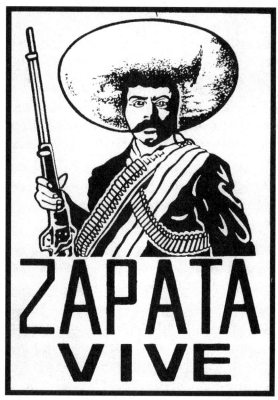

Zapata lives! Legendary figures such as Mexican Revolutionary Emiliano Zapata inspire great admiration and emulation. After Zapata became the inspiration and namesake for the Zapatistas, pictures and Zapata decals like this one were freely circulated in Chiapas and other parts of Mexico.

enters the new millennium more people live in poverty than did twenty years ago and the gap between the richest and poorest Latin Americans grows wider. Nearly half of the region's 500 million people are poor, an increase of 70 million in one decade. The regimes that took power during Latin America's recent turn to democratic rule did not seem to make any significant progress in the arena of social justice, with the result that the neoliberal economic models triumphant at the start of the decade of the 1990s were increasingly being called into question. If it is a reality that the need for social change will remain on the agenda in the twenty-first century in Latin America, then the next question to be asked is whether or not the traditional forms of revolution and rebellion will remain relevant. In the 1990s there has been a considerable literature on the rising importance of social movements. In recent years, throughout the region groups have formed around a wide range of issues, including gender, ecology, housing, land, political repression, and indigenous rights. Buoyed by contacts made both within the region and internationally, these organizations took advantage of democratic openings to forcefully press their case and win important victories. However, it might be a mistake to view these important movements, which fall within the long-standing existence of powerful reformist movements worldwide, as a replacement for the phenomenon of revolutionary change. Latin America's ruling elites have rarely demonstrated a great tolerance for such political opposition, and it is unlikely that will change overnight. The social movements themselves, often with their single-issue focus, are not necessarily capable of articulating the broader vision for societal change that the region's social and political inequalities demand. For this reason the continued appearance of revolutionary movements may be inevitable.

Bibliography

Colburn, Forrest. *The Vogue of Revolution in Poor Countries*. Princeton, NJ: Princeton University Press, 1994.

Debray, Regis. *Revolution in the Revolution?* New York: Grove Press, 1967.

Hodges, Donald C. *The Latin American Revolution: Politics and Strategy from Apro-Marxism to Guevarism*. New York: William Morrow, 1974.

Lefeber, Walter W. *Inevitable Revolutions: The United States in Central America*. 2nd ed. New York: Norton, 1994.

Liss, Sheldon. *Marxist Thought in Latin America*. Berkeley: University of California Press, 1984.

McClintock, Cynthia. *Revolutionary Movements in Latin America*. Washington, DC: United States Institute of Peace Press, 1998.

Montgomery, Tommie Sue. *Revolution in El Salvador: From Civil Strife to Peace*. 2nd ed. Boulder, CO: Westview Press, 1995.

Palmer, David Scott. *Shining Path of Peru*. 2nd ed. New York: St. Martin's Press, 1992.

Selbin, Eric. *Modern Latin American Revolutions*. Boulder, CO: Westview Press, 1993.

Skocpol, Theda. *States and Social Revolution*. Cambridge, England: Cambridge University Press, 1979.

Vanden, Harry E. *Latin American Marxism: A Bibliography*. New York: Garland, 1991.

Vanden, Harry E., and Gary Prevost. *Democracy and Socialism in Sandinista Nicaragua*. Boulder, CO: Lynne Reinner Publishers, 1993.

Wickham-Crowley, Timothy. *Guerrillas and Revolution in Latin America*. Princeton, NJ: Princeton University Press, 1992.

FILMS AND VIDEOS

Americas in Transitions. U.S., 1982.
El Salvador: Another Vietnam. U.S., 1981.
Seven Dreams of Peace. U.S., 1996.
Tupamaros. U.S., 1996.
Ya Basta! The Battle Cry of The Forceless. U.S., 1997.

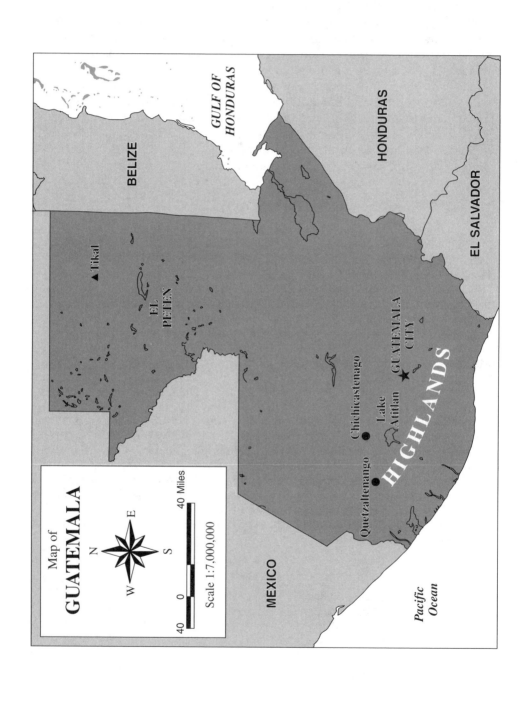

TEN

GUATEMALA

Susanne Jonas

How is it possible that a country as small as Guatemala has taken on such grandiose and dramatic proportions in Latin America? Already in the mid-1960s, Uruguayan writer Eduardo Galeano referred to Guatemala as "the key to Latin America" and "a source of great lessons painfully learned." Beyond its dramatic, tortuous political history, Guatemala is distinguished by being one of the few Latin American countries with an indigenous majority of the population. During the second half of the twentieth century, Guatemala has also loomed large in the saga of United States-Latin America relations. Guatemala has suffered Latin America's longest and bloodiest Cold War civil war, lasting thirty-six years and leaving some 200,000 civilians dead or "disappeared." And at the beginning of the twenty-first century, Guatemala's peace process holds important lessons for the entire hemisphere.

Located just to the south of Mexico, slightly smaller than Tennessee (42,042 square miles), Guatemala is the most populous Central American country, its population having reached well over 11 million by 1999 and constituting over 30 percent of Central America's total. (It is worth noting that, by the end of the twentieth century, up to 10 percent of that population has migrated to the United States for political or economic reasons.) The diversity of its population, which is over 60 percent Mayan, is both a rich human/cultural resource and a source of the country's particularly turbulent history: The extreme polarization of Guatemala's social structure stems largely from the compounding of class divisions and exploitation with ethnic divisions and discrimination, which during some periods reached genocidal proportions.

The Mayan population (subdivided into twenty-two language groups) is dispersed today throughout almost all regions of Guatemala, but historically it was concentrated in the western highlands, or *altiplano*, which stretch from Mexico on the north into Honduras and El Salvador on the south. The highlands area, world famous for its spectacular beauty, contains a chain of volcanos, some of them sloping directly down into the also world-famous Lake Atitlán. The country's other major regions are the southern Pacific coastal lowlands, site of major agro-export plantations, and the large lowlands Petén area in the north, home to one of the continent's major tropical rainforests as well as the major Mayan ruins at Tikal. In the eastern half of the country the Sierra de las Minas and Lake Izabal on the Rio Dulce lead to an Atlantic coastal lowland; this area has remained primarily *ladino* (mestizo), with Garifuna and Xinca indigenous populations on the Atlantic coast. Guatemala City, the capital, is located on a mesa surrounded by the central highlands.

About half of Guatemala's population is still rural, and 52 percent of its labor force is in the countryside (in part because of the scarcity of stable, permanent, full-time jobs in the cities). Guatemala City has come to concentrate 35 percent of the entire population, with Quetzaltenango at 11 percent, and Los Angeles, California, at around 5 percent. The urban primacy of Guatemala City is even more striking in regard to political power and provision of social services.

Precolonial, Colonial, and Neocolonial History

Pre-Hispanic indigenous Guatemala was by no means "primitive"; what the Spanish conquerors found in 1524 was a complex, stratified, proto-class society torn by multiple social tensions. Despite these class divisions, the population was unified by a common belief system. The ruling elites were priests rather than warriors, which explains the predominance of temples in the Mayan ruins. Preconquest Mayan society had developed sophisticated technologies—more advanced and scientific in some areas (e.g.,mathematics and astronomy) than those of Europe during the Middle Ages. By the sixteenth century, it was a society in transition; had it not been interrupted by the conquest, it might well have developed into a society as advanced as those in Western Europe.

Despite the class divisions in pre-Hispanic Guatemala, at no time before the conquest did the Mayas suffer the systematic material deprivation that has characterized Guatemala since 1524. Malnutrition, for example, was not a chronic condition of the population, as it is today. Prior to 1524, Guatemala was a primarily agricultural society in which land was cultivated both individually and communally to produce food and other necessities for the population itself—rather than for export to the world market, i.e., for consumption and profit by foreigners thousands of miles away. In this sense, underdevelopment as we know it today did not exist in Guatemala prior to 1524, but was the direct outcome of the conquest and Guatemala's integration into an expanding capitalist world economy.

The Spanish conquest itself, a violent clash of two socioeconomic systems and two cultures, forcibly integrated the Mayas into "western civilization": several million were killed immediately, and by 1650, an estimated two-thirds to six-sevenths of the indigenous population in Central America and Mexico had died, largely through disease epidemics. Following the military conquest, the colonization of Guatemala was carried out by Spanish state functionaries, Spanish settler planters and merchants, and the Catholic Church, which maintained a very close relation with the state.

The conquest and the subsequent three centuries of colonialism (1524–1821) integrated Guatemala into an expanding capitalist world market that determined the colony's production priorities and systematically channeled its surplus into the pockets of foreign ruling classes. This dependent relationship also left internal legacies that endured far longer than the colonial relation to Spain itself: agricultural mono-export (at the expense of food production, tying the ups and downs of the entire economy to the fortunes of export prices), concentration of landholding in the hands of a small minority, and various forms of unfree/forced indigenous labor as the underpinning of the entire socioeconomic structure. The overlap between the degrees of class and racial oppression was notable: unlike *indios*, as they were disparagingly called by the *criollo* (European) elites—and unlike African slave labor imported into areas where the indigenous populations had been exterminated—the *ladinos* or mixed-origin populations acquired greater freedom and social mobility, and eventually formed the nuclei of urban working and middle classes.

Independence from Spain in 1821 (led by the elites, but supported by nearly all sectors of the population, each for its own reasons) brought little change in internal structures, although it initiated a diversification of Guatemala's external contacts. Spain's previous economic/commercial monopoly was replaced by British interests and (later in the nineteenth century) by German and U.S. interests. Within Guatemala, power alternated between Liberals and Conservatives from 1821 until the Liberal "Revolution" of 1871. Both the Liberal and Conservative parties were dominated by *criollo* elites, but they differed on issues such as the state's relation to the Catholic Church and the degree of centralization/federalism.

The 1871 triumph of the Liberals led by General Justo Rufino Barrios came in the wake of the rise of coffee as the dominant export. The land for the coffee estates, which required large concentrations of land and labor, came from the newly consolidated Liberal (anticlerical) state's confiscation of Catholic Church properties, once that Church had been disestablished, and from a major new wave of expropriations of indigenous communal lands. The Liberal Revolution also saw the consolidation of the army as the principal labor mobilizer and enforcer; the army viewed its mission as maintaining "order" in the countryside. Ironically, the Liberal Revolution, touted as a necessity for development, modernization, and "progress," proved far more costly than previous governments to the indigenous populations, which were now subjected to harsher forms of forced labor. Except for a brief democratic interlude in the early 1920s, Liberal military dictators ruled with an iron hand on behalf of the coffee oligarchy and foreign investors for over seventy years.

The other major change during the late nineteenth and early twentieth centuries was the expansion of U.S. private corporate interests into Guatemala and several other Central American countries. The most notable of the U.S. corporate investors in Guatemala, the United Fruit Company (UFCo), began monopolistic operations in banana production; UFCo became the largest landowner in Guatemala, writing its own contracts with the government and operating virtually unrestricted by any Guatemalan government regulations—functioning, in essence, as "a state within a state." UFCo also owned the only railroad and hence could dictate transportation prices. U.S. interests reinforced the interests of Guatemala's coffee growers: concentration of land ownership and coercion applied to the subjugated indigenous labor force.

This period also saw the rise of the United States as a world power and a great expansion of U.S. influence over internal Guatemalan political affairs, in alliance with the local landed oligarchy. This alliance was the key to the longevity of the Liberal dictatorships. Washington's support was crucial to the last of these dictators, Jorge Ubico, who ruled from 1931 to 1944. The Ubico regime contained social tensions, particularly after the world depression left hundreds of thousands of rural workers unemployed during the 1930s, through top-down repression rather than reform. The model of the "pressure cooker" in Guatemala and other Central American nations contrasted sharply with the "safety valve" reforms and industrialization programs of the 1930s in larger Latin American countries such as Mexico, Chile, and Brazil. Although the purely repressive Central American model gave the appearance of guaranteeing stability, subsequent events revealed the fragility of that model.

The Revolution of 1944–1954 and the 1954 CIA Intervention

Under the weight of the economic and social crises caused by the world Depression of the 1930s, Guatemala's neocolonial order cracked in 1944, when a broad middle- and working-class coalition (including young army officers) overthrew the Ubico dictatorship. Thus was initiated the Revolution of 1944–1954, the only genuinely democratic experience in Guatemala's entire history. The two governments of Juan José Arévalo (1945–1950) and Jacobo Arbenz (1951–1954) for the first time guaranteed basic democratic liberties (including free elections and the formation of political opposition parties), abolished forced labor (which had been nearly universal for the indigenous population), granted minimum wages and basic organizing and bargaining rights for workers and peasants, and established basic institutions of social welfare. In addition, the Revolution modernized Guatemalan capitalism, undertaking agricultural diversification and industrialization programs, fomenting national enterprises and regulating foreign investment to serve national priorities.

Most significant in this nationalist democratic revolution was Arbenz' far-reaching (but capitalist) agrarian reform of 1952, which distributed land to over 100,000 peasant families. The principle underlying the land reform was the government's expropriation of large tracts of land that were not being used by their owners, with compensation based on the value declared for tax purposes. The land would be used to produce, and the large numbers of landless would own enough land to have some disposable income; in short, the producers could become consumers, forming the basis for an internal market and reducing dependence on the world market. (This basic principle has always associated industrialization and modernization of the economy with labor guarantees and land reform.)

Coming on top of other nationalistic moves by Arbenz, the expropriation of unused land belonging to UFCo (the largest landowner in Guatemala, which had been using a mere 15 percent of its holdings) prompted an angry response from the U.S. government. (Not so coincidentally John Foster Dulles, Secretary of State beginning in 1953, and CIA director Allen Dulles had been major lawyers for UFCo.) More broadly, Washington feared the spread of the "example" of reform and popular mobilization from Guatemala to other Central American countries. The fact that the Guatemalan Revolution was occurring at the height of the Cold War enabled the U.S. to charge that Guatemala was serving as a "beachhead for Soviet expansion" in the Western Hemisphere (although in reality the Soviets were virtually uninvolved in Guatemala), and gave the CIA the justification it needed to plan the ouster of Arbenz.

After mid-1952, the CIA worked with Guatemalan Rightist opposition forces (e.g., many of the large landowners, Rightist politicians, and the Catholic Church) to organize the overthrow of the Arbenz government in June 1954 and install in its place a pro-U.S. counterrevolutionary regime led by (U.S.-chosen) Colonel Carlos Castillo Armas. In general, the "Liberation," as its Guatemalan supporters called it, marked the first major U.S. Cold War covert intervention in the Western Hemisphere. Many elements of that CIA covert operation have subsequently been used against other leftist governments in Latin America—e.g., the Castro government in Cuba (1961), the Allende government in Chile (1973), and the Sandinista government in Nicaragua (1980s).

Aftermath: Chronic Crisis

The Castillo Armas regime immediately reversed the democratic and progressive legislation of the Revolution, including everything from the land reform and labor laws to literacy programs that were deemed "pro-communist indoctrination." All pro-Revolution organizations and political parties were declared illegal; under direct U.S. supervision, the government also unleashed a wide-ranging witch hunt and McCarthy-style repression cam-

---

THE U.S. COVERT OPERATION IN GUATEMALA, 1954

- Sent a team of ambassadors to Central America instructed to collaborate with the ouster of Arbenz; head of the team was John Peurifoy as Ambassador to Guatemala, an extreme anti-communist with prior experience in defeating the rebels in the Greek civil war
- CIA chose Colonel Carlos Castillo Armas to be the Guatemalan pointman to lead the anti-Arbenz operation
- CIA fully trained, equipped, and funded the anti-Arbenz mercenary army (in Honduras) of Guatemalan rightists, led by Castillo Armas
- CIA carried out psychological warfare through clandestine "Radio Liberty" in Guatemala and through aerial propaganda leaflets dropped from planes
- Funded and worked with anti-Arbenz elements in the Guatemalan military leadership while neutralizing those loyal to Arbenz
- Maneuvered on the diplomatic front to get the Organization of American States to approve a resolution (March 1954) condemning Guatemala as posing a threat of "Communist agression" against the entire hemisphere
- Imposed embargo on arms to Guatemala by all U.S. allies, and subsequently used the shipment of (obsolete) arms from Czechoslovakia as pretext for final move against Arbenz
- Helped Castillo Armas' mercenary army "invade" Guatemala from Honduras on June 18, 1954; as soon as they were over the border, flew Castillo Armas (in Ambassador Peurifoy's private plane) to Guatemala City
- Simultaneously, CIA planes, manned by U.S. pilots, strafed and bombarded Guatemala City and other cities, to demoralize Arbenz and get him to resign (which he did on June 27)
- Despite having promised to allow pro-Revolution military officers to take charge following Arbenz' resignation, the United States doublecrossed them and installed Castillo Armas in power
- Organized powerful lobby (largely UFCo-orchestrated) in the U.S. Congress, media, and elsewhere to secure "consensus" in U.S. public opinion supporting the coup and suppress criticism of the operation (this was the height of the McCarthy era in the United States)

(Note: Many members of the CIA team that organized the Guatemalan "Liberation" went on to organize the Bay of Pigs invasion against Cuba (1961) and other covert operations.)

---

paign that cost the lives of some 8000 supporters of the Revolution and forced thousands of others into exile or hiding. The legacy of the Revolution and its violent termination was to compound the social polarization already characteristic of Guatemala, throwing the country into permanent crisis.

Nevertheless, even under the post-1954 counterrevolutionary order, history could not be "reversed," since the same underlying structural dynamics and contradictions that had caused the Revolution continued to develop. The Guatemalan economy, like that of all Central America, enjoyed a thirty-year period (1950–1980) of growth based on the expansion and diversification of agricultural exports to the world market; a minimal industrialization program during the 1960s and 1970s was carried out mainly by U.S. companies within the context of the Central American Common Market. But even export-led growth generated turmoil because of the extreme inequities in resource and income distribution. To take the most telling indicator for Guatemala as an example, after the reversal of the land reform, 2 percent of the population controlled 67 percent of the arable land. In the 1970s, the diversification of agricultural exports brought significant new land expropriations from peasants and new concentrations of land tenure; the main beneficiaries were army generals using their control over the state apparatus to accumulate personal wealth. Thus, impoverishment stemming from land concentration intensified exponentially, as Guatemala became virtually the only country in Latin America not to have sustained even minimal land reform.

At the social level, the diversification of the productive structure significantly modified Guatemala's traditional class structure and reshaped the ruling coalition between the army and economic elites—the latter being represented in a tightly knit umbrella organization, the Coordinating Committee of Agricultural, Commercial, Industrial and Financial Associations (CACIF). Among other things, diversification of the ruling class meant incorporation of the upper ranks of military officers and a redefinition of the alliance between the army and the bourgeoisie (economic elites). Rather than "opening up" the class structure, these modifications only accentuated its overall polarization.

At the bottom pole of Guatemalan society, meanwhile, industrialization and agricultural diversification did not significantly expand the proletariat as a fully employed labor force. Rather, the countryside saw the growth of a semi-proletariat: land-starved peasants from the highlands were forced to work on southern coast plantations as seasonal migrant laborers during part of the year. In the cities, migrants from rural areas swelled the ranks of an underemployed informal proletariat. As a consequence, the "development" of the 1960s and 1970s actually left a decreasing proportion of the economically active population fully employed on a permanent basis. These tendencies were disastrously compounded during the 1980s, Latin America's "Lost Decade."

The profound changes in society after 1954 produced new generations of social movements (labor, peasant, indigenous, student, community, human rights)—first in the 1960s, then in the late 1970s and (after they were destroyed in the late 1970s and early 1980s) again in the second half of the 1980s. In the absence of any serious attempt to meet the needs of the poor or the indigenous or to use the benefits of growth during the 1960s and 1970s to redistribute wealth, these movements continually exerted new pressures upon the state and the established social order. These pressures were con-

This billboard was at the entrance to Chichicastenango until after the signing of the Peace Accords at the end of 1996. It shows the degree of control by the army and the Civilian Self-Defense Patrols (PACs), misnamed "Comites Voluntarios," since there was nothing voluntary about them. *(Photo by S. Jonas)*

tained by a level of repression at times unmatched anywhere else in Latin America; one generation after another of social movement leaders and activists, as well as moderate Leftist political opposition leaders, was eliminated by the army and illegal paramilitary forces. Even systematic repression failed to stop the reemergence of popular movements in one or another form, although it severely restricted their functioning.

These massive social conflicts defined Guatemalan politics during the last four decades of the twentieth century. Within an overall framework of direct military rule, there was a civilian interlude under President Julio César Méndez Montenegro (1966–1970) and a more definitive return to civilian rule beginning in 1986; in both cases, the army dominated politics from behind the scenes. But largely as a legacy of the experience of the 1944–1954 Revolution and its violent overthrow, hardline regimes, whether military or civilian, faced constant challenges. It was precisely the refusal to permit even moderate reformist political options that created the conditions for the growth of a revolutionary guerrilla movement attempting to repeat the experience of the 1959 Cuban Revolution. Quite literally, there was no alternative "within the system."

The first wave of guerrilla insurgency, during the 1960s, was centered in the Eastern region, where the peasants were *ladino* rather than Mayan. Although small and without a base among the indigenous population, the insurgency of the Fuerzas Armadas Rebeldes (FAR) was contained only after a major counterinsurgency effort (1966–1968), organized, financed, and run directly by the United States along the lines of its operations in Vietnam. This was a turning point in Guatemala, with U.S. military advisers playing a decisive role in transforming the Guatemalan army (previously "weakened" in Washington's view by nationalist tendencies and inefficiency) into a modern, disciplined counterinsurgency army. The military grew to some 46,000 troops during the 1980s; it became known as the most brutal in Latin America—a literal "killing machine"—and during the 1970s and 1980s it came to dominate the state directly.

The counterinsurgency state was institutionalized after 1970, when the head of the 1966–1968 army campaign, Colonel Carlos Arana Osorio (the "butcher of Zacapa") used that victory to win the 1970 presidential election. Since the goal of this first "dirty war" had been to eradicate the civilian support base of the guerrillas, it cost the lives of over 8000 civilians. It was also within this context, in Guatemala, that Latin America first experienced the artifacts of counterinsurgency war: semiofficial death squads (based in the security forces and financed by economic elites, with such names as "White Hand" and "An Eye for an Eye") and "disappearances" of civilian opposition figures. Since that time, Guatemala has had more than 40,000 civilian disappearances, accounting for over 40 percent of the total for all Latin America. Thus ended the first phase of Guatemala's thirty-six-year civil war, with the army's temporary victory by 1968 over FAR insurgents.

Insurgency and Counterinsurgency in the 1970s–1980s

As suggested earlier, the structural transformations of the 1960s–1980s caused Guatemala's Mayan populations to redefine their class identity. These same factors profoundly affected their self-conceptions and identities as indigenous. Economic growth followed by economic crisis broke down the objective barriers that had kept the Mayas relatively isolated in the highlands. This was greatly intensified by the economic and political crises of the 1970s and 1980s, when growing numbers of Mayas were forced to migrate to the southern coast as seasonal laborers and to Guatemala City. These changes and displacements brought them into increased contact with the *ladino*, Spanish-speaking world. Rather than "ladinizing," or acculturating, them, however, these experiences reinforced their struggle to preserve their indigenous identity, although in new forms—as Guatemalan Jesuit priest/scholar/activist Ricardo Falla put it, to discover "new ways of being indigenous." These factors form the background for understanding why Guatemala's Mayan peoples became one of the powerful social forces driving the insurgency of the 1970s and 1980s.

In the countryside, structural contradictions—the crisis in subsistence agriculture, compounded by a massive earthquake in 1976—uprooted and displaced thousands of indigenous peasants, causing them to redefine themselves in both class and cultural terms. As producers, they were being semi-proletarianized as a seasonal migrant labor force on the plantations of the southern coast, meanwhile often losing even the tiny subsistence plots of land they had traditionally held in the highlands. The combination of their experiences of being evicted from their own lands and their experiences as a migrant semiproletariat radicalized large numbers of highlands Mayas. Even the more developmentalist influences were contradictory, in that they raised hopes and expectations in the 1960s, only to dash them in the 1970s. The clearest examples of this dynamic were those peasants who received land from the government's colonization programs in the 1960s, only to have it taken away again in the 1970s, as powerful army officers grabbed profitable lands in colonization areas.

Culturally, highlands indigenous communities were being transformed and redefined throughout the 1960s and 1970s, as they opened up to contact with the *ladino* world. Increased contact had the paradoxical effect of reinforcing their defense of their ethnic/cultural identity, and this became a factor in mobilizing their resistance to the *ladino* state. Politically, "reformist" parties such as the Christian Democrats came into indigenous communities, raising expectations of change—only to leave those hopes unfulfilled for most people. Meanwhile, Mayan organizations were defined by the government as "subversive" and excluded from "normal" political expression. Even their self-help organizations, formed in response to the devastating 1976 earthquake, were viewed as a threat.

Finally, increased army repression against indigenous communities had contradictory effects: Rather than terrorizing the Mayas into passivity, by the late 1970s it stimulated some of them to take up arms as the only available means of self-defense against state violence. All of these contradictory experiences of the 1970s occurred in interaction with the transformation of grassroots organizations of the Catholic Church, the rise of Christian base communities, and the gradual emergence of a "Church of the Poor." These new religious currents became central to the radicalization of the Mayan highlands.

All of these strands were woven together by 1976–1978 in the emergence of the Comité de Unidad Campesina (CUC) as a national peasant organization, including both peasants and agricultural workers, both Mayas and poor *ladinos*, but led primarily by Mayas—by definition a "subversive" organization from the viewpoint of the ruling coalition. CUC came into the limelight after a major massacre at Panzós, Alta Verapaz in 1978 and the 1980 massacre at the Spanish embassy, in which Guatemalan security forces burned alive over three dozen indigenous protesters. Among the victims was Vicente Menchú, father of Rigoberta Menchú. In February 1980, CUC staged a massive strike of workers on the southern coast sugar and cotton plantations; from the viewpoint of landowners and the army, this strike was their worst nightmare come true.

Equally important in the growth of a politicized indigenous movement was a change in the stance of the revolutionary insurgents vis-à-vis the Maya population, within the context of a broader reevaluation of strategy and organizational recomposition after the defeat of 1968. This involved a recognition of the failures of the *foco* strategy of the 1960s as fundamentally militaristic and not rooted in a solid mass base. Even more serious, the insurgents had virtually ignored the indigenous population during the 1960s. By the time of their resurgence in the early 1970s, the three major organizations had generally come to understand some of these errors in their organizing strategies; two of them, Ejército Guerrillero de los Pobres (EGP) and Organización del Pueblo en Armas (ORPA), spent several years being educated by the indigenous population and organizing a political support base in the western highlands (and other areas) before renewing armed actions later in the 1970s.

In sum, veterans of the 1960s insurgency were able to reorganize and reinitiate their struggle in the early 1970s, this time in the western indigenous highlands, and with Mayan communities becoming central participants. The active involvement of up to 500,000 Mayas in the uprising of the late 1970s and early 1980s was without precedent in Guatemala, indeed in the hemisphere. Coming in the wake of the 1979 Sandinista victory in Nicaragua and the outbreak of civil war in El Salvador, also in 1979, this remarkable "awakening" in the indigenous highlands provoked a revolutionary crisis, threatening the army's century-old domination over rural Guatemala.

The guerrilla military offensive reached its height in 1980–1981, gaining 6000–8000 armed fighters and 250,000–500,000 active collaborators and supporters and operating in most parts of the country. In the context of the Sandinista triumph in Nicaragua and the outbreak of civil war in El Salvador, (both in 1979), the new wave of armed struggle in Guatemala was taken very seriously by the ruling coalition as heralding a possible seizure of power by the insurgents. In early 1982, the various guerrilla organizations united in the Unidad Revolucionaria Nacional Guatemalteca (URNG), overcoming years of sectarian divisions.

Even as unity was proclaimed, however, and even as the revolutionary movement achieved its maximal expression during 1980 and 1981, a change in the balance of forces between the insurgents and the army began during the second half of 1981, as the army initiated an all-out "scorched-earth" counteroffensive. By the spring of 1982, the revolutionary movement had suffered serious losses to its infrastructure in the city, where security forces had already previously, in 1978–1980, decimated the leadership and ranks of the unions and other popular movements and political opposition forces. In the highlands, the army unleashed a virtual holocaust upon the indigenous communities. Blinded by its own triumphalism, the URNG had in fact lost the initiative, and some of its fundamental weaknesses came to the surface. As a result of the URNG's weaknesses and of major changes within the ruling coalition, the army gained the upper hand and dealt decisive blows against the insurgents. For the next several years, the URNG was on the defensive; it did not recover a capacity to take new initiatives until the late 1980s.

A major reason for this second defeat of the guerrillas and the suffering inflicted on its supporters among the population was the failure to have anticipated the scorched-earth, genocidal war unleashed by the Guatemalan security forces in mid-1981; hence, tens of thousands of highlands Mayas were left unprepared to defend themselves. The statistics are staggering: From mid-1981 to 1983 alone, 440 villages were entirely wiped off the face of the map and up to 150,000 civilians were killed or "disappeared." There were over 1 million displaced persons (1 million internal refugees, up to 200,000 refugees in Mexico). Accompanying these massive population displacements was the deliberate destruction of huge areas of the highlands (burning of forests, etc.), causing irreversible environmental devastation. The aim of these genocidal policies was not only to elminate the guerrillas' popular support base but also to destroy the Mayan culture, identity, and communal structures.

The army carried out these goals in the first stage (1981–1983) through scorched-earth warfare and in the second stage (after 1983) through the imposition of coercive institutions throughout the countryside that were designed to consolidate military control over the population. Among these institutions were mandatory paramilitary "civilian self-defense patrols," or PACs (at one point involving 1 million peasants, one-quarter of the adult population); "development poles," rural forced resettlement camps where every aspect of people's lives was subject to direct army control; and militarization of the entire administrative apparatus of the country. These counterinsurgency institutions were legalized in the new constitution of 1985, which provided the juridical framework for civilian government in the late 1980s.

Transition to Restricted Civilian Rule

As discussed earlier, the beginning of revolutionary insurgency in Guatemala during the 1960s generated a counterinsurgent response on the part of the United States and the Guatemalan ruling coalition, which was institutionalized in state power after 1970. During the late 1970s, the ability of the military regimes to govern Guatemala deteriorated seriously, as a consequence of relatively weakened internal cohesion within the ruling coalition and the lack of any consensual basis or societal legitimacy. The clearest examples were the openly fraudulent elections of 1974, 1978, and 1982. By 1982, these divisions were serious enough to spark recognition of the need for a change in the nature of military rule; to recover some modicum of legitimacy, at least among the ruling sectors; and to end Guatemala's international isolation as a pariah state, and hence its restricted access to international financial assistance.

The shift is generally seen as beginning with the military coup of March 1982 (following the third successive electoral fraud), which brought to power the regime of General Efraín Ríos Montt. The Ríos Montt government (March 1982–August 1983) presided over the bloodiest era and the majority of the massacres. It was only after this most brutal phase of the counterinsurgency war had accomplished its goals under Ríos Montt that army leaders and their civilian allies, now under the military government of General Oscar Mejía Víctores (1983–1985), took concrete steps toward a return to civilian rule. They recognized that a facade of constitutional democracy was needed to overcome the contradictions of direct military dictatorship. This understanding was the background for the political process of 1983–1985, during which a Constituent Assembly was elected to write a new constitution containing basic guarantees of citizens' rights, at least on paper (alongside institutionalization of PACS, etc.). Finally, presidential elections were held in late 1985.

The 1985 presidential election, although free of fraud, was severely restricted and unrepresentative of large sectors of the population, as only Rightist and Centrist parties that had reached agreement with the military were allowed to participate. Aside from the exclusion of the Left, there were no real choices on substantive issues. Nevertheless, the election did permit nonmilitary candidates for the first time in fifteen years; it was overwhelmingly won by Christian Democrat Vinicio Cerezo, the most progressive of the candidates. Cerezo's victory was greeted with high hopes for a real change from the many years of military dictatorship.

Despite these hopes and despite having come into power with a significant popular mandate, however, Cerezo chose not to fully use the space that he had—that is, not to wage the struggle that would have been needed to achieve a real transfer of power from the military to civilians. His government did very little to control the army or address the country's underlying social/economic problems; he accepted the army's priority of defeating popular and revolutionary forces, and this significantly limited the possibility for genuinely pluralistic politics or for ending the civil war. In this regard, the Cerezo period (1986–1990) turned out to be not so much a genuine "transition to democracy" as a necessary adjustment for trying to deal with Guatemala's multiple crises and reestablish minimal international credibility. It evolved into a civilian version of the counterinsurgency state, in some respects a continuation of what had been imposed in the late 1960s.

A second nonfraudulent election was held in 1990; it was viewed as significant insofar as it established the continuity of civilian rule, between Cerezo and newly elected Jorge Serrano. Nevertheless, abstention was extremely high, with only 30 percent of eligible voters participating, and once again, no Leftist opposition parties were permitted. By 1990, however, there were new currents in the "informal" arena of Guatemalan civil society (outside the electoral process), and these began to undermine the foundations of the counterinsurgency state. One major expression of these currents was an emerging national consensus, articulated primarily in dialogues led by the Catholic Church, for an end to the civil war. Virtually all political sectors began to recognize that Guatemala could not be truly democratized until the civil war was ended through political negotiations (rather than a military victory by either side), until the country was demilitarized, and until

underlying structural inequalities and ethnic discrimination were acknowledged and addressed.

Social Crisis and Reemergence of Social Movements

Structural social crisis—ironically, a product of macroeconomic growth during the 1970s—was compounded during the 1980s when the international
capitalist crisis hit Central America (and all of Latin America) as severely as
the Depression of the 1930s had. Among its principal manifestations were
rising prices for all industrial imports (largely a consequence of the "oil
shocks"), coupled with falling prices for Central American exports. These
crises left the Guatemalan economy suffering negative growth rates during
the 1980s; both unemployment and inflation soared to unprecedented levels. As a result, purchasing power in 1989 was 22 percent of what it had
been in 1972, and the overall poverty levels of 1980 jumped markedly during the late 1980s.

The central social characteristic of Guatemala during the 1980s (and into
the 1990s) remained increasing concentration of wealth amid pervasive
poverty. All of the Central American countries shared this characteristic, but
Guatemalan poverty has been particularly extreme on several counts. First,
the inequality of resource and income distribution has been greater, and no
measures have been taken since the overthrow of Arbenz to alleviate it
(i.e., there has been no land or tax reform). The second particularity of
Guatemalan poverty has been the number of social indicators on which it
ranks worst (illiteracy, physical quality of life, infant mortality). The third
particularity is the ethnic component of poverty, with all statistics for the
Mayan population being far worse than the national average. As elsewhere,
there has also been a marked feminization of poverty, with increasing numbers of women becoming heads of household as well as low-wage workers
(see details below).

These characteristics of extreme underdevelopment and inequality were
not new to Guatemala, but a number of things did change dramatically during the 1980s. First, under the impact of the international crisis of the 1980s,
all of Guatemala's economic and social problems were seriously aggravated.
Even at the macro-economic level, Guatemala lost over fifteen years of
growth during the 1980s, reversing the growth pattern of the previous thirty
years. Second, after the mid-1980s, the government began to implement austerity policies more aggressively, culminating in the neoliberal structural adjustment measures of the late 1980s and early 1990s; these policies further
aggravated the grave social crisis. Third, informalization of the urban economy left only slightly over one-third of the workforce fully and permanently
employed.

This last indicator was among the important modifications in Guatemala's
class structure during the 1980s, which left close to 90 percent of the population living below the official poverty line by the end of the decade (up

from 79 percent in 1980); nearly three-quarters of the population lived in extreme poverty and were unable to afford a basic minimum diet. During the late 1980s, the impact of the economic and social crisis in regenerating social ferment among the poor proved greater than the ability of the counterinsurgency state to repress such ferment. Despite the reescalation of repression against labor and other popular movements, the constitution of this huge majority of the population that was united by being poor led to a slow rebuilding and reemergence of popular movements after the disasters of the early 1980s; a stream of austerity protests began even under the military government in 1985 and continued with suprising vigor.

Guatemala's new popular movements were the product not only of austerity measures but also of the country's multiple crises, including the many crises of uprooted populations. The war alone left over 10 percent of the population displaced. Natural disaster (the 1976 earthquake), war, and economic crisis during the late 1970s and 1980s brought significant migration to the capital, causing its population to double. Increasingly, the urban poor were indigenous, and more than half of the households came to be headed by women. A significant number of the new urban poor (250,000 to 500,000 people) lived in the city's massive shantytowns in precarious squatter settlements. The absence of basic social services (running water, sewage, electricity, transportation) sparked new community struggles that became as important as more traditional labor union struggles among organized sectors of the labor force. Residents of one such community protested by leaving the body of a child who had died from typhoid on the steps of the National Palace.

In the rural areas, meanwhile, hundreds of thousands of those displaced within the highlands or to the southern coast joined together with the landless already living there to form a national movement for land. The reconstituted popular movements of primarily rural Mayas also included human rights groups organized around demands that were openly political and directly related to the ongoing counterinsurgency war: for example, the Grupo de Apoyo Mutuo (GAM), an organization of wives and mothers of the "disappeared" and other human rights victims; the mainly indigenous widows' organization, the National Coordinating Committee of Guatemalan Widows (CONAVIGUA); CERJ Runujel Junam (Council of Ethnic Communities, "Everyone is Equal"), founded to empower highlands Mayas to resist service in the PACs; and the Council of Displaced Guatemalans (CONDEG), representing internal refugees. Many thousands of Mayas also defied army relocation and control programs by fleeing to remote mountain areas and forming permanent "communities in resistance" (CPRs), which began to gain formal recognition nationally and internationally in the early 1990s.

Among the main new characteristics of Guatemala's social movements in the late 1980s/early 1990s were the following: The first and most important was the centrality of the indigenous population and its double condition of exploitation and ethnic discrimination in both rural and urban settings. This was reflected in the rise of diverse movements and organizations fighting for a broad range of indigenous rights. These movements were bolstered by working with indigenous organizations throughout the Americas (the 1991 continental meeting was held in Guatemala) and by the awarding of the 1992 Nobel Peace Prize to Guatemalan Mayan and political opposition leader Rigoberta Menchú. The second novelty was the growing role of the Catholic Church alongside Guatemala's social movements. Liberation theology was a major influence throughout the 1970s and 1980s, and even after the appearance and rapid growth of evangelical Protestant groups during the 1980s (reaching up to one-third of the population), the Catholic Church remained a leading force in articulating the demands of the popular movements.

The third new element of the late 1980s and 1990s movements was the slowly emerging and increasingly visible protagonism of women. (By this time, women were also becoming more central to the labor force and as single heads of household.) Women had been excluded from traditional politics in Guatemala (voting as well as office-holding), and their political activities had generally been very limited. Traditional political parties had excluded women from virtually all positions of political leadership. Only in the late 1980s did women begin to increase their participation in electoral (and nonelectoral) politics—although such participation remained limited by the traditional problems of discrimination and illiteracy.

On the economic front, women began to organize in workplaces where they were overrepresented (e.g., *maquiladora* industries, schools), although their presence in union leadership remained less visible. In their communities, by contrast, women became visible as the principal organizers of austerity protests in the 1980s and ongoing community mobilizations in the 1990s (e.g., for social services in shantytown neighborhoods). Women were also very prominent in human rights organizations such as GAM and indigenous human rights organizations such as CONAVIGUA, CERJ, and CONDEG. It was only in the 1990s, however, that Guatemalan women founded organizations designed explicitly to achieve their rights as women and began to demand equal participation for their organizations in broader coalitions.

In short, Guatemala experienced the gradual emergence of a bloc of popular and indigenous organizations. The notion of a "bloc" indicates that the social subject is not one class in the traditional sense, but a combination of exploited and dominated sectors whose political expression is a coalition, or "front," of popular and indigenous movements; it incorporates conditions related to (ethnic) identity and (gender-based) reproduction as well as (class-based) exploitation. Guatemala's popular and Mayan organizations continued to suffer from many serious weaknesses—above all, continued vulnerability to the endless stream of kidnappings, disappearances, death threats, and assassinations. Their articulation as a social force was also hindered by continuing problems of disunity and inability to organize among the huge informal proletariat. Because repression forced them to operate semiclandestinely, their advances were often imperceptible. Nevertheless, their continued existence and growth was in itself a form of defiance of the counterinsurgency state.

By the late 1980s the context for political action was also shaped by the resurgence of the URNG. Even while having destroyed much of the URNG's social base in the highlands in the early 1980s, the army had been unable to inflict a "final" defeat upon the insurgent forces or to "win" the war definitively. Hence, the organizations of the URNG survived the holocaust; they remained the nuclei of future resistance even at their low point and gradually began to recover their ability to take initiatives, both militarily and politically. Nevertheless, their inability to resist the army's counteroffensive of the early 1980s, combined with the "civilianization" of the counterinsurgency state in the mid-1980s, required once again a profound reorganization and redefinition of strategy.

This redefinition became necessary, first, in response to the clear lesson of the early 1980s that "taking state power" through military victory over the counterinsurgency forces was a totally unthinkable objective—and that the cost of the second round of the war for the civilian population had been so high as to preclude a strategy based simply on continuing the war. Guatemala was one of the few countries in Latin America where the armed insurgent movement operated continuously since the 1960s. But armed struggle is not what people choose; after thirty years of counterinsurgency war, and particularly after the holocaust of the early 1980s, the URNG could not simply propose another decade of war. (In fact, the mid-1980s saw several splits within the organizations of the URNG, with dissidents arguing that the insurgents should have laid down their arms after the defeat of 1981–1983.)

Second, in view of the 1985 election and transition to civilian rule, that is, to a potentially legitimate government, the Left had to find new ways of becoming a significant force in civil society. Hence, shortly after the 1985 election, the URNG began to propose dialogue/negotiations for a political settlement to the war. For the URNG, the emphasis on negotiations was part of several larger modifications of strategy: giving more weight to political aspects of the struggle while at the same time maintaining a military capacity, broadening its social and political alliances, slowly beginning to recognize the role of popular and indigenous sectors acting autonomously, and realizing the importance of an ideological pluralism that would allow the social movements to follow their own organizational dynamic. This was also a response to the growing protagonism, complexity, and plurality of interests in Guatemalan civil society.

To summarize, because of its profound contradictions, the Guatemalan counterinsurgency project could not be stabilized. In the first place, it did not and could not win the battle for legitimacy, given its intrinsic brutality. Second, its basic premise, that the army had definitively won the war against the guerrilla insurgency, was disproven in practice, causing discontent and destabilization within the ruling coalition. Finally, this was combined with neoliberal economic policies designed to expand the economy solely through world market–oriented "nontraditional exports." Aside from intensifying social conflicts, these policies limited economic growth precisely because they did nothing to develop the internal market.

By the late 1980s, then, Guatemala was by no means in an insurrectionary situation or "ungovernable," but it was in a chronic social crisis. The counterinsurgency state made reformism by itself unviable by precluding partial solutions to the staggering problems of poverty and racism. Gradualist approaches to change simply were not permitted. But faced with the deepening of these problems, important sectors of the population made continual efforts to organize in self-defense, as seen above. Meanwhile, the URNG was experiencing another resurgence, but even while continuing armed actions, its main strategic goal after 1986 was to pressure the government and army into negotiating a political settlement to the war.

For four years the Guatemalan government stubbornly insisted that the insurgents must "lay down their arms" and disarm unilaterally without negotiating any substantive issues. They maintained this stance even after the 1987 Central American Peace Accords negotiated (in Guatemala City) primarily to end the Contra War against the Sandinista government in Nicaragua, but also to address the need for negotiated peace in El Salvador and Guatemala. Only several years later did Guatemalan army and government spokesmen finally acknowledge the significant upsurge in guerrilla actions. The implicit admission that the war could not be "won" militarily by either side created the conditions, for the first time beginning in 1990–1991, for serious discussions about ending the war.

Guatemala's Peace Process (1990–1996)

This section summarizes the saga of the Guatemalan peace process and the accords signed in December 1996. It is important to keep in mind that as recently as 1992–1993, hardliners among Guatemala's military and civilian elites were determined not to negotiate a settlement permitting a legal presence or political participation by the insurgent Left or its allies, and they regarded virtually all of the organizations of civil society as the guerrillas' allies or "facades." Particularly after the signing of a negotiated peace in neighboring El Salvador in January 1992, the elites vowed "never" to tolerate such an outcome in Guatemala. The extraordinary story of how and why, from 1994 to 1996, the Guatemalan army and government found themselves involved in very much the same kind of process as the Salvadorans, with the United Nations as moderator and verifier of the process, is chronicled in detail elsewhere (Jonas 2000).

By 1990, considerable political pressure for peace had built up within Guatemala as well as internationally. During 1989, the National Reconciliation Commission (established by the 1987 Central American Peace Accords) sponsored a National Dialogue. Although boycotted by the army, the government, and the business elites, this Dialogue expressed a clear national consensus among all other sectors in favor of a substantive political settlement to the war. The dialogue process projected a series of URNG meetings with the political parties, "social sectors" (private enterprise, popular and religious movements), and finally with the government, and the army. The

1990 sessions included a September meeting between the URNG and CACIF—an unthinkable event during the previous thirty years. Beyond the formal meetings, the dialogue process opened up spaces within a repressive context for public discussion of issues that had been undiscussable for decades; in this sense, it became an important avenue for beginning to democratize Guatemala.

In early 1991 the newly elected government of Jorge Serrano opened direct negotiations with the URNG. For the first time, top army officials agreed to participate in meetings to set the agenda and procedures for peace talks without demanding that the URNG first disarm—although they still hoped to win URNG demobilization in exchange for minimal, pro forma concessions. During the next year, there were agreements in principle on democratization and partial agreements on human rights. The precariousness of the process became evident when it stagnated in mid-1992 and moved toward total breakdown during the last months of Serrano's crisis-ridden government.

The entire peace process was derailed by the May 1993 "Serranazo," or attempted *auto-golpe*. Serrano's suspension of the constitution and dissolution of Congress in order to seize absolute control (initially but briefly supported by some factions of the army) unleashed a major political and constitutional crisis. After being repudiated by virtually all sectors of civil society and the international community, the *Serranazo* was resolved in June through the (most unexpected) ascendance of Human Rights Ombudsman Ramiro de León Carpio to the presidency. But the peace process remained at a standstill during the rest of 1993. The new government, closely allied with the dominant wing of the army high command, presented unrealistic negotiation proposals that would have discarded previously signed agreements and, in essence, would have required the URNG to disarm without any substantive settlements. These proposals were widely rejected throughout Guatemalan society and were viewed as totally nonviable by the international community.

In January 1994, with these tactics having run their course, the negotiations were resumed, this time on a significantly different basis. During the 1991–1993 rounds, Guatemala's peace talks had been moderated by Monsignor Rodolfo Quezada Toruño of the Catholic Bishops' Conference, with the United Nations in an "observer" role. As of January 1994, both sides agreed that the United Nations should become the moderator; this paved the way for significantly increased involvement by the international community, raising the stakes in the negotiations and giving the entire process a less reversible dynamic.

Furthermore, the January 1994 Framework Accord established a clear agenda and timetable. This accord also formalized a role for a broad-based multisector Assembly of Civil Society (ASC), which included virtually all organized sectors of civil society (even, for the first time, women's organizations) as well as the major political parties. Only the big business sectors represented in CACIF decided not to participate. Having gained new experience during the Serranazo, grassroots organizations had become increasingly vocal in demanding participation in the peace process. The ASC was also striking in the diversity or plurality of political/ideological positions represented within its ranks; unlike El Salvador's popular organizations in relation to the FMLN, the ASC was by no means a simple instrument of the URNG. As the main agreements were being hammered out, the ASC—after itself engaging in a fascinating process of consensus-building among widely divergent positions—offered proposals to the negotiating parties on each issue. While not binding, their proposals had to be taken into account by the two parties, and the URNG adopted many of the ASC proposals as its own negotiating positions. The formation of the ASC also gave Guatemala's organized popular sectors their first sustained experience of participating in the political process and was the precursor to the eventual participation by many of those sectors in the 1995 election.

The breakthrough Human Rights Accord was signed in late March 1994, calling for the immediate establishment of international verification mechanisms to monitor human rights. After the mandated U.N. Verification Mission (MINUGUA) finally arrived in November 1994, its functioning on the ground throughout Guatemala created a political climate that was much more positive for ending systematic human rights violations (as well as mechanisms for denouncing such violations—an important change in a country previously dominated by fear). At the negotiating table, meanwhile, two new accords were signed in June 1994 on the Resettling of Displaced Populations (mainly Guatemalan refugees returning from Mexico) and a Truth Commission empowered to *esclarecer*, or shed light, on past human rights crimes, but without judicial powers and without naming the individuals responsible—which sparked fierce criticism from popular and human rights organizations.

The next theme on the agenda, Identity and Rights of Indigenous Peoples, was the subject of negotiation for nine months, until March 1995. The signing of this accord was a landmark achievement for a country whose population is 60 percent indigenous. This accord went far beyond antidiscrimination protections for Guatemala's indigenous majority to mandate a constitutional reform redefining Guatemala as a multiethnic, multicultural, and multilingual nation. If fully implemented, this agreement would require profound reforms in the country's educational, judicial, and political institutions. It laid the formal basis for a new entitlement of Guatemala's indigenous majority and established their right to make claims upon the state—all of which is a precondition for democracy and genuine pluralism in Guatemala. This accord, together with independent initiatives by a variety of indigenous organizations, also created a new context for social and political interactions and for a more democratic political culture. As an example of this new culture, after its signing, the residents of Sololá, a town in the heart of the conflict zone, decided to base the 1996 competition for the "Queen of Sololá," traditionally a beauty contest, on who could best explain the Accord on Indigenous Rights.

Nationally, the peace process was directly impacted by the dynamics of the campaign for the November 1995 general election—and vice versa. The most important novelties of this electoral process were the URNG's early 1995 call, urging participation in the vote, and the formation of a left-of-center electoral front of popular and indigenous organizations (the "left flank" of the ASC), the New Guatemala Democratic Front (FDNG), to participate in the elections. In the November 1995 general elections, no presidential candidate received an absolute majority. The major surprise was the stronger-than-expected showing of the newly formed FDNG, which won six seats in congress; additionally, alliances between the FDNG and locally based indigenous "civic committees" (unaffiliated with the traditional political parties) won several important mayoralties, including Xelajú (Quetzaltenango), Guatemala's second largest city, whose residents are half *ladino*, half indigenous. A January 1996 run-off for president pitted modernizing conservative Alvaro Arzú of the Partido de Avanzada Nacional (PAN) against a stand-in for the Rightist former dictator Efraín Ríos Montt of the Frente Republicano Guatemalteco (FRG), who opposed the peace process. Arzú won by a scant 2 percent margin.

Even before taking office, Arzú had already held several direct, secret meetings with the URNG. Shortly after taking office, Arzú immediately signaled his intention to bring the ongoing peace talks to a successful conclusion. Once the formal peace negotiations were reinitiated, and following intensive consultations with the private sector, an Accord on Socio-Economic Issues was signed in May 1996—this time, finally, with CACIF support. The accord did not directly resolve Guatemala's most fundamental problems, such as grossly distorted land ownership and income distribution, widespread poverty, and un/underemployment. However, it did commit the government to increase spending on health and education and to carry out a much-needed tax reform—the latter being the key to financing virtually all of the reforms from the peace accords and the minimum basis for any future change. Meanwhile, the most difficult issues of social justice were deferred to the future.

The crowning achievement of the peace process came in September 1996, with the signing of the Accord on Strengthening of Civilian Power and Role of the Armed Forces in a Democratic Society. This accord mandated constitutional reforms subordinating the army to civilian control and restricting the army's role to the sole function of external defense—a stark contrast to the army's past practices of involving itself in all areas of government. Most importantly, the accord created a new civilian police force to handle all internal security matters. The army's size (46,000) and budget were also to be reduced by one-third; the PACs and other counterinsurgency units were to be eliminated. This accord also contained important provisions for reforms of the corrupt and dysfunctional judicial system.

After a serious crisis in October 1996 that nearly derailed the entire process, the talks were resumed and operational accords were signed in December. These dealt with a definitive cease fire, constitutional and electoral reforms, the legal reintegration of the URNG (entailing a partial amnesty for both the URNG and the army), and a timetable for fulfillment of all of the accords. Following the dramatic return of the URNG leadership to Guatemala on December 28, the historic Final Peace Accord was signed in Guatemala's National Palace on December 29, 1996, amid considerable national celebration and international attention. Thus ended the first phase of the peace process that the Guatemalan elites had vowed "never" to permit in Guatemala.

How did this "never" turn into acceptance? The United Nations played a role that no other mediating force could have played in facilitating agreements between the government and the URNG, making the peace process less reversible and beginning crucial measures of verification. In addition, six governments played an important supportive role as the "Group of Friends" of the peace process—the main "friends" being Mexico, Spain, Norway, and the United States. And within Guatemala, slowly but surely, despite fierce resistances and significant delays, the peace process acquired credibility. Even the recalcitrant army and CACIF could no longer afford to resist the process openly and found themselves having to defend their interests by participating in the negotiations. In short, none of the major Guatemalan players could afford to boycott the process.

Seen in its totality, the peace process was a great step forward for Guatemala's democractic development—although not for social justice. Rather than being imposed by victors upon vanquished, the negotiations represented a splitting of differences between radically opposed forces, with major concessions from both sides. In addition, most of the accords contained provisions for citizen participation in decision making—including *comisiones paritarias* (with equal representation from the government and indigenous organizations) and a host of other multisectoral commissions. Accord implementation also gave rise to a widespread practice of *consultas*, involving some (not all) policy makers in direct interchanges with citizens and social organizations, even outside the capital city (also a novelty). Finally, the accords provided innovative mechanisms, such as the Women's Forum, for training and participation by those who have never had such opportunities. (Although there was no accord on women's rights, several of the main accords contained provisions specifically designed to expand women's rights.)

Taken as a whole, the accords and the provision for U.N. verification of government compliance represented an *adios* to forty-two years of painful Cold War history and provided the framework for institutionalizing political democracy. If fully implemented, the accords had the potential to open up an opportunity for significant transformations of Guatemalan society. But even after the signing and initial implementation of some accords, the road remained full of mine fields: The efforts to fully implement the accords were bound to encounter very serious resistances from those who held power in the old system.

Postwar Guatemala (1997–2000)

By the beginning of the twenty-first century, four years after the signing of the final peace accords, it remained evident that the implementation phase of Guatemala's peace process was just as difficult and dangerous as the negotiations had been. Guatemala's "peace resisters" lost no time in sharpening their knives to defend the old order, taking every opportunity to challenge the substance and the continuity of the peace process. Just getting the entire complex of new laws and constitutional reforms through Congress sparked battles on many fronts. The Arzú government, which had taken such bold initiatives to finalize the peace negotiations, was much more timid—on many occasions resistant—with regard to compliance with the accords. This became particularly evident in early 1998, when it pulled back from its commitment to carry out a reasonable tax reform that was to have been a long-range mechanism for internal financing of the peace accords. Meanwhile, the rise in common crime, a problem intrinsic to postwar situations around the world, provided a pretext for keeping the army involved in policing and other internal security matters, in violation of the demilitarization accord.

The most difficult moment for postwar Guatemala came in May 1999, with the referendum on constitutional reforms required to put into effect some of the most significant provisions of the accords on indigenous rights and on strengthening civilian power (limiting the functions of the army and making judicial reform). Although polls had shown ahead of time that the reforms were likely to be approved, a well-financed last-month blitzkrieg campaign by peace resisters (who urged a "No" vote, using blatantly racist arguments) succeeded in defeating the reforms—that is, in getting a 55 percent majority for the "No" among the bare 18.5 percent of the electorate that voted. Clearly, the main winner of this vote was abstention, and the main loser was the peace process itself. This political disaster raised a basic question as to whether Guatemala's fragile democracy could be consolidated. (For a detailed analysis, see Jonas 2000, Chapter 8.)

The late 1999 general elections gave a strong victory to Alfonso Portillo, the presidential candidate of FRG, the party founded by ex-dictator Efraín Ríos Montt. Politically, the FRG's victory resulted from an astute populist campaign by Portillo, combined with a "punishment vote" against the Arzú government—primarily for the PAN's failure to take even the most basic measures to improve people's daily lives (socioeconomic situation and personal security), while maintaining the privileges of the rich. In this sense, it was a vote about people's most immediate concerns, not about the long-range structural issues addressed in the peace accords. Within the FRG delegation that was to dominate the new Congress were former army officials who had been key architects and henchmen of the scorched-earth dirty war of the 1980s—not to mention Ríos Montt himself, who was to preside over Congress.

PRESIDENTS/REGIMES SINCE 1930s

- Jorge Ubico (1931–1944) (military dictatorship)
- Juan José Arévalo (1945–1950) (freely elected)
- Jacobo Arbenz (1951–1954) (freely elected, overthrown)
- Col. Carlos Castillo Armas (1954–1957) (military coup)
- Gen. Miguel Ydígoras Fuentes (1958–1963) (military dictatorship)
- Col. Enrique Peralta Azurdia (1963–1966) (military coup and dictatorship)
- Julio César Méndez Montenegro (1966–1970) (freely elected) (Partido Revolucionario)
- Col. Carlos Arana Osorio (1970–1974) (elected, military dictatorship)
- Gen. Kjell Laugerud García (1974–1978) (electoral fraud, military dictatorship)
- Gen. Romeo Lucas García (1978–1982) (electoral fraud, military dictatorship)
- Gen. Efraín Ríos Montt (1982–1983) (military coup and dictatorship)
- Gen. Oscar Mejía Victores (1983–1985) (military coup and dictatorship)
- Vinicio Cerezo Arévalo (1986–1990) (freely elected) (Democracia Cristiana Guatemalteca)
- Jorge Serrano Elías (1990–1993) (freely elected, 1993 attempted auto-golpe) (Movimiento de Acción Solidarista)
- Ramiro de León Carpio (1993–1995) (appointed transition government)
- Alvaro Arzú (1996–1999) (freely elected) (Partido de Avanzada Nacional)
- Alfonso Portillo (2000–2004) (freely elected) (Frente Republicano Guatemalteco)

At the same time as this contorted shift from a moderate Rightist to an extreme Rightist government, the election also featured a stronger than expected showing of the Alianza Nueva Nación (ANN), the Leftist coalition constructed by the newly legalized URNG together with other progressive forces. Despite its scarce resources, internal divisions, and many other disadvantages, the Alianza won 13 percent of the national vote and nine seats in Congress. Structurally, the consolidation of the Left as the third force was a major step toward "normalizing" Guatemalan politics; for the first time since 1954, all political/ideological tendencies were represented. Furthermore, pro-peace forces in Guatemalan civil society—particularly Mayan and women's organizations—continued to pressure the government to honor and implement the peace accords. Although their efforts gained limited immediate results, they established for the first time the presence of counter-hegemonic forces in a society where traditionally the only social sector to exercise any real power was the business elite (CACIF). Given the weakness of pro-peace forces within Guatemala, concerted international pressure—above all, a conditioning of international aid on compliance with the accords—remained a necessary complement to internal pro-peace efforts.

**PRINCIPAL POLITICAL PARTIES REPRESENTED IN
CONGRESS AS OF 1999–2000**

Frente Republicano Guatemalteco (FRG)
Partido de Avanzada Nacional (PAN)
Alianza Nueva Nación (ANN), includes former guerrilla organization URNG
Democracia Cristiana Guatemalteca (DCG)

*Parties Previously Important but Now in Decline, Defunct,
or Subsumed within Other Parties*

Movimiento de Liberación Nacional (MLN)
Unión del Centro Nacional (UCN)
Partido Institucional Democrático (PID) (party of the army)
Partido Revolucionario (PR)
Frente Democrático Nueva Guatemala (FDNG)
Partido Socialista Democrático (PSD)
Partido Guatemalteco de Trabajo (PGT)—Communist Party

(Whether or not key international actors, particularly the United States, would exercise such leverage consistently was another question.)

Despite these pressures for change, Guatemala's political and social institutions remained weak and dysfunctional (beyond the capacity to conduct fraud-free elections after 1985). A major legacy of the counterinsurgency state was the decades-long subordination of all state institutions to the army. Although this ongoing institutional weakness became clear with the 1993 Serranazo, its failure was one of the first steps toward establishing, as a starting point, a strong defense of the constitutional order—an achievement that in Guatemala could never be taken for granted.

As late as the mid-1990s, Guatemala's institutions were still unable to guarantee basic rights in practice. The peace process was a crucial mechanism for attempting to reform previously dysfunctional institutions. The accords mandated reform of the legislative and judicial branches, as well as the executive, and thorough reform of the electoral system. No less important than what the accords prescribed on paper, the U.N. Verification Mission (MINUGUA), the U.N. Development Program, and other agencies of the United Nations and the international community invested huge amounts of resources and energy into institutional strengthening programs. Among the most important focuses was creation of a new Civilian National Police force (independent of the army) and reform of the weak and corrupted justice system, which was characterized by pervasive impunity (nonpunishment of blatant crimes, including human rights crimes).

By mid-2000, these efforts had yet to yield positive results. The most heinous peacetime crime was the April 1998 assassination of Bishop Juan Gerardi just two days after the Archbishop's Human Rights Office (which

GOVERNMENT INSTITUTIONS

Executive: President (elected every 4 years), cabinet, and armed forces (technically subordinated to the president as commander-in-chief, but actually has functioned autonomously, including a host of subunits such as the presidential guard, military intelligence, etc.—all of which is slated by the peace accords to be radically changed)

Legislative: One-chamber Congress, with 113 members

Judicial System: Regular court system consists of sixty-five courts with jurisdictions for different regions of the country, appeals courts, and Supreme Court. Members of the Supreme Court are elected by Congress, and other court judges are nominated by the Supreme Court and approved by Congress. There is also an active Public Prosecutor's Office. In addition, Guatemala has a Constitutional Court that has far reaching powers in matters reaching far beyond traditional constitutional issues (e.g., new taxes).

The peace accords mandate thorough overhaul and reform of the judicial system, to eliminate ingrained problems of corruption and impunity, vulnerability to threats, incompetence, and so on. Additionally, the accords mandate incorporation of Mayan customary law (*derecho consuetudinario*) into the legal system. All of these reforms are under discussion, but most reforms have not yet been made.

Semi-Government Institutions: Supreme Electoral Tribunal, Constitutional Court (see above), Ombudsman for Human Rights

Local Government: Twenty-two departments, 330 municipalities; departmental governors are appointed by the executive, while municipal mayors are elected

he had founded) released a report attributing 85 percent of the killings during the war to state security forces (the armed forces and PACs). The Gerardi assassination, along with other major assassinations and crimes from the thirty-six-year war, remained unsolved and unpunished. The official Truth Commission (Historical Clarification Commission) established by the peace accords released a far-reaching report in February 1999, based on 9000 interviews; the report attributed 93 percent of the human rights crimes committed during the war to the army and its paramilitary units (vs. 3 percent to the URNG), and established that some actions and policies of the Guatemalan government during the 1980s were genocidal in nature. The report also sharply criticized the U.S. role in supporting the apparatus of terror. But implementation of the Truth Commission's follow-up recommendations would require new battles.

Furthermore, like the rest of Central America, Guatemala was in the throes of neoliberal "reform," with all of its negative consequences for income distribution and social justice. The structural problems that had given rise to the thirty-six-year war were farther than ever from being resolved; poverty statistics were geometrically higher than in the 1950s and 1960s, and the official wisdom no longer even promised a "trickle-down" effect to eradicate

---

INTEREST GROUPS

By far the most powerful is the umbrella organization for big business, CACIF; labor unions and peasant federations have existed since the Revolution of 1944, but since the 1954 coup, they have been relatively weak. During the 1980s and 1990s, interest groups became organized in the following additional areas: human rights organizations, both general and those representing indigenous organizations (reflecting the fact that the Maya population was the main target of state repression); indigenous organizations, working on a series of cultural, political, and economic issues; community organizations, particularly in the urban shantytowns; student organizations, at both the high school and university levels; women's organizations, both as part of the broader popular movement and (more recently) for specifically women's issues; and an association for small and medium businesses, as well as "guilds" of lawyers and other professionals. By far the most effective interest group activities during the 1990s have been those undertaken in broad cross-sector coalitions, such as the Assembly of Civil Society during the peace negotiations.

---

poverty. Indeed, to mention just one example, while agrarian reform had been considered a "pro-communist" idea during the Arbenz era in the 1950s, it has simply disappeared from the vocabulary of the new world order of the twenty-first century.

In sum, emerging from a war that had cost over 200,000 civilian lives, Guatemala at the turn of the century remained very much a society in transition—with the outcome uncertain. Although the continuity of the constitutional order and of the peace process appeared intact, many other long-standing problems remained unresolved. The words of Salvadoran writer Roberto Turcios (in 1997) capture an essential dilemma of interpreting postwar transitions such as those of El Salvador and Guatemala: "Looking back over the past 25 years, you can see a gigantic leap forward; but looking ahead, what stands out is uncertainty."

Chronology

1524 Spanish conquest; beginning of colonial era
1821 Independence from Spain
1871 "Liberal reform" begins under presidency of General Justo Rufino Barrios; disestablishment of the Church
1901 United Fruit Company (UFCo) arrives in Guatemala
1931 Jorge Ubico takes over the presidency
1944 Ubico overthrown in military coup; civilian-military uprising subsequently ousts military junta and begins Revolution of 1944–1954
1945 Juan José Arévalo elected president; new democratic constitution is promulgated

1947 New labor code establishes basic workers' rights

1949 Formation of Partido Guatemalteco de Trabajo (Communist Party), not legalized until 1951

1950 Jacobo Arbenz Guzmán elected president

1952 Agrarian Reform Law passed

1954 (June) Arbenz overthrown in CIA-organized "Liberation"; Carlos Castillo Armas takes power

1957 Castillo Armas assassinated

1958 General Miguel Yidígoras Fuentes elected president

1959 Cuban Revolution

1960 (November) Major military uprising against Ydígoras suppressed; some participants take to the mountains

1962 Massive student and labor demonstrations, formation of MR-13 and Rebel Armed Forces (FAR), and beginning of guerrilla insurgency

1963 Overthrow of Yidígoras in coup led by Colonel Enrique Peralta Azurdia to prevent 1963 elections

1966 Julio César Méndez Montenegro (Revolutionary Party) elected president

1966–1968 United States sends Green Berets, finances and directs counterinsurgency campaign led by Colonel Carlos Arana Osorio; founding of MANO Blanca and other death squads; by 1970, 8000 unarmed civilians killed by security forces

1970 Arana elected president

1972 Entry of EGP guerrillas into Guatemala

1974 General Kjell Laugerud becomes president through electoral fraud

1975 Guerrilla activities resume

1976 (February) Massive earthquake; formation of National Committee of Trade Union Unity (CNUS), increased popular organizing

1977 Massive protest march by mineworkers from Ixtahuacan to Guatemala City

1978 (March) General Romeo Lucas García becomes president through electoral fraud; (April) Formation of Committee of Campesino Unity (CUC); (May) Massacre of Kekchi Indians at Panzos; U.S. bans arms sales to Guatemalan government

1979 (July) Sandinista victory in Nicaragua

1979 (September) ORPA guerrillas launch first military operation

1980 (January) Government massacre and burning of the Spanish Embassy; Spain breaks diplomatic relations; great increase in guerrilla activity in Mayan highlands

1981 Beginning of army counteroffensive, involving numerous massacres and destruction of over 400 Mayan villages by 1983

1982 (February) Formation of Guatemalan National Revolutionary Unity (URNG) by EGP, ORPA, FAR, and PGT Nucleus; (March) General Angel Aníbal Guevara "wins" presidency through fraudulent election, but discontented army officers led by Efraín Ríos Montt seize power in coup; Ríos Montt becomes president; counterinsurgency campaign escalates

1983 (January) United States resumes military sales to Guatemala; (August) General Oscar Mejía Víctores seizes power in military coup; counterinsurgency war continues

1984 Constituent assembly draws up new constitution

1985 Official U.S. economic and military aid resumed; formation of Mutual Support Group (GAM); (December) Christian Democrat Vinicio Cerezo wins presidency in national election; takes office in January 1986

1987 (August) Espuipulas II, Central American Peace Accords signed in Guatemala; (September) Guatemalan army begins "Year's End" counterinsurgency offensive

1988 (May) Abortive military coup attempt by Rightist civilians and military officers

1989 (May) Another failed coup attempt

1990 Beginning of "Dialogue" process of discussions between URNG and political and social sectors; (November) Presidential election, first round; (December) Massacre at Santiago Atitlán

1991 (January) Jorge Serrano wins runoff election; (April) Beginning of Government/URNG peace negotiations and establishing of agenda and procedures; (October) Massive continental indigenous conference held in Guatemala, with march from Quetzaltenango to capital

1992 (October) Awarding of Nobel Peace Prize to Guatemalan Mayan and political opposition leader Rigoberta Menchú.

1993 (May–June) Jorge Serrano attempts *auto-golpe*, or "Serranazo," reversed/resolved by ascendance to presidency of Ramiro de León Carpio, former human rights ombudsman

1994 (January) Framework Accord signed, establishing United Nations as moderator of peace negotiations and formation of Assembly of Civil Society; (March) Human Rights accord signed; (June) Signing of accords on Resettlement of the Uprooted and Truth Commission (Historical Clarification Commission); (November) Arrival of MINUGUA, United Nations verification mission

1995 (March) Signing of accord on Identity and Rights of Indigenous Peoples; (March) Eruption of scandal involving CIA-paid Guatemalan army officers in previous assassinations of U.S. citizen Michael Devine and guerrilla husband of U.S. lawyer Jennifer Harbury, Efraín Bámaca; (November–January 1996) In second round, Alvaro Arzú wins presidential election; first-time participation of center-Leftist FDNG in election

1996 (January) New President Alvaro Arzú takes office; (March) Informal cease fire between army and URNG; (May) Signing of Accord on Socio-Economic Issues; (September) Signing of Accord on Strengthening of Civilian Power and Role of Armed Forces in a Democratic Society; (December) Operational accords signed (definitive cease fire, constitutional and electoral reforms, reintegration of URNG, and timetable); (December 29) Final Peace Accord signed in Guatemala City, ending thirty-six-year civil war

1997 (January) International community (donor nations and agencies) pledge $1.9 billion to implement peace accords, conditioned on Guatemalan government compliance with accords

1998 (February) Government retreat on tax reform; (April) Assassination of Auxiliary Bishop Juan Gerardi two days after release of major human rights report under his supervision; (October–November) Central America, including Guatemala, hit by devastating Hurricane Mitch

1999 (February) Historical Clarification Commission releases report on human rights crimes during the war; (March) U.S. President Clinton, in Guatemala, apologizes for U.S. role in Guatemalan counterinsurgency war; (May) Constitutional reforms defeated in referendum; (November–December) In second round, Alfonso Portillo and FRG (party of exdictator Ríos Montt) win election; first-time participation of (now legal) URNG in election, as part of Coalition Alianza Nueva Náción

Bibliography

This bibliography includes only references in English, although many of the best analyses written by Guatemalans are available only in Spanish; wherever possible, I am including translated works by Guatemalans and other Latin Americans. (Students who read Spanish should read, for example, the works of Edelberto Torres Rivas, Gabriel Aguilera, Ricardo Falla, and a host of Mayan analysts.) For reasons of space, this bibliography includes only books, not articles.

Adams, Richard. *Crucifixion by Power*. Austin: University of Texas Press, 1970.

Barry, Tom. *Inside Guatemala*. Albuquerque, NM: Inter-Hemispheric Education Resource Center, 1992.

Carmack, Robert, ed. *Harvest of Violence*. Norman: University of Oklahoma Press, 1988.

Chase-Dunn, Christopher, Susanne Jonas, and Nelson Amaro, eds., *Globalization on the Ground: Post-Bellum Guatemalan Development and Democracy*. Boulder: Rowman & Littlefield, 2001.

Falla, Ricardo. *Massacres of the Jungle*. Boulder, CO: Westview Press, 1994.

Galeano, Eduardo. *Guatemala: Occupied Country*. New York: Monthly Review Press, 1969.

Gleijeses, Piero. *Shattered Hope: The Guatemalan Revolution and the U.S.* Princeton, NJ: Princeton University Press, 1991.

Immerman, Richard. *The CIA in Guatemala*. Austin: University of Texas Press, 1982.

Jonas, Susanne. *The Battle for Guatemala: Rebels, Death Squads and U.S. Power*. Boulder, CO: Westview Press, 1991.

———. *Of Centaurs and Doves: Guatemala's Peace Process*. Boulder, CO: Westview Press, 2000.

Jonas, Susanne, and David Tobis, eds. *Guatemala*. Berkeley, CA: NACLA, 1974.

Menchú, Rigoberta, with Elisabeth Burgos-Debray. *I . . . Rigoberta Menchú*. New York: Verso Press, 1980.

Payeras, Mario. *Days of the Jungle*. New York: Monthly Review Press, 1983.

Perera, Victor. *Unfinished Conquest: The Guatemalan Tragedy*. Berkeley: University of California Press, 1993.

Schlesinger, Stephen, and Stephen Kinzer. *Bitter Fruit*. New York: Doubleday and Anchor Books, 1983.

Smith, Carol, ed. *Guatemalan Indians and the State: 1540–1988*. Austin: University of Texas Press, 1990.

Warren, Kay. *Indigenous Movements and Their Critics: Pan-Mayanism and Ethnic Resurgence in Guatemala*. Princeton, Princeton University Press, 1998.

CENTRAL AMERICAN CONTEXT

Booth, John, and Thomas Walker. *Understanding Central America*. Boulder, CO: Westview Press, 1999.

Dunkerley, James. *Power in the Isthmus*. New York: Verso Press, 1988.

LaFeber, Walter. *Inevitable Revolutions*. New York: Norton, 1984.

Pérez Brignoli, Hector. *A Brief History of Central America*. Berkeley: University of California Press, 1989.

Torres Rivas, Edelberto. *Repression and Resistance*. Boulder, CO: Westview Press, 1989.

Vilas, Carlos. *Between Earthquakes and Volcanoes: Market, State, and the Revolutions in Central America*. New York: Monthly Review Press, 1995.

Walker, Thomas and Ariel Arimony, eds., *Repression, Resistance, and Democratic Transition in Central America*. Wilmington: Scholarly Resources, 2000.

LITERATURE, POETRY, AND PHOTOS

Arias, Arturo. *After the Bombs*. Trans. Asa Zatz. Willimantic, CT: Curbstone Press, 1990.

Asturias, Miguel Angel. *The President*. Trans. Frances Partridge. Prospect Height, IL: Waveland Press, 1997.

Castillo, Otto René. *Let's Go*. Trans. Margaret Randall. Willimantic, CT: Curbstone Press, 1971.

Goldman, Francisco. *The Long Night of White Chickens*. New York: Atlantic Monthly Press, 1992.

Montejo, Víctor. *Testimony: Death of a Guatemalan Village*. Trans. Victor Perera. Willimantic, CT: Curbstone Press, 1987.

Simon, Jean-Marie. *Guatemala: Eternal Spring, Eternal Tyranny*. New York: Norton, 1987 (photos).

Zimmerman, Marc. *Literature and Resistance in Guatemala*. Athens: Ohio University Center for International Studies, 1995.

FILMS AND VIDEOS

Devils Don't Dream. Guatemala, 1995.

Dirty Secrets: Jennifer, Everardo and the CIA. Guatemala, 1948.

El Norte. U.S./Guatemala, 1985.

Mayan Voices/American Lives. Guatemala, 1994.

Men with Guns. U.S., 1997

When the Mountains Tremble. Guatemala, 1983.

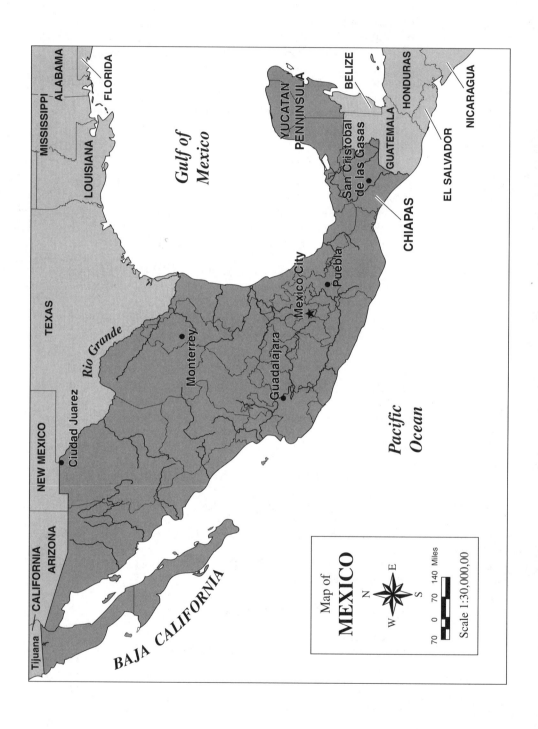

ELEVEN

MEXICO

Nora Hamilton

Introduction

Mexico is a country of approximately 100 million people and 1,958,000 square kilometers, the second largest of Latin America in both population and size. Geographically part of North America, Mexico is characterized by a varied terrain, ranging from northern desert to temperate valleys in central Mexico, with tropical and semitropical zones in the southeast and east. Mountain ranges dissecting Mexico from north to south have made transportation and communication difficult for much of its history. Mexico is also part of the Pacific earthquake zone; in 1985 two severe earthquakes in Mexico City killed thousands of people and demolished a number of buildings.

Mexico's population has grown rapidly during most of the twentieth century, although levels of growth have been reduced from 2.8 percent per year in the 1970s to 1.8 percent in the 1990s. Its urban population is now over 75 percent of the total, up from 40 percent in 1950, with 30 percent of the total population in cities of over 1 million and over 20 million in greater Mexico City. The concentration of economic, political, and cultural life in Mexico City has been a major factor in its attraction of people from other parts of Mexico and has resulted in the attendant problems of pollution, overcrowding, traffic congestion, and shortages, including water and electricity. Other major cities include Monterrey, a northern industrial city, and Guadalajara, a more traditional colonial city of small and medium industries. Some decentralization has occurred in recent years with the growth of cities of the interior and particularly along the U.S. border.

Several factors have been important in shaping Mexico's history as well as its contemporary political, social, and economic life. First, it has a rich

INDIGENOUS GROUPS

Although the Mexican population is predominantly *mestizo*, there is a large indigenous population, which has been variously estimated at from 10 to nearly 30 percent of the population, with most estimates at approximately 15 percent. The difficulty of ascertaining the exact number reflects the fact that indigenous designation is based less on race than on culture, with the acquisition of Western clothing and Spanish language often considered indicative of incorporation into the predominantly *mestizo* society (although this designation has been questioned by indigenous groups and some anthropologists). There are an estimated fifty-six different groups, among which the best known are the Yaqui in the northwest, Otomi in central Mexico, Mixtec and Zapotec in the south (particularly the state of Oaxaca), Tarascans in western Mexico, and various Mayan groups, among them the Mam, Tzotzil, and Tzeltal in the southeast.

The Mexican revolution led to a new emphasis on Mexico's indigenous past, evident in the works of Mexico's muralists in the 1920s and 1930s, but the policy of the post-revolutionary governments was based on the assumption that assimilation and cultural homogeneity were necessary for economic success. Areas of indigenous concentration in southern Mexico are the poorest in the nation. Indigenous groups in Mexico linked with indigenous movements in other parts of the Americas during the 1980s and succeeded in winning some concessions, including a reform of Article 4 of the Constitution to recognize the "pluricultural composition" of Mexico and protecting the languages and cultures of the indigenous people.

The Zapatistas, an indigenous revolutionary group based in the state of Chiapas, have given preeminence to indigenous rights, demanding political and cultural autonomy for Mexico's Indian nations. This was agreed upon in the 1996 Indigenous Rights and Culture (San Andrés) Accords, but the Zedillo administration resisted implementing it. The administration of Vicente Fox has been more receptive to the Zapatista demands and has sent the proposed reforms to Congress.

and varied cultural heritage largely due to the substantial number of indigenous populations that inhabited the area for centuries prior to the arrival of the Spanish. Evidence of the artistic achievement and complexity of these pre-Colombian civilizations can be found at archaeological sites in various parts of Mexico and in Mexico's museums, especially the National Museum of Anthropology in Mexico City. As a result of the mixture of indigenous populations with the Spaniards, Mexico is today a predominantly *mestizo* country. However, some Mexicans claim pure European heritage, and there is a substantial minority of indigenous populations, approximately 15 percent of the total, chiefly in the southern and western regions. Mexico also has a small Afro-Mexican population, whose ancestors had been brought to Mexico to work on plantations during the colonial period.

Second, Mexico has had a special, unequal, and often difficult relationship with the United States, in part due to geographic contiguity. Prior to the Mexican-American War in the mid-nineteenth century Mexico extended into what is now the southwestern United States. Following the U.S. victory and its annexation of half of Mexico's territory, Mexicans continued to live in the area, and their number has been substantially increased through Mexico-United States migration, facilitated by the 2000-mile border shared by the two countries. Although the threat of U.S. military intervention continued to be a real one until the 1930s, Mexico's current relationship with the United States is largely economic. Mexico is dependent on the United States for more than 60 percent of its foreign investment and trade, a relationship now formalized in NAFTA, which incorporates Canada, Mexico, and the United States. Other issues of concern between Mexico and the United States are Mexican migration, the treatment of Mexicans in the United States, and the war on drugs.

A third factor distinguishing Mexico is the Mexican Revolution in the early part of this century, a cataclysmic event that resulted in the decimation of 10 percent of Mexico's population and has shaped Mexico's economic, political, and social life since that time. Although the goals of the various groups that fought in the revolution—democracy, land reform, social justice, and national sovereignty—have been only partially met, they have constituted the prevailing ideology in twentieth-century Mexico. The dominant political party of Mexico since the revolution, the PRI continues to base its legitimacy on its claim to represent these values.

The political structure emerging from the revolution has been an important element in Mexico's long-term political stability, a fourth factor distinguishing Mexico from most other countries of Latin America. Termed the "perfect dictatorship" by Peruvian writer Vargas Llosa, Mexico's dominant party system combined authoritarian controls with flexibility in responding to its constituencies and was for the most part successful in neutralizing protests and dissident groups.

The PRI is based on a corporate structure, composed of three sectors—labor, peasant, and popular—which incorporate major labor confederations and unions, peasant organizations, and, in the case of the popular sector, a range of groups including organizations of state workers and teachers. Sectoral leaders amassed enormous power through control of the respective organizations, which received various favors in return for political support and/or payoffs. Opposition parties have been tolerated but until recently were prevented from winning elections through widespread fraud. At the same time, the president, although very powerful, could not succeed himself, and the politically ambitious and able could aspire to high office by joining and working within the PRI.

Mexico's political stability also benefited from its economic growth between the 1940s and the 1970s. Mexico is one of the most industrialized countries of Latin America, and prior to the 1980s it was one of the most dynamic, with growth rates averaging 6 percent annually (8 percent annually for industrial growth). Industrial growth has been a factor in Mexico's urbanization and in the emergence of middle-income groups in a range of occupations, including small and medium farmers, business owners and industrialists, state workers, professionals, and upper levels of the working class.

Nevertheless, the benefits of growth have been unevenly distributed. In the agricultural sector the relatively prosperous commercial farms of the northern states producing for export contrast dramatically with the impoverished *minifundia* and communal farms of southern Mexico, particularly in the southern states of Chiapas, Guerrero, and Oaxaca. Within the private sector as a whole, a small number of economic groups, consisting of industrial and commercial firms, banks, real estate companies, and other assets, and controlled by a small number or networks of investors, have traditionally shared economic control with public sector firms and transnational corporations. Workers have been divided between those organized in corporate or independent unions, which have benefited at least to some extent by economic growth, and those in smaller firms or the informal sector, whose economic situation is much more precarious.

As in other Latin American countries, Mexico is undergoing rapid transformations in the economic and political spheres, which are having social and cultural repercussions. Economic globalization and the economic crisis of the 1980s have resulted in a rejection of old economic models and an acceptance of neoliberalism by Mexican policy makers. This new model is based on opening the economy to foreign trade and investment and the reduction of state intervention in the economy, a process institutionalized when Mexico joined NAFTA in 1994.

Economic crisis and the embrace of economic liberalism have in turn led to painful economic and social dislocations and adjustments due to loss of jobs, reduced wages, and the elimination of previous economic safeguards, in turn leading to new individual, household, and collective initiatives. Individuals and households rely increasingly on the informal sector and/or migration to the United States, and new forms of organization and mobilization have emerged, ranging from demonstrations by debtors to crossborder organizing among labor groups. On January 1, 1994, the day NAFTA went into effect, indigenous peasants in Chiapas staged a revolt targeting the new economic model as well as accumulated economic and political grievances at the local and regional levels. The worsening economic situation has undermined one of the major pillars of PRI stability, leading to pressures for political reform and increased support for opposition parties.

International opening, internal economic changes, and social mobilization have in turn been factors in a process of democratization, which has resulted in increased opposition representation in municipal governments, the national congress, and among individual state governors. A major milestone in this process was reached on July 2, 2000, as Mexicans elected opposition candidate Vicente Fox of the National Action Party (PAN) as president, ending the seventy-one-year hegemony of the PRI.

Historical Background

EARLY HISTORY

Long before the coming of the Spaniards, the area that is now Mexico was the home of numerous different populations ranging from nomadic hunting societies in the northern plains to highly complex civilizations that achieved high levels of artistic, scientific, and technological sophistication, notably in architecture, sculpture, mathematics, and astronomy. These civilizations were prominent in central and southern Mexico, particularly during the classic period (roughly 150–900 A.D.), when the major cities of Teotihuacán, Monte Albán, Palenque, and others were built and flourished.

The classic civilizations were succeeded by warrior groups. By the early fourteenth century, the Aztecs, a military group, had established a foothold in central Mexico, where they built their capital, Tenochtitlán. From here they conquered the neighboring populations and established an empire that extended from the Gulf of Mexico to the Pacific and from central Mexico into Guatemala. The Aztecs assimilated many of the religious beliefs and cultural practices of the populations they conquered, which were able to maintain their cultural autonomy. A hierarchal governing system was established through which the Aztecs collected tribute and commissioned labor from the subject populations.

The Spaniards, led by Hernán Cortés, arrived in Mexican territory in 1519 and by 1521 had completed the conquest of the Aztec empire with the assistance of some of the subject populations. Because of the immense wealth of the capital city, Tenochtitlán, it became one of the two major centers of the Spanish empire in the Americas, the Viceroyalty of New Spain. The colonial period was characterized by the struggle of the Spanish conquerors and their *criollo* descendants to extract the wealth of the colony, on the one hand, and to circumvent the political and economic restrictions of the Spanish crown, which was attempting to prevent the rise of a rival economic power in the colonies, on the other.

Three hundred years of Spanish colonialism had a profound effect in shaping Mexico's future. For the native populations and civilizations the effects were devastating: Aside from loss through war, contact with the Spaniards brought diseases such as smallpox, which devastated much of the population, and many died through overwork in silver mines or on plantations. Many elements of pre-Colombian culture were destroyed or lost, among them the temple of Tenochtitlán, which was demolished and replaced by a cathedral.

The hierarchical system of the Aztecs was reinforced by the Spaniards with the addition of strong racial components. Initially, large areas were given to the Spanish conquerors in the form of *encomiendas*, a type of trust that gave the trustee the right to collect tribute from the incorporated indigenous communities. As the mines were depleted, the Spaniards and *criollos* began to take over the lands of the indigenous communities and forced their inhabitants to work for them. The major strategy was a form of debt

RELIGION

The Catholic Church has been a major force in Mexican history since the colonial period, although its role has been an ambiguous one. On the one hand, the official Church has been for the most part conservative, upholding authoritarian and hierarchical values, and has generally reinforced the status quo. On the other, individual members of the clergy and Catholic laity have actively defended the rights of downtrodden sectors, evident in the role of priests such as Miguel Hidalgo and José María Morelos in the early independence movements, and more recently in the work of catechists influenced by liberation theology in areas such as Chiapas, where they have had a role in the organization of indigenous peasants since the 1970s. Prior to his retirement in 1999, Bishop Samuel Ruíz of San Cristóbal de las Casas worked tirelessly on behalf of the indigenous groups of Chiapas and played a leading role in efforts to mediate the conflict between the Zapatistas and the government.

Its economic and spiritual power, and its social and political conservatism, made the Church a major target of reformist groups and governments. In the mid-nineteenth century, the Liberal government succeeded in undermining the economic power of the Church through the expropriation of its landholdings and encouraged Protestant missionaries to come to Mexico in an effort to counter its spiritual influence. In the early twentieth century, the revolutionary governments restricted its ideological role through the establishment of state control of education. Draconian measures against the Church in the 1920s resulted in the Cristero rebellion, which ended with an agreement curtailing state persecution of the Church in return for non-interference of the Church in politics, with the result that the political role of the Church has been quite limited throughout most of the twentieth century.

Nevertheless, Catholicism has retained a considerable following; according to a 1989 poll, 92 percent of the population consider themselves Catholic. Bishops and other members of the clergy have increasingly spoken out on political and social issues, including human rights violations, electoral fraud, and the gap between the wealthy and the poor. In 1991, the Salinas government proposed legislation that would reverse many constitutional restrictions on the Church, which was passed in 1992, and government representatives increasingly consult Church authorities on issues of mutual interest.

Approximately 5 percent of the Mexican population consider themselves Protestant. Evangelical movements have had a more limited role in Mexico than in some other Latin American countries, but have been growing in recent years. Both Evangelical and mainstream Protestant groups have been particularly active in certain areas, such as eastern Chiapas, where they have introduced more democratic forms of religious practice and broken down ethnic and gender barriers to participation. Friction between Catholics, Protestants, and evangelical Christians has overlapped with political and social conflicts in the region, but the Zapatista movement incorporates members of all religious groups.

peonage, through which the Indians incurred debts from the landowners in order to pay tribute, which they were then forced to pay off by working for the landowners, a form of servitude that was often passed on to succeeding generations.

As elsewhere in Latin America, the Catholic Church had an ambiguous role. Following the conquest several religious orders established houses in New Spain with the mission of converting the Indians to Christianity; while some were benevolent, if paternalistic, and attempted to modify the exploitative behavior of the Spaniards toward the Indians, others were extremely harsh. Ultimately a form of Christianity emerged that incorporated elements of indigenous customs and rituals, including the Indian Virgin of Guadalupe and the celebration of the Day of the Dead. Many religious orders became wealthy owners of land, and the official Church became associated with the conservative elements of society, reinforcing the strict hierarchal social order. There have been exceptions throughout Mexican history, however, of dedicated priests and some bishops who worked in the poor communities and sympathized with their needs and interests.

INDEPENDENCE AND THE MEXICAN REPUBLIC (1810–1910)

The initial independence movements in the early nineteenth century were in fact led by priests, Miguel Hidalgo, a creole, and José María Morelos, a *mestizo*, and incorporated Indian and *mestizo* peasants, mineworkers, artisans, and unemployed as well as some of the lower clergy. These movements were oriented not only toward political independence but also toward the abolition of slavery and of tributes paid by the Indians. The threat of social revolution frightened many of the *criollo* population as well as the Spaniards, who crushed the initial revolts. When independence from Spain was eventually achieved in 1821 under General Agustín de Iturbide, it left the existing social system intact. It is Hidalgo, however, who is remembered as the father of Mexican independence and the date of his call to arms, September 16, 1810, that is commemorated as Mexico's Independence Day.

The legacy of the independence movement was a weak state and an oversized military, resulting in several decades of anarchy characterized by internal and external wars, military coups, and economic devastation. Mexico was poorly prepared to defend its borders or to prevent the westward expansion of the United States. In 1834, Texas seceded, and in the 1848 Mexican-American War Mexico lost most of what is now the U.S. southwest.

Politically power was contested by Conservatives, representing elite groups who wanted a centralized state and the retention of the colonial socioeconomic hierarchy, and Liberals, a mostly urban middle class who opposed land concentration, Church power, and monopoly control of trade. In 1855, the Liberals came to power and under the leadership of Benito Juárez, a Zapotec Indian, passed a series of laws, and subsequently the constitution of 1857, to end the prerogatives of the Church and the military. Catholicism was no longer the official religion; the prerogatives of military and ecclesiastical courts were eliminated; and corporate property, including not only that of the Church but also communal indigenous property, was abolished, with peasants receiving individual titles. The government hoped that the elimination of corporate property would result in an agrarian middle class of family farms along the lines of the United States, but most of the land was eventually taken over by wealthy landowners, mineowners, and merchants.

This period, the *Reforma*, was interrupted by a Conservative revolt assisted by the French, who took advantage of U.S. involvement in the Civil War to occupy Mexico from 1863 to 1867, when they were finally defeated by the Liberals. But a decade of intermittent war had left economic devastation, a weak central state, and, despite the defeat of the Conservative army, an unruly military, this time the Liberal army. Ironically it was only after another military revolt, this one led by a Liberal general, Porfirio Díaz, and under the subsequent Díaz regime, that the centralization of state power and conditions for political order and economic growth were achieved.

Following his successful revolt Díaz was elected president in 1876 and re-elected after an interim term in 1884 after which he held on to power, through largely fraudulent elections, until 1910. This period, subsequently known as the *Porfiriato*, was characterized by the physical, economic, and political integration of the country, the consolidation of the Mexican state, and economic growth through increased integration with the world economy. Railroad construction and the elimination of regional tariffs opened up the national market, in the process eliminating a major power base of regional generals and *caciques* and facilitating the centralization of state power.

Díaz sought to modernize Mexico on the basis of foreign investment and European immigration. Generous concessions were given to U.S. and European investors in infrastructure, mining, agriculture, and petroleum. Mexican mineral and agricultural exports expanded dramatically, and manufacturing, based on light industries, also grew. But the benefits of economic growth were highly concentrated by foreign investors and a small number of domestic groups. Díaz' favoritism to foreigners irked domestic investors, and many were genuinely concerned at the growth of foreign, and particularly U.S., control of major sectors of the economy, including mineral resources, finance, and agriculture. The small industrial proletariat that worked in the railroads, mines, and manufacturing industries often received low wages for work in difficult and even harsh conditions and was subject to prohibitions against forming independent labor organizations.

The most exploited group was undoubtedly the rural sector, which included the majority of Mexico's population. The growth of Mexico's exports and domestic markets resulted in an expansion of agricultural production, often leading to landowner takeovers of the agricultural land of neighboring peasants and indigenous communities. Peasant revolts were ruthlessly crushed by guards hired by landowners or by federal troops. By the end of the *Porfiriato* an estimated 97 percent of the rural population had no land. Labor conditions on the plantations and *haciendas* were often extremely harsh.

By the first decade of the twentieth century, there was a growing movement for democracy, including journalists and intellectuals demanding a return to the principles of nineteenth century liberalism, as well as regional elites—landowners, mineowners, bankers, and industrialists of the north and northwest—resentful of the concentration of political power by a small coterie around Díaz. The first group, which included the Flores Magón brothers, formed the Liberal party and expanded their program to incorporate the rights of rural and urban workers, including the expropriation of unproductive land, land grants to rural workers, an eight-hour day, minimum wage, and other benefits. Linked to the International Workers of the World (IWW) and to anarchist movements in Mexico, the Liberal party supported some of the major strike movements in the last decade of the Díaz regime.

The second group was composed of regional landowning, mining, industrial, and banking elites, who decided to contest the presidential elections of 1910. They formed the Anti-Reelectionist Party, with Francisco Madero as their presidential candidate, and campaigned under the slogan, "Effective suffrage, no reelection." However, Díaz had Madero arrested; Madero escaped and fled to the United States, where he issued a call on Mexicans to take up arms against the discredited Díaz regime, a signal for uprisings in several states. Madero also obtained the assistance of a small group of peasant guerrillas under the leadership of Emiliano Zapata by promising a return of land usurped by landowners under Díaz.

THE MEXICAN REVOLUTION (1910–1934)

The revolt against Díaz succeeded in defeating the Porfirian army, and Madero easily won the subsequent elections. But he failed to restore lands taken from the peasants in southern Mexico, which had the effect of turning Zapata and his followers against Madero and also radicalizing their goals. With the Plan de Ayala, issued in 1911, Zapata expanded the call to return the land expropriated from peasant proprietors to incorporate demands for agrarian reform that would expropriate one-third of large landholdings and distribute them to landless workers.

Madero also failed to dismantle state institutions, notably the Porfirian army, led by General Victoriano Huerta. In 1913 Huerta, with the complicity of the U.S. Ambassador Henry Lane Wilson, carried out a coup against Madero. Madero was assassinated, members of congress were arrested, and Huerta took control of the government.

This action reunited the heterogeneous forces that had opposed Díaz, who now attacked the counterrevolutionary government of Huerta. The Constitutionalist Army was formed under the leadership of Venustiano Carranza, a landowner from Coahuila; among his division leaders were Pancho Villa and Álvaro Obregón. In the rural central and southern regions, Zapata led the army of the south, incorporating peasants and rural workers from the *haciendas*. The revolutionary armies defeated Huerta in 1914.

With victory, however, the fragile unity of the revolutionary forces ended. While the leaders of the Constitutionalist army wanted a return to democracy and national sovereignty, Zapata and Villa (who joined him) wanted more fundamental social reforms, particularly a redistribution of land, and distrusted the Constitutionalists. Unable to reach agreement, the revolutionary armies fought each other until the assassination of Zapata in 1919 and the defeat of Villa in 1920. By 1916, however, the Constitutionalists had gained control of the capital city and most of the country; Carranza became provisional president and called for a constitutional congress that would formalize the new regime.

To a remarkable degree, the constitution that emerged in 1917 reflected the heterogeneous goals of the different revolutionary groups. The Constitutionalists were themselves divided between the more conservative followers of Carranza and more radical groups who called for basic reforms, due to genuine sympathy with radical goals or pragmatic recognition that social peace could not be achieved without them. The constitution incorporated various provisions of the 1857 constitution, including a federal system with a separation of powers and no reelection, but it also called for an interventionist state that would in effect implement the goals of various revolutionary groups. It reinforced state control of education, eliminating Church-controlled education; called for national control over land and natural resources; enabled the state to expropriate and redistribute land in the public interest; and outlined extensive rights for labor, including an eight-hour day, a forty-hour week, and the right to organize and strike.

The years of violent revolution had resulted in the decimation of an estimated 10 percent of the population. The immediate post-revolutionary period was one of continued instability, as various groups among the revolutionary leadership jockeyed for power. In the aftermath of the revolution, the revolutionary leadership confronted three immediate challenges: to establish the institutions of an effective state and political system, to rebuild the economy and institute the basis for national economic control, and to establish the legitimacy of the new system by carrying out the political, social, and ideological principles incorporated in the new constitution.

This process pitted various groups against each other: The revolutionary leadership itself was in dispute as those who had established control over the central government were forced to defend their position against other military leaders ambitious for power. Carranza was elected president in 1917, but an attempt to impose his chosen candidate in 1920 was defeated (and Carranza was subsequently assassinated). Álvaro Obregón, representing a more reform-oriented group within the revolutionary movement, was elected in 1920. He was succeeded by Plutarco Elías Calles in 1924; Obregón was reelected in 1928 but assassinated before he could take office. Over the following six years (1928–1934) three presidents served, but Calles controlled power behind the scenes, earning the title "*Jefe Máximo*"; this period became known as the *Maximato*.

There were also confrontations between the Mexican government and foreign interests over issues involving subsoil rights and mining concessions; peasants and their supporters within the state opposed landowners and their advocates over the expropriation of land; and workers struggled against business groups (and both against the state) over labor rights and organization. The most serious conflict was the Cristero rebellion, a violent struggle resulting from government efforts to implement draconian anticlerical measures. The rebellion was instigated by the clergy and landowners of the Bajío region, but fought for the most part by peasants, particularly debt *peones* on the estates, whose religion was the basis of their way of life.

Education gradually became a means to promote an alternative national culture, particularly targeting the peasantry and indigenous populations. Contact with the peasantry resulted in the radicalization of many of the teachers, who pushed for educational programs relevant to the population and actively promoted land reform. Their radicalism and anticlericalism brought them into confrontation with the landowners and the Church and in some cases the workers on the traditional *haciendas*. Many were killed during the Cristero rebellion and the later Sinarquista revolt in the late 1930s.

By 1930, the government had succeeded in consolidating the Mexican state; political power was concentrated in the central government; the Cristero rebellion had been contained. The formation of a government party, the National Revolutionary Party (PNR), brought together different factions of the revolutionary leadership and provided for periodic changes in government leadership through regular elections without reelection. But the electoral process was far from democratic. An opposition campaign for the presidency in 1929 was defeated with the help of stuffed ballot boxes and graveyard voters.

Social reforms had also been limited. A labor law was passed permitting workers to organize and even strike under certain circumstances, but it also instituted state control through the creation of tripartite federal labor boards giving the government final say in labor-management disputes. Agrarian reform had been intermittent and limited; in 1930 Calles proposed that it be ended. Efforts to enforce legislation protecting national resources and subsoil rights was effectively resisted by foreign mining and petroleum companies backed by the U.S. government, including the threat of military force.

The limited reforms of this period can be in large part attributed to a conservative trend within the Mexican leadership, reflecting increased U.S. influence as well as rapprochement with pre-revolutionary business elites. While the U.S. oil and mining companies had vociferously opposed Mexican efforts to limit concessions to foreign companies, calling for U.S. military intervention, the International Banking Commission, formed to negotiate with Mexico regarding its outstanding debts to European and U.S. banks, was more conciliatory. Negotiations over the debt and other outstanding issues also reinforced contacts between Mexican government officials and private bankers and their U.S. counterparts. The Calles government and its successors also collaborated with Mexican business groups to promote economic development and encourage foreign investment, particularly in manufacturing, and revolutionary generals and government officials took advantage of their position to acquire land or business ventures.

By the early 1930s, an informal alliance could be identified between members of the "revolutionary elite" of government officials and revolutionary generals, some of the larger Mexican business groups, and U.S. interests, united in the goal of limiting revolutionary change in the interests of protecting investment and property rights and promoting economic growth. At the same time, a potential alliance also existed among "agrarians," progressive sectors of the government, including governors who carried out land distribution programs and other reforms in their respective states, and members of the state bureaucracy who identified with peasant groups and workers in pushing for reform.

LÁZARO CÁRDENAS AND THE REVOLUTIONARY AGENDA (1934–1940)

The progressive sectors within the government party obtained control of the 1933 nominating convention and proposed a six-year plan (influenced in part by the Soviet five-year plan and Roosevelt's New Deal as well as the yet unfulfilled promises of the revolution) that set the parameters for the subsequent administration. Among other measures it gave priority to agrarian reform and reinforced the concept of a strong state role in directing the economy, promoting union organization, and ensuring national control of natural resources. Their candidate was Lázaro Cárdenas, one of the "agrarians" who as governor of Michoacán had carried out a land reform program and promoted education.

Although Calles had assumed that he could continue to control Cárdenas as he had the previous presidents, Cárdenas' support for workers in labor conflicts led to a protracted showdown between the two, which culminated in the expulsion of Calles from the country. The Cárdenas victory marked an important step in institutionalizing the presidential office as the center of executive power. It also consolidated labor support for Cárdenas, who continued to support workers in their conflicts with business groups, and encouraged labor organizing, including the establishment of an independent labor confederation, the Mexican Labor Confederation (CTM).

The Cárdenas government carried out an extensive agrarian reform, distributing land to individual peasants and to communities in the form of *ejidos*, owned by the villages, which could be farmed by individual peasant families or collectively. Land reform targeted not only traditional *haciendas* but also commercial estates, which were distributed to rural workers as collective *ejidos*, and continued to be worked as an economic unit with the government providing credit and other inputs. The *ejidos* could not be bought, sold, or rented, in effect removing substantial amounts of land from the capital market—a measure that (in theory at least) would protect peasants from losing their land to landowners, as had occurred following the 1857 reform. Cárdenas also encouraged peasant organization, including the formation of a National Peasant Confederation (CNC).

The Cárdenas government also took on the United States and British-owned petroleum companies in a conflict that began when the petroleum workers' union attempted to obtain a collective contract and eventually went to the Mexican Supreme Court. It was the refusal of the companies to follow the ruling of the Court that resulted in the government decision to expropriate and nationalize the companies. The move had significant internal and international repercussions: Britain broke off relations with Mexico, the United States suspended a silver purchase agreement with Mexico as well as negotiations for loans to Mexico, and the petroleum companies succeeded in having Mexican petroleum exports boycotted in the United States and major European markets. The move was very popular in Mexico, however, where it was seen as a blow for Mexican sovereignty against an industry that had not only exploited the workers but had also consistently disregarded Mexican law.

Shortly after the expropriation, and in the interests of consolidating his support, Cárdenas restructured the government party, changing its name to the Party of the Mexican Revolution (PRM) and creating four sectors: labor, incorporating the CTM as well as other confederations and independent unions; peasant, which would be dominated by the CNC; popular, which drew in different groups and organizations, including federations of teachers and state employees as well as organizations of women, students, professionals, and small farmers; and military, incorporating elected representatives from each military zone (this sector was subsequently dropped). Membership in the party would be based on membership in one of the organizations in the relevant sector. Ostensibly a mechanism for popular input into the party and government, including selection of party candidates for office, the party in fact became a mechanism for controlling the member organizations.

The reforms of the government aroused the opposition of powerful groups within the private sector and led to considerable anxiety among conservative groups within the party and government. A conservative opposition party, the National Action Party (PAN), was formed in 1939, incorporating pro-Church and pro-Hispanic groups opposed to Cárdenas' reforms and particularly "socialist" education. In the central and southern states of the Bajío region, where the Cristero movement had emerged in the 1920s, a new paramilitary group, the Sinarquistas, attacked peasants as well as rural teachers associated with land reforms and the "socialist" values of the revolution.

In the meantime, the pending war in Europe and U.S. fears of a two-front war with Germany and Japan led to U.S. efforts to ensure support and reinforce defenses in Latin America. The Cárdenas administration had pursued an independent foreign policy relative to the United States; it had taken the initiative to push for a nonintervention policy in the Americas at the Pan American Conference in 1936 specifically aimed at preventing U.S. military involvement in the region. It had also supported the republicans in the Spanish Civil War, opened Mexico to Spanish exiles when the republicans lost, and provided refuge for Trotsky when he was expelled from the Soviet Union. Nevertheless, the Cárdenas administration had maintained relatively good relations with the United States even through the petroleum conflict and was prepared to collaborate in mutual defense against fascism.

Thus involvement in hemispheric defense and the need to appease business groups and foreign investors, as well as conservative groups within the government and party, in the interests of political and economic stability were factors in a shift in the government policy in the latter years of the Cárdenas administration. Strikes and other forms of labor protest were discouraged, and the progress of land distribution was slowed. A moderate, Manuel Avila Camacho, was selected as presidential candidate for the PRM and defeated an independent opposition candidate; as in the past, however, the government party used fraudulent means to ensure the victory of Avila Camacho.

In retrospect, the Cárdenas government succeeded to a greater extent than any of its predecessors (or successors) in implementing the social goals of the revolution. The agrarian reform provided land for a substantial number of peasants and was responsible for relative social peace in the countryside for several generations. More than any other government, it recognized the rights of labor and encouraged labor organization. The nationalization of Mexico's oil reserves asserted Mexico's sovereignty and established a precedent for the nationalization of other key economic sectors, generally through negotiated sale rather than expropriation. Mexico also continued to exercise independence in its foreign policy, albeit at a more symbolic level. Finally, the actions of the Cárdenas government affirmed the activist role of the state in social reform and economic development.

The 1920s and 1930s were a period of cultural foment and artistic creativity. It was during this period that Mexico's muralists, among them Diego Rivera, José Clemente Orozco, and David Álfaro Siqueiros, rejecting elitist notions of art and culture, produced their monumental murals in schools, hospitals, government buildings, and other public places. Writers such as Mariano Azuela (*Los de abajo*/The Underdogs) also broke with European traditions in favor of a more direct, raw style that portrayed the brutal lives and exploitation of Mexico's poor. Painters such as Orozco as well as writers often portrayed not only the victimization of the poor by the wealthy or the Church but also the brutality and corruption of some of the revolution's leaders and government officials, themes that were later taken up by Carlos Fuentes (*The Death of Artemio Cruz*) and Juan Rulfo (*The Burning Plain*).

Economic Development and "The Mexican Miracle": 1940–1982

Under the conservative presidents that followed Cárdenas, the focus of government programs shifted to an emphasis on economic development and particularly the promotion of industry. Agrarian reform was neglected, and party control over the member organizations of the labor and peasant sectors was tightened. In some cases government or party officials removed democratically elected leaders of unions or other sectoral organizations if they threatened the status quo, and imposed more compliant leaders.

Mexico's economic development was based on the ISI model followed by several Latin American countries, providing high levels of protection and tax relief for manufacturing industries oriented primarily to the domestic market. This model was partly the result of circumstances; the dramatic fall in exports of primary commodities during the Depression demonstrated the danger of excessive dependence on primary commodity export, while the cutbacks in manufacturing imports during World War II reinforced the validity of an industrialization strategy. A mixed economy evolved with substantial state involvement and an expanding public sector, which included strategic industries such as telecommunications, railroads, airlines, electric power, steel, mining, and, of course, petroleum and petrochemicals. Many services provided by public sector industries were subsidized to keep domestic industry costs low.

Foreign investment was encouraged although subject to certain restrictions: Areas such as petroleum, mining, and banking and finance were off limits to foreigners; foreign subsidiaries operating in Mexico were required to be at least 51 percent Mexican-owned (although this regulation was often weakly enforced); and performance requirements were established for certain industries, such as the automobile industry, which was required to obtain an increasing percentage of its inputs in Mexico and to achieve a balance of trade in the industry, increasing vehicle and parts exports to the level of auto-related imports.

In contrast to state promotion of industry, rural development, particularly of the small farm, peasant and *ejidal* sectors, was relatively neglected. Government promotion of agriculture tended to be concentrated on irrigation programs and technologies beneficial to large and middle-sized farms located in northern Mexico, most of them oriented to export. While agricultural exports did increase substantially during this period, food production for the domestic market stagnated, leading to increased dependence on food imports. Although several programs were instituted to help small farmers and improve domestic food production in the 1970s, their effectiveness was limited and most were discontinued with the economic crisis of the following decade.

The Mexican economy grew rapidly between 1940 and 1970 and more unevenly during the 1970s. Economic growth averaged 6 percent annually, and industrial growth increased at a rate of 8 percent. By the 1970s Mexico, along with Brazil, was one of the most dynamic countries of Latin America and was recognized as a semideveloped industrial economy. But economic growth was accompanied by growing inequality; by 1977, the lowest 20 percent of the households controlled 2.9 percent of the income, while the upper 20 percent controlled over 57 percent. Disparities were also evident within sectors. In agriculture, there was a striking contrast between the large and middle-sized commercial farms oriented to export, often highly mechanized and for most part located in northern Mexico, and a large number of relatively poor *ejidos* and small peasant holdings in southern Mexico. In industry, a limited number of large firms controlled the majority of assets.

The economy was dominated by what has been referred to as a triple alliance of state-owned firms, private domestic firms, and multinational corporations. Firms of the public sector tended to be in infrastructure and strategic industries. MNCs were dominant in automobiles, electric machinery, and chemicals. Private domestic firms tended to be concentrated in consumer industries; many of these were part of economic groups, which combined banks, manufacturing industries, real estate agencies, construction firms, insurance companies, and other assets and were generally controlled by a small number of investors, often a few families, through interlocking ownership and directorates. The economic groups as well as the large state-owned firms had growing access to foreign capital and technology through joint ventures, loans, and technology transfers.

The economic groups, and to some extent the domestic private sector in general, tended to be divided between those dependent on close links with the state and those that were more independent. The former included small and middle-sized manufacturers, many of them organized in the National Chamber of Industries, as well as powerful economic groups in areas such as construction, that benefited from state contracts. The latter included some middle-sized firms located outside the federal district as well as powerful economic groups in the city of Monterrey. The prototype for the independent business sector was the Garza Sada group, which began with a brewery established in the late nineteenth century, expanded into glass manufacturing, initially to make glasses for the brewery, subsequently in steel production, and later into chemicals and other industries. By the 1970s there were four major groups, each with vertically integrated industries, banks, and other institutions and for most part run by third-generation descendants of the original founders.

With the growth of the urban and industrial working class, divisions emerged between those able to secure a job in the larger unionized industries, particularly foreign or state-owned companies; those in small and medium firms or shops; and those unable to obtain regular jobs, who became part of the growing informal sector. The first group, in party-controlled or independent unions, generally benefited from higher wages, job security, and in some cases additional benefits such as subsidized housing, but the second and particularly the third group lacked job security and a dependable wage income.

The combination of industrial growth, centered in the major cities, particularly the federal district, and stagnation of the rural area was a factor in growing rural-urban migration and the massive growth in the population in and around Mexico City, putting a major strain on its resources. Squatter settlements were formed in the periphery of the city by new migrants as well as groups from crowded central city tenements. Some of these eventually became overcrowded satellite cities in their own right; the largest of these, Nezahualcóyotl, had 4 million inhabitants by the 1980s and is one of the largest cities in Mexico. The inability of industry to absorb many of these migrants was a major factor in the growth of the informal sector, which included skilled workers who contracted out their labor as well as street vendors and employees of small workshops that subcontracted with factories and other businesses.

This was also a period of substantial migration to the United States, encouraged by the *bracero* program, initiated during World War II, which contracted Mexican workers for specified periods of time to work in U.S. industry and agriculture. This led to a process of cyclical migration whereby Mexican workers, chiefly from the western states of Michoacán, Jalisco, Guanajuato, and Zacatecas, came to the United States as farm workers for part of the year, returning to their homes during the remaining months. By the 1950s Mexican migrants were also working in industry and staying longer; some settled in the United States and brought their families.

Political Power and Interest Groups: Mexico's Perfect Dictatorship

Mexico's political system has been characterized as one of "flexible authoritarianism"—its flexibility an important factor in its longevity and the political stability that Mexico enjoyed relative to other Latin American countries throughout much of the twentieth century. Political control was exercised through the government party, the Institutional Revolutionary Party, or PRI, which was closely integrated with the state. Party membership was based on membership in labor, peasant, or other organizations, which in turn belonged to the labor, peasant, or popular sectors of the party. Through its corporate structure the party was able to penetrate virtually all sectors of society.

Clientelistic relations linked party, state, and member organizations. Party and government officials provided favors in return for political support, such as voting for PRI candidates, participating in PRI-sponsored demonstrations, and working in political campaigns. Favors ranged from bribes (often used among peasant organizations in return for votes or participation in PRI rallies) to special institutional privileges, such as hospitals and medical insurance for state workers or subsidized housing programs for members of designated unions.

However, party-client relations went beyond political support. Corporate unions often controlled access to jobs, particularly in the state sector, and in some cases, such as the Oil Workers Union, workers "bought" their jobs. Street vendors paid a regular quota to political patrons for a particular space; the patron in turn paid off officials above him. Bribes were also paid to the police to prevent harassment of various kinds. PRI leaders with connections to the informal sector took in an estimated $21 million monthly.

State control was centralized in the federal government and particularly the presidency. Despite constitutional checks and balances, the president (prior to 1997) controlled legislative as well as executive functions. And although governors and municipal officials are formally elected, the president often has a hand in their selection as well as their removal and/or replacement. With 85 percent of public funds, the federal government also exercised monetary control and could withhold funds from opposition or dissident state or local officials. At the same time, state governors and local officials could exercise considerable and even arbitrary power at the state and local level, which has been a particular problem in the southern rural states.

Access to high levels of government and party ran along two parallel tracks. Career politicians, or *políticos*, rise through the party and/or electoral system, while highly trained specialists, or *técnicos*, generally have careers in the federal bureaucracy. *Políticos* generally hold party positions; elected offices, such as municipal officers, state governors, or members of the legislature; and certain cabinet posts, such as Interior (*Gobernación*). *Técnicos* have been important in economic organizations such as the Banco de Mexico (central bank), development banks, and cabinet posts such as Treasury. Until the 1970s the president has held an elected position in the past and has come from a political position, such as Secretary of the Interior. The shift began with Luis Echeverría (1970–1976), who had never held an elected office prior to becoming president, and Jóse López Portillo (1976–1982), the first president from the Ministry of the Treasury.

Political success generally depended on membership in *camarillas*, cliques that form around individuals in a leadership position. At a given point, a political aspirant attaches himself (or herself) to the *camarilla* of a specific leader as a means of getting ahead. When the leader is elected or selected for a post in government, he brings his *camarilla* with him to fill subordinate posts in the same bureaucracy. Family connections and education, especially at the university level, are important in the formation of *camarillas*. Until recently the National Autonomous University of Mexico (UNAM), the major university in the country, and those in particular faculties such as law, were important for political contacts. Beginning in the 1980s education in private universities has become more important, and especially those abroad, chiefly in the United States, such as Yale, Harvard, and MIT.

An important element in the flexibility of Mexico's political system is the fact that the president could not succeed himself, although he generally chose his successor, in consultation with party and private sector leaders. This means that aspiring politicians, by following one of the indicated trajectories and attaching themselves to a *camarilla*, could eventually aspire to a high-level government post. But because of the turnover in top government positions with each new presidential election, high-level office could also be short-lived. One unfortunate consequence was that high-level office was often seen as a one-time opportunity to ensure one's economic future through legal or nonlegal means, such as generous government contracts to family-owned companies or close business associates. Corruption reached unprecedented levels during the oil boom of the late 1970s when several members of the López Portillo government amassed billions of dollars through contracts with their own companies.

Opposition parties have existed throughout much of the post-revolutionary period, providing a veneer of political pluralism, but prior to the late 1980s PRI control over the election process guaranteed that their candidates rarely achieved political office even at the lower levels of government. The most

MAJOR PARTIES, INTEREST GROUPS, AND OTHER ORGANIZATIONS PARTIAL LISTING

Political Parties	*Chamber of Deputies 1997–2000*
PRI (Institutional Revolutionary Party)	239
PAN (National Action Party)	122
PRD (Democratic Revolutionary Party)	125
PVEM (Green Party)	8
PT (Labor Party)	6
Total	500

MAJOR GOVERNMENT INSTITUTIONS

Armed Forces (240,000 members as of 1999)
CONACYT (National Council for Science and Technology)
Chamber of Deputies (500 members)
Senate (128 members)
Supreme Court (11 members)

SECTORS OF PRI AND MAJOR AFFILIATES

Labor Sector
  CT (Labor Congress)
  CTM (Mexican Workers' Confederation)
Peasant Sector
  CNC (National Peasant Confederation)
Popular Sector
  UNE, formerly CNOP (National Congress of Popular Organizations)

MAJOR BUSINESS GROUPS

CCE (Businessmen's Coordinating Council)
CMHN (Mexican Council of Businessmen)
Coparmex (Mexican Employers Confederation)
Concamin (Confederation of Chambers of Industry)
Concanaco (Confederation of National Chambers of Commerce)
Canacintra (National Chamber of Manufacturing Industries)
ABM (Mexican Bankers Association)
AMIS (Mexican Insurance Association)

LABOR ORGANIZATIONS

Corporate Sector

CT (Congress of Labor), umbrella organization
CTM (Mexican Labor Confederation), member of CT
SNTE (National Union of Teachers)

Independent Organizations

UNT (National Union of Workers)
FAT (Authentic Labor Front), member of UNT
STIMAHCS (Union of Metal and Allied Industry Workers), affiliate of FAT
El Foro (National Trade Union Forum)
TELMEX (Telephone Workers Union), member of El Foro

PEASANT ORGANIZATIONS

CNC (National Peasant Confederation), member of Peasant Sector of PRI
UNORCA (National Union of Autonomous Regional Peasant Organizations), independent

GUERRILLA/REVOLUTIONARY ORGANIZATIONS

EZLN (Zapatista Army for National Liberation)
ERP (Popular Revolutionary Army)

OTHER ORGANIZATIONS

El Barzón, debtors' organization
CONAMUP (National Council of the Urban Popular Movements)
Alianza Cívica, network of civic organizations
National Indigenous Congress
CND (National Democratic Convention)
CNM (National Women's Convention), member of CND
CNI (National Indigenous Convention), member of CND

important opposition party before 1988 was PAN, a conservative, pro-Church, and generally pro-business party. There were also several left-wing parties, including the Mexican Communist party, as well as a few parties that could be characterized as "loyal" opposition.

The government and the PRI were generally very skilled at co-opting opposition groups and neutralizing dissent, through tactics ranging from payoffs to limited reforms that responded to some opposition demands, a process that often succeeded in dividing the opposition. The revenues generated through Mexico's economic growth also enabled the government to expand services in areas such as health and education. Infant mortality declined from 91 per 1000 in 1960 to 35 per 1000 in 1993; most of the population has at least a sixth grade education, and the percent of the relevant age group in secondary school increased from 11 percent in 1960 to 55 percent in the early 1990s. Increased economic resources also facilitated special services to the sectoral constituencies of the PRI.

For opposition and dissident groups that could not be co-opted, the government did not hesitate to use repression, particularly in the rural areas, where assassinations were rarely publicized. Guerrilla movements that emerged in the 1950s and 1970s in southern Mexico were brutally repressed. But the fact that repression was for most part "hidden" enabled Mexico to retain the reputation of a relatively benign authoritarian regime throughout most of this period.

This changed with the student revolt in 1968, a series of protests of high school and university students that was met with escalating violence by police forces. On the evening of October 2, 1968, military forces fired into a demonstration of students and other dissidents gathered at Tlatelolco Plaza in Mexico City, killing an estimated total of 200–400 students. Although the student movement was silenced, it raised awareness of the poverty and inequality accompanying Mexico's economic miracle and revealed the coercion and repression underlying the party's "perfect dictatorship."

Economic Liberalization and Political Transition: 1982–2000

The past fifteen to twenty years have been characterized by accelerated changes in Mexico's economic trajectory, which in turn have led to the creation of new social groups and changes in existing ones. While some groups have been strengthened as a result of the new economic model, others have suffered severe dislocations, which have had economic, social, and ultimately political repercussions. In conjunction with changes in the international context, including the process of economic globalization, the demise of the Soviet bloc, and the transition from authoritarian to democratic regimes in Europe and particularly Latin America, these changes resulted in diluting PRI hegemony, strengthening opposition movements and parties, and a gradual, although convoluted, process of democratization.

THE "MIRACLE" UNRAVELS: 1970–1982

After 1968 the Mexican government confronted two challenges: to restore the legitimacy of the system, especially for groups "left out" of the Mexican miracle, and to cope with the stagnation and problems of the growth model. The government of Luis Echeverría (1970–1976) pursued a "democratic opening" in an effort to establish or reestablish dialogue with different groups. Political prisoners, including labor leaders arrested in the 1950s and student leaders arrested in 1968, were released, and some of the latter joined the government; the government also increased expenditures on health, housing, and social welfare and increased the number of Mexicans covered by social security.

On the economic front, Echeverría pursued a nationalist and statist agenda in an effort to stimulate the economy in the context of low savings and a slowdown in private investment. The government took control of a range of industries, including some in areas such as textiles and sugar refining that were confronting bankruptcy, in order to maintain employment. It also expanded investment in steel, chemicals, fertilizers, and heavy industry. The number of firms in the public sector increased from 277 to 845, and public investment increased from 37 to 51 percent of the total. Efforts to raise taxes to pay for increased investment were resisted by the private sector as well as groups within the government, but the government was able to take advantage of the increasing availability of foreign loans, raising the foreign debt from $280 million to $3 billion between 1970 and 1975.

Nevertheless, the economic situation continued to deteriorate. Despite efforts to promote exports, the trade deficit tripled between 1970 and 1976. Dependence on loans and deficit spending led to growing inflation, which, combined with the negative trade balance, resulted in a 50 percent devaluation of the peso in 1976 (from 12.5 to 25 to the dollar), the first devaluation since 1954. Business sectors, concerned about increasing state intervention as well as inflation, began to withdraw investment and to export capital.

In the meantime, Echeverría's efforts to dialogue with different social groups were offset by his inability to cope with continuing social unrest. He initially supported a movement for democracy that emerged in several of the major unions, including electricians and automobile workers, in an effort to get rid of leaders imposed by the labor bureaucracy, but later backed down under pressures from corporate labor leaders. Police forces and hired thugs attacked student movements, and military forces crushed a guerrilla movement that emerged in southern Mexico.

Under Echeverría's successor, José López Portillo, the critical economic situation was temporarily relieved by an oil boom, the result of the discovery and development of Mexican petroleum in the southwestern part of the country and in the gulf region at a time of high and growing international oil prices. The government used the increased revenues from the growth of Mexico's oil exports, as well as foreign loans attracted by Mexico's growth potential, to expand oil production and petrochemical industries as well as other industries.

During the three-year period between 1978 and 1981, the GDP increased by 8 percent annually; total investment, much of it foreign, jumped by 16.2 percent a year; and urban employment grew by 5.7 percent annually, with 4 million new jobs created in oil, public works, and industry. But the net result was to make the economy even more vulnerable. The massive growth in oil exports ironically shifted what had become a diversified export sector, with manufactured goods constituting 47 percent of the total in 1976, to mono-exports, with oil exports increasing from 15 to 75 percent of the total between 1976 and 1981. At the same time, the increase in oil exports was more than offset by imports of the new technology needed to develop oil reserves as well as necessary inputs for expanding industries and imports of consumer goods for the rapidly expanding domestic market. Increased loans necessitated by industrial expansion and the negative balance of trade increased the foreign debt to $86 billion by 1982.

High spending levels and the influx of foreign capital in turn resulted in an overheated economy and a dramatic growth in inflation. The overvalued peso and fear of devaluation led to massive capital flight to banks in the United States and Switzerland and real estate investments in the United States and Europe.

Mexico's vulnerability became evident with the worldwide recession of the early 1980s, which led to a reduction of commodity prices, particularly oil, on the world market by 1981. At the same time, U.S. interest rates had increased from 6.5 percent to 16.7 percent between 1977 and 1981, a further factor in capital flight, as well as the increased costs of servicing the debt. In August 1982, Mexico announced that it was unable to meet its debt obligations, portending the economic crisis that would engulf most countries of Latin America in the 1980s.

Because several major U.S. banks (such as Citibank and Bank of America) were heavily overextended in Latin America, default would have led to a crisis and possibly a collapse of the international banking system. Foreign creditors; the governments of the United States, Europe, and Japan; and the International Monetary Fund provided loans to Mexico and other debtor countries that attempted to stabilize their economies, instituting austerity programs that severely penalized the more vulnerable sectors of the population. The Mexican government immediately closed down 105 state firms and agencies, while many small and medium private firms were forced to close or dismiss workers. In 1982 alone 1 million Mexican workers lost their jobs.

Blaming the domestic banks for capital export and speculation, López Portillo nationalized the banking system, a move that was very popular among certain sectors, including small and middle-sized industries, since the large banks were seen as having monopoly privileges and focusing their lending on their own economic groups. But the nationalization provoked the distrust and hostility of business groups, which became increasingly active politically during the 1980s and 1990s.

DEBT NEGOTIATIONS, AUSTERITY, AND RESTRUCTURING: 1982–1988

The contours of the new economic system were not immediately evident. The initial priority was to stabilize the economy and to renegotiate external debt and obtain loans in order to maintain interest payments. Since debt repayment was the priority of foreign lenders, debt relief generally involved only sufficient funds to enable debtor countries to repay their debt, which as a result actually increased during most of the 1980s. At the same time, the austerity measures, involving the continued closing down of public agencies, the removal of price controls resulting in increased prices, and substantial declines in real wages, led to a deepening recession. Finally, renegotiations in 1989–1990 resulted in an agreement based on the Brady Plan (named for the U.S. Treasury Secretary), which reduced Mexico's external debt and provided some relief.

In the meantime, major international lending agencies such as the World Bank and the International Monetary Fund, as well as U.S. government agencies, began to pressure for a more thoroughgoing economic restructuring in the direction of economic liberalization, or neoliberalism. Among other measures, the new model called for a reduction of the state role in the economy, including the privatization of public sector firms; trade liberalization and increased exports; an opening of the economy to foreign investment; and tax reform.

Other factors were also important in Mexico's economic transformation. The globalization of production and finance, as well as dramatic technological developments, led to a widespread perception by Mexican policy makers of the need for links with the world market. The policy makers themselves had changed: The *técnicos* were now a majority; President Miguel de la Madrid (1982–1988) and key members of his cabinet had received advanced degrees from major U.S. universities, and the architect of the new economic strategy, Secretary of Budget and Planning (and later president) Carlos Salinas de Gortari, had a Ph.D. in economics from Harvard. Several private sector groups, notably the more independent groups in the north, as well as a growing number of export-oriented firms in other cities, had also been long-term advocates of a reduction of state economic intervention and an opening of foreign trade. Finally, de la Madrid and Salinas gave priority to attracting investment, especially foreign capital and Mexican flight capital from abroad, in promoting Mexico's economic recovery.

In 1986, Mexico joined GATT, the General Agreement on Tariffs and Trade (now the World Trade Organization), thus committing itself to reduce tariffs and other barriers to trade. By December 1989, Mexico had moved beyond GATT requirements, decreasing its maximum tariff from 100 percent to 20 percent, and had reduced other import barriers. Manufactured exports were promoted, and automobile exports and *maquiladores*, both predominantly foreign owned, became particularly important. Auto exports increased from $81 million in 1982 to over $1 billion in 1988; and Ford, General Motors, and Chrysler, along with the government-owned PEMEX, constituted the four top exporters in 1991. The number of *maquiladoras* increased from 454 in 1975 to 1954 in 1992, employing nearly 500,000 people; employment was over 760,000 by 1997.

The economic crisis had a devastating effect on wages, which were reduced to half their pre-crisis levels during the 1980s. As elsewhere, economic restructuring also resulted in the "flexibilization" of labor, undermining the role of unions in the workplace and giving employers greater discretion in the hiring, firing, and placement of workers. The downsizing and closing of firms have led to increased employment in the informal sector, and efforts of both employers and corporate party unions to eliminate independent unions have further undermined the labor movement. Government control over union recognition and the legality of strikes has been used arbitrarily on behalf of employers, and in several cases labor activists have been fired and blacklisted. Union membership declined significantly. While there has been a rapid job increase in the *maquila* sector, these jobs are low paying, with limited benefits, and are characterized by difficult working conditions and high turnover, making the *maquilas* difficult to organize.

Not surprisingly, migration to the United States also increased; according to the 1990 U.S. census over half of the foreign-born Mexicans in the United States at that time had come in the preceding decade. The new migrants were also more heterogeneous in social composition and geographic origin, with an increasing number from urban and middle-class sectors and a substantial contingent from Mexico City, previously a center of attraction for rural migrants. There was also a growing number of migrants from the impoverished indigenous regions of southern Mexico and other rural areas.

At the same time, social movements and popular grassroots organizations, some of which had their roots in earlier organizing efforts, have played an important role in representing the grievances of various population sectors. In the late 1970s and early 1980s three coordinating committees (*coordinadoras*) were formed linking independent regional and local organizations: the National Coordinating Committee Plan de Ayala (CNPA), which joined rural credit organizations, *ejidal* unions, and other peasant movements; the National Coordinating Committee of Urban Popular Movements (CONAMUP) incorporating tenant rights groups, neighborhood organizations, and associations of self-employed workers as well as other grassroots movements; and the National Coordinating Committee of Education Workers (CNTE), a democratic movement within the teachers' union.

In September 1985, two devastating earthquakes in Mexico City and the inadequacy of government response galvanized a massive popular movement around issues ranging from housing for those who lost their homes to the need for democratic government. The women's movement also grew significantly during this period as more women entered the labor market and women's role in family and household survival strategies led to increasing activism. Women's committees were formed in several grassroots organizations in addition to organizations at the national level; their goals included giving women greater voice in existing organizations, empowerment and leadership training for women, and combatting patriarchy in its various forms.

Dissatisfaction with the new trajectory of the government also emerged within the PRI itself. In 1987, a group of dissidents formed the "democratic current" and campaigned unsuccessfully for the democratization of the internal nomination process for the 1988 presidential candidate. Several left

WOMEN

Like many Latin American countries, Mexico has traditionally been characterized by patriarchy, which often translates into fierce protectionism by men of their wives, sisters, and daughters. In extreme cases (notably in the countryside) the social life of women may be restricted to the private sphere of home and church. This syndrome is gradually breaking down under the pressures of industrialization, urbanization, and, increasingly, women's political organizing. The percentage of Mexico's labor force who were women grew from 18 percent in 1978 to 27 percent in 1993, although many of these jobs are in Mexico's growing *maquiladora* sector, often characterized by low wages, few benefits, and long hours.

Women's organizations are increasingly questioning existing gender relations. Women also constitute a large proportion of the leaders in nongovernmental organizations active in community organizing, civic action, and mobilization around human rights issues. In 1982, Rosario Ibarra de Piedra, a former housewife who became an activist on behalf of political prisoners and the "disappeared" when her own son was arrested and disappeared in the 1970s, became the first woman to run for president of Mexico, as a candidate of the small Trotskyist Revolutionary Workers' Party. As this case demonstrates, women are frequently at the forefront of movements for reform, and they have played a significant role in the Zapatista movement in Chiapas.

Beginning in the López Portillo administration (1976–1982), an increasing number of women have been recruited into top administrative positions in the government. In the administration of Ernesto Zedillo (1994–2000), women held several cabinet-level positions, including Rosario Greene, appointed to the important post of Secretary of Foreign Relations in 1998. Following the 1997 congressional elections, the Chamber of Deputies had eighty-five women (of a total of 500), or 17 percent of the total—still low, given the fact that women are 51 percent of the population, but a significant increase from only ten years ago. This total declined, however, in the 2000 elections. (Women represent only 11.5 percent in the U.S. House of Representatives.) Women control an increasing proportion (although still a minority) of positions in the national executive committees of the three major parties. The PRD and PRI have both pledged to increase the proportion of women in the executive committees to at least 30 percent of the total, and as of August 2000 both parties were headed by women (Dulce María Sauri, president of PRI, and Amalia García, president of PRD).

the party and organized around an opposition candidate, Cuauhtémoc Cárdenas, son of Lázaro Cárdenas, who was also supported by a number of leftist and other small parties as well as some of the resurgent popular movements and grassroots organizations.

Cárdenas was a very popular candidate, drawing immense crowds wherever he campaigned. However, in an election characterized by spectacular fraud (including a computer breakdown during the vote-counting process) the PRI candidate, Carlos Salinas, was declared the victor with 50.7 percent of the vote; Cárdenas officially received 31.1 percent, and the candidate of PAN, Manuel Clouthier, 16.8 percent. Groups and parties supporting Cárdenas formed the PRD, protesting the election fraud and calling for democratic reforms and a return to the principles of nationalism and social justice that they felt had been abandoned by the PRI government.

THE TRIUMPH OF THE TECHNOCRATS: 1988–1993

The denationalization of state-owned firms, which had begun gradually under de la Madrid, was accelerated in the early 1990s under Salinas. Between 1990 and 1992, the giant telecommunications firm TELMEX (Telefonos de Mexico), the eighteen nationalized banks, mining companies, airlines, and other government assets were privatized or reprivatized, resulting in a one-time windfall for the state of $20 billion (used to pay off internal debt and for Pronasol, a government poverty relief program). Between 1982 and 1992 the number of state enterprises was reduced from 1155 to 232.

Mexico has also substantially reduced its restrictions on foreign capital. The 1994 Foreign Investment Law formalized reductions on domestic content requirements and eliminated other performance criteria. Companies may be 100 percent foreign owned, and areas previously off limits to foreign investment are gradually being opened to minority foreign ownership. In the early 1990s Salinas began negotiating with the United States and Canada to join NAFTA, an agreement that would eventually eliminate all trade barriers between the three countries, creating a single market and enhancing Mexico's attractiveness as an investment site combining cheap labor and direct access to the U.S. market. The NAFTA agreement was approved by the U.S. Congress in 1993 and went into effect on January 1, 1994.

Perhaps the most controversial initiative of the Salinas government was the Agrarian Law of 1992, which in effect reversed the agrarian reform, considered one of the pillars of Mexico's revolutionary legacy. Peasants are no longer able to petition for land, and the *ejidos*, which by law could not be sold or rented (although this did occur in practice), can now be divided among individual *ejiditarios*, permitting their sale to domestic or foreign corporations as well as the use of land as collateral for loans. The purpose was to promote agro-exports, either through joint ventures between agribusiness interests and former *ejiditarios* or through direct sale or rental of their land to agribusiness. However, few former *ejiditarios* have the necessary training and technological inputs for agro-export production, and in small farmer-agribusiness ventures, it is often the small farmer who bears the risks. Combined with NAFTA, which is expected to undermine small peasant producers unable to compete with grain imports from the United States, the new agrarian law deals a devastating blow to the small peasant and *ejidal* producer.

At the macro-economic level, economic liberalization appeared to have been successful by the early 1990s. Following a downturn in 1986 (due to a sharp drop in oil prices), growth resumed, and exports increased from $16.8

NORTH AMERICAN FREE TRADE AGREEMENT

The North American Free Trade Agreement (NAFTA), which was negotiated by the governments of Canada, Mexico, and the United States during the early 1990s and went into effect in 1994, calls for the elimination of tariffs and other barriers to trade between the three countries (for products meeting local content requirements) over a fifteen-year period, removes performance requirements for most investment, and protects intellectual property rights. For the Salinas government, it was a means to institutionalize, or "lock in," Mexico's new market model based on an opening to international trade and investment and to attract foreign investment to Mexico, where it would have access to the U.S. market at much lower labor costs.

One of the more controversial aspects of the negotiations was the secrecy that surrounded them. Efforts of Canadian, U.S., and Mexican labor, environmental, and human rights organizations, and of cross-border alliances among them, to promote the inclusion of regulations with respect to labor laws and environmental protection in the agreement were unsuccessful. The governments did agree to relatively weak side agreements addressing some of the issues, however. Labor unions have had some success in using the labor side agreement to challenge company practices contrary to the labor laws in the respective countries, as when companies in Mexico have tried to block the formation of unions or U.S. companies have violated the rights of migrant workers.

Because it has been embedded in a complex set of national policies and its implementation has been accompanied by dramatic changes resulting from the 1994 peso crisis and subsequent recovery, it is difficult to assess the effects of NAFTA. NAFTA does appear to have had a significant impact in increasing the level of foreign investment in Mexico and facilitating exports to the United States. Direct foreign investment between 1995 and 1999 was an estimated $54 billion, twice as much as in the previous five years. United States–Mexico trade has increased significantly, much of this intraindustry trade, and Mexico's total exports increased from $60.4 billion in 1994 to $136.7 billion in 1999. However, as trade liberalizes, resulting in competition from low-cost imports, some small and medium producers have been forced out of business. Small farmers producing corn for the domestic market have been particularly hard hit, forcing many to leave their farms and migrate to uncertain jobs in the cities or to the United States.

---

billion to $70.3 billion by 1993. Furthermore, the composition of exports had shifted from primarily oil (75 percent) to 80 percent manufactured goods, especially automobiles, other vehicles, vehicle parts, and electronics and electrical machinery. By this time inflation had also been reduced to single-digit numbers. Foreign investment, which reached a low point of $183 million in 1987, was up to $33.3 billion by 1993.

However, there were several danger signs. Most foreign investment— $28.9 billion—was in portfolio investment, attracted to the Mexican stock market and to the high interest rates of government treasury bonds. Imports, largely supplies and other inputs for restructuring existing industry or the establishment of new industries oriented to export, increased even more rapidly than exports, resulting in an $18.5 billion deficit by 1994. The auto industry and *maquiladoras*—two of the major exporters, were also major importers; in fact, much of Mexico's trade with the United States was intra-industry and even intra-firm trade within transnational corporations and their subsidiaries or contracting companies. High interest rates drew foreign capital but made loans prohibitively expensive for domestic businesses lacking access to foreign credit.

In the meantime, economic restructuring resulted in significant social transformation. In effect, both agriculture and industry are characterized by both increasing complexity, with the emergence of new middle groups oriented to export, on the one hand, and increased polarization—the result of concentration or reconcentration of wealth, deteriorating conditions for many middle- and working-class groups, and the increased poverty and destitution of poorer sectors—on the other.

The larger economic groups, temporarily weakened by the economic crisis and the 1982 bank nationalization, succeeded in reconstituting themselves with significant help from the government, and several new groups formed through buying firms very cheaply during the crisis of the 1980s. Both old and new groups subsequently benefited from the reprivatization of the banks and the privatization of other major firms such as the Cananea Mining Company, Azteca Television, and Teléfonos de Mexico.

The reconcentration of wealth and economic power in a small number of economic groups became evident in the growth in the number of Mexican billionaires identified in the annual reports of *Forbes* magazine: In 1994 Mexico had twenty-four billionaires, more than any other country with the exception of the United States, Germany, and Japan. These groups have also become more cohesive, linked by various networks including cross-group investing, membership on different boards of directors, and intergroup alliances to buy controlling interest in privatizing industries. Finally, the private sector, and particularly the large economic groups, have become more fully integrated with foreign and particularly U.S. corporations through joint ventures, marketing arrangements, franchises, and technical agreements, which now encompass virtually every sector of the economy.

Export promotion and trade liberalization did lead to the strengthening of some smaller firms, including subcontractors to larger manufacturing firms producing for export and to foreign (especially U.S.) manufacturers to produce specific brands, for example, in the apparel industry. But trade liberalization has taken a toll on industries producing for the domestic market. Increased imports of consumer goods, while offering benefits to consumers, forced many small and medium businesses to close down, especially in such areas as textiles, clothing, shoes, and furniture; other businesses shifted from production to import. In both cases, job losses resulted.

Although the new Salinas government gave priority to the continuation of economic reforms, the declining legitimacy of the PRI and the weakening of its labor and peasant base as well as the growing strength of the opposition demanded attention to political reform and restructuring as well. During the Salinas administration several laws were passed to reform the electoral process (e.g., through the appointment of neutral electoral officials to oversee the elections) and to permit greater participation by minority party representation. There were also efforts to weaken the sectoral bases of the PRI, enabling individuals to join the party without being members of sectoral organizations. However, the corporate leaders fought changes, and their role in enforcing measures such as wage control and mobilizing electoral support diluted internal reforms.

To restructure the party base, Salinas continued a strategy begun by de la Madrid of encouraging individuals in business to participate in the party and become candidates for elections and worked closely with the major business groups. Previously business groups had not been welcome in the party or directly involved in PRI electoral politics. The government also established contact with some of the independent social organizations and grassroots movements, offering support for some of their demands in return for promises of political support for the PRI or at least pledges not to support the opposition.

The government took separate tacks with the two major opposition parties, working with PAN, many of whose members supported the government's economic program as well as its political reforms, while attempting to neutralize the PRD. The Salinas government recognized PAN victories in several elections, including gubernatorial races, but generally refused to recognize electoral victories claimed by the PRD. Elections in some of the southern states, often controlled by the more corrupt and repressive PRI officials, also resulted in considerable violence, including the assassination of several PRD candidates and militants.

One of Salinas' most effective strategies in reviving support for the PRI was the National Solidarity Program, or PRONASOL, an anti-poverty program that drew on resources from the privatization of major banks and industries to provide subsidized food for urban and rural neighborhoods as well as potable water, street paving, and other infrastructure for poor municipal communities. It also had a political agenda, targeting areas, such as the state of Michoacán, where the PRD had significant support.

The Salinas government also benefitted from economic conditions in the early 1990s: Growth rates were increasing after nearly a decade of declining and negative growth, the inflation rate was reduced, foreign investment was growing. In 1990 negotiations began for Mexico's inclusion in NAFTA, which was presented to the people of Mexico as a highly beneficial arrangement that would result in increased jobs and broad economic improvements and would symbolize Mexico's incorporation into the "first world." The approval of the agreement by the U.S. Congress at the end of 1993 marked the culmination of Salinas' economic success, and his administration seemed to be headed to a triumphant conclusion.

Economic Collapse, Partial Recovery, and the Rise of the Opposition: 1994–2000

The following year brought an end to illusions. It began with the revolt of indigenous peasants in the southern state of Chiapas organized in the EZLN on January 1, 1994, the day NAFTA went into effect. The causes were complex, but a central factor was the worsening economic conditions of the peasantry as a result of economic restructuring and a history of political repression by state and local government officials. The reversal of the agrarian reform and the threat posed by NAFTA to small peasant producers were additional factors in the uprising and its timing.

When the government sent troops to crush the revolt, repression by the government forces was widely publicized, resulting in widespread national and international protest. Both the publicity and the reaction were in large part a consequence of Mexico's increased international visibility as a result of NAFTA negotiations, as well as the emergence of grassroots human rights organizations throughout the country that had established links with international human rights movements.

The government ended the military assault and formed a commission to begin negotiations with the Zapatistas, a protracted process stalemated over disagreements over indigenous autonomy, the increased military presence in the region, and continued violations of human rights, including the assassinations of Zapatistas carried out by paramilitary forces linked to the PRI. At the same time, events in Chiapas, and the communiques of the Zapatistas' charismatic spokesman, Subcomandante Marcos, have continued to be available to a large audience via newspapers, TV, and the Internet; solidarity groups, human rights delegations, and international sympathizers have visited the area in an effort to provide some protection to the population.

The uprising in Chiapas was followed in less than three months by the assassination of PRI presidential candidate Luís Donaldo Colosio on March 23, 1994. Although a young migrant worker was arrested, few believe he was acting alone, and suspicion has fallen on drug cartels, corrupt PRI officials opposed to political and economic reforms, and even high levels of government. In the meantime several kidnappings of prominent businessmen heightened the sense of insecurity and crisis. Both foreign and domestic groups began withdrawing investment and exporting capital from Mexico.

The presidential elections took place in September. Ernesto Zedillo, another technocrat with a Ph.D. from Yale, had been selected by Salinas to replace Colosio, and he defeated both Cárdenas of the PRD and the PAN candidate in what most national and international observers considered relatively honest elections, despite some fraud, particularly in the rural areas. Electoral reforms enacted during the Salinas administration had increased the independence of the Federal Electoral Institute (responsible for overseeing the electoral process and the vote count), and the presence of grassroots observers throughout much of Mexico was in fact a major factor in the honesty of the elections compared with past elections.

Zedillo's victory could be attributed to a number of factors. The PRI's control of the government gave it greater access to campaign funds and media coverage; it also received large donations from major business interests. Neither of the two opposition parties ran an effective campaign, and the PRD had been further undermined by internal conflicts and differences regarding strategy as well as deliberate efforts of the government and the PRI to neutralize its effectiveness. In addition, PRI hegemony guaranteed that neither of the two major opposition parties had had much experience in governing, and it was probably felt that despite its problems, the PRI was the only party with sufficient experience for the difficult situation in which Mexico found itself.

The election was followed by another high-level assassination even before Zedillo came to office—this time the Secretary General of the PRI—in which high levels of the party and government were implicated. In the meantime, the hemorrhage of capital continued, with the result that foreign exchange reserves became dangerously low, confronting Zedillo with a major crisis shortly after he came to power. Zedillo attempted to float the peso, but instead it plummeted by 55 percent, immersing Mexico in another economic disaster just as it appeared to have been recovering from the previous one. The devaluation and declining value of the peso on the international market revealed the precariousness of Mexico's earlier economic recovery. Far from joining advanced industrial countries, Mexico now confronted another severe economic crisis.

With the help of the Clinton administration, Zedillo secured $48.8 billion in foreign loans from the United States, the International Monetary Fund, and other countries and international lending agencies. Zedillo instituted an austerity program, and Mexico's macro-economic balance was quickly restored: After a negative growth of 5 percent in 1995 the economy grew by 5 percent in 1996 and 7 percent in 1997. Inflation was reduced, and increased investor confidence enabled Zedillo to issue government bonds at lower rates of interest and repay Mexico's debt to the United States by the end of 1996. Foreign investment again began to climb, with an increasing proportion in direct investment rather than the more volatile portfolio investment. Mexico's industrial growth reached 9 percent in 1997.

However, the combined costs of the crisis and the austerity program were again borne by the lower and middle sectors of the Mexican population, and income distribution has again worsened. Real wages, which by 1993 had begun to recover to their 1980 levels, dropped substantially, and as of 1997 were still 20 percent below the 1994 levels. An estimated 46 percent of the population is still in poverty, 15 percent (nearly 14 million people) in extreme poverty (i.e., earning less than $1 a day). The rural sector and those in the southern states have particularly high levels of poverty. Regional and sectoral contrasts between industrial cities and northern states on the one hand, and poor rural states such as Chiapas, Guerrero, and Oaxaca on the other, have widened.

The first years of the Zedillo administration were marked by increased demonstrations, marches, and other forms of protest. Sharp increases in interest rates charged by private banks led to a debtors' revolt under the impetus of Barzón (its name denoting part of the yoke for oxen), a militant organization composed initially of farmers confronting the loss of their farms and subsequently expanding to include small business owners and middle-class consumers, which staged dramatic demonstrations throughout Mexico. In the countryside, peasants and *ejiditarios* carried out a series of land invasions, and in several instances groups of peasants attacked freight trains or raided warehouses for grain and other food supplies. In the middle of 1996 a second guerrilla group emerged, the Popular Revolutionary Army (ERP), in the southern state of Guerrero, which had been the scene of a massacre of seventeen *campesinos* by police forces the previous year.

Charges and revelations of corruption have affected all levels of government and party as well as business groups, including Raúl Salinas, brother of the former president; ex-president Carlos Salinas, widely blamed for Mexico's economic problems, has left the country for voluntary exile in Ireland. Mexico's role as the major cocaine route to the United States has been a further factor in corruption and violence. In 1996, in keeping with the United States–Mexico strategy of militarizing the drug war, President Zedillo named General José de Jesús Gutiérrez Robello as head of the National Institute to Combat Drugs, shifting control over the drug war from the corrupt federal police force to the military, believed to be relatively free of corruption. Less than three months later, however, Gutiérrez Robello was arrested for collaborating with Mexico's largest drug cartel, and subsequently other high level military officers have been implicated in the drug trade and protection of the cartels.

Human rights violations have continued. According to human rights organizations, there were over 300 politically motivated assassinations in the 1994–1997 period, including members and leaders of political parties and social organizations, journalists, government officials, guerrillas, soldiers, and policemen. The worst massacre occurred at Acteal, in Chiapas, in December 1997 when forty-five men, women, and children were killed by paramilitary troops. Subsequently, the government clamped down on foreign observers in the area, expelling several sympathizers of the Zapatistas accused of "revolutionary tourism."

Repeated economic setbacks and profound disillusion with the PRI resulted in increased support for the political opposition evident in several opposition victories in gubernatorial, municipal, and legislative elections. Initially the PAN was the major beneficiary, winning several key states in 1995 and 1996. The PRD subsequently staged a comeback from its poor showing in the 1994 elections, partly the work of the new party leader, Andrés Manuel López Obrador. In the 1997 midterm elections, the PRI lost control of the legislative assembly to the opposition, and PRD candidate Cuauhtémoc Cárdenas became the first elected mayor of Mexico City (a post previously appointed by the president). Results in the 1998 gubernatorial races were mixed, with the PRI winning five out of eight of the elections, in some cases after holding primaries. However, the PRD won two gubernatorial elections for first time; the eighth went to the PAN.

Although the experience of opposition government has been mixed, both the PAN and the PRD have gained experience in governing at the state and municipal levels, as well as in the legislature, where the combined opposition has been in the majority in the assembly since 1997. Zedillo continued to recognize opposition victories and enacted further electoral reforms that among other measures provide government funding and media access to opposition parties, enabling them to compete more effectively with the PRI. In November 1999 the PRI held an open primary to select its presidential candidate for the first time, eliminating the practice of presidential selection of the candidate and thus an important source of presidential power.

Toward the Future: The 2000 Elections

In the subsequent July 2 presidential elections Vicente Fox of PAN won a sweeping victory, obtaining 42.5 percent of the vote to 36.1 percent for Francisco Labastida of the PRI and 16.6 percent for PRD candidate Cuauhtémoc Cárdenas. The PAN also became the leading party in Congress, although it does not control a majority. Fox has indicated that he will seek alliances with other parties.

Although Fox, a previous Coca-Cola executive and governor of Guanajuato, has given some indication of his presidential agenda in the pre-election campaign and his post-election initiatives (as well as his previous experience as governor), the full implications of the PAN victory—and the PRI defeat—will become clearer over the next several years and will depend on several factors. Fox has distanced himself from PAN to some extent, forming a separate base in the Amigos de Fox (Friends of Fox) during the electoral campaign and running as the candidate of an alliance that also included the small Green party (PVEM—Ecological Green Party of Mexico) as well as PAN, but the conservative social record of PAN governments in other states as well as Guanajuato has worried some observers.

Much of the vote for Fox and PAN was undoubtedly a vote against PRI and a vote for change. Although Fox has promised change and has reached out to various sectors of the population, including the Zapatistas and indigenous groups, he will continue the free market policies of his PRI predecessors (also favored by PAN). He therefore confronts a major challenge to respond to the needs of those sectors—an estimated 30 to 40 percent of the population—that have been marginalized by these economic policies.

In addition, the formidable apparatus of control developed by the PRI over the years may not be easily dismantled, particularly in states—nineteen out of thirty-two—where PRI controls the government. Fox has pledged to continue decentralization of power, which could benefit entrenched PRI governors. At the same time, the deep internal divisions within the PRI (aggravated as a result of its resounding defeat) will not be easily overcome. The PRD, which won the Mexico City mayor's race by a narrow margin but generally did poorly otherwise, also confronts the problem of rebuilding its base and reconciling the different tendencies within the party.

President-elect Fox took several initiatives suggesting efforts toward innovation in foreign policy. On a visit to several South American countries, he promoted closer ties between Mexico and MERCOSUR, the trade alliance of the Southern Cone countries. He also made several proposals during a trip to Canada and the United States aimed at easing restrictions on Mexican migration to the United States and promoting a long-term vision of open borders (which was met with considerable skepticism by Mexico's two NAFTA partners), as well as suggestions for increased U.S. and Canadian financial assistance to Mexico that would reduce the need for Mexicans to migrate.

Whatever the long-term implications of the July 2, 2000, elections, the defeat of the PRI represents an important milestone in Mexico's long process of democratization. Electoral reforms enacted during the Salinas and Zedillo administrations leveled the playing field and made the opposition victory possible. But the most significant factor has been the growth of civil society and pressures enacted by its component groups, which will continue to be essential for the continuation and progression of democracy in Mexico.

Conclusion

The twentieth century was one of profound change for Mexico, from a largely poor rural society with a few industrial enclaves governed by a personalist dictatorship to a dynamic, relatively industrialized urban society with a large middle class and a modern state controlled for over 70 years by a hegemonic government party. But it was also one of strong continuities: Economic growth and development increased the complexity of Mexico's social structure, but the gap between the wealthy and the poor continues to be extreme. Foreign economic domination has been replaced by growing integration with the global economy and particularly the United States, which may prove to be no less constraining.

The goals enshrined in Mexico's revolution and constitution for national sovereignty and social justice are still elusive. Many feel that they have been undermined by the new economic agenda and see striking similarities with the modernization promoted by the Díaz regime at the turn of the century. At the same time, like the Mexican revolution in the early part of the century, the Chiapas revolt and the growing importance and visibility of social movements challenge the assumption that modernization can go forward without taking into account historic demands for social justice.

Perhaps the most important change is the fact that democracy is part of both the international agenda and that of many Mexicans in a way that it was not at the time of the Mexican revolution. Not only is there broad consensus among social movements and opposition parties of its significance, but there is also a social infrastructure for democracy—in the form of civic action groups, human rights organizations, and other grassroots movements, as well as international links with parallel groups in the United States and other parts of the world. Whether these conditions will evolve into a participatory political system that can transform Mexico's inequitable economic and political structures constitutes a major challenge confronting Mexicans as they enter the twenty-first century.

Chronology

150–900 Classic period of Ancient Meso-American culture; rise of major cities including Teotihuacán, Palenque, Monte Albán

900 Decline of classic culture, rise of warrior tribes

1325 Building of Tenochtitlán, Aztec capital, now the center of Mexico City

1521 Conquest of Aztec empire by Spaniards under Hernán Cortés

1521–1821 Spanish Colonial Period

1812–1815 Revolt against Spain led by *criollo* priest Miguel Hidalgo; put down by the Spanish, but date (September 15) commemorated as Mexican independence day

1821 Mexican independence

1846–1848 Mexican-American War, culminating in Mexico's defeat; in the Treaty of Guadalupe Hidalgo, Mexico loses half its territory to the United States

1857 Beginning of the Reforma; Liberals come to power and a new constitution is adopted

1862 French intervention on behalf of Conservatives, who defeat the Liberal army

1864 Archduke Ferdinand Maximilian appointed by Napoleon III as emperor of Mexico

1867 Maximilian and the Conservatives are defeated by the Liberals under the leadership of Benito Juárez in 1867; the Liberal republic is reestablished

1876–1910 Porfiriato; coup carried out by General Porfirio Díaz, who controls power for the next thirty-four years

1910 Formation of the Anti-Reelectionist Party; revolt against Díaz, led by Francisco Madero; beginning of the Mexican Revolution

1911 Success of revolt with abdication of Díaz; Madero elected president

1913 Madero assassinated by Victoriano Huerta, who becomes president, dissolving congress; Constitutionalist army formed under leadership of Venustiano Carranza; Army of the South under Emiliano Zapata and Constitutionalist Army battle Huerta

1914–1916 Huerta defeated; victorious forces meet at convention of Aguascalientes, but different parties are unable to come to agreement, and there is a split between Constitutionalists and forces of Zapata and Pancho Villa, leading to conflict between two sides. In 1915 Carranza gains control of Mexico City, and in 1916 calls a constitutional convention

1917 New constitution approved

1927–1929 Cristero rebellion: uprising of pro-Catholic groups, especially rural populations in central Mexico, against anticlerical provisions of the government

1929 Establishment of government party, PNR

1934–1940 Lázaro Cárdenas president

1938 Expropriation of U.S.- and British-owned oil companies, which come under state control; Government party restructured on corporate basis; name changed to PRM (Party of the Mexican Revolution); name changed to PRI (Institutional Revolutionary Party) in 1947

1939 Formation of PAN

1940–1970 "Mexican Miracle"

1968 Student mobilization repressed when government agents and military surround student demonstration at Tlatelolco plaza, firing into the crowd and killing an estimated 200–400 people

1982 Debt crisis; beginning of economic restructuring; nationalization of banks under José López Portillo

1988 Opposition candidacy of Cuauhtémoc Cárdenas in presidential election; formation of PRD

1988–1994 Salinas president; acceleration of process of economic restructuring, including privatization of government assets and negotiation of NAFTA with Canada and the United States

1989 PAN wins gubernatorial election in Baja California—the first time an opposition candidate becomes a state governor

1994 (January 1) Uprising of EZLN in Chiapas; (March) Assassination of PRI presidential candidate Luís Donald Colosio; (September) Election of Ernesto Zedillo in relatively open elections; (December) Foreign exchange crisis and peso devaluation, again plunging country into major recession

1996 Emergence of another guerrilla group, ERP, in southern state of Guerrero

1997 Midterm elections, with Cárdenas becoming mayor of Mexico City, and loss of PRI control of Chamber of Deputies for the first time since the party was formed

1999 (November 7) First PRI primary in history; former Interior Minister and economist Francisco Labastida becomes presidential candidate

2000 (July 2) Vicente Fox, candidate of PAN, elected president, defeating PRI candidate Labastida and Cuauhtémoc Cárdenas of the PRD and ending seventy-one years of PRI dominance

Bibliography

Bennett, Douglas C., and Kenneth E. Sharpe. *Transnational Corporations vs. the State: The Political Economy of the Mexican Auto Industry.* Princeton, NJ: Princeton University Press, 1985.

Bethell, Leslie, ed. *Mexico since Independence.* Cambridge, England: Cambridge University Press, 1991.

Camp, Roderic A. *Politics in Mexico: The Decline of Authoritarianism.* 3rd ed. New York: Oxford University Press, 1999.

———. *Entrepreneurs and Politics in Twentieth Century Mexico.* New York: Oxford University Press, 1989.

Centeno, Miguel Angel. *Democracy within Reason: Technocratic Revolution in Mexico.* 2nd ed. University City: Pennsylvania State University Press, 1997.

Cockcroft, James D. *Mexico's Hope: An Encounter with Politics and History.* New York: Monthly Review Press, 1998.

Collier, George. *Basta! Land and the Zapatista Rebellion in Chiapas.* Rev. ed. Oakland, CA.: Institute for Food and Development Policy, 1999.

Collins, Ruth Berins. *The Contradictory Alliance: State-Labor Relations and Regime Change in Mexico.* Berkeley: International and Area Studies, University of California, 1992.

Cook, María Lorena, Kevin J. Middlebrook, and Juan Molinar Horcasitas, eds. *The Politics of Economic Restructuring: State-Society Relations and Regime Change in Mexico.* La Jolla. Center for U.S.-Mexican Studies, University of California, San Diego, 1994.

Cornelius, Wayne, Judith Gentleman, and Peter H. Smith, eds. *Mexico's Alternative Political Futures.* La Jolla: Center for U.S.-Mexican Studies, University of California, San Diego, 1989.

Cornelius, Wayne A., and David Myhre, eds. *The Transformation of Rural Mexico: Reforming the Ejido Sector.* La Jolla: Center for U.S.-Mexican Studies, University of California, San Diego, 1998.

Cornelius, Wayne A., Todd A. Eisenstadt, and Jane Hinley, eds. *Subnational Politics and Democratization in Mexico.* La Jolla: Center for U.S.-Mexican Studies, University of California, San Diego, 1991.

Eckstein, Susan. *The Poverty of Revolution: The State and the Urban Poor in Mexico.* Princeton, NJ: Princeton University Press, 1988.

Foweraker, Joe, and Ann Craig, eds. *Popular Movements and Political Change in Mexico.* Boulder, CO: Lynne Reinner Publishers, 1991.

Fuentes, Carlos. *The Death of Artemio Cruz.* New York: Noonday Press, 1971.

Hamilton, Nora. *The Limits of State Autonomy: Post-Revolutionary Mexico.* Princeton, NJ: Princeton University Press, 1982.

Harvey, Neil. *The Chiapas Rebellion: The Struggle for Land and Democracy.* Durham, NC: Duke University Press, 1998.

Hellman, Judith Adler. *Mexican Lives.* New York: The New Press, 1994.

Knight, Alan. *The Mexican Revolution.* Volumes 1 and 2. Lincoln: University of Nebraska Press, 1986.

Lustig, Nora. *Mexico: The Remaking of an Economy.* 2nd ed. Washington, DC: The Brookings Institution, 1998.

Massey, Douglas, et al. *Return to Aztlan: The Social Process of International Migration from Western Mexico.* Berkeley: University of California Press, 1987.

Maxwell, Sylvia, and Ricardo Anzaldua Montoya, eds. *Government and Private Sector in Contemporary Mexico.* La Jolla: Center for U.S.-Mexican Studies, University of California, San Diego, 1987.

Meyer, Lorenzo. *Mexico and the United States in the Oil Controversy: 1917–1942.* Austin: University of Texas Press, 1977.

Middlebrook, Kevin J. *The Paradox of Revolution: Labor, the State and Authoritarianism in Mexico.* Baltimore: The Johns Hopkins University Press, 1995.

Monsivais, Carlos. *Mexican Postcards*. London: Verso, 1997.

Otero, Gerardo, ed. *Neoliberalism Revisited: Economic Restructuring and Mexico's Political Future*. Boulder, CO: Westview Press, 1996.

Paz, Octavio. *The Labyrinth of Solitude: Life and Thought in Mexico*. New York: Grove Press, 1985.

Pozas, María de los Angeles. *Industrial Restructuring in Mexico: Corporate Adaptation, Technological Innovation, and Changing Patterns of Industrial Relations in Monterrey*. San Diego: Center for U.S.-Mexican Studies, University of California, 1993.

Randall, Laura, ed. *Changing Structure of Mexico: Political, Social and Economic Prospects*. London: M.E. Sharpe, 1996.

Rodriguez, Victoria E., ed. *Women's Participation in Mexican Political Life*. Boulder, CO: Westview Press, 1998.

Ruiz, Ramón Eduardo. *Triumphs and Tragedy: A History of the Mexican People*. New York: W.W. Norton and Company, 1992.

Rulfo, Juan. *The Burning Plain and Other Stories*. Austin: University of Texas Press, 1996.

———. *Pedro Paramo*. New York: Grove Press, 1994.

Vaughan, Mary Kay. *Cultural Politics in Revolution: Teachers, Peasants and Schools in Mexico: 1930–1940*. Tuscon: University of Arizona Press, 1997.

Wise, Carol, ed. *The Post-NAFTA Political Economy: Mexico and the Western Hemisphere*. University Park: Pennsylvania State University Press, 1998.

Womack, John, Jr. *Zapata and the Mexican Revolution*. New York: Vintage Books, 1968.

FILMS AND VIDEOS

The Five Suns: A Sacred History of Mexico. U.S., 1996. A film by Patricia Amlen, University of California, Berkeley, Center for Media and Independent Learning.

Mexico: Dead or Alive. Canada, 1996. Film examining human rights and politics in Mexico through the experience of Mexican doctor, by Mary Ellen Davis, produced by the National Film Board of Canada.

The Mexican American War. U.S., Four-hour video. Paul Espinosa, Espinosa Productions, 4800 Marlborough Drive, San Diego, CA 92116. Tel. 619 284-9811; espinosa@electriciti.com.

The Sixth Sun: Mayan Uprisings in Chiapas. U.S., 1996. An excellent documentary on Chiapas uprising by Saul Landau.

Ya Basta! The Battle Cry of the Faceless. U.S., 1997. Documentary film by Thierry Zeno on Zapatistas in Chiapas.

WEB SITES

Latin American Government Documents Project, http://www.library.cornell.edu/colldev/ladocshome.html. Includes texts of presidential messages, other documents, and content pages of Mexican journals.

University of Texas LANIC, http://www.lanic.utexas.edu. Major gateway to information on Mexico as well as other Latin American countries.

Instituto Nacional de Estadística Geográfica e Informática (INEGI), http://ags.inegi.gob.mx. Official statistical agency.

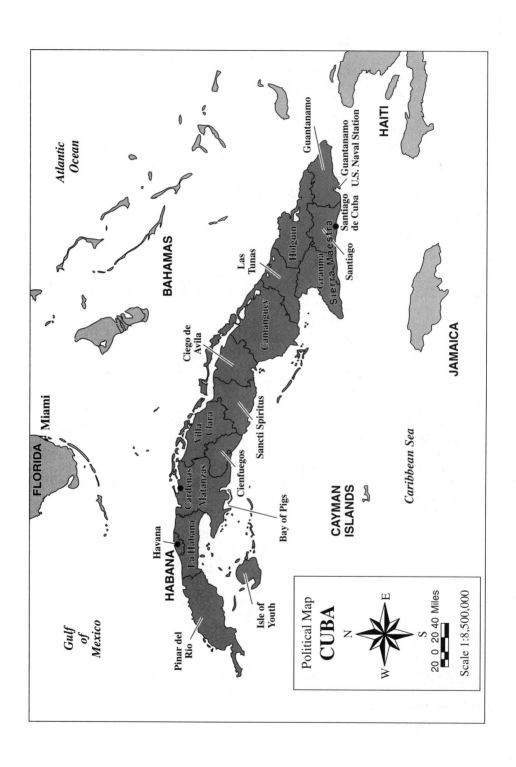

Political Map
CUBA

Scale 1:8,500,000

TWELVE

CUBA

Gary Prevost

Introduction

Cuba is an archipelago of two main islands, Cuba and the Isle of Youth, and about 1600 keys and inlets. The total area of 42,803 square miles is nearly as large as Pennsylvania. Cuba lies just ninety miles south of Key West, Florida; flying time between Miami and Havana is just forty-five minutes. Low hills and fertile valleys cover more than half of the country. Tropical forests and high mountains in the east, which sheltered the revolutionary movement in the 1950s, are contrasted with the prairies and western hills and valleys. Cuba's subtropical climate is warm and humid, with an average annual temperature of 75 degrees. The climate contributes to Cuba's attraction as a year-round tourist destination.

In 1959 Cuba began a social revolution under the leadership of the 26th of July movement, named for the date in 1953 when movement leaders tried to overthrow the dictatorial regime of Fulgencio Batista with an ill-fated attack on the Moncada army barracks in Santiago, the country's second largest city. The movement, under the leadership of Fidel Castro and Che Guevara, carried out profound changes in Cuban society including the establishment of a socialist economic system. Today the revolutionary movement that took control in 1959 is still in power despite a nearly forty-year economic blockade by the government of the United States and the collapse of Cuba's main trading partner, the Soviet Union. It is the character of Cuba's revolution and its success in resisting years of efforts by the United States to regain control of the island that have made Cuba far more prominent in world affairs than its small size would indicate.

Cuba's current population is 11.3 million, with an annual growth rate of 1 percent. More than 70 percent of the population live in urban areas, with the capital Havana having 2.5 million residents. Cubans of Spanish descent make up 66 percent of the population, while 12 percent have African ancestry and 21.9 percent are of mixed heritage. There is a small community of persons of Asian heritage (less than 0.1 percent). More than half of all Cubans are under the age of thirty—born and raised since 1959. Just under 1 million Cubans live in the United States, primarily in south Florida, where they have a major impact on political, social, and economic life. The core of this Cuban-American community was middle- and upper-class Cubans who left between 1959 and 1961 during the dramatic changes brought on by the revolution. The community has been augmented through the years by thousands of others who have migrated for both political and economic reasons. The government of the United States treats all refugees from Cuba who arrive on U.S. soil as political, a privilege extended to no other Latin American nation. Such a designation grants them the right to live and work in the United States.

Education is a priority in Cuban society, and the state provides free primary, secondary, technical, and higher education to all citizens. Cuba has an average of one teacher for every forty-five inhabitants, and the literacy rate of 96.4 percent is one of the highest in Latin America. Recent economic hard times have made for a shortage of supplies, but no children are without schooling. Cuba's health care system has been a priority for the revolution and is a well-regarded model for the developing world, with more than 260 hospitals and 420 clinics. Family doctors are assigned to each community, and there is a doctor for every 260 Cubans. The average life expectancy is seventy-six years, and the infant mortality rate is 7 per 1000—both the best in Latin America.

Women and Cuban citizens of African descent suffered from widespread discrimination prior to 1959, and the increased prominence of both groups in Cuban society is one of the major achievements of the revolution, although racism and sexism are still prevalent factors in society. Racism is rooted in the importation of millions of slaves to Cuba to cultivate sugar cane from the eighteenth century onward. Prior to 1959 women worked outside the home only as domestic servants and prostitutes, but today women have been integrated fully into the workplace and have equal access to education and equality before the law. Women also have much greater control over their lives through the widespread availability of contraceptives and abortion. As a result of the equal access to education at all levels since 1959, women now occupy prominent positions in almost all institutions of the society, especially in financial institutions, academia, and management of enterprises. The prominence of women leaders in society has continued to grow as the post-revolutionary generation assumes power. However, women remain underrepresented at the highest levels of the Communist party, the country's only party, and in the government.

Racial discrimination was formally outlawed at the outset of the revolution, and long-standing customs that barred black Cubans from many public facilities were overcome. As the result of equal access to education Afro-

Cubans have risen to high places in the government, armed forces, education, and commerce. Recent years have seen a significant increase in the study and appreciation of the contributions made by persons of African heritage to the development of Cuba's distinctive culture. The links of this community to Africa were strengthened during the 1970s and 1980s when Cuba developed close political and military ties with the African nations of Angola and Ethiopia. However, racist attitudes still persist in the society and although no formal statistics are available, black Cubans seem to make up a greater percentage of those at the bottom end of the economic ladder.

Cuba is a predominately secular society, the result of both a relatively weak Catholic Church prior to 1959 and policies of the revolution. Among the believers, Catholicism is the dominant faith, although many people combine it with ideas of African origin to form beliefs known as Santería. Santería is probably the most widely practiced religion in the country, and in recent years it has benefited the most from a more tolerant attitude toward religion by the government. A number of Protestant churches also function, but there is no significant presence of the evangelicals who have become important players in other parts of Latin America. At the time of the revolution in 1959 the Catholic Church sided with the Batista regime and many foreign priests, especially Spanish priests, were expelled from the country. While guaranteeing freedom of religious practice, the government actively discouraged religious participation for many years, barring believers from membership in the Communist party and promotions in most areas of Cuban life until 1991. The changing role of religion in Cuban society was embodied in the visit of Pope John Paul II in January 1998. Church attendance and baptisms have risen significantly in recent years, but the number of practicing Catholics still probably numbers under 400,000.

History

Prior to the arrival of Columbus in 1492 Cuba was inhabited mainly by the indigenous Taino, Siboney, and Guanajatadey people. In 1511 a Spanish colony was established and the indigenous were forced into slavery and wiped out, mostly by disease. As a result, contemporary Cuba, unlike much of Latin America, retains no indigenous subculture. In 1519 the Spanish governor of Cuba sent Hernán Cortés to conquer Mexico. Cuba became the last stop before Spain for ships delivering the riches of Spanish America and the Philippines. In 1762 Havana fell into British hands for a short period until it was returned to Spain in exchange for Florida the following year. Generally the Spaniards had little interest in the island until the increased demand for sugar in Europe resulted in its selection for significant cultivation in the eighteenth century when African slaves were brought to work on the plantations. By the nineteenth century sugar production became the basis of the economy, a factor that has remained constant to the present day.

When Napoleon invaded the Iberian peninsula in 1807, Latin American nations began to use the occasion to gain independence, but Cuba remained

A Park (Parque de la Iglesia) in San Antonio de los Baños, Cuba. Bust of 1959 Cuban revolutionary hero Camilo Cienfuegos is seen against the background of a colonial-style church (La Iglesia Villa Ariguanado) built in 1826. *(Photo by Miguel Collazo)*

Spanish, in significant measure because of the successful sugar industry and the close identification of the local elites with Madrid. However, Spanish control was resisted as three wars for independence were fought in the last decades of the century. The first, known as the Ten Years War, had an abolitionist component. It began in 1868 with the leadership of landowner Carlos Manuel de Céspedes, who freed his own slaves, and ended with minor Spanish concessions in 1878. Slavery was abolished two years later. A second inconclusive war lasted a year and ended in 1880. The final struggle began in 1895 led by Cuba's national hero, writer-poet José Martí, who was killed early in the war, and by General Antonio Maceo, an Afro-Cuban who had become a hero when he refused to accept the earlier peace agreement with the Spanish.

When the fight for independence seemed almost won, the U.S. battleship Maine blew up in Havana harbor. The resulting war with the United States ended Spanish rule in 1898. Cuba expected immediate independence but instead gained only American occupation. Most European governments expected the United States, which had several times tried to buy Cuba in the middle of the nineteenth century, would annex the island along with Puerto Rico, Guam, and the Philippines, but Washington promised independence, primarily to avoid the payment of reparations to Spain.

The occupation government of General Leonard Wood began reordering Cuban life along the lines of North American society. The University of Havana was moved to a prominent location overlooking the city, other schools were organized, public health programs were initiated, and a presidential political system was installed, complete with checks and balances following the U.S. model. A capitol building, copied from the one in Washington, DC, completed the picture. Congress made the provision that an amendment to an appropriations bill introduced by Senator Orville H. Platt be incorporated in the Cuban constitution of 1901. The amendment limited Cuban sovereignty in fiscal and treaty-making matters and allowed the United States to intervene at any time to maintain a "government adequate for the protection of life, property, and individual liberty." The Platt Amendment also provided for a North American naval base at Guantanamo, a site still occupied by the United States against the objections of the Cuban government. Cuban products now went to North American markets, and the island became, in essence, a political protectorate of the United States. Twice, in 1905 and in 1917, the United States intervened militarily under the Platt provision.

A British-American agreement set up an International Sugar Committee to control the sale of Cuban sugar, dividing the export market exclusively between the two countries and giving them the power to establish the price. U.S. investment in Cuba, in addition to sugar refineries and lands, included mining, communications, and the railways. The U.S. Federal Reserve Bank established its only foreign branch in Havana. By 1926 U.S. direct investment on the island totaled nearly $1.4 billion.

Two political parties developed, the Liberals and the Conservatives. In 1924 Liberal candidate Gerardo Machado was elected president for a four-year term. In 1927, Machado changed the constitution, extending the presidential term to six years and had himself reelected, which in essence destroyed the party system in Cuba. During the Machado presidency, student and university activism grew. Julio A. Mella, a law student and secretary-general of the Student Federation, organized a national student congress. He later founded the Popular University José Martí, patterned on the Popular University González Prada, established by Haya de la Torre and José Carlos Mardátequi in Peru, to expand education to the working class. Strongly anti-imperialist and highly critical of the role of the United States, Mella worked with the Mexican Enrique Flores Magón to organize the Cuban Communist party in 1925. Through Mella's efforts students began to attack the increasingly dictatorial government of Machado, who responded by jailing Mella. After his release Mella left for exile in Mexico. Opposition to the Machado dictatorship continued in the University of Havana, where students organized the University Student Directorate, which focused anti-Machado sentiment in Havana. The directorate leadership was ousted from the university, ending the first phase of struggle against Machado.

However, the economic collapse of 1929 caused a precipitous drop in the world price of sugar, followed by political unrest and severe repression. The assassination of Mella in Mexico and the increased repression by Machado led to a second directorate in 1930, which began organizing open demonstrations against the government. The new leadership included future president Carlos Prío Socarras, Raúl Roa (later foreign minister under Fidel Castro), and Eduardo Chibas, future founder of the Cuban People's Party (Orthodox). A clash with police killed one of the student leaders and brought the closing of the university by Machado. Now known as the Generation of 1930, the students turned to urban violence. Directorate leaders were arrested, as were most of the faculty, including physiology professor Ramón Grau San Martín. Other groups developed in opposition to the increasingly unpopular Machado. U.S. Ambassador Summer Welles tried to mediate the conflict between Machado and his opposition, but failed, and a general strike, uprisings among the unionized sugar workers, and an army revolt forced Machado into exile in August 1933. He was replaced by Carlos Manuel de Céspedes, son of the hero of 1868, who restored the 1901 constitution. The new government immediately received U.S. backing aimed at isolating the most radical forces.

Directorate leaders continued to agitate against the government, accusing Céspedes of being too close to Machado and the United States. Students demanded a new constitution, plus social and economic reforms. Government plans to freeze army promotions and reduce pay led to a takeover of the army by noncommissioned officers headed by Sergeant Fulgéncio Batista. Batista, who had worked as a stenographer at the military trials of the students under the Machado regime, invited directorate leaders to a meeting. Together they agreed to a coup and on the composition of a new government, ousting Céspedes in September 1933. Although Batista did not accept a post in the new government, the action placed Batista in a position where he dominated politics through the control of the army for the next twenty-six years.

The new government was headed by Professor San Martín, whose short-lived government initiated important social and nationalist legislation. For example, Antonio Guiteras, Minister of Government, nationalized the Cuban electrical system. Simultaneously a series of workers' protests, land confiscations by peasants, and a takeover of sugar mills by sugar workers resulted in strong opposition to the new government from Cuba's wealthy elites and U.S. Ambassador Welles. Behind the scenes Batista and Welles conspired to bring down the new government as the army withdrew its support of San Martín.

Prior to Batista's election in 1940 a new progressive and democratic constitution was enacted. Like Mexico's 1917 constitution it was oriented toward social and economic rights. In the second elections held under the new constitution, Grau San Martín was elected president in 1944. He ran on the ticket of the Cuban Revolutionary Party (Auténtico), a party that was an outgrowth of the student movements of the 1930s. He had been living in exile in Miami and returned only after his election. A second Auténtico President, Carlos Prío Socarras, a student leader of the 1930s, was elected in 1948.

The Auténtico program stressed progressive policies but quickly became identified with extremes of corruption. A new political party, the Cuban Peoples' Party (Orthodox), formed around the leadership of Eduardo Chibas, also a member of the Generation of 1930. University students, critical of the Auténtico corruption, became a source of support and leadership for the Ortodoxos. The party's youth wing was led by Fidel Castro, a law student at the University of Havana. The popularity of the new party indicated that it would win the presidency in the 1952 election, even though Chibas had committed suicide a year earlier. Castro was an Ortodoxo candidate for congress.

In a surprise move, Batista launched a military coup in March 1952, removing Prío Socarras. He canceled the upcoming election and appointed himself president. The new Batista government catered to U.S. policy interests by adopting an anti-Communist position and by breaking formal diplomatic relations with the Soviet Union. Washington responded with military assistance grants of $1.5 million annually from 1954 to 1956 and doubled this figure during the 1957–1958 period. A military mission assisted in training Batista's army. Cuba was opened up to increased American investment, and Havana became an ever more popular gambling and nightclub center just a few miles off the Florida coast. American fascination with Cuba had begun in the 1920s during U.S. prohibition times when U.S. citizens went to Cuba to drink and gamble in facilities operated by North American mobsters. In the 1950s organized crime and the Batista government cooperated in personal enrichment.

Revolution

The opposition to the new Batista government was centered in the urban areas. Following the example of the Generation of 1930, students organized urban guerrilla warfare, using the universities as sanctuaries from the national authorities. In Havana students formed the Revolutionary Directorate under the leadership of José Antonio Echeverría. On the other end of the island in the city of Santiago de Cuba, Frank País, son of a Protestant minister, organized students at the University of Oriente.

Fidel Castro gathered a number of students and workers around him and sought to begin a national uprising by capturing the army barracks at Moncada, Santiago, and the Céspedes barracks in Bayamo. They attacked on July 26, 1953. In the ensuing battles most of the attackers were killed, and Castro was captured. At his trial Castro defended himself, saying, "History will absolve me." He was sentenced to prison on the Isle of Pines (now renamed the Isle of Youth) but was released after twenty-two months as a part of a general amnesty by Batista under popular pressure. An agreement between Castro and Frank País created the 26th of July movement (M-26-7), named for the date of the Moncada barracks attack. After Castro had made a number of appearances in continued opposition to Batista, he was advised to leave the country and began to enlist and train a guerrilla army in Mexico. There he met and began work with an Argentine doctor, Ernesto "Che" Guevara, who had been in Guatemala with the government of Jacobo Arbenz until the CIA-backed overthrow of that government in 1954. After successful fund-raising among anti-Batista Cubans, Castro bought a yacht, the *Granma*, from a retired American couple. In November 1956 he loaded the *Granma* with eighty-two men and sailed for Cuba, landing in Oriente Province. In a coordinated effort Frank País tried to divert the attention of Batista's forces to the city of Santiago, but the invaders were met by army units and were almost completely defeated. The survivors, including Castro, his brother Raúl, and Che Guevara, took refuge in the Sierra Maestra mountains.

For the next two years the war against Batista proceeded on two fronts, the 26th of July movement guerrilla campaign in the Sierra Maestra of Eastern Cuba and an urban resistance campaign consisting of several different political groupings. During 1957 the guerrillas worked to consolidate their position in the mountains by recruiting local peasants to join them and to provide logistical support. During this period the 26th of July movement articulated its political program and publicized it with the aid of a small radio transmitter and the favorable coverage given their movement by a *New York Times* reporter, Herbert Matthews.

Meanwhile many Cubans were already bombing government installations, executing police, and undermining confidence in the Batista government. In March 1957 the Revolutionary Directorate under the leadership of José Antonio Echeverría tried to kill Batista in an armed attack on the presidential palace. The attempt failed and resulted in the death of Echeverría and most of the directorate leadership. Other nonstudent armed revolutionary groups included the Civic Resistance (affiliated with the 26th of July movement); the Montecristo movement of progressive army officers led by Colonel Ramón Barquín, which attempted a failed coup against Batista; and the Puros, who briefly held the Cienfuegos naval station in September 1957. Batista responded to the rebellion with widespread repression. Close to 20,000 Cubans would die in the struggle between 1953 and 1959, mostly civilians.

The ultimate military success of the 26th of July movement was surprising both in the quickness of its triumph and the small numbers of its starting point. Of the eighty-two men who boarded the *Granma* in Mexico only twelve made it to the mountains. After a year of accumulating a few hundred cadre, the guerrillas launched their first attacks in early 1958, just a year before their ultimate triumph. Batista's defeat began in May 1958 when his army carried out an ill-fated all-out offensive against the rebels in the Sierra Maestra. The turning point was a ten-day battle in Jigue when the rebels surrounded a government unit of greater firepower and defeated them. Following that defeat, the morale of Batista's primarily conscript army was very low. Seizing the moment, the 26th of July movement went on the offensive. In the decisive battle at Santa Clara in December 1958 the rebel forces under the leadership of Che Guevara and Camilo Cienfuegos totally routed Batista's forces, and the army collapsed. Batista had no reliable de-

The Museum of the Revolution, located on the edges of Old Havana, is the former presidential palace. It was constructed between 1913 and 1920. Tiffany's of New York decorated the interior. The palace was the site of an unsuccessful assassination attempt on Fulgencio Batista in March 1957. *(Photo by Catherine A. Kocy)*

fenses around him in Havana and on December 31, 1958, he fled the country. Victory came to the 26th of July movement even sooner than it had expected.

Beyond the broad outlines of the military campaign just detailed, the triumph of the 26th of July movement was a complex phenomenon. It was not a mass-based revolutionary war by a peasant army like those that occurred in China or Vietnam. Peasants were recruited to the 26th of July movement and gave it important support, but the guerrilla army, 800 as late as September 1958, was primarily a force of students, professionals, and workers from Cuba's middle sectors. The Cuban insurrection was not an urban proletarian revolution. Organized labor, whose ranks were heavily influenced by the Communist Party (PS), opposed the 26th of July movement until almost the very end, when the communists gave their belated support.

The 26th of July movement also carried out a broad alliance strategy that culminated at a July 1958 meeting in Caracas, Venezuela, where the Revolutionary Democratic Civic Front was organized encompassing almost all of the anti-Batista forces. The front, combined with the military weakening of Batista, eroded U.S. government support for the regime. In March 1958 under pressure from the Senate, the U.S. State Department placed an arms embargo on Cuba. In December the Eisenhower administration repeatedly placed pressure on Batista to step down. However, the U.S. opposition to

Batista was predicated on the assumption that the moderate anti-Batista forces would dominate the new government. That assumption proved to be erroneous.

Revolution in Power

On January 8, 1959, Fidel Castro and the 26th of July movement entered Havana. He noted that the U.S. military had prohibited the Liberator Army under General Calixto García from entering Santiago de Cuba in 1898 and commented that history would not be repeated. Castro took no position in the new government but set about consolidating Cuba's military forces under his command. He sent one of his trusted lieutenants, Camilo Cienfuegos, to relieve Barquín, who had taken command of Batista's remaining troops. Forces of the directorate initially refused to disarm and had to be persuaded to accept Castro's authority.

Castro and his allies from the Sierra Maestra were committed to a program of radical social and economic reform, and they soon set out on a course to consolidate control over state power. The victory over Batista came so quickly that most of the old political structures were intact. Only a few thousand of Batista's closest allies left the country. Most of the landowning elite, businesspeople, professionals, and clergy stayed hoping that they could influence the course of the new government, protecting their considerable privileges. Well aware that their radical plans would encounter stiff resistance among those committed to only minor change, Castro and his allies moved to isolate his opponents one by one. In mid-February 1959 Fidel accepted the position of prime minister and began to push through measures that would distribute wealth and increase support in the rural areas. In May, an agricultural reform act limited the size of most farm holdings to under 1000 acres. This measure destroyed the largest holdings, including U.S.-owned sugar properties, several of which exceeded 400,000 acres. Land was distributed to thousands of rural workers, and the government moved to improve conditions on the large farms it now controlled. As a result, support for the revolution increased throughout the countryside. The passage of the Rent Reduction Act resulted in the transfer of about 15 percent of the national income from property owners to wage workers and peasants.

A literacy campaign sent thousands of young volunteers to rural areas. Literacy was increased, and the young supporters of the revolution learned firsthand about the conditions of the rural areas. The government also began building hundreds of new schools and training thousands of additional teachers. Health care was extended to the entire population for the first time with the construction of rural clinics and hospitals. Many private and racially segregated facilities such as clubs and beaches were opened to the public. These radical social and economic measures carried out in the first year of the revolution often involved mass mobilizations, which served to unite the poor majority of Cuban citizens behind the government. These measures also served to identify the movement's political enemies, who exposed themselves through their vociferous opposition to the changes. Moderates in the government, such as acting President Manuel Urrutia, resigned in protest in June 1959, taking much of the leadership of the old democratic parties and landed elite into exile with them. Simultaneously the use of revolutionary tribunals to judge and then execute approximately 500 members of Batista's police and security agencies was popular with the Cuban masses but forced many of those who had been associated with the old regime to seek refuge abroad. One by one those political forces that opposed the radical direction of the revolution dropped away until only the revolutionary core remained, primarily the cadre of the 26th of July movement from the Sierra Maestra and a few allies from the Revolutionary Directorate who increasingly assumed key cabinet posts and took control of the government bureaucracy. The final element in the revolutionary coalition was the Cuban Communist Party (PSP). Castro made a formal alliance with them in late 1959, not completely trusting them, but desirous of using their organizational skills in the reconstructed government bureaucracies. Their inclusion in the government also served to drive out the remaining anti-communist elements.

The increasingly radical direction of the revolution in 1959–1960 led to a direct confrontation with Washington. The U.S. government had first begun to realize that it had a potential major problem with Cuba when Castro left Washington following a visit in 1959 without requesting significant U.S. aid. Up until that point U.S. officials had expected to control Cuba through the normal give-and-take of foreign aid. By April 1959 the Cuban leadership had already decided on a series of radical changes in Cuba and were not seeking approval in Washington. At the time Castro left Washington, Cuba still maintained the Batista policy of nonrecognition of the Soviet Union. However, this policy began to change, and in December 1959 an official Soviet journalist was admitted to Havana. In February 1960 U.S.S.R. First Deputy Premier Anastasias Mikoyan paid a visit, and a Soviet-Cuban trade agreement was signed. Che Guevara went to Eastern Europe soon after and lined up $100 million in credits for industrialization in Cuba. Relations with the Soviet Union offered a balance and an alternative to dominance of American power in Cuban affairs. Formal diplomatic relations were reestablished between the two countries in May 1960.

The Cuban economy depended on sugar. A U.S. quota system had allocated Cuba a 2.8-million-ton market at a predetermined and subsidized price considerably above the world market. This amounted to significant U.S. governmental aid to Cuba. One of the first actions of friendship by the Soviet Union was the February 1960 purchase of Cuban sugar. As United States-Cuba relations worsened, the U.S.S.R. agreed to purchase 2.7 million tons of Cuban sugar if the American government reduced its quota. The Soviet Union also began to supply Cuba with oil. Cuba has a small domestic supply of petroleum, but only enough to meet about 15 percent of national needs. With a shortage of foreign exchange, Cuba found it increasingly difficult to keep refineries supplied with imported oil, mostly from Venezuela. In April 1960 the first shipment of Soviet oil arrived in exchange for Cuban products. American oil companies, who owned Cuba's refineries, advised by the U.S. Secretary of the Treasury, refused to refine the oil. The refineries were taken over by the Cuban government, and Washington responded by eliminating Cuba's sugar quota, the backbone of the Cuban economy.

The confrontation between Havana and Washington had been building throughout 1959 and 1960. The Cuban government began regulating the U.S.-owned Cuban Telephone Company in March 1959. The confrontation over the oil refineries resulted in the first nationalizations in July 1960, and they were followed quickly by the seizing of U.S.-owned sugar plantations in August, foreign banks in September, and more businesses in October. Late in 1960 the United States broke diplomatic relations with Cuba, and in January 1961 the Eisenhower administration instituted an embargo on most exports to Cuba. The Agrarian Reform Law of May 1959 laid the groundwork for eventual seizure of many large American properties with an offer of twenty-year bonds for payment; the United States, rejecting the bonds, demanded "prompt, adequate, and effective compensation." By December 1959 the CIA began to recruit Cuban exiles, and in March 1960 Eisenhower decided to arm and train an exile force for the purpose of invading the island and precipitating the overthrow of the Castro government.

John Kennedy assumed the presidency of the United States in January 1961 and with it the responsibility for the group of Cuban exiles, now training in Central America under CIA direction. In Cuba, Castro had inaugurated the Committees for the Defense of the Revolution (CDR), organized block by block in the cities, to guard against opposition and to enlist support for the government. In the mountains of Escambray a group of anti-Castro guerrillas maintained harassment of government troops, but at U.S. request they stopped action until the exile forces were ready. In April the exiles invaded Cuba at the Bay of Pigs but were stalled by local militias, while in the cities the CDRs quickly pointed out persons in opposition, who were immediately arrested before any of them could support the invasion. The major result of the American intervention was the consolidation of Castro's position by creating a solid identification between the anti-imperialism of Cuban tradition and the victory of the forces under Fidel Castro. Soon after the defeat of the exile force at the Bay of Pigs, Castro declared the "socialist" character of the Cuban revolution. Socialist countries supported Cuba, with the U.S.S.R. honoring its promise to buy 2.7 million tons of sugar. The People's Republic of China bought a million tons; other socialist nations, 300,000 tons.

From the declared commitment to socialism in April 1961 to the campaign to produce 10 million tons of sugar cane in 1970 the Cuban revolution moved through its most idealistic period. Domestically the revolution sought to create a thoroughly home-grown socialist economy marked primarily by lack of market incentives. Shared sacrifice and a drive for self-sufficiency were the primary driving forces in economic development. The leadership sought to diversify the Cuban economy while instituting a policy of industrialization. New products such as cotton were introduced to the island with the hope of reducing the island's dependency on foreign inputs. At the time of the revolution the United States had $1 billion invested in Cuba. U.S. companies controlled 40 percent of the sugar crop and 55 percent of the sugarmill capacity; more importantly, the United States was the major buyer of Cuban sugar. In return for preferential entry of its sugar into U.S. markets Cuba was required to open its market to the U.S. manufactured goods; this undercut the development of domestic industries. There were numerous distortions—Cuba exported raw sugar but imported candy. It produced vast quantities of tobacco but imported cigarettes. Cuban economic policy of the 1960s was designed to reverse this reality. The determination to end dependence on sugar production took the extreme form of plowing over vast acreage of sugar lands and planting new crops, but these efforts largely failed due to the lack of expertise and appropriate climatic conditions.

During the 1960s the Cuban government also borrowed a strategy of heavy industrialization from the Soviet Union, but these efforts yielded only limited success because of Cuba's particular conditions and the lack of trained personnel. Following the failure of the "balanced growth" model Cuba turned to an approach labeled the "turnpike model." Instead of seeking to diversify the economy immediately, Cuba would give priority to sugar production by increasing the cultivated acreage and increasing mechanization. Earnings from sugar export would be used to import machinery to diversify agricultural and industrial production on a sounder basis. Other sectors were also developed, especially the production of cattle, fishing, and citrus fruit. Cement, nickel, and electricity were also expanded with assistance of machinery from the Soviet Union. During this period (1964–1970) the nationalization of the Cuban economy was completed. All industry, commerce, and finance and 70 percent of agricultural land were controlled by the state. This period was marked by a great ideological debate over socialist economic strategy. The basic question debated was whether a largely underdeveloped country like Cuba could primarily use moral incentives to motivate greater productivity in the workforce or whether it was necessary to use some sort of material incentives. Cuban Communist leader Carlos Rafael Rodríguez argued that given Cuba's low level of development, the workers could not be expected to have sufficient consciousness for appeals to the good of the society; increased productivity needed to be rewarded with higher wages and bonuses. This "market socialism" position was also advocated by Soviet advisers.

The more radical position, argued by Guevara, was that economic organization could be totally centralized with resources allocated to enterprises according to plan rather than market forces. Central to this argument was that workers could be motivated without material incentives to work for the collective, the common good. After some experimentation with both models, Castro endorsed Guevara's approach in 1966 and that period culminated in the revolutionary offensive of 1968–1970, which focused on a large-scale investment in sugar with the aim of harvesting and processing 10 million tons of sugar in 1970. The concentration of resources on production entailed further sacrifices from the populace, but the primary goal was to finance industrialization without further debt. It was also hoped that the success of the campaign would be paid off in higher levels of production throughout the society from increased industrialization.

The 1970 sugar harvest was a massive undertaking that involved workers from all sectors and volunteers from around the world; although close to 10 million tons were cut, major processing problems cut the final harvest to 8.5 million tons, far short of the goal. It was a significant blow to the prestige of the revolution, and production dropped in several key sectors outside of sugar. The failure of the revolutionary offensive led to a reassessment of the goals and strategies of the revolution in economic development as well as in other areas. It was recognized that more attention had to be paid to productivity, perhaps at the sacrifice of some egalitarian goals. It was also realized that economic independence from the Soviet Union could not be achieved in the short run.

Concurrently to the changing economic realities, the end of the 1960s brought some changes in the international front. During the 1960s the Cuban leadership advocated an uncompromising stance toward Latin American elites and the United States. Castro's Second Declaration of Havana saw revolution as inevitable in Latin America due to class oppression, economic exploitation, and oligarchical domination by pro-U.S. repressive regimes. Havana sympathized with such prospects and saw it as "the duty of every revolutionary to make the revolution." As a strategy Castro called for armed revolution on a continental scale. The Cubans gave direct material support to revolutionary movements in Nicaragua, Guatemala, Venezuela, and Colombia. Guevara, a leader of Cuba's own revolution, went to fight in Bolivia, where he was killed in 1967. Two conferences during this era epitomized the commitment of the Cuban leadership to the strategy of revolutionary guerrilla warfare. In 1966 Castro convened the Conference of Solidarity of the Peoples of Asia, Africa, and Latin America, where, in his keynote speech, the Cuban leader attacked U.S. imperialism, Latin American elite governments, and all political movements that opposed the necessity of armed struggle, including communist parties. The strategy of guerrilla warfare was confirmed at the Latin America Solidarity Conference the following year in Havana. While this strategy struck a responsive chord among revolutionaries throughout the Americas, the policy did isolate Cuba within the hemisphere. Its support for armed guerrilla movements made normal relations with most governments in Latin America impossible and even served to bring Castro in conflict with significant Leftist forces in the region. Castro directly attacked the reform-oriented approach of the region's communist parties as a betrayal of revolutionary principles. Most communist parties in the hemisphere had renounced armed struggle as a viable strategy for power and were pursuing reforms within existing Latin American political structures.

Decade of the 1970s—Economic Changes

The decade of the 1970s in Cuba saw a more sober approach in economic policy making, internal governance, and foreign affairs. In hindsight, this was the decade where the Cuban revolution was successfully institutionalized. The longevity of the Cuban revolutionary project was secured in a series of crucial policy shifts following the failure of the sugar harvest. As a starting point, the party and Castro himself took full responsibility for the shortfall. There was no significant scapegoating, nor did the events result in a purge of party leadership. The response to the failure was policy initiatives in economics and politics that were probably long overdue. The changes were not instituted hastily but rather introduced gradually over the course of the next decade.

The changes in the economic arena were considerable. The failure of the economic projects of the 1960s led the Cuban leadership to reluctantly conclude that the only viable economic strategy was to move toward economic integration with the East European Council of Mutual Economic Assistance (CMEA). This was a difficult decision for the revolutionary leaders because it meant that the diversification of the Cuban economy that they had so desperately sought in the 1960s would have to be placed largely on hold. Integration into the CMEA meant that Cuba would primarily concentrate on the production of sugar, nickel, and citrus products in return for oil, manufactured goods, and canned foods. This arrangement worked in large measure because Cuba received a guaranteed return for its exported primary products, something it could not likely have obtained in the open world capitalist market. Cuba received an especially favorable exchange rate on Soviet oil for its sugar. This arrangement essentially shielded Cuba from the dramatic rise in world energy prices that occurred between 1973 and 1982, devastating many Third World economies. The Soviet demand for Cuban sugar was high, and by the early 1980s Cuba was importing more Soviet oil than it needed, allowing for the resale of millions of barrels into the world market for hard currency. This export of oil became a valuable project for Cuba and allowed for the further raising of the Cuban standard of living. By the mid-1980s, 85 percent of Cuba export-import was with the CMEA countries. The only major trade that remained with the capitalist world was the prized Cuban tobacco. During this period Cuba did not abandon its goal of increasing food self-sufficiency and developing more domestic industries, but inevitably these efforts did take a back seat to meeting the production goals for the economic activity with the East.

The growing certainty of the economic deals made with the CMEA on a multiyear basis allowed for a new emphasis on planning that included the reactivation of the state Central Planning Board (JUCEPLAN). Prices and investments were centrally controlled, although in the 1970s there was some decentralization of economic planning to local and regional authorities. Without great fanfare there was also a shift away from the 1960s emphasis on solely moral incentives toward the use of material incentives to raise levels of production. The shift clearly had ideological overtones that were welcomed by the Soviet advisers, but the change also occurred because unlike in the 1960s, the improved state of the economy gave the government a much greater ability to carry out a program of worker bonuses. Even with all of these changes, the period of 1970–1989 was not one of unbroken progress for the Cuban economy. After a brief period of accelerated growth in the early 1970s the first five year plan (1975–1980) fell far short of its goals. The economy did grow again in the first half of the 1980s, buoyed in part by the profitable reexport of Soviet oil during a period of high world oil prices. Throughout this period there continued to be problems of lower than expected worker productivity.

During this time, the Cuban consumer did not always directly benefit from the overall growth of the economy because of its primary export orientation, but the wealth redistribution policies of the revolution did result in a significant sharing of the benefits of CMEA membership. In 1970 virtually all consumer goods were rationed, but by the mid-1980s only 30 percent of income was being spent on rationed goods and by 1989 the ration had all but been eliminated. By the end of the 1980s, Cuba had constructed one of the most egalitarian societies in the world, free of the malnutrition and hunger that marked most of its Central American and Caribbean neighbors. However, even at Cuba's height, the Cuban consumer still suffered from a lack of variety and quality of goods available to buy. When the economic shocks of 1989 intervened, Cuba had not yet achieved a fully developed socialist economy.

Political Process

The 1970s saw an overhaul of the Cuban political process with the institutionalizing of the formal organs of government power, known as People's Power. These institutions, created islandwide in 1976, represented a shift in governance structures from the first phase of the revolution. The 1960s had seen the consolidation of the Cuban Communist Party and the utilization of the neighborhood-based CDRs as dual governing organs. The CDRs were designed in 1960 for security purposes, reporting on the activities of counterrevolutionaries and supporting governmental policy. At their peak they numbered 3 million members, but as the 1960s wore on active membership declined somewhat and they became primarily responsible for neighborhood ideological education and social organization and communicating government decisions to the masses. The leadership recognized that the CDRs could not rule the country and that task was given to the Cuban Communist Party (PCC) created in 1965. The PCC's origins can be traced to 1961 when the alliance with the old Communist Party (PSP) was formalized with the creation of the Integrated Revolutionary Organization (ORI). It was viewed as temporary and with 16,000 members it was reorganized in 1963 into the United Party of the Socialist Revolution (PURS). The PURS was then acknowledged by the Soviet Union as a legitimate Communist party. The final stage of party development began in October 1965 with the launching of the PCC, an organization modeled after the Soviet one. It had a small politburo at the top composed primarily of Sierra Maestra veterans and a handful from the old PSP, a central committee of a few hundred members, and a National Party Congress that was to meet every five years to establish broad policy guidelines. Actually there was little change in governance style for several years. The first Party Congress was not convened until 1975; in the interim, decision making revolved almost exclusively around the small core of 26th of July movement veterans who had led the revolution from its beginning. But after 1975 the party and its formal structures grew in importance. By 1980 party members occupied nearly all of the important positions with the state ministries, the armed forces, and the education system. Like other communist parties it was a limited membership organization never encompassing more than 5 percent of the population. Party members are selected carefully to ensure that they are fully dedicated to the tasks of the revolution. They are expected to be model citizens and modest in their personal lives. Most of them start early, beginning as Young Pioneers when teenagers, then becoming Young Communists when they enter adulthood, and finally party membership a few years later. Their material rewards are generally limited, yet they have always been favored by somewhat easier access to housing and consumer goods and are able to travel more abroad.

The Cuban government never functioned as smoothly nor as efficiently as the creators intended. During the early years, costly planning and administrative mistakes were made, some the result of inexperience, others the results of the adopting of inappropriate Soviet models. The limitation of the CDRs as a feedback mechanism was also acknowledged after the failure of the 10-million-ton campaign in 1970. In response, popular participation in policy implementation was proposed through newly created government organs called People's Power. Following a trial run in Matanzas province in 1974 the institutions were established nationwide in 1976. Still in operation today People's Power is composed of municipal, provincial, and national assemblies that are assigned the task of supervising government agencies within their jurisdictions and at the national level, formulating laws and regulations for the society as a whole. The first People's Power elections were held in 1976 following the ratification in a national referendum of a new constitution. The country is divided into 169 municipalities and then into electoral districts where roughly every 3500 people elect one representative to a Municipal Assembly of People's Power. In each of these constituent districts an electoral committee is appointed to oversee the nomination of candidates. The district is broken down into subdistricts of 300–400 persons, each of which can propose a candidate. This process usually produces several candidates from each district, and by law there must be at least two nominees; an uncontested election is not permitted. The electoral commission investigates all candidates and publishes its results. Candidates are not permitted to campaign and can be disqualified if they are judged to be doing so. Runoff elections are often necessary to obtain a majority vote.

Municipal deputies must spend part of each week available to their constituents to receive their complaints or opinions. Deputies are not professional politicians and are generally given time off from their full-time jobs to carry out these functions. Some have compared their position to that of county supervisors in the U.S. system, providing a link to the local population with only limited powers of their own. In the original system, the municipal deputies were also responsible for electing provincial and national deputies in indirect elections. They elected delegates from lists provided by a nominating committee headed by a representative of the Communist party and made up of members of a wide range of civic organizations. This indirect system was replaced by significant electoral reform carried out for the 1993 elections.

The Provincial People's Power Assemblies can propose projects and assign priorities to housing, hospitals, and other projects. The provincial legislatures and their executives act as an intermediary between national policy and its execution at the local level. The provincial government allocates its budget, received from the national level, among the various municipal units. This is done by collecting requests and advice from the lower levels. The Assemblies are responsible for selecting the directors for industries, for moving personnel from one job to another, and for replacing persons who are removed or retire. However, not all enterprises report to the provincial level; some report directly to the national level.

The highest organ of government is the 601-member National Assembly of People's Power. As the legislative body of Cuba, the Assembly passes the budget, confirms heads of ministries, makes laws, selects Supreme Court Justices, and sets basic economic policies. The Assembly meets only infrequently to ratify decisions and draw public attention to national issues. The primary work of the Assembly, as in many other legislative bodies worldwide, is done in standing committees. The Assembly, whose deputies are elected for five-year terms, also appoints a thirty-one-member Council of State to run the government on a day-to-day basis between Assembly sessions. The President of the Council (Fidel Castro) was chosen by the Assembly and is both Head of State and Head of Government. This gives him the power to nominate the first vice president (Raúl Castro, brother of Fidel), five other vice presidents, and members of the Council of Ministers, all of whom are subject to confirmation by the Assembly. In addition to its executive functions, the Council of State can legislate by issuing decree laws when the Assembly is not in session. The Council of State also is responsible for the court system. The composition of the National Assembly is interesting. The largest single group of 173 are leaders of local levels of government, but the second largest group, of 145, are workers, peasants, cooperative workers, educators, health service employees, and others directly linked to production and services. Thirty-five are members of the armed forces, and thirty are writers or other cultural workers. Not surprisingly, the Communist party apparatus is well represented with sixty-four functionaries.

The Communist Party of Cuba (PCC) is not legally an institution of the government, but by constitutional mandate and in political practice it rules the country. Over half of those originally elected at the municipal level were party members, and of the 481 delegates first elected to the National Assembly, 441 were party members. The Council of State has always been dominated by the veterans of the Sierra Maestra and now by the younger generation of Communist leaders. The direction of the Communist party officially lies in its National Congress, which meets every five years to adopt new national plans and to elect the Central Committee, the ongoing policy-making body of the party. The committee meets in plenary session at least once every year and officially is the highest body of the party between sessions of the party Congresses. Selection to the committee is prized, a mark of honor and prestige in Cuban society. The 126-member Central Committee works as a planning body and shadows the implementation of party policies by the government. Virtually every person of importance in Cuba is a member or alternate member of the Central Committee, from generals and provincial heads to top medical people and administrators. Little is known about the internal workings of this body, but it is said to operate on the basis of consensus since the formal existence of factions is prohibited. It has surely been the scene of important political policy discussions, especially in the time period since 1989.

The Secretariat, selected from the membership of the Central Committee, is officially its executive body and is responsible for carrying out the committee's policies between yearly meetings. To oversee the work of the Secretariat, a Political Bureau (Politburo) is elected from the Central Committee to run the party. In the Political Bureau lies the political power of decision. The Political Bureau's twenty-four members control both the party and important posts in the government. Fidel Castro is not only the first secretary of the party but also commander-in-chief and president of the Council of State and the Council of Ministers. His brother Raúl is second secretary, first vice president, and minister of the armed forces. Members of the Political Bureau also head the Ministry of Culture, the Confederation of Cuban Workers, and the Sugar Industry, Ministry of Agriculture, and Ministry of Interior.

The unions, with a special place in Cuban politics, differ from other organizations and interest groups. The unions' general secretary is a member of the Political Bureau, and the national committee of the Confederation of Cuban Workers (CTC) and its national directorate have the right to initiate laws, a power otherwise restricted to government organs. Normally the minister of labor is a member of the CTC and the trade unions are guaranteed positions on the Central Committee and in the leadership of the provincial and municipal party organizations. Within the National Assembly and other government bodies, the CTC acts as an interest group, not independent of the Communist Party, but sometimes representing an alternate perspective.

The special role of unions flows in part from Cuba's self declaration as a workers' state and also because the unions predate the revolution (the CTC was founded in 1939) and have played a historical role in Cuban politics. Further, support of organized labor is vital to the Cuban economy. Workers are especially encouraged to become party members where they make up the majority. In theory the unions have the right to strike, but in practice it has never been exercised. However, there is a natural tension between the unions and the state-run management over wages and work rules. Management wants to increase production quotas and keep work rules flexible while the unions express contrary interests. It is often the party organization that mediates such conflicts, but disagreements can be taken to municipal courts for resolution.

Formal, legal political opposition in Cuba does not exist. The Communist Party is the only legal political party and throughout the years of the revolution those persons who have sought to pursue a political position against the Communist Party have faced significant state repression usually in the form of jail terms. Even today Amnesty International acknowledges 400 political prisoner cases. The great majority of the political dissidents have gone into exile, and as a result the political opposition inside Cuba today is very weak. Beyond a formal political opposition is it possible to speak of a civil society in Cuba independent of the Communist Party and the government. In the mid-1980s the government permitted society to form new associations "from below." It was a recognition that neither the huge mass organizations (CDR, CTC, etc.) nor the specialized professional associations provided for the diversity of Cuban society. The civil associations grew slowly at first and then during the economic crisis of the 1990s grew rapidly. Today there are some 2200 associations registered in Cuba. The greatest number are fraternal-philosophical, including 420 Masonic lodges. The others range from sports clubs to scientific and technical groups. Two hundred of them are nationwide. To receive legal recognition from the state, an association must also be approved by the state organization in the sphere related to the new association. The number of successful new associations approved demonstrates that barriers are not insurmountable, but the approval of new civil associations has been limited since February 1996 because of the intensification of the U.S. economic pressure on Cuba and the subsequent hardening of Cuba's domestic policies. This slowing of the pace of growth in civil society demonstrates the wariness with which such independence is viewed in party circles.

International Relations

The 1970s and 1980s also saw a reorientation of Cuba's foreign relations. The 1960s had been marked by an uncompromising revolutionary internationalism that clearly aligned Cuba with revolutionary causes throughout the world, especially in Latin America. As a consequence Cuba was largely in a position of diplomatic isolation except for its growing political and economic ties with the Soviet Union and its allies. All of Latin America, with the exception of Mexico, had broken relations with Cuba in the 1960s. Exceptions to Cuba's isolation included normal relations with Mexico, Canada, and Spain, despite U.S. pressure on those countries. However, two events in the late 1960s helped foster a shift in Cuba's international relations. First, in 1967 Fidel's confidant, Che Guevara, was killed in Bolivia attempting to lead revolutionary forces in that country. Guevara's death came at the end of a series of defeats suffered by revolutionary groups that the Cubans had backed in Latin America. Che's defeat lead to a reevaluation of the perspective that had argued that the Cuban model of insurrection could be easily copied elsewhere in Latin America. Simultaneously, Soviet pressure on Cuba began to take effect. The Soviets had always been uneasy about support for guerrilla warfare and Cuba's outspoken criticism of reform-oriented Latin American Communist parties, but the pressure did not become severe until Castro was brought into line following the Soviet invasion of Czechoslovakia. Castro's first instinct was to criticize Soviet behavior in that invasion, but it quickly became clear that deviations from Moscow's perspective would have severe economic consequences for Cuba.

Soon after, the election of Richard Nixon brought the prospect of U.S-Soviet détente and with it a strong desire by the Soviet Union to downplay revolutionary rhetoric in the Third World. Cuba largely complied with Soviet pressure and began to stress diplomatic initiatives in Latin America, resulting in the reestablishment of relations with Argentina, Peru, and Chile. These three countries had undergone shifts to the left and saw the reestablishment of relations with Cuba as part of a foreign policy shift away from total domination by the United States. Later political changes, particularly the military coups in Chile and Argentina, damaged these relations, although ties with Argentina were never suspended. By the mid-1970s Cuba had shifted its own policy toward more normalized relations with other countries of the Americas, but the general political circumstances, particularly the domination of Latin America by military regimes, made a significant breakdown of isolation difficult. It was within that context that Cuba began to project itself more aggressively within the Non-Aligned Movement (NAM) and within Africa.

Cuba's role in Africa in the 1970s signaled the beginning of a new era of foreign policy that was to be marked by an expansion of Cuban power and influence—an end to Cuba's isolation. Cuba had aided Algeria and Zanzibar in the 1960s, but the actions of the 1970s were qualitatively different. By the end of the decade Cuba had 35,000 troops on the continent aiding the revolutionary governments of Ethiopia and Angola against foreign invasions while also providing wide-ranging civilian support from medicine to education. Crucial to the respect Cuba gained throughout the Third World was the role that 10,000 Cuban troops played in repelling a South African incursion into Angola in 1975. Similarly, more than 13,000 Cuban troops were instrumental in 1978 in repelling a Somalian invasion of Ethiopia that had been inspired by the United States. These actions would not have been possible without the political and financial support of the Soviet Union, but they allowed the Cuban government a visible opportunity to project its commitment to revolutionary internationalism on world scale. The Cuban shift now focused more on the defense of revolutionary governments in power rather than the support of insurgent movements.

Cuba's successes in Africa led directly to a prominent role for Castro in NAM, an organization of Third World countries that grew in prestige during the 1970s. In 1979 at the ministerial conference of NAM, Cuba received strong endorsement of its Africa policies and in September 1979 at the sixth NAM Summit in Havana, Castro was elected to the presidency of the organization. The presidency of NAM represented a new high of prestige for Castro and revolutionary Cuba, yet Castro's term as president was not without its setbacks. Cuba lost prestige within the organization when it backed the unpopular Soviet invasion of Afghanistan. However, Cuba's setbacks over Afghanistan were reversed during the crisis over the Falklands/Malvinas in 1982. Overt U.S. support for the British during that brief war gave Cuba the opportunity to rally Latin American nations on a nationalistic basis against the United States, thus helping to break down Cuba's isolation from Latin America. A major trade deal with Argentina ensued soon after the crisis, and the systematic reestablishment of relations with the rest of Latin America proceeded throughout the 1980s. By the end of the decade Cuba was extending its trade with most of Latin America, and Cuban leaders, including Castro, were welcomed and prominent participants in Latin American and Caribbean political meetings.

Parallel to successes in Africa and with NAM, Cuba also played an important role in the Central American/Caribbean region in the early 1980s as a supporter of the revolutionary governments that emerged in Grenada and Nicaragua in 1979. Cuba's relationship with the Nicaraguan revolutionaries was long-standing, going back to the founding of the Sandinista National Liberation Front (FSLN) in 1961. During the dark days of the FSLN its leaders often lived in exile in Cuba before returning in the late 1970s to lead a successful revolution against the Somoza dictatorship. The Sandinista uprising received more direct support from countries such as Costa Rica and Venezuela, but once the FSLN attained power, Cuba and Nicaragua established a close relationship. Cuba provided important material support and considerable revolutionary advice. Similarly, the Cubans developed close ties with Maurice Bishop's New Jewel Movement in Grenada, especially by providing labor and technical support for the new international airport under construction there.

By 1983 Cuba's fortunes in the international arena were on a strong upward path, but there was a cost for these gains. As it had in earlier times, Cuba became a target of the United States because of its successes. There had been a brief thaw in United States-Cuba relations after 1977 when diplomatic missions were reopened in each country and the ban on U.S. citizens traveling to Cuba was lifted. However, the long-standing trade embargo was not lifted and by 1979 Cuba was being harshly attacked for its policies in Africa. When Ronald Reagan assumed the White House in 1981 Cuba's relations with Grenada and Nicaragua were attacked and the ban on U.S. citizen travel to Cuba was reinstated. Cuba suffered a major setback in 1983 when the United States invaded Grenada after a coup d'etat killed Cuba's ally, Maurice Bishop. Cuba's deep involvement continued in Nicaragua through the decade, but the Sandinistas lost power in the 1990 elections after a long and debilitating war with the United States.

Recent Developments

Dramatic changes began in Cuba with the fall of the Berlin Wall in November 1989 and were accelerated by the collapse of the Soviet Union at the end of 1991. These events impacted Cuba so strongly because at the beginning of 1989 virtually all of Cuba's foreign trade (87 percent) was with the Soviet Union and other socialist countries of CMEA. Cuba was dependent on CMEA for most of the country's energy supplies, fertilizer, machine tools, and canned foods. The CMEA arrangement to purchase Cuban sugar, nickel, and other primary production had given Cuba significant economic and social progress after 1970, but the sudden and unexpected loss of these markets wrecked the Cuban economy. In 1989 Cuba imported 13 million tons of oil from the Soviet Union, but by 1992 it was able to import only 6 million tons, all of it at world market prices. The importing of canned food from Eastern Europe was ended altogether. By 1993 Cuba had lost 75 percent of its import capacity, and the country's economic activity contracted by 50 percent. Outside of the context of war, no modern economy had been so devastated in the twentieth century. The destruction of the economy resulted in the return of rationing for basic necessities. Rationing was not new to revolutionary Cuba, but in the 1980s it had been largely eliminated and a system of "parallel markets" allowed consumers to add to the food available in the subsidized state markets. Since these "parallel markets" depended to a large measure on food imported from Eastern Europe, they disappeared virtually overnight in 1991 as rationing was reintroduced.

The return to a ration was clearly a setback for Cuba, but it also meant that the country was not abandoning its socialist principles. The hardships were to be shared, and no one was to be left on his or her own. The equitable rationing of goods was in stark contrast to most of the rest of Latin America, where "structural adjustment programs" often resulted in food prices beyond the means of the majority who are poor and in subsequent malnutrition. In addition to rations other dramatic measures were introduced to rescue the economy and maintain the productivity of the people. To maintain food production in the context of fuel shortages more than 80,000 oxen were imported to take the place of tractors. The stated goal was food self-sufficiency, but that was unlikely as ownership patterns initially remained the same and no significant incentives were introduced. In an attempt to deal with the dramatic reduction in public transportation, 600,000 bicycles were imported from China into a country where there was no tradition of cycling. In Havana the conservation of electricity was quite dramatic, with power shut off for a period of time each day in each neighborhood. To earn immediate hard currency, a program to dramatically increase the tourism industry was implemented despite the social problems, such as drugs and prostitution, that came along with it. From just a $165 million industry in 1989, tourism revenues grew to $850 million in five years as successful foreign investments in new facilities were attracted from Europe and Latin America.

Parallel to the tourism expansion in the early 1990s was Cuba's attempt to cash in on the extensive long-term investments it had made in medical technology. Two products in particular were marketed, a hepatitis-B vaccine and an anti-stroke medicine. Cuba targeted Third World markets with some modest successes in the $200-million-per-year range, but the competition in the markets with U.S. and European multinationals made significant inroads in the arena difficult. In 1992–1993 Cuba also stabilized trade relations with its formerly socialist partners in Russia and the other formerly Soviet republics. Initially it appeared that the Russians would totally turn their backs on Cuba out of deference to the West, but when large-scale Western aid for the Russians did not materialize, Cuba and Russia signed new trade agreements that continue on a much reduced scale the bartering of Russian oil for Cuban sugar, an economic arrangement that benefits both countries. Russia also continues to pay for a radar installation in Cuba against the wishes of the United States, although the last Soviet troops left the island in 1993. At the height of the Cold War there had been 40,000 Russian troops in Cuba.

To spur foreign investment, changes were made in Cuban law to allow full recovery of investments in three years and relatively easy repatriation of profits. Taxation in the first years of investment was also sharply reduced. Latin American businesspeople, particularly Mexicans, were seriously courted by the Cuban government. An early fruit of this initiative was the decision by Domos, a Mexican telecommunication company, to invest heavily in updating the Cuban phone system. By 1994 over 150 foreign-Cuban joint ventures were underway, comprising over $1.5 billion invested from many other countries, including Spain, Canada, Germany, and Israel. The bulk of the activity was in tourism, where investors have insisted on a quick turnaround of profits in hard currency, thus limiting the positive impact on the economy. These efforts have been limited by the aggressive efforts of the U.S. government to prevent foreign business investment in Cuba. First the Torricelli Bill in 1992 and then the Helms-Burton legislation of 1996 tightened the long-term U.S. embargo on Cuba by punishing firms that make investments on the island. Although the legislation, especially Helms-Burton, has caused friction between the United States and its allies, its presence does represent an obstacle to Cuba's further reintegration into the current world economy.

By the middle of 1994, the economic freefall continued and the Cuban economy and society seemed to be headed for disaster. In practice the ration was not providing enough for people to eat, and the amount of time spent in lines obtaining the basic necessities was further undermining the remaining economic production. Discontent with the economic situation boiled over during the summer of 1994 as several incidents surrounding the hijacking of boats in Havana harbor brought out people in demonstrations against the government for the first time since 1959. However, ultimately the Cuban leadership was successful in defusing the situation and beginning a slow turnaround of the economy that continues to the present day. The Cuban government opened up its ports in August 1994 and allowed thousands of discontented Cubans to go to the United States, where their arrival created a political crisis for President Bill Clinton. The crisis ended with a new immigration agreement between the United States and Cuba in September 1994, and the United States ended its long-standing policy of granting political asylum to all arriving Cuban refugees. Under the new policy, refugees reaching U.S. soil are still granted the right to apply for asylum, but those intercepted at sea are returned to Cuba. A new agreement, signed in May 1995, allows for the legal immigration of up to 20,000 Cubans per year to the United States.

On the economic front, the Cuban government initiated a series of reforms that were designed to encourage private investment. The most important and successful project has been the reopening of private agricultural markets where the producers sell directly to the public. Begun in late 1994, these markets resulted in a better food situation for the average Cuban and also served to restore the value of the Cuban peso. Another important reform allowed the licensing of a wide range of individual service businesses from tailors to barbers to small restaurants in private homes. A major economic decision in 1993 allowed for the legalization of the dollar for use by the Cuban population as a whole. The circulation of the dollar had become too widespread for the government to ignore, so the decision was made to legalize it for the purposes of better control. It is now estimated that $600 million–$800 million a year flows into the Cuban economy from Cubans living in the United States. Dollar legalization had a sound economic foundation, but the political and social ramifications have been negative. Pursuit of the dollar increases prostitution, overvalues jobs in the tourist sector, and privileges those in the society who have the good fortune to have relatives in the United States.

The other aspect of Cuban economic recovery was the attraction of modest amounts of foreign capital into Cuba's main production areas of sugar and nickel mining. Although the investments are small, they helped Cuba reverse its economic freefall, with a gain of 2.5 percent in 1995 followed by more substantial gains of 7.8 percent and 2.5 percent in 1996 and 1997, Cuba's growth rate slowed in 1998 to 1.2 percent but rebounded to a 6.2 percent gain in 1999. However, at this rate it will take Cuba another decade to return to its economic position of the late 1980s. Despite the modest economic growth, the daily lives of the average Cuban revolve around obtaining the basic necessities of life. Waiting in long lines to obtain rationed food and commuting by bicycle or waiting for inconsistent public transportation cuts sharply into worker productivity, which must improve if the Cuban economy is to prosper. These difficulties of life are not unique to Cuba, but what makes it an interesting place to study is that Cuba has gone through this dramatic crisis while trying to maintain its socialist principles. In Cuba, unlike the former Communist countries in Europe, there is no full-scale embracing of a market economy. In speech after speech Castro has reiterated that Cuba will not return to a capitalist past. This has meant that the sacrifice has been shared. The free medical and educational systems have been maintained. In part because there has been shared sacrifice, there has been no social explosion, which many predicted.

Modest political reform is also under way in Cuba, although the process is primarily a top-down one initiated by the leadership of the Communist party. The changes were promulgated at the Fourth Congress of the Cuban Communist Party, held in October 1991. This meeting, the first congress after the demise of the Soviet Communist party, took several important initiatives in the political arena. The most important change was in Cuba's formal government structure. Since the system was established in the mid-1970s, Cubans had gone to the polls every four years to elect their local municipal delegate in a secret ballot vote. However, the remainder of the Cuban political officials were chosen by indirect election. Under the reforms implemented in the 1992–1993 elections, Cuban citizens voted for the first time directly for candidates to the Provincial Assemblies and the National Assembly, in addition to their customary vote for a municipal delegate.

The process was completed on February 24, 1993, when 1190 provincial delegates and 589 deputies to the National Assembly were elected for five-year terms. Cuban election officials reported a record 99.6 percent turnout. The highest previous turnout had been for the 1984 municipal election, in which 98.7 percent of registered voters participated. The first round of the municipal voting in December 1992 had drawn a 97 percent voter turnout. Under the new system for selecting the provincial and national legislators, lists were put together by nominating commissions made up of delegates representing trade unions as well as farmers', women's, and students' organizations. Each organization, representing its constituency, held meetings to solicit potential nominations. Over 70,000 names emerged from these meetings. The nominating commissions made their recommendations to the Municipal Assemblies, which decided on the final list of candidates.

Under the new Cuban electoral rules, National Assembly candidates are nominated by municipalities at a ratio of one for roughly 20,000 inhabitants, and voters may choose all, several, or none of the names on the ballot. To win, a candidate must receive a majority of the votes cast. The system at the national level does not allow the voter to choose one candidate over another, but it gives the voter the option of rejecting a nominated candidate. In contrast, at the municipal level the voters choose among two to eight candidates. The February 1993 election results were significant when opponents of the Cuban government had called for an electoral boycott or the casting of blank ballots. Some in the Cuban community of Miami had predicted that up to 50 percent of the Cuban electorate would heed the call for a boycott, but it did not. In addition to the 99 percent turnout, the Election Commission reported that 92.8 percent of the ballots were valid, with only 7.2 percent spoiled or blank. None of the 589 national candidates received less than 87 percent of the vote, and 88.5 percent of the ballots went for the entire slate. The Cuban government did not permit international observers to monitor the process, reasoning that the elections would not be accepted as valid in any case by the United States.

At its inaugural session in March 1993, the National Assembly elected the foreign minister, Ricardo Alarcón, as president of the Assembly, replacing Juan Escalona. It also elected a new Council of State, with Fidel Castro continuing as President. The thirty-one-member Council of State, including sixteen members who were new to the body, exercises legislative power between Assembly sessions. Its significantly changed composition served to ratify the personnel changes that had been evident in the elections of the Communist party's highest bodies at the October 1991 Congress. The trend is clearly in favor of younger leaders: The average age of the legislators is forty-three, making it one of the youngest legislatures in the world, elected by one of the world's youngest electorates with a minimum voting age of sixteen. Most prominent among the young leaders is Roberto Robaina, leader of the Communist Youth League who became foreign minister after Ricardo Alarcón's election to head the National Assembly. These reforms, together with other moves such as opening the membership of the ruling Communist party to religious believers, are designed to increase participation in the Cuban political process within the carefully drawn lines of the Communist leadership. If the reforms are to succeed, they will have to go beyond these tentative steps and include bolder measures such as multicandidate direct elections for the National Assembly.

The trends evidenced in the 1993 elections continued in 1998. There was an overall participation rate in excess of 98 percent. Nationally, 95 percent of the votes cast were judged to be valid, with only 3.3 percent blank and 1.7 percent spoiled. As in 1993 there had been strong calls from those outside Cuba who oppose the revolution for voters to use the occasion to voice opposition to the process; there is no evidence that such a protest occurred. The process of passing on political power to a new generation continued, as two-thirds of the National Assembly delegates were elected for the first time; 28 percent were women. The transition at the level of top leadership also continued, with 45 percent of the Council of State becoming members of this body for the first time. However, in the midst of the changing faces there was also continuity. Ricardo Alarcón remained president of the Assembly, Raúl Castro was reelected to be first vice president of the Council of State, and Fidel Castro was elected president. To underscore that continuity Castro addressed the first session of the new Assembly for seven and one-half hours to dispel reports that his health was fading. There appears to be no significant pressure for serious political reforms from either within Cuba's political establishment or from the wider society.

Cuba underwent significant changes in the 1990s, but those changes generally did not extend to its relations with the United States. As Cuba plunged into economic crisis at the beginning of the decade U.S. policy focused on attempting to prevent Cuba from reintegrating into the world economy. In 1992 Congress passed and President Bush signed the Cuba Democracy Act, which sought to tighten the thirty-year-old embargo by cutting off third-country trading to Cuba by U.S. companies. The legislation also specified that the only acceptable political change in Cuba was the total removal of the Communist party from power. U.S. policy makers fully expected the revolutionary government to fall quickly in the absence of its socialist allies in Europe. When the collapse did not occur, new legislation drafted in Congress by Jesse Helms and Dan Burton sought an even tighter embargo on Cuba by punishing virtually every enterprise from any country that sought to make new investments on the island. Initially opposed by the Clinton administration because of vigorous opposition from U.S. allies, the Helms-Burton legislation was passed into law in 1996 following an incident in the Straits of Florida when the Cuban Air Force shot down airplanes of a Miami-based exile group that had entered Cuban airspace. Tensions between the two governments also grew over continued U.S. government support for groups seeking the overthrow of the Cuban government. However, opposition to the embargo within the United States continued to build. In early 1998 the U.S. Chamber of Commerce began a public campaign against the embargo, citing worldwide opposition to it and its inconsistency in light of U.S. trade with China and Vietnam, other countries where the Communist party remains in power. As a result of the campaign many Republican lawmakers, especially in Midwest farm states, began calling for a lessening of the embargo to allow for the sale of food and medicines. In 2000, legislation permitting the sale of food and medicine was passed by the U.S. Congress and signed by President Clinton. However, a clause barring any U.S. government financing of such sales limited its practical effectiveness. The incoming Bush administration showed no sign of a change in U.S. policy toward the island.

Cuba entered the new millennium as controversial as ever. Fidel Castro, now the aging revolutionary, commands attention and respect almost everywhere he travels in the world. The United States, the world's only remaining superpower, still works for his destruction. Cuba has changed dramatically in many ways since 1989 as it constructs a new economy out of the ruins of its ties with the socialist East. Steadfastly refusing to renounce its past, Cuba seeks to define socialism for the new century by retaining the significant social achievements of the revolution in the framework of an economy fueled by foreign investment and private initiative. It is not yet clear that Cuba can successfully find that path, especially in the context of a U.S.-dominated world, but the Cuban revolution and Fidel Castro have successfully defied the odds so many times before that betting against their success may be a risky proposition.

Chronology

1898 Cuba achieves independence from Spain during Spanish American War; Cuba occupied by U.S. troops until 1902

1901 Platt Amendment to new Cuban constitution gives the United States the right to intervene in Cuba to "maintain government adequate for the protection of life, property, and individual liberty"

1906 American governor appointed to replace Cuban president

1925 Gerardo Machado becomes president and rules in dictatorial manner

1933 Machado overthrown by popular revolt

1934 U.S. President Franklin Roosevelt abrogates Platt Amendment; Provisional government overthrown by "sergeants' revolt" led by Fulgencio Batista

1940 Batista elected president under a new constitution

1944 Opposition candidate, Grau San Martín, elected president

1948 Carlos Prío Socarras elected president

1952 Batista takes over government in a coup

1953 Young rebels, led by Fidel Castro, attack Moncada military barracks in Santiago and are captured and jailed

1955 Batista declares amnesty; Castro flees to Mexico

1956 In July, rebels led by Castro travel by boat to east end of Cuba; only a dozen escape battles with armed forces and take refuge in Sierra Maestra Mountains

1958 Guerrilla war starting in mountains spreads and defeats Batista's force at end of year

1959 Castro creates coalition government in January; in June moderates in cabinet resign, leaving effective control to Castro and the 26th of July movement

1961 In January, United States breaks relations with Cuba and imposes trade embargo; Invasion at Bay of Pigs by CIA supported by Cuban exiles defeated by Cuban Army

1962 United States confronts Soviet Union over its placement of missiles in Cuba; "Missile Crisis" ends with Soviets pulling missiles out in exchange for U.S. promise never to invade Cuba

1965 Cuban Communist Party formed

1970 Failed 10-million-ton sugar harvest leads to economic and political reform

1975 First Communist Party Congress called

1976   New system of local, provincial, and national assemblies create People's Power
1986   Cuban Communist Party begins "rectification" plan in response to economic slowdown and bureaucratic inefficiencies
1989   Collapse of Communist regimes in Eastern Europe begins process of economic reform
1994   Confrontation with the United States over refugee exodus; private agricultural markets reinstated
1998   Visit of Pope John Paul II

Bibliography

Anderson, Jon. *Che Guevara: A Revolutionary Life*. New York: Grove Press, 1997.

Castro, Fidel, and Frei Betto. *Fidel and Religion: Castro Talks on Revolution and Religion with Frei Betto*. New York: Simon and Schuester, 1987.

Chaffee, Wilber, and Gary Prevost, eds. *Cuba—A Different America*. Savage, MD: Rowman and Littlefield, 1992.

Erisman, Michael. *Cuba's International Relations: The Anatomy of a Nationalistic Foreign Policy*. Boulder, CO: Westview Press, 1985.

Franklin, Jane. *The Cuban Revolution and the United States: A Chronological History*. Melbourne: Ocean Press, 1997.

Guevara, Ernesto Che. *Episodes of the Cuban Revolutionary War*. New York: Pathfinder Press, 1996.

Kirk, John. *Between God and Party: Religion and Politics in Revolutionary Cuba*. Tampa: University of South Florida Press, 1989.

Lechuga, Carlos. *In the Eye of the Storm—Castro, Krushchev, Kennedy, and the Missile Crisis*. Melbourne: Ocean Press, 1995.

Liss, Sheldon. *Fidel Castro's Political and Social Thought*. Boulder, CO: Westview Press, 1994.

Lutjens, Sheryl. *The State, Bureaucracy and Cuban Schools: Power and Participation*. Boulder, CO: Westview Press, 1996.

Matthews, Herbert. *Revolution in Cuba*. New York: Charles Scribner's, 1975.

Murphy, Catherine. *Cultivating Havana: Urban Agriculture and Food Security in Years of Crisis*. San Francisco: Food First Books, 1999.

Pérez, Louis A. *Cuba: Between Reform and Revolution*. New York: Oxford University Press, 1988.

Roman, Peter. *Cuba's Experience with Representative Government*. Boulder, CO: Westview Press, 1999.

Sarduy, Pedro Pérez, and Jean Stubbs. *AfroCuba: An Anthology of Cuban Writing on Race, Politics, and Culture*. Melbourne: Ocean Press, 1993.

Smith, Wayne S. *The Closest of Enemies: A Personal and Diplomatic Account of U.S.–Cuban Relations since 1957*. New York: Norton, 1987.

Szulc, Tad. *Fidel: A Critical Portrait*. New York: William Morrow, 1986.

FILMS AND VIDEOS

Fidel. Cuba, 2000.
If You Only Understood. Cuba, 1998.
The King Does Not Lie: The Initiation of a Shango Priest. U.S., 1992.

Memories of Underdevelopment. Cuba, 1968.
The Uncompromising Revolution. U.S., 1992.

WEB SITES

Granma International (newspaper of the Communist Party), www.granma.cu
Radio Havana, www.radiohc.org/index.html
Cuban government (official), www.cubagov.cu

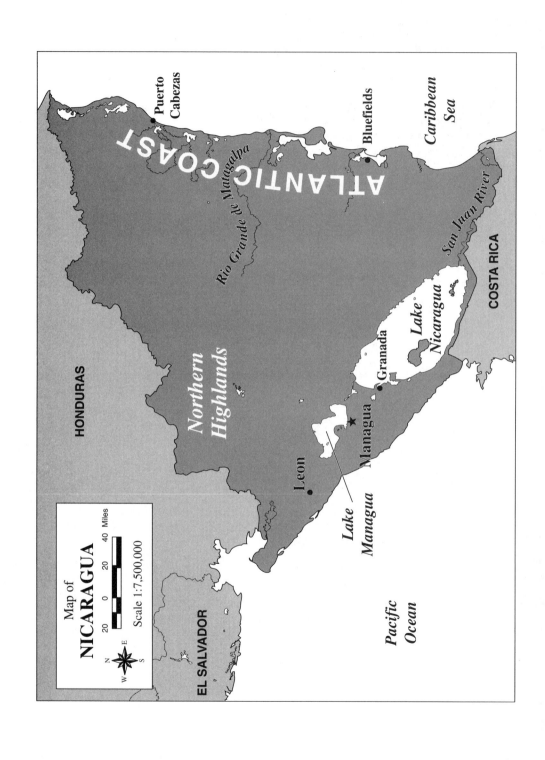

THIRTEEN

NICARAGUA

Gary Prevost and Harry E. Vanden

Introduction

Nicaragua, located at the geographic center of Central America, is the largest and most sparsely settled of the Central American republics. Its 57,143 square miles make it about the size of the state of Iowa. Its population of 4.5 million—which has grown rapidly in the last two decades—is concentrated on the Pacific Coast side of the country. It has three distinct geographic regions: mountains in the north, a narrow Pacific coastal plain containing two large lakes, and a wider Atlantic coastal plain. The Pacific plain is part of a trough that connects the Atlantic and Pacific Oceans through the San Juan River Valley. For more than a century this region has been viewed as having great potential for a new interoceanic canal. There is considerable volcanic activity in the northwestern part of the country, with three volcanos reaching 5000 feet emerging from Lake Nicaragua.

Most of Nicaragua has considerable potential for agricultural production. Occupying nearly half of the country, the Caribbean lowlands are composed primarily of hot, humid tropical rainforest and swamps. They are not conducive to long-term productive agriculture, and less than 10 percent of the population lives there. The central highlands and western lowlands have been much more hospitable to human habitation and agricultural production. The central region is especially good for coffee production, while the western lowlands support a wide range of agricultural products such as cotton, rice, and sugar.

Nicaragua is favored not only with above-average natural resources and climatic conditions but also with several other favorable characteristics. Unlike some Latin American countries, it is not overpopulated. Arable land is adequate for the size of the population. Much of the country has a relatively homogeneous population, with no significant racial, linguistic, or religious differences. Most Nicaraguans are Roman Catholic, speak Spanish, and are *mestizo* (mixed Spanish and Indian ancestry). The exception to this homogeneity is the Atlantic Coast region, which is quite different. This region has an English-speaking black population with a Caribbean heritage and a small native indigenous population of Sumo and Miskito Indians. Despite its abundant natural resources Nicaragua has remained one of the poorest countries in the hemisphere throughout the twentieth century, with low per capita income and short life expectancy. It is also a country that has had more than its share of political violence and oppression. However, Nicaragua also falls within a select group of countries worldwide that has experienced a highly unusual phenomenon—social revolution. The events of the 1970s and 1980s in Nicaragua, the era of the Sandinista revolution, warrant Nicaragua's inclusion as a case study in this volume. It shares many characteristics with its Central and Latin American neighbors, but it was the brief period of revolutionary fervor that makes Nicaragua stand out. Yet, in order to understand the historical context of the events of 1978–1990 it is necessary to review Nicaraguan history.

As Thomas Walker has observed in his treatment of Nicaraguan history, the patterns of conflict that have marked modern Nicaragua did not begin with the Spanish conquerors of the sixteenth century. The region was inhabited by indigenous groups of South American origin that occupied the less hospitable eastern regions, while the western side was colonized by Meso-American groups from the north. There was little contact between the two groups, but within the western region there were clear patterns of warfare, slavery, and involuntary servitude. Spanish conquerors reached Nicaragua from Panama in 1522, making their first contact with indigenous people on the western plains. The expedition under the leadership of Gil González was seeking to obtain gold and converts to Christianity and was apparently successful on both counts. It also discovered the apparent water link between the Atlantic and Pacific. The initial contact was not without violence, however, as a legendary chief, Diriangen, offered armed resistance to the Spanish. In 1524, under the leadership of Francisco Hernández de Córdoba, the Spanish imposed their control over the region and founded the settlements of Grenada and León.

The Spanish conquest of Nicaragua had a profound and devastating impact. The existing indigenous population of around 1 million was reduced within a few decades to just tens of thousands. Some deaths occurred in battles with the Spanish, but most came from diseases that the Spanish introduced, such as measles and influenza, for which the local population had no immune defenses. Slavery was also a factor in reducing the population. As many as 400,000–500,000 natives were put in bondage during the early period; many were shipped out of the country. Demand for slaves was especially high from Peru. By the 1540s the Indian population of western Nicaragua dropped below 50,000 and continued to decline afterward. The legacy of this devastation is that the more populated western part of Nicaragua is predominantly a *mestizo* culture with little trace of the indigenous past except for a significant number of cities and towns with native names. Today, few contemporary residents understand the significance of the long-forgotten histories behind these names.

Another legacy of the colonial period is the rivalry between the cities of León and Grenada. Grenada was originally designated by the Spanish to be the administrative center. As a result it was populated by the aristocratic class, while colonizers of lower social status settled León, which was projected to be primarily a fortress city on the northern reaches of the colony. However, León emerged as the administrative capital and aristocratic Grenadans had to endure centuries of rule by a city they viewed to be inferior. This resentment boiled into open warfare on occasion as the two cities also developed an economic rivalry. Wealth in aristocratic Grenada was based primarily on cattle, while the León economy was more commercially oriented and included international trade. For much of the colonial period Nicaragua was an underpopulated, impoverished corner of the Spanish empire. The economy, with its severe labor shortages, supported the wealthy lifestyles of the upper class in León and Grenada but was insufficient for more widespread prosperity.

The end of the colonial era did not bring any great relief to Nicaragua's difficult position. It won its independence in stages, first as a part of the Mexican empire in 1821. It then became a member of the Central American Federation in 1823 and finally emerged as a sovereign state in 1838 when it withdrew from the federation. Internally most of the nineteenth century after independence was marked by constant battles between León and Grenada for control of the country. By then the Leonese had come to call themselves Liberals, and the Grenadinos identified themselves as Conservatives. In a pattern that was to repeat itself, the chaos created by the internal conflict combined with the departure of the Spanish allowed outside forces to exert significant influence over Nicaragua.

British interests established a protectorate over the Atlantic region, known as the Autonomous Kingdom of Mosquitía, which lasted for most of the nineteenth century. U.S.-based Commodore Cornelius Vanderbuilt's transit company became involved in moving California-bound gold prospectors across Nicaragua in 1849. Simultaneously, the British claimed control over the mouth of the San Juan River on the Atlantic Coast, threatening the Vanderbuilt operations. In 1850 the United States and Great Britain attempted to diffuse the conflict by signing the Clayton-Bulwar Treaty, in which they agreed to cooperate on the development of any transoceanic transit route. The treaty was negotiated and signed without involving the government of Nicaragua, establishing a pattern of disregard for Nicaragua's sovereignty that has continued to the present.

The Clayton-Bulwar Treaty did not end conflict in Nicaragua. In 1855 the liberals of León hired an American soldier of fortune, William Walker, to lead their army against Grenada. Under Walker's leadership the liberal army triumphed and Walker became the de facto president of Nicaragua. He instituted liberal reforms, including the encouragement of foreign investment and development of Nicaragua's natural resources. Initially Walker's activities were supported by the U.S. government. However, the British and other Central American governments were taken aback by what seemed to be a bold imperialist act by the United States. Nicaraguans of both political parties also began to turn against Walker when he legalized slavery and established English as the country's official language. Now seen as a hated foreigner, Walker came under attack from forces armed by the British, other Central American governments, and even private U.S. interests who feared he had become a liability to stable commerce in the region. In 1857 the U.S. government brokered a deal that sent Walker into exile. He returned in 1860, but was unsuccessful in regaining control and was defeated and executed. The final defeat of Walker in 1860 by a combined Central American force ushered in a thirty-year period of rule by the Conservatives who quelled numerous uprisings and established a semblance of a stable, yet traditional, government.

The Modern Era

The beginning of a modern national consciousness in Nicaragua that included the Indian and *mestizo* masses only emerged toward the end of the nineteenth century. Only then did a few intellectuals begin to look toward their distant indigenous past to rediscover the nation's historic identity and transcend the narrow Hispanicism that had often constrained national politics, thought, and literature. Although the Liberal reform movement did not develop in Nicaragua until the late nineteenth century, it carried a vision of society similar to movements in Mexico (under Benito Juárez) and elsewhere in Latin America. José Santos Zelaya's Liberal revolution of 1893 marked the beginning of the modern Liberal movement in Nicaragua. Although constrained by traditional European-style liberalism, Zelaya endeavored to centralize state power. He introduced some progressive ideas and began to challenge the traditional oligarchy and the power of the Catholic Church. His successful drive to recover the Atlantic Coast from British colonialism also stimulated the growth of a national consciousness. Supported by elements of the national bourgeoisie, Zelaya introduced reforms that soon alarmed the Conservative forces and threatened the interests of U.S. capital, which was antagonistic to the growth of a vigorous, independent national capitalist class in Nicaragua.

As Zelaya faced increasing internal and external pressure, his regime degenerated into a dictatorship. In 1909, Washington forced him to resign before he could implement his plans to modernize Nicaragua. Using various pretexts, the United States sent Marines in 1909 to reinstate Conservative rule and ensure the dominant position of U.S. capital. As U.S. intervention increased over the next years (the Marines, again landed in 1912 to prop up the regime of Adolfo Díaz, did not leave until 1924), anti-interventionist sentiment grew among the Nicaraguan people. With the outbreak of a new Liberal uprising against a Conservative coup in 1925 and the U.S.-inspired reinstallation of Adolfo Díaz as president, the struggle began to take on clear nationalist and anti-imperialist overtones. The Marines once again intervened. It was at this point that Augusto César Sandino returned from Mexico and joined the now strongly nationalist Liberal struggle. Although Sandino, a mechanic, encountered open hostility from the upper-class head of the Liberal army, José M. Moncada, he was able to arm and organize his own Liberal band and participate in the increasingly successful offensive.

Sandino was born into poverty in southern Nicaragua in 1895. As a young man his nationalist instincts were fueled when he witnessed the humiliation of Liberal general Benjamín Zeledón by U.S. Marines in 1912. Between 1923 and 1926 Sandino worked in Mexico as a mechanic in the oil industry of Tampico; it was there that his eclectic political philosophy was formed through contacts with anarchists, Free Masons, and supporters of the Mexican Revolution. The Liberal struggle was met with enthusiastic support from the masses, who participated in growing numbers. But as these forces were in sight of a clear military victory, the United States arranged a compromise solution that was accepted by Moncada and eventually supported by all the Liberal generals, save one—Sandino. Thereafter, large numbers of peasants, miners, artisans, workers, and Indians who had fought with Sandino followed him to the Segovias, a remote mountain region in the north. From here he began a guerrilla war.

The first Sandinista struggle continued from 1927 to 1933, and Sandino's growing army of miners, Indians, peasants, artisans, and workers made life very difficult for the Marines. Their political work and the increasing sophistication and tenacity of their popular guerrilla war had gained the support of many Nicaraguans, growing numbers of Latin Americans, and a few informed North Americans. The intensity of the conflict with the Marines forced Sandino and his followers to upgrade their military tactics and strengthen their ties with the rural masses who supported their struggle.

This was one of the first modern examples of the power of a guerrilla army with popular support against a technologically superior invader, even when the latter was bolstered by a significant national mercenary military force. Mobile guerrilla bands as the components of an egalitarian people's army, political as well as military organization, integrated political and military actions, close ties to the peasants, and, most importantly, popular support and involvement—such were the legacy from Sandino's war. More than three decades later these lessons were put to use by the leadership of the next generation—the FSLN.

Yet although Sandino's political support had enabled him to gain a military victory, he disbanded his army before he could achieve far-reaching political and economic change. After his death at the hands of Anastasio Somoza's National Guard (1934), most of Sandino's followers were soon killed by the U.S.-trained National Guard. Some Sandinist columns fought on for a few more years in remote areas, but they too were eventually forced to abandon systematic armed resistance. All that remained was the legacy of Sandino and the example of his army, which lived on in the popular mind for some time, nourished by eyewitness accounts and firsthand stories from Sandinist survivors.

Nicaragua returned to more traditional authoritarian rule as Somoza took direct control of the Nicaraguan government in 1936. He instituted an increasingly repressive family dictatorship that—mostly because of its close ties to the United States—would endure until militarily defeated by the FSLN in 1979. The Nicaraguan people were restricted from power and largely disenfranchised. Further, Somoza realized that the memory of Sandino and his Army to Defend National Sovereignty represented a threat to his rule. Not content to have ordered Sandino's execution, Somoza attempted to distort the popular memory of Sandino and his followers by having an anti-Sandino book published under his name. Somoza's efforts achieved some success, in that it was soon very difficult for most of Nicaraguans to obtain any favorable written accounts of the Sandinist struggle within the country. However, despite bloody repression and the intense vilification of Sandino and his followers, sporadic popular struggle continued through the 1930s, 1940s, and 1950s, although at a relatively low level. This period of struggle included military actions by both old Sandinists and younger patriots such as the "Generation of '44." Somoza proved to be one of the best friends of the United States and was warmly received by Franklin Roosevelt in Washington. By the 1950s Nicaragua was a fully dependent producer of primary goods (mostly coffee and cotton) and was an integral part of the U.S. system of political and economic control in the Western Hemisphere. There were occasional armed actions by old Sandinists and other Nicaraguans who could no longer countenance the heavy-handed political and economic manipulation that characterized the Somozas and their friends. Students and workers occasionally demonstrated against the regime, but they lacked any clear ideological perspective in which to place their efforts. Opposition to the dictatorship came to be symbolized by the sincere, but elitist, Conservative party. Even the Nicaraguan Socialist Party (founded as a pro-Moscow Communist party in 1944) often collaborated with the traditional politicians and Somoza-controlled unions, at the workers' expense. Somoza had taken over the Liberal party and even went so far as to make pacts (in 1948 and 1950) with the Conservative party in an attempt to co-opt the only major focal point of opposition to his regime.

Carlos Fonseca and the Roots of the FSLN

It has been said that Nicaragua is a land of poets and that poets often reflect the popular will. Rigoberto López Pérez was one of the Nicaraguan intellectuals who directly felt the far-reaching cultural implications of a dependent dictatorship that was subservient to the United States. He, like Cuban poet José Martí, felt compelled to exchange pen for pistol to liberate his country. In 1956 the young poet assassinated Somoza. In so doing he not only avenged Sandino but also spurred a reexamination of national conscience that increasingly challenged the status quo. The dictator's eldest son Luis took over the reigns of power and became the next Somoza to rule. A new wave of guerrilla activities broke out in the countryside; one of the more famous of these was led by Ramón Raudales, a veteran of Sandino's army. The university students also began to show a new militancy and, for the first time, a small group began to study Marxist theory. Previously, the Nicaraguan Socialist Party (PSN) had been founded in 1944 and maintained the closest of ties to the Soviet Union. Like most Latin American Communist parties prior to the 1960s, its ideology was modeled after that of Soviet Stalinism. It was thus ill-equipped to creatively fuse Marxism with the national reality of Nicaragua. Nonetheless, the party was virtually the only institution in the country where Marxist ideas were taken seriously. As such, it attracted the attention of emerging young student radicals like Carlos Fonseca Amador and Tomás Borge.

Fonseca Amador was born in Matagalpa in northern Nicaragua. His mother was a cook, his father a worker in an American-owned mine. Borge was a secondary school classmate and close friend. Fonseca Amador became a political activist at an early age. At sixteen he participated in a strike at his school demanding the removal of a medallion depicting Somoza from the school's crest. At seventeen he and Borge discovered the writings of Marx and Engels in the bookstore of poet Samuel Meza and read and studied these philosophers. He soon drifted toward the PSN. First he sold *Unidad*, the PSN's paper, throughout Matagalpa; in 1955, at the age of nineteen, he joined the party. Fonseca Amador enrolled in law school in Leon the following year and, with Silvio Mayorga and Borge, formed a cell of the PSN's youth group.

Fonseca began studying Nicaraguan history that year, and later traced the roots of the rebellion to the numerous attempts of the Indians to resist Spanish conquest. He also identified with the rebellion in 1821 led by Cleto Ordoñez against the annexation of Nicaragua by Augustín de Iturbide, the Emperor of Mexico. Other nineteenth-century Nicaraguans that Fonseca Amador identified with included those who sought a united Central America, particularly Francisco Morazán; those who fought the American adventurer William Walker in the 1850s; and those who participated in the War of the Indians in 1881. Fonseca Amador saw the latter, an uprising of Indian and *mestizo* people against the ruling elite of Matagalpa, as a forerunner to Sandino's war. Fonseca Amador also carefully studied Sandino's thought and politico-military activities. He found great inspiration in Sandino's struggle against the Marines and also in his strong class consciousness and internationalism.

Although enthralled with the revolutionary actions of the Nicaraguan people, Fonseca Amador did not limit his study to Nicaraguan history. He was becoming a Marxist and an internationalist. In 1957 he traveled to the Soviet Union and wrote *A Nicaraguan in Moscow*, a positive, almost uncritical acceptance of the Soviet model of socialism. However, he began to be disillusioned by the reformist approaches of the PSN and sought a new vehicle for change based on the methodology of armed struggle. The key turning point was the shooting of four students during anti-Somoza demonstrations in 1959 and the tepid response of PSN leaders to the National Guard's actions.

His disenchantment with the PSN did not involve a rejection of Marxism but rather a belief that the PSN was abandoning the use of Marxism as a dynamic philosophy. Fonseca Amador achieved an important theoretical break with the strategy of the PSN and with almost all of Latin American Marxism at the time. The Nicaraguan PSN argued that, in the absence of fully developed capitalism in Nicaragua and an industrial working class, the main task of the revolutionary party, outside of the trade union work in the embryonic working class, was to seek alliances with the "national bourgeoisie" in pursuit of a "bourgeois-democratic" era in Nicaragua. This strategy, which downplayed the revolutionary potential of the Nicaraguan people, led Fonseca Amador to break with the PSN.

The guerrilla war in Cuba and the example of the Cuban Revolution had already inspired guerrilla activity in the late 1950s. Like many young Latin American revolutionaries, Fonseca and his collaborators were much taken by Fidel Castro's 26th of July movement and believed that guerrilla warfare was the best method of achieving political change. Deported to Guatemala in April 1959 following student demonstrations in León, Fonseca went briefly to Cuba. Then, with advice from Che Guevara and practical assistance from the Cuban government, he joined up with the Rigoberto López Pérez column in the Honduran border region. The column was composed of a group of fifty-five Nicaraguans, Cubans, and other Latin Americans. The column was surprised and massacred; Fonseca Amador was wounded but made his way to Cuba for convalescence. He became convinced of the need for a new political formation, and in July 1961 the FSLN was formally launched in Tegucigalpa, Honduras, by Fonseca, Tómas Borge, and Silvio Mayorga. The FSLN consisted of just twelve militants, including Colonel Santos López, a veteran of the Sandino-led struggle against the U.S. Marines in the late 1920s, and Victor Tirado López, later like Tómas Borge, one of the nine members of the FSLN's National Directorate. According to Borge's prison writings, the name of the organization and its clear link to Sandino was suggested and fought for by Fonseca Amador. However, it is clear that there was not unanimity on the question of the name of the organization, which points to the fact that Sandino was not the only root of the new revolutionary struggle. However, his influence was not small. On the contrary, the figure of Sandino was and continued to be a significant factor in shaping the political philosophy of the FSLN.

Drawing heavily on the Cuban revolutionary experience and the writings of Che Guevara and Fidel Castro, the Sandinistas reinterpreted Sandino. They drew on the revolutionary thought of other Latin Americans such as Peruvian José Carlos Mariátegui. By studying Nicaraguan circumstances in light of similar wars in Cuba, Vietnam, and elsewhere, the Sandinistas were able to build on Sandino's tactics and infuse their movement with a coherent ideology. The Sandinistas believed that the only road to power was through armed struggle. Like other young Fidelistas throughout Latin America, they felt that launching rural guerrilla warfare was all that was necessary to convince the people, beginning with the peasantry, to take up arms and join the guerrillas. In Nicaragua, as elsewhere in the region, this was a fundamental and very costly error, and the FSLN's first attempts at guerrilla warfare met with defeat. The new Sandinistas had failed to do what their namesake had done well—mobilize the local populace on the side of the guerrillas through well-planned political and organizational activity coordinated with and part of the armed struggle. Some of the FSLN's best cadres became isolated and surrounded at Pancasán in mid-1967. Most were killed as the National Guard closed their trap on the guerrillas. Like the Fidelista guerrilla currents all over Latin America, they suffered a disastrous military setback. Things were even worse in the cities. In Managua in January 1967 Conservative leader Fernando Agüero took advantage of a large peaceful demonstration against the dictatorship to attempt an ill-planned and unorganized putsch against Somoza that resulted in a heavy loss of life. However, even in defeat the tenacity of the resistance waged by the FSLN focused national attention on their struggle and helped turn a military defeat into a political victory. Unlike many other guerrilla movements in Latin America, the Sandinistas were able to learn from their early mistakes. They demonstrated a great capacity for self-criticism and were thus able to transcend their initial error of isolating themselves from the masses. They were able to fashion a strategy that eventually would bear fruit.

In the period after Pancasán the FSLN's increased prestige brought many new recruits, especially from among students and youth in the cities. At this time the organization focused mainly on developing a base among the *campesinos* in the north central part of the country. It was there that the urban recruits were sent. The work bore fruit and became the axis of the "prolonged people's war" concept that dominated Sandinista thinking at that time. Increased attention was also being paid to urban work that was necessarily clandestine. The FSLN began to establish what it called "intermediate organizations"—student, worker, neighborhood, and Christian movements. The success the Sandinistas were having in winning *campesinos* to their cause in the mountains alarmed Somoza and his U.S. advisers. Large-scale counterinsurgency operations were launched. Peasants suspected of collaborating with the FSLN "disappeared," were tortured, and were murdered. The counterrevolutionary terror became so intense that the guerrillas were forced further and further back into the mountains and progressively separated from the inhabited areas where they had been gaining support.

Simultaneously, other powerful sectors of Nicaraguan society were beginning to undergo change. Progressive sectors within the Catholic Church became more and more concerned with the conditions of the lower classes. Motivated by this concern and the ideas of liberation theology, they intervened actively in the process of social change. As discussed in Chapter 6, after the Latin American bishops meeting at Medellín in 1968, a section of the Latin American Church began to become involved in the struggle for social change. In Nicaragua the key institution was the Institute for Human Advancement (INPRHU), which began to organize using the methodology that Brazilian educational philosopher Paulo Freire had developed. Numerous Christian popular organizations emerged in the 1970s as the struggle against Somoza deepened. Eventually, an important unity was struck between the FSLN and these forces when prominent church figures such as Ernesto and Fernando Cardenal and Miguel D'Escoto became part of the FSLN. Such unity was not easily achieved because for a long period Christians and the Marxist-oriented leaders of the FSLN were wary of each other. The Christian forces perceived an antireligious orientation in traditional Marxist movements, while the mainstream of the FSLN questioned the revolutionary credentials of the Christian forces. What is most significant about the Nicaraguan case and the FSLN is that this historic gulf between Marxist and Christian forces was bridged not simply through a brief tactical alliance but through the integration of progressive Christians into the revolutionary movement. The result of this unity was that the political philosophy of the FSLN, and in particular its attitude toward Christianity, became unique among revolutionary parties with Marxist origins.

The growing strength of the political opposition coincided in the late 1960s and early 1970s with a growing crisis within the ruling Somoza dynasty. In June 1967 the third Somoza, Anastasio Jr., came to power in a blatantly rigged election. This election came on the heels of the death of Luis Somoza, who had ruled since the death of his father. Luis ruled in a manner that allowed for economic modernization under the aegis of the Kennedy administration's Alliance for Progress and for modest political reform that gave the presidency to two Liberals outside of the Somoza family, René Schick Gutiérrez and Lorenzo Guerrero. Unlike his brother Luis, Anastasio Jr. was a military man and his arrival at power signaled the end of an era of cosmetic liberalization and a return to more blatant authoritarian dictatorship. This approach was underscored by the bloody suppression of a protest rally shortly before the 1967 election. Once in power, Anastasio turned away from the civilian power base of the Liberal party that his brother had rejuvenated and turned much more to the use of military power to maintain family rule. Positions throughout government that were filled with technocrats by his older brother came increasingly to be filled by officers of the National Guard loyal to the Somoza family but without governing expertise. By 1970 corruption and incompetence became more widespread as the family more openly used public office for private enrichment. Anastasio also more blatantly ignored the Nicaraguan constitution. According to that document he was to step down when his term expired in 1971, but through a pact with Conservative leader Fernando Agüero he circumvented the rules and was elected to a new presidential term that was to last until 1981.

Turning Point for Revolution

Most observers argue that a key turning point for the regime was the Christmas earthquake of 1972, which cost the lives of 10,000 people and destroyed central Managua. Passing on the opportunity to be magnanimous with the family fortune in the face of the disaster, Somoza chose to turn the catastrophe to short-term personal advantage. He and his associates used their control of the government to channel international relief funds into their own pockets, primarily through the self-awarding of government contracts and the purchase of earthquake-damaged land and industries. Popular resentment against the government began to build among all classes when it became clear that Somoza used the tragedy to his own advantage. Donated international relief supplies were often sold by the government or given to friends of the Somoza family. Emergency housing funds from the U.S. government went disproportionately into the construction of luxury homes for Guard officers, while the homeless poor had to settle for wooden shacks they constructed themselves. Reconstruction of the city's roads and drainage system was also badly mismanaged. Somoza lost not only whatever support he may have had among the poorer classes but also the loyalty of the country's economic elite. Somoza's competitors in the business world were outraged by the manner in which he largely shut them out of the earthquake reconstruction. He also levied new taxes and then proceeded to exempt his own businesses. After 1973, large segments of the business community went elsewhere with their political support, eventually to the revolutionaries.

The political crisis of the Somoza regime and the earthquake came at a time when the FSLN was not well poised to take advantage. After Pancasán the movement survived but it did not prosper. By 1972 the revolutionaries had fewer than 500 cadres within Nicaragua, and much of the leadership, including Fonseca Amador, was living in exile in Cuba. Realizing that popular sentiment against the dictatorship was building, the FSLN made a spectacular reentry into Nicaraguan politics on December 27, 1974, with the seizure of the home of a wealthy Somoza supporter who was hosting a party for the U.S. ambassador. An FSLN commando unit held more than a dozen foreign diplomats and Nicaraguan political leaders hostage for several days, and forced Somoza to release Sandinista political prisoners, pay a large sum of money, and broadcast and publish FSLN communiqués. This action surprised many Nicaraguans since Somoza had declared the guerrilla challenge to be dead.

Somoza's response to the FSLN action served to deepen the crisis of his regime. He imposed martial law and sent his National Guard into the countryside to destroy the FSLN. In pursuit of that objective the Guard carried out arbitrary imprisonment, torture, and murder of hundreds of peasants. These brutal acts were not the first committed by the Guard, but the political landscape had changed. Catholic priests in the rural areas documented these actions, and the Nicaraguan Church hierarchy, which had previously supported the Somoza dynasty, denounced its human rights violations. The Church's changed stance gave international notoriety to Somoza.

However, even as the regime weakened, the path to political change was not entirely clear. For its part, the FSLN was severely divided over the proper strategy to employ against Somoza. Three tendencies emerged, formalized at a meeting of the National Directorate in Cuba in 1975, the first convening of that body since 1970. The three tendencies were called Prolonged People's War, Proletarian, and Insurrectionalist or Tercerista. The Prolonged People's War group, which included Ricardo Morales and Tomás Borge, had strategy and concrete political work that emphasized rural guerrilla warfare. They advanced beyond the guerrilla war theories of the 1960s but downplayed political work in the cities except as a recruiting ground for guerrilla fighters. As the decade of the 1970s developed, this tendency was probably the slowest to arrive at the judgment that a revolutionary situation was at hand.

The Proletarian tendency, which included Luis Carrión and Jaime Wheelock, based itself in large measure on dependency theory and the traditional Marxist-Leninist emphasis on the industrial working class. This tendency saw the Nicaraguan revolution as unfolding along more traditional lines as a confrontation between the owners and the working class. Political work in the cities was emphasized, and this group also built a base among students.

The Insurrectionalist tendency, which included Daniel and Humberto Ortega, was the last one to emerge. In reality it did not represent an entirely new approach; rather, it served primarily as a mediator between the two existing tendencies. The Terceristas (or Third Force, as they were called) did not draw a sharp distinction between a rural and urban emphasis, seeing the need for action in both arenas. They also argued that a broad alliance of all anti-Somoza forces was needed, similar to the work done by the 26th of July movement on the eve of the Cuban Revolution.

The three tendencies finally converged around the tactical and strategic questions brought to the fore by the upsurge of mass struggle that opened in late 1977 and as the urban masses moved into action after the murder of Conservative opposition leader and well-respected newspaper publisher Pedro Joaquín Chamorro in early 1978. After the first serious confrontation between the urban masses and the National Guard—the uprising in the Indian community of Monimbó in February 1978—the Insurrectionalist tendency shifted its strategy almost exclusively to prepare for insurrection in the cities. The Insurrectionalists also participated in the Broad Opposition Front (FAO) through their supporters in the "Group of Twelve." The twelve were prominent middle- and upper-class opponents of Somoza, including Sergio Ramírez, later elected vice president on the FSLN ticket in 1984. All opposition forces soon united under the banner of the National Patriotic Front (FPN). The FPN took on the character of a united front, drawing in the trade unions, two of the three factions of the old PSN, student groups, and organizations such as the Popular Social Christian and Independent Liberal parties—all under FSLN hegemony. Finally, the experience of the September 1978 attempt at insurrection—which the Insurrectionalist tendency spearheaded most enthusiastically—taught the need for better organization and preparation. The cumulative effect of these lessons, and the massive organized mobilization that resulted, paid off in June 1979 as the FSLN coordinated a massive popular insurrection.

As the summer of 1979 approached, the Somoza dictatorship became increasingly isolated. The only significant Nicaraguan sector that continued to support the dictator was the National Guard. Meanwhile, the FSLN continued to score important victories in the rural areas, and its forces were also gaining significant influence among the city-dwelling poor. Despite his increasingly dismal prospects, Somoza was unwilling to compromise and launched what proved to be a fatal strategy. He ordered the bombing of civilian areas in order to deny his adversaries food and shelter. It failed because the FSLN suffered few casualties and bombing served to further rally popular support behind the rebels. Faced with imminent defeat Somoza fled the country on July 17, 1979. He went first to the United States and then into exile in Paraguay, where he was assassinated fourteen months later by Argentinian revolutionaries. His demise ended one of the most durable dictatorships–forty-six years—in Latin American history.

On July 19, 1979, the Sandinistas marched into Managua and established a revolutionary government that was dominated by the FSLN, but also contained political actors from the non-Sandinista opposition to Somoza. The new government reflected the relationship of forces that existed at the time that the guerrilla war triumphed. The FSLN, confident that it had a mandate for significant social, political, and economic change, set about the process of creating a Nicaraguan revolution. The Sandinistas remained in power for eleven years until 1990, when, following an electoral defeat at the hands of a coalition headed by Violeta Chamorro, the FSLN handed over power and retreated to the position it held through the 1990s, that of leading opposition party.

The FSLN in Power

As the Sandinistas consolidated their political control after July 1979, more moderate elements of the victorious coalition left the government. After the initial euphoria of the revolutionary victory died down, the revolutionary leadership engaged in actions that suggested the participation and grassroots democracy that had been initially envisioned as part of the Sandinista program might be sidetracked. Power became concentrated in the upper echelons of government and in the FSLN's National Directorate. Later, as the United States and its allies pressured the Nicaraguan leadership to bring the regime more in line with Western-style political systems, steps were taken toward a system of representative democracy that the dominant group in the Sandinista leadership hoped would satisfy many of its detractors and thus increase the legitimacy of the Nicaraguan government in the eyes of the West, a legitimacy that was never received.

The political challenge that faced the Sandinistas as they assumed political power in July 1979 was significant. The revolutionaries had come to power at the head of a broad anti-Somoza front that had many different conceptions about the future of Nicaragua. The middle- and upper-class opponents of Somoza grounded in the nation's traditional opposition parties—Conservatives, Independent Liberals, and Social Christians—were interested primarily in gaining political power for themselves within traditional Nicaraguan political structures. Their commitment to social change was limited at best. They were largely interested in perpetuating the traditional authoritarian system but without the dictator Somoza and his Liberal party.

The Sandinistas and their supporters in the peasantry and the urban poor were interested in a far more radical transformation. They were more interested in the end product of social change than in the particular forms of political structures. However, much of the Sandinista leadership was skeptical of a narrow definition of democracy that reinstated the traditional party system, minimized direct popular participation, and did not include a social and economic dimension. Sandinista leaders believed that democracy did not begin or end with elections. Because the Sandinistas were primarily interested in social change they initiated a political process that would favor newly formed mass organizations of workers, peasants, women, and youth. Their direct involvement was embodied in the Council of State, which exercised legislative authority from 1979 to 1984. The Council, which would eventually expand to fifty members, included representatives from the traditional political elites (e.g., Conservative party), COSEP (business organizations), and the Catholic Church. However, while the Sandinistas sought input from these groups the majority of the Council were representatives of organizations loyal to the Sandinistas and committed to comprehensive social change. Key groups included AMNLAE (the national women's organization), Sandinista Youth (JS 19-J), the ACT (the peasants' organization), and the CST (a union organization). In granting a majority of seats to these grassroots organizations the Sandinistas were virtually guaranteeing the projection of significant social change through the legislative process while at the same time breaking the hold of the traditional elites on the Nicaraguan political process. Fully aware of the political direction that the Sandinistas were taking the revolution and the consequences for their political and economic interests, key elite members of the broad anti-Somoza front, including Violeta Chamorro, widow of Pedro Joaquín Chamorro, withdrew from the provisional government in protest over the composition of the Council of State. Faced with that challenge, the FSLN leadership restructured the executive branch with a smaller representation of non-Sandinistas and began to move the revolutionary process in a more radical direction. In the first four years of Sandinista power the revolutionary government recognized trade unions, organized significant land reform, passed measures guaranteeing women's rights, expanded health care and education, and broadened its diplomatic contacts to include the East European socialist countries and the Non-Aligned Movement (NAM). These actions served to galvanize opposition to the Sandinistas both within Nicaragua from the former elites and from the United States government.

Consolidating Political Institutions

Despite its obvious advantages to the furtherance of a revolutionary program, especially the involvement of grassroots organizations, the Sandinistas did not consider the Council of State to be a permanent body but rather a transitional one until elections could be held. Elections were promised in 1979, but the Sandinistas argued that significant preparation was needed for them to accurately reflect the will of the Nicaraguan people. International pressures grew on the FSLN to hold the elections sooner rather than later. The context for the elections also changed with the full-scale launching of the Contra War against Nicaragua by the United States in 1981–1982. Hoping to utilize the elections to legitimize Sandinista political power, the FSLN modeled their government and electoral process after Western examples. The president would be directly elected for a six-year term and, as in the French system, would dominate over the legislative branch. The National Assembly was created as a unicameral body with selection primarily by proportional representation (the number of seats is directly proportioned to the party percent of the vote). Very little consideration was given to retaining a direct legislative role for the mass organizations. Some Sandinistas privately raised concerns about the loss of grassroots initiative, but by 1983–1984 defeating the counterrevolution had become the dominant task. Priority was ultimately given to gaining support in the Contra War from Western governments—something that was never achieved to any significant degree. Ironically, the primary support for the FSLN in the Contra War came from Cuba and the U.S.S.R., neither of whom saw Western-style elections in Nicaragua as a positive. Within Nicaragua the FSLN sought to legitimize its policies by defeating the traditional parties in the electoral arena. Ultimately, key elite actors, who were by now supporting the war against the Sandinistas either overtly or covertly, boycotted the elections and thereby undermined their legitimacy in the eyes of much of the Western world. In any case, the November 4, 1984, elections in Nicaragua were significant in that a revolutionary party competed for political power with elite-oriented parties. The negotiated electoral law defined parties as entities that could vie for political power, a far cry from the special status reserved for the Vanguard party in Marxist–Leninist states. The result was also a rare event in Nicaraguan history—an honest election. There was real electoral competition among seven different parties, three to the right of FSLN and three to the left. After a history of rigged elections and limited suffrage, the 1984 elections, open to all Nicaraguan citizens sixteen years of age and above, helped embed in the Nicaraguan nation a notion of representative democracy that had been severely lacking. Despite the boycott of Rightist parties, armed threats by the contras, and a U.S. government campaign against the legitimacy of the elections, participation was extremely high: 93 percent of those eligible registered and of these 75 percent voted on election day. The big winners were the Sandinistas, who garnered 62.9 percent of the votes for president and vice president and 62.3 percent of the National Assembly votes. Although political conditions prior to the election were not perfect, the voting itself did not see the type of corruption and vote fraud that had been so common in countries like Guatemala and El Salvador. The government and its policies were openly criticized during the campaign, and the opposition was able to win one-third of the seats in the National Assembly.

The 1984 elections also laid the groundwork for successful national elections in 1990 and 1996 that saw the defeat of the Sandinistas and in both cases the successful transfer of political power from one party to another. However, the 1984 elections were not an unqualified success for democracy. As was pointed out earlier, grassroots organizations lost their direct representation and now were dependent almost exclusively on representation through the FSLN party. If the FSLN party had been capable of giving that participation, the loss of direct representation may not have been as crucial, but the FSLN did not prove to be that vehicle. Throughout its years in power, pressed by its continuing war with the U.S.-backed contras, the FSLN operated as a top-down vanguard revolutionary movement. Party leaders rejected the idea of creating a mass party in 1979, and through the 1980s decision making was tightly controlled through the nine-member National Directorate; party ranks remained small, only a few thousand. Potential new members had to go through a lengthy membership process that was tightly controlled by the few hundred combatants of the war against Somoza. This hierarchical control extended to the mass organizations, which had almost no independence from the Sandinista party. With control of the government definitively in the hands of the FSLN, most national decisions were made within the party's inner circles with little input from the outside. This hierarchical functioning would eventually come to haunt the Sandinistas in the period leading up to the 1990 elections.

The eleven years that the Sandinistas were in power were tumultuous ones both in Nicaragua and throughout Central America. Within Nicaragua the FSLN attempted revolutionary transformation on a scale rarely seen in Latin America. At the same time in the 1980s, civil wars raged in nearby El Salvador and Guatemala as rebel movements similar to the FSLN made serious bids for power. The region also became a prime battleground for the implementation of a U.S. conservative vision of a continuation of a Cold War between the United States and the Soviet Union. U.S. president Ronald Reagan made the defeat of the Sandinistas and their removal from power a high priority of the United States government. To this end the United States armed and financed a counterrevolutionary war against Nicaragua throughout the 1980s, utilizing primarily the forces of the defeated dictator Somoza operating out of bases in Honduras. By the end of the decade the FSLN, with significant Soviet assistance, defeated militarily the counterrevolutionaries (contras), but at great costs. More than 30,000 lives were lost and the country's economy was devastated. Weary of the war and facing the continued hostility of the United States, the Nicaraguan people voted the FSLN out of power in the February 1990 elections. To the surprise of many observers the

Sandinistas handed over the reigns of power to the incoming Chamorro administration in April 1990. In doing so the FSLN became the first revolutionary group in Latin American history to cede power to an opposition force through an election.

The decade of the 1990s saw two conservative governments that sought to reverse the policies and programs of the Sandinistas. Violeta Chamorro's National Opposition Union (UNO) and Arnoldo Alemán's Constitutional Liberal Party (PLC), elected in 1996, have succeeded in a significant measure in undermining FSLN programs, but they have not succeeded in their goal of marginalizing the FSLN. The Sandinistas emerged from both the 1990 and 1996 elections as the leading opposition force with political control in several municipalities. As a result the FSLN and its supporters have maintained political space for the Left in Nicaraguan politics, thereby protecting some of the achievements of their revolution, especially in agrarian reform, workers rights, women's rights, and Atlantic Coast autonomy.

The 1990 Election and the End of One-Party Dominant Rule

The 1990 election was held after more than a decade of Sandinista rule and after the general outlines of a transformed Nicaraguan society were already in place. During these years, many traditional values had been challenged, if not replaced, by modern values in some sectors of the population. There were also many external factors that were brought to bear on the electoral process and the ensuing Chamorro administration. The vote occurred as the United States was poised to again extend its power through the region and—as became apparent—to further project it in much of the rest of the world. As it turned out, the election occurred in an international and regional context over which the Nicaraguan government had only limited control despite its often brilliant use of diplomacy and the international legal system. From 1982 on, the United States had used military, diplomatic, and economic means to impose its will on the Sandinista government and the Nicaraguan people. Although the Republican administrations were not able to realize their primary objective of overthrowing the Sandinistas through the Contra War, they could make sure that the new government had very difficult going, had very limited options, and was hard-put to claim it could be a model for other Central or Latin American countries.

Although the FSLN had been able to maintain unity while it was in power, most of the other parties had not been able to overcome the traditional Nicaraguan proclivity for factionalism and internecine struggle. Although only six opposition parties had opposed the FSLN in the 1984 election (encouraged by the United States, the Coordinadora Democrática boycotted the elections), by the beginning of 1988 there were fourteen opposition parties plus a few opposition political groupings. The Reagan administration had pushed the military side of low-intensity conflict and discouraged parties from participating in 1984. However, as Bush took office, U.S. policy began to emphasize an electoral challenge to the Sandinistas.

If traditional factionalism had held sway, there would have been some twenty opposition parties on the ballot. This would have splintered the opposition vote and allowed the FSLN an easy victory. Realizing this, the Bush administration pushed for a unified opposition coalition and strongly encouraged the selection of a fresh opposition candidate who could serve as a symbol around which the opposition could rally. Although lacking political experience, Violeta Chamorro filled this role very well. With U.S. support, she was able to edge out Enrique Bolaños, a traditional political leader and head of COSEP, and become the UNO candidate. By the time of the election, the U.S.-supported unity of UNO had held. Included in the new coalition were parties that traced their origins to the old Conservative and Liberal parties as well as social democratic parties, Social Christian parties, a party tied to Contra leaders, and even two Communist parties—the Nicaraguan Socialist Party (PSN) and the Communist Party of Nicaragua (PC de N).

The 1990 campaign proved to be lively, and the besieged Sandinista leadership was thrown into a different kind of battle. In order to be able to successfully compete against the U.S.-supported UNO coalition, the Sandinista leadership had to devote its organizational and human resources to an expensive electoral contest that ate up better than $7 million in very scarce funds. The cost of preparing and administering the election was itself enormous (this would also be the case for the 1996 election). The Supreme Electoral Council, the independent government body responsible for overseeing and running the election, spent in excess of $15 million. Given the miserable economic conditions in which most workers and peasants found themselves by 1989, they might have well preferred to forgo the election in favor of a direct dispersal of funds that would have guaranteed jobs, increased real wages, and thus gained relief from hyperinflation.

The Sandinista leadership knew that conditions were bad, but they thought their political base could endure a little longer while they employed the human and material resources at their disposal to win the election. They mobilized their followers well and spent $7 million on a very fancy campaign that not only featured door-to-door organizing and mass rallies but also gave away FSLN baseball caps, straw hats, T-shirts, backpacks, and cigarette lighters. The FSLN used outside media and public relations consultants to develop a very slick, rock star–like presentation of Daniel Ortega. The Sandinistas reasoned that such extravagant spending was necessary to win the election, secure their position, and legitimize their political system in the eyes of the West. They also realized that they were playing a high-stakes game and that the United States had designated huge sums of money for the UNO campaign. This was epitomized by the 1989 U.S. congressional authorization of $9 million in overt funding for the opposition. It was to be dispensed through the National Endowment for Democracy. The result was, however, that the Sandinista campaign was in stark contrast to the austere, impoverished conditions in which most Nicaraguans found themselves. This was clearly a contributing factor to the Sandinista defeat.

Up to the time of the February election it seemed that the Nicaraguan revolution might be able to build on the experiment with socialist democracy that developed in Chile in the early 1970s. The Sandinistas reasoned that they would give an expanded electorate the opportunity to decide if they wanted to continue in the process of socialist construction or opt for another type of régime. Down to the eve of the election most opinion polls suggested that the Nicaraguan people would ratify the socialist, mixed economy experiment and continue with Sandinista democracy. However, the Sandinistas' stunning defeat at the hands of the U.S.-sponsored UNO suggested that the *demos* (the people) were not entirely satisfied with Sandinista rule, or the type of socialist democracy that was developing in Nicaragua. Careful analysis of the facts suggests the low intensity conflict that the Bush administration waged against Nicaragua had disastrous effects on the economy. Nor was the Nicaraguan government well prepared to manage the deteriorating economic conditions.

By 1988 inflation had reached some 36,000 percent, real wages had fallen to 29 percent of their 1980 value, milk consumption had fallen by 50 percent, and production reached levels that were abysmally low. In that same year, the deteriorating economy began to heavily impact daily life and increasingly became a subject of intense public concern. The government clearly assigned blame to the U.S. actions. However, like the neoliberal policies the Chamorro administration later followed, the government response was an austerity program that was modeled on the programs that Brazil and Argentina employed in 1985 and 1986 and as such fell disproportionately on the poor. This marked a shift in Sandinista policy because it was the first time since the Sandinista insurrection that the Nicaraguan government had begun a program of economic reforms that did not include steps to protect the poor, the social base of the Sandinistas, from its harshest effects. By mid-1988, prices for basic commodities had risen 600 percent, while the government lifted price controls on most goods and services, with devastating results for wage-earners.

By the late-1980s, the harm had been done and there was a growing perception that the Sandinistas were not in control or were selling out their poor supporters to gain the economic cooperation of middle- and upper-class commercial interests. It seemed that the only response to the economic crisis that the Sandinista leadership could agree to implement was one that sought to activate traditional commercial groups in the hope that they would lead the recovery. But by the end of 1989, it seemed to many that the economic dimension of the Contra War, coupled with internal deficiencies in management and allocation, had caused the Sandinista government to ignore the economic plight of the masses.

To diminish any remaining Sandinista support, the Bush administration cranked up the Contras again in summer 1989. As they rampaged through the countryside they spread political messages for the election: "Only UNO can end the economic crisis" and "There will be no peace under a Sandinista government." The Contras became an active part of the anti-Sandinista campaign organized by the United States. The sophisticated low-intensity conflict campaign was clearly having a dual effect. By January 1990, 52 percent of those registered voters surveyed believed that the economy was the most important issue for them in deciding how to vote in the coming election. By comparison, 37 percent thought the Contra War was the most important issue.

As economic conditions deteriorated and the political support for the direct, participatory democracy of the mass organizations was diminished by their exclusion from the legislative body after 1984 and their frequent subordination to FSLN control, there were fewer channels through which the masses could effectively communicate the gravity of their plight. Thomas Cronin suggests one reaction to such a situation is that when there is growing suspicion that privileged interests exert far greater influences on the typical politician than does the common voter, there is a demand for more democracy. But neither the official party nor the mass organizations seemed willing or able to provide greater democratic participation. And by lauding the election and the connected Western-style representative democracy, the Sandinistas themselves seemed to be telling the people that this (and not participatory democracy) was the only democratic instrument through which they could express themselves. Meanwhile, the UNO coalition was arguing that its fundamental objective was to "construct democracy" and that it planned to democratize the nation and the society. UNO was the only party on the ballot that had any chance of challenging Sandinista political hegemony. Since Sandinista dominance appeared to many to be ever less responsive to popular democracy, there were very limited choices for most voters.

Many felt that the Sandinista leaders were isolated from the hardships of the masses and that their political position facilitated access to goods that the poor could no longer afford. Many were also angered by what they perceived as increasing bureaucratization in government offices. They saw the formation of a bureaucratic class that was not particularly sympathetic to popular needs and was the beneficiary of a disproportionate share of scarce resources. This created a considerable amount of resentment. Thus it seemed to many that the vanguard party had lost contact with the very people it was supposed to represent and consequently was not responding to their needs and feelings.

When the results of the election were counted UNO had won a landslide victory, with 54.7 percent of the votes compared to 40.8 percent for the FSLN. The FSLN was defeated throughout the country, even in previously strong FSLN working-class districts in Managua. UNO gained fifty-one of the ninety-two National Assembly seats and control of 101 of 132 municipal councils.

Careful analysis suggests that it was the U.S.-induced economic crisis and the ineffective way it was handled that most hurt the Sandinistas in their

President Daniel Ortega (left, wearing hat and bandana and shaking hands) campaigning in the 1990 Nicaraguan elections. Recast in jeans, cowboy boots, and bandana, Ortega was portrayed by FSLN as a rock star–like friend of the people. He lost to UNO candidate Violeta Chamorro. *(Photo by H. Vanden)*

traditional bastions of working-class support. Further, the war extracted a huge economic as well as human toll. By ignoring those aspects of direct, participatory democracy that were part of the initial Sandinista program and by failing to economically support its mass base (and natural constituency), the FSLN left open a more formal Western-style institutional democracy as an avenue of popular expression. In this way the Sandinista leadership undermined the dominance of their party in the Nicaraguan political system and set the stage for the creation of a multiparty system where no party dominated.

The newly refined electoral framework was imperfect, but it still provided a mechanism by which a growing desperation with conditions could be registered. The 1990 election proved to be a very effective means of registering a massive protest vote. Many political observers celebrated the 1990 election as a return of democracy and the end of one-party dominance. One could equally argue that it was the beginning of an imposed régime that resulted from economic and military pressure from the United States and its allies and from pro-U.S. conservative groups inside Nicaragua. During the election, these forces employed a variety of tactics to induce a majority of the population to vote against the Sandinista government. In all, the United States had invested heavily in supporting opposition forces in Nicaragua— some $26 million in overt and covert aid since the 1984 election. *Newsweek* suggested that $5 million in covert funds had been used for the 1990 election alone. Overt funding for the election was estimated at $12.5 million. Many Nicaraguan voters came to believe that the only way things were going to improve was if they removed the Sandinistas from office. The authoritarian decision-making style by the government and the arrogance of many government and FSLN party leaders also convinced many other voters to sanction the party in office the only way they could: by voting for the only viable opposition—UNO.

In an action that further reduced the possibility of a return to a one-party-dominant régime under Sandinista control, the Sandinista government engaged in what came to be a very controversial action. Soon after the 1990 election they rushed legislation through the National Assembly that granted title to confiscated property to those who had occupied it during the Sandinista years. While this did give title to some peasants and cooperatives and other small property owners, it also gave quite a few Sandinista leaders title to expensive properties they had used or been awarded as compensation for their years of service and sacrifice. Known as the Piñata, it came to be regarded as a way for the Sandinista leadership to enrich themselves before leaving office. As time progressed and poverty among the masses increased, the Piñata bred increasing resentment, helped erode support for the Sandinistas, and seemed to confirm the growing popular perception that government, while paid for by the many, was by and for the few.

The Chamorro Years

In retrospect, it would seem that the 1990 election marked the beginning of a return to political decision making by political and economic elites that was conducted far from institutions in which the masses could exercise any real power. Indeed, the next six years saw the development of a political system that was increasingly characterized by intense competition among political elites—sometimes about issues that were often irrelevant to the daily lives of the Nicaraguan masses. Nor were important concerns addressed; as unemployment and poverty became more generalized and income and wealth more concentrated, it became increasingly clear those aspects of economic democracy that had grown during the earlier years of Sandinista rule were severely eroded by successive waves of neoliberal policies.

The popular expectation was, however, quite different. It was expected that the new government would heed the democratic mandate, utilize the bountiful aid and support that would surely be offered by the U.S. government, and begin to listen to popular political demands and respond to the masses' often desperate needs. In reality, it seemed that the real electors were not the majority who voted for UNO, but the external and internal economic elites who had engineered the Sandinista electoral demise. It was their demands—and not those of the common people—that would get the greatest attention. What the majority that voted for UNO did not realize was that Violeta Chamorro had been chosen as an electoral tool to unseat the Sandinistas. Thus, there would be strong pressure to dismantle the type of state apparatus that had developed under Sandinista rule, implement a conservative neoliberal economic program, strengthen traditional parties, and further reduce the power and size of the mass organizations and the Sandinista party. Nor would these changes give the masses any appreciable power in the new system.

As the new president began her term, she initially relied on the Mayorga Plan, which was designed to revise the structure of the Nicaraguan state and fully reintegrate Nicaragua into the world economy on terms that would be favorable to foreign investors and the dependent Nicaraguan bourgeoisie. This process continued over the next six years and was buttressed with the election of Alemán in 1996. Initially, however, it was tempered and at times blocked by the political power that the FSLN had developed. The FSLN was able to allude to its institutionalized power in state structures like the Sandinista Army and supported sporadic popular mobilizations. The mass mobilizations at the time of the revolution and during the first years of Sandinista rule also set the stage for an often tenacious popular resistance against many of the unpopular economic policies that the Chamorro government tried to implement. As resistance was worn down, elements of the new policies were, however, gradually put in place. Meanwhile, other political parties occupied more and more political space.

Nor did the FSLN prove to be an adequate channel for popular resistance. The initial Sandinista commitment to participatory democracy was never reinstitutionalized in the party or in its ties to mass organizations. By 1991 it was becoming increasingly apparent that the Chamorro government was unable to solve basic economic problems for the common people. The fact that conditions actually deteriorated after the 1990 election did little to convince the masses of the ultimate utility of Western-style representative democracy. Nor were conflicts and centripetal forces limited to the Sandinista party.

An uneasy alliance between Violeta Chamorro and her vice presidential candidate, Virgilio Godoy, barely endured through the electoral victory. Godoy was rapidly eclipsed by Chamorro's son-in-law, Antonio Lacayo. Upon her inauguration, he assumed the office of minister of the presidency. Thereafter Lacayo operated as de facto head of government, performing most of the executive functions for the president (who was more head of state than head of government). This left Vice President Godoy not only outside the decision-making process, but literally outside the presidential office building. Eventually, UNO members in the National Assembly divided into two often hostile camps: One group, led by Conservative leader Miriam Argüello, was aligned with Godoy, and the other, led by Alfredo César, was allied with the president.

The National Assembly became a focal point for political competition and deal making. While the economy continued to deteriorate, political conflict increased. A dispute between the president and many Assembly members of her own UNO coalition in 1992 worsened the situation. This angered the other UNO delegates who questioned the legitimacy of the institution and began to boycott Assembly sessions. They believed that the understanding on which their coalition was based had been betrayed and further accused Chamorro and Lacayo of collaborating with the Sandinistas in a co-government. On the Left, worker and peasant organizations and the increasingly militant ex-Sandinista fighters (*Recompas*), who had still not received land, accused the Sandinista leadership of collaborating with the government at their expense. Former Contras (Recontras) who had not received their promised land also became increasingly militant.

1994 Constitutional Crisis

Many factors converged in 1994 to precipitate a crisis that shook the Nicaraguan state to its very foundations. Unemployment and underemployment were at horrendous levels (well over 50 percent) and economic conditions generally were approaching those of Haiti. But the political deterioration was equally bad. Coalitions and alliances that had been forged previously continued to unravel as the political setting became ever more contentious. The common vision and collective dedication that had characterized the uprising against Somoza and the first years of Sandinista rule were gone. Also forgotten by the leadership of the FSLN was how much of the revolutionary victory was owed to the masses' involvement in the insurrection and how important unity had been to their victory. Virtual government had tied the FSLN to many government policies, and the continuation of autocratic decision-making policies by the Sandinista party leadership had angered many party loyalists. The perception that elements of the leadership—and not the movement generally—had most benefited from the Piñata added to dissatisfaction.

There was a movement to reform the 1987 constitution. Pushed by a coalition made up of parties and individuals who currently did not have easy access to power, it envisioned increasing the power of the National Assembly at the expense of the executive. The constitutional reforms would take away the president's power to tax and spend by decree without legislative approval, prohibit nepotism, expand constitutional liberties, abolish the draft, clarify the right to private and other forms of property, reduce the presidential term from six to five years, and stipulate that a second round of voting would need to be held in those elections where the leading candidate did not get at least 45 percent of the vote. The net effect would have been to considerably strengthen the legislature at the expense of the presidency and (through the prohibition against nepotism) to eliminate Antonio Lacayo from future governmental positions, including that of the presidency. Begun in 1993, this process gained momentum during 1994. It led to much heated discussion between the two branches of government, but no consensus or compromise was reached.

When the package of constitutional reforms was finally sent to the executive in January 1995, President Chamorro did not promulgate them (by publishing them in the official newspaper) in the required fifteen-day period and then announced in February that her government did not recognize them. The next day several of the national newspapers published the texts of the reforms as signed by president of the National Assembly Luís Humberto Guzmán, thus—it could be argued—promulgating them. This led to months of wrangling and mutual recrimination. For a while there were two constitutions, with each of the two branches declaring that theirs was the legal one. The situation worsened when the legislature would not accept Chamorro's recommendations for supreme court justices, and instead sent their own list back to the executive, who in turn refused to appoint them. This left the nation's highest court without a quorum.

The severity of the crisis was such that it took the combined effort of the major donor nations to convince the governmental institutions that cooperation was necessary to move beyond the breach. The impending June 1994 Paris meeting of donor nations acted as a catalyst. But the political immaturity of the political actors was so great that the U.S. Embassy had to pressure both sides, and recourse to the offices of Cardinal Obando y Bravo was necessary to force both parties to resolve their differences. Many saw this as a serious erosion of fledgling democratic political institutions, since it was necessary to go to foreign brokers and extra government actors and to employ extralegal political deals to resolve the crisis. This further increased the general population's negative perception of the political class and their confidence in Nicaraguan democracy.

The 1996 Elections and the Evolving Party System

As the 1996 elections approached, the FSLN began to ally itself with Minister of the Presidency Antonio Lacayo's newly formed National Project. The Sandinista Renovation Movement (MRS) was making common cause with the Christian Democratic Union, Virgilio Godoy's Independent Liberal Party, Miriam Argüello's Popular Conservative Alliance, the Nicaraguan Democratic Union (MDN), and the National Conservative Party (PNC). The strongest contender for the 1996 presidential election was Managua's conservative mayor, Arnoldo Alemán. Alemán was using his Constitutionalist Liberal Party (PLC) to gain control of the now factionalized old Liberal Party (including Liberal groups who were allied with Somoza). In the end this strategy and his successful public works campaign in Managua combined to give him victory in the first round of the election. Amid fears that Alemán would bring back the Somocistas and allow them to retake their confiscated land and properties and reconstitute Liberal Party dominance, there was a surge in support for Daniel Ortega and the FSLN in the final months of the campaign. Some polls even mistakenly gave FSLN an edge on the eve of the election. The final results proved otherwise. Alemán won the October 20 contest. There were, however, charges of tampering with the transmittal of the returns from the polling places to the central tallying point in the Supreme Electoral Council (a part of the process not overseen by the electoral observers). Some seven parties requested that the electoral results for Managua be annulled. Nonetheless, the Supreme Electoral Council finally tallied the votes and declared that Alemán received 51 percent of the votes to Ortega's 38 percent. Alemán's Liberal Alliance was also a big winner elsewhere, winning many municipalities, including Managua, and forty-two of ninety-three seats in the National Assembly. The FSLN won thirty-six seats in the assembly; the smaller parties, fifteen.

In 1996 it was the vestiges of the old Liberal party reorganized as the Liberal Alliance that had again united to claim victory. The FSLN's eleven years of party dominance had been refuted in the 1990 and again in the 1996 elections. Although still a power contender, it was far from being the dominant party in Nicaragua. The Sandinista Renovation Movement, led by Sergio Ramírez, ran as a separate party, but it only got a small percentage of the vote. Other political groupings were fractionalized as well. There were twenty-four parties on the ballot, but Alemán's Liberal Alliance and the FSLN secured 89.8 percent of the votes. It still, however, may be said that Nicaragua maintained some aspects of a one-party-dominant system. Not only was the FSLN a major contender for power, but it also had been defeated by none other that a recast coalition of Liberal party groupings, which included strong participation from the Somoza faction of the Liberal party. The political hegemony of the FSLN had been broken, and the Liberal Alliance had gained power. There was a possibility that a one-party-dominant system under Liberal hegemony would develop under Alemán's rule. Yet the Nicaraguan proclivity for factionalism and FSLN strength continued to threaten this project.

It remained to be seen if the old Somoza-dominated Liberal party could claim party hegemony once again. Alemán campaigned on returning property taken during Sandinista rule to its previous owners, most of whom benefited from, or were strongly tied to, the Somozas. In the first months of Alemán's rule there was a strong upsurge in returning Somocistas, and shortly after the election Somoza's nephews returned to Nicaragua to reclaim much of Somoza's property.

As of 2001, Nicaragua was no longer a one-party-dominant system. Yet the survival of the newly restructured competitive party system will depend on many factors. Apart from whether the Liberal coalition holds, there was the question of economic conditions. As this and other questions came to the fore, the evolving system was challenged to provide effective democratic representation and participation for the masses. If it became a mechanism for competition among the political elites to the exclusion of popular participation and popular concerns, the probability of system breakdown and eventual return to some form of hegemonic, authoritarian rule would increase dramatically.

The combination of the policies of the U.S. government and the political actions of Chamorro and her successor Liberal Arnoldo Alemán have gone a long way to returning Nicaragua to its political and economic position prior to the 1979 Sandinista revolution. However, in certain ways Nicaragua still bears the marks of its revolutionary period, and the FSLN, while defeated in both the 1990 and 1996 presidential election, remained a formidable political force, holding more than one-third of the legislative seats in the National Assembly and the mayor's position in a number of significant cities and towns. In November 2000, the FSLN won a surprising victory in the Managua mayor's race, but it was unclear whether this renewed momentum would lead to success in the 2001 presidential election.

Nicaraguan Government Structures

Similar to other Latin American governments Nicaragua has four independent branches of government: executive, legislative, judicial, and electoral. As is often the case in Latin America, the executive branch is the most powerful. The state's administrative apparatus is rather large, with sixteen ministries and thirty-five independent agencies having cabinet rank. The appointive powers of the president are extensive, including all ministers and vice ministers of the state and numerous other high-level functionaries. The president chooses the chief and associate justices of the supreme court, but from a list provided by the National Assembly.

The National Assembly is composed of ninety members elected by proportional representation from nine administrative regions, plus the defeated presidential candidates of any party receiving at least 1.1 percent of the national vote. The Assembly's most important powers are budgetary oversight, the ability to summon the president and ministers, and its role in naming supreme court justices, members of the electoral council, and the controller general. The National Assembly also has an extensive system of standing and special committees, although the work of the body has been weakened by limited resources. When the assembly acted primarily to back up the president during the Sandinista years it never developed an independent stance. However, divisions within UNO between 1990 and 1996 allowed the Assembly to become more of a player in its own right. In 1995 reforms also strengthened the hand of the assembly *vis-à-vis* the executive branch.

Courts in Nicaraguan and Latin American history have not played a role similar to those of their North American neighbors. As a unitary state Nicaragua does not have a formal checks and balances system. The lack of judicial review of laws leaves the Nicaraguan courts with the role of applying and interpreting laws rather than making them. The Supreme Court has twelve magistrates and is organized into four divisions, each responsible for a specific realm of law: civil, criminal, constitutional, and administrative.

The fourth branch of government, the Supreme Electoral Council, is intended to ensure that electoral administration is nonpartisan. Established in 1983, it performed well in the 1984 elections and was in significant measure responsible for the legitimacy of the hotly contested 1990 elections. Under the leadership of Sandinista Mariano Fiallos, it set a high standard for honesty and competence. Unfortunately this organ's reputation was damaged by widespread irregularities in the 1996 election.

Interest Groups

The Sandinistas have been out of political power at the level of the national government for a decade, but any discussion of interest groups in contemporary Nicaragua must bear a strong input from the Sandinista era. Many of the key sectors and organizations that influence politics in Nicaragua today emerged during the 1980s. Many were originally a part of FSLN structures, but after 1990 they moved to a more independent position. As is true elsewhere in Latin America, the most powerful traditional groups, such as large landowners and large-scale entrepreneurs, did not work through organizations but maintained direct links with the governments of Chamorro and Alemán that ruled in the 1990s. Our focus is on interest groups that have worked from the grass roots seeking to defend gains that were made in the 1980s.

WOMEN

In the area of women's rights, the gains of the 1980s were numerous, including paid maternity leave; equal access to education; legal equality in relation to divorce, adoption, and parental responsibility; a measure of economic independence; and the inclusion of sex education in the school curriculum. Of course, these gains occurred in the context of a very traditional male-oriented society and with a Sandinista government that often resisted women's demands out of a lack of commitment to women's rights and a deference to the Roman Catholic hierarchy. However, even with those limitations, women had emerged by 1990 as much greater players in Nicaraguan politics and society than ever before.

The gains for women achieved during the Sandinista period were undermined in the 1990s. On the positive side, the legal framework was largely maintained. Successive post-Sandinista regimes and the Catholic Church have sought to restrict the right to unilateral divorce by either party, but so far the Sandinista-era law has been sustained. However, the legal framework put in place by the Sandinistas had many serious limitations for women's rights, and now Nicaraguan women's organizations are seeking to strengthen their rights but are doing so in a generally unfavorable political climate. Examples of loopholes in the legal code of the revolutionary period included abortion, violence against women, democratization of the family, lack of an equal pay provision, and protection for gays and lesbians. Despite pressure from some women, abortion was never decriminalized. The Sandinista leadership made it clear that it was unwilling to go against the Catholic Church on this issue. However, during the 1980s abortion became widely tolerated and few prosecutions occurred. Since 1990 the Managua women's hospital stopped performing therapeutic abortions, and the procedure has been driven entirely underground. The pro-government media presented powerful anti-abortion measures, and these dovetailed with the traditional Catholic Church's wider campaign of promoting a more traditional role for women. Nicaragua also took a backward step with the passage of anti-sodomy laws in 1999. Prior to this measure, Nicaraguan law had been silent on such questions. The conservative framework of laws on women and the family allowed the Nicaraguan delegation at the U.N. Population Conference in Cairo in 1994 to line up with the Vatican against the mildly progressive majority document.

Nonetheless, the greater involvement of women in the public life of Nicaragua, an important advancement of the 1980s, remained strong. The women's movement is probably stronger today than ten years ago, with the Nicaraguan Women's Association (AMNLAE) strengthened and many new organizations on the scene, including several that have clearly labeled themselves as feminist. However, on many fronts the position of women was under strong attack in Nicaragua. The country's economic crisis bore heavily on women because so many were heads of households and because they bore a disproportionate burden of household production and reproduction. Desperate economic circumstances resulted in the greater occurrence of prostitution. AMNLAE's service orientation benefited some women, but there was little defense of women's rights in the political arena. The now conservative-dominated Catholic Church and its allies in government had the upper hand in implementing their anti-feminist agenda. Countering this trend were a variety of new groups organized around concrete issues such as violence against women and women's health, including abortion.

WORKERS

A significant expansion of workers' rights, especially the right to form unions and engage in collective bargaining, was a definitive achievement of Sandinista power. Prior to 1979, only about 30,000 Nicaraguans (less than 10 percent of the workers) were trade union members, and strikes or even collective bargaining were made virtually impossible by the Somoza regime. By the end of the 1980s there were more than 2000 workplace unions, with some 55 percent of the working population unionized. New laws enacted by the National Assembly guaranteed the right to strike and collective bargaining. Some trade union rights, including the right to strike, were suspended during the Contra War, but strikes occurred throughout the 1980s. Most labor confrontations were settled through dialogue with the FSLN.

The arrival in power of the Chamorro government in 1990 brought new challenges for the labor movement. The privatization process was not limited to the agricultural sector; state-owned manufacturing, utility, and service industries were also targeted. As in the rural areas, the initial instinct of the union movement was total opposition to privatization, and large demonstrations, including factory occupations, occurred during the summer of 1990. However, divisions within the working class and the absolute commitment of the government led to the privatization process going forward. The union movement concentrated on winning agreements allowing all workers to purchase all or part of the privatized enterprises. This process of full and partial workers' ownership turned out to be highly controversial and contradictory. An agreement between the government and the FSLN in 1991 established the principle that when an enterprise was privatized a minimum of 25 percent of the value of the enterprise must be available for pur-

chase by the employees. No provision of the agreement blocked full purchase of the enterprise if the workers could raise the capital.

Union leaders were convinced that full and partial worker ownership represented an important achievement and a primary battleground for the
union movement, but it proved to be a questionable position. By compro-
mising their initial demand against privatization, the union movement for-
feited the momentum and bargaining power that it had in 1990. When the
union movement entered the arena of ownership and management, it was
not playing its strongest card. In the arena of financial capital, the government and the private sector had both the money and the expertise. The
unions worked hard to adjust to their new role, but it seems that the amount
of time and resources devoted to privatization came at the expense of their
representation of workers in traditional owner-management situations. The
Sandinista-affiliated National Workers' Front (FNT) mobilized often during
the Chamorro presidency, mounting big strikes in 1990, 1991, 1992, and 1995.
These mobilizations delayed but did not stop the government's austerity
programs. However, by the end of the Chamorro period organized labor
was worn out. Their decline in influence continued under the Alemán government so that today they maintain a presence in Nicaraguan politics but
with a significantly smaller role than during the Sandinista period. A decade
after the Sandinistas lost power the labor movement is considerably weakened but remains a force in Nicaraguan society capable of direct action for
either political or economic goals.

BUSINESS

The last twenty-five years have seen considerable swings in the strength of
this traditional interest group. After holding considerable influence during
the long years of Somoza family rule, the business community was largely
marginalized during the Sandinista years. However, the power of the Sandinistas did force the business community to form an organization to articulate its interests, the Superior Council of Private Enterprise (COSEP). During the early years of its existence following the Sandinista revolution COSEP
was one of many organizations given representation in the Council of State,
which served as Nicaragua's legislature from 1979 to 1984. However, COSEP
was marginalized in that assembly and was unable to prevent the Sandinistas from dramatically reorienting the country's economy to the interests of
the majority poor. However, the Sandinistas did maintain a mixed economy
and those business owners who stayed in Nicaragua were generally able to
operate their businesses at a profit, but clearly their political power was
sharply curtailed. After the 1984 elections eliminated the Council of State
the business community saw its interests represented by the opposition Conservative and Independent Liberal parties, each of whom had several seats
in the Sandinista-dominated National Assembly.

The influence of COSEP and the business community improved with the
election of Chamorro, but not as quickly as might have been expected. First
of all, COSEP failed in its bid to have its leader Enrique Bolaños as the UNO

candidate. Almost immediately after Chamorro's election their influence was reduced when they sided with Vice President Godoy in his attempt to immediately marginalize the revolutionary forces. Chamorro rejected Godoy's approach and engaged in an ongoing series of negotiations with the FSLN that largely left COSEP on the sidelines. Although marginalized from the negotiations, the end result of Chamorro's success in returning the Nicaraguan economy to a free-market model placed the business community in a strong position to retain its former status. The election of Arnoldo Alemán in 1996 with Enrique Bolaños as his vice president completed the business community's return to its former status. The disposition of the property question in 1997 demonstrated that strength. The Alemán-dominated National Assembly passed a new property law that strengthened the position of former owners to an even greater degree than the 1995 law had. However, it should be noted that the FSLN remained a key player in the negotiations over the final legislation. Business is clearly once again a major player in Nicaragua, but the clock has not been rolled back to 1978.

RURAL GROUPS

Agrarian reform would be at the top of the list of Sandinista achievements because it is often cited as the single most important development of the 1980s in Nicaragua. Nicaragua was primarily an agrarian country. By 1990 the agrarian reform had affected more than half of the country's arable land, benefiting some 60 percent of all rural families. Also, by 1990 the majority of farms were in the hands of small- and medium-sized producers, in contrast to the historic maldistribution of land going back to colonial times. Initially the Sandinista land reform had concentrated on creating a significant state sector for agro-export, but, beginning in 1985, much greater emphasis was placed on land distribution to individual *campesinos*, and by 1989 the small private producers and the cooperatives were responsible for 47 percent of all agricultural production. The *campesino* sector benefited from the government's policy of easy credit terms and technical assistance along with state-run processing and storage facilities. This step forward was partially offset by commercial policies that kept producer prices low. In one of its final acts in 1990, the outgoing Sandinista-led National Assembly passed laws designed to protect the agrarian reform from its possible dismantling by the future governments. While the laws could not make up for ten years of failure to grant the necessary titles, they provided a legal basis to struggle for the maintenance of this gain.

However, the agrarian reform program was attacked by both Chamorro and Alemán, and this achievement remains in jeopardy. Formally, Chamorro was committed to respecting the land tenure arrangements of the Sandinista government. In practice the counterreform began almost immediately. Decrees 10–90 and 11–90 of May 1990 created a commission charged with reviewing the land confiscations of the previous government. Former landlords were given six months to petition for the return of their lands, although lands confiscated from Somoza were to be excluded.

The large-scale return of former owners, mainly self-exiles who had developed business interests in Miami, led to many confrontations and mobilizations. These mobilizations led to the July 1990 general strike, which demanded the repeal of Decrees 10–90 and 11–90. The National Workers' Federation (FNT) received assurances that no further land would be returned, but in reality the government continued its privatization and land-return policies behind the scenes. The ability of the rural union movement to carry out a resolute struggle against the return of lands was undermined by cross-cutting interests. In some instances farm workers welcomed former landlords, hoping that their return would bring new capital into their farms. In other instances, the government's firmness in moving forward with privatization persuaded some farmers to accept what they thought was the best deal they could get.

At the end of the Sandinista period, nearly 12 percent of the country's farmland was state-owned under the rubric of the Area of People's Property (APP). This area was declining slowly after 1985 as Sandinista agrarian policy shifted toward the distribution of individual plots, but it remained largely intact and became a key target of the Chamorro counterreform. Many of the 70,000 workers on state farms were affiliated with the Sandinista-led Rural Workers' Association (ATC) and were seen as a significant Sandinista power base to be attacked.

Initially, the ATC sought to prevent the privatization process entirely, but it retreated from this position as the result of the division within its ranks. Eventually, the union accepted the government's policy with several stipulations. No property was to be returned to people who had close links with Somoza, and smallholders and cooperatives who had benefited from agrarian reform would be protected. In the latter case, former owners were compensated with shares in public utility companies (water, electricity, and telecommunications). After considerable negotiation, the union agreed to a formula for the privatization of APP lands—workers (32 percent), demobilized army personnel (17 percent), ex-Contras (21 percent), and former owners (30 percent). However, the workers on many farms that were to be returned to their former owners refused to accept the agreement. They argued that they were the legitimate owners and feared the loss of their jobs, homes, and personal plots. This led to serious conflicts in which former owners tried to take possession of the disputed properties with the aid of the police and army. The speed with which this privatization was carried out is demonstrated by the fact that by the end of 1993 the ATC reported that the agricultural APP had been 100 percent privatized. In the face of these policies and pressures, it is not clear how long Nicaragua's relatively democratic distribution of land can be maintained.

ARMED FORCES

Sometimes overlooked in recitations of revolutionary achievements, especially by outside observers, was the elimination of the repressive apparatus of the Somoza regime and its replacement by an army and police force under civilian political control. The brutality of Somoza's National Guard is well chronicled and one of the Sandinista government's first acts was the establishment of the Sandinista Army and the Sandinista Police without any involvement of persons connected to the National Guard. In many bureaucratic areas the Sandinistas were forced to depend on some Somoza holdovers, but not in the police and army. As a result, when the Sandinistas handed over state power in 1990, they left behind army and police institutions imbued with a revolutionary consciousness and insulated from penetration by North American institutions. The Sandinista army and police were not immune from human rights abuses. Rather, they were under strict political supervision, and their human rights record compared quite favorably with that of their Central American neighbors. Disappearances and killings by government forces were commonplace in the 1980s in El Salvador, Guatemala, and Honduras. This simply did not happen on any comparable scale in Nicaragua.

The elimination of Somoza's National Guard and the repressive police force of his rule was clearly an important achievement of the Sandinista revolution. Maintenance of Sandinista influence in the army and the police was at the center of the transition negotiations after the February 1990 elections. Sandinista leaders were fearful that the Chamorro administration would bring former Contras directly into the government apparatus and exact revenge on their people for the military defeat that the Contras suffered at the hands of the Sandinista army. Aware of the importance of the issue to the FSLN and mindful of their considerable power even in defeat, Chamorro allowed Sandinista Humberto Ortega to remain as the head of the army. The president herself assumed the position of minister of defense. Chamorro argued that retaining Ortega as head of the army would maintain social peace and allow for an orderly reduction in the size of the military. The reductions were dramatic. At the time of the 1990 elections there were about 96,000 soldiers and by mid-1994 the number stood at 17,000. The retirement of Humberto Ortega in early 1995 and his replacement by a less controversial Sandinista officer, General Joaquín Cuadra, was hailed by many as a further depoliticizing of the armed forces. Cuadra is from a Nicaraguan oligarchic family and is a cousin of Antonio Lacayo, influential adviser to President Chamorro. By the end of 1995, the Sandinista label had been removed from the organization.

The maintenance of the army as a progressive force was only partially successful. On the positive side, the army was not absorbed into the framework of U.S. domination that was true for virtually every other Latin American army except that of Cuba. The army did not engage in the systematic human rights abuses so common in Nicaragua's northern neighbors in Central America. Nicaraguan citizens did not have to fear arbitrary death or detention as they did during the Somoza era. The army also remained strictly neutral during the protracted political stalemate between the executive and legislative branches in 1994 and 1995. The professionalism of the army helped defuse the potentially volatile confrontation. In numerous incidents, the army was deployed in labor disputes, especially in the countryside, where it has acted in support of former landowners attempting to recover their land from occupying workers. There was also a developing bitterness within the Sandinista ranks toward senior army officers who have apparently acquired considerable amounts of land.

The deterioration of the police as a progressive force occurred with even greater speed. The Ministry of Interior was renamed the Ministry of Government, and the Sandinista Police became the National Police. Chamorro appointee Carlos Hurtado became the new high official, replacing Tomás Borge. New uniforms were issued, and police units in riot gear were commonly deployed in the capital, a departure from the Sandinista era. In 1992 Managua mayor Arnoldo Alemán created a new municipal police force (highly visible in the capital with their red berets). After initial hesitation, the police were used as strikebreakers. In the most dramatic confrontation to date, three people were killed when a force of over 600 anti-riot policemen opened fire on protesters in the Managua neighborhood of Villa Progresa during a transportation strike in May 1995. During the 1980s the Sandinista police gained a reputation for honesty and discipline. Much of that reputation is now gone. Bribery and corruption have developed on a widespread basis in the context of the desperate economic situation and low police salaries.

INDIGENOUS PEOPLE

After initial serious mistakes, the Sandinista government enacted an autonomy statute for Nicaragua's Atlantic Coast that is a significant achievement for the rights of the indigenous peoples of the Americas. Nicaragua's eastern coast, rich in minerals and other natural resources, had long been exploited with no care for the environment or the non-Hispanic population that lived there. The region encompasses 56 percent of Nicaragua's territory but with a population of some 350,000 it has less than 10 percent of the population. Roughly two-thirds of the region's people are *mestizo* immigrants who have come to the region from the west in search of land. However, the rest of the population is indigenous, with the largest group (75,000) being Miskitos who live in small communities throughout the Atlantic Coast region. There are also small communities of Creoles, the name used by descendants of Africans. Initially the Pacific Coast–based Sandinistas continued the same pattern of dominant relations with the coast. After serious confrontation with CIA-sponsored Indian rebel groups in the early 1980s, however, the government entered into dialogue with the Atlantic Coast residents. This dialogue resulted in a 1987 Autonomy Statute that guaranteed the rights of the indigenous groups to their own language, culture, and communal forms of land ownership. In addition, the statute recognized the rights of the different groups in regard to the development of natural resources. Also established were regional government assemblies with direct representation from each ethnic group. The statute intended for the transference of considerable authority to these governments, especially in the areas of taxation and resource development.

Both governments in the 1990s challenged the autonomy process. Basically, Managua used flanking tactics to undermine the rights of the residents of Nicaragua's Atlantic Coast. Rather than seeking any formal reversal of the Autonomy Statute, the central government simply ignored the law and created its own approach to the region. In April 1990, Chamorro created the Institute for the Development of the Atlantic Coast (INDERA). For four years the meager resources allotted for the coast were channeled through INDERA rather than the regional Autonomous Councils. The Managua government used INDERA to divide the different coast groups by pitting them against each other. With shifting political alliances, both Atlantic Coast regional governments passed motions rejecting INDERA in 1994, and the central government eliminated the agency and proceeded to carry out all programs for the coast through national-level ministries.

The greatest challenges to the coast today are growing environmental destruction and the lack of control over its natural resources—fishing, forestry, and mining. According to the spirit of the autonomy law, control over the coast's resources was to be vested with the regional government bodies. The central government ignored this aspect of the law or used local leaders sympathetic to the central government to conclude deals on the exploitation of resources that are detrimental to the region's interests.

POLITICAL PARTIES

A review of the contemporary political parties in Nicaragua needs to be grounded in the country's history. From the time of independence to 1979 Nicaraguan politics were largely dominated by two parties—Liberals and Conservatives. The Liberals had their base in the university town of León with a tenuous link to the ideas of democracy and progress. The Conservatives were based in Grenada and its traditional Catholic values. Their rivalry was fierce, often escalating to civil war. Few, if any, honest elections were conducted prior to 1979. The Somozas captured the Liberal Party. The Conservatives were his main opposition, tolerated only as long as they were no real threat to the family's entrenched power.

As David Close has written, the creation of a competitive political party system came in 1982 when the FSLN-dominated Council of State passed a political parties law. The passage of this law was significant because it moved FSLN away from Leninist principles and opened the legal possibility of a Sandinista electoral defeat. Under the law the number of parties in Nicaragua grew rapidly with seven contesting the 1984 election. By 1990 more than thirty parties had been registered, although the election turned into a two-way contest when the parties opposed to the Sandinistas came together under the banner of UNO. UNO succeeded in defeating the Sandinistas in 1991 but suffered deep divisions during its years in power. FSLN also survived the Chamorro period but had its own problems and divisions. The difficulties of the two main contenders in the 1990 elections allowed the revival of the Liberal current within Nicaraguan politics and the subsequent election of its leader, Arnoldo Alemán, to the presidency in 1996. Nicaragua approached its next election cycle in 2001. The state of the major parties follows.

FSLN. The FSLN remains the largest and best-organized political party in Nicaragua, but the election defeat and its aftermath have taken a heavy toll on the organization, making its long-term prospects unclear. Sandinista success in the war against Somoza and in the years of state power was nurtured by a broad unity built around certain basic principles. This unity emerged from years of factional warfare in the 1970s and held up fairly well until the election defeat. However, since 1990 the divisions have reemerged, although not along the same lines as in the 1970s. After a bitterly divisive party congress in May 1994, the FSLN broke into two separate political organizations in January 1995 with the departure from the party of several key figures, including former Vice President Sergio Ramírez. Many prominent intellectuals, including Ernesto and Fernando Cardenal, also left the party. Many of those who left formed the Sandinista Renovation Movement (MRS), which was formally launched as a political party at a congress in May 1995. The gulf between those who stayed in the FSLN and the newly formed MRS was quite wide.

During 1992 and 1993, divisions developed within the party over the political course that the party's National Directorate was pursuing as an opposition party. Arguing that the main threat to the gains of the revolution was the activity of the far-right Godoy/Alemán forces, FSLN leadership pursued a tactical alliance with Chamorro and Lacayo against the far Right. The policy was implemented through an ongoing national dialogue and through an alliance in the National Assembly that removed Alfredo César as parliamentary leader in January 1993. This alliance resulted in considerable political cost to the Sandinistas. The alliance gave the FSLN no real control over Chamorro government policies (it was not co-governance), but it meant that the FSLN was seen as bearing some of the responsibility for the dire economic circumstances of the country. In practice, FSLN support for social and economic stability meant that the economic interests of the popular sectors took a back seat in the political priorities of the FSLN. Important elements in the resurgent popular movements, especially the trade unions, showed marked displeasure with the FSLN leadership. This opposition came out into the open in July 1993 with the publication of an open letter signed by twenty-nine prominent Sandinistas that called for the party leadership to distance itself definitively from the Chamorro government and resume close affiliation with the social base of the FSLN, the workers and peasants.

Following the publication of the letter of the Group of 29, Daniel Ortega made an important tactical shift. Fearing a challenge from the Left, Ortega began to reposition himself within the party debates. Ortega began to identify more closely with popular sectors and to distance himself somewhat, at least in rhetoric, from Chamorro and Lacayo. Ortega's shift to the Left made FSLN leaders with more clearly social democratic tendencies (i.e., Ramírez, Carrión, and Téllez) vulnerable. Two events in autumn 1993 heightened the division. At a meeting of the National Directorate, Ramírez declared an interest in running for the presidency in light of his positive standing in the polls in comparison to Ortega. In hindsight, Ortega may have seen this declaration by Ramírez as the signaling of a power struggle for control of the party. In addition, sharp divisions of opinion within the National Directorate raged publicly over a national strike that had turned violent. Ramírez and others criticized the tactics of the strikers, while Ortega clearly sided with those in the streets. These differences were formalized with the emergence of two tendencies prior to the special May 1994 party congress. Ramírez formed the group "For the Return to a Sandinista Majority," and Ortega led the "Democratic Left" tendency. The Ramírez group made it clear that it felt that the FSLN needed to move toward the political center if it was to regain political power in the 1996 elections, a task that was considered to be of the highest priority. In reality, the Ortega group had reestablished its revolutionary credentials without really questioning or changing its conservative alliance strategy.

The May 1994 congress represented a solid victory for the Democratic Left tendency, which dominated the elections to the new Sandinista Assembly and National Directorate. The congress, however, also laid the groundwork for the split that occurred several months later. The spirit of the congress was deeply divisive and marked by harsh personal attacks. In a seemingly vindictive act, Ramírez was excluded from an expanded National Directorate despite his prominent position in the party and his leadership of an obviously important minority grouping. Many rank-and-file Sandinistas were shocked by the harshness of the divisions at the congress and hoped that the differences would not lead to a split, but such a break-up may have been inevitable. Since the Sandinista movement incorporated the relatively conservative Group of Twelve in 1978, it had been a broadly heterogeneous political party. That heterogeneity had been suppressed during the years of state power, but the disorientation caused by the electoral defeat and the challenges of being a revolutionary party in the post–Cold War era were too great to overcome without a split.

The party's alliance strategy was not the only locus of discontent with FSLN. The party was still suffering from the widespread belief, both inside and outside the party, that individual members of the party unfairly benefited from the distribution of goods that occurred during the transition to the Chamorro government. Known as the Piñata, this process apparently resulted in the transfer of considerable property and goods to the leadership ranks of the FSLN throughout the country. Many of the transactions may well have been justified by years of low-paid services, but it was ultimately viewed as unjust by many rank-and-file Sandinistas who did not materially benefit during the transition and by the wider population. The long-term impact of the Piñata is difficult to assess, but it appeared to significantly undercut the moral authority of the Sandinista movement and helped magnify class divisions within the FSLN. Such divisions made it almost impossible for the party to mount a sustained alternative to the neoliberal economic policies of the government. The split, combined with the FSLN's loss of moral authority and failure to articulate a credible alternative to the neoliberal economic policies of the government, made the FSLN's defeat at the hands of

Alemán in the 1996 elections a nearly foregone conclusion. The victory of FSLN candidate Herty Lewites in the 2000 mayoral election in Managua lifted the party's prospects, but its long-term effect is not clear. Today, most Nicaraguans see the FSLN as part of the political elite that has failed to solve their problems. Divided as it now is, it will be hard for the FSLN to change that image and return to the national leadership of Nicaragua.

Liberal Parties. With the disintegration of the anti-Sandinista UNO coalition in the mid-1990s a liberal party—the Liberal Constitutional Party (PLC)—emerged as the key anti-Sandinista force. The PLC broke with the official Liberal party of the Somozas, the PLN, in the late 1960s over Anastasio Somoza's decision to assume the presidency in the 1967 elections. It participated as part of the FSLN's opposition in the Council of State but before the mid-1990s was not a significant force. However, solid party building activities after 1990, previously unused by any party other than the Sandinistas, quickly catapulted the party into a strong position. Its first national presence came with its 1994 victories in the Atlantic Coast regional elections.

Although Arnoldo Alemán became the party central leader and won the presidency in 1996 under the PLC banner, he was not a longtime member. The PLC recruited Alemán, the mayor of Managua under the UNO government, calculating that his reputation as a strong leader who got things done would make him an excellent candidate. Today the PLC has a strong party organization and may remain at the head of Nicaraguan government in the foreseeable future.

The other strong partner of the Liberal Alliance that contested the 1996 election was the Independent Liberal Party. Founded in 1944 to oppose the continuation of the Somozas in power, this party had strong anti-Somoza credentials and participated in the revolutionary struggle and the first revolutionary government. Its senior leader, Virgilio Godoy, was elected vice president under Violeta Barrios de Chamorro in 1990, although sharp divisions with the UNO coalition sharply reduced the power of the vice president.

Conclusion

Where did Nicaragua stand a decade after the electoral defeat of the FSLN? It can be said that the future course of Nicaragua was yet to be definitively determined but that conservative forces had clearly gained the upper hand in the context of a world situation favorable to their neoliberal program and the continuing failure of the FSLN leadership to provide a coherent alternative. As the new millennium began, Nicaragua continued to slide back to many of its traditional ways:

- The great majority of Nicaraguans were living in grinding poverty with little immediate hope of redemption. The average per capita income for the country was some $450 per annum, making Nicaragua the poorest country in the hemisphere after Haiti.

- Reminiscent of its traditional dependency, Nicaragua was ever more closely tied to the advanced industrial countries of the West as a producer of primary products and recipient of their aid. It had followed State Department IMF and Work Bank advice to implement neoliberal reforms only to gain one of the highest per capita debts in the world (the external debt was some $6 billion).
- With the presidential term of Arnaldo Alemán, the country returned to traditional personalistic politics marked by increasing authoritarian tendencies, frequent accusations of blatant favoritism and corruption, and ever more partisan party politics conducted by the political elite.
- Power and personalism were overshadowing government and party institutions. Pacts and political arrangements often defined the rules of political competition and law making more than the courts or constitution.
- Strikes and demonstration against unpopular policies still characterized political life, and the populace displayed high levels of political alienation and disillusionment with political institutions.
- Mass organization and popular mobilizations seemed to be two of the few remaining ways for the masses to meaningfully participate in the political process.
- Liberation theology and the Popular (Catholic) Church continued to come under attack from the conservative Catholic Church hierarchy and had lost a great deal of their previous influence.

However, the final chapter of the Nicaraguan revolution has yet to be written. Some crucial gains of the revolution, especially in land tenure and democracy, remain alive. Nicaragua's population, while beaten down, has shown considerable willingness to struggle. The biggest question mark may be the FSLN itself. The split in the party made its return to power difficult in the short term. It is not clear whether the party can recover to again become an inspiration for the majority of Nicaraguans seeking fundamental social change. At the base of the party there remain many dedicated people through whom the organization may be able to recover its lost credibility, but it is not clear that a national leadership exists to formulate a strategy for the return to power. The FSLN was seen as part of the political problem by most Nicaraguans and therefore not looked to as a solution. Those who left to form the MRS believed that they could rebuild the people's trust, but their limited base among the country's intellectuals made this unlikely. The grassroots movements alone, however well-organized, were not capable of defending the gains of the Sandinista revolution. Organizations like unions, cooperatives, and women's movements were all capable of militant struggle within their own sectors, but they face an enemy that has control of the state apparatus and the backing of powerful foreign governments and international organizations. As a result of this relationship of forces, the grassroots organizations could be isolated and in some instances played off against each other. Because of Nicaragua's unsolved social and economic problems, radical change could return to the agenda in Nicaragua and build on the gains of the Sandinista period. However, it would require a new political force. It could be a revitalized FSLN, or it could be a new political movement that would come from the militancy of the current grassroots organizing.

Chronology

1522 Spanish reach Nicaragua

1821 Nicaragua becomes independent

1823–1838 Nicaragua part of Central American Federation

1855 William Walker takes over Nicaragua

1908 Marines occupy Bluefields

1912–1924 Marines occupy Nicaragua

1926–1933 Marines again occupy Nicaragua; Sandino leads guerrilla war

1934 Sandino assassinated

1936–1957 Anastasio Somoza dictatorship

1957 Anastasio Somoza assassinated, son Luis becomes president

1961 FSLN founded in meeting in Tegucigalpa, Honduras

1967 Anastasio Somoza Jr. becomes president

1960s FSLN guerrilla fronts repeatedly destroyed forcing shift to coordinated political and military action

1974 Reemergence of FSLN guerrilla activity with seizure of Somoza associates at a holiday party

1975–1977 Carlos Fonseca Amador killed; the FSLN splits into three factions; Insurrectionalists (Tercerista faction) shift strategy from rural guerrilla warfare to urban insurrection and broad alliances

1978 FSLN commandos seize National Palace; September insurrection in major cities defeated by National Guard

1979 Reunification of the FSLN; final offensive defeats Somocista forces and Junta of National Reconstruction takes power on July 19

1980 National Literacy Crusade; Violeta Chamorro and Alfonso Robelo leave JGRN; Council of State, dominated by Sandinista mass organizations, assumes legislative power

1981 U.S. government begins covert financing of the ex-National Guardsmen

1982 Nicaraguan government imposes state of emergency after Contra attacks

1983 Visit of Pope John Paul II highlights conflict between official church and revolution; Nicaragua joins Contadora peace process

1984 Elections held; Daniel Ortega elected president and Sandinistas win 63 percent of the seats in the National Assembly elections

1985 Daniel Ortega and Sergio Ramírez are inaugurated as president and vice-president of Nicaragua; United States declares economic embargo against Nicaragua and unilaterally ends the Manzanillo talks

1986 World Court rules that United States is in violation of international law for its support of the Contras; National Assembly elaborates new constitution

1987 Constitution approved; National Assembly passes autonomy statute for the regions of the Atlantic Coast

1988 Nicaraguan government institutes harsh austerity measures in the face of declining productivity and 36,000 percent inflation; Sapoa agreement is signed between the Contras and the Nicaraguan government; Hurricane Joan devastates the country, particularly the Atlantic Coast region

1989 Central American presidents meeting in El Salvador agree to joint plan for demobilization of the Contras; Nicaraguan government moves up the election date to February 1990; economic conditions continue to worsen

1990 Elections are held in Nicaragua, and the final results give 55 percent to UNO and 41 percent to the FSLN; Violeta Chamorro assumes the presidency; the Nicaraguan Workers' Front (FNT) is formed with 200,000 members

1991 The FSLN holds its first party congress

1996 Arnoldo Alemán elected president

Bibliography

Black, George. *The Triumph of the People*. London: Zed Books, 1981.

Close, David. *Nicaragua: The Chamorro Years*. Boulder, CO: Lynne Reinner Publishers, 1999.

Gilbert, Dennis. *Sandinistas*. Oxford, England: Blackwell, 1988.

Millett, Richard. *Guardians of the Dynasty*. Mary Knoll, NY: Orbis Books, 1977.

Norsworthy, Kent. *Nicaragua—A Country Guide*. Albuquerque, NM: Inter-Hemispheric Education Resource Center, 1990.

Prevost, Gary, and Harry E. Vanden, eds. *The Undermining of the Sandinista Revolution*. London: MacMillan, and New York: St. Martin's Press, 1999.

Robinson, William. *A Faustian Bargain*. Boulder, CO: Westview Press, 1993.

Schoultz, Lars. *Beneath the United States, A History of U.S. Policy Toward Latin America*. Cambridge, MA: Harvard University Press, 1998.

Spalding, Rose. *Capitalists and the Revolution in Nicaragua*. Chapel Hill: University of North Carolina Press, 1995.

Vanden, Harry E., and Gary Prevost. *Democracy and Socialism in the Sandinista Nicaragua*. Boulder, CO: Lynne Reinner Publishers, 1993.

Vilas, Carlos. *State, Class, and Ethnicity in Nicaragua*. Boulder, CO: Lynne Reinner Publishers, 1989.

Walker, Thomas, ed. *Nicaragua without Illusions*. Wilmington, DE: Scholarly Resources, 1997.

———. *Nicaragua: The Land of Sandino*. Boulder, CO: Westview Press, 1991.

FILMS AND VIDEOS

Deadly Embrace: Nicaragua, the World Bank and the International Monetary Fund. U.S., 1999. [Available through Ashley Eames, Wentworth, NH, 03282.]

Fire From the Mountains. U.S., 1987.

Nicaragua: From the Ashes. U.S., 1982.

Thank God and the Revolution. U.S., 1981.

BOLIVIA

PARAGUAY

BRAZIL

Pacific
Ocean

Rio de la Plata

●Córdoba

Rosario

URUGUAY

★
Buenos Aires

CHILE

Map of
ARGENTINA

N

W   E

S

100   0   100   200   300   Miles

Scale 1:45,000,000

Falkland Islands
(Islas Malvinas)

FOURTEEN

ARGENTINA

Aldo C. Vacs

Argentina at a Glance

Argentina is located in the Southern Cone of South America. The country is shaped like an inverted triangle, with the northern base bordering on Bolivia, Paraguay, and Brazil; the eastern side on Brazil and Uruguay; the western side on Chile, and the apex pointing toward Antarctica. Its territory comprises about 2.8 million square kilometers, making it the eighth largest country in the world and the second largest in Latin America (after Brazil). The Andes mountains run from the Bolivian border to Tierra del Fuego and separate Argentina from Chile. Argentina exhibits a great diversity of physical features, productive capacity, and demographic patterns. The northern region has subtropical weather, the central has a temperate climate, and the southern areas display cold temperatures. The northwest is quite arid and poor but has small subtropical areas and a string of fertile valleys where most of the population—including a substantial *mestizo* component—resides. Cuyo, in the Western central region, is also arid but contains a number of oasis settlements that facilitate fruit and wine production and in which most of the population—largely from Spanish and Italian descent—is concentrated. The Gran Chaco, which includes savannas and subtropical forests, is located in the north central and eastern region where most of the small remnants of the indigenous population live together with groups of European descent devoted to the production of cotton, tobacco, tea, and *yerba mate*. Patagonia, in the south, contains arid plateaus where sheep are raised and fertile valleys where fruit is produced but remains scarcely populated. The Pampas, in the central eastern portion of Argentina, are among the most fertile grasslands in the world, and their temperate climate and adequate rainfall facilitate the large-scale production of grains and the raising of live-stock. Most of the country's population live in large urban concentrations located in the Pampas region, including the capital city, Buenos Aires, as well as Rosario, La Plata, Mar del Plata, Bahía Blanca, and their respective suburban areas and satellite cities.

Argentina has a population of about 35 million people, most of them from European ancestry. In the late nineteenth and early twentieth centuries massive waves of immigrants from Italy, Spain, Central Europe, Russia, and the Middle East substantially altered the size and composition of the Argentine population. Between 1870 and 1914 the population grew from about 2 million to 8 million people, of whom close to one-third were foreign born. After 1930, European immigration declined, but the country attracted large numbers of immigrants from neighboring countries. Most of these immigrants, together with large contingents of the existing rural population, settled largely in the cities, making Argentina one of the most urbanized countries in Latin America. By 1914 more than 50 percent of the population was living in urban concentrations; by the early 1990s it was estimated that close to 90 percent of the total population lived in urban areas.

From an economic perspective, Argentina has been a relatively rich country, particularly in the Latin American context. Between the 1870s and 1930 the country experienced a rapid economic growth, which led to the emergence of a large middle and urban working class and an expansion of political participation. The Great Depression brought about the end of economic prosperity, political stability, and social progress and inaugurated a period of growing confrontation during which Argentina's situation steadily declined. Between the 1940s and the early 1980s the fluctuations between populist and fragile liberal democratic regimes and increasingly repressive military dictatorships contributed to economic stagnation, growing concentration of income and wealth in the hands of the elites, and worsening poverty and marginality among the working and middle-class sectors. In the early 1980s, the establishment and seeming consolidation of liberal democracy ended the darkest period of Argentina's political history, restoring the respect for human rights and providing for popular participation and political stability. However, the implementation of stringent free market policies has reinforced inequitable patterns of income distribution, fostered unemployment, led to a continuous increase in poverty, and fostered the multiplication of social problems.

Political Evolution

FROM COLONY TO OLIGARCHIC REPUBLIC

Most of the territory currently occupied by Argentina was settled throughout the sixteenth and seventeenth centuries by two groups of Spanish colonizers: One arrived by land from Peru, occupying the northwestern area of current Argentina and spreading toward the south and the southeast; another came by sea from Spain and colonized the areas comprising the Río de la Plata basin. The inhabitants of the northwestern region remained linked to the viceroyalty of Peru, supplying food, beasts of burden, and textiles demanded by the Peruvian and Upper Peruvian (Bolivian) silver-mining economy. The colonists who settled in the margins of the Río de la Plata and in the areas along the Paraná and Uruguay rivers produced hides for export to Spain and engaged in legal as well as illegal commercial activities, including the smuggling of goods to and from Great Britain.

From the Spanish crown's perspective, the economic importance of both regions was limited: There were neither precious metals nor other valuable raw materials, there was only a scarce number of sedentary Indians whose labor could be exploited in agricultural activities, and the lack of conditions for a plantation economy prevented the introduction of large numbers of slaves. However, the strategic and commercial importance of the Río de la Plata area and specifically of Buenos Aires, its main city, increased in the late colonial period as it became a barrier against Portuguese territorial expansion and an entry point for commercial transactions with the hinterland. The continuous territorial disputes with Portugal transformed Buenos Aires into a crucial defensive outpost and led to the creation of local military forces. The commercial role of the city and the Pampa region was bolstered during the eighteenth century by the increasing demand for hides in Europe and, in the late eighteenth and early nineteenth century, by the export of salted meat, particularly to the slave plantations of Brazil and the Caribbean.

The creation in 1776 of the viceroyalty of the Río de la Plata (comprising current Argentina, Uruguay, and portions of Bolivia, Paraguay, and Chile) with Buenos Aires as the government seat reinforced this trend and permanently shifted the balance of power in favor of the *porteño* (port city) elites. At the same time, this shift in the balance of power sharpened the conflict between the oligarchies of the interior, who zealously defended their political autonomy and tried to protect the regional economies from foreign competition, and the Buenos Aires elites, who tried to attain political supremacy and championed free trade.

Argentina's independence from Spain, secured between 1810 and 1816, was the culmination of a process involving growing tensions between the creole landed and commercial oligarchies, who had gradually concentrated most economic resources in their hands, and the Spanish rulers and administrators of a declining empire, who excluded these elites from political participation and wanted to preserve an outmoded mercantilist system. The first two decades after independence were marked by a succession of civil wars between the Unitarians—supporters of the prerogative of Buenos Aires to establish a centralized national government and promote free trade—and the Federalists—regional groups who steadfastly defended provincial autonomy and espoused economic protectionism. The confrontation between these two groups resulted in a period of tremendous political instability accompanied by rapid economic decline.

This violent stalemate was temporarily broken after the inauguration in 1829 of Juan Manuel de Rosas as governor of Buenos Aires, a position he occupied with only a brief interruption until 1852. Rosas, a rich landowner from Buenos Aires province who defined himself as a Federalist, was able to establish his ascendancy on the federal *caudillos* (political-military strongmen) of the interior and to quell successive unitarian challenges. Rosas' peculiar brand of federalism embodied the interests of the traditional cattle ranchers and exporters of hides and salted meat from Buenos Aires, who wanted a peaceful climate in which they could export their products, import manufactures, profit from the customs revenues generated by the port of Buenos Aires, and control the conduct of foreign relations. In exchange for this they were inclined to leave provincial authority in the hands of local *caudillos*, maintaining harmonious relations with the provincial elites that shared their aversion to any change in the economic status quo, traditional class structure, and forms of political domination.

However, after two decades of dictatorial rule, the inability of the Rosas regime to promote the kind of political and economic changes that many among the elites believed were necessary to overcome the country's isolation and relative stagnation led to an alliance between interior and coastal groups interested in fostering a process of capitalist agrarian development. The fall of Rosas in 1852 was followed by a short period of internal conflict as the Buenos Aires and provincial elites clashed over the definition of the political and economic design of the emerging state. Finally, through a suitable combination of military force, political concessions, and economic might, the agrarian and commercial exporting elites of Buenos Aires were able to assert their hegemony and establish new conditions for political stability and economic growth, completing the occupation of the national territory, implementing free market and free trade policies, and creating a stable oligarchic political regime. This group consolidated its supremacy and prevented internal discord by forging an alliance between the Pampean and regional elites and appealing to the use of force and fraud when necessary to win elections.

Political stability facilitated Argentina's economic modernization and reinsertion into the world political economy as a producer and exporter of grains and beef. Between 1862 and 1916 successive administrations confronted the problems of the scarcity of labor, capital, skills, infrastructure, and technology by promoting massive immigration, attracting foreign investment, fostering education, implementing an ambitious program of public works, and encouraging the introduction of new techniques for cattle-raising and grain cultivation, food processing, storage, and transportation. Thus, by World War I, Argentina had become a major world exporter of beef, grains, and wool. The population had increased fivefold and was becoming mainly urban. There was a growing number of middle- and working-class people concentrated in the largest cities, especially in Buenos Aires, and the per capita income was higher than in several European countries.

However, the emergence of a politically disenfranchised middle-class and urban working-class sectors and the existence of some provincial elites who felt excluded from the economic bonanza resulted in growing opposition to the oligarchic regime. Middle-class and marginal elite groups converged in the creation in 1892 of the Unión Cívica Radical (UCR, Radical Civic Union), the first and oldest mass party in Argentina, which fought for the expansion of political participation. In turn, the increase in the number of immigrants and urban workers led both to the rise of the anarchist movement and to the creation in 1894 of the Socialist party, which sought significant political and socioeconomic changes.

THE ASCENT AND FALL OF MASS DEMOCRACY

Between 1892 and 1912, the Radicals, under the leadership of Hipólito Yrigoyen, engaged in armed revolts and practiced electoral abstention to force the Conservative elite to make political concessions. The emergence of militant labor and Leftist political organizations, the growing pressure coming from the middle-class opposition, and the realization on the part of the oligarchy that the Radicals, despite their name, did not intend to alter the existing economic and social structures prompted the decision to liberalize the political system. In 1912, the reformist wing of the ruling Conservative party passed a law instituting obligatory universal male suffrage and enacted guarantees to make voting secret and unconstrained. Afterward, the Radical party began to participate successfully in a series of contests that culminated in 1916 with the election of Yrigoyen as president.

The period of 1916–1930 was one of democratic political stability characterized by the predominance of the Radical party at the national and provincial levels. The Radical administrations focused their initiatives on the political arena, promoting the enlargement of the electorate and the displacement of conservative groups from power positions, but they introduced only minor changes in the socioeconomic domain. Federal interventions reduced the influence of the Conservative political groups that, unlike other Latin American traditional elites, could not rely on the electoral manipulation of a pliable peasantry, whose presence was practically negligible in the Argentine agrarian capitalist system. However, the oligarchic groups did not attempt to eliminate the democratic regime as long as the Radicals were able to use their political dominance to protect the existing socioeconomic structures. The Radical administrations' policies were limited to favor the urban and rural middle sectors through state patronage and social and educational policies and to satisfy some of the demands of the urban workers by favoring the creation of a social security system, controlling the prices of wage goods, and mediating in labor conflicts. This moderate income redistribution was tolerated by the agrarian elites as long as Argentina's export-oriented economy continued to grow.

This period of political stability and social peace ended when the crash of 1929 and the ensuing Great Depression led to an abrupt decline in export revenues. The collapse of the economy led to an acute fight for economic shares between different socioeconomic groups. At the same time, the crisis reduced the margin of maneuver of the Radical administration, which was unable to sustain its state patronage or to overcome the structural causes of the economic crisis. Moreover, in his old age, President Yrigoyen seemed to have lost the ability to deal effectively with the growing political and economic problems challenging his administration. In these circumstances, the landed and commercial elites were able to mobilize part of the discontented middle class and to incite some army officers to overthrow the elected government. The coup d'etat of September 1930—orchestrated by the traditional oligarchy, supported by middle-class groups, and implemented by the armed forces—signaled the end of the era of Argentina's political stability and the beginning of more than five decades of continuous disarray.

The leader of the 1930 coup, General José F. Uriburu, attempted between 1930 and 1932 to establish an authoritarian regime whose corporatist features resembled Italian fascism. However, the oligarchy and a substantial portion of the military and middle sectors opposed Uriburu's project and forced him to allow the emergence of a façade democracy. The banning of the Radical party and the use of electoral fraud and coercion facilitated the coming into power of Conservative administrations that attempted to restore the old oligarchic regime by limiting political participation and favoring export-oriented economic growth based on a close commercial association with Great Britain.

Throughout the so-called "infamous decade" (1930–1943) the ruling Conservative groups attempted to re-create the "paradise lost" of the oligarchic regime when their political domination was uncontested, and the export-import model of growth reigned supreme. However, it soon became clear that in the international and domestic circumstances engendered by the Great Depression, this goal was unattainable. The Conservative governments of the 1930s and early 1940s realized that even the substantial economic concessions made to Great Britain were not able to revive the prosperity based on the traditional export-import model. The rise of a new model of economic growth, import substituting industrialization, became inevitable as the decline in export revenues and the consequent scarcity of hard currency reduced the capacity to import and created opportunities and incentives for the rise of local manufacturing. This economic transformation would have significant social and political consequences that ultimately would lead to the end of Conservative rule.

The emergence of an industrial elite producing consumer goods for the domestic market, the decline in agricultural exports and the consequent rural stagnation, the escalating pace of rural-urban migration associated with the new employment opportunities in the emerging industrial sector, the influential political role played by the military after 1930, the growing discontent of the middle sectors with the Conservative electoral fraud and economic policies, the demands of labor organizations, and the rise of nationalism created a volatile situation that could not be adequately controlled by the conservative regime. The beginning of World War II reinforced some of these trends—such as the need to produce domestic manufactures, the growing importance of the military, and the rise of democratic and nationalistic demands by different groups—and created the opportunity for the military to oust the Conservative administration without significant opposition.

THE RISE AND DECLINE OF PERONISM

The 1943 coup was plotted by a secret military lodge—the United Officers Group—made up of nationalistic and authoritarian officers who sympathized with the fascist ideology and wanted to maintain Argentina's neutrality during World War II. Among those who participated in the coup, colonel Juan D. Perón rapidly emerged as the most skillful political figure. Palace coups engineered by the lodge controlled by Perón removed the two initial military presidents from office. Finally, a close Perón associate, General Edelmiro Farrell, became president (1944–1946) and, with his backing, Perón concentrated in his hands the vice presidency, the ministry of war, and the newly created secretariat of labor and social welfare. Afterward, using the power and resources of these offices, Perón organized a coalition that included his military supporters and an emerging state-controlled labor movement. Faced with Perón's growing power, his military and civilian adversaries tried to oust him, but this attempt failed when, after a few days of incarceration, Perón was rescued by a massive mobilization of workers who demanded his release on October 17, 1945. Eva Duarte, a young actress who had become Perón's companion in 1944, offered him continuous support during the crisis, and they married shortly afterward. Eva Perón—Evita, as she became popularly known—rapidly emerged as a prominent political figure on her own right, helping gather support for Perón among the poorer sectors of the population.

After being forced to release Perón, a divided military heeded the growing demands for democratization and called for elections to be held in early 1946. Both Perón and his adversaries tried to mobilize and organize their supporters into broad political coalitions. On the Peronist side, the state-supported labor organizations created the Partido Laborista (Labor Party), while some former Radical and Conservative politicians established the so-called Renovating Junta of Radicalism, which counted on the support of some nationalistic middle-class groups and provincial political organizations. Both parties endorsed Perón as their presidential candidate but maintained separate lists of candidates for other offices. The opposition front included Radicals, Socialists, Communists, and some Conservatives that conformed an electoral alliance called Unión Democrática (Democratic Union). Alliance members agreed to support the presidential candidate nominated by the Radicals but presented their own candidates for other offices. In the February 1946 elections, Perón won the presidency with 54 percent of the vote and his supporters carried most provinces, securing substantial majorities in congress.

A new political era, the era of populism, had started. The 1946 elections signaled the end of the Radical electoral predominance, the Conservative ability to manipulate the political process, and the capacity of minor parties, such as the Socialists, to gain congressional seats. Perón's victory rested on the support of the new urban working-class electorate fostered by the internal migrations and industrialization, the rural population and the inhabitants of the poorer provinces, and sectors of the lower middle class grate-

Evita, in a characteristic gesture, addressing her followers from the balcony of the Casa Rosada during Peronist rallies in Buenos Aires' central square, the Plaza de Mayo. *(Photo provided by the Department of Documentary Photographs, Argentine National Archive)*

ful for his economic and social initiatives. After his inauguration, Perón cemented a state-dominated populist alliance whose fundamental pillars were organized labor, the industrialists producing for the domestic market, and the nationalistic military groups favorable to rapid industrialization. This populist regime favored a strong state intervention in the economy to promote industrialization, income redistribution policies favorable to organized labor and civilian and military bureaucracies, and the nationalization of crucial sectors of the economy (public utilities, transportation, and foreign trade).

The Peronist government maintained the democratic forms (periodic elections, division of powers, and political party competition) but engaged in a number of semi-authoritarian practices, such as restricting the freedoms of expression, assembly, and strike; controlling the judiciary; manipulating the mass media and the educational system; imposing political constrains on public employees, union leaders, and education workers; and harassing and persecuting adversaries. In this context, the chances of the opposition parties to compete successfully for power were considerably reduced, and they began to favor a military coup as the only alternative to what they defined as an increasingly "totalitarian" regime.

The Peronist economic policies and political practices were relatively successful in the early postwar years as Argentina benefited from the use of war-accumulated reserves and the recovery of the international economy while workers, industrialists, and the military remained united behind a government that satisfied their demands. Meanwhile, Peronism expanded its basis of electoral support by extending the franchise to women in 1947 and establishing the women's branch of the party. Evita played a central role in encouraging these decisions and became the leader of the women's branch of the Peronist party. She also performed a crucial role in strengthening the regime by offering social welfare services through the Eva Perón Foundation, overseeing organized labor, and promoting the public veneration of Perón's leadership in her speeches and publications.

In 1949 Perón called for a constitutional convention that, amid strong objections from the opposition, instituted the possibility of presidential reelection, an option that had been forbidden by the 1853 constitution. Peronist union leaders, women activists, and some elected officials tried to nominate Evita as vice presidential candidate, but faced with strong military opposition and affected by failing health, she was forced to decline the nomination. In 1951, Perón was reelected president, gathering 65 percent of all votes cast.

At the time of his second inauguration in 1952, Perón confronted growing difficulties as changes in the international economic situation, decline in domestic agricultural production, balance-of-payments deficits, inflation, and economic stagnation led to a renewed fight for economic shares among the members of the Peronist coalition. Perón's inability to restore economic prosperity and satisfy the conflicting demands of his followers reinforced the trend toward authoritarianism. The increasingly repressive characteristics of his political initiatives—declaration of a state of siege and internal war, takeover of newspapers and growing censorship, forced membership in the Peronist party and other organizations, and an open confrontation with the Catholic Church—weakened his regime and strengthened the resolve of the opposition to remove him by any means. Evita's death in 1952, the multiplication of the allegations of corruption, and a number of scandals involving Perón and his associates contributed to undermine the regime's popularity and made it increasingly difficult to mobilize supporters in its defense. Perón's misguided policies that fluctuated between using more repression and making concessions fostered the unity of the anti-Peronist forces. Finally, in September 1955, after a series of failed revolts a faction of the military supported by the opposition parties and the Catholic Church succeeded in overthrowing the regime. Perón fled the country and was replaced by a military administration that very rapidly became involved in internal feuds concerning how to deal with the defeated Peronists and what kind of program to implement to replace Perón's populist policies.

AUTHORITARIANISM AND LIMITED DEMOCRACY

After the fall of the Peronist regime a succession of anti-populist civilian and military governments attempted with scarce success to overcome Argentina's political, economic, and social crisis by introducing a new political economic model able to foster growth and political stability. The forces that overthrew Perón agreed that the decline of the classic import substitution industrialization model required the rejection of Perón's income redistribution and nationalistic policies and a new economic strategy that would include adjustment programs to reduce the growing balance-of-payments deficits, incentives for foreign investment in order to attract new capital and technology, and stabilization plans to eliminate inflation. Notwithstanding their different origins, composition, and ruling styles, the governments established during this period practiced exclusionary or repressive policies toward important sectors of the population, particularly against Peronism, which until 1973 was totally or partially banned from participating in elections. Meanwhile, to different degrees, these governments maintained the state intervention in the economy while trying to shift the country's industrialization strategy in a new direction, one that combined relative protection and support for local producers with incentives for foreign investment and the welcoming of financial capital in an attempt to promote exports (especially of manufactures), foster international competitiveness, and modernize the most dynamic sectors of the economy.

These attempts failed due to a number of economic situations, including the relative scarcity of foreign investment, inflationary pressures, hard currency shortages, and state mismanagement. More important yet, the groups favored by the populist regime, such as organized labor and state-dependent industrialists, were able to outlast its fall and struggled to preserve or augment their respective shares of a dwindling economic pie while looking at the state as the means for the attainment of their sectoral goals. Ultimately this confrontation led to growing inflation, social conflict, and a progressive government paralysis that intensified the economic crisis and heightened political instability.

Between 1955 and 1976 Argentina had a succession of authoritarian military and partially democratic civilian governments that were unable to overcome this stalemate. This failure affected the military administrations established in 1955–1958, 1962–1964, and 1966–1973, all of which were forced to step down and allow for a transition to civilian rule to escape political and economic disaster. The civilian governments of Arturo Frondizi (1958–1962) and Arturo Illia (1964–1966) were elected thanks to the military ban on Peronism, but they were overthrown by the military after they were unable to solve the country's problems.

Finally, in the 1970s, faced with urban insurrections and the rise of guerrilla movements, the military and their allies allowed the electoral participation of Peronism—but not of Perón himself—in an attempt to restore some degree of stability. This led to the election in March 1973 of Perón's personal delegate, Héctor J. Cámpora, who resigned three months after his inauguration so a new election, in which Perón could participate, could be held. Faced with the internal divisions affecting the Peronist movement, Perón attempted to maintain a neutral position by nominating his wife, María E. Martínez de Perón (Isabel Perón), as the vice presidential candidate. The formula of Perón-Perón won the October 1973 presidential elections with 62 percent of the votes, but Juan Perón died in July 1974. He was succeeded by his widow, who contributed, through a combination of governmental mismanagement, corruption, and authoritarian practices, to exacerbate the domestic strife. In early 1976 Argentina was in complete turmoil with Peronist and Marxist guerrilla groups fighting against the military and paramilitary organizations while strikes, lockouts, and demonstrations proliferated in a context of economic stagnation, spiraling inflation, and political crisis.

MILITARY REGIME AND STATE TERROR

In March 1976 the armed forces overthrew Isabel Perón and started the so-called "Process of National Reorganization." This Argentine version of bureaucratic authoritarianism lasted until 1983. The military junta closed congress and provincial legislatures, removed all elected officials and supreme court justices, banned the activities of political parties, placed labor and some business organizations under military control, and enacted other measures aimed at controlling political life. The new regime also unleashed a wave of repression that surpassed all previous authoritarian experiences. A brutal system of state terror was institutionalized, with multiple military, paramilitary, and police groups trying to annihilate the opposition. This campaign of extermination, which the military itself called a "dirty war," was aimed at eliminating not only the armed guerrilla groups and their sympathizers but also any kind of dissent. To achieve this end the regime used multiple terrorist methods, including murder, "disappearance," incarceration in clandestine concentration camps, jailing, torture, exile, and looting opponents' property. More than 10,000—according to some estimates, as many as 30,000—"disappeared" after being abducted, tortured, and assassinated by the security forces. Hundreds were killed in armed confrontations, while thousands more were forced into exile.

The military rulers were also determined to eliminate the socioeconomic and political factors that led to Argentina's economic decline, social strife, and political instability. They agreed with a number of influential members of the elite and technocratic experts that the roots of the crisis were found in the existence of an interventionist state and a semiclosed economy typical of the import substitution industrialization strategy. These advisers believed that the loosening of free market forces would not only create the conditions for renewed economic growth but also discipline the social actors'

Members of the military junta that ruled after the 1976 military coup and waged a "dirty war" against their opponents, which resulted in thousands of assassinations and "disappearances." From left to right: Admiral Emilio Massera, General Jorge Videla, and Brigadier Orlando Agosti. *(Photo provided by the Department of Documentary Photographs, Argentine National Archive)*

behavior, destroying the socioeconomic and political basis for the emergence of populist regimes. After a free market and trade liberalization program had been fully implemented, the different socioeconomic and political groups would perceive the futility of trying to influence public policies in their favor because the market, not the state, would assume the role of allocating resources and distributing income. As a result, the main cause of Argentina's high level of social conflict and political mobilization would be eliminated and governability would be restored. Once this happened, the military and their civilian allies envisioned the establishment of a more stable and less participatory political regime in which some form of restricted electoral competition would finally be authorized.

However, the military regime was unable to attain its goals. The restrictions imposed by the armed forces on the monetarist economic team, which included a ban on reducing military budgets and privatizing military-controlled state enterprises, the formulation of misguided economic policies (especially those that led to the overvaluation of the local currency), the persistent refusal of the economic agents to modify their state-oriented expectations and behaviors, and the worsening external financial conditions, led to economic disaster. At the same time, growing domestic and foreign condemnation of the dictatorship's atrocious human rights violations con-

tributed to isolate and weaken the military regime. Domestically, this opposition was spearheaded by several human rights organizations led by the
Mothers of the Plaza de Mayo, a group of mothers of the "disappeared" that
since 1977 began to congregate every Thursday at Buenos Aires' main public square in front of the presidential palace demanding information about
their relatives and an end to illegal repression. Internationally, the courageous activities of the human rights groups and the shock generated by a
number of state terrorist activities—such as the kidnapping of Jacobo Timerman, director of the newspaper *La Opinión*, and the disappearance and assassination of several priests and well-known personalities—resulted in the
condemnation of the Argentine regime by nongovernmental human rights
organizations (such as Amnesty International and Americas Watch), the
United Nations and OAS human rights commissions, and several developed
nations' governments, including the United States under the Carter administration and Western European governments.

In 1982, faced with a foreign debt crisis, economic stagnation, and growing domestic discontent, the government attempted to solve their problems
by embarking upon an anti-colonial military adventure. The recovery of the
Falkland/Malvinas islands, controlled by the British and claimed by Argentina, appeared to offer the perfect chance to unify the nation behind the
government, regain some prestige for the military, and legitimize the regime.
However, the confrontation with Great Britain ended in a complete Argentine defeat, and the domestic backlash forced the military to call for elections and transfer power to the civilians.

The authoritarian regime had failed to attain its ultimate goals but succeeded, through brutal repression and the application of regressive economic
policies, in changing Argentina's socioeconomic structure; reducing the
power of organized labor; weakening the middle sectors; creating conditions
for the growth of large, diversified domestic economic groups and foreign
corporations devoted to export activities; and reducing the state economic
role and its commitment to policies aimed to protect low- and middle-
income groups. The Argentine society that emerged from the military process was much more heterogeneous and fragmented than the one that had
facilitated the rise of populism. These new economic and social conditions
facilitated the acceptance of liberal political and economic prescriptions to
promote stability and growth.

THE RETURN TO DEMOCRACY

The collapse of the military government convinced a majority of the Argentine population not only that authoritarian regimes were unable to solve
the country's problems but also that they inflicted a staggering cost in human lives, civil rights, and social welfare. This majority was inclined to support parties and candidates that offered the highest likelihood of consolidating a stable democracy and rejecting authoritarian deviations. Even those
groups that had supported the military regime and benefited from its policies recognized that without a solid political foundation the free market

model they favored was not going to last, particularly if its survival depended on the arbitrary decisions made by military rulers. At the same time, the acknowledgment that earlier state-led experiences had been unable to overcome the country's structural deficiencies and the simultaneous perception that socialist and populist regimes were crumbling the world over resulted in an expectation that more liberal economic policies would be better able to solve the crisis.

The democratically elected administrations of Raúl Alfonsín (1983–1989) and Carlos S. Menem (1989–1995, reelected 1995–1999) enjoyed the advantage of political legitimacy but confronted numerous economic obstacles inherited from the military. The basic elements of a liberal democracy, such as periodic elections, party competition, and majority rule with constitutional limitations, were preserved. However, there was also a growing concentration of power in the executive branch, which limited legislative participation and judicial control over important decisions as the country completed its turn toward a free-market economy.

The Radical party led by Alfonsín won the 1983 elections by a wide margin of votes. It was favored in that occasion by the popular feeling that the Radicals would maintain their traditional respect for democratic liberties, the presidential candidacy of a relatively charismatic leader, and the fear that the Peronists would persist in embracing some of the authoritarian practices used in the past. Moreover, the military government's policies had promoted a process of deindustrialization that eroded Peronism's traditional basis of electoral support by substantially reducing the number of industrial workers and weakening the strength of organized labor. In these conditions, it was possible for the Radicals to consolidate their basis of electoral support among the middle sectors and to make inroads among the growing number of self-employed and nonunionized workers.

Initially, the Alfonsín administration implemented an economic plan that combined orthodox liberal stabilization measures with some unorthodox ones aimed at protecting middle- and low-income sectors. At the same time, the Alfonsín administration attempted to fulfill its promises to bring the military personnel responsible for human rights violations to trial and to depoliticize the armed forces. However, the economic policies failed to overcome the domestic resistance of the Peronist party and organized labor to free-market policies and the business groups' refusal to accept government controls on wage, fiscal, and exchange policies. As the civilian opposition grew, the military also defied the human rights policies of the administration and engaged in a series of revolts that compelled Alfonsín to make concessions, greatly reducing the number of officers that could be punished for their deeds during the "dirty war." Moreover, foreign banks, the IMF, and the governments of developed countries gradually withdrew their economic support for the administration, making it impossible to solve the debt crisis.

The disenchantment of large sectors of the population with the economic, social, and human rights policies of the Radical administration led to a decline in its popularity. Meanwhile, the Peronists were able to complete their process of internal reorganization on a more democratic basis, eliminating some unpopular figures from the party's leadership and projecting an image of moderation that attracted the support of not only the working class but also some middle-class sectors. On the Right, other groups were also able to increase their appeal among middle- and upper-class groups by denouncing the Radicals' vacillating economic policies and by calling for a more coherent strategy of economic liberalization. In the economically ravaged provinces, Peronist gains were accompanied by the growth and consolidation of local opposition groups. In 1987, the Radicals were soundly defeated by the Peronists in the midterm congressional elections and lost a number of important governorships.

In 1988, Carlos S. Menem won the Peronist primaries and became the party's presidential candidate. Throughout his campaign, Menem, the governor of one of the poorest provinces, projected a traditional Peronist image, emphasizing populist themes that appealed to the majority of the members of the party. Meanwhile, as the 1989 presidential elections approached, government attempts to regain control over the situation failed. The dollar rose, interest rates skyrocketed, prices increased out of control, strikes and lockouts proliferated. In this context, Menem secured his victory with 51.7 percent of the votes, and the Peronists won a majority of the gubernatorial and congressional positions in dispute.

After the elections, the paralysis of the Alfonsín administration combined with the misgivings concerning Menem's populist economic and social promises worsened the crisis. The already high rate of inflation was replaced by hyperinflation, with prices rising more than 120 percent per month. Real wages collapsed, igniting a social explosion and forcing the presidential declaration of a state of siege. Finally, Alfonsín resigned in late June to facilitate Menem's early presidential inauguration a few days later.

LIBERAL DEMOCRACY AND FREE MARKETS

To the surprise of his followers and adversaries alike, the new president appointed a cabinet and team of advisers that embraced economic and political ideas opposed to the traditional Peronist policies. The populist promises of a "productive revolution" and huge wage raises made during the electoral campaign were replaced by a free-market economic program executed by some of the most representative figures of Argentina's economic and technocratic elites. The traditional Peronist approach, which favored active state intervention in the economy to promote the development of the industrial sector as well as the implementation of redistribution policies and social legislation to expand the domestic market, was abandoned in favor of a view that considered the state interference in the market as the main cause of Argentina's economic decline. Menem's project—the construction of a "popular market capitalism"—required the dismantling of the interventionist state conceived in the 1940s by Perón, which had survived the assault of successive military and civilian administrations. Under Menem, the Peronist tradition of personalistic leadership and the subordination of the Peronist party and unions to the government continued, facilitating the concentration of power in the hands of a charismatic president. Meanwhile, the hyperinflation had generated a strong longing for economic stability that fostered support for the implementation of stringent economic policies.

The Menem administration formulated a series of ever more radical neoliberal economic and social policies that resulted in sweeping market reforms. All state enterprises and services were privatized and transferred to domestic or foreign owners, including the phone, airline, railroad, shipping, coal mining, highway, steel, armaments, and petrochemical companies, the postal and insurance services, the public television and radio stations, and an array of other public utilities and firms controlled by the state. Most economic activities were deregulated, a number of regulatory agencies were eliminated, and there were massive dismissals of public employees. Government monetary control was minimized and a new currency was created that was freely convertible in dollars at a parity rate of 1 for 1. Tax reforms and massive cuts in public expenditures resulted in a balanced budget. In the external sector, the opening of the economy included the implementation of free trade policies—such as the removal of tariff and nontariff barriers and the elimination of most subsidies, the liberalization of rules concerning financial and investment flows, and the acceptance of a foreign debt-for-equity approach.

These economic policies succeeded in accomplishing some impressive results: Inflation was contained (declining from an annual average of 5000 percent in the last few months of the Alfonsín administration to around 1.5 percent in 1995), the economy grew at a significant rate (the GNP average annual growth went from −0.9 percent in the 1985–1989 period to 6.1 percent in 1990–1994), the rate of exchange remained unchanged, and capital inflows increased (foreign direct investment grew from $826 million in 1990 dollars between 1985 and 1989 to $3.44 million in the period 1990–1995). At the same time, the program reinforced the trends toward regressive income distribution, higher unemployment, concentration of wealth, oligopolization of the economy, growing trade deficits, decline of the provincial economies most affected by federal budget cuts, and increasing unemployment. Nevertheless, electoral support for the administration among the population increased significantly as these measures generated economic stability and made the return of inflation unlikely. Moreover, these policies fostered a number of structural, market-oriented transformations that appeared to be irreversible: The interventionist state and distributive socioeconomic coalitions that had fostered the populist and other state-led experiences of the past no longer seemed viable.

In other areas, Menem followed a course that bolstered his political preeminence. In the labor movement, strong opposition against the economic program prevailed among unions and employees in the public sector while labor leaders and workers in the private sector were more reluctant to confront a Peronist government. Perceiving these divisions, the administration reacted forcefully against its opponents, dismissing state workers, imposing obligatory arbitration in private sector conflicts, and giving legal recognition only to the pro-government organizations. The right to strike was limited by presidential decree, and other executive measures further weakened organized labor by weakening collective bargaining, tying wage and salary raises to increases in productivity, and limiting union control of the health and other worker social services.

Inside the Peronist party, Menem supporters were appointed to the leading positions, securing tight control by the administration over the nomination of candidates and reinforcing the subordination of the Peronist party to the president and congressional delegation. The nomination and appointment of judges sympathetic to the administration eliminated many of the potential obstacles to the use of executive decrees to implement controversial policy initiatives. A law increasing from five to nine the number of justices packed the supreme court with Menem loyalists, reducing the chances of judicial opposition to the administration's policies.

Menem cemented good relations with influential military officers by pardoning the former members of the ruling juntas and other military personnel still incarcerated for their responsibility in human rights violations. Although internal military divisions and frictions were not completely eliminated, the concessions made by Menem and the promotion of more professionally oriented officers to high command positions made it possible to defeat new revolts of small discontented groups and considerably reduced military pressures on the administration.

In 1994, Menem considered that the time was ripe to promote a constitutional reform that would permit his reelection. Negotiations with the president of the UCR, Alfonsín, resulted in an agreement in which, in exchange for supporting the reform, the opposition obtained the president's promise to replace three pro-Menem supreme court justices with less partisan personalities and a commitment to support constitutional provisions aimed at limiting executive power, shortening presidential and senatorial tenures, creating the post of chief of cabinet, reforming the judiciary, and reinforcing controls on the administration. A combined Peronist-Radical majority in the constitutional assembly secured the passage of the reform, including the presidential reelection amendment.

The 1995 general elections resulted in a major victory for Menem, a tremendous defeat for the Radicals and an encouraging outcome for an emerging center-Left coalition, the FrePaSo, made up of Leftist groups, Peronist dissidents, and some provincial organizations. Menem was reelected for the 1995–1999 term with close to 50 percent of the votes, while the Peronists won most congressional and gubernatorial races. The Radicals gathered less than 17 percent of the votes, falling to the third position in electoral terms and losing a number of congressional seats and provincial governorships. FrePaSo obtained close to 30 percent of the votes, doubling its congressional representation. Other smaller parties and coalitions performed badly, and few provincial parties were able to gain any congressional seats.

The 1995 vote confirmed the preference of the population for the continuity of an administration that had secured economic and political stability. It also showed the Radical's inability to overcome the negative consequences of the hyperinflation, social turmoil, and political debacle characteristic of the final months of the Alfonsín administration. The electoral rise of the FrePaSo made it clear, however, that a significant portion of the population opposed the administration policies and would prefer the application of a less orthodox economic strategy aimed at generating employment and income redistribution; less stringent social, educational, and health programs; different military and human rights policies; and more control over the executive's actions.

Throughout the early part of his second administration Menem was faced with a decline in economic growth, a dramatic rise in unemployment, and severe socioeconomic crises in some of the provinces. In 1995, in part as a reflection of the Mexican crisis of December 1994, Argentina experienced a severe capital flight ($8 billion dollars) that led to rising interest rates and falls in investment and consumption, which resulted in a 4.4 decline in the GNP. At the same time, unemployment rose to 16 percent by the end of the year. Although the economy slightly recovered in 1996 (3 percent GNP growth), unemployment remained very high (17 percent). These developments forced Menem to promise new policies able to generate jobs and improve social conditions. The feasibility of these policies, however, was limited by the constraints that the neoliberal economic program imposed on the state actions.

As the congressional elections of 1997 approached, the main opposition forces—the Radical party and FrePaSo—realized that an electoral alliance would have excellent prospects of defeating the Peronists. The rise in unemployment, numerous allegations of corruption and police brutality, and the growing insecurity and distrust of the judiciary affected the government's popularity, particularly in the larger cities and most populated provinces. Thus, the leaders of the two main opposition groups agreed on establishing an electoral front—the Alliance for Work, Justice and Education—that presented common candidates in most electoral districts and advocated a program calling for the creation of jobs, elimination of corruption, and the increase of educational, health, and other social expenditures. This political approach succeeded, and the Alliance obtained more than 45 percent of the votes, versus 36 percent for the Peronists—who lost their absolute majority in the Chamber of Deputies—and 18 percent for other minor parties.

These results opened a period of intense political competition in anticipation of the presidential elections of 1999. The Peronists became involved in an internal struggle for the presidential nomination that pitted the governor of Buenos Aires province, Eduardo Duhalde, against President Menem, who indicated his interest in running for a third period. Menem's attempt to remove the constitutional ban on a third consecutive presidential term ultimately failed, but it exposed deep divisions inside the party and weakened Duhalde's electoral chances. In contrast, the Alliance organized an orderly presidential primary in which the Radical party nominated the mayor of the city of Buenos Aires, Fernando de la Rua, while FrePaSo supported Graciela Fernández Meijide, a senator representing the Federal District. De la Rua won the primary with a substantial majority and became the Alliance's presidential candidate. Carlos Alvarez, a leader of FrePaSo, was the vice presidential candidate. In turn, Fernández Meijide became the Alliance's candidate for governor of Buenos Aires province.

Throughout the presidential campaign, the Alliance benefited from the dissensions inside the Peronist party; the Menem administration's inability to overcome the economic recession, reduce unemployment, and eliminate corruption; and Duhalde's incapacity to prevent a number of police scandals in Buenos Aires province. At the same time, de la Rua and Alvarez were able to present themselves as moderate and responsible candidates able to preserve political and economic stability while fighting corruption, implementing progressive social policies, and strengthening public security. On October 24, 1999, the Alliance won the presidential elections with 48.5 percent of the votes, versus 38.1 percent for the Peronists. At the same time, the Alliance increased its representation in the Chamber of Deputies to 124 seats (five less than the majority) while 103 seats remained controlled by the Peronists. The Alliance was able to win in some provinces previously held by the Peronists, but its candidate for governor was defeated in the largest electoral district, the Province of Buenos Aires, where the Peronist candidate, Carlos Ruckauf, obtained 48 percent of the votes, versus 41 percent for Fernández Meijide.

On December 10, 1999, Fernando De la Rua became president of Argentina for the period 1999–2003, marking the third time since 1983 that a constitutionally elected civilian was inaugurated. The De la Rua administration included Radical and FrePaSo members but the most important offices—among them, the ministries of economics, interior, defense, and foreign relations—were held by Radicals while some FrePaSo representatives, including Fernández Meijide, were appointed in the social welfare ministries and in other secondary positions. The alliance began to be affected by internal dissensions as it became clear that the president and the Radical leaders were neither going to alter substantially the economic, social, and foreign policies followed by Menem nor engage in a strong anti-corruption campaign. In October 2000, Vice President Alvarez resigned after his calls for a stronger stance against corruption in the Senate and the executive branch were ignored by the president. The alliance remained in place but was considerably weakened by this resignation as well as by a ministerial reshuffle that, in March 2001, resulted, among other changes, in the removal of Fernández Meijide, the appointment of Domingo Cavallo as chief of the ministerial cabinet, and the appointment as new minister of economics Ricardo López Murphy, who was determined to maintain and deepen the neoliberal course followed by his predecessors. All these internal problems affecting the coalition, together with the inability of the De la Rua administration to end the recession and eliminate corruption, affected the government's popularity and created new opportunities for a Peronist electoral resurgence.

Nevertheless, although political conflict, social tensions, and economic problems continue to affect Argentina, the orderly transfer of power from the incumbent Peronists to the opposition Radical–FrePaSo alliance and the continuous use of legal means to state dissent and discontent tend to confirm that liberal democracy had been largely consolidated in Argentina. Instead of reacting to the existing difficulties in the manner that was characteristic in the past—for instance, by engaging in confrontational actions and calling for authoritarian solutions—a large majority of the population has chosen to use suffrage and other constitutional means to convey its dissatisfaction and opposition to political authorities.

Politics and Power

Constitutional Framework and Political Institutions

The Argentine constitution promulgated in 1853 and amended on different occasions is currently in effect after having been rescinded or suspended during different periods of authoritarian rule. The 1853 constitution instituted a republican and representative political system with moderate federal features. It provided for a division of powers between the executive, legislative—divided into a Chamber of Deputies and a Senate—and judicial branches while upholding a presidentialist regime. The president is both the head of state and of government and was appointed by an Electoral College whose members were chosen by popular vote. Senators were appointed by the provincial legislatures, while deputies were directly elected by popular vote. Members of the federal judiciary were nominated by the president and confirmed by the Senate. The provinces could establish their own government structures, but the national government could assume control in a number of cases, limiting in practice the extent of their autonomy.

The constitution guaranteed a number of individual rights, among them freedom of association, speech, and press; protection of domicile, correspondence, and private activities against unwarranted government searches and interference; equality before the law; right to a public trial; and prohibition of retroactive application of any laws. Freedom of religion and of public worship were also sanctioned, but the Catholic Church maintained a privileged position, enjoying economic support from the federal government. In economic terms, the 1853 constitution was extremely liberal, establishing the inviolability of private property, espousing free trade and market principles, promoting foreign immigration and investment, and opening internal rivers to free navigation.

The 1853 constitution was amended but remained largely unchanged until 1949, when a convention convened by President Perón—in circumstances defined as illegal by the opposition—introduced substantial reforms including the possibility of presidential reelection and endorsing state economic intervention, limitations on private property rights, the nationalization of natural resources, public utilities, credit, and foreign trade. After Perón's overthrow, the military government declared the 1949 constitutional reform null and void and summoned a new constitutional convention that adjourned after having approved a single new article guaranteeing workers' rights, minimum wages, and social security benefits. In 1994, under Menem, a constitutional convention shortened the duration of the presidential and vice presidential mandate to four years and allowed for reelection. It also introduced new constitutional rights and guarantees including consumer, children's, and the indigenous population's rights and endorsed legislation establishing women's right to occupy at least one-third of all elected positions.

The executive branch consists of the president, the vice president, and the cabinet. Executive power is vested in the president, who can appoint and remove the ministers at will, except the chief of cabinet, who is answerable to the president but politically responsible to Congress and can be removed through a nonconfidence vote. The president and vice president are elected directly by popular vote through a run-off system for a four-year term with the possibility of immediate reelection for one additional period. The president is the "supreme chief of the nation" whose powers include the general administration of the country, the appointment of administration officials, the implementation of the laws, the right to introduce laws before Congress and to veto or approve legislation in part or as a whole, and the conduct of foreign relations. The president is the commander-in-chief of the armed forces and nominates Supreme Court Justices and members of the diplomatic corps for confirmation by the Senate. The president can also declare, with the approval of the Senate, a state of siege, temporarily suspending some civil liberties in case of external attack. Argentina followed a presidentialist tradition, concentrating in the presidents a large amount of power that made it possible for them to often dominate the legislative and judicial branches. Also, the fact that elected presidents were many times charismatic individuals and leaders of major political parties reinforced the subordination of congress and the judiciary to the presidential will and the neglect of their independent roles.

The legislative branch consists of two houses: the Chamber of Deputies and the Senate. According to the constitution, the deputies represent the nation as a whole while the senators represent the provinces and the federal district. Congress has the power to make all laws and regulations, levy taxes and establish the budget of the central government, ratify or reject treaties and integration accords, authorize the executive to declare war, declare a state of siege and intervene in a province, and accept or reject the resignation of the president and vice president. Both chambers possess similar powers, and their approval is required to pass most legislation. To override a presidential veto, two-thirds of the votes in both chambers are required.

Judicial power at the national level is exercised by a Supreme Court of Justice and the lower courts created by Congress. The judicial branch is formally independent but, in practice, has been affected by external interferences and internal problems. The judiciary has often been subordinated to political authorities; judges and judicial personnel have been removed and replaced for political reasons, and the executive has disregarded judicial decisions. Compounding these problems, the judiciary has been plagued by slow procedures, frequent reversals of precedents, lack of citizen access, occasional corruption, and political disagreements between its members.

Until the early 1990s, Argentina had a significantly large and diversified public sector composed of the central administration, decentralized agencies, and state enterprises. Since the rise of Peronism in the 1940s, the public sector grew very rapidly as the regulatory, distributive, and productive functions of the state expanded. The central administration has been highly bureaucratic in its procedures and clientelistic in its recruitment and composition. Attempts made by successive civilian and military governments to increase efficiency, reduce size, and attract better-qualified candidates were contradicted and frustrated by the inability of these same administrations to forego clientelistic practices and risk political and social confrontations. Menem was more successful in reducing the size of the state, but clientelistic practices, bureaucratic procedures, and corruption still plague some areas of the public administration.

According to the constitution, the twenty-three provinces and the Federal District retain all power not delegated to the federal government. Each province elects its own legislature and governor, but the constitution makes governors the "natural agents" of the federal government in charge of enforcing the national constitution and laws. Contributing to reinforce the subordination of the provinces to the central authority is the federal government's power to take over and replace the local officials with federal appointees when the "republican form of government" is endangered by internal conflicts. Because the courts have declined to define the notion of "republicanism," arguing that it is a political matter, federal authorities can define these circumstances very broadly and assume control of a province without judicial interference.

MAIN POLITICAL PARTIES AND COALITIONS

The Radical Party. The Radical party emerged as the first Argentine modern mass party demanding the end of the oligarchic regime and renewal and moralization in the political, electoral, and administrative spheres. It was supported by diverse groups, including university students, marginal members of the elite, and middle- and low-income creole sectors. In 1896 Hipólito Yrigoyen became the leader of the party and began to expand its basis of support by recruiting new members among the immigrant-descent urban middle sectors and workers. The promulgation, in 1912, of an electoral law that guaranteed free, universal male, obligatory suffrage facilitated Yrigoyen's presidential victory in 1916.

In power, the Radical party emphasized the virtues of liberal democracy, the significance of popular sovereignty, and the importance of universal and free suffrage. Under Yrigoyen, the Radicals also favored some nationalistic and statist policies and implemented moderate redistributive and social policies, although without affecting the essential characteristics of the agriculturally based export-import model.

In the 1930s, the Radicals were prevented from coming back to power by the use of repression, proscription, and fraud. After being defeated by the Peronists in 1946, Radicalism remained the main opposition party and adopted a program calling for nationalization of natural resources, strategic industries and services, state intervention in the economy, income redistribution, and an independent foreign policy while denouncing the Peronist violations of civil liberties and political freedoms.

After supporting the military coup that ousted Perón, the Radicals split into two different parties: the Intransigent faction led by Arturo Frondizi and the People's faction led by Ricardo Balbín. In the elections of 1958, after having reached an agreement with Perón, Frondizi was elected president with Peronist support but rapidly lost it and was overthrown in 1962. In 1964, taking advantage of the proscription of Peronism, the People's Radicals won the presidential elections. The new president, Arturo Illia, implemented some modest nationalistic and redistributive policies while respecting most constitutional freedoms and guarantees until he was overthrown by the military in 1966.

In the 1970s, the People's faction was able to obtain the exclusive use of the Radical name. Two major internal groups emerged during this period competing for control over the party: One led by Balbín embraced moderate positions, favored alliances with other political parties, and maintained a friendly approach toward Perón; another, led by Raúl Alfonsín, favored more nationalistic and redistributive economic policies and opposed collaboration with Perón. Although losing two successive presidential elections to the Peronists in 1973 and being unable to prevent the military coup of 1976, Balbín remained leader of the party until his death in 1981. In 1982, when the military announced the call for elections, Alfonsín gained control over the party and became its successful presidential candidate. The Radical defeat in the 1989 presidential elections, hyperinflation, the electoral decline in successive congressional elections, and the secret negotiations with Menem on constitutional reform eroded Alfonsín's popularity but were not enough to completely upset his control over the party machine. In the late 1990s, the Radicals were able to regain some of their popularity among the middle sectors by denouncing the socioeconomic difficulties and corruption associated with the Menem administration. The conformation of the alliance with the center-left FrePaSo helped to facilitate this recovery and, by 1998, the Radicals were once again in a competitive political position. In November 1998, Fernando De la Rua, the president of the Radical party and mayor of the city of Buenos Aires, won the open primaries organized by the Alliance and became its presidential candidate for the 1999 elections. De la Rua's victory in the presidential elections strengthened the Radical party's unity, but its popularity was affected by the inability of the new administration to overcome the economic recession, deal effectively with the problem of corruption, and implement the social policies promised during the electoral campaign. Disagreements with its FrePaSo partners also contributed to create internal difficulties that weakened the De la Rua administration and the Radicals' electoral chances.

Peronist Party. The Peronist party was created in 1946 after Perón's victory in the presidential elections. Throughout Perón's first presidency (1946–1952) the party—which after the introduction of women's suffrage in 1947 was divided into male and female sections—played a secondary role compared with the labor confederation, state agencies, the armed forces, and other organizations such as the Eva Perón Foundation. The party was reduced to mobilize Peronist voters at election times and to disseminate the Doctrina Justicialista—an ideology advocated by Perón that represented a third option between capitalism and communism and called for social class cooperation, state intervention, nationalistic policies, and nonalignment in order to build an Argentina that would be economically independent, socially just, and politically sovereign. During Perón's unfinished second presidency (1952–1955), the party's importance increased as Perón's authoritarian turn led to attempts to establish partisan control on the civil service and socioeconomic organizations.

After Perón's fall, the party became an underground political organization subordinated to the exiled leader, conveying Perón's orders to his followers. However, Perón was unable to prevent the emergence of the so-called neo-Peronist parties that with the support of some union leaders were determined to develop a "Peronism without Perón." Most of these parties had a brief existence, but a few of them established provincial roots and remained active into the 1990s.

In the 1970s, Peronism was formally reorganized as the Justice Party (Partido Justicialista—PJ). Perón remained the party chief, with the right to appoint or remove the party authorities and select its electoral candidates. However, internal factions—including the union leadership, guerrilla groups, professional politicians, and youth organizations—were vying for power. Perón tried to reestablish his authority and prevent further divisions by becoming president and nominating his wife for vice president, but his death in 1974 cleared the way for violent internal confrontations.

After the 1976 military coup, Peronism was banned and many of its leaders were jailed, persecuted, or killed by the military. The party resurfaced in 1982 but split into a so-called *verticalista* faction—interested in maintaining the power of the traditional political and union bosses and continuing the tradition of hierarchical control from the top as practiced by Perón—and a number of *antiverticalista* groups—which tried to introduce more democratic procedures and elect a new leadership. The *verticalistas* succeeded, appointing Isabel Perón president of the party and nominating traditional politicians and union bosses as candidates for most elective offices. The nondemocratic features of this process, the unsavory personalities and activities of some of the Peronist candidates, and the growing popularity of Alfonsín combined to produce the defeat of the PJ in the 1983 elections. The confrontation between *verticalistas* and *antiverticalistas* resumed, with the former considerably weakened and the latter strengthened by these results. By the late 1980s, Carlos Menem, a provincial governor and vice president of the party, appealed to populist and nationalistic rhetoric to prevail in the first open party primaries and went on to win the presidential election of 1989. After his inauguration, Menem reasserted his control over the party by becoming its president. Attempts made by groups opposed to Menem to maintain some influence failed, and the party remained under the control of the president's supporters, although new internal divisions began to emerge as Menem's second presidential term was coming to an end. In 1998 and 1999, Menem tried unsuccessfully to nullify the constitutional article that made it impossible for him to run for a third presidential term but confronted growing opposition on the part of important party figures such as Eduardo Duhalde, the governor of Buenos Aires province, who finally became the Peronist presidential candidate in the 1999 elections. Duhalde's defeat left the party in disarray, and a number of Peronist leaders, including the elected governor of Buenos Aires, Carlos Ruckauf; other governors; and Menem himself began to compete to gain control over the party machine in anticipation of the 2003 presidential elections. At the same time, the chances of a Peronist electoral recovery were improved by the inability of the De la Rua administration to overcome the recession and solve the disputes inside the Alliance with its FrePaSo partners.

FrePaSo. In 1991, a group of eight Peronist deputies led by Carlos "Chacho" Alvarez left the party, denouncing Menem's decision of pardoning the jailed members of the military juntas. This group joined forces with a number of progressive Christian Democrats, Leftist union leaders, and human rights activists (led by Graciela Fernández Meijide) to create the Movement for Democracy and Social Justice, which participated, with scarce success, in the 1991 midterm elections. In 1993, the movement merged with the Leftist Southern Front, formed by sectors of the Communist, Socialist, and other Leftist groups, to create a Leftist coalition, the Great Front, which opposed Menem's economic, social, and human rights policies. In the 1993 midterm elections, the Front was able to elect its two first national deputies (Alvarez and Fernández Meijide), but its appeal was mainly restricted to the progressive constituencies of the city of Buenos Aires. By 1994, however, the Front was able to capitalize on the discontent of Peronist and Radical voters who felt disenfranchised by the turn toward conservative, free-market positions taken by both major parties, and obtained a substantial number of votes in that year's constitutional convention elections. After these elections, the Front formed an alliance, the FrePaSo—Front for a Country in Solidarity—with other dissident Peronist groups, the Socialist Unity and the Christian Democracy, which agreed on a moderate Leftist platform with redistributive, nationalistic, and anti-corruption components.

In the 1995 presidential elections, FrePaSo gathered close to 30 percent of the votes, displacing UCR from the second position and electing a number of representatives to congress. Afterward, FrePaSo was able to broaden its influence, particularly in the largest electoral districts. Human rights activist Graciela Fernández Meijide remained one of its most popular and influential leaders, and she was elected senator representing the Federal Capital. In 1997, FrePaSo established the Alliance for Work, Justice, and Education with the Radical party and defeated Peronism in that year's congressional elections. Fernández Meijide headed the Alliance's list of candidates in the largest electoral district, Buenos Aires province, and was able to secure an impressive victory with more than 48 percent of the votes, versus 41 percent for the Peronists. In the Alliance's open primaries to nominate a presidential candidate for 1999, conducted in November 1998, Fernández Meijide was defeated by the Radical De la Rua, but she was nominated candidate for the governorship of Buenos Aires. The president of FrePaSo, Carlos "Chacho" Alvarez, was selected as the vice presidential candidate of the Alliance. The October 1999 elections had mixed consequences for FrePaSo: On one hand, Alvarez became vice president and the party increased its number of seats in congress and provincial legislatures; on the other hand, Fernández Meijide lost the gubernatorial election in the province of Buenos Aires, reducing the influence of the party. The alliance with the Radicals made it possible for a number of FrePaSo leaders to become members of the cabinet, including Fernández Meijide, who was appointed minister of social action. However, disagreements with the Radicals concerning the economic and social policies and the fight against corruption led to internal tensions in the Alliance. Finally, in October 2000, Alvarez resigned the vice presidency denouncing the lack of effective anticorruption policies and the activities of some corrupt senators and cabinet officials. Alvarez's departure did not mark the end of the FrePaSo–Radical alliance but weakened it considerably while highlighting the inability of the FrePaSo to modify the administration's policies.

INTEREST GROUPS

The Military. The modern Argentine armed forces were organized as a professional institution during the late nineteenth century and remained subordinated to the civilian authorities until 1930. Since then, the military have not only organized coups and established authoritarian regimes but have also played a crucial political role under most civilian administrations, exercising indirect control and vetoing government initiatives. Most officers embraced conservative positions and supported the creation of a political system characterized by limited participation, hierarchical order, and an emphasis on domestic national security. However, agreement of these basic points has not prevented the emergence of factions that disagreed on the best methods to attain these goals or that were motivated by personalistic and group ambitions.

After overthrowing Perón in 1955, the coup leaders purged Perón's supporters from the officer corps but split into moderate and radical anti-

Peronist factions, a division that would linger until the 1970s. The continuous capacity of Peronism to obtain electoral majorities and the civilian administrations' inability to suppress it resulted in the military coups of 1962 and 1966. In 1966, General Juan Carlos Onganía banned all political parties and established a bureaucratic authoritarian regime. However, growing economic and social problems accompanied by urban revolts and the rise of guerrilla movements led to Onganía's removal by his fellow officers and to a call for elections in which Peronism was finally allowed to participate.

In 1976, the armed forces overthrew Isabel Perón and inaugurated an authoritarian regime that, unlike previous ones, divided power equally among the three branches and attempted to create a system in which the military as an institution exercised power. However, as the difficulties accumulated the military split once again into opposing factions: One group tried to implement less orthodox economic policies while establishing closer ties with conservative and provincial parties in order to coopt their support; another group favored market policies and opposed any kind of political opening. The latter tried to overcome the crisis by increasing repression and arousing nationalistic feelings through the recovery of the Falklands/Malvinas Islands. The defeat on the islands forced the military to call for elections that resulted in the Radical victory.

Under Alfonsín the military budget was greatly reduced and the power of the civilian authorities was strengthened. The members of the three military juntas were tried and sentenced to prison for human rights violations. However, as the number of officers brought to trial increased, the military multiplied their demonstrations of discontent and refused to testify before civilian judges. Faced with growing disobedience, Alfonsín tried to limit the number of military under judicial investigation by supporting a law that extinguished any penal action against officers if they were not indicted within sixty days after the promulgation of the law. When this was not enough to satisfy the military and a revolt erupted, Alfonsín supported a "due obedience law" that exempted most officers from trial, with the exception of those who had been top commanders during the "dirty war."

The concessions made by Menem, especially the pardons for the members of the juntas, satisfied most of the military and diminished support for the rebellious groups, making it possible to defeat and expel them from the ranks. After this, the military remained subordinated to the civilian government, performing their professional activities and exhibiting no signs of being interested in meddling in the political arena. This stance was not modified even when, in early 2001, a judge declared the unconstitutionality of the laws passed under Alfonsín, renewing the possibility of bringing to trial those officers accused of human rights violations. Although vehemently opposed to this decision, the military did not revolt as they had done in the past, preferring in this case to appeal the decision to higher courts.

The Catholic Church. The Catholic Church has played an influential role in Argentine politics, either as a supporter or opponent of specific policies implemented by different governments, particularly in the educational and social areas. The 1853 constitution instituted freedom of belief but granted Catholicism a privileged position by requiring the federal government to finance the Church and the president and vice president to be Catholic.

The Catholic Church has supported those governments, which promised to implement policies that corresponded to a conservative interpretation of Catholic teachings, disregarding the authoritarian or democratic origins of these administrations. When some governments formulated policies that clashed with these notions, the Church conducted political campaigns aimed at reversing these measures and sometimes to remove the governments responsible for them. For example, the Church supported Perón because he promised to maintain religious education in public schools and to follow Catholic social teachings, but when Perón decided to eliminate religious education, promulgate a divorce law, and legalize prostitution, the Church became a crucial participant in the coalition that overthrew him.

The majority of the bishops and cardinals have been consistently conservative, even during the 1960s and 1970s when less traditional attitudes proliferated in the rest of Latin America. The emergence in Argentina of a group of progressive priests who embraced liberation theology was a phenomenon restricted mainly to the rank and file. Most Church authorities welcomed the military coups of 1966 and 1976, especially because right-wing nationalistic figures associated with the Church were appointed to important positions.

Throughout the 1976–1983 period, most Church dignitaries supported the military regime or adopted neutral positions and only a few bishops and archbishops openly opposed the authoritarian government. After the restoration of democracy in 1983, the most conflictive aspects of Church-state relations were focused on family, cultural, and educational issues. Under Alfonsín, the Church hierarchy unsuccessfully opposed the passing of a divorce law and a more liberal family code. This defeat strengthened the influence of a more moderate group of bishops who emphasized the moral role of the Church but distanced themselves from open political actions. Under Menem, the Church hierarchy initially adopted a more supportive attitude than during the Alfonsín administration in the expectation that the new president—who had opposed the divorce law and advocated the application of the Church's social teachings—would follow a less secular course. However, some members of the hierarchy criticized the application of economic policies that affected the poor and generated unemployment, while others denounced the pardons given by Menem to the military.

Organized Labor. Argentina's long tradition of well-organized and relatively powerful labor organizations started in the late nineteenth century. The first unions were formed by European immigrants, particularly skilled workers, who embraced anarchist and socialist ideologies. In the 1940s, Perón was able to skillfully manipulate the labor movement through a combination of rewards for his supporters (collective bargaining, official recognition, social benefits) and elimination of his opponents (denial of legal recognition and benefits and removal from office). By 1945, the General Confederation of Labor (CGT) was under the control of Peronist union leaders, many of them newly elected, and the numbers of unionized workers increased rapidly. In October 1945, a workers' mobilization forced the release of Perón from confinement and cleared the way for his presidential campaign. After Perón's inauguration, union membership became obligatory for most workers, the number of unionized workers greatly increased, and their wages and benefits improved. The CGT remained firmly under the control of Perón, who eliminated political dissidents and appointed loyal members of small unions to lead the organization.

After Perón's fall the CGT and most unions were taken over by the military, but in elections held in 1956 a majority of the unions elected Peronist leaders and, in the early 1960s, the Peronists regained control of the CGT. Although persecuted and banned by different military and civilian governments, organized labor became an important political actor able to use its mobilization capacity to support Peronism and strengthen or weaken the administrations established between 1958 and 1976.

Under the 1976–1983 authoritarian regime, the CGT was taken over by the military and some influential labor leaders who tried to oppose the military rulers were kidnapped and killed or forced into exile. As the economic crisis erupted, union leaders led some demonstrations and strikes but remained weak and disorganized. Only after the Falklands/Malvinas crisis were the multiple labor factions able to overcome part of their differences and to reestablish a unified CGT under Peronist control.

After the defeat of the PJ in the 1983 elections, confrontations within the CGT became more acute and created the chances for the rise of new labor leaders. In 1986, the CGT regained legal status and pursued a number of goals, among which the most important were the recomposition of real wages, the control of social services, and the promulgation of a new law on trade unions, but its ability to exact concessions from the government was limited by its lack of internal unity.

Some labor leaders negotiated with the Radical government and secured the appointment of one of them as minister of labor. The Alfonsín administration sent to congress a package of labor legislation reestablishing collective bargaining, maintaining union-provided social services, and strengthening the rights of organized labor. However, after the Radical electoral defeats, this alliance collapsed and most union leaders went back to the Peronist fold and organized several general strikes.

After his inauguration, Menem saw in an independent CGT as an obstacle for the smooth implementation of a neoliberal program. Collaborationist union leaders were appointed to government positions and tried to gain control over the CGT, which split into rival organizations. One of them stated its complete loyalty to the administration and supported the neoliberal economic plan; the other declared its support for Peronism but opposed the economic policies and warned that it would continue to fight for higher wages and against dismissals. In late 1992, public employees and teachers' unions joined by other smaller organizations formed a new labor organization that strongly opposed the neoliberal economic policies, denounced the official CGT as collaborationist, and established political links with the opposition. In 1994, a group of Peronist unions, led by the transportation workers' union, broke away from the CGT and formed another organization—the Movement of Argentine Workers (MTA)—demanding a tougher opposition to the government's labor and welfare policies. Meanwhile, the CGT remained the largest labor confederation, comprising labor organizations whose leaders backed most government initiatives, although they occasionally requested changes in the administration policies, mainly to reduce unemployment, protect social benefits, and prevent wage cuts.

In 2000, sectors of organized labor confronted the De la Rua administration and called for strikes to oppose a new labor law that would weaken job stability and curtail the application of collective bargaining agreements. However, the divisions inside the labor movement prevented the creation of a unified front, and the labor reform promoted by the government was passed with the support of CGT's moderate union leaders against MTA resistance.

Business Associations. Argentine business associations are organized along sectors of economic activity, including agricultural, industrial, commercial, and financial interests. Among the agricultural associations the most powerful are the Argentine Rural Society, which represents the interests of the largest and wealthiest landowners—cattle raisers and grain producers—and the Argentine Rural Confederations, which represent the interests of the medium to large agricultural producers, including cattle breeders and grain producers. Both organizations strongly defend private property rights—opposing any land reform—and advocate free-market and trade policies. In the 1990s, they became the strongest supporters of Menem's economic policies, particularly welcoming the elimination of exchange controls, the elimination of regulations and agricultural state boards, and the measures directed to reduce labor costs.

The Argentine Agrarian Federation initially represented tenant farmers and afterward small and medium-size farmers engaged in mixed agricultural and cattle-raising activities that produce mostly for the domestic market. Politically, it has usually opposed authoritarian regimes and supported democracy, favoring some degree of state intervention to enlarge the domestic market and protect small producers. It has been less supportive of neoliberal policies, expressing concern about the decline of the domestic market and the increase in agricultural imports.

The most important industrial association is the Argentine Industrial Union, whose membership and influence expanded as the import substitution industrialization process developed. The organization was controlled by the large industrialists from Buenos Aires who opposed Perón's labor policies. After becoming president, Perón dissolved the organization and replaced it with another that represented the interests of the smaller industrialists of the interior and those that emerged as a result of the Peronist industrializing policies. After Perón's fall the Industrial Union was restored and continued to represent the larger domestic and foreign industrial companies that supported a moderately liberal economic approach, although it also favored some state intervention and protection to promote their interests.

The 1976–1983 military regime recognized the Argentine Industrial Union as representative of all industrial groups, but two factions emerged: one that represented the large industrial groups with liberal economic positions and another that represented the smaller industrial groups of the interior and favored some degree of state intervention. Under Menem, the former backed most of the neoliberal policies while the latter expressed reservations concerning the rapid opening of the economy and the decline of the domestic market.

The Argentine Chamber of Commerce represents the interests of the commercial sector but also includes among its members insurance, transportation, and financial companies. It has always defended the free-market system, advocated free trade, and called for the lifting of price controls and state regulations. In political terms, it has traditionally supported conservative civilian and military governments while opposing those that followed populist and state-led strategies. In the 1990s, it became one of the strongest supporters of Menem's neoliberal policies.

Bank organizations include the Association of Banks of the Argentine Republic, the Association of Argentine Banks, and the Association of Banks of the Interior of the Argentine Republic. The first represents the interests of the largest banks, more than half of which are foreign owned. The other two associations represent the interests of smaller banks mostly of local capital. All of them support liberal economic principles, including free financial and exchange markets, but differ on the roles to be played by foreign capital and the state. While the first one supports unrestricted free movement of capital and complete lifting of most financial regulations, the other two favor some regulations to prevent the concentration of capital in the largest foreign and national banks.

WOMEN'S ROLE

Women's participation in Argentina's labor force has been increasing steadily since the 1940s, but the proportion of women in the paid labor force remained around 29 percent in 1990, with more than two-thirds of female workers concentrated in the service sector. Wages for women were estimated to be on average one-third lower than those for men. In educational terms women have fared better, having attained a higher level of literacy and high school attendance than men and representing a substantial proportion of university students, including those in traditional male-dominated careers such as law, medicine, and engineering.

In the political realm, women have played an increasingly important role, particularly since their enfranchisement in the late 1940s. Since the turn of the century, Argentine women fought for the right to vote and participated in political party activities, particularly in Left and center-Left parties. The emergence of Peronism in the 1940s was associated with the rise to prominence of Eva Duarte de Perón (Evita), who became one of the twentieth century's leading political figures and has remained a revered icon for a substantial sector of the population. Evita was instrumental in securing the extension of the right to vote to women in 1947 and became the leader of the women's sector of the Peronist party until her death in 1952. After 1947, women became active participants in many of the political parties, were elected to the national and provincial legislatures, and were appointed members of different cabinets, although in a lesser proportion than men. In 1973, Isabel Perón—Juan D. Perón's third wife—was elected vice president of the country in a formula headed by her husband. After Perón's death in 1974, Isabel Perón became the president of the country until she was overthrown by the military coup of March 1976.

Women played a crucial role during the last military dictatorship (1976–1983) in the struggle for human rights and democracy. The Mothers (and Grandmothers) of the Plaza de Mayo became the main opponents of the military junta, openly denouncing the terrorist tactics of the regime and demanding the return of the disappeared. Through their brave actions, which cost them heavily in terms of repression and persecution, the Mothers were able to call world attention to the brutality of the military government and mobilize sectors of the Argentine population in the demand for respect for human rights and the establishment of democracy. After the transition to democracy, the Mothers and other human rights organizations in which women play a fundamental role have continuously demanded the investigation and condemnation of those responsible for terrorist practices and the return of the children of the disappeared.

In the 1990s, in order to increase women's formal political representation, a constitutionally endorsed law required that political parties reserve every third place on their lists of candidates for women. The implementation of this quota law, the first in the world of its kind, led to a rapid increase in the number of women elected to office; currently more than 30 percent of the seats in congress are occupied by women representing different parties. Also, there has been an increase in the number of women in ministerial and secretarial positions and running for executive office at the provincial level since the reestablishment of democracy, but the proportion of women appointed and elected to these offices remains very low.

Looking Forward: Argentina's Political Prospects

Since the early 1980s, the Argentine political economic situation has been characterized by the gradual consolidation of a liberal democratic regime and the implementation of neoliberal economic policies. This development has surprised many analysts familiar with the country's evolution in the twentieth century. In the past, these elements were clearly antagonistic: Liberal democratic governments felt threatened by the local versions of populism and were unable to stand the negative reactions generated by the attempts to implement free-market policies; populist regimes were perceived as incompatible with liberal democracy and neoliberal economic programs because they often engaged in authoritarian practices and favored state intervention in the economy; and economic liberal programs were implemented through authoritarian means by the elites and the military due to their inability to gain electoral support and popular backing for free-market policies. The inability to reconcile these three elements became an important factor in fostering the periodic outbursts of political, economic, and social instability that resulted in Argentina's traditional merry-go-round of military and civilian governments since 1930.

The current situation, characterized by the relative stability of a constitutional liberal democratic regime; the strengthening of an administration led by a president who appeals to personalistic patterns of mobilization, representation, and communication; and the successful implementation of strict neoliberal economic policies, represents a scenario that would have been considered implausible in the past. Notwithstanding these circumstances favorable to the consolidation of elected governments with neoliberal programs, the concern over the stability of the emergent Argentine liberal democracy is still an issue when considering the strength and durability of the commitment to this regime by different domestic groups. In Argentina support for liberal democracy depended on a number of political variables, such as the degree of devastation brought about by authoritarian regimes and the intensity of the population's revulsion against these regimes, the depth of the popular belief in the legitimacy of democracy, the ability of democratic governments to establish effective institutional arrangements, and the existence of representative political parties. But there is another crucial element that must be present to guarantee the stability of liberal democracy: continuous support for the socioeconomic features of the system, namely private property, free markets, consumer sovereignty, and minimal state intervention in the economy. If a situation arises in which the political and economic sides of the liberal democratic equation no longer complement each other—for instance, if parties opposed to the neoliberal policies come to power and maintain their electoral promises or, even while in opposition, are able to hinder the application of these policies—the commitment to free-market capitalism might take precedence over the allegiance to political democracy. When confronted with the rise of these tensions between market and democracy the elected administrations of Alfonsín and Menem turned to solutions that, without completely eliminating the liberal democratic features of the regime, represented a consistent effort to concentrate political power in the executive branch, limit the participation or influence of organized political and socioeconomic groups in the decisions, and establish direct relations between personalistic leaders and an atomized civil society.

However, the fact that the concentration of power in the executive and the implementation of neoliberal policies has facilitated a rise in corruption and generated unprecedented levels of unemployment and poverty among the population may lead to some political changes in the future. Election results in the late 1990s seem to indicate that these problems are leading to the growth of a center-Left opposition interested in implementing some policies aimed at reducing arbitrariness and corruption while lessening unemployment and poverty. These changes, if they occur, do not seem to foretell any radical transformations of the existing economic framework and would not provoke reactions that could threaten political stability. In these conditions, the prospects for the consolidation of liberal democracy in Argentina are brighter than they were since the turn of the century, although this stability may be preserved at the cost of perpetuating many of the socioeconomic inequities and problems that have multiplied in the last decade because of the application of free-market policies.

Chronology

1516 First Spanish expedition arrives at the Río de la Plata
1536 First foundation of Buenos Aires; the city is abandoned in 1540
1580 Second foundation of Buenos Aires
1776 Creation of the viceroyalty of the Río de la Plata
1806–1807 British invasions repelled by criollo militias
1810 Crillo government junta replaces Spanish authorities
1816 Declaration of Independence
1816–1829 Civil wars between federal and centralist factions
1829–1852 Dictatorship of Juan Manuel de Rosas
1853 National constitution molded on U.S. presidentialist system adopted
1853–1861 Sporadic civil war between Buenos Aires elites and provincial leaders
1862–1880 Consolidation of oligarchic regime led by agro-exporting Buenos Aires elites
1880–1916 Economic prosperity generated by export-import growth model and political stability under oligarchic regime
1916–1930 Mass democracy under elected middle-class Radical administrations: Hipólito Yrigoyen (1916–1922, 1928–1930) and Marcelo T. de Alvear (1922–1928)

1930–1943 Great Depression and economic crisis in Argentina; military coup overthrows Yrigoyen, return of oligarchy to power and beginning of import substitution industrialization

1943–1955 Rise and fall of Juan D. Perón's populist regime

1955–1966 Political instability characterized by succession of military governments and limited democratic regimes

1966–1973 Military regime in power; socioeconomic crisis, urban explosions, and guerrilla warfare

1973–1976 Return to democracy under Peronist elected government; President Perón dies in office (1974) and is replaced by his widow and vice president María E. Martínez de Perón (Isabel Perón); growing socioeconomic and political tensions; violent confrontations between guerrilla groups and military

1976–1983 Military regime, "dirty war," and economic crisis; invasion of Falkland/Malvinas islands and defeat (1982); military call for elections (1983)

1983–1989 Radical party wins elections; Raúl Alfonsín elected president; growing economic and social problems; hyperinflation and political crisis

1989–1995 Peronist candidate Carlos S. Menem elected president for period 1989–1995; Menem implements free-market economic policies and attains political preeminence; constitution amended allowing for presidential reelection (1994)

1995–1999 Menem reelected president; consolidation of market economy; growing socioeconomic problems and accusations of corruption

1999 Electoral Alliance between Radical party and FrePaSo wins presidential election; Fernando De la Rua and Carlos Alvarez elected president and vice president, respectively, for period 1999–2003

2000 Vice President Carlos Alvarez resigns in October denouncing lack of effective governmental action against corruption. Alliance between Radicalism and FrePaSo remains but is considerably weakened.

Bibliography

Brysk, Alison. *The Politics of Human Rights in Argentina: Protest, Change, and Democratization*. Stanford, CA: Stanford University Press, 1994.

Corradi, Juan. *The Fitful Republic: Economy, Society and Politics in Argentina*. Boulder, CO, and London: Westview Press, 1985.

Epstein, Edward, ed. *The New Argentine Democracy: The Search for a Successful Formula*. Westport, CT: Praeger, 1992.

Hodges, Donald C. *Argentina's "Dirty War": An Intellectual Biography*. Austin: University of Texas Press, 1991.

James, Daniel. *Resistance and Integration: Peronism and the Argentine Working Class, 1946–1976*. Cambridge, England: Cambridge University Press, 1988.

Lewis, Paul. *The Crisis of Argentine Capitalism*. Chapel Hill: University of North Carolina Press, 1990.

O'Donnell, Guillermo. *Bureaucratic Authoritarianism: Argentina, 1966–1973, in Comparative Perspective.* Berkeley: University of California Press, 1988.

Page, Joseph. *Perón: A Biography.* New York: Random House, 1983.

Peralta Ramos, Mónica, and Carlos Waissman. *From Military Rule to Democracy in Argentina.* Boulder, CO: Westview Press, 1987.

Potash, Robert. *The Army and Politics in Argentina, 1928–1945: Yrigoyen to Perón.* Stanford, CA: Stanford University Press, 1969.

———. *The Army and Politics in Argentina, 1945–1962: Perón to Frondizi.* Stanford, CA: Stanford University Press, 1980.

Rock, David. *Argentina, 1516–1987: From Spanish Colonization to Alfonsín.* 2nd ed. Berkeley: University of California Press, 1987.

———. *Politics in Argentina, 1890–1930: The Rise and Fall of Radicalism.* London: Cambridge University Press, 1975.

Simpson, John, and Jana Bennet. *The Disappeared and the Mothers of the Plaza.* New York: St. Martin's Press, 1985.

Smith, William C. *Authoritarianism and the Crisis of the Argentine Political Economy.* Stanford, CA: Stanford University Press, 1989.

Snow, Peter, and Luigi Manzetti. *Political Forces in Argentina.* 3rd ed. Westport, CT: Praeger, 1993.

Timerman, Jacob. *Prisoner without a Name, Cell without a Number.* New York: Vintage Books, 1982.

FILMS AND DOCUMENTARIES

Americas (Program 1): The Garden of Forking Paths. U.S., 1993. Documentary examining Argentina's political, economic, and social development in the twentieth century.

Las Madres: The Mothers of Plaza de Mayo. U.S., 1985. Documentary about the courageous role played by the mothers of the "disappeared".

The Official Story. Argentina, 1985. On the "dirty war," the "disappeared," and their repercussions on Argentine society.

La República Perdida I. 1983; *La República Perdida II.* Argentina, 1985. Documentaries focused on the twentieth-century political history of Argentina that explore the causes for instability.

Tango Bar. Argentina, 1988. The story of the tango is narrated against the background of Argentina's 1976–1983 dictatorship.

WEB SITES AND OTHER SOURCES

Information on current Argentine events is available in English through the *Foreign Broadcast Information Service—Latin America* as well as the foreign news sections of the *Miami Herald, New York Times, Wall Street Journal,* and *Washington Post.* Access to the main Argentine newspapers and magazines is easily secured through the Internet on a daily and weekly basis.

Among the main newspapers are the following: *Clarín* (www.clarin.com.ar), *La Nación* (www.lanacion.com.ar), and *Página/12* (www.pagina12.com.ar).

Political information can be obtained at different sites, including the Latin American Network Information Center (LANIC) maintained by the University of Texas, which offers a wealth of data and numerous links to different sites in Argentina and abroad dealing with governmental institutions, political parties, human rights, media and academic research centers (http://info.lanic.utexas.edu/la/argentina/).

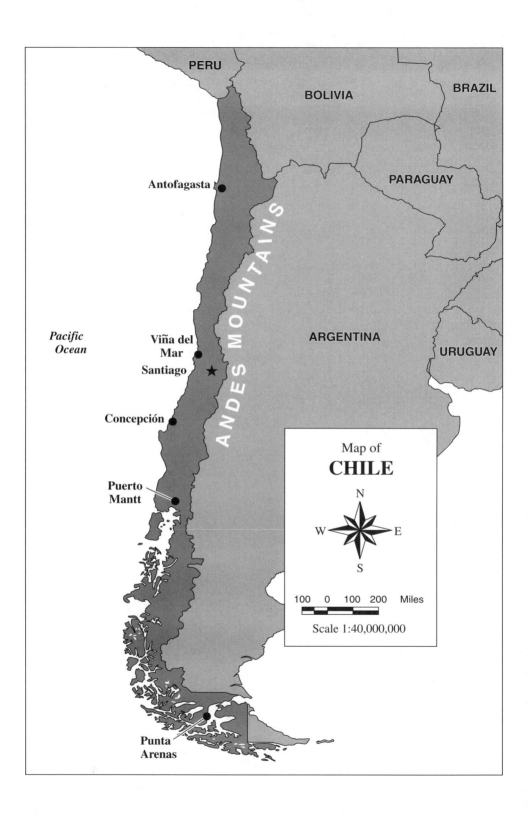

PERU

BOLIVIA

BRAZIL

PARAGUAY

Antofagasta

*Pacific
Ocean*

ARGENTINA

URUGUAY

Viña del
Mar
Santiago

A N D E S   M O U N T A I N S

Concepción

Puerto
Mantt

Map of
CHILE

N

W ★ E

S

100 0 100 200   Miles

Scale 1:40,000,000

Punta
Arenas

FIFTEEN

CHILE

Eduardo Silva

Introduction

Long and narrow, Chile clings to the western edge of South America's Southern Cone. Hugging approximately 3000 miles of Pacific coastline from Peru to Tierra del Fuego and separated from Argentina by the majestic Cordillera de los Andes, the country only averages about 100 miles in width. Chile's territory also includes possessions in Oceania and Antarctica. It is a truly eccentric geography.

The country's length ensures a great variety of climate over its 292,257 square miles (about twice the size of California). The arid, mineral-rich, sparsely populated, northern third (Arica to Atacama) is home to one of the driest deserts in the world. The climate in the central third (Coquimbo to Llanquihue), where the bulk of the population lives, ranges from semiarid to mild mediterranean to wet temperate. Scrub brush tends to be the dominant natural vegetation in the semiarid valleys of the Norte Chico and the mediterranean zone of the central valley that begins just south of Santiago. Here, rainfall is largely confined to a few winter months. The temperate zone enjoys copious, year-round precipitation (even heavier than the Pacific Northwest of the United States) and is home to dense temperate rainforests. The beautiful lake region—carved out by ice-age glaciers—thrives on domestic and international tourism. Together, the mediterranean and temperate zones are the agricultural heartland, dairy center, and timber capital of the nation, although minerals such as copper and coal are also mined. Temperate climate continues to the extreme south, dominated by a spectacular geography of islands and fjords as the continent breaks up. Most of the sparse population lives in the Magallanes region, where sheep ranching, fishing, oil, and timber extraction are the major economic activities.

Most analysts describe Chile as a country with a strong democratic tradition that overcame near civil war in the early 1970s, economic chaos, and a harsh military dictatorship through the 1980s to emerge as a model of economic and political stability in the 1990s. In 1973, the armed forces, in alliance with socioeconomic elites and conservative middle classes, overthrew the constitutionally elected socialist government of Salvador Allende. Thousands lost their lives, and tens of thousands went into exile (forced or self-imposed) as the military violently purged Leftists and Marxists from Chilean institutional life. Exercising autocratic rule, general Augusto Pinochet imposed a radical free-market economic restructuring of Chile's economy and society that yielded rapid, sustained economic growth from the mid-1980s to the year 2000. The military government oversaw a transition to civilian rule in the late 1980s, and the democratic regime established in 1990 was remarkably stable during the first decade of its existence. It avoided many of the ills that plagued other Latin American democracies, such as temporary breakdowns, guerrilla movements, putsches, impeachments, electoral volatility, and debilitating corruption. Instead, regular, peaceful elections, the rule of law, constitutional order, and reasonably well-functioning public administration were the norm. Equally encouraging, democratically elected governments managed the economy in a manner that ensured continued high growth.

This rosy assessment, however, must be tempered by the darker legacies of Chile's military government. A decade after the end of military rule, Chile's constitution was still full of antidemocratic clauses that protected the interests of the socio-political forces that supported the dictatorship: socioeconomic elites and the armed forces. The constitution engineered by the dictatorship permitted conservative political parties to block any legislation they strongly opposed. It also ensured the military an influential role in policy making on issues that should be the exclusive domain of civilian rulers, issues such as human rights and constitutional reform. Moreover, the emphasis on economic growth masked glaring socio-economic problems. In the year 2000, Chile was a more unequal country than it was before the dictatorship's imposition of the free-market economic model. Thanks to those economic and social policies, in the late 1990s Chile had one of the worst income distributions in all of Latin America. Not only did the upper income brackets receive more of the nation's wealth than before 1970, but general poverty and indigence rates were higher, real wages just managed to pass those of the early 1970s, and few of the hard-earned labor rights abolished by the military government had been reinstated. These inequalities extended to the provision of health services, education, and housing. In addition to these problems, for all its growth Chile's economy had not developed beyond the agro-mineral export profile of traditional underdeveloped nations and paid a heavy cost in terms of environmental degradation and natural resource depletion.

In sum, Chile may well be a model for free-market economics and political stability. But it suffers from the socio-economic and environmental imbalances that radical free-market models generate. Moreover, its political stability rests, in part, on anti-democratic institutions. Those institutions protect the privileges of upper class social groups from meaningful reforms to the inequalities of the marketplace. The true test of Chile's vaunted stability must await attempts at socio-economic reform after the restoration of full political democracy.

Chile is a heavily urbanized country; 85 percent of its approximately 14.3 million people live in cities and towns, mostly in the central part of the nation. Over a third (5 million) live in metropolitan Santiago, the capital city. At 1.5 percent, the annual population growth rate is on the lower end for Latin America as a whole, but still higher than that of other Southern Cone countries. Most Chileans are *mestizos*, the descendants of sixteenth and seventeenth century Iberian European conquistadors and the local native population. In contrast to Argentina and Brazil, waves of non-Iberian European immigrants did not contribute greatly to the Chilean nationality. Between 1889 and 1914 only about 55,000 reached Chile. Unlike other countries, however, most of those immigrants became part of the upper middle class and a commercial strata inserted between *mestizo* employees and white persons of Spanish heritage who comprise the upper classes. Lacking a plantation economy, persons of African descent are a negligible component of the population. As in most of Latin America, racism manifests itself in a strong correlation of skin color and native American features to socioeconomic status. In general, the more European-looking, the higher the status. Since the 1980s, Asians have also arrived in Chile in greater numbers following Chile's opening to international trade.

Native Peoples

Although the vast majority of Chileans are *mestizos* or of European heritage, some 3 percent of the population are native peoples, mostly Araucanian or Mapuche. They inhabited the dense forests of south central Chile, approximately from the Itata to the Toltén rivers (the present day regions of Bío-Bío and Araucanía). In the mid-1500s, Alonzo de Ercilla immortalized them in the epic poem *La Araucana*. This proud warrior nation had preserved their independence from the Inca empire and, with considerable success, fought to retain their freedom from Spanish colonial rule. The Mapuches continued armed resistance until the 1880s.

Over those three and a half centuries of armed resistance against Spanish rule the Araucanos, nevertheless, slowly lost territory. When subjugated, they were sent to work in mines, fields, and households. In the twentieth century, the vanquished Mapuches suffered from widespread discrimination and second-class citizenry. Until the military government of 1973–1989, close-knit Mapuche communities based on family groupings retained common lands called *reducciones*, which they worked communally or as individual family parcels. Communal property and a separate identity for indigenous peoples clashed with the dictatorship's free-market ideals. In 1978 it broke up the *reducciones* and replaced them with the family farm, which could be bought, mortgaged, and sold to cultivate individualistic, competitive, and economic maximizing behavior among the Mapuche. The democratic governments of Patricio Aylwin and Eduardo Frei Ruiz-Tagle have attempted to redress some of the worst discriminatory policies of the military government and earlier. A vibrant indigenous peoples' movement has also emerged. All told, approximately 900,000 people claiming Mapuche heritage currently live in Chile, most of them exploited and poor.

Women

Chilean women have also suffered from a long history of second-class citizenry and discrimination, albeit in relation to men. However, as the twentieth century progressed they made advances. After World War II they won the right to vote (1949) and obtained wide access to education, including university education. Yet even well into the 1960s, debates over whether women should have unrestricted access to higher education were common. Many men argued that because of marriage women frequently did not finish their degree programs; thus, given the limited size of entry classes, they represented a waste of scarce educational resources. Such views notwithstanding, women have steadily gained entry into the professions. Women have also become more visible in the business world at the midmanagerial level, although the board room still remains a predominantly male preserve. Female participation in the nonprofessional labor force has also increased since the 1970s, especially in nondomestic services (food services, sales, secretarial) and nontraditional industry (fruit packing, canneries, poultry dressing and packaging). Thus, traditional gender roles are increasingly under challenge among both the middle and working classes.

Women have become an important political force in Chile as well. At the most basic level, since obtaining the right to vote in 1949 they have had a significant impact on elections. But they have also played a more direct role in politics as of late. To begin with, the women's movement was a vital force in the opposition to the military regime, especially in organizing the vote that defeated Pinochet in the decisive plebiscite of October 5, 1988. In newly redemocratized Chile, female politicians in municipalities and in the national legislature are more numerous than ever before, representing the full political spectrum. They also occupy numerous government posts, although not the most sensitive and visible ones.

Despite these advances, women still suffer from gender discrimination, not only in the workplace but also socially. Women, and married women in particular, are subjugated to men where property and the legal guardianship of children are concerned. Consequently, the lack of a divorce law disproportionately affects women, especially after married couples separate.

Given the influence of the Catholic Church on this burning sociopolitical issue, it seems unlikely that divorce will be legal for some time.

Political Economy

Since 1975, Chile has applied a free-market economic model, which has delivered sustained, high economic growth rates since the mid-1980s. Its economy is very open to international trade and finance, and its structure has changed substantially since the 1960s. Openness to trade significantly diversified the economy. Once dependent on copper for over 80 percent of export earnings, the emphasis on comparative advantage has intensified agro-exports in fruits, timber, fish, and wine. Other minerals, such as molybdenum, also enter the mix. Consequently, copper now supplies less than 50 percent of export earnings. The financial services, construction, and commercial sectors have also expanded significantly. Manufacturing, after a period of decline due to the dismantling of protection and subsidies, has been restructured, stabilized, and is even exporting products. In addition to these modifications, rapid economic growth has stimulated a tight labor market. This, together with low inflation, has contributed to rising wages. Privatized pension funds and health insurance, in addition to capital inflows from abroad, provide ample investment funds for the Chilean economy.

The governing center-Left coalition (now in its third term) is committed to the maintenance of macro-economic stability, with a special emphasis on inflation control. Due to extensive privatization, with the exception of copper mining (10 percent of export value goes to the military), the state has renounced public enterprise as a development tool. It mainly relies on fiscal and monetary policy as arm's-length policy instruments to direct the economy. Increased spending for public health and to combat poverty has decreased the number of poor people, especially those in the category of extreme poverty. These improvements have been touted as great successes for the social market economy, as Chileans (taking a page from the Germans) like to call their economic model.

Justifiably proud of their accomplishments, official Chile (the government and those close to it) and Conservatives alike see little need for change; in fact, many live in great fear of it. Nevertheless, there are lingering problems that perhaps should receive more attention than they do. Although growing and more diversified, the economy is extremely vulnerable to fluctuations of the world economy. For example, the Asian economic crisis hit the country hard. The commitment to inflation control tends to overvalue the currency, hurting exporters and suppressing policies that reactivate economies during downturns. Lack of state direction has also inhibited a transition from an agro-mineral extractive economy to one capable of adding value to the products and developing technology in those sectors. And, although poverty levels may be declining, the highly unequal distribution of the nation's wealth has not changed since the military government, when it became even more concentrated than before. Moreover, Chile's education policy and other barriers limit opportunity for social mobility for the majority who are not members of the relatively small middle class or the tightly knit circles of the rich, the well born, and the powerful.

Political History

Geography, natural resource endowments, and fierce armed resistance by the Araucanian people left their stamp on the social, political, and economic development of Chile. In colonial times, Chile was a far-flung outpost of the Spanish empire that began at the valley of the Acongagua river, considerably south of its contemporary northern border. Diego de Almagro was the first conquistador to arrive in 1536. Finding little mineral wealth he returned to Peru at the end of the year. A few years later Pedro de Valdivia set out to conquer Chile and founded numerous settlements, beginning with Santiago in 1541. Initially part of the viceroyalty of Peru, it later became an independent captaincy general.

In contrast to Peru, Bolivia, and Mexico the relative absence of gold and silver gave the social and economic structures of colonial Chile a decidedly agrarian foundation. Most creole wealth, power, and privilege flowed from control over large estates: the *encomienda* and the *hacienda*. This system engendered a highly rigid class structure with harsh labor exploitation. These characteristics are key to understanding the nation's contemporary history.

During colonial times, seignorial land owners of Spanish descent lorded over an Indian and *mestizo* workforce. Under highly arbitrary working conditions, workers owed unlimited days of labor and service to the *hacendado* or *encomendero* in return for a plot of land from which to eke out a living. These were the origins of the institution of the *inquilinaje*, which, in its essential features, persists today. *Inquilinos* were sharecroppers who owed unrestricted fealty to the landlord, had to be at his beck and call, and worked his land for a small wage. Ranching, and later wheat farming, were the principal land uses. Shipments of tallow, hides, and small amounts of gold and copper to Peru constituted Chile's major exports. This was true even into the eighteenth century, when European ports opened to Spanish American trade.

In addition to the *encomenderos* (conquistadors and their descendants who received land grants and rights to the labor of the natives on it), public officials, the high clergy, and merchants rounded out the colonial elite. Constant warfare against the Mapuches and a frontier mentality heavily influenced the politics of these elites and their relationship to subordinate social groups. The Indian wars contributed to authoritarian politics, harsh repression, and rigid social stratification. Successful Araucanian resistance eliminated the prospect of stable landholdings south of the Bío-Bío River. In colonial times, land scarcity concentrated holdings in a relatively small, closely knit agrarian elite who continually faced a scarcity of Indian labor due to the Mapuche's fierce love of freedom. This led to the enslavement of Araucanians defeated in battle or captured in slaving raids. These conditions caused even harsher exploitation of Indian labor than in other colonies. Native people who wished to escape the worst conditions took on *mestizo* culture in order to become tenant farmers or *inquilinos*.

This stratified and repressive social system was extremely rigid, a characteristic that still endures today. From colonial days until the present, elites have defended the exploitative underpinnings of their wealth and privilege vigorously. For example, in colonial times landowners undermined and resisted periodic attempts by the Spanish colonial governments to ban the worst features of labor oppression. In the 1960s and 1970s they fought against land reform. In the 1990s they vehemently opposed peasant mobilization and unionization.

Chile secured its independence from Spain in 1818. Between then and 1830 family, personal, and ideological conflicts contributed to a period of political instability marked by a succession of government experiments. The last one, based on the liberal constitution of 1828, challenged some of the privileges of the traditional patrician landowning and merchant oligarchy. Following a period of chaotic public finances, the Conservative oligarchy defeated the Liberals in the civil war of 1829–1930, paving the way for the autocratic republic (1831–1871).

Diego Portales was the behind-the-scenes architect of the conservative restoration, which became known as the Portilian state. He emphasized law and order and fiscal discipline. Rigged elections ensured the victory of the "right" presidential candidate; censorship and repression of the opposition was the rule. Conservatives then legitimated their rule by drafting the constitution of 1833, which established a centralized and authoritarian government. A successful war against the Peru-Bolivian confederation, the assassination ("martyrdom") of Portales in 1837, and, after a peaceful transfer of power, the state-crafting of second president Manuel Bulnes (1841–1851) consolidated the autocratic republic. Bulnes' support for legislative and judicial branch institution-building—especially congressional coresponsibility for the national budget—solidified the remarkable stability of the autocratic republic, a feature that set Chile apart from the rest of Latin America. Electoral fraud and other repressive measures, however, continued. A series of constitutional reforms eroded the autocratic republic between 1870 and 1875. Those reforms limited presidential terms from a total of ten years (two five-year terms) to one six-year term with no immediate reelection. Civil liberties and greater congressional power—control over government operations and the military—were also introduced.

President José Manuel Balmaceda challenged the considerable power of the legislature (which overrepresented the oligarchy) when legislators blocked his reform-minded economic and social policies. This challenge erupted in the civil war of 1891, ending fifty years of political stability and ushering in the parliamentary republic (1891–1924) after Balmaceda's defeat. The parliamentary republic simply reinterpreted the 1833 constitution to mean congressional dominance over the presidency. The political and fiscal disorder that reigned during this period sparked constitutional reform that culminated in the constitution of 1925, a document that reestablished presidential dominance over the legislature, introduced direct popular elections for both chambers of congress, and lasted until 1973.

Chile underwent substantial socioeconomic change between 1860 and the early twentieth century, principally with the emergence of the mining industry. This change began in earnest after Chile's second war against Peru and Bolivia: the War of the Pacific (1879–1884). Victorious, Chile annexed the Bolivian province of Atacama and the Peruvian provinces of Tarapacá and Arica. This act deprived Bolivia of its access to the Pacific ocean and gave Chile vast mineral wealth—first nitrate and then copper.

Mining brought three changes. First, it created a new, very wealthy social group, mineowners, who became part of the socioeconomic elite of Chile. Second, mining ushered in an enduring characteristic of Chile's economic system: control of its principal export product by foreign economic interests. After the War of the Pacific, the British gained control of nitrate mining. They allied themselves with Chilean mineowners in defense of economic liberalism (free trade and the night-watchman state, a state devoted almost exclusively to the maintenance of internal order and external defense) and fiercely opposed state efforts to tax and regulate them. In fact, such efforts had been one of the catalysts for the civil war of 1891. Third, mining necessitated miners, most of whom came from rural Chile. Miners were ruthlessly exploited and became increasing militant in their demands for fairness and social justice. Laboring under harsh working conditions in repressive company town systems, miners provided the foundation for the more activist and radical sectors of the working class. Chilean governments violently suppressed their attempts to organize in the first two decades of the twentieth century. These clashes cost hundreds, sometimes thousands, of lives.

Landowners, financiers, and merchants—the traditional socioeconomic elite of Chile—also supported the free-trade economic model. Although no longer exported in large quantities, agricultural products (with the exception of cattle) competed with imports. Landowners also had family links to the financial sector and a growing industrial sector dominated by import-competitive food and beverage industries. These elites supported labor repression. With the export boom in nitrates, rapidly expanding trade, and incipient industrialization came urbanization and a growing service and industrial labor force. It too attempted to organize and had to be kept under control.

Between 1891 and 1920, the parliamentary republic served Chile's agromineral, financial, and merchant oligarchy and British economic interests well. Free trade, a minimalist state almost entirely devoted to the maintenance of internal order, and brutal labor repression were the order of the day. But socioeconomic change pressured the stability of this political regime. Urbanization and the expansion of mining, industrial, and service wage labor under harsh working conditions generated spontaneous labor organizing. These early, illegal, and often militant unions could be repressed, but they could not be eliminated. Urbanization and Chile's nitrate-fueled economic boom also swelled the ranks of the middle classes. Since the political system excluded their interests as well, the middle class helped build reformist political parties that forged links to labor. Such was the case of the populist Democratic party and the Radical party. The Democratic party, founded in 1887, appealed to the lower middle class and labor. This populist political party supported labor reform, public education, tariff barriers to stimulate industrialization, more taxes on land and business, and direct election of the president. More middle-of-the road reformist parties, such as the anti-clerical Radical party (founded in 1863), also expanded. Both parties had congressional representation.

After World War I, the Democratic and Radical parties seriously challenged the parties of the oligarchy: the Conservative and Liberal parties. Chile fell into a deep economic depression during the worldwide economic slump that followed the end of the Great War. The precipitous fall of nitrate prices due to the invention of synthetic nitrates during the war aggravated matters. Labor and the middle class clamored for government action to ease the hardship caused by the Depression. Socialists, communists, and anarcho-syndicalists made significant in-roads in the labor movement. Their militancy threatened social and political stability.

The Conservative government remained inflexible in its defense of economic liberalism and violent labor repression. This stance encouraged another enduring feature of Chilean politics: electoral coalitions. A minority sector of the Liberal party allied with the Radical and Democratic parties to form the Liberal Alliance. This was Chile's first populist electoral coalition, one that brought together the middle class, significant sectors of labor, and a breakaway segment of the upper class. Their leading light, young firebrand Arturo Alessandri of the Liberal party, became president in 1920 on a platform of educational, labor, and economic reform. The Liberal Alliance defeated the National Union, a coalition formed by the Conservative party and most of the Liberal party.

Although his government also violently repressed the more militant factions of labor, it did propose paternalistic labor code and social welfare reforms. However, oligarchs used the congress, especially their control of the powerful senate, to block his efforts. Conservative obstructionism and the ensuing economic disorder, high inflation, and social unrest caused Alessandri to resign his presidency in 1924.

The ungovernability of Chile prompted the demise of the parliamentary republic and ushered in the return of presidential dominance with the constitution of 1925. Political stability, however, eluded Chile until 1932. Between 1924 and 1925 a military junta established paternalistic labor code reforms that gave government control over unions and introduced social welfare modeled after the German program established by Otto von Bismarck in the 1880s. However, disgruntled military officers overthrew the junta in early 1925. This second military government supported organized labor even more, frequently intervening on its behalf in labor disputes. To further court urban labor, the junta asked Alessandri to take over the presidency in March

1925. Unfortunately, Alessandri did not share the junta's pro-labor position. His anti-labor stance and continued economic hard times brought him into conflict with the military, and he resigned the presidency in October 1925.

Colonel Carlos Ibáñez del Campo emerged from the ensuing political instability as the strong-man of Chile. After his formal election to the presidency in 1927, he established a dictatorship that lasted until 1931. Ibáñez jailed opponents, especially labor leaders, and suspended civil liberties. However, he also favored state activism in the economy. Borrowing heavily from abroad, the government stimulated railroad construction, road-building, and the erection of power utilities. The Great Depression that began with the stock market crash in 1929 put an end to that economic program as foreign loans dried up and the price of nitrate and other commodities fell precipitously. A wave of protest that united professional members of the middle class and labor forced Ibáñez to resign in 1931.

Political instability engulfed Chile once again. A dizzying array of governments came and went over the next year, including the 100-day "Socialist Republic" led by Marmaduque Grove and Carlos Dávila, who alternated in power with support from military factions. Although brief, this regime established the newly formed Socialist party as a force to be reckoned with. Economic chaos and a lack of consensus among civilian and military leaders brought the Socialist Republic (which had seen a succession of six governments) down. The period ended with a military coup designed to get the armed forces out of government, the high command being disillusioned with politics. At the head of a provisional government, General Bartolomé Blanche scheduled elections to return Chile to full political democracy. Arturo Alessandri won those elections and began his second presidency in late 1932. His administration marked the beginning of forty years of uninterrupted democratic rule, a period that ended with the violent overthrow of Salvador Allende in 1973.

Conservatives, Reformers, and Revolutionaries

The political system that emerged from the ruins of the parliamentary republic had a number of well-defined features. It was a highly presidentialist and centralized system; the presidency initiated most of the significant legislation, and all important decisions for the country—including education—were made in the capital, Santiago. The congress mainly negotiated bills with the presidency, fine-tuning them to the interests of the political parties and their constituencies. However, the congress had the power to kill bills. When no candidate won a clear majority in presidential elections, the congress nominated the president from the top two vote-getters. This occurred with some frequency and a tradition formed in which the congress ratified the candidate with the most votes.

Chile had long had a multiparty instead of a two-party political system. During this period, however, it was a solidly tripolar system when measured on an ideological spectrum from Left to Right. On the Right were the

Conservative and Liberal parties. The Radical party and later the Christian Democrats occupied the Center; the Socialist and Communist parties dominated the Left. This party system reflected the cleavages of Chile's rapidly changing socioeconomic system. Urbanization and the expansion of mining had generated middle-class and labor groups that demanded inclusion in the policy process. They chafed at the rigid socioeconomic system that reserved so much privilege and opportunity for only the elite. In this context, the Right mostly represented the interests of socioeconomic elites (the upper and upper-middle classes), although social Conservatives of the middle and even working classes, usually staunch Catholics, also gravitated toward the Right. For the most part, the middle and lower-middle classes supported Centrist parties, although anticlerical forces from the upper class also swelled the ranks of the Radical party, and some sectors of organized labor later backed the Christian Democrats. Usually, however, urban labor and much of the lower middle class sustained the Socialist and the Communist parties. Meanwhile, because of the social institution of the *inquilinaje*, rural labor remained a captive voting block for Conservatives.

Each pole of this party system advocated different policies to promote economic development and social peace. The Right supported maintaining a good business climate, one that favored investment opportunities over redistribution of some of the national wealth to less advantaged social groups. By and large, Conservatives also opposed labor rights. The Center was more reformist. Centrists proposed greater state involvement in the economy to promote industrialization through public ownership, planning, and regulation, and they sought land reform to modernize agriculture. Centrists also championed social reforms in education, health, and housing and pledged support for organized labor. The Left advanced the same causes; the difference was in their ideological and programmatic emphasis. Influenced by Marxism, Leftists unabashedly pronounced that private property—its concentration in the hands of a few—was the root of social and economic inequality in Chile. Therefore, state involvement in the economy should be greater than that advocated by more middle class–oriented Centrist parties, and more radical land reform was required. Revolutionaries called for the abolition of most or all private businesses. Leftists believed in strong support for organized labor (higher wages, benefits, and rights) and generous fiscal expenditures for social reforms.

One of the keys to political stability in a polarized, multiparty political system in which each pole musters roughly a third of the votes lay in the flexibility of the Centrist parties. Since they frequently won the highest plurality, they had to be willing to enter into governing coalitions with either the moderate Right or Left, depending on circumstance. This ensured policy moderation and majorities in the congress with which to pass legislation. Knowing that they might become part of governing coalitions also kept the Right and Left poles of the system from radicalizing and, thus, from destabilizing the system. However, because presidents could only win by pluralities, when parties of the Right and Left won, they too had to be flexible and enter into governing coalitions with centrist parties.

Arturo Alessandri's second administration (1932–1938) followed the logic of this political system. He took office determined to restore political order, to generate economic recovery from the Great Depression, and to implement mild labor reforms based on the Labor Code passed during his first administration. No longer the firebrand reformer of the early 1920s, Alessandri allied with the forces of the Right, the socioeconomic elites in particular, to establish a governing coalition. Minister of Finance Gustavo Ross, a prominent financier, was the most visible symbol of the alliance. Austere fiscal and monetary policies, recovery of copper and nitrate prices in world markets, mild support for commerce and industry, and generous tax concessions to builders revived the economy and cut unemployment to virtually nothing.

Alessandri's administration also undertook modest social programs. He vigorously implemented the Labor Code of 1925 to channel class conflict and supported the formation and recognition of legal unions in a framework that carefully controlled them, especially their strike activity. However, in an enduring implicit pact with socioeconomic elites, Alessandri did not support unionization of agricultural workers and allowed landowners to resist all attempts to do so by the workers themselves. In a further break from orthodoxy, Alessandri controlled prices for food in response to the growing strength of the Socialist and Communist parties. In return, he compensated landowners with subsidies for their lost income. Alessandri's government, however, did not address the nagging questions of economic nationalism and income distribution. International companies controlled most of Chile's mineral export sectors (copper and nitrates), as well as much of the financial and commercial sectors. The concentration of wealth limited opportunities for the middle class and virtually eliminated them for the lower class.

The Radical party saw these circumstances as impediments to industrialization, the key to economic modernization. Therefore, Alessandri's rightward shift induced the Radical party to seek support from the Left. This was the birth of the Popular Front, an electoral and governing coalition dominated by the Centrist Radical party that included the Socialist and Communist parties, among others. This electoral strategy ushered in three Radical party administrations between 1938 and 1952 that progressively drifted to the Right.

Pedro Aguirre Cerda's Popular Front government (1938–1941) broke with economic orthodoxy and laid the foundation for the nation's economic and social policy for the next twenty-five years. His administration's economic policy focused on the industrialization of Chile. To achieve that goal, it initiated an industrial policy that increased the role of the state in the economy significantly. First, it created a state development corporation, the Corporación de Fomento (Development Corporation, CORFO), which targeted economic sectors for development. In sectors that required large investments, such as utilities, basic industry, and transportation, the state created public enterprises or joint ventures with the private sector. Second, in other sectors, such as light manufacturing, the state (through CORFO, the central bank, and the state bank) offered subsidies such as preferential credit, interest rates, and foreign exchange rates. Third, the government also erected high trade barriers to protect domestic industry from import competition. Thus, the Popular Front government established the basis for a mixed economy, rather than a state-dominated socialist one, in which the state gave incentives for the development of private industry. Successive governments to 1970 built on this model.

The Popular Front was a broad coalition of middle-class reformist and labor parties. As such, it espoused an ideological commitment to redistributive policies and the strengthening of organized labor. In practice, however, only the middle class (the constituency of the Radical party) benefited from redistributionist policies such as increased income, health, education, and housing. Social policy for workers (the constituency of the Socialist and Communist parties) largely flowed from the government's nationalistic economic policy. The emphasis was on full employment with job creation in the state sector, manufacturing, construction, and the urban service sector. Redistribution for labor was not addressed until the middle of the 1960s. Although labor had to postpone immediate rewards for future benefits during the Popular Front, it did not come away empty-handed. It advanced institutionally. The number of legal unions almost tripled and consolidated a confederation dominated by the Socialist party. Meanwhile, the Socialist party became an electoral rather than a revolutionary party and expanded rapidly. The Socialist party also gave CORFO its developmentalist cast.

Import substitution industrialization discriminated against agriculture. Landowners also feared the economic, social, and political consequences of unionization in the countryside. To appease this powerful conservative sector of Chile's socioeconomic elite, the Popular Front adopted a dual strategy. Tax breaks and low import duties on imported agricultural machinery compensated for the Popular Front's low food price policy for urban workers. The Radical party also continued, and enforced, the hands-off policy on unionization for rural labor begun under Alessandri. This protected landowner profits, the social institution of the *inquilinaje*, and captive votes.

To summarize, the Popular Front established the foundations of Chile's political economy for the next twenty-five years. It cemented an enduring, albeit implicit, multiclass coalition of industrialists, middle classes, and urban labor that supported import substitution industrialization with redistribution and the promotion of labor rights. Reformist centrist and left political parties mediated that coalition and established policies that appeased landowners. However, redistributive measures were a constant source of tension. Making good on the promise of greater social justice in a country with high levels of social inequality proved to be extraordinarily difficult. Successive administrations struggled with the problem.

After Aguirre Cerda's death in office in 1941, successive Radical party–led administrations drifted to the Right. Under pressure from the United States and the right wing of the Radical party, the government of Gabriel González Videla (1946–1952) outlawed the Communist party, despite the fact that he had accepted their electoral support to win the presidency. He also purged communists from his cabinet. Feeling betrayed, the Left vented its anger against the administration with labor unrest and by opposing the government in the Congress. From then on, socialists and communists put their differences aside and ran their own presidential candidates.

A disenchanted electorate, augmented by the female vote, put an end to fourteen years of Radical party–led Popular Front coalition tactics with the election of independent Carlos Ibáñez del Campo to a second presidency. His center-Right presidency marked the tone of political conflicts for the next twenty years. First, the center-Right feared the electoral resurgence of an independent Left. Second, in three-way presidential elections with candidates from the Right, Center, and Left, minority governments in which presidents won by a plurality were the rule (Ibáñez del Campo claimed 47 percent of the vote). Third, inflation and a sluggish economy were the principal economic issues, generating fierce political maneuvering over fiscal, monetary, foreign exchange, and trade policy. Balance of payment deficits in the national accounts fueled inflation. Fighting inflation required stabilization policies—tight fiscal and monetary policies (reducing government expenditures and increasing interest rates). It also meant borrowing from the International Monetary Fund (IMF). The IMF's loan conditions and oversight of the national economy to ensure compliance fueled nationalist economic sentiment, especially against the United States, due to its significant influence over IMF policy.

Ibáñez del Campo's government floundered over stabilization policy because tight fiscal policy meant cutting government subsidies for public utilities and transportation. This increased prices for consumers and hit low-income groups particularly hard, giving the Left ample political ammunition. The perception of center-Right governments selling out the nation to the interests of the United States further bolstered the center-Left.

The next presidential election was a five-way race won by Jorge Alessandri (son of Arturo Alessandri), who ran as an independent backed by the Conservative and Liberal parties. However, Alessandri won with less than one-third of the ballots cast (31.6 percent), an alliance of the Socialist and Communist parties headed by Salvador Allende came in a close second (28.9 percent), and a new centrist political force, the Christian Democratic party under Eduardo Frei Montalva, garnered 20.7 percent. The Radical party candidate and an eccentric priest accounted for the rest.

Alessandri's administration (1958–1964) ushered in a period in which successive minority governments of the Right, Center, and Left each attempted to impose their own solutions to Chile's socioeconomic problems. For programmatic and electoral reasons, governing parties refused coalitions with a sector of the opposition, either to the Right or the Left. One by one, they also broke with the understandings that held together the broad social base that supported Chilean democracy. These conditions fueled a leftward drift, radicalization, and polarization of Chilean politics.

Although the reformist political parties that helped bring Alessandri to power did not control the Congress, he refused to invite representatives of the center-Right into his cabinet. Instead, he used the power of the presidency to implement a free-market economic model of development as much as possible. He imposed economic stabilization plans (budget-cutting), instituted a single fixed exchange rate, reduced the level of protection for domestic industries to boost efficiency, encouraged foreign direct investment, and curbed labor rights. He also began a very modest agrarian reform program and failed to get U.S. copper companies to invest more in processing the ore in Chile to boost the value of exports. Copper by then accounted for about 80 percent of hard currency earnings. Alessandri's policies did little to solve Chile's socioeconomic problems, but they did alienate the center-Left and the Left because they perceived those policies to be an onslaught against hard-earned gains.

Certain they could not win the presidency in 1964, and fearful of the Left's chances in a serious three-way race, the Conservative and Liberal parties decided not to present a candidate. This electoral strategy boosted the center-Left, now dominated by the Christian Democratic party under Eduardo Frei, which won handily with 56 percent of the vote. Salvador Allende, again the standard-bearer of the Communist-Socialist alliance, garnered 39 percent. The candidate of the Radical party finished a poor third.

The Christian Democrats came into office with a reformist socioeconomic program. The "Revolution in Liberty" addressed the social problems of the urban poor by stressing housing, education, and neighborhood self-help organizations. Land reform would aid the rural poor and, it was hoped, boost agricultural productivity. A controlled opening of the economy to imports, partial nationalization with compensation of U.S.-dominated copper mines, and promotion of export diversification into fishing and timber were intended to invigorate the Chilean economy.

The Frei administration began to implement much of this platform during its first three years. But the manner in which it proceeded only served to deepen the nation's ideological polarization. Although the Right had helped elect the new government, and although they lacked a majority in congress, the Christian Democrats decided to rule alone. Neither Conservative nor Liberal party members were invited to serve in the cabinet. This hampered agrarian reform and killed trade liberalization policies. Business sectors also opposed increased regulation of their activities. In short, property owners suspected that the administration's policies were simply disguised socialism. Meanwhile, the left feared that the Christian Democrats were trying to displace them by organizing new social groups that they considered to be their natural constituencies: shantytown dwellers and the rural poor. Thus, the Communist, and especially the Socialist party began to outbid the Christian Democrats by espousing more radical programs. This stepped up revolutionary rhetoric.

Political opposition and renewed inflation hampered the implementation of the Revolution in Liberty for the last half of the Frei administration. Polarization deepened as the Conservative and Liberal parties united in the National party in 1966. This was a response to the leftward drift in the center of gravity of the Chilean party system. The more radical wing of the

Christian Democratic party gained ascendancy, and revolutionary splinter groups of the Communist and Socialist parties gathered visibility.

Confident that center-Right Christian Democratic voters would abandon the party's center-Left candidate Radomiro Tomic—whose platform was very similar to that of the traditional Left—the National party ran Jorge Alessandri for the presidency in 1970. He offered honesty, austerity, and proven ability to govern. The Left, now in a coalition of parties dominated by socialists and communists called Unidad Popular (Popular Unity) offered their perennial candidate Salvador Allende. Unidad Popular also included the Radical party, the firebrand Revolutionary Movement of the Left (Movimiento Revolucionario de Izquierda), and a breakaway faction of the Christian Democrats. Their platform promised a democratic, peaceful road to socialism. It stressed nationalization, income redistribution, a reform of labor relations in favor of workers, creation of a unicameral congress, and reform of the education and judiciary system. Tomic was expected to run a distant third or to withdraw his candidacy altogether. To the shock of the overconfident Right and the surprise of the Left, Unidad Popular won the presidential election, albeit with a plurality of the slimmest margin 36.3 percent to Alessandri's 34.9 percent. The event was one of the defining moments of Chile's contemporary political history. Allende's government and defeat are still key reference points for contending political forces.

Maneuvers to block Allende's ascension to office began immediately. A U.S.-backed plan to induce a coup d'etat by kidnapping the commander-in-chief of the armed forces, René Schneider, failed when the general was killed in the bungled attempt. Conservatives tried to get the Christian Democratic party to join with them in ratifying runner-up Jorge Alessandri as president, a legal move within the rules set by the constitution of 1925. Christian Democrats declined the invitation. Instead, they extracted acquiescence to a reduction in presidential powers from Unidad Popular. With this, Christian Democrats believed they could moderate the new government's policy proposals.

Unidad Popular took office in early 1971 amid great expectations by both supporters and detractors. Initial policies for the Chilean path to socialism followed three tracks. One track stressed demand-stimulus measures to increase the purchasing power of wage labor, thereby boosting the sales of manufactured goods and services to the benefit of industrialists and merchants. The idea was to ally the fears of upper and middle classes by fueling economic growth that all could benefit from while simultaneously wooing labor votes away from centrist parties, especially the Christian Democrats. The strategy worked in 1971 as Chile experienced strong wage and GDP growth. The second component involved nationalization of industry. Unidad Popular sought to build up the state sector, encourage joint ventures between the public and private sectors, and maintain a substantial private sector. Initial efforts concentrated on foreign concerns in mining, manufacturing, and services. These led to strong confrontations with U.S.-owned Anaconda and Kennecott mining and the International Telegraph and Telephone company. But Chilean property owners, with the exception of the small, underdeveloped financial sector, were not affected and, for the most part, raised no alarm. Accelerating agrarian reform and the organization of the peasantry was the third major policy area. This immediately created friction between the landed oligarchy and Unidad Popular, although for most of 1971 these tensions remained isolated.

Conflict, however, sharpened progressively from mid-1971 on, as Unidad Popular directed nationalization policy more and more toward large-scale domestic companies. In part, Unidad Popular wanted to break the economic power of the Chilean business sectors that opposed their government, believing that would break their political power as well. Nationalization of major textile firms and forestry industries in May and June 1971 and the attempted nationalization of a leading pulp and paper firm that also published the major conservative newspaper in Chile, *El Mercurio*, galvanized upper-class opposition to Allende's government.

Meanwhile, an economic crisis fueled by deficit spending and falling investment began to engulf Chile. This began to turn the middle class and medium and small business against Unidad Popular. Mounting labor strife and the creation of an alternative commercial distribution system for basic consumer goods to counter mounting scarcity, the Juntas de Abastecimiento Popular, further stiffened opposition by those groups.

In December 1971, confrontation over all of these pressing issues culminated in the formation of a broad coalition of the middle class, medium- and small-scale businesspeople, and large-scale business groups against Unidad Popular: the Private Sector National Front. To break the back of the bourgeoisie, Allende's government responded with a nationalization policy targeted against the nation's most important consumer durables, food processing, pulp and paper, beverages, construction, and fishing companies. Meanwhile, the Christian Democratic party's efforts to negotiate nationalization policy with Unidad Popular finally collapsed in mid-1972.

Class conflict mounted quickly afterward. Business staged a massive lockout, the "Bosses' Strike" that began in August 1972. Labor countered by breaking into factories and running down inventory to keep production going. A monthlong trucker's strike—clandestinely financed by the U.S. Central Intelligence Agency—broke out in October in tandem with more massive lock-outs. Labor answered by organizing alternative transportation systems. After this, Conservative political parties and the Christian Democratic party united in an electoral alliance, the Democratic Confederation, to sweep the March 1973 congressional elections. The plan, to gain a two-thirds majority in congress to impeach Allende, failed as Unidad Popular increased its popular vote from 36 percent to 44 percent. Electoral support for opposition parties dropped from 64 percent during the 1970 presidential election to 54 percent.

These electoral results and the violent social conflict that engulfed Chile afterward, set the stage for the military's intervention. It should be added that from the very beginning the U.S. government did everything in its power to help set that stage. The United States contributed to economic destabilization—making the economy scream—by denying loans to Chile from the U.S. Agency for International Development, the Export-Import Bank, the Inter-American Development Bank, and the World Bank. Its intelligence services helped organize Chilean Rightists and financed the survival of crucial conservative news media (*El Mercurio*) as well as key events, such as the trucker's strike. Yet despite high levels of confrontation, the ferocity of the military's coup against Allende on September 11, 1973, took everyone by surprise. It was a well-orchestrated combat operation against a revolution that was mostly rhetoric with respect to its capacity for armed resistance. In the terror that followed, thousands lost their lives, thousands more were arrested and tortured, and tens of thousands went into forced or voluntary exile. Chile's largest sports venue, the National Stadium, became a symbol of that terror. That was where famed folk singer Víctor Jara was brutally murdered along with U.S. citizen Charles Horman. General Sergio Arellano Stark's whirlwind helicopter tour through several northern cities— the "Caravan of Death"—became another icon of terror. His committee left a wake of dead to place both moderates in the military and the Chilean people on notice that this military government was committed to zealous repression.

Military Government

The Popular Front, the Christian Democratic government, and Popular Unity were reformist political moments in a secular trend that, however modestly at times, progressively chipped away at the privileges of the well-born and powerful and increased the well-being of middle and laboring classes. Land reform, economic nationalism, and labor rights were at the center of the struggle. That trend came to a head in the sharp political polarization and escalating class conflict of Allende's government. The military government that replaced democracy in September 1973 reversed the trend. It restored the privileges and prerogatives of the propertied classes, albeit not those of the traditional upper-class groups.

The Chilean armed forces had intervened in politics to resolve a deep societal crisis, which they attributed to the failings of a developmental model that fed class conflict. Therefore, during its first year of rule the military junta searched for a development model altogether different from Chile's past. The junta found it in neoconservative free-market economics. This economic ideology offered a vision of the economy, society, and the state capable of eradicating state-led development and Marxism. The military had largely achieved its goal when it handed the reins of power over to civilians in 1990. Since the second half of the 1980s, Chile has enjoyed a healthy, growing market economy and political stability in a political system in which traditional Leftists have little place.

The military inherited a chaotic economy. Extravagant fiscal deficits fed hyperinflation, expropriation had left much of industry and commerce paralyzed, and domestic and foreign investment was nonexistent. The U.S.-trained neoconservative economists that advised the junta argued that sound, sustained economic growth depended on monetary stability, reestablishing a free-market economy in which the private sector was the engine of growth, and building an economy open to international competition and foreign investment. To wring inflation and other price distortions out of the economy, they implemented an orthodox economic stabilization program. Between 1975 and 1978 price controls were lifted, interest rates were increased, and fiscal spending was slashed. Constructing a free-market economy, however, required additional measures. The junta's economic team privatized a considerable portion of Chile's mixed economy (especially the industrial and financial sectors but not the nationalized mining sector) and deregulated the financial system. Thoroughgoing trade reform, especially tariff barrier reduction, restructured Chile's economy from industries producing for domestic markets toward sectors with a comparative advantage: mining, fishing, fruits, and timber. The commercial sector (import-export business) and construction sectors also boomed. Generous conditions for foreign investors lured external capital back into the country.

How did the military government accomplish the economic transformation of Chile? First, the military government insulated the neoconservative economic team from pressure groups. The absence of democratic institutions and the labor-repressive character of the regime meant that wage-earners and the salaried middle classes had no defense. The closed nature of the authoritarian regime meant that Chilean industrialists who suffered under international competition lacked access to policy makers. Second, there were no differences of opinion over what to do among the cohesive, socially well-connected members of the neoconservative economic team that became the chief advisers to the government, who were known as the "Chicago Boys" because most of them had received graduate degrees from the economics department of the University of Chicago, where they studied with Milton Friedman, a Nobel prize–winning monetarist. Third, the core of the Chicago Boys was also connected to Chilean businessmen who supported their policies. They saw a chance to build economic empires.

The military government also restructured Chilean politics. The junta established a highly centralized closed authoritarian political system. It closed congress indefinitely, banned all political parties, and purged state institutions and universities. Socialists, communists, and other far-left groups were persecuted mercilessly and many died or suffered torture, imprisonment, and exile at the hands of the consolidated intelligence services of the armed forces and the national police force. The Christian Democratic party at first sought to collaborate with the military and wanted to quickly restore democracy, but they were rebuffed. Instead, General Augusto Pinochet, commander-in-chief of the army, centralized power in his person and became president of the nation. He accomplished his goal of establishing one-man rule after ousting air force General Leigh, his chief opponent, from the junta and replacing him with the more pliant General Matthei.

Thus, Pinochet maintained order with iron-fisted rule and brooked no opposition to the economic policies of the Chicago Boys. After very difficult
economic times from the end of 1973, the economy rebounded in 1979, and
the private sector, which had always backed his labor-repressive policies,
enthusiastically supported his economic policies. Pinochet, and his civilian
supporters, however, also wanted to legitimate authoritarian rule. They accomplished this goal by writing a new constitution that was submitted to a
plebiscite in 1980. The constitution was approved by a wide margin under
very questionable electoral conditions. The constitution of 1980 was designed
to guide Chile through a transition from military rule to a protected democracy. The new constitution awarded the military guardianship over the
political system and safeguarded the privileges of property by making it virtually impossible to reform the free-market economic system. This constitution, with a few superficial amendments, still rules Chile today.

How did the constitution of 1980 accomplish these goals? The transition
itself began in 1988 with a plebiscite to decide whether General Pinochet
would continue as president or not. If the plebiscite ratified him for another
eight-year period (to 1997), elections for Congress—the legislative branch of
government—would be held in 1989. If the plebiscite rejected Pinochet, then
open elections for the presidency and for Congress would be held in 1989.
Naturally, Pinochet and his supporters fully expected to win. Moreover,
thinking beyond Pinochet's incumbency, once in the new political system,
presidencies would be advised by a national security council in which the
military had the dominant representation. The legislature and the electoral
system were designed to strengthen Conservative interests, and extraordinary majorities were required to amend the constitution, making the document virtually unamendable, given the overrepresentation of Conservatives
in the legislature.

From the vantage point of 1980, 1997 seemed a long time in the future.
Repression, economic good times, the weight of official propaganda in the
controlled press, and defeat in the 1980 plebiscite had left the banned political parties disheartened and in disarray. They resigned themselves to suffering Pinochet for another seventeen years, certain in the knowledge that
they would not be able to mount effective opposition from the legislature
after 1989. In the meantime, Pinochet's economists privatized the pension
system, health care insurance, and the educational system. They also decentralized political administration by giving regions and municipalities
more authority over local issues.

The economic crisis that beset Chile, and the rest of Latin America, in
1982–1983 changed the gloomy political prospects of the opposition. Chile's
economy—like that of Argentina, Brazil, and Mexico—had boomed at the
cost of a mountain of debt, much of it owed to foreign creditors. When international financial centers sharply raised interest rates to fight inflation
and to shore up the flagging U.S. dollar, Chile's economy went into a tail-
spin. Between 1982 and 1983 the GDP plunged by 15 percent. The financial system collapsed as firms and banks became insolvent and went bank-

rupt because they could no longer turn over their debt at cheap interest rates. Unemployment soared to 33 percent. The middle classes lost their savings.

This economic crisis shook Pinochet's regime to the core. His support for the Chicago Boys and their unflagging adherence to orthodox deflationary policies in a depressed economy aroused a powerful opposition movement. As discontent mounted, the union movement began to mobilize protests. The first mass mobilization, held in May 1983, was successful beyond the wildest dreams of its organizers. Opposition political parties quickly took over the protest movement, and mass demonstrations against Pinochet's rule were held on an almost monthly basis until 1986. Two blocs quickly vied for control of this movement: the Christian Democratic–led Democratic Alliance and the Communist-led Popular Democratic Movement.

The military government, however, managed to defuse the political opposition. It played for time by engaging the Democratic Alliance in negotiations for a transition from authoritarian rule. The Democratic Alliance wanted to substantially amend the 1980 constitution to remove the tutelary powers of the military and overrepresentation of conservatives. Pinochet temporized, fighting for time to blunt the political impact of mass mobilization. He accomplished this by retaining the loyalty of the armed forces, the private sector, and much of the middle class. He divided the opposition by insisting that, as a condition for negotiation, the Democratic Alliance remain steadfast in its rejection of the Popular Democratic Movement. The restoration of vigorous economic growth as of 1984 further dulled the power of the opposition. After a failed attempt on Pinochet's life in 1986, mass mobilization ended. As the opposition movement spent its force, it missed an opportunity to change the conditions of the transition and the political system that was to replace military rule. Thus, the transition followed the timetable and institutional structure set by the junta.

Despite these setbacks, the opposition to Pinochet did not come away completely empty-handed. It struggled successfully for free and fair elections for the 1988 plebiscite, a significant accomplishment as it turned out. Moreover, the Democratic Alliance emerged as the more important of the two opposition movements, and its member parties learned how to work together more efficiently. This political force, now calling itself the Coalition of Parties for the No (the "no" vote was a ballot against Pinochet), soundly defeated him in the plebiscite (54.7 to 43 percent). The military, agreeing to abide by the terms of the 1980 constitution, accepted defeat and set presidential and congressional elections for December 1989.

The resurrection of political parties in the mid-1980s also extended to the center-Right, which, being in full agreement with the military government, had disbanded their political organizations. The more traditional conservatives of the old National party formed National Renovation, while libertarians (free-marketeers connected to the military government) established the Independent Democratic Union. Military hard-liners formed the fleeting National Vanguard (Avanzada Nacional).

These conservative political parties had little difficulty forming a solid electoral front for the plebiscite. However, presidential and congressional elections have been a different story. For the 1989 presidential election, National Renovation and the Independent Democratic Union supported the candidacy of Hernán Büchi, the architect of Chile's strong economic recovery based on more flexible management of free-market economics. But a populist banker-businessman, Francisco Javier Errázuriz, also ran on the Right. Meanwhile, the seventeen-party center-Left opposition bloc, now calling itself the Coalition for Democracy (Concertación de Partidos por la Democracia) backed the candidacy of Patricio Aylwin, a conservative Christian Democrat who as president of the senate in 1973 had staunchly opposed Allende.

The presidential election results closely mirrored those of the plebiscite. Aylwin won with 55.2 percent of the vote. Conservatives garnered 44.8 percent. But those votes were split between Büchi (29.4 percent) and Errázuriz (15.4 percent). The far Left, by contrast, fared poorly. For example, the Communist party did not gain a single seat in the new congress. Aylwin and the Concertación took office in March 1990.

Power and Politics

During the 1990s, redemocratized Chile became a paradox. On the positive side, it has enjoyed remarkable economic and political stability, making Chile the envy of many other Latin American nations. Between 1986 and 2000, the free-market economy installed by the military government produced rapid, sustained economic growth of approximately six percent per year with low inflation, virtually balanced budgets, and an investment rate of about 25 percent of GDP. The nation reduced its foreign debt, attracted significant quantities of foreign capital, and exported capital to neighboring countries. Moreover, in 2000, Chile overcame the recession of the late 1990s that had been induced by an Asian financial crisis. Chile's political system has also enjoyed a remarkable degree of political stability in a hemisphere plagued by instability. Historically, Chile's basic state institutions—the executive, the legislature, the courts—have functioned reasonably well and, in comparison to other Latin American countries, have been relatively free of corruption. Redemocratized Chile's smaller, leaner state continued that tradition. Moreover, after 1990 Chile has enjoyed regular, fair, and free elections that truly decide "who governs" among well-established, institutionalized, programmatic political parties. Furthermore, the country became free of constant, debilitating political disorder, with few restrictions on freedom of expression and association.

Yet Chile's prosperity and political stability came at a high price. Socioeconomically, Chile was a more unequal country by the year 2000 than it was before 1970; employees were more at the mercy of their employers and the labor market than before the military government; and environmental degradation and natural resource depletion had increased exponentially. Moreover, the political system fell considerably short of being fully democratic. It was a "protected" democracy full of undemocratic institutions, authoritarian enclaves, and reserve domains of power for the military meant to constrain the "sovereign" will of the people. These institutions conferred extraordinary powers on conservative political forces to defend the orthodox free-market socio-economic model implanted by the military government, along with all of its inequalities. The social democratic political forces that have governed Chile since 1990 (and will govern until at least 2006) found legislating social, economic, and political reform a tough uphill battle. They discovered that it was virtually impossible to repeal the undemocratic institutions that consistently discriminated in favor of the economic and social interests of a conservative minority.

Administratively, the decentralization program of the military government divided Chile's territory into twelve numbered regions (*regiones* I to XII) and the Santiago metropolitan area. Each region is headed by an intendant (*intendente*) appointed by the president. Regions were divided into the traditional 51 provinces, each headed by a governor also appointed by the president. In November 1991 the Congress approved constitutional changes to local government whereby appointed mayors would be directly elected.

The 1980 constitution established a political system in which executive power is vested in the president, who, according to constitutional reform measures of February 1994, serves a six year term. Successive reelection is not allowed. Presidents are directly elected by absolute majority; in the absence of a clear-cut majority, the two top vote-getters compete in a run-off election (or second round) vote. The president of the republic is aided by a cabinet of his or her choosing composed of 20 ministers and the president of the National Energy Commission and the comptroller-general of the republic. The executive branch is also assisted by a National Security Council that includes the president of the republic, the presidents of the supreme court and the senate, and the heads of the armed forces (army, navy, air force) and the national militarized police (Carabineros). The presidency is the strongest branch of the political system. It initiates most bills, and the presidency's full weight behind a bill can overcome opposition through compromise. Moreover, the presidency has a strong role in the maintenance of internal order.

The legislative branch consists of a bicameral Congress located in the port city of Valparaíso (about an hour and a half by road from Santiago). It is not as powerful an institution as it had been before 1973: it is located in a city other than the capital, it meets fewer days than it did before, and its oversight capacity and the competence of its committees are diminished. The 47-seat Senate has 38 elected members plus nine designated senators; all serve for eight year terms with half of the Senate up for reelection every four years. Four of the designated senatorial positions are reserved for ex-heads of the armed forces and Carabineros who have held the post for at least two years.

These are selected by the National Security Council. The Supreme Court names two from the ranks of former members of the court and one who has served as comptroller general of the republic. The President of the Republic designates two senators, one who has been a university president (*rector*) and the other, a government minister. In addition to these 47 members, former presidents of the republic are automatically senators for life. The lower house of the Congress, the Chamber of Deputies, has 120 members drawn from sixty two-member electoral districts and serve four-year terms.

The judicial branch of government consists of a 21-member Supreme Court, sixteen appellate courts, major claims courts, and local courts. Supreme Court justices are appointed by the president of the republic from a slate of five names proposed by the court itself. Each appellate court has jurisdiction over one or more provinces, and most have three members. However, the largest have thirteen members and Santiago's appellate court has twenty-five. The Supreme Court exercises its duties in separate chambers consisting of at least five judges each. These chambers are presided over by the most senior member or the president of the court. The judicial system also includes special courts, such as juvenile courts, labor courts, and military courts in time of peace.

Chile's presidential political system is based on the 1980 constitution, which kept Chile from achieving a transition to full political democracy. The constitution of 1980 established a protected democracy in which a number of antidemocratic institutions allow conservative political forces to limit the power of the presidency and congressional majorities should they fall into the hands of center-left political coalitions. Conversely, center-Right presidencies would enjoy assured support for most policy initiatives. The point was to protect from any meaningful reform of the socio-economic order based on private property rights and free markets established by the military government.

How is this protected democracy structured? To begin with, a number of features of the 1980 constitution grant the armed forces tutelary power over civilian political forces, especially center-left ones. The armed forces themselves retain significant autonomy from civilian control. Their budgets cannot fall below the levels they were in 1989 (the last year of the military government), and to avoid civilian claims of financial exigency in meeting those targets they are guaranteed ten percent of export revenues from copper. Military doctrine and promotion of general officers are free of civilian oversight. The president of the republic may nominate the commander-in-chief of the armed forces only from a list of five names submitted by the military, and can only remove him before the four year term is up under the most extraordinary of circumstances. Moreover, internal security laws give military courts expanded jurisdiction over judicial issues that are usually the purview of civilian courts. This has hampered the investigation of human rights abuses committed during the military government. The military's dominance of the National Security Council gives them a strong institutional voice in national policy-making beyond matters of national security. The National Security Council names two members to the Constitutional Tribunal, which resolves constitutional disputes. It also has the authority to give its opinion on any matters that may "gravely undermine the basis of the institutional system" (articles 95 and 96).

The background of the Supreme Court justices also favors the interests of the upper class socioeconomic groups that supported the military government. Towards the end of his rule, Pinochet offered generous retirement incentives to the most senior members to ensure the appointment of relatively young judges who were friends of the outgoing regime. Thus, on constitutional issues, the Supreme Court generally supports the conservative position. For example, it has consistently taken a narrow interpretation of private property rights in which any expropriation—which the state can only undertake for reasons of public utility or national interest—must be compensated at full market value, in cash, and in advance. The Supreme Court's Conservative bias has also hampered the investigation and prosecution of human rights violations during the military government.

The powers of the Senate and the electoral system round out the tether with which the 1980 constitution ties the democratic regime to the free market socio-economic order built by the military government. All legislation must have the approval of both chambers of the Congress. Thus, the Senate can kill a bill if it is unwilling to compromise with the house of deputies. The designated senators generally give Conservatives a majority over supporters of the center-left on core issues. As a result, center-Left governments must compromise strongly with Conservatives, to the point of gutting bills at times, as has been the case with constitutional reform efforts and labor law reform. Even then, when Conservatives do not wish to compromise they simply veto bills. Some analysts have argued that the President of the Republic's capacity to appoint some of the designated senators eventually will change the balance of forces. This may be overly optimistic, however, because the institutions they must be drawn from are notorious for their conservatism.

The electoral system also favors Conservative political forces by overrepresenting them. First, the boundaries of electoral districts for both the Chamber of Deputies and the Senate were gerrymandered to give more weight to areas that had voted heavily for Pinochet in the 1988 plebiscite. For example, electoral districts for deputies give greater representation to rural areas than urban areas which voted for the democratic opposition. Thus, Santiago, which accounts for 40 percent of the nation's population receives only 26 percent of the deputies. Further, in 1989, twenty rural districts with approximately 1.5 million people elected forty deputies while six urban areas with the same population elected only fourteen. Second, the binomial electoral system also benefits Conservatives in lower house elections. Each district elects two deputies. A party coalition must obtain double or more votes than the competing coalition to win both seats. If it does not, the minority coalition automatically wins a seat. This system ensures that the second highest list, frequently supporters of Pinochet and conservative parties, obtain maximum representation, certainly more than under first past the post or straightforward proportional representation. In other words, the second largest bloc can win one out of every two contested seats with only one third of the vote, which is the historic percentage of the vote for the Right.

Completing Chile's transition to full political democracy—deepening democracy—has proven difficult. Constitutional amendments require two-thirds support of all deputies and senators. This means that constitutional amendments require support from Conservatives in the legislature who, to date, only have approved relatively minor changes. The first set of reforms were negotiated in 1989 after Pinochet's defeat in the October 1988 plebiscite and before the first general election in December 1989. Fifty-four mostly minor reforms were approved in a plebiscite on July 30, 1989, largely with the help of the center-Right Renovación Nacional party. Among the more significant ones was the restoration of full electoral competition by lifting the ban on the Communist party and other erstwhile left-wing revolutionary parties. Furthermore, the leadership of labor unions and interest group associations were once again permitted to be militants of political parties. The number of elected senators was increased from 26 to 38, which reduced the proportion of designated senators in that chamber. The president would no longer have the power to dissolve the Chamber of Deputies, and civilian representation was increased on the National Security Council to reach parity with military members. During Patricio Alywin's administration, in November of 1991, the Congress approved amendments to local government. They provided for the replacement of presidentially appointed local officials with directly elected mayors. In February of 1994, the length of the presidential term was reduced from eight to six years. All other attempts at modifications, especially with respect to clauses affecting human rights issues, have not prospered. The government of President Ricardo Lagos, which took office in March 2000, pledged to continue efforts to reform the constitution.

Chile has a strong, well institutionalized political party system. It remains a tripolar multiparty system with many of the traditional parties still active, although, of course, there are new parties as well, several of which are principal. The core of the old National Party formed Renovación Nacional (RN), a center-Right party based on traditional Conservative values that includes some moderates and occasionally is willing to negotiate key policy issues with center-Left administrations that have dominated Chilean politics since the transition. A "new Right" also developed. Close collaborators of the military government, especially among the economic technocrats, formed the Unión Democrática Independiente (UDI). The UDI, a libertarian party, is less inclined to compromise with centrist or center-Left political parties. The RN and UDI have managed to form electoral coalitions for presidential races, but relations between the two parties are usually strained. However, they formed a more lasting coalition for the 1999 elections. The Alianza por Chile survived as a legislative bloc after the 2000 run-off election won by Ricardo Lagos of the Concertación. The Unión de Centro Centro emerged as a third right-wing party that is somewhat more populist and nationalistic than the other two. It frequently runs its own presidential candidate.

The Center is dominated by the Christian Democratic party (PDC). The PDC retains its traditional factions: conservatives (guatones), leftists (chas-cones), and centrists (renovadores). Ideologically, the PDC continues to rely on Social-Christian doctrine. Yet the party has evolved in that it is no longer a confessional party. The Radical party is another traditional centrist party that remains on the political scene. It has moved to the center-Left ideologically and has joined the Socialist International.

The Left changed substantially, especially the Socialist party (PS). After significant internal turmoil, dissention, and splits, the PS has undergone an ideological transformation by renouncing Marxism, the class struggle, and becoming a European-style social democratic party. It is, essentially, a moderate center-Left party styled after the Labour Party of Tony Blair and the Socialist parties of Spain under Felipe González, France under Francois Mitterand and Jaques Jospin, and Germany under Gerhardt Schroder. These parties are searching for a "third way," a middle ground between free-market capitalism and orthodox Socialism. The Party for Democracy (Partido por la Democracia, PDD) is another moderate center-Left party that formed following one of the initial splits of the PS. Both the PS and the PPD renounced social revolution and socialist state-building. They no longer supported nationalization, extensive industrial policy, the strong mixed economy, full employment, or the comprehensive welfare state. They softened their commitment to labor rights and more equal distribution of the national wealth. Party leadership accepted free-market economics and settled for putting a human face on capitalism. Meanwhile, the Communist Party of Chile (PCCh) retains its Marxist roots, although it no longer actively advocates violent revolution. In that sense, it seems to have embraced an ideological posture similar to that of Euro-Communists in the 1980s. Further to the left, but also, for the moment, eschewing revolution, are the Revolutionary Movement of the Left (MIR) and the Movimiento Patriótico Manuel Rodríquez, whose origins lay in the armed resistance to the military government.

In a significant departure from the past, the electoral system encourages coalition-building among political parties. Ironically, the center-Left has forged the most enduring one: the Concertación de Partidos por la Democracia (CPD), the successor to the Alianza Democrática and the Concertación de Partidos por el NO. The CPD has won three successive presidential races (1989, 1993, 1999). As of the mid 1990s, it included four major political parties: the Christian Democrats, the Socialist party, the Party for Democracy, and the Radical party. The more notable element of this coalition was the taming of the left, including the strongly reformist wings of both the Christian Democrats and the Radical party. Some of the original members of the CPD have left because they feel the coalition does not pursue their key issues with significant force. These have been smaller less significant parties, such as the Alianza Humanista-Verdè, which supports New Age and ecological causes. The Communist party and other left-wing parties form their own blocs if they can or run separately, garnering between five and nine percent of the vote.

Right-wing political parties have had more difficulties forging enduring electoral pacts. Generally, Renovación Nacional and the Unión Democrática

Independiente join forces for presidential races and go their separate ways afterwards. Not winning the presidency may be part of the problem; there are fewer incentives for long-term concerted action. However, substantial differences in conservative ideology and willingness to negotiate with the center-Left also divide them. Finally, the Unión de Centro Centro usually goes its own way due to its right-wing brand of national-populism. Nevertheless, by the year 2000, RN and UDI managed to keep their electoral coalition—the Alliance for Chile—together for policy purposes. The victory of Socialist Ricardo Lagos for the CPD probably provided the glue that bound them. Conservatives reckoned they would forge a more united front to contain a more reform-minded government.

Chile also boasts a number of well-organized interest groups that participate in politics and policy-making. The most influential ones are those of business, finance, and agriculture. Each of the major economic sectors has a sectoral peak association. The most powerful ones are the Sociedad de Fomento Fabril (SFF), the Sociedad Nacional de Agricultura, and the Cámara Nacional de Comercio, which organize industrialists, landowners, and merchants respectively. The SFF takes a very hard line with respect to the maintenance of Chile's protected democracy. The Sociedad Nacional de Minería, Cámara de la Construcción Chilena, and the Asociación de Bancos e Instituciones Financieras round out the most important business interest groups. In practice, these associations mostly represent the interests of large-scale business people. The six major sectoral associations have formed an encompassing peak association, the Confederación de la Producción y Comercio (CPC). The CPC defends the general interests of business in the policy process. Its views represent a consensus of those of its six member organizations.

Labor organizations have emerged significantly weakened after 18 years of military rule and repression. The old, Marxist-dominated Central Unica de Trabajadores (CUT) was broken up by the military government, which only allowed labor organizations at the plant level. An unofficial, Christian Democrat-led, anti-Marxist confederation—the Central Democrática de Trabajadores (CDT)—was tolerated. The Confederación de Trabajadores del Cobre remained the most militant union. It spearheaded the protest movement of 1983 and it formed the core of the Comando Central de Trabajadores and the Coordinadora Nacional de Sindicatos (CNS). In 1988, the CNS became the Confederación Unitaria de Trabajadores, which remains Chile's principal labor confederation. It is a grouping of industrial, professional, and mining unions led by leftist Christian Democrats and elements of the Left, including the Communist party. Overall, the union movement is not as strong as it was before the military government. Restricted collective bargaining, weak strike laws, open shops, low membership (11.5 percent of all employed workers in 1997), and other measures have limited organized labor's ability to represent its interests.

The Catholic Church, students, and intellectuals also play a role in Chilean politics. During the Pinochet period, the Church promoted human rights and gave aid to the poor and dispossessed. Its political role has declined with redemocratization, dedicating itself mainly to assuring the defeat of abortion and divorce laws. Chile is one of the few countries of the world that forbids divorce. The student movement is not as active as it has been historically in Chile, but its organizations continue to produce future leaders of the major political parties. By contrast, intellectuals, especially those with advanced degrees from foreign universities (with a heavy concentration in economics) have become very influential. They swell the ranks of the technocracy that advises all elected political leaders in and out of government. Lastly, the environmental, women's, and indigenous people's movements have also gained more recognition.

To a large extent, Chile's political stability after 1989 rested on antidemocratic institutions and a biased electoral system that were a legacy of a transition to democracy in which the military government had the upper hand. Those institutions protected the chief interest of right-wing forces: the maintenance of the extreme free-market socio-economic system installed during the military dictatorship. That system insured a good business climate at the expense of other social groups (middle class and, especially, urban and rural labor) whose interest in a more egalitarian order remained firmly subordinate to the inegalitarian orientation of propertied groups. Under these conditions, conservative socio-political forces did not need to resort to capital flight and mobilization (or the threat of such actions) to destabilize the economic and political system to defend themselves from their political enemies, a credible threat given the radicalization of right-wing political groups between 1970 and 1989. Upper class social groups— who were less tolerant of reforms than they were in the 1950s and 1960s—could stop unwanted change legally. Their extreme interpretation of property rights after 18 years of military rule led them to reject virtually all legislative proposals that diminished their ability to use market power to dominate the rest of society. As will be seen, this occurred despite the fact that proposed reforms were well within the norm of democratic capitalism; they were not attempts to install socialism.

The moderation of center-Left socio-political forces also played a significant role in the stability of Chile's post authoritarian political system. The top leadership of the political parties in the Concertación developed a remarkable consensus over free-market economic principles. The policy consensus was extraordinary because little over a decade and a half before, all preferred a mixed economy and a strong, nationalist industrial policy; the differences between them were only a matter of degree. Socialist ideals of nationalization and state planning were completely abandoned. As a result, serious challenges to conservatives on the issues that had torn Chile apart in the past—property, profits, and the social order—were no longer on the political agenda.

A number of international and domestic factors influenced this shift in the leadership of the center-Left. On the external front, the failure of alternative models to generate sustained economic growth was a powerful stimulant.

These included such disasters as the heterodox stabilization plans of Argentina, Brazil, and Peru in the mid-1980s, as well as the collapse of the Soviet Union in the early 1990s, and the end of Communism. Moreover, the world economy had expanded dramatically and was more tightly integrated through commodity chains, trade, and the explosive growth of international finance. These conditions made it difficult for nations (and especially developing nations with heavy foreign debt loads) to pursue economic models based on state-led developmentalist planning and economic nationalism. On the domestic front, electoral laws encouraged coalition-building among political parties, which blunted more extreme ideological posturing in the center-Left. Moreover, during the transition from authoritarianism, the Concertación had promised the military government it would not substantively alter the free-market socio-economic system. This became a fundamental point of trust between the forces of the opposition to the dictatorship and the right wing, a trust which was not broken through 1999. The very success of that model in generating sustained economic growth meant that no government could run the electoral risk of ruining such stellar performance. By the same token, the authoritarian enclaves of the 1980 constitution reinforced moderation in socio-economic policy. The veto powers of the Senate obliged the Concertación to obtain the support of some conservative political party members to get its legislation passed. Conservative forces exacted a heavy toll for that support.

Given all three of these domestic conditions, the politics of consensus-building dominated policy making in Chile throughout the 1990s. In Chile's strongly presidentialist system, the executive initiated most legislation. But the policy-making process involved extensive negotiation with the socio-economic and political forces directly affected. The result was generally a compromise bill in which the core interests of the center-Right were strongly protected, or else the bill died (as occurred with some environmental policy related to forests). During such negotiations, National Renovation was the party most amenable to negotiation and compromise with the Concertación. In any event, its leaders seemed to be more pragmatic and flexible than those of the Independent Democratic Union. Business organizations and labor unions also participated in the policy formulation process. Generally, business interests received a much more favorable hearing than did labor and other groups.

Despite these constraints, the two Concertación governments (1990–1999) were mildly reformist, which differentiated them strongly from the military dictatorship or a government of the center-Right. They addressed many issues that required urgent attention because they were ignored by the previous regime. Human rights and poverty were high on the list. New social issues, such as the rights of women and ethnic minorities and environmental degradation, were also taken into account. A third term for the Concertación, under the administration of Ricardo Lagos, continued in the same vein and renewed efforts for constitutional reform.

Human rights were a pressing matter, given the state terror the military unleashed, especially between 1973 and 1977. The issue divided the Chilean polity, arousing strong passions on either side: Conservatives who felt the violence was justified and Leftists and reformists who suffered it. The Concertación built its approach on three principles: truth, justice, and reparation. Truth involved the investigation and full public disclosure of the extent of human rights violations with respect to victims and methods. Justice referred to the military: making the perpetrators accountable. Reparation entailed compensating victims and their families.

By these definitions, justice was not done. The Concertación did not have the political power to bring human rights violators to trial. Given the nature of Chile's transition to democracy, the armed forces remained politically strong, and there was no question of overturning the amnesty the military government had decreed for itself in 1978. Thus, the principle of justice gave way to that of reconciliation. To that end, the Aylwin administration established the Truth and Reconciliation Commission, also known as the Retting Commission. The commission investigated human rights violations that involved deaths and disappearances. It gave a full accounting of victims, the methods used by the security branches of the armed forces and the police, and the judiciary's condoning of state terror. It was hoped that this public accounting, and an amnesty for most of the remaining political prisoners in Chile, would begin the process of reconciliation.

In addition to the truth component of its human rights policy, the Aylwin government also addressed reparations and, in a small measure, justice. With respect to reparations, the state compensated the families of victims who had died or disappeared. It also helped persons and families that had suffered through exile or loss of employment with relocation programs and with payments for former state employees who had been fired by the military government. With respect to justice, the Concertación pushed through pardons for most of the remaining political prisoners. It also managed a slight reorientation of military justice: Some cases would be tried by civilian rather than military courts.

Combatting poverty was another high priority for the Concertación, especially during the Aylwin administration. Although the Concertación took a proactive stance, it achieved only mixed success in addressing the sharp increase in social inequality that was one of the darker legacies of the dictatorship's free-market economic and social reforms. Reducing poverty and indigence was a major priority. In the late 1960s, the percentage of Chileans living in poverty and indigence stood at 22 and 6 percent respectively. Towards the end of the military government those rates soared to 38 and 17 percent. Social policy under Aylwin reduced those numbers to 24 and 7 percent in 1994. The fact that the figure was still higher than those of the late 1960s highlights the problems Chile faces in becoming a more egalitarian society. Moreover, successive Concertación governments failed to alter Chile's highly skewed distribution of national income, which became one of the most unequal in Latin America during the military government.

Still, the fall in poverty and indigence rates was a welcome improvement and was made possible through several policy instruments. For the most part, the Concertación relied on the expansion of the labor market (higher employment), increases in minimum wages, and job training programs. Other measures included channeling resources to a social investment fund (Fondo de Solidaridad e Inversión Social, FOSIS). FOSIS provided funds for community projects in small business start-ups, neighborhood improvement, and small-scale rural projects. The Aylwin and Frei administrations have also increased public spending on health care and education. For example, during Aylwin's government expenditures on public health rose by 70 percent compared to the military dictatorship. These were mainly channeled into the public health system, on which 75 percent of Chileans rely. Still, public hospitals had deteriorated so much during the military government that actual service increased only moderately. The private health insurance system, which only about 25 percent of Chileans can afford, remained unaffected by the change. It was one of the "social modernizations" of the Pinochet era.

Tax hikes financed increased social spending. The Aylwin administration negotiated tax increases with the center-Right, which used its majority in the Senate to set new rates at levels that were comfortable for business. Although the manufacturer's association (Sociedad de Fomento Fabril) opposed any new taxes, most business groups and National Renovation were more pragmatic. In fact, they insisted that the corporate tax portion of those increases be earmarked for social expenditures. Progressive tax reform raised overall government expenditures for social purposes from 9.9 percent of the GDP under Pinochet to 11.7 percent under Aylwin. Congress renewed the tax reform law, which had a short sunset clause, toward the end of the Aylwin administration. Although the rates were now lower than in the early 1990s, they remained higher than under the military government. It is worth noting that services to lower income sectors did not necessarily increase by much. Much of the spending went to improve deteriorated infrastructure rather than direct service. Moreover, many of the high-cost items in the social service category did not involve direct assistance to lower income groups. These included payments to an expanded battery of consultants and rebuilding the institutional capacity of government agencies that provide the services, such as hiring more personnel, providing more office equipment, and facilitating transportation.

Severe repression of workers and their organizations during the military government placed labor relations high on the Concertación's policy agenda. Reform of the military government's labor code, however, suffered a worse fate than the fight against poverty. In a united front, business organizations and right wing political parties used the institutions of Chile's protected democracy to reject the central propositions of the government and labor movement through two Concertación administrations, and the battle lines have been drawn again in their third administration under Ricardo Lagos. The key issues were the strengthening of union organization, finances, membership, and expanding the right to strike.

In the wake of the military dictatorship, the labor movement, a major constituency of the Concertación, had one fundamental demand: to strengthen job security and collective negotiation. To address these issues, the Aylwin administration proposed a bill to reform three key aspects of the military government's labor code. First, the Aylwin bill sought to make it more difficult and expensive to fire workers. The old code allowed employers to fire workers without showing cause and to hire replacements during strikes. Second, the bill sought to establish collective negotiation by economic sector (rather than on a company-by-company basis as under existing law) and to expand items for collective negotiation. Third, the bill mandated that nonunion employees would be obligated to pay union dues if they benefitted from union-negotiated contracts. This stopped short of a key CUT demand: mandatory union enrollment.

The Chilean private sector, represented by the Confederación de la Producción y Comercio, along with conservative political parties, consistently opposed all of these measures. Their majority in the Senate—aided by the appointed senators—forced the Concertación to negotiate point by point and the bill soon bogged down in the legislature. Meanwhile, the CPC took advantage of its privileged access to government officials to strenuously lobby against the bill. Their efforts gutted the proposed reforms, which already represented the bare minimum of organized labor's agenda. Collective negotiation by sector was not approved, nor would non union members have to pay fees for union-negotiated benefits. Issues subject to collective negotiation were expanded a little. Labor won the most with respect to job security clauses through the imposition of higher severance pay.

Organized labor did not fare any better under the second Concertación administration of Eduardo Frei, Jr. His government introduced a bill intended to strengthen unions and collective bargaining in January 1995. Even less inclined to negotiate than during the Aylwin administration, conservatives exercised their veto power in the Senate to stall the bill permanently. Direct lobbying on the presidency by the CPC prevented the cautious Frei administration from pushing the bill more forcefully through the legislative process.

On balance, then, the first two Concertación administrations sought to strengthen job security, unions, and their ability to conduct collective bargaining. The Aylwin administration had a little more success than Frei's government, but the private sector and conservative parties won on most core issues in both. During Aylwin's government both the private sector and CUT were willing to negotiate on some issues, but the membership of these organizations resented the "softness" of their leadership, which contributed to a hardening of more polarized postures by both the CPC and the CUT in the Frei government. Moreover, the Concertación's lack of unqualified and vigorous support of labor's core demands has cooled relations between organized labor and the governing coalition. It remains to be seen whether Ricardo Lagos' government will have more success than his predecessors.

The upshot of these legislative disputes was that unionized labor initially increased after democratization, only to suffer a clear decline. As a percentage of the employed labor force, unionized workers increased from 10 percent in 1986 to 15 percent in 1992, and steadily declined to 11.3 percent in 1998. The figures look slightly better when calculated for regular wage-earning workers. In 1986, 14.2 percent of wage earners were union, reaching a high of 22 percent in 1992 and dropping to 16.3 percent by 1997.

Lack of success in reforming the military government's labor laws—especially with respect to sectoral negotiation and collective bargaining—

certainly contributed to this decline. Contemporary labor law does little to reverse employer hostility to union labor, union fragmentation, and limits on union activities. About the only significant advance has been a law permitting the existence of labor confederations. Changes in the composition of the economy also mitigate against organized labor. These include the expansion of seasonal labor (in agriculture and the fishing and tourist industries, for example); deindustrialization as a result of Chile's free-market economic model; the stagnation of economic sectors with a tradition of strong unions, such as the mining sector; and the growth of economic sectors with a tradition of weak unionization, such as services and commerce.

In addition to these traditional issues, the Concertación also embraced new social movements whose issues had received scant, if any, recognition by the military government. During the military government, the feminist, environmental, and indigenous people's movements mostly aligned with opposition political forces. They survived by establishing nongovernmental organizations that carried out research and organized people. The military government suffered their presence, kept them under close surveillance, and usually ignored their policy recommendations. But because of their connections to the political parties of the Concertación, once Chile redemocratized many of these researchers and activists were called upon to formulate policy in their respective areas of expertise. They headed and staffed the technical commissions that drafted the electoral platform and governing program of the Concertación on gender, environment, and indigenous peoples. Later, they entered public service in government agencies created by the Aylwin administration to address these issues.

However, both the issues and the new state agencies were well subordinated to traditional socioeconomic and political concerns such as economic growth and the consolidation of political democracy. None gained cabinet status and some had only administrative budgets, meaning they could not execute policy. They could only propose policy to the relevant ministries, which may or may not act upon those proposals.

The feminist movement played an important part in the mass mobilization against the military government and in generating support for the Concertación during the 1988 plebiscite. In the governments of the Concertación, gender issues have received far more attention than in the past. In January 1991, the Aylwin administration created the National Women's Service (Servicio Nacional de la Mujer, SERNAM). Its mandate was to incorporate a gender perspective into public policy. SERNAM's immediate focus was to reduce discrimination against women in access to employment, housing, education, and credit. Longer term objectives were aimed at improving the position of women with respect to men. They included dismantling institutionally rooted gender inequalities that hindered equal rights for women, easing the responsibility of females for home and childcare, and stopping the sexual division of labor by integrating women into the labor market.

SERNAM did not gain cabinet rank and only had an administrative budget. During the Aylwin administration SERNAM proposed gender-specific changes to the reform of the labor law. Many of the provisions were directed toward the mainly female seasonal labor in the burgeoning fruit industry. Issues included housing, transport, and the establishment of hygienic facilities. SERNAM had also sought to rescind laws that block married women's access to credit without their husband's consent. Moreover, the agency sponsored a childcare program for women entering paid employment in the private sector, again with emphasis on seasonal female labor in the fruit industry. The emphasis on this sector stems from the sharp increase in this workforce due to the success of this new export industry and the fact that labor laws biased toward employer interests make it susceptible to high rates of exploitation.

SERNAM focused more on urban areas, even in rural districts. In part, this prompted the National Institute for Agricultural and Husbandry Development (Instituto Nacional de Desarrollo Agropecuario, INDAP) of the Ministry of Agriculture to establish a women's department (Area Mujer). This agency attended to the needs of peasant women who were not employed as seasonal labor in the fruit industry; thus, it was more urban-centered because it revolved around packing operations.

Overall, SERNAM did not succeed in promoting its longer term goals or, sadly, many of its shorter term ones, either. This was largely due to the agency's firmly subordinated place on the Concertación's policy agenda. Consequently, SERNAM concentrated on forming working teams with the departments of other ministries relevant to its work. These teams generated research that its members hoped would be useful in policy debates. Under these conditions, and in the interests of compromise with conservative political forces, SERNAM played a more limited role than its staff envisioned. Existing programs operated mainly as government services rather than as foci to encourage the empowerment, organization, and participation of women in the community, unions, and social organizations. Thus, SERNAM lacked a strongly organized social base to help push its agenda forward.

A similar situation occurred with the environmental movement. The military government had formed a small agency to address environmental problems. However, that agency, for all intents and purposes, had no mandate and most environmentalists avoided it because they opposed Pinochet. This changed with redemocratization. The Concertación welcomed environmentalists into their fold and vowed to address Chile's environmental problems. The Aylwin administration created the National Commission for the Environment (Comisión Nacional del Medio Ambiente, CONAMA) and in 1994 passed the Comprehensive Environmental Act. CONAMA did not gain cabinet rank. Instead, it is an interministerial commission chaired by the top trouble-shooter and right hand to the President of the Republic, the minister of the General Secretariat of the Republic.

CONAMA is a small agency. It has a permanent staff of fewer than seventy employees and hires consultants for special projects. Its heart is the technical secretariat, whose principal function is to oversee the implementation of environmental impact reports for new public and private economic development projects. Pollution abatement rather than natural resource extraction are CONAMA's principal focus. Meanwhile, all of the ten line ministries with environmental functions have retained their jurisdictions and implement resolutions taken in the interministerial meetings of CONAMA. CONAMA's consultative council incorporates civil society and business in the policy process.

The Comprehensive Environmental Act turned mandatory environmental impact reporting into the main instrument of environmental policy. The "polluter pays" principle is the second major instrument to force compliance with environmental regulations. However, the requirement is weak because the burden of proof rests with the prosecution. The act emphasizes gradualism. This means prioritizing problems and applying only small, incremental changes to deal with the most urgent ones.

Overall, CONAMA and the Comprehensive Environmental Act are weak institutional and legislative instruments to tackle Chile's formidable environmental problems, which include high levels of pollution in urban and rural areas and rapid rates of extraction of natural resources, such as fisheries. CONAMA does not have the mandate, political backing, or staff to effectively tackle environmental problems. The Comprehensive Law reinforces this condition. Why? Because political leaders are fearful that more vigorous environmental action may hamper economic growth. Thus, Concertación administrations bow to pressure from conservative political forces. Still, CONAMA represents official recognition of the issue and is an advance over previous conditions.

In addition to gender and environmental issues, the Concertación also addressed the plight of its indigenous peoples. The Mapuches had gained some ground under Allende's socialist government, helping to formulate legislation that promoted multiethnicity. His government also used agrarian reform to secure title for land rights. But the military government reacted violently against indigenous people. It broke up Mapuche organizations by subjecting its leadership to death, imprisonment, and exile and sought to obliterate Mapuche identity and communities in 1978 by destroying indigenous property rights through the conversion of communal land to private land ownership based on areas traditionally farmed by individual families (*hijuelas*). In the end, the military government's strategy did not work, for legally the *hijuelas* did not become alienable property—could not be sold—for twenty years after the date of the decree that established them. The Concertación acted quickly to reverse the situation with the most vigorous action occurring between 1989 and 1993. In 1989, while Patricio Aylwin was still a candidate for the presidency, the Concertación signed an agreement with the indigenous peoples of Chile. In it, the Concertación committed itself to the promulgation of a new law that would recognize ancestral culture and rights. Alywin's government partially delivered on this promise by passing a new Indian Law in 1993. The law recognized ancestral lands. It protected them by making them inalienable and established a fund to buy back lands that had been usurped by Chileans since the beginning of the century, when the reservations originally had been established. The law also promoted multiethnicity, legally recognized Indian communities, encouraged participation in policy making, and acknowledged the need for socioeconomic development. A National Indigenous Peoples Development Corporation (CONADI) now administrates indigenous affairs.

The Indian Law was an important progressive step, but, of course, much remains to be done. For one, CONADI would benefit from more independence from the presidency. The removal of directors who sided too openly with indigenous communities against the development projects of important private firms hurt the legitimacy of the institution among indigenous peoples and their allies. It transformed the Indian representatives on CONADI's council into state functionaries. The commitment to socioeconomic development for indigenous peoples was lukewarm at best. That, combined with festering, at times violent, land conflicts (especially by Mapuches) forced the Frei administration to address the issue in July 1999. With great fanfare he committed about U.S. $280 million over three years. His effort, however, was seen as largely cosmetic, as most of those funds were not fresh. He mostly called on monies already earmarked for public works and education in regions with heavy indigenous populations to the formal Indian budget. Finally, the all-important issue of autonomy for indigenous peoples had barely been touched upon by the end of the Frei administration.

On balance, in the transition from authoritarianism, the first two governments of the Concertación accomplished a great deal. Their policies helped to consolidate civilian rule and maintain economic stability, and addressed social equity and the concerns of new social movements. However, the process of overcoming the dark legacies of military rule was far from complete in 2000. An intransigent center-Right (and a frequently complacent Concertación) blocked progress on a number of vital issues. Constitutional reform to restore Chile to full political democracy proved beyond the powers of the Concertación, and the antidemocratic institutions it created remained. The designated senators, most of whom had to be chosen from conservative institutions, undercut the play of party politics in representative democracy. The Chilean military enjoyed a great deal of autonomy from civilian leaders. The core of their budget was fixed (10 percent of copper exports), and military doctrine and promotions were their prerogatives. They also dominated the National Security Council, which gave them direct institutional channels for participation in government policy making. Substantive amendments to the Constitution were not possible without support from conservative political parties. But their interest in the maintenance of military guardianship and veto power over economic policy rendered them uncooperative. To be fair, however, on relatively minor issues Renovación Nacional was more flexible than the Democratic Independent Union, and a small number of conservatives, led by Andrés Allamand, even supported restoration of full political democracy.

The Concertación made equally little headway in protecting the rights of employees by strengthening the labor movement. First, the Concertación's pro-market and pro-business posture induced it to place only the most fundamental of labor's demands on its policy agenda and to ignore most of labor's other concerns. Second, even on those few selected issues, the Concertación failed to pass legislation that significantly reformed the labor code. Thus, organized labor's ability to engage in collective bargaining from a position of strength was stymied at every turn. Here, intransigent right-wing politicians—exercising their veto power in the Senate—and direct lobbying by big business were the main culprits. Yet the Concertación's readiness to cave in to business opposition raised doubts about the coalition's allegiance to labor, a presumably important constituent of the center-Left governing coalition. This contributed to serious tension between organized labor and the Concertación.

Deepening economic development and social equality presented further challenges. Although Chile succeeded in diversifying the commodities it exports, its economy was still essentially an agromineral extractive one. In 2000, as in the 1950s and 1960s, the challenge was to add value to those commodities and generate whole new industries in Chile, increase wages, build service industries, and accelerate economic growth. The Asian economic crisis-induced recession of 1999, which ended Chile's record of uninterrupted high economic growth since the mid-1980s, exposed Chile's vulnerability to agro-export and market specialization. As a result, the recession helped place industrial policy on the agenda again. Moreover, after years of dormancy due to the complacency that economic success had generated, the economic crisis also focused attention on the persistence of unequal income distribution (in 1994 Chile ranked among the most unequal in Latin America) and the high price of services (education, health, housing, utilities). Consequently, there was a sharp upswing in the debate over the tax and regulatory policies necessary to deal with those issues.

In March 2000, the third government of the Concertación renewed the center-Left coalition's commitment to confront the darker legacies of the military government. The December 1999 election was unique in that the Concertación's candidate was Socialist Ricardo Lagos, a former cabinet member of the Allende government. Joaquin Lavín ran for a conservative coalition (RN and UDI) that called itself the Alliance for Chile. Although nominally from UDI, Lavín conducted an independent minded campaign. The vote was close and the presence of candidates from several other parties kept either of them from obtaining an absolute majority. This forced a run-off election in January 2000, which Lagos won with 51.3 percent of the vote to Lavín's 48.7 percent.

The Lagos campaign's platform pledged the administration to renew efforts to resolve the human rights question, to reform the constitution and the labor code, to improve access to higher quality health and education, and to reduce social inequality. What are the chances that Lagos' government may have more success than its predecessors? To begin with, the human rights question runs like a thread through many of the issues central to institutional reform. Thus, advances on that front may open opportunities for further reforms that are key to the restoration of full political democracy.

Right wing forces look to the military—and Pinochet personally—as the saviors of Chile and the guardians of the extreme free-market socio-economic order they cherish. Conservatives viewed attacks on the armed forces as assaults on all the (antidemocratic) institutions that protected their privileges. The military themselves used their considerable influence and institutional powers to defend themselves from prosecution. In 1998, Pinochet's and the military's position seemed unassailable. But by mid-2000, Pinochet's political fortunes had declined dramatically due to efforts to prosecute him for his role in human rights violations. Efforts by lower courts to open investigations in other instances had also flourished. In the process, Chile learned it could function perfectly well without Pinochet's protection; it would not descend into chaos and violence. Moreover, forward-looking conservative political figures distanced themselves from him and the Alliance for Chile offered its own constitutional reform bill.

How did this startling turn of fortune come about? In October of 1998, Senator Pinochet travelled to Great Britain for medical reasons. Due to his affinity with the neoconservatives that had dominated British politics since 1979, he had long considered the nation a safe haven. But things had changed with the election of the Labour Party's Tony Blair to the Prime Ministership. While Pinochet was in London, British authorities arrested him pending extradition to Spain for human rights violations. Spanish courts had requested the extradition based on a case put together by Chilean and Spanish survivors of leftist political activists killed by the military, allegedly with Pinochet's full knowledge. Pinochet languished under house arrest for 16 months in Britain. The Frei administration scrambled to establish negotiations between all parties involved, while the justice system apprehended officers who had taken part in the 1973 "Death Caravan" to northern Chile. Meanwhile, the Frei administration strenuously labored to have Pinochet released from custody and returned to Chile, arguing that his homeland was the only rightful venue for a trial, and that the Chilean justice system would indeed look into whether grounds existed to proceed against Pinochet for human rights abuses. Those efforts bore fruit in March 2000 when Pinochet was pronounced medically unfit for extradition and trial in Spain and flown back to Chile. Although his supporters gave him a hero's welcome, the new Lagos administration upheld the government's commitment to let the courts decide whether Pinochet should stand trial. The legal machinery began to operate. In August 2000, the Supreme Court of Chile upheld a lower court decision that stripped Pinochet of the diplomatic immunity he enjoyed under the constitutional provision that allowed former presidents of the republic to be senators for life. The first few months of 2001 saw General Pinochet declared mentally and physically fit to stand trial, and a lower court reduced the charges from conspiracy to commit kidnapping and murder to conspiracy to cover up kidnappings and murder.

The appeals process will delay results, but the fact that these events are taking place at all demonstrates the degree to which Chilean political elites of both the center-Left and, especially, the center-Right, are gaining confidence in the nation's ability to overcome the conflicts of yesteryear. The Pinochet affair was very salutory for Chile. On the human rights front, his absence precipitated renewed calls for truth (full disclosure of where bodies were buried and who killed them) and justice (trials for some of the perpetrators). Once Pinochet was back in Chile, the Lagos administration established a negotiating committee (mesa de diálogo) that included representatives from the military. Initial agreements centered on the issue of disclosure. Persons with knowledge of where bodies were buried were not required to reveal who had committed the killings. Human rights organizations saw this as an attempt to protect the perpetrators from prosecution. However, there was nothing they could do to oppose the agreement, which became the basis for a bill that sailed through the legislative process. The matter of prosecutions, including that of Pinochet, would be addressed in due course. Meanwhile, the military has begun to make public startling, painful, and highly embarrassing accounts of what happened to many of the disappeared.

Some progress was also made on the constitutional reform front. The Lagos administration reiterated the Concertación's commitment to abolish all of the antidemocratic institutions and to bring the military firmly back under civilian control. This was an improvement over the Frei administration's footdragging. Moreover, in a significant turnaround, the center-Right Alliance for Chile agreed to one major change: to abrogate the designated senators, including those who held the office by virtue of having been President of the Republic. The concession was based on the pragmatic realization that eventually most of those seats would be held by supporters of the Concertación (two presidents so far, a third one in six years, and the right to either appoint more directly or to influence the composition of the institutions from which they are drawn). In May 2000, the legislature amended the constitution, abolishing the right of former presidents to become senators for life. Unfortunately, this change of heart did not mean the right wing felt comfortable leaving socio-economic policy up for democratic debate. The Alliance for Chile sought to protect the socio-economic system by proposing a clause that gave key socio-economic policy (that related particularly to property) constitutional protection, and at the same time significantly raised the number of congressional votes necessary to approve changes on those matters.

In its first year in office the Lagos administration has presided over a resumption of economic growth after the steep recession of 1999, albeit at a slower pace than had been the norm in the 1990s. Stimulated by interest rate cuts and a partial lifting of controls on the capital account for international firms, gross domestic product expanded by about 5 percent in 2000 and was estimated at slightly higher for 2001. Employment lagged behind growth figures but finally responded, falling from a high of approximately 11 percent in 2000 to 8.5 percent in the first quarter of 2001. True to the pragmatism of "Third Way" renovated socialism, the Lagos government has kept the privatization of utilities on track.

In addition to market-friendliness, renovated socialism also affirmed a concern for social equity. To that end, the Lagos administration revived efforts to reform that labor code in an effort to remove its worst pro-business biases. It has also introduced a mild tax reform bill that primarily affects business to raise revenue for proposed increases in spending for education and health. Business groups and conservative political parties have bitterly opposed the Lagos administration's bills, as well as its intention to put some teeth into environmental policy. They have threatened the government with investment strikes that would stymie economic recovery. The Lagos administration has countered citing evidence that investment rates have not been adversely affected by the proposed reforms. It then accused the private sector of deliberately misleading the public over the consequences of those bills, strongly implying that business had overreacted to mild and just reforms by raising the specter of the shadow of the past.

Despite these tensions between the private sector and the Lagos administration, on balance, recent events suggest that by 2001 Chile had less to fear from the conflicts of the past than many Chileans thought when the transition to democracy began in 1989. Conflicts over potentially destabilizing issues such as human rights, constitutional reform, economic development, and social policy were institutionally channeled. For example, human rights and constitutional questions wound their way through the legal and legislative systems or were settled in executive branch-sponsored negotiations between the parties involved. The debate over economic development and social equity did not, by and large, exceed the normal political differences over levels of taxation and regulation common in developed democratic countries. The venue for such debates was the proper one: the legislature, rather than rule by presidential decree.

However, these positive steps fell short of advancing the cause of social justice in Chile, of helping Chile to become a more egalitarian society, of ameliorating its environmental degradation, and of restoring full political democracy. Chile's income distribution remained one of the most unequal in Latin America; its labor code was one of the most regressive; and access to decent health, education, and housing were restricted to 25 percent of the population that could afford it. On many of these measures, Chile had not recovered to standards that existed before military rule, although the figures were an improvement over those prevalent during the dictatorship. Chile achieved political and economic stability, but at the cost of undemocratic institutions and of making a fetish of economic growth. Restoring Chile to full political democracy and achieving a more equitable distribution of the fruits of economic growth depend, in no small measure, on more flexibility among conservatives. They must lose their fear that normal debates and give and take over taxes, regulation, labor relations, and mild limits to property rights are somehow threats to the basic socio-economic order. To the contrary—as is the case in advanced capitalist democracies—they are ways of preserving it.

Chronology

1536 Diego de Almagro extends Spanish conquest to Chile; colonial period shapes social and economic systems; perennial Indian wars in central Chile against Mapuches

1810 Chile begins independence movement from Spain

1818 With help from Argentine general José de San Martín, general Bernardo O'Higgins finally liberates Chile from Spain; Chile becomes a republic

1833 Autocratic republic begins when Diego Portales' new authoritarian constitution ends political instability and sets the groundwork for the Portilian state, which lasts until 1898

1837 Portales assassinated

1839 Chilean military defeats Peru-Bolivia Confederation in a war that began in 1836

1851 Rebellion to democratize autocratic republic defeated

1879 War of the Pacific against Peru and Bolivia over mining concessions breaks out

1884 Chile wins War of the Pacific and permanently gains provinces of Arica, Tarapacá, and Antofagasta; Bolivia loses access to Pacific Ocean

1888 Mapuches finally defeated; Indian law allocates inalienable reservations—*reducciones*—to Indian communities

1891 Civil war against president José Manuel Balmaceda ends autocratic republic; beginning of parliamentary republic

1925 Chile's Portilian constitution replaced by the constitution of 1925; political instability engulfs Chile

1932 Political stability returns with election of Arturo Alessandri to presidency

1938 Popular Front government, devoted to progressive socioeconomic reform

1942 Popular Front officially dissolved, but center-Left coalitions keep reformist Radical party candidates in the presidency

1946 Under pressure from the United States, President Gabriel González Videla outlaws Communist party—which had been a part of his electoral and governing coalition—in 1948; Chile becomes a Cold War battleground

1949 Women receive the right to vote

1952 Independent Carlos Ibáñez elected president on an anti-political platform; he relegalizes Communist party and is plagued by economic difficulties in the aftermath of the Korean War

1958 Jorge Alessandri becomes president; Chile has three democratic administrations that try global reform of Chile's economic, political, and social institutions; Alessandri's is the conservative attempt

1964 Eduardo Frei, Sr., becomes president; he heads a progressive Christian Democratic administration that introduces many social and economic programs, for example, partial nationalization of copper and land reform

1970 Salvador Allende elected president at the head of Popular Unity, a coalition of Leftist political parties; Chile begins the peaceful, democratic road to socialism; political and social polarization over nationalization of industry and land reform and other sociopolitical issues tear the country apart

1973 On September 11, the armed forces overthrow Unidad Popular and a U.S.-backed military junta takes political power; several years of state terror follow

1974 In December, General Augusto Pinochet becomes president of Chile

1975 Radical neoconservative experiments in economic and social reform begin

1978 Military government approves an amnesty law for all security personnel involved in human rights violations

1980 A new constitution with many authoritarian enclaves is approved in a highly questionable plebiscite

1982 Beginning of an economic depression that revived moribund opposition political parties and a broad opposition movement

1983 In May, once-a-month mass mobilizations against the military regime begin demanding democracy; opposition political parties and organized labor lead the protest

1986 The economy stabilizes; crackdown on political opposition after failed assassination attempt on General Pinochet

1988 End of military rule; the Christian Democrat–led opposition coalition, with help from U.S. government, defeats general Pinochet in a plebiscite on his continued rule in October of that year

1990 Christian Democrat Patricio Aylwin becomes president of redemocratized Chile at the head of a broad center-Left coalition of political parties known as Concertación; his government introduces progressive legislation to redress the worst excesses of the military government; extends presidential terms to six years; record economic expansion continues

1994 Christian Democrat Eduardo Frei, Jr., begins a second Concertación administration

1998 Asian economic crisis triggers recession in Chile; Pinochet taken into custody in Britain pending extradition charges to Spain for human rights violations

1999 Ricardo Lagos, a moderate European-style Socialist becomes the presidential candidate for the Concertación after internal primaries, ending Christian Democratic domination of the governing coalition

2000 Lagos wins run-off election and begins third government of the Concertación; Pinochet released from custody in Britain returns to Chile to face legal proceedings for human rights violations; economic growth resumes

2001 Pinochet, 85 years old, legally declared fit to stand trial

Bibliography

Angell, Alan, and Benny Pollock, eds. *The Legacy of Dictatorship: Political, Economic, and Social Change in Pinochet's Chile*. Liverpool, England: The University of Liverpool, 1993.

Bauer, Arnold J. *Chilean Rural Society from the Spanish Conquest to 1930*. New York: Cambridge University Press, 1975.

Collings, Joseph. *Chile's Free Market Miracle: A Second Look*. Monroe, OR: Institute for Food and Development Policy, 1995.

Drake, Paul. *Socialism and Populism in Chile, 1932–1952*. Urbana: University of Illinois Press, 1978.

Drake, Paul W., and Iván Jaksic, eds. *The Struggle for Democracy in Chile, 1982–1990*. Rev. ed. Lincoln: University of Nebraska Press, 1995.

Edwards, Sebastián, and Alejandra Cox-Edwards. *Monetarism and Liberalization: The Chilean Experiment*. Cambridge: Ballinger, 1987.

Ellsworth, P. T. *Chile: An Economy in Transition*. New York: Macmillan, 1945.

Fleet, Michael. *The Rise and Fall of Chilean Christian Democracy*. Princeton, NJ: Princeton University Press, 1985.

Foxley, Alejandro. *Latin American Experiments in Neoconservative Economics*. Berkeley: University of California Press, 1983.

Garretón, Manuel Antonio. *The Chilean Political Process*. Boston: Unwin Hyman, 1989.

Gil, Frederico. *The Political System of Chile*. Boston: Houghton-Mifflin, 1966.

Gil, Frederico, Ricardo Lagos, and Henry Landsberger, eds. *Chile at the Turning Point: Lessons of the Socialist Years, 1970–1973*. Philadelphia: Institute for the Study of Human Issues, 1979.

Hojman, David. *Chile: The Political Economy of Development and Democracy in the 1990s*. Pittsburgh, PA: Pittsburgh University Press, 1993.

———, ed. *Neoliberalism with a Human Face? The Politics and Economics of the Chilean Model*. Liverpool, England: University of Liverpool, 1995.

Kaufman, Edy. *Crisis in Allende's Chile: New Perspectives*. New York: Praeger, 1988.

Kaufman, Robert. *The Politics of Land Reform in Chile, 1950–1970*. Cambridge, MA: Harvard University Press, 1972.

Kay, Cristóbal, and Patricio Silva, eds. *Development and Social Change in Chilean Countryside: From the Pre-Land Reform Period to the Democratic Transition*. Amsterdam: Centrum voor Studie en Documentatie van Latijns Amerika, 1992.

Kirsch, Henry W. *Industrial Development in a Traditional Society: Entrepreneurship and Modernization in Chile*. Gainsville: University of Florida Press, 1977.

Loveman, Brian. *Chile: The Legacy of Hispanic Capitalism*. 2nd. ed. Oxford, England: Oxford University Press, 1988.

Mamalakis, Markos. *Growth and Structure of the Chilean Economy: From Independence to Allende*. New Haven, CT: Yale University Press, 1976.

Martínez, Javier, and Alvaro Díaz. *Chile: The Great Transformation*. Washington, DC: The Brookings Institution, 1996.

Montecinos, Verónica. *Economists, Politics, and the State: Chile 1958–1994*. Amsterdam: Centrum voor Studie en Documentatie van Latijns Amerika, 1998.

Monteón, Michael. *Chile and the Great Depression: the Politics of Underdevelopment, 1927–1948*. Tucson: Arizona State University Press, 1998.

Moran, Theodore H. *Multinational Corporations and the Politics of Dependence: Copper in Chile*. Princeton, NJ: Princeton University Press, 1974.

O'Brian, Philip. *Allende's Chile*. New York: Praeger, 1976.

―――. *The Pinochet Decade*. London: Latin American Bureau, 1983.

Oppenheim, Lois Hecht. *Politics in Chile: Democracy, Authoritarianism, and the Search for Development*. Boulder, CO: Westview, 1993.

Oxhorn, Philip D. *Organizing Civil Society: The Popular Sectors and the Struggle for Democracy in Chile*. Philadelphia: The Pennsylvania State University Press, 1995.

Petras, James. *Politics and Social Forces in Chilean Development*. Berkeley: University of California Press, 1970.

Petras, James, and Fernando Leiva, with Henry Veltmeyer. *Democracy and Poverty in Chile: The Limits of Electoral Politics*. Boulder, CO: Westview, 1994.

Roxborough, Ian, Philip O'Brien, and Jackie Roddick, eds. *Chile: The State and Revolution*. London: Macmillan, 1977.

Scully, Timothy. *Rethinking the Center: Party Politics in Nineteenth and Twentieth Century Chile*. Stanford, CA: Stanford University Press, 1992.

Sigmund, Paul. *The Overthrow of Allende and the Politics of Chile, 1964–1976*. Pittsburgh, PA: Pittsburgh University Press, 1977.

Silva, Eduardo. *The State and Capital in Chile: Business Elites, Technocrats, and Market Economics*. Boulder, CO: Westview Press, 1996.

Spooner, Mary Helen. *Soldiers in a Narrow Land: The Pinochet Regime in Chile*. Berkeley: University of California Press, 1994.

Stallings, Barbara. *Class Conflict and Development in Chile*. Stanford, CA: Stanford University Press, 1978.

Stevenson, John Reese. *The Chilean Popular Front*. Westport, CT: Greenwood Press, 1945.

Tulchin, Joseph, and Augusto Varas. *From Dictatorship to Democracy: Rebuilding Political Consensus in Chile*. Boulder, CO: Lynn Rienner, 1991.

Valenzuela, Arturo. *Chile: Politics and Society*. New Brunswick, NJ: Transaction, 1976.

―――. *The Breakdown of Democratic Regimes: Chile*. Baltimore: Johns Hopkins University Press, 1978.

Valenzuela, Arturo, and Samuel Valenzuela, eds. *Military Rule in Chile: Dictatorship and Oppositions*. Baltimore: Johns Hopkins University Press, 1986.

Verdugo, Patricia. *Chile, Pinochet, and the Caravan of Death*. Coral Gables, FL: North-South Center Press, 2001.

Vylder, Stephen de. *Allende's Chile*. Cambridge, England: Cambridge University Press, 1976.

White, Judy, ed. *Chile's Days of Terror: Eyewitness Accounts of the Military Coup*. New York: Pathfinder Press, 1974.

Winn, Peter. *Weavers of Revolution*. New York: Oxford University Press, 1986.

Wright, Thomas C. *Landowners and Reform in Chile: The SNA 1919–1940*. Urbana: University of Illinois Press, 1982.

FILMS AND VIDEOS

The Battle of Chile. U.S., 1976.
Chile, Obstinate Memory. U.S., 1997.
Details of a Duel: A Question of Honor. Chile/Cuba, 1988.
In Women's Hands. U.S., 1993.
Microchip al Chip. Chile, 1991.

VENEZUELA

GUYANA

SURINAME

FRENCH
GUIANA

COLOMBIA

Amazon River

AMAZON RAINFOREST

Recife

PERU

*BRAZILIAN
HIGHLANDS*

San Francisco River

Salvador

BOLIVIA

Brasília
★

Belo Horizonte

CHILE

Rio de Janeiro

PARAGUAY

São Paulo

Map of
BRAZIL

N
W   E
S

150 0 150 300 Miles

Scale 1:24,000,000

URUGUAY

ARGENTINA

SIXTEEN

BRAZIL

Wilber Albert Chaffee

Introduction

A continental nation, Brazil dominates South America, occupying half of the territory and bordering on all the other South American nations except Ecuador and Chile. One of the giants among nations, Brazil is fourth largest in area, the third largest democracy, and the largest Catholic country. If Brazil were turned 180 degrees on the globe, its southernmost point would reach as far north as the border between North and South Carolina. The Amazon River, draining much of the land east of the Andes, carries twelve times the volume of water of the Mississippi and is navigable by ocean freighter across the width of Brazil, making the Peruvian city of Iquitos a seaport. The Amazon region is the world's largest rainforest.

With 170 million people, half of South America's population, Brazil is the fifth largest in the world. Starting originally as a group of Portuguese colonies, today's population is a mix of the indigenous Amero-Indians; descendents of slaves brought from Africa; members of originally European immigrant families, especially Portuguese, Germans, and Italians; and over 1 million of Japanese ancestry. As a result, Brazil is second only to Nigeria in terms of persons of African ancestry, and has the largest Japanese population outside of Japan. Sixteen of Brazil's cities have a population of a million or greater, including its capital Brasília. The cities of Rio de Janeiro and greater São Paulo have 6 million and 17 million people, respectively.

Thanks to my class in Latin American politics and to John Wirth, Brasilio Sallum, Jr., and J. A. Lindgren Alves for going through various drafts. Special thanks to Diva for careful editorial work.

The Brazilian economy, eighth largest in the world, exceeds those of South Korea, Taiwan, or Russia and approaches the size of countries like Canada, Italy, and Great Britain. Brazil, traditionally known for its exports of primary products, is often identified with coffee. Although coffee remains an important export and Brazil is the world's largest coffee producer, Brazil is also a major producer of soybeans, orange juice, cacao, sugar, frozen chickens, diamonds, gold, and iron ore. Today, industrial manufactures exceed the value of primary products, with exports of steel, airplanes, automobiles and automotive parts, consumer durables, and electronic equipment.

Brazil today publishes 60 percent of the literature of South America and has an important national literature generally unknown in much of the rest of the world. Authors include Euclides da Cunha, Machado de Assis, Rachel de Queiroz, Carlos Drummond de Andrade, Guimarães Rosa, Jorge Amado, and Clarice Lispector. Brazil's Globo television system is the fourth largest commercial network in the world, exceeded in size only by three North American networks, and its programming is seen the world over.

Proud of their country, Brazilians will tell you, "God is a Brazilian."

A Brief Political History

European contact with what is today Brazil came with the landing in 1500 of Pedro Álvares Cabral at Coroa Vermelha in today's state of Bahia while sailing from Portugal to Asia via the Cape of Good Hope. The first permanent Portuguese settlement was not founded until 1532 at São Vicente in São Paulo. Subsequently, Portugal established colonies, called *capitanias* (captaincies) to harvest brazilwood for textile dyes, beginning in the northeast, the territory that bulges east toward Africa. Brazilian land proved to have good soil to expand the cultivation of sugar cane, brought from the Azores, which was followed by a massive slave trade from Portuguese colonies in Africa to tend the sugar cane and its processing in giant *engenhos* (sugar mills).

Political power was centered in *municipios* (municipalities) dominated by agricultural elites, who also controlled the politics of the captaincies. Although the Portuguese crown eventually established a viceroyalty, first in Bahia and later in Rio de Janeiro, the captaincies essentially reported directly to Lisbon. Border conflicts developed with Argentina, beginning a tradition of competition over leadership in South America.

In 1808, as a result of Napoleon's invasion and conquest of Iberia, the Portuguese royal family fled from Lisbon and established the new capital for their empire in Rio de Janeiro. For the first time, national politics in Brazil was centralized, technical schools were established, and printing presses were brought in. A sense of nationhood began to develop as the captaincies became provinces. With the defeat of Napoleon, the royal family returned to Lisbon in 1821, leaving the crown prince, Dom Pedro de Bragança, as regent. At the urging of the Brazilians, Dom Pedro proclaimed the independence of Brazil in 1822, becoming its first emperor, Dom Pedro I. Under the constitution of 1824 the emperor had *moderating power*, allowing him to "watch over the maintenance of the independence, equilibrium, and harmony of the other Political Powers." The moderating power allowed him to dissolve the Congress and form a new government. The declaration of independence under the emperor maintained Brazil as a single country, avoiding the disintegration that happened with Spanish colonies.

Dom Pedro I abdicated in favor of his five-year-old son, Dom Pedro II, in 1831, and the country was ruled by a regency until the young emperor reached the age of fifteen in 1840 and assumed full royal powers. Dom Pedro II reigned rather than ruled. A national assembly was established with representation from the various provinces. Under Dom Pedro II the now independent country was centralized in name, but the control from Rio de Janeiro was light-handed, seldom interfering with the politics of the states. Two political parties developed, the Liberal party and the Conservative party, representing the patriarchal oligarchies that controlled the states. The parties alternated in forming the government and served at the emperor's pleasure.

During the later part of the Portuguese colonial rule and much of the Brazilian monarchy, the British dominated Brazilian trade and its economy under special treaty rights. They supplied English manufactured goods and bought most of Brazil's exports, which were primary products, especially cotton, sugar, and minerals.

One of the few national actions was the war with Paraguay (1865–1870), which gave what may be the first real sense of nationalism; a national military hero, the Duque de Caixas; and the first counterweight to the extreme federalism of Brazil in the form of an active national military. At the same time, the states maintained their own military forces under the control of their governors. The Paraguayan War also highlighted the essential military weakness of Brazil; its lack of infrastructure, especially in its interior; and the difficulties in executing a war even against a nation as small and weak as Paraguay. The need for national economic development, as a result, came from the military, which saw itself as the only force really interested in the good of the nation as a whole.

Slavery became a continuingly contentious political issue, with the British pressuring Brazil to end the slave trade, and in 1871 the Law of the Free Womb made anyone born after that date free. Professional groups from the cities and military positivists, followers of French positivist leader Auguste Comte—who believed that scientific methods could be applied to society and to politics—led the fight for emancipation of the slaves, establishment of the republic, and development. In 1888, while the emperor was visiting Europe, his daughter, Princess Isabel, as regent and under pressure from the army that had declared that hunting escaped slaves was beneath its honor, abolished slavery. The following year the military, headed by Marshall Deodoro da Fonseca, overthrew the monarchy and declared Brazil a republic. The positivist slogan "Order and Progress" became part of the new flag.

The republic adopted a constitution, modeled on the American constitution, with a nationally elected president permitted one four-year term. Federal funds began to be used to create a national infrastructure of roads and railways, initiating a long period of economic growth. By 1894, politics became the politics of the governors, with no national political parties, each state having a Republican party. By tacit agreement between the two major states, São Paulo and Minas Gerais, the presidency was traded between them every four years in *café com leite* (coffee with milk) politics; São Paulo's economy dominated through the growing of coffee and Minas as a producer of dairy goods. In this strongly federal system, the congress served as a meeting place where legislation covered only those points agreed to by the states, in negotiation with the federal president. Although there was a federal military, the states all had their own militias under the command of the governors, in some cases rivaling the national army in power. Opposition to the power of the two states included attempts by Brazil's best-known statesman, Rui Barbosa, who had been a part of the Second Hague Conference in 1907, to win the presidency. Other opposition came from a group of military officers, dominated by young lieutenants (*tenentes*), who revolted against the government in the 1920s but failed to overturn the system. The 1929 Depression brought about the loss of income from coffee exports and increasing discontent with the traditional politics of the Old Republic. Defeated in 1930 as presidential candidate, Getúlio Vargas of the state of Rio Grande do Sul, along with dissident military including many of the *tenentes*, successfully ousted the old government and inaugurated the Second Republic. Vargas was made provisional president by the congress.

Vargas dominated Brazilian politics from 1930 until his suicide in 1954, navigating among conflicting interests of the states, of differing military factions, and of ideological political parties such as the Integralistas, modeled on Europe's fascism, and the Communists, led respectively by Plinio Salgado and by former *tenente* leader Luis Carlos Prestes. Centralization of Brazilian politics became a reality for the first time since the early 1800s as Vargas replaced elected governors who did not support him with appointed *interventors*, but he faced a rebellion in 1932 that lasted several months when the state of São Paulo reacted against the imposition of *tenente* João Alberto as *interventor*. Vargas, who believed in the virtues of a rural culture and economy, faced a strong internal migration from agricultural workers that were streaming to the cities. An increasing urban population without jobs threatened political order. He sought ways of increasing industrial employment to absorb the growing urban workforce, a process that developed into a strategy of import substitution reflecting his xenophobia. This fit the nationalist and developmentalist sentiments of the military that increasingly became the major support of Vargas. In 1934 a new constitution was written and the Congress elected Vargas to the presidency. The constitution, which did not allow for reelection, called for elections in 1938. As the election approached, political parties began to support candidates. But in 1937, backed by the army, Vargas declared the *Estado Novo* (New State), officializing his dictatorship. He presented a new constitution, eliminated political parties, and further increased his authority by centralizing fiscal power. A corporative system of state-sponsored unions kept labor both under control and supportive of the government. A system of labor courts, modeled on the Italian system, was created to eliminate industrial conflict. Both strikes and lockouts were declared against the public interest, while other legislation established a minimum wage and protection for labor. Vargas cultivated his image to become the *pai dos pobres* (father of the poor).

As World War II approached, Vargas sensed the eventual victory of the Allies and negotiated Brazilian involvement in the war with the United States. With American financial and technical support, he gained the construction of the first integrated steel plant in Latin America at Volta Redonda, in the state of Rio de Janeiro, and the training of a Brazilian Expeditionary Force, which then sailed to Europe and fought alongside American troops in the Italian campaign.

The involvement of the Brazilian military alongside U.S. troops created a long-term relationship between officers of the two militaries. The technological and industrial resources available to the American troops impressed upon the Brazilians the need for accelerated economic development. Additionally, strong friendships were developed that extended into the mid-1980s and resulted in close cooperation between the armed forces along with acceptance of North American views of global ideological conflict.

A strong argument erupted, which continues today, dominating economic policy debate in the late 1940s. Industrialists, with Roberto Simonsen as their spokesman, wanted protection from foreign competition, including high tariff barriers and restriction of the entry of foreign capital. Opposing him, economist Eugenio Gudin believed that Brazil's future lay in the export of primary products and called for low tariffs and foreign investments. The debate took place in the newspapers, but Simonsen's position mirrored the sentiments of Vargas and the arguments coming from the Economic Commission for Latin America (ECLA) in Santiago, Chile.

Democratic Interlude

At a time when Brazilian troops were fighting in Europe against dictatorship, the *Estado Novo* of Vargas seemed out of place to many Brazilians and pressure for elections built. Vargas began the process of developing political parties, encouraging the organization of the Social Democratic Party (PSD) by a group of *interventors* representing the interests of their states, but also including industrialists and large landowners, and the Brazilian Labor Party (PTB) built around urban labor and a system of control over workers. Opposition to Vargas, including many of the *tenentes*, created the National Democratic Union (UDN). General Eurico Dutra was launched as a candidate of a PSD-PTB coalition, while UDN nominated Brigadero Eduardo Gomes, a *tenente* hero and head of the air force during World War II. Vargas was forced to resign in October 1945, and Dutra was elected president by popular vote. A new constitution, written in 1946, completed the move to democratic rule.

Vargas returned to the presidency in 1950, winning election as the PSD-PTB candidate, easily defeating Eduardo Gomes' second attempt as a candidate. His term in office was marked by a tilt toward economic nationalism, especially the creation of Petrobras, the national oil company. The Vargas presidency was full of allegations of corruption, much of it coming from the pen and voice of the Carlos Lacerda, newspaper publisher and governor of Rio de Janeiro. Told by the military leadership that he was no longer acceptable as president, Vargas committed suicide in the presidential palace in 1954, leaving behind a statement blaming his death on a "sea of mud" and a "campaign of international groups joined with national groups" seeking control of Brazilian resources. Vargas became a political martyr, which turned the tables on his tormentors.

Scheduled presidential elections went forward, pitting Minas Gerais governor Juscelino Kubitschek, the PSD-PTB candidate, against UDN candidate and *tenente* leader, Marshal Juarez Tavora. Kubitschek, a physician of Czech ancestry, campaigned with the slogan "Fifty years progress in five years," winning the presidency. With his inauguration in 1956, Kubitschek quickly set out a "Program of Targets," including the construction of a new capital, christened Brasília, to be located in the country's interior. Much of the program was authored by Celso Furtado, an economist who had been working for ECLA. An automobile industry came into being, encouraged by special treatment of foreign manufacturers who were given a protected market, bringing a major surge of import substitution. A program of roads and other infrastructure changed the map of Brazil. The fast-paced growth brought employment, increasing inflation, and charges of corruption. Kubitschek finished his term with a display of confidence and accomplishment, moving the capital from Rio de Janeiro to the newly constructed Brasília. However, rural unrest was beginning and labor felt left out.

In early 1961, UDN candidate and São Paulo governor Janio Quadros became Brazil's new president, defeating PSD-PTB candidate Marshall Henrique Lott. Quadros had campaigned with a broom as the symbol of his pledge to sweep the country clean of corruption. A major attempt to stabilize the economy failed, mostly due to the refusal of the congress to approve harsh austerity measures. In August, after only seven months in office, Quadros tendered his resignation, apparently in an attempt to gain stronger presidential powers, but was surprised when the congress accepted it. João "Jango" Goulart, minister of labor under Vargas and Kubitschek's vice president, had been elected vice president again under Quadros. At the time of the president's resignation, Goulart was visiting the People's Republic of China, lending credence to the belief that he was sympathetic to communist ideas. The generals refused to permit Goulart to assume office on his return, but after negotiation and a quickly legislated parliamentary system, Goulart was sworn in as president, with the leader of the Chamber of Deputies as prime minister. Goulart then won a national plebiscite in January 1963, returning Brazil to a presidential system and gaining full executive powers for himself. Dissatisfaction with Goulart, the result of recession, increasing inflation, fears of his Leftist rhetoric, and his failure to punish a military mutiny, resulted in a joint military-civilian coup at the end of March 1964, a coup hailed by the United States as saving Brazil from communism.

The Military in Politics

The involvement of the military in Brazilian politics certainly did not begin with the 1964 coup. The history of Brazil is one that includes intimate inclusion of the military beginning with the Paraguayan War in the middle of the nineteenth century. Later military officers eliminated the monarchy, with military officers taking over the presidency for the first two post-imperial administrations, those of Generals Deodoro da Fonseca and Floriano Peixoto. At that time the officers assumed the *poder moderador* (moderating power) earlier exercised by the emperor, beginning a long history of insertion into politics. The federal military, seeing itself as the only political force above regional interests and rival civilian factions competing for power, gave itself the right to involve itself in politics any time the nation seemed in danger. Such was the presidency of General Hermes da Fonseca (1910–1914). This was followed by the *tenente* uprisings, first in 1922 with the "18 of the Fort" at Copacabana in Rio de Janeiro and two years later with the 1924 revolt centered in São Paulo. The revolt was followed by the march of the young military officers, led by Captain Luis Carlos Prestes, through the interior of the country trying to overthrow the landed oligarchy in an attempt to correct perceived maladies in the political system. It was the same beliefs that led to a split in military ranks in 1930 and support for the overthrow of the lame-duck presidency of Washington Luis, placing Getúlio Vargas in Rio de Janeiro's Catete Palace (then Brazil's White House).

Later, it was the military that became the opposition to Vargas, and every presidential election from 1945 until 1980 had a military officer as one of the two major presidential candidates. When Vargas was pressured out of the presidency in 1945, his elected replacement was army chief of staff General Eurico Dutra, opposed by Brigadeiro Eduardo Gomes, survivor of the Copacabana Fort uprising of 1922 and hero of the Italian campaign of the Brazilian Expeditionary Force during World War II. Four years later Vargas won the presidency, with Gomes again being defeated. In 1955 Kubitschek was elected president, opposed by former *tenente* leader Marshal Juarez Távora, one of the founders of the Escola Superior de Guerra (Superior War College); four years later Jânio Quadros won the presidency against opposition candidate Marshal Henrique Lott.

Generals as Presidents

Following the overthrow of President Goulart, Army Chief of Staff General Humberto Castelo Branco was made president by vote of congress, with the expectation that he would fill out the remainder of the Quadros-Goulart term and allow new elections in 1965. However, the military was not about to hand power back to civilian politicians, who were seen as corrupt and working for particular advantages of the states rather than the nation. The presidential term of Castelo Branco was extended until 1967. The generals abolished old political parties and replaced them with an official party, the National Renovating Alliance (ARENA), and a single opposition party, the Brazilian Democratic Movement (MDB). Political power was centralized in the executive, who could make decree laws without the consent of congress, and congress was temporarily closed. Election of presidents was transferred from popular vote to indirect election by an electoral college made up of members of congress. Election of governors and mayors of major cities was also made indirect. A major shift in power occurred when the federal government reduced the distribution of tax revenues, retaining more in Brasília and controlling expenditures. Before 1964, close to 55 percent of federally collected revenues were passed on to the states and municipalities; in the next twenty years that dropped to 30 percent.

Castelo Branco began the process of taming inflation, then running at more than 50 percent a year, by fiscal reform and monetary restriction. A veteran of the Brazilian Expeditionary Force in Italy, he aligned Brazil with the policies of the United States in a doctrine of national security that included repression of the suspected communists. A series of institutional acts, decrees that bypassed legislative approval, centralized control of the government and suspended political rights for many prominent citizens, including former political allies of the military such as Carlos Lacerda and former president Kubitschek, both of whom had hoped to run for the presidency in the next election.

A hard-line military faction, critical of the administration of Castelo Branco, controlled the next election and made General Arthur Costa e Silva the president in 1967. He brought a new economic team into the government headed by a young professor of economics from the University of São Paulo, Antônio Delfim Netto. Delfim Netto increased available credit, especially in agriculture, and began a process of fast economic growth that lasted from 1968 to 1974, averaging almost 11 percent a year, the "Brazilian Miracle." Production costs were reduced by control of wages, and exports were promoted. Costa e Silva personally took on writing a new constitution that fit the needs of the military. A massive cerebral hemorrhage incapacitated the president in mid-1969, but the military leadership refused to allow the civilian vice president to take office and instead selected General Emílio Médici as the new president.

Médici continued the economics of Delfim Netto and additionally began a project to develop the Amazon. Opposition to the government, including urban guerrilla warfare and the kidnapping of foreign diplomats, was met with increased repression, including the disappearance of suspects. At the same time, the rapid growth of the economy brought increased social mobility and national pride. The continued growth in the economy served to legitimize military rule despite a rising vote for the opposition MDB.

General Ernesto Geisel, part of the same military group as former president Castelo Branco, became president in 1974 with an announced policy of moving the country back toward democracy. He brought in a new economic team that faced problems of increasing inflation and price increases in the purchase of petroleum. International borrowing and increased investment by the state sought to rekindle the growth pattern, as the opposition politicians increased in strength. State-owned companies dominated the economy, running much of industry, mining, and banking. Geisel restored the political rights of many who had been exiled, only to find them winning contested elections for governorships and other offices. General João Figueiredo, selected by Geisel to succeed him in 1979, faced continuing deterioration of the economy, with slowed growth and increasing inflation. A serious recession began in 1982 as foreign investment stopped and the servicing of Brazil's debt, now the largest among developing countries at $120 billion, overwhelmed the budget. A new independent labor union formed under the leadership of autoworker Luís Inácio da Silva, "Lula," breaking the control that the government had maintained over workers since the administration of Vargas. Professional groups and the Catholic Church openly expressed the realities of military repression of civilians.

A new election law attempted to split the opposition by allowing new political parties to form, and required all parties to have the word "Party" in their name. ARENA became the Party of Social Democracy (PDS) and the MDB the PMDB. At the same time new parties were organized. Lula organized the Workers' Party (PT) and Leonel Brizola, governor of Rio de Janeiro, founded the Party of Democratic Workers (PDT). Massive popular demonstrations, *diretas ja!* (direct elections now!), filled the streets with demands for election of the president by popular vote. Figueiredo refused, and PDS split over the issue, with some members leaving the party to form the Party of the Liberal Front (PFL). In the next presidential election, both candidates were civilians, and the opposition won the indirect election with a coalition of PMDB and PFL, called the Democratic Alliance, that included a vice president who had previously been president of the promilitary majority party, PDS.

The "New Republic"

The day before the inauguration in March 1985, president-elect Tancredo Neves of the PMDB underwent emergency surgery and vice president-elect, José Sarney, temporarily took over the office, shortly thereafter assuming the presidency when Neves died. Brazil now had a civilian president who had earlier been head of the military-aligned PDS and a congress controlled by the leadership that had opposed the military.

Sarney faced a serious economic crisis of high inflation and slow growth. A group of young economists came forward with new theories on how to halt the inflation without the orthodox recessionary measures normally prescribed. At the end of February 1986, the theories were put into effect with the Cruzado Plan, which froze wages and prices while increasing the income of the lowest paid workers. The resulting new demands brought new employment as industry used existing capacity for production. The plan's immediate success catapulted Sarney's popularity, while preparations went ahead for an election of congressional deputies, many senators, and governors. Despite recommendations of economists that the plan be modified since demand exceeded productive capacity, Sarney refused. The great importance of the election was that the combined deputies and senators would also become a constituent assembly, writing a new constitution to replace that of the military's. Sarney's allies overwhelmingly won the election, but the Cruzado Plan collapsed immediately after the election as inflation soared and growth came to a halt by the end of the year.

The new 1988 constitution provided liberal benefits for many formerly left out of social services and distributed a larger portion of the federal tax receipts to the states and municipalities. A split in the PMDB resulted in the creation of the Brazilian Social Democratic Party (PSDB), led by senators displeased with the rightward swing of the PMDB resulting from former ARENA members who had switched parties. Sarney, who had successfully campaigned for a five-year presidency (later changed to four years), completed his term in March 1990, while inflation soared to over 80 percent a month.

The new president, Fernando Collor de Mello, had beaten labor leader and organizer of the PT Luís Inácio "Lula" da Silva in the first direct election for a president since 1960, winning 52.6 percent of the run-off election. Governor of the small northeastern state of Alagoas, Collor was the youngest president in Brazil's history, campaigning against corruption in politics and established politicians and running as a candidate of a new party he created solely for the election. He promised that no one who had served previous governments would be in his cabinet. His most audacious appointment was a thirty-six-year-old woman, Zélia Cardoso de Mello, as minister of economics, a combination of the former ministries of finance and planning.

To control inflation, Collor immediately froze all saving accounts in the country, temporarily lowering inflation. Additionally, Collor believed that Brazil's import substitution strategy needed to be replaced with an economy open to the global market. He began a process of privatization of the state-owned industries, beginning with the National Steel Company at Volta Redonda. A scheduled lowering of tariffs on imports reduced the barriers that protected Brazilian industry from international competition. Thus Brazil embarked on a new economic course, sloughing off decades of state-led growth and protectionism.

Collor, secure in his popular election and coming into office as the Cold War's abrupt ending invalidated the national security doctrine, began to reduce the influence of the military, including the cutting of their budget and the elimination of nuclear weapons research. He also continued reducing the long-standing antagonisms with Argentina. In the spring of 1991, Collor signed the Treaty of Asunción creating a common market among the countries of Argentina, Uruguay, Paraguay, and Brazil. Known by its abbreviated name, Mercosul (Market of the Southern Cone) effectively increased the internal market for the products of the two largest economies in South America.

The economic stabilization policies of the new government were ineffective, as inflation increased. At the same time, two of the ministers were accused of corruption and congress refused to go along with many of Collor's proposals to restructure the economy. A cabinet reshuffle brought back the ambassador to the United States, Marcílio Marques Moreira, an economist with a strong banking background, who was made the economics minister.

In spring 1992, Fernando Collor's younger brother, Pedro, publicly stated that the president was receiving funds in exchange for political favors. A congressional investigation produced evidence that resulted in the impeachment of Collor, followed in December by his resignation and a vote by the congress to remove his political rights for ten years. The impeachment proceedings of Collor were the first time in Latin American history that a president had been legally removed from office through constitutional processes. Brazil's fledgling democratic institutions had passed a major test.

Vice President Itamar Franco, succeeding to the presidency, continued Collor's privatization initiative and other neoliberal programs. The most important action he took was the appointment of Senator Fernando Henrique Cardoso, first as foreign minister, then as finance minister. The president gave Cardoso full support in a program to end the longstanding inflation that had plagued Brazil for decades and was then running at more than 20 percent a month. The new finance minister brought together a team of economists, many of whom had developed the Cruzado Plan in the Sarney administration, and with them instituted a new stabilization program, the Real Plan, named after the new currency put into circulation. By July 1994 the Real Plan had brought inflation down dramatically, and Cardoso became a candidate for the presidency in the fall elections.

In the election, the only two significant candidates were Cardoso, leader of PSDB in coalition with PFL, and Workers' Party candidate Lula, who had narrowly lost to Collor in the previous election. Cardoso won the election and enjoyed marked popularity as the continued success of the Real Plan meant a better standard of living for much of the population, especially the urban poor.

Cardoso had an international reputation as a scholar, having coauthored a book in the 1960s that examined the problems of economic development in Latin America in relation to its dependency on the capitalist economy of the industrialized nations of Europe and North America. He believed that dependent economies like Brazil could develop associated with the industrialized world, "associated-dependent development." During the military regime, he had been removed from his position as a professor of sociology and spent a number of years in exile, teaching in France and the United States. One of the founders of the left-of-center PSDB, Cardoso was now president, elected in a coalition with the right-of-center PFL.

Much of the legislation for the restructuring of Brazil's economy came through the extensive use of provisionary measures, allowing a president to legislate for thirty days unless the Congress rejects the measure. Provisionary measures could be reissued every thirty days as long as Congress did not act. It was with provisionary measures that the Real Plan was instituted and continued every thirty days for thirteen months until the congress enacted the necessary legislation.

Cardoso came to office as the man who defeated inflation, and his continuing legitimacy largely depended on continuing success at holding inflation down. Successive governments in Brazil had used inflation to pay for budget deficits, and the deficits in turn fed inflation. A major issue has been the necessity of reforming the budget in order to hold down inflation and balance the budget. Even though the government's coalition in the congress enjoyed sufficient votes to pass reforming legislation, party loyalty has not been adequate for fiscal reform, as deputies often voted contrary to their parties' position. The Congress did agree to amend the constitution to permit the president, governors, and mayors to run for a second consecutive term, a break with Brazil's past, and allowing Cardoso to run for reelection, claiming the need for a second term to finish the job of restructuring the economy.

Political Economy

In many ways, Brazil's politics have been defined by its economy. Initial European interest in Brazil, especially by the Portuguese, focused on the export of primary products including brazilwood as a dye, sugar, gold, diamonds, coffee, and rubber. By the first part of the twentieth century coffee had become synonymous with images of Brazil. Even today, primary products remain a major part of the export economy, with iron ore, soybeans, orange juice, and frozen chickens taking their place alongside coffee.

By the 1930s Brazilian economists and planners began to realize that the future development of the country required diversification and industrialization. The ability to compete in the international market of industrial goods was questioned, and Brazil began implementing a strategy of import substitution with its allied policy of trade barriers, including high tariffs, to protect the new industries. Much of the new strategy came from theoretical studies by the United Nation's Economic Commission for Latin America (ECLA), which claimed lack of development resulted from a structural dependence on Europe and the United States. This required restrictions on trade and foreign investment while building an import substitution industry and erecting tariff barriers to protect the new national industries. Brazilian governments, starting with construction of the National Steel Company at Volta Redonda in the 1940s, began the development of state-owned industry, soon followed by the creation of a state-owned oil company, Petrobras. Electric power and telephones also were taken over by the government, and there was major investment in transportation and many other areas. The government became the major owner of industry and employer in the country as the import substitution strategy was pushed with low-interest loans.

In the private sector, the development of the automobile industry brought with it many associated companies as parts suppliers and service industries grew. Brazil went from being a supplier of coffee to a highly diverse industrializing country, producing aircraft, weaponry, subway cars, electronics, pharmaceuticals, petrochemicals, textiles, and footwear.

Diversification of industry by import substitution was accompanied by diversification in agricultural exports. The military governments gave negative interest loans to agribusiness for expansion and new products, knowing that it was the fastest way of increasing exports. Part of the increase came with the development of the alcohol-from-sugar program for automobile fuel in response to the dramatic rise in imported petroleum prices in the 1970s.

The military, needing legitimacy, strongly pushed economic growth as a means of gaining popular support. During the late 1960s and early 1970s, rapidity of economic growth earned Brazil considerable international attention. The strategy of import substitution, begun under Vargas and continued with the advice of the dependency theory advocates, was expanded by the military, giving the federal government control over a major portion of the economy. The growth was financed by reducing the labor value of production through limiting wage increases, through funds from the national pension program, and from foreign loans. Beset with persistent balance of payment problems, Brazil was able to finance growth through foreign lending in the 1970s. Banks pushed loans as a result of the glut of petrodollars they were accumulating from oil producers who had raised prices dramatically. The ability to borrow ended with the oil price collapse of the late 1970s drying up the ready availability of foreign loan capital.

Inflation became a characteristic of the Brazilian economy, fed in part by federal and state expenditures exceeding tax revenues. Much of industry was oligopolistic, faced little competition domestically, and was protected by high tariffs from less expensive foreign products. As a result, prices could be set to guarantee profits without regard to quality or costs. Wages were indexed to inflation, their value set by government standards rather than by collective bargaining.

During the 1980s the economy stagnated as inflation increased, the worst conditions since the 1929 Depression, creating the "Lost Decade." The combination of depression and inflation was a major factor in the loss of power of the military and their decision to allow a return to democratic rule. The civilian governments of Sarney and Collor tried unsuccessfully to stabilize the economy with various anti-inflation plans.

The Collor government changed Brazil's economic policies, privatizing state-owned companies, inviting greater foreign investment, and lowering tariff barriers to imports. These actions continued under the brief administration of President Itamar Franco and were followed by the first successful stabilization effort headed by Franco's Finance Minister, Fernando Henrique Cardoso—an action that propelled him to the presidency.

Geography of Inequality

Brazil is divided into twenty-seven states, varying geographically in size from the huge state of Amazonas to small states like Alagoas. Populations of the states also represent great differences, with a population of more than 30 million in the state of São Paulo and only 300,000 in Amapá. Elected governors and state legislatures govern states, which, in turn, are divided into some 5000 municipalities, in some ways equivalent to U.S. counties, each with its own mayor and municipal council.

Brasília is the site of the federal government, located in a Federal District near the center of the southern part of the country. Constructed in the late 1950s in an area long allocated for a new federal capital, it was designed by Brazilian architects Oscar Niemeyer and Lucio Costa. Today the region of the Federal District has over 2 million people and has become a hub that connects the interior of the country with the industrialized southeast.

The Brazilian Institute of Geography and Statistics (IBGE) divides the country into five regions: north, northeast, southeast, center-west, and south. The north, comprised of the states of Pará, Amazonas, Acre, Rondonia, Roraima, Amapa, and Tocantins, is the area of the Amazon basin with the cities of Manaus and Belém the only two major cities. This is the area of Brazil's vast rainforest, the home of most of Brazil's remaining Indians. This region borders the Guianas, Venezuela, Colombia, Peru, and Bolivia, yet has few roads or other land transport. The northeast, a region of drought, desert, and poverty, has long existed with a sugar economy and subsistence farming. An Office for the Development of the Northeast, SUDENE, is charged with improving the living condition among the northeastern states, but it has not made a significant difference in its forty years of existence. All the states have an Atlantic coast, with the cities of Fortaleza, Recife, and Salvador major ports and state capitals. Northeastern states are Maranhão, Piauí, Ceará, Rio Grande do Norte, Paraíba, Pernambuco, Alagoas, Sergipe, and Bahia. The northeast's population includes many descendants from the African slave trade and Salvador, Bahia, is known as the capital of African Brazil. The southeast consists of the states of Rio de Janeiro, Espírito Santo, Minas Gerais, and São Paulo and is the economic powerhouse of Brazil, as well as the region with the greatest population. The center-west, a new frontier for Brazil, contains the states of Mato Grosso, Mato Grosso do Sul, and Goias, along with the Federal District of Brasília. The south is comprised of the states of Rio Grande do Sul, Santa Catarina, and Paraná, the most European part of Brazil, with much of the population tracing ancestry back to Germany and Italy.

Brazil's geography of inequality underpins its system of economic and political power. The northeast is poor, literacy is low, and infant mortality high. Much of the political power still resides in the hands of traditional families, while much of the population lives by subsistence farming and the area is devastated every few years by drought. The southeast and south are industrialized, with the state of São Paulo's economy exceeding that of Argentina and that of the state of Minas Gerais being greater than that of Chile or Peru. Banking, agribusiness, and service industries are also centered in São Paulo.

A shift in the population has taken place, changing the major locus of poverty. In the last fifty years Brazil has gone from an agrarian to an overwhelmingly urban society—now 80 percent of the population—with peasants pushed off the land, especially in the northeast, by drought and capital-intensive agriculture, moving to the major cities seeking work in the increasingly industrialized economy. The result is seen in the thousands of *favelas*, the squatter housing built on swamps, vacant lots, and hillsides, which are a prominent and permanent part of the urban landscape. Often lacking adequate running water or sewage, their populations run into the millions.

The geography of inequality is not only regional but also appears in the cities and their *favelas*, in deep class divisions, in great differentials of educational opportunity, and in income maldistribution. The income of the upper 10 percent of society is twenty-six times the income of the lowest 40 percent. Brazil has the greatest wealth inequality of any major nation in the world.

A Culture of Discrimination

AFRO-BRAZILIANS

To the first-time visitor to Brazil, the apparent lack of racial discrimination in a population that exhibits every human color seemingly demonstrates a color-blind society. In the 1940s Brazilian anthropologist Gilberto Freyre gave legitimacy to the concept of racial democracy with his studies of social history encapsulated in his book *The Masters and the Slaves* (*Casa-Grande & Senzala*). Census takers have found over 100 words used to express the multitude of ethnotypes resulting from relations among the many races present in the society. Possibly the most popular and best-known Brazilian is soccer star Edson Arantes do Nascimento, better known as Pelé, an Afro-Brazilian; a mulatto, Machado de Assis, founder of the prestigious Brazilian Academy of Letters, is perhaps Latin America's greatest literary figure.

But behind this surface lies a pervasive racism. Classified employment ads in newspapers ask for persons of "good appearance," code words meaning Afro-Brazilians need not apply. Despite the fact that a majority of Brazilians have some African ancestry, persons of color are poorly represented in politics and in business. A cursory examination of poverty shows income levels decreasing as complexion darkens. A visit to the universities finds few of color among either the faculty or the students. The officer corps of the military, and especially the navy, is almost exclusively white.

Organized reaction against discrimination exists in muted form, not emerging as a significant interest group. Racial discrimination is constitutionally illegal. Furthermore, since the end of slavery in 1888, there have been no "Jim Crow" laws in Brazil. A result is that Afro-Brazilians have not had a focus in their battle for equality. There are, however, a series of Afro-Brazilian organizations that are pressing for greater consciousness and full equality.

Advances have been made in recent years. An Afro-Brazilian was elected governor of one of the smaller states, and another was elected mayor of Brazil's largest city, São Paulo, in 1996. In 1999, the second Afro-Brazilian was promoted to the rank of general. One of the most important politicians in Rio de Janeiro is Benedita da Silva, an Afro-Brazilian woman from the *favelas* who has been federal deputy, senator, and vice governor of the state.

WOMEN

Traditionally, Brazilian culture calls for the man as breadwinner and the woman as housewife and mother. Men control Brazilian society, but with women entering the workforce in rapidly increasing numbers, this culture has been changing. Two forces have brought this change. First is the decreasing value of labor in production, partly the result of the "wage squeeze" during the military regime and partly due to restructuring of the economy. Both have exacerbated income inequality and require more than one income to feed and sustain a family. Second, an increasing number of educated women are claiming the right to personal careers and professions. On an average, the income of a black woman is one-quarter that of a white man.

The changing role of women also appears in Brazil's political life. It was only in the decade of the 1990s that women emerged onto the political scene as elected officials and decision makers. The Workers' Party (PT) has been a vehicle for a number of them, including the election of women as mayors, Luiza Erundina in São Paulo and Maria Luiza Fontanelli in Fortaleza, congresswoman Marta Suplicy from São Paulo, and Benedita da Silva, vice governor of Rio de Janeiro. Luiza Erundina subsequently served in the cabinet of President Itamar Franco, and Maria Luiza Fontanelli was elected as a congresswoman from the state of Ceará. Marta Suplicy, best known for her books on sexology, became mayor of Sao Paulo in 2000, and Benedita da Silva earlier was elected federal senator from Rio de Janeiro. In 1994 the state of Maranhão elected Rosane Sarney, the daughter of former president José Sarney (1985–1990), as the first woman governor; she was subsequently re-elected in 1998. A few women have been appointed to cabinet positions in Brasília; the most notable is the appointment of Zélia Cardoso de Mello to the most powerful position as minister of the economy by President Collor de Mello (no relation) in 1990.

A significant change in gender politics is the election law that required that 20 percent of the candidates fielded by political parties in the 1998 election be women, rising to 30 percent in the next election. Of course, candidature does not necessarily translate into increased election of women, but it strongly increases the probability that women will assume a greater role among public officials.

The Political System

Brazil, unlike most Latin American countries that gained their independence from monarchical European countries shortly after the independence of the United States and became republics, adopted a constitutional monarchy system including a bicameral legislature with a population-based lower house of deputies and a senate representing states. The legal system, carried over from the Portuguese colonial period, was based on the Napoleanic code rather than on English common law, as in the United States. As mentioned, Brazil, too, became a republic but only at the end of the nineteenth century, in 1889.

During the military regime (1964–1985), elections continued and Congress was briefly shut down twice. Generals who became president took off their uniforms and served only five-year terms. The military manipulated election laws, created and joined states, and used the economy in order to maintain control, especially where their dominance of voting in the smaller northeastern states meant a majority in the senate.

A major problem in Brazilian elections is the manner in which federal deputies and state legislatures are elected; Brazil has an open-list, proportional election. Deputies and members of the state legislatures are not elected from individual districts, but at large, from the state, each state acting as a single election district. The candidates with the most votes win the seats of the state. As a result, candidates compete against other members of their own party. While it is necessary to be affiliated with a party in order to be a candidate, winners have little loyalty to their parties and often change party to gain an improved position. Additionally, this method of proportional representation strengthens various interest groups that would not be able to elect a representative in a local district but can win sufficient votes in the states to elect a favored candidate. This puts a premium on coalition-building while weakening party structure; party discipline is episodic at best.

Election to executive positions, the president, governors, and mayors, requires a majority of valid votes cast. If no candidate obtains a majority on the first ballot, the two candidates with the most votes compete in a run-off election.

Voting is required in Brazil, and the 1988 constitution extended the franchise both to illiterates and to sixteen-year-olds. This total opening was gradually obtained in different intervening constitutions until the one of 1988, which marked a final and major shift away from the restricted franchise adopted in 1891, when only literate males could vote.

1988 Constitution

The congress, serving as a constituent assembly, wrote a new constitution in 1988. Written in an atmosphere of reaction against the centralization and excesses of the military regime, the new constitution has a strong liberal content, including bringing rural workers into the social security system for the first time and expanding labor rights.

The most important decentralizing provision of the new constitution requires that substantial federal revenues be passed on to the states and municipalities. At the same time, the constitution failed to provide for funding of the new expenditures or the transfer of some of the responsibilities to the states and municipalities. An additional result of the constitutional redistribution of revenues is the greatly enhanced power of governors, who control spending of funds within their states and with it pork for deputies who seek reelection. With power and patronage tilted to the states, governors have strong influence over their state delegations to congress. Municipalities have been the largest benefactors of the new funds, with many mayors initiating new projects as a result. It has made mayorships a valuable political position, often giving incumbents sufficient popularity to select their successor. The advantages falling to municipalities have resulted in the splitting of many of them, creating new municipal governments.

Presidents have sought to amend the constitution in order to change the distribution of funds so as to balance the federal budget, as a balanced budget is essential to the control of inflation. But governors, enjoying the new power that comes from the constitutionally mandated funds, have often successfully prevented amendments that would reallocate monies.

The President

The president and vice president are elected directly every four years with the right of a single reelection. If a candidate does not receive a majority of the votes, a run-off election between the top two candidates decides the winner. The presidential residence is the Palácio da Alvorada (Palace of the Dawn), and presidential offices are in the Palácio do Planalto (Palace of the High Plain) in the capital of Brasília.

Historically the President of Brazil has been able to function largely independent of the congress. The 1988 constitution reduced the power of the presidency in relation to the Congress, giving the congress virtual veto of any presidential action. In reality, however, the faction-ridden congress has not used its power effectively and the president has been able to use provisionary measures to legislate, which the Congress has accepted despite their power to overturn the measures. A leader of the government in the congress introduces legislation for the executive and tries to shepherd it into law. The president has the right of legislative veto but can be overridden by a second congressional vote.

The president constructs his cabinet in order to give representation to various interest groups, political bosses, or parties, expecting support in the Congress as a result of the offices. The Ministries of Finance (Fazenda) and Planning (Planejamento), which, along with the president of the Central Bank, determine the economic policies of Brazil, are the most important. Often there is serious rivalry between the two ministers, the president and the personalities of the ministers determining which one of them dominates policy. Usually the business community of São Paulo, expressed by the São Paulo State Federation of Industries (FIESP), is consulted before the president makes his choice of economic ministers. The Ministry of Labor will go to someone who has links to unions. Cabinet positions may be used to bring different parties into the government, with deputies and senators given positions. In this manner, a president can form a legislative coalition to support his policies, with the expectation that the cabinet members will be able to obtain their parties' votes for executive-sponsored legislation. Accepting a cabinet or other executive position does not mean losing a legislative seat, but only temporarily surrendering it to an elected alternate legislator and reclaiming the seat when he/she returns to the legislature. The Foreign Ministry, known as Itamaraty, is very professional and operates largely independent of the foreign minister, who acts more as a spokesman for foreign policy.

A major new change has been the creation of a single Ministry of Defense, replacing the traditional Ministries of the Army, Navy, Air Force, and Chief of Staff of the Armed Forces. The new Ministry is a political position headed by a civilian, and the military forces report to the minister, while the military officers focus on the professionalism of their units rather than on politics. This change lessens the role of the military in Brazilian politics, which has given up de facto the moderating power they assumed at the empire's end in 1889.

A constitutionally created Council of the Republic, composed of the Minister of Justice and representatives from the House and the Senate, advises the president on legislation. Similarly, a Council of National Defense advises on questions of "national sovereignty," membership coming from the military commanders; the ministers of justice, foreign relations, and planning; and representatives of the house and senate.

The president also nominates federal judges. If the president leaves the country, the vice president, followed by the presidents of the Senate and the House, becomes acting president until his return.

The 1988 constitution expanded the role of the office of the General Prosecutor of the Republic, giving him the ability to investigate and prosecute crime independent of political pressures. The office is in many ways equivalent to the attorney general in the United States. But in other ways the General Prosecutor's Office is a fourth branch of government, as it has constitutionally guaranteed functional and administrative autonomy. However, its relatively recent definition by the constitution has meant that it is still determining its full role as a safeguard of democratic rule.

The Legislature

Brazil has a bicameral legislature: a lower House of Deputies (Câmara dos Deputados) with representation based on the population of each state and an upper house, the Senate (Senado), with three elected from each state. All deputies are elected every four years. The Federal District and territories also have congressional representation. In addition to legislation, the houses of Congress can initiate Parliamentary Commissions of Inquiry (CPIs) to investigate possibly legal irregularities. The constitution stipulates that each state has a minimum of eight and a maximum of seventy deputies. This distribution strongly favors the smaller and poorer states of the north and center-west over the more populous and richer state of São Paulo.

Senators are elected for eight years, half of them every four years. Each senator is elected with a first and second alternate senator, who replaces the senator if he/she leaves office, either through death, removal, or to accept another position. Senators frequently leave their seats, often to run for mayor or governor or to become a member of the cabinet. If a senator wishes to return to his/her seat, the alternate reverts to his/her previous position.

Like the United States, the House of Deputies has the right of impeachment and the Senate, the trial of the impeachment.

The Courts

The Supreme Court has eleven judges, nominated by the president and confirmed by the Senate. It deals with federal issues, constitutionality of legislation, and is the final court of appeal. Additionally there is a Supreme Court of Justice, which rules as a final court of appeal on criminal cases. The judiciary also includes a number of separate courts systems to deal with specific areas of jurisdiction.

A National Labor Court system arbitrates between labor and management. All the courts have regional and local lower courts. Labor courts were set up in the 1930s under the administration of Getúlio Vargas to reduce the cost of strikes and to use labor unions as an arm of presidential power. Today the courts still serve to mediate industrial conflict, being a holdover of the corporatist institutions set up at that time. An Electoral Court system controls elections, making sure that candidates have the necessary credentials, that voting is honest, and that the elections take place in accordance with the law. A military court system, as its name implies, handles cases involving members of the armed forces, which has its own system of military law.

The judicial system of Brazil is the weakest of the branches of government. This is partly a result of a lack of a tradition of judicial independence and partly the result of the fact that law is based on the Napoleonic code rather than on judicial interpretation as in the common law system. Lower courts do not always honor Supreme Court decisions, and decisions often are not final, as there are a number of ways to appeal rulings.

Political Parties

Several parties have a significant representation in Brazil. The Party of the Brazilian Democratic Movement (PMDB) is a centrist party that originated as the opposition party that the military allowed during its regime. In addition to membership traced back to its anti-military origin, a number of former members of the military's ARENA, following its lack of popularity, changed party loyalty and joined the PMDB.

ARENA underwent a number of changes, first becoming the Party of Social Democracy (PDS), then incorporating a smaller party to become the Brazilian Progressive Party (PPB). The PPB is the most conservative of Brazil's major parties and is dominated by former governor of São Paulo and businessman Paulo Maluf.

The Party of the Liberal Front (PFL) resulted from a 1984 split in the PDS over the demand for direct election of the president. The new party included the last vice president under the military and the president of the PDS who supported direct election. Today the right-of-center PFL is dominated by Antonio Carlos Magalhães of Bahia and generally represents the political elite of the northeastern states and landowner interests, but it is enjoying increased representation in the south and southeast.

The present president of Brazil, Fernando Henrique Cardoso of São Paulo, leads the Brazilian Social Democratic Party (PSDB), a left-of-center party that split off from PMDB in 1988. Cardoso won the presidential election in coalition with the PFL, with one of its leaders, Marco Maciel, as the vice presidential candidate.

Leonel Brizola organized the Democratic Worker's Party (PDT) shortly after being permitted to return to Brazil after a military-imposed exile. Brother-in-law to ex-president Goulart and former governor of both the states of Rio Grande do Sul and Rio de Janeiro, Brizola was elected a vice president of the world Social Democratic organization. The PDT has been very much the personal vehicle of Brizola, and it takes a nationalist and left-of-center political position. The party is strongest in the states of Rio de Janeiro and the southern states.

The Workers' Party (PT) is the furthest left of the major parties, adopting an openly socialist stance. Its leader and principal organizer is Lula, former automobile worker and three times the runner-up presidential candidate. There are strong links between the PT and the Central Union of Workers (CUT) labor confederation. The greatest support for the PT lies in the industrial cities of São Paulo, in the south, and major urban areas. It is the only political party with party discipline and has grown in importance consistently since its organization. The PT tends to focus opposition to the government in Brasília and maintains initiatives to reduce inequality.

In addition to these larger parties, there are many smaller parties with a few deputies in the congress. Among them is the former Brazilian Communist party, which changed its name to the Popular Socialist Party. In the 1998 presidential election, its candidate, Ciro Gomes, came in third. Gomes earlier had been a member of PSDB, governor of Ceará, and minister of finance. The Communist Party of Brazil, which earlier had split from the Brazilian Communist Party, remains. Pernambuco leader Miguel Arraes leads a Brazilian Socialist Party. The Brazilian Labor Party, taking its name from the earlier party created by Getúlio Vargas, was organized by his grandniece Ivete Vargas.

Throughout these permutations, it bears repeating that the Brazilian genius for short-term coalition-building at the expense of party-building is the dominant style of political action, while federalism continues as the institutional matrix of its politics.

Interest Groups

Major interest groups have organized delegations within the legislature, largely made possible by the system of proportional representation that allows candidates identified with the group to receive sufficient votes in a state to win a seat. Many of these groups cross party lines and are formally organized in the legislature. Among the organized groups are the agricultural interests, banking, soccer clubs, the construction industry, private schools, evangelical churches, and retired persons.

BUSINESS

Business in Brazil is organized within each state by federations of industry, another holdover from the corporatist 1930s. The São Paulo State Federation of Industries (FIESP) is the most powerful of these federations, as the state has close to half the country's industry. FIESP maintains a major research office and financially supports particular political candidates. More than any other group, FIESP represents the interests of Brazilian business and presidents usually ask the advice of the federation in selecting finance and planning ministers and consult with it in matters of the economy. The Brazilian-American Chamber of Commerce wields considerable influence as a result of investment by multinational corporations.

UNIONS

Parallel to business are the labor unions, which function under a consolidation of labor laws originally created by Getúlio Vargas in 1943. The General Federation of Workers (CGT) is the official confederation of unions, based on the corporate structure put in place by Vargas and funded by union dues required from all unionized labor. Unions recognized by the Ministry of Labor receive income from government-required union dues, equivalent to a single day's pay each year, collected and dispersed by the Ministry. The system of official unions gave the government virtual control of labor for almost fifty years. A second major confederation is the Central Union of Workers (CUT), an independent union originally organized under the leadership of Lula by the metal workers of São Paulo's automobile industry in the early 1980s. The CUT has grown at the expense of the CGT as unions feel that their interests are better represented by the independent nature of the new federation. The CUT has been affiliated with the PT, but over time it developed an independent policy position. A union economic research institute, the Interunion Department of Statistics and Social Economics (DIEESE), sponsored by CUT in São Paulo, has been able to challenge government statistics on wages, employment, and buying power of wage earners. A third confederation is the Union Power (Força Sindical), which takes a less militant position than the CUT and has developed, in part, from efforts of the AFL-CIO to create a labor leadership modeled on the North American experience. Rural workers, generally left out of traditional industrial unions, are represented by a National Confederation of Workers in Agriculture (CONTAG), growing first under military sponsorship and later independently, using the right to administer government social programs for its membership as a means of enlisting members. CONTAG affiliated with the CUT in 1996.

BANKING

Banking is big business in Brazil. Until the Real Plan stabilization, banking profits were extremely high, and with their financial power came political power. With inflation under control, many private banks went bankrupt and the political power of the banking industry has diminished, but they still maintain a substantial voice. A serious problem was the state banks, controlled by governors, who often used their financial power for political purposes. The restructuring of private banking and privatization of state banks required a major federal program in the mid-1990s to save the financial system; it cost over $50 billion.

PUBLIC EMPLOYEES

Public employment is well organized in Brazil at all levels. Federal employees are particularly well positioned and effective in protecting their jobs and salaries through the trade union lobby, the Interunion Department of Legislative Staff (DIAP). On a number of occasions presidents of Brazil have tried to reduce federal expenditures by cutting the oversized bureaucracy, but they have often had their attempts defeated as members of congress have responded to the lobbying of the legislative staff.

AGRARIAN REFORM

Much-needed land reform has been a long-standing lack in Brazil. A number of governments have placed laws on the books or made statements about its need, including the newly instituted military regime in 1964, but nothing adequate has yet been done to make land and agricultural credits available to the many who seek it. In the 1950s the Peasant Leagues gained headlines in their occupation of land in the northeast. Much of Brazil's agricultural land is held for investment and lies fallow, and ownership is highly concentrated. Other land is part of large agribusiness companies. A Landless Movement (MST) has organized and become a potent political force in Brazil. They have taken over land, called for a land-reform program, and created dramatic demonstrations of their demands, including a massive march on Brasília and the occupation of government buildings. Battles with landowners have resulted in a number of deaths. The PT and the CUT have recognized the legitimacy of the claims of MST and allied with them, and the Catholic Church has called for recognition of their needs.

LANDOWNERS

Strong opposition to land reform comes from *fazendeiros* (landowners) and the *coroneis* (colonels), traditional political bosses in the northeastern states. Well organized in the Rural Democratic Union (UDR), owners' interests are well represented in the congress as the Parliamentary Front of Agriculture. It can count on more than a third of the votes in the two houses and has successfully prevented any effective land reform. During the writing of the 1988 constitution, they were a part of a coalition called the Big Center (Centrão), which wrote effective protection of their interests. Their continuing power comes from their ability to control voting in rural areas, particularly in the smaller states of the northeast that dominate the senate because of their number. As a result, the UDR can block any legislation contrary to their interests, yet they are necessary for any action that the executive wishes to get through congress.

STUDENTS

Politics in Brazil, as in most of Latin America, begins in the universities. Students seeking political careers first enter university politics, usually associating themselves with a national political party. One of the first organizations to be repressed by the military was the National Union of Students, operating since the 1930s, which reappeared as civilian rule returned. Students were in the forefront of the protests calling for the impeachment of President Collor and can get a hearing in the highest levels of the government on issues pertaining to education. A political party will offer outgoing presidents of the union backing for election to congress and a subsequent political career.

ORGANIZED RELIGION

Brazil is the most populous Catholic country, and the Church remains an important force. The Church historically has been identified with the social and political elite, and demonstrations by the faithful against the Goulart government were an important factor in legitimizing the 1964 coup. During the 1960s much of the Church became strongly committed to liberation theology with its championing of the poor. Under the leadership of the Brazilian National Confederation of Bishops (CNBB), "base communities" were developed for worship and to provide needed services. The base communities fostered the organization of new groups that made demands on the government. Among the new groups that found their inspiration in the base communities was the new trade union movement. During the military regime, priests often were spokesmen of opposition to authoritarian rule. The archdiocese of São Paulo gathered reports on human rights violations that were published in 1985 under the title *Brasil: Nunca Mais* (Brazil: Never Again), which went to fourteen editions. The military governments came to view many priests and bishops as supporters of left-wing policies and antithetical to their intentions of cleansing the country of communism. Some priests were killed or exiled as a result, although the repression in general never went as far as in Chile or Argentina. Like the military governments, the Vatican has seen danger in liberation theology. Liberal priests have been silenced, and the archdiocese of a powerful cardinal who supported the new theology was reduced in size and influence. Over the last decade, as the older generation of Brazilian bishops retired, new bishops opposed to liberation theology have replaced them. Yet the Church is by no means monolithic, as the Council of Bishops, like Brazilian federalism itself, has proved a flexible institution capable of accommodating its different factions.

The Church speaks out on questions of morality, and during the Sarney administration it successfully petitioned the government to ban the commercial distribution of the film *Hail Mary* as sacrilegious. At various times presidents have called on the Vatican to give backing for political policies, including a religious rationale for land reform. Yet the Church has not wanted to form its own political party.

The lack of an adequate number of priests along with a well-financed effort by evangelical groups has resulted in the fast growth of non-Catholic churches, especially evangelicals. The most prominent of them is the Brazilian-born Universal Church of the Reign of God, with over 2500 congregations, which has successfully used television to promote membership and has expanded abroad, including to the United States. With the open-list proportional elections, the evangelical churches have elected a significant number of representatives who represent an important interest bloc in the Câmara dos Deputados.

Another religious interest in Brazil comes through African-based Umbanda and Candomblé, based on West African Yoruba religion brought by slaves. Not well organized politically, its influence cannot be measured due to the blending of many of its rituals and gods with Catholic worship. Yet politicians carefully honor its expression and accept its voice when raised.

The Amazon

The Amazon region makes up almost 60 percent of Brazil's territory; thinly populated except for a few cities like Manaus, the Amazon is important in terms of its biodiversity and effects on the global climate. Brazil's borders with ten other countries run through the Amazon, and vast areas are set aside as homelands for Amero-Indians. The indigenous peoples have suffered dramatically as disease and occupation by persons seeking gold have decimated their populations. Politically, the military has focused on the region in terms of national security and control of drug trafficking. Others have seen the area in terms of potential economic development with the building of vast mining and hydroelectric projects.

Part of the concern has been the destruction of vast areas of the rainforest, amounting to 14 percent of the area in ten years, for lumber, minerals, or farm land. During the military governments an ill-conceived road building project, the Trans-Amazon Highway, tried to open the area for agriculture. In response, environmental groups have tried to save the Amazon, most significantly by promoting sustainable development. Conflict between ranchers and the environmentalists climaxed in the 1988 assassination of Chico Mendes, a leader of the rubber tappers (*seringueiros*), by a local landowner and his son. Mendes had lobbied hard nationally and internationally, winning the "Global 500" award given by the United Nations for his work in organizing extraction reserves that restricted the destruction of the rainforest. He had also organized the tappers into a union and helped found the National Council of Rubber Tappers. His lobbying led to the suspension of a loan from the InterAmerican Development Bank for road building in the area. Mendes' killing sparked an expansion and coordination of environmental groups in Brazil and the winning of political offices by allies.

Brazil Today

Brazil must be counted as one of the world's great emerging markets, with a maturing democracy and a stabilized and growing economy after forty years of inflation. The country has embraced the global economy and the political consequences of that choice. The transition to democratic rule was managed successfully, with increased power to the legislature and the judiciary and measures that reduce the role of the military in domestic politics. Corruption is less acceptable. Economically the tradition of inflation, debt-financing, and oligopolistic industry has been broken. New social programs in education, social security, and public health have been put into place. Internationally, Brazil has emerged as the leading power in both the politics and economy of South America, with almost no historic differences with neighbors and leadership in a regional economic bloc that has significant political ramifications.

Despite these advances, Brazil remains with a legacy of social problems that threaten its future. Poverty, inequality, and ignorance require resources not presently available to the government. Urban infrastructure continues to fall behind need as droughts and mechanization of agriculture drive rural populations into cities. Land reform and agricultural credits for small landholders are part of an unfulfilled agenda. Northeast Brazil still lacks adequate opportunities for employment, and infant mortality rates are among the world's worst. Unfortunately, what Brazilians call "the social debt" and inequities in wealth have no immediate solution. What are required are actions to redistribute income and heavy government expenditures in health, education, and land reform. This comes at a time when the budget is already stretched and increased expenditures could again trigger inflation, a condition that particularly inflicts the poor. Additionally, Brazil must address the growing environmental issues, among them serious urban pollution and the burning of the rainforest.

Growth is returning as investment pours into Brazil. The only question is whether the growth will be sufficient to both absorb the increasing numbers of persons entering the workforce each year and at the same time begin to give jobs to the many already out of work or underemployed. Industrial restructuring as a result of privatization and international market competition reduced blue-collar jobs and brought a wave of unemployment. At the same time, protectionist barriers in industrialized countries limit purchase of Brazil's exports.

Brazil is a nation of superlatives, but one that threatens the nation is the reality of the greatest wealth and income inequality among major nations of the world. The great question is whether Brazil's democracy and economic reforms can be maintained and advanced at the same time that great problems remain. Can successive governments pay the "social debt"?

Chronology

1500 Sighting and landing of Brazilian territory by Pedro Álvares Cabral

1808 Portuguese royal family arrives in Brazil and makes Rio de Janeiro the capital of the Portuguese empire

1822 The Portuguese crown prince, Dom Pedro I, declares Brazil an independent nation and himself emperor

1888 Elimination of slavery

1889 Overthrow of emperor and establishment of the first republic by the military

1922 Week of Modern Art; revolt of Copacabana Fort

1924 Revolt of the *tenentes* in São Paulo and the beginning of the Prestes Column's march through the interior

1930 Overthrow of the first republic and assumption of the presidency by Getúlio Vargas

1937 Vargas establishes the Estado Novo (New State)

1945 Vargas forced out of office; General Dutra elected president

1954 Vargas, elected president in 1950, commits suicide

1956 Election of Juscelino Kubitschek and the beginning of the construction of Brasília

1961 President Jânio Quadros resigns; succeeded by Vice President João Goulart

1964 Military coup ousts Goulart; generals assume presidency, beginning twenty-one years of military rule

1985 Civilian elected president

1988 New constitution written

1990 Election of Fernando Collor de Mello, defeating Luís Ignacio "Lula" da Silva

1992 Collor de Mello impeached and resigns; succeeded by Vice President Itamar Franco
1994 Real Plan stabilizes economy; Fernando Henrique Cardoso elected president, defeating Lula
1998 Cardoso elected for a second term, again defeating Lula
1999 Devaluation of the real; military ministries replaced by a single civilian minister of defense

Bibliography

The following books in English give a broad picture of various aspects of Brazil. Additionally, there is a vast Portuguese-language literature for those able to read it. Fortunately, Spanish speakers can read Portuguese materials relatively easily.

Ames, Barry. *The Deadlock of Democracy in Brazil.* Ann Arbor: University of Michigan Press, 2000.
Birdsall, Nancy, and Richard H. Sabot, eds. *Opportunity Foregone: Education in Brazil.* Washington, DC: Inter-American Development Bank, 1996.
Bresser Pereira, Luis Carlos. *Economic Crisis and State Reform in Brazil: Toward a New Interpretation of Latin America.* Boulder, CO: Lynne Rienner Publishers, 1996.
Chaffee, Wilber Albert. *Desenvolvimento: Politics and Economy in Brazil.* Boulder, CO: Lynne Rienner Publishers, 1998.
Cohen, Youssef. *Radicals, Reformers, and Reactionaries.* Chicago: University of Chicago Press, 1994.
Eakin, Marshall C. *Brazil: The Once and Future Country.* New York: St. Martin's Press, 1997.
Evans, Peter. *Dependent Development: The Alliance of Multinational, State, and Local Capital in Brazil.* Princeton, NJ: Princeton University Press, 1979.
Furtado, Celso. *The Economic Growth of Brazil: A Survey from Colonial to Modern Times.* Berkeley: University of California Press, 1968.
Geddes, Barbara. *Politician's Dilemma: Building State Capacity in Latin America.* Berkeley: University of California Press, 1994.
Graham, Lawrence W., and Robert H. Wilson, eds. *The Political Economy of Brazil: Public Policies in an Era of Transition.* Austin: University of Texas Press, 1990.
Hagopian, Francis. *Traditional Politics and Regime Change in Brazil.* New York: Cambridge University Press, 1996.
Hunter, Wendy. *Eroding Military Influence in Brazil: Politicians against Soldiers.* Chapel Hill: University of North Carolina Press, 1997.
Keck, Margaret. *The Workers' Party and Democratization in Brazil.* New Haven, CT: Yale University Press, 1992.
Kingston, Peter R. *Crafting Coalitions for Reform: Business Preferences, Political Institutions, and Neoliberal Reform in Brazil.* University Park: The Pennsylvania State University Press, 1999.
Lewin, Linda. *Politic and Parentela in Paraiba: A Case Study of Family-Based Oligarchy in Brazil.* Princeton, NJ: Princeton University Press, 1987.
Mainwaring, Scott. *The Catholic Church and Politics in Brazil, 1916–1985.* Stanford, CA: Stanford University Press, 1986.

Moreira Alves, María Helena. *State and Opposition in Military Brazil*. Austin: University of Texas Press, 1985.

Page, Joseph A. *History and Cultures: The Brazilians*. Reading, MA.: Addison-Wesley, 1995.

Scheper-Hughes, Nancy. *Death without Weeping: The Violence of Everyday Life in Brazil*. Berkeley: University of California Press, 1992.

Schneider, Ben Ross. *Politics within the State: Elite Bureaucrats and Industrial Policy in Authoritarian Brazil*. Pittsburgh, PA: University of Pittsburgh Press, 1991.

Silverstein, Ben, and Emir Sader. *Without Fear of Being Happy: Lula, the Workers Party in Brazil*. New York: Verso, 1991.

Skidmore, Thomas E. *Politics in Brazil: 1930–1964, An Experiment in Democracy*. New York: Oxford University Press, 1967.

———. *The Politics of Military Rule in Brazil, 1964–85*. New York: Oxford University Press, 1988.

Stepan, Alfred, ed. *Democratizing Brazil: Problems of Transition and Consolidation*. New York: Oxford University Press, 1989.

Wirth, John D., Edson de Oliveira Nunes, and Thomas E. Bogenschild, eds. *State and Society in Brazil: Continuity and Change*. Boulder, CO.: Westview Press, 1987.

FILMS

Brazil has an active film industry, and a number of films are available on videotape, some in English, but most with subtitles. The following are suggested.

Black Orpheus. Brazil, 1958.
Dona Flor and Her Two Husbands. Brazil, 1977.
Central Station. Brazil, 1998.
Peixote. Brazil, 1981.
Bye Bye Brazil. Brazil, 1979.
Four Days in September. Brazil, 1998.

WEB SITES

In addition to bibliographical resources, the Internet offers a vast library of material in both English and Portuguese. The following are addresses of a few of the most useful sites for further reading.

Brazilian Embassy, www.brasil.emb.nw.dc.us
Brazilian Senate, www.senado.gov.br
Brazilian Finance Ministry, www.fazenda.gov.br
Latin American Network Information Center (LANIC), lanic.utexas.edu
Brazilian Studies Association, brasa.unm.edu
Political Data Base of the Americas, www.georgetown.edu/LatAmerPolitical/nome.html
Brazilian American Chamber of Commerce, www.brazilcham.com/brazweb.html

APPENDIX 1
RECENT PRESIDENTIAL ELECTIONS

Argentina

1995 Presidential Election

Candidate	Party	Percentage
Carlos Saúl Menem	Justice Party (PJ)	47.5
José Bordón	Front for a Country in Solidarity (Frepaso)	27.8
Horacio Massaccesi	Radical Civic Union (UCR)	16.2

1999 Presidential Election

Candidate	Party	Percentage
Fernando de la Rúa Bruno	Alliance (UCR-Frepaso)	48.5
Eduardo Alberto Duhalde Maldanodo	Justice Party (PJ)	38.1
Domingo Felipe Cavallo	Action for the Republic (AR)	10.1

Bolivia

1997 Presidential Election

Candidate	Party	Percentage
Hugo Banzer Suárez	National Democratic Alliance (ADN)	22.3
Juan Carlos Durán Saucedo	Nationalist Revolutionary Movement (MNR)	17.7
Jaime Paz Zamora	Movement of Revolutionary Left (MIR)	16.7
Remedios Loza	Conscience of the Fatherland (Condepa)	15.9
Ivo Mateo Kuljis Fuchtner	Citizens' Solidarity Union (UCS)	15.9

Brazil

1994 Presidential Election

Candidate	Party	Percentage
Fernando Henrique Cardoso	Brazilian Social Democratic Party (PSDB)	44.0
Luís Inacio "Lula" da Silva	Workers' Party (PT)	17.7
Enéas Carneiro	National Order Redefinition Party (PRONA)	5.9

1998 Presidential Election

Candidate	Party	Percentage
Fernando Henrique Cardoso	Brazilian Social Democratic Party (PSDB)	53.1
Luís Inacio "Lula" da Silva	Workers' Party (PT)	31.7
Ciro Gomez	Popular Socialist Party (PPS)	11.0

Chile

1994 Presidential Election

Candidate	Party	Percentage
Eduardo Frei Ruiz-Tagle	Christian Democrat Party (PDC)	58
Arturo Alessandri	Independent	24.4

1999–2000 Presidential Election: Round 1

Candidate	Party	Percentage
Ricardo Lagos Escobar	Party for Democracy (PPD)	48.0
Joaquín Lavín Infante	Independent Democratic Union (UDI)	47.5

1999–2000 Presidential Election: Round 2

Candidate	Party	Percentage
Ricardo Lagos Escobar	Party for Democracy (PPD)	51.3
Joaquín Lavín Infante	Independent Democratic Union (UDI)	48.7

Colombia

1994 Presidential Election: Round 1

Candidate	Party	Percentage
Ernesto Samper Pizano	Liberal Party (PL)	45.3
Andrés Pastrana Arango	Social Conservative Party (PSC)	45.0

1994 Presidential Election: Round 2

Candidate	Party	Percentage
Ernesto Samper Pizano	Liberal Party (PL)	50.6
Andrés Pastrana Arango	Social Conservative Party (PSC)	48.5

1998 Presidential Election: Round 1

Candidate	Party	Percentage
Horacio Serpa Uribe	Liberal Party (PL)	34.6
Andrés Pastrana Arango	Social Conservative Party (PSC)	34.4
Noemi Sanin	Independent	26.9

1998 Presidential Election: Round 2

Candidate	Party	Percentage
Andrés Pastrana Arango	Social Conservative Party (PSC)	52.0
Horacio Serpa Uribe	Liberal Party (PL)	48.0

Costa Rica

1994 Presidential Election

Candidate	Party	Percentage
José María Figueres	National Liberation Party (PLN)	49.6
Miguel Ángel Rodríguez	Christian Social Unity Party (PUSC)	47.7

1998 Presidential Election

Candidate	Party	Percentage
Miguel Ángel Rodríguez	Christian Social Unity Party (PUSC)	46.9
José Miguel Corrales	National Liberation Party (PLN)	44.4

Dominican Republic

1996 Presidential Election: Round 1

Candidate	Party	Percentage
José Francisco Peña Gómez	Dominican Revolutionary Party (PRD)	45.9
Leonel Antonio Fernández Reyna	Dominican Liberation Party (PLD)	38.8
Jacinto Bienvenido Peynado Garrigosa	Social Christian Reformist Party (PRSC)	14.9

1996 Presidential Election: Round 2

Candidate	Party	Percentage
Leonel Antonio Fernández Reyna	Dominican Liberation Party (PLD)	51.2
José Francisco Peña Gómez	Dominican Revolutionary Party (PRD)	48.8

2000 Presidential Election

Candidate	Party	Percentage
Hipólito Mejia	Dominican Revolutionary Party (PRD)	49.9
Danilo Medina	Dominican Liberation Party (PLD)	24.8
Joaquín Balaguer	Social Christian Reformist Party (PRSC)	24.7

Ecuador

1998 Presidential Election: Round 1

Candidate	Party	Percentage
Jamil Mahuad Witt	People's Democracy (DP)	35.3
Álvaro Fernando Noboa Pontón	Ecuadorian Roldosist Party (PRE)	26.9
Rodrigo Borja Zevallos	Party of the Democratic Left (ID)	15.9
Freddy Ehlers Zurita	Pluri-National Pachakutik Movement (MUPP)—New Country (NP)	14.3

1998 Presidential Election: Round 2

Candidate	Party	Percentage
Jamil Mahuad Witt	People's Democracy (DP)	51.3
Álvaro Fernando Noboa Pontón	Ecuadorian Roldosist Party (PRE)	48.7

El Salvador

1994 Presidential Election

Candidate	Party	Percentage
Armando Calderón Sol	National Republican Alliance (ARENA)	68.3
Ruben Zamora	National Liberation Front Farabundo Martí (FMLN)—Christian Social Union (USC)	31.4

1999 Presidential Election

Candidate	Party	Percentage
Francisco Flores	National Republican Alliance (ARENA)	52.0
Facundo Guardado	National Liberation Front Farabundo Martí (FMLN)—Christian Social Union (USC)	28.9
Rubén Zamora Rivas	United Democratic Center (CDU)	7.6
Rodolfo Parker	Christian Democratic (PDC)	5.8

Guatemala

1999 Presidential Election: Round 1

Candidate	Party	Percentage
Alfonso Antonio Portillo Cabrera	Republican Guatemalan Front (FRG)	47.8
Óscar Berger Perdomo	National Progress Party (PAN)	30.3
Álvaro Colom Caballeros	Guatemalan National Revolutionary Unity (URNG)	12.3

1999 Presidential Election: Round 2

Candidate	Party	Percentage
Alfonso Antonio Portillo Cabrera	Republican Guatemalan Front (FRG)	68.3
Óscar Berger Perdomo	National Progress Party (PAN)	31.7

Haiti

1990 Presidential Election

Candidate	Party	Percentage
Jean-Bertrand Aristide	National Front for Change and Democracy (FNCD)	67.5
Marc Bazin	National Alliance for Democracy and Progress (ANDP)	14.2

1995 Presidential Election

Candidate	Party	Percentage
René García Préval	Organization of the People in Struggle (OPL)	87.9
Léon Jeune	Independent	2.5
Victor Benoît	National Committee of the Congress of Democratic Movements (KONAKOM)	2.3

2000 Presidential Election

Candidate	Party	Percentage
Jean-Bertrand Aristide	Lavalas	91.7

Honduras

1993 Presidential Election

Candidate	Party	Percentage
Carlos R. Reina	Liberal Party (PLH)	53.0
José O. Ramos	National Party (PN)	43.0

1997 Presidential Election

Candidate	Party	Percentage
Carlos Roberto Flores Facussé	Liberal Party (PLH)	52.8
Alba Nora Gúnera Osorio Viuda de Melgar	National Party (PN)	42.7

Mexico

1994 Presidential Election

Candidate	Party	Percentage
Ernesto Zedillo Ponce de Léon	Institutional Revolutionary Party (PRI)	48.8
Diego Fernández de Cevallos	National Action Party (PAN)	25.9
Cuauhtémoc Cárdenas Solórzano	Democratic Revolution Party (PRD)	16.6

2000 Presidential Election

Candidate	Party	Percentage
Vicente Fox	National Action Party (PAN)	42.5
Francisco Labastida Ochoa	Institutional Revolutionary Party (PRI)	36.1
Cuauhtémoc Cárdenas	Democratic Revolutionary Party (PRD)	16.6

Nicaragua

1990 Presidential Election

Candidate	Party	Percentage
Violeta Barrios de Chamorro	United Nicaraguan Opposition (UNO)	54.7
José Daniel Ortega Saavedra	Sandinista National Liberation Front (FSLN)	40.8

1996 Presidential Election

Candidate	Party	Percentage
José Arnoldo Alemán Lacayo	Liberal Alliance (AL)	51.0
José Daniel Ortega Saavedra	Sandinista National Liberation Front (FSLN)	37.7

Panama

1994 Presidential Election

Candidate	Party	Percentage
Ernesto Pérez Balladares	Democratic Revolutionary Party (PRD)	32.0
Mireya Moscoso de Gruber	Arnulfista Party (PA)	29.7
Rubén Blades	Motherland Movement (MPE)	17.4
Rubén Carles	Molirena	16.4

1999 Presidential Election

Candidate	Party	Percentage
Mireya Moscoso de Gruber	Arnulfista Party (PA)	44.9
Martín Torrijos Espino	Democratic Revolutionary Party (PRD)	37.6
Alberto Vallarino Clement	Christian Democratic Party (PDC)	17.5

Paraguay

1998 Presidential Election

Candidate	Party	Percentage
Raúl Alberto Cubas Grau	Republican National Alliance (ANR)	55.4
Domingo Isabelino Laíno Figueredo	Democratic Alliance (AD)	43.9

Peru

1995 Presidential Election

Candidate	Party	Percentage
Alberto Keinya Fujimori	Change '90	64.4
Javier Peréz de Cuellar	Union for Peru (UPP)	21.8

2000 Presidential Election: Round 1

Candidate	Party	Percentage
Alberto Keinya Fujimori	Peru 2000	49.9
Alejandro Toledo	Possible Peru (PP)	40.2

2000 Presidential Election: Round 2

Candidate	Party	Percentage
Alberto Keinya Fujimori	Peru 2000	74.3
Alejandro Toledo	Possible Peru (PP)	25.7

2001 Presidential Election

Candidate	Party	Percentage
Alejandro Toledo	Possible Peru (PP)	36.5
Alan García	Partido Aprista Peruano	25.8
Lourdes Flores	National Unity	24.3

Uruguay

1994 Presidential Election

Candidate	Party	Percentage
Julio María Sanguinetti	Colorado Party (PC)	31.4
Alberto Volonte	National Party—Whites (PN)	30.2
Tabaré Ramón Vásquez Rosas	Progressive Encounter (EP)	30.0
Rafael Michelini Dellepiane	New Space (NE)	5.0

1999 Presidential Election: Round 1

Candidate	Party	Percentage
Tabaré Ramón Vásquez Rosas	Progressive Encounter (EP)	38.5
Jorge Luis Batlle Ibáñez	Colorado Party (PC)	31.3
Luis Alberto Lacalle de Herrera	National Party—Whites (PN)	21.3

1999 Presidential Election: Round 2

Candidate	Party	Percentage
Jorge Luis Batlle Ibáñez	Colorado Party (PC)	54.1
Tabaré Ramón Vásquez Rosas	Progressive Encounter (EP)	45.9

Venezuela

1993 Presidential Election

Candidate	Party	Percentage
Rafael Caldera	National Convergence (CN)	30.5
Claudio Fermín	Democratic Action (AD)	23.6
Oswaldo Alvarez Paz	Social Christian Party (COPEI)	22.7
Andrés Velásquez	Radical Cause (CR)	22.0

1998 Presidential Election

Candidate	Party	Percentage
Hugo Rafael Chávez Fríaz	Movement for the Fifth Republic (MVR)	56.5
Henrique Fernando Salas Römer	Independent	39.5

2000 Presidential Election

Candidate	Party	Percentage
Hugo Rafael Chávez Frías	Movement for the Fifth Republic (MVR)	59.5
Francisco Arias	Independent	37.5

Sources: Georgetown University and Organization of American States Political Database of the Americas, http://www.georgetown.edu/pdba/; Wilfried, Derksen, "Elections around the World," http://www.agora.stm.it/elections/election.htm.

APPENDIX 2
RECENT LEGISLATIVE ELECTIONS

Argentina

1999 Chamber of Deputies Elections

Party	Percentage	Number of Seats
Alliance (Radical Civic Union— Front for a Country in Solidarity)	43.6	124
Justice Party (JP)	33.7	101
Action for the Republic (AR)	7.6	12

Bolivia

1997 Chamber of Deputies and Chamber of Senators Elections

Party	Percentage	Number of Seats (Deputies/Senators)
Nationalist Democratic Alliance (ADN)	22.3	33/13
Nationalist Revolutionary Movement (MNR)	17.7	26/3
Movement of Revolutionary Left (MIR)	16.7	25/6
Citizens' Solidarity Union (UCS)	15.9	21/2
Conscience of the Fatherland (Condepa)	15.9	17/3

Brazil

1998 Chamber of Deputies and Federal Senate Elections

Party	Percentage	Number of Seats (Deputies/Senators)
Brazilian Social Democratic Party (PSDB)	53.1	106/20
Workers' Party (PT)	31.7	99/16
Popular Socialist Party (PPS)	11.0	82/27

Chile

1997 Chamber of Deputies Election

Party	Percentage	Number of Seats
Christian Democratic Party (PDC)	23.0	39
National Renewal (RN)	16.8	23
Independent Democratic Union (UDI)	14.4	17
Party for Democracy (PPD)	12.6	16
Socialist Party (PS)	11.1	11
Communist Party of Chile (PCC)	6.9	0

1997 Senate of the Republic Election

Party	Percentage	Number of Seats
Christian Democratic Party (PDC)	29.2	24
Independent Democratic Union (UDI)	17.2	16
National Renewal (RN)	14.8	9
Socialist Party (PS)	14.6	5
Communist Party of Chile (PCC)	8.4	0

Colombia

1998 Chamber of Representatives Election

Party	Percentage	Number of Seats
Liberal Party (PL)	54.0	98
Social Conservative Party (PSC)	27.0	52

1998 Senate of the Republic Election

Party	Percentage	Number of Seats
Liberal Party (PL)	55.9	51
Social Conservative Party (PSC)	24.5	26

Costa Rica

1998 Legislative Assembly Election

Party	Percentage	Number of Seats
Christian Social Unity Party (PUSC)	41.3	29
National Liberation Party (PLN)	34.9	22
Democratic Force (FD)	5.7	2

Dominican Republic

1996 Chamber of Deputies and Senate Elections

Party	Percentage	Number of Seats (Deputies/Senators)
Dominican Revolutionary Party (PRD)	51.4	83/24
Dominican Liberation Party (PLD)	30.4	49/4
Social Christian Reformist Party (PRSC)	16.8	17/2

Ecuador

1998 National Congress Election

Party	Number of Seats
People's Democracy—Christian Democrat Union (DP—UDC)	35
Social Christian Party (PSC)	26
Ecuadorian Roldosista Party (PRE)	25
Party of the Democratic Left (ID)	17
Pluri-National Pachakutik Movement—New Country (MUPP—NP)	6

El Salvador

1999 Legislative Assembly Election

Party	Percentage	Number of Seats
National Republican Alliance (ARENA)	36.0	29
National Liberation Front Farabundo Martí (FMLN)	35.2	31
Party of National Conciliation (PCN)	8.8	13
Christian Democratic Party (PDC)	7.2	6
United Democratic Center (CDU)	5.4	3

Guatemala

1999 Congress of the Republic Election

Party	Number of Seats
Republican Guatemalan Front (FRG)	63
National Progress Party (PAN)	37
Guatemalan National Revolutionary Union (URNG)	9

Haiti

1995 Chamber of Deputies and Senate Elections

Party	Number of Seats (Deputies/Senators)
Lavalas	68/17
National Front for Changes and Democracy (FNCD)	2/0
National Committee of the Congress of Democratic Movements (KONAKOM)	1/0

Honduras

1997 National Congress Election

Party	Percentage	Number of Seats
Liberal Party of Honduras (PLH)	49.7	67
National Party (PN)	41.3	54

Mexico

2000 Chamber of Deputies and Chamber of Senators Elections

Party	Percentage (Deputies/Senators)	Number of Seats (Deputies/Senators)
Institutional Revolutionary Party (PRI)	42.0/45.3	210/58
Alliance for Change (PAN)	44.8/41.4	224/53
Alliance for Mexico (PRD)	13.2/13.3	66/17

Nicaragua

1996 National Assembly Election

Party	Percentage	Number of Seats
Liberal Alliance (AL)	46.0	42
Sandinista National Liberation Front (FSLN)	36.5	37

Panama

1999 Legislative Assembly Elections

Party	Percentage	Number of Seats
New Nation (NN)	57.7	42
Union for Panama (UPP)	33.8	24
Opposition Action (AO)	8.5	6

Paraguay

1997 Chamber of Deputies Election

Party	Percentage	Number of Seats
Republican National Alliance (ANR)	53.8	45
Democratic Alliance (AD)	42.7	35

1997 Chamber of Senators Election

Party	Percentage	Number of Seats
Republican National Alliance (ANR)	51.7	24
Democratic Alliance (AD)	42.1	20

Peru

2000 Congress of the Republic Election

Party	Percentage	Number of Seats
Peru 2000	42.2	52
Possible Peru (PP)	23.3	26
Moralizing Independent Front (FIM)	7.5	9
We Are Peru (SP)	7.2	8
American Revolutionary People's Alliance (APRA)	5.5	6

Uruguay

1997 Chamber of Deputies and Chamber of Senators Elections

Party	Percentage	Number of Seats (Deputies/Senators)
Progressive Encounter (EP)	38.5	40/12
Colorado Party (PC)	31.3	32/10
National Party—Whites (PN)	21.3	22/7

Venezuela

2000 National Assembly Election

Party	Number of Seats
Movement for the Fifth Republic (MVR)	76
Democratic Action (AD)	29
Movement towards Socialism (MAS)	21
Project Venezuela (ProVen)	7
Social Christian Party (COPEI)	5

Sources: Georgetown University and Organization of American States Political Database of the Americas, http://www.georgetown.edu/pdba/; Wilfried Derksen, "Elections Around the World," http://www.agora.stm.it/elections/election.htm.

AUTHORS AND CONTRIBUTORS

Authors

Gary Prevost is Professor of Political Science at St. John's University in Minnesota. He received his Ph.D. in political science from the University of Minnesota and has published widely on Latin America and Spain. His books include *Democracy and Socialism in Sandinista Nicaragua*, coauthored with Harry E. Vanden; *The 1990 Nicaraguan Elections and their Aftermath*, coedited with Vanessa Castro; *The Undermining of the Sandinista Revolution*, coedited with Harry E. Vanden; and *Cuba: A Different America*, coedited with Wilber Chaffee, in addition to numerous articles and book chapters on Nicaragua and Spanish politics. His research on Latin America has been supported by a number of grants, including a Fulbright Central American Republics Award.

Harry E. Vanden is Professor of Political Science and International Studies at the University of South Florida, Tampa. He received his Ph.D. in political science from the New School for Social Research and also holds a graduate Certificate in Latin American Studies from the Maxwell School of Syracuse University. He has lived in several Latin American countries, including Peru, where he was a Fulbright Scholar and later worked in the Peruvian government's National Institute of Public Administration. His scholarly publications include numerous articles and book chapters and the following books: *Mariátegui, influencias*; *National Marxism in Latin America*; *A Bibliography of Latin American Marxism*; *Democracy and Socialism in Sandinista Nicaragua*, coauthored with Gary Prevost; and *The Undermining of the Sandinista Revolution*, coedited with Gary Prevost.

Contributors

Wilber Albert Chaffee is Professor of Politics at Saint Mary's College of California, a Senior Research Associate at the Instituto Universitário de Pesquisas do Rio de Janeiro, and a participant in the Brazil Working Group at Bolívar House, Stanford University. He received his Ph.D. in government from the University of Texas, Austin. In addition to his numerous articles and book chapters, he has published *The Economics of Violence in Latin America*; *Cuba, A Different America*, coedited with Gary Prevost; and his latest book, *Desenvolvimento: Politics and Economy in Brazil*.

Nora Hamilton is Associate Professor of Political Science at the University of Southern California. She received her Ph.D. in sociology from the University of Wisconsin. She has published *The Limits of State Autonomy: Post-Revolutionary Mexico*; *Crisis in Central America* (editor); *Modern Mexico, State Economy and Social Conflict*, coedited with Timothy Harding; and several articles and book chapters on political and economic change in Mexico and Central America. She has also published on Central American migration and recently published *Seeking Community in a Global City: Guatemalans and Salvadorans in Los Angeles*, coauthored with Norma Chinchilla.

Susanne Jonas is Professor of Latin American and Latino Studies at the University of California, Santa Cruz. She received her Ph.D. in political science from the University of California, Berkeley, and has been an expert on Central America, particularly Guatemala, and on U.S. policy in the region, for thirty-three years. Her most recent book is *Of Centaurs and Doves: Guatemala's Peace Process*. Among her other recent books are *Immigration: A Civil Rights Issue for the Americas*, *Beyond the Neoliberal Peace: From Conflict Resolution to Social Reconciliation*, *Latin America Faces the 21st Century*, and *The Battle for Guatemala*. She has also written dozens of related journal articles and book chapters as well as op-ed articles for major U.S. newspapers. She is currently working on issues of comparative peace processes around the world as well as Guatemalan and Salvadoran migrant communities in California and the United States.

Eduardo Silva is Associate Professor of Political Science and a Fellow of the Center for International Studies at the University of Missouri–St. Louis. He received his Ph.D. in political science from the University of California, San Diego. He is author of *The State and Capital in Chile: Business Elites, Technocrats and Market Economics* and coeditor of *Organized Business, Economic Change and Democracy in Latin America* and *Elections and Democratization in Latin America, 1980–1985*. He has also published over thirty articles that have appeared in professional journals, edited volumes, and public affairs outlets.

Aldo C. Vacs is Professor and Chair of the Department of Government, Skidmore College, a Research Associate at the University of Pittsburgh, and a contributing editor for the *Handbook of Latin American Studies*. He holds a Ph.D. in political science from the University of Pittsburgh. Dr. Vacs has published many articles and book chapters and has authored *Discreet Partners: Argentina and the USSR since 1917*; *The 1980 Grain Embargo Negotiations: The U.S., Argentina and the USSR*; and *Negotiating the Rivers*. He is currently researching political democratization, economic liberalization, and the process of political economic transformation in Latin America.

INDEX

Index compiled by Betilde Muñoz and Patrice E. Olsen